JAHANGIRI
OR
MEMOIRS OF JAHANGIR

JAHANGIRI
OR
MEMOIRS OF JAHANGIR

TRANSLATED BY
ALEXANDER ROGERS, I.C.S. (Retired)

EDITED BY
HENRY BEVERIDGE, I.C.S. (Retired)

GYAN

Published by

Gyan Publishing House
5, Ansari Road
Daryaganj, New Delhi-110002
Phone: 011-47034999, 9811692060
E-mail: books@gyanbooks.com

Distribution Network
gyanbooks.com
India, USA, Canada, UK, Australia, France

ISBN : 978-81-212-2347-8 (PB)
First Published, 1929

2nd Impression 2021

Printed at: Gyan Press, Delhi.

Jahangiri or Memoirs of Jahangir
Translated by: Alexander Rogers

TABLE OF TRANSLITERATION.

ا (Hamza)	not represented at the beginning or end of a word; ’ in the middle of a word.
ب	b
پ	p
ت	t
ٹ	ṭ
ث	s̤
ج	j
چ	ch
ح	ḥ
خ	kh
د	d
ڈ	ḍ
ذ	z̲
ر	r
ڑ	ṛ
ز	z
ژ	zh
س	s
ش	sh
ص	ṣ
ض	ẓ
ط	ṭ
ظ	z̤
ع	‘
غ	gh
ف	f
ق	q
ک	k
گ	g
ل	l
م	m
ن	n (m before ب and پ)
و	w (v in Hindu names)
ه	h (not represented at the end of a word except when radical)
ی	y

VOWELS — ـَ a. ـَا ā. ـَىٰ (alif maḳṣūra) ā.

ـِ i. ـِی ī; e in some Hindu names. ـِیّ iyy; ī at the end of a word.

ـُ u. ـُو ū; o in some Hindu names. ـُوّ uww; ū at the end of a word.

DIPHTHONGS — ـَو au. ـَوّ aww. ـَی ai. ـَیّ ayy.

The ‘Izāfat’ is rendered by ‘-i-’.

The Persian copulative particle و is transliterated by ‘u’.

The ل of the Arabic article is assimilated according to rule, the final vowel of the preceding word being preserved.

PREFACE.

Mr. Rogers translated the Memoirs of Jahāngīr several years ago from the edition which Sayyid Aḥmad printed at Ghazipur in 1863 and at Allyghur in 1864. Orientalists are greatly indebted to the Sayyid for his disinterested labours, but his text seems to have been made from a single and defective MS. and is often incorrect, especially in the case of proper names. I have collated it with the excellent MSS. in the India Office and the British Museum, and have thus been able to make numerous corrections. I have also consulted the MS. in the Library of the R.A.S., but it is not a good one. I have, with Mr. Rogers's permission, revised the translation, and I have added many notes.

There is an account of the Memoirs in the sixth volume of Elliot & Dowson's "History of India," and there the subject of the various recensions is discussed. There is also a valuable note by Dr. Rieu in his "Catalogue of Persian MSS.," i, 253. It is there pointed out that there is a manuscript translation of the first nine years of the Memoirs by William Erskine in the British Museum. I have consulted this translation and found it helpful. The MS. is numbered Add. 26,611. The translation is, of course, excellent, and it was made from a good MS.

A translation of what Dr. Rieu calls the garbled Memoirs of Jahāngīr was made by Major David Price and published by the Oriental Translation Committee of the Royal Asiatic Society in 1829. The author of this work is unknown, and its history is an unsolved problem. It is occasionally fuller than the genuine Memoirs, and it contains some picturesque touches, such as the account of Akbar's deathbed. But it is certain that it is, in part at least, a fabrication, and that it contains statements which Jahāngīr could never have made. Compare, for instance, the account of the death of Sohrāb, the son of Mīrzā Rustam, near the end of Price's translation, pp. 138–9, with that given in the genuine Memoirs in the narrative of the fifteenth year of the reign, p. 293, and also in the Iqbāl-nāma, p. 139. Besides being inaccurate, the garbled or spurious Memoirs are much shorter than the genuine work, and do not go beyond the fifteenth year. Price's translation, too, was made from a single and badly written MS.[1] which is now in the R.A.S. Library. Dr. Rieu remarks that it is to be regretted that so poor a fabrication as the garbled Memoirs should have been given to the world as a genuine production of Jahāngīr. This being so, it is appropriate that the present translation of the genuine Memoirs should be published by the Royal Asiatic Society.

When Jahāngīr had written his Memoirs for the first twelve years of his reign he made them into a volume, and had a number of copies made and distributed (Elliot, vi, 360). The first of these he gave to Shāh Jahān, who was then in high favour. The present publication is a translation of the first volume of the Memoirs, but the translation of the whole Memoirs, together with the additions of Mu'tamad Khān and Muḥammad Hādī, has been completed, and it is to be hoped that its publication will follow in due course.

Jahāngīr reigned for twenty-two years, but ill-health and sorrow made him give up the writing of his Memoirs in the seventeenth year of his reign (see Elliot, vi, 280). He then entrusted the task to Mu'tamad Khān, the author

[1] It is owing to the crabbed writing of Price's MS. that at p. 21 Jahāngīr is made to say that the Prince of Kashmir belonged to the society of Jogīs. The real statement is that the prince belonged to the Chak family.

of the Iqbāl-nāma, who continued the Memoirs to the beginning of the nineteenth year. He then dropped writing the Memoirs in the name of the emperor, but he continued the narrative of the reign, to Jahāngīr's death, in his own work, the Iqbāl-nāma. Muḥammad Hādī afterwards continued the Memoirs down to Jahāngīr's death, but his work is little more than an abridgment of the Iqbāl-nāma. Sayyid Aḥmad's edition contains the continuations of the Memoirs by Mu'tamad and Muḥammad Hādī, and also Muḥammad Hādī's preface and introduction. But this preface and introduction have not been translated by Mr. Rogers, and I do not think that a translation is necessary. Muḥammad Hādī is a late writer (see Elliot, vi, 392), his date being the first quarter of the eighteenth century, and his introduction seems to be almost wholly derived from the Ma'āṣir-i-Jahāngīrī of Kāmgār Ḥusainī (Elliot, vi, 257). It consists mainly of an account of Jahāngīr's life from his birth up to his accession.

It is perhaps unnecessary to say anything about the importance of Jahāngīr's Memoirs. They give a lively picture of India in the early decades of the seventeenth century, and are a valuable supplement to the Akbar-nāma. I may be allowed, however, to end this preface with the following remarks which I contributed to the *Indian Magazine* for May, 1907:—

"The Royal authors of the East had more blood in them than those kings whose works have been catalogued by Horace Walpole. To find a parallel to them we must go back to Julius Cæsar, and even then the advantage is not upon the side of Europe. After all, the commentaries of the famous Roman are a little disappointing, and certainly the Memoirs of Bābar and Jahāngīr are far more human and fuller of matter than the story of the Gallic Wars. All Muhammadans have a fancy for writing chronicles and autobiographies, and several Muhammadan kings have yielded to the common impulse. Central Asia has given us the Memoirs of Tamarlane, Bābar, and Ḥaidar, and the chronicle of Abu-l-ghazi; Persia has given us the Memoirs of Shah Ṭahmasp, and India the Memoirs of the Princess Gulbadan and Jahāngīr. In modern times we see the same impulse at work, for we have the biography of the late Ameer of Afghanistan and the diary of the Shah of Persia.

"The contributions to literature by Royal authors which come to us from the East form a department by themselves, and one which is of great value. Nearly all Eastern histories are disfigured by adulation. Even when the author has had no special reason for flattery and for suppression of truth, he has been dazzled by the greatness of his subject, and gives us a picture which no more reveals the real king than does a telescope the real constitution of the Morning Star. But when Eastern monarchs give us chronicles, the case is different. They have no occasion for fear or favour, and mercilessly expose the failings of their contemporaries. Not that they are to be trusted any more than other Orientals when speaking of themselves. Bābar has suppressed the story of his vassalage to Shah Isma'īl, of his defeat at Ghajdawān, and his treatment of 'Ālam Lodi; and Jahāngīr has glossed over his rebellion against his father, and the circumstances of Shīr-āfgan's death. But when they have to speak of others—whether kings or nobles—they give us the whole truth, and perhaps a little more. An amiable Princess like Gulbadan Begam may veil the faults and weaknesses of her brothers Humāyūn and Hindāl; but Bābar strips the gilt off nearly every one whom he mentions, and spares no one—not even his own father.

"The Memoirs of Bābar, Ḥaidar, and Gulbadan have been translated into English, and those of Ṭahmasp have been translated into German; but unfortunately Jahāngīr's have never been fully translated,[1] though there are extracts in Elliot & Dowson's History, and Major Price many years ago gave us from an imperfect manuscript a garbled account of a few years of his Memoirs. Yet in reality Jahāngīr's Memoirs are not inferior in interest to those of Bābar. Indeed, we may go further and say there is twice as much matter in them as in Bābar's Memoirs, and that they are by far the most entertaining of the two works. Not that Jahāngīr was by any means as remarkable a man as his great-grandfather. He was a most faulty human being, and his own account of himself often excites our disgust and contempt. But he had the sense not to confine his narrative to an account of himself, and he has given us a picture of his father, the great Akbar, which is a bigger 'plum' than anything in Bābar's Memoirs. But his account of himself has also its charm, for it reveals the real man, and so he lives for us in his Memoirs just as James VI—to whom, and to the Emperor Claudius, he bears a strange and even ludicrous resemblance—lives in the 'Fortunes of Nigel' or Claudius in Suetonius and Tacitus. Jahāngīr was indeed a strange mixture. The man who could stand by and see men flayed alive, and who, as he himself tells us, put one man to death and had two others hamstrung because they showed themselves inopportunely and frightened away his game, could yet be a lover of justice and could spend his Thursday evenings in holding high converse. He could quote Firdūsi's verse against cruelty to animals—

> 'Ah! spare yon emmet, rich in hoarded grain—
> He lives with pleasure, and he dies with pain';

and be soft-hearted enough to wish that his father were alive to share with him the delicious mangoes of India. He could procure the murder of Abu-l-faẓl and avow

[1] A translation was begun by the Rev. Mr. Lowe for the Asiatic Society of Bengal, but only one fasciculus was published. This was in 1889.

the fact without remorse, and also pity the royal elephants because they shivered in winter when they sprinkled themselves with cold water. 'I observed this,' he says, 'and so I ordered that the water should be heated to the temperature of luke-warm milk.' And he adds: 'This was entirely my own idea; nobody had ever thought of it before.' One good trait in Jahāngīr was his hearty enjoyment of Nature and his love for flowers. Bābar had this also, but he was old, or at least worn out, when he came to India, and he was disgusted by an Indian attempt to poison him, and so his description of India is meagre and splenetic. Jahāngīr, on the other hand, is a true Indian, and dwells delightedly on the charms of Indian flowers, particularises the palās, the bokūl, and the champa, and avows that no fruit of Afghanistan or Central Asia is equal to the mango. He loved, too, to converse with pandits and Hindu ascetics, though he is contemptuous of their avatars, and causes the image of Vishnu as the boar avatar to be broken and flung into the Pushkar lake.

"It is a remark of Hallam's that the best attribute of Muhammadan princes is a rigorous justice in chastising the offences of others. Of this quality Jahāngīr, in spite of all his weaknesses, had a large share, and even to this day he is spoken of with respect by Muhammadans on account of his love of justice. It is a pathetic circumstance that it was this princely quality which was to some extent the cause of the great affront put upon him by Mahābat Khān. Many complaints had been made to Jahāngīr of the oppressions of Mahābat in Bengal, and crowds of suppliants had come to Jahāngīr's camp. It was his desire to give them redress and to punish Mahābat for his exactions, together with his physical and mental weakness, which led to his capture on the banks of the Jhilam.

"One of the many interesting observations in his Memoirs

is his account of an inscription he saw at Hindaun. He says that in the thirteenth year of his reign, as he was marching back to Agra, he found a verse by someone inscribed on the pillar of a pleasure-house on an islet in the lake at Hindaun. He then proceeds to quote it, and it turns out to be one of Omar Khayyam's! This is FitzGerald's paraphrase:—

'For some we loved, the loveliest and the best
That from his vintage Time hath prest,
Have drunk their Cup a Round or two before,
And one by one crept silently to rest.'

"The same quatrain has also been quoted by Badayūnī in his history, and the interesting thing about Jahāngīr's quotation of it is that he could see the beauty of the verse and at the same time did not know who was the author. There is also an interest in the fact that the third line contains a different reading from that given in Whinfield's edition of the text. Hindaun is in the Jaipur territory, and one would like to know if the inscription still exists.

"Among other things in Jahāngīr's Memoirs there is the description of the outbreak of the Plague, given to him by a lady of his court [which has been quoted by Dr. Simpson in his book upon Plague], and there is a very full account of Kashmir, which is considerably superior to that in the Ayin Akbarī, which Sir Walter Lawrence has praised."

With reference to the portrait of Jahāngīr prefixed to this volume, it may be interesting to note that it appears from Mr. E. B. Havell's "Indian Sculpture," p. 203, that the British Museum possesses a drawing by Rembrandt which was copied from a Moghul miniature, and which has been pronounced by Mr. Rouffaer to be a portrait of Jahāngīr. Coryat (Purchas, reprint, iv, 473) thus describes Jahāngīr's personal appearance:—"He is fifty and three years of age, his nativity-day having been celebrated with wonderful pomp since my arrival here. On that day he weighed himself in a pair of golden scales, which by great chance I saw the same day; a custom he observes most inviolably every year. He is of complexion neither white nor black, but of a middle betwixt them. I know not how to express it with a more expressive and significant epitheton than olive. An olive colour his face presenteth. He is of a seemly composition of body, of a stature little unequal (as I guess not without grounds of probability) to mine, but much more corpulent than myself."

As regards the bibliography of the Tūzuk-i-Jahāngīrī, I have to note that there is an Urdu translation by Munshī Aḥmad 'Alī Sīmāb of Rāmpūra, that is, Aligarh in Tonk. It was made from Muḥammad Hādī's edition under the patronage of Muḥammad Ibrāhīm 'Alī Khān Nawāb of Tonk, and was published by Newal Kishor in 1291 (1874). There is also a Hindi translation by Munshī Debī Prasād which was published in 1905 at Calcutta by the Bhārat Mitra Press. The Urdu translation referred to by Mr. Blumhardt in his Catalogue of Hindustani MSS., p. 61, and noticed by Elliot, vi, 401, and Garcin de Tassy, iii, 301, is, as the two latter writers have remarked, a translation of the Iqbāl-nāma. The MS. referred to by Elliot, vi, 277, as having been in the possession of General Thomas Paterson Smith, and which is described in Ethé's Catalogue of the India Office MSS., No. 2833, p. 1533, was made by Sayyid Muḥammad, the elder brother of Sayyid Aḥmad. As the end of the MS. the copyist gives some account of himself and of his family. He made the copy from copies in the Royal Library and in the possession of Rajah Roghū Nāth Singh *alias* Lāl Singh Jālpūr. He finished it in October, 1843. Sayyid Muḥammad was Munsif of Hutgām in the Fatḥpūr district. He died young in 1845. My friend Mr. T. W. Arnold, of the India Office, informs me that Sayyid Aḥmad told him that he found a valuable illustrated MS. of the Tūzuk in the débris of the Delhi Royal Library, and took it home, but that it was lost when his house was plundered by the mutineers. There is in the Bodleian a copy in Sayyid Aḥmad's own handwriting. He states that he made use of ten good MSS. The Englishman at whose request he made the copy was John Panton Gubbins, who was once Sessions Judge of Delhi. This copy is described in the Bodleian Catalogue, p. 117, No. 221. The MS. No. 220 described on the same page was brought home by Fraser, and is a good one, but only goes down to the end of the 14th year.

H. BEVERIDGE.

March, 1909.

POSTSCRIPT.—Since writing this Preface I have been enabled by the kindness of Mr. Irvine to examine the Hindi Jahāngīr-nāma of Debī Prasād. It is not a translation, but an abstract, and I do not think it is of much value. Being a Jodhpūr man he has been able, perhaps, to correct some spellings of places, but he does not seem to have consulted any MSS., and when he comes to a difficulty he shirks it. The most valuable adjunct to the Tūzuk, after the Iqbāl-nāma, is the Ma'āṣir-i-Jahāngīrī of Kāmgār Ḥusainī. It is important as giving the early history of Jahāngīr, that is, of the time when he was Prince Selīm. There are three copies of his work in the British Museum, but the so-called Maāthir-i-Jahāngīrī of the India Office Library, No. 3098, or 324 of the new Catalogue, is only a copy of the Iqbāl-nāma.

I regret that the number of Errata and Addenda is so large, but when I began the revision I did not know that Sayyid Aḥmad's text was so incorrect. It will be seen that at pp. 158 and 162 I have made two erroneous notes.

H. B.

JAHĀNGĪR'S MEMOIRS.

In the Name of God, the Merciful, the Clement.

CHAPTER I.

BY the boundless favour of Allah, when one sidereal hour of Thursday, Jumādā-ṣ-ṣānī 20th, A.H. 1014 (October 24th, 1605), had passed, I ascended the royal throne in the capital of Agra, in the 38th year of my age.[1]

Till he was 28 years old, no child of my father had lived, and he was continually praying for the survival of a son to dervishes and recluses, by whom spiritual approach to the throne of Allah is obtained. As the great master, Khwāja Mu'īnu-d-dīn Chishtī, was the fountain-head of most of the saints of India, he considered that in order to obtain this object he should have recourse to his blessed threshold, and resolved within himself that if Almighty God should bestow a son on him he would, by way of complete humility, go on foot from Agra to his

[1] That is, he was 37 years 3 months by the lunar calendar, and 36 years 1 month by solar reckoning (Pādshāhnāma, i, 69). Elliot and all the MSS. have 8th Jumādā-ṣ-ṣānī as the date of the accession, but this is clearly wrong, as Akbar did not die till 13th Jumādā-ṣ-ṣānī. Evidently the copyists have, as is so often the case, misread *bistam* as *hashtam*. See Blochmann's remark, p. 454, note 3. That Jahāngīr was not at this time 38 is shown by his stating at p. 37 that he celebrated his 38th birthday at Lahore after the capture of Khusrau.

blessed mausoleum, a distance of 140 *kos*. In A.H. 977, on Wednesday, 17th Rabīʿu-l-awwal (August 31st, 1569), when seven *gharī* of the aforesaid day had passed, when Libra (Mīzān) had risen to the 24th degree, God Almighty brought me into existence from the hiding-place of nothingness. At the time when my venerated father was on the outlook for a son, a dervish of the name of Shaikh Salīm, a man of ecstatic condition, who had traversed many of the stages of life, had his abode on a hill near Sīkrī, one of the villages of Agra, and the people of that neighbourhood had complete trust in him. As my father was very submissive to dervishes, he also visited him. One day, when waiting on him and in a state of distraction, he asked him how many sons he should have. The Shaikh replied, "The Giver who gives without being asked will bestow three sons on you." My father said, "I have made a vow that, casting my first son on the skirt of your favour, I will make your friendship and kindness his protector and preserver." The Shaikh accepted this idea, and said, "I congratulate you, and I will give him my own name." When my mother came near the time of her delivery, he (Akbar) sent her to the Shaikh's house that I might be born there. After my birth they gave me the name of Sultan Salīm, but I never heard my father, whether in his cups or in his sober moments, call me Muḥammad Salīm or Sultan Salīm, but always *Shaikhū Bābā*. My revered father, considering the village of Sīkrī, which was the place of my birth, lucky for him, made it his capital. In the course of fourteen or fifteen years that hill, full of wild beasts, became a city containing all kinds of gardens and buildings, and lofty, elegant edifices and pleasant places, attractive to the heart. After the conquest of Gujarāt this village was named Fatḥpūr. When I became king it occurred to me to change my name, because this resembled that of the Emperor of Rūm. An inspiration from the hidden world brought it into my mind that, inasmuch as the business of kings is the controlling of the world, I should give myself the name of Jahāngīr (World-seizer) and make my title of honour (*laqab*) Nūru-d-dīn, inasmuch as my sitting on the throne coincided with the rising and shining on the earth of the great light (the Sun). I had also heard, in the days when I was a prince, from Indian sages, that after the expiration of the reign and life of King Jalālu-d-dīn Akbar one named Nūru-d-dīn would be administrator of the affairs of the State. Therefore I gave myself the name and appellation of Nūru-d-dīn Jahāngīr Pādshāh. As this great event took place in Agra, it is necessary that some account of that city should be given.

Agra is one of the grand old cities of Hindustan. It had formerly an old fort on the bank of the Jumna, but this my father threw down before my birth, and he founded a fort of cut red stone, the like of which those who have travelled over the world cannot point out. It was completed in the space of fifteen or sixteen years. It had four gates and two sally-ports, and its cost was 35 lakhs of rupees, equal to 115,000 *tomān* of current Persian coinage and to 10,500,000 *khānī* according to the Tūrān reckoning. The habitable part of the city extends on both sides of the river. On its west side, which has the greater population, its circumference is seven kos and its breadth is one kos. The circumference of the inhabited part on the other side of the water, the side towards the east, is 2½ kos, its length being one kos and its breadth half a kos. But in the number of its buildings it is equal to several cities of 'Irāq, Khurāsān, and Māwarā'a-n-nahr (Transoxiana) put together. Many persons have erected buildings of three or four storeys in it. The mass of people is so great, that moving about in the lanes and bazars is difficult. It is on the boundary of the second climate. On its east is the province of Qanauj; on the west, Nāgor; on the north, Sambhal; and on the south, Chanderī.

It is written in the books of the Hindus that the source

of the Jumna is in a hill of the name of Kalind,[1] which men cannot reach because of the excessive cold. The apparent source is a hill near the pargana of Khiẓrābād.

The air of Agra is warm and dry; physicians say that it depresses the spirits (*rūḥrā ba taḥlīl mībarad*) and induces weakness. It is unsuited to most temperaments, except to the phlegmatic and melancholy, which are safe from its bad effects. For this reason animals of this constitution and temperament, such as the elephant, the buffalo, and others, thrive in its climate.

Before the rule of the Lodī Afghans, Agra was a great and populous place, and had a castle described by Mas'ūd b. Sa'd b. Salmān in the ode (*qaṣīda*) which he wrote in praise of Maḥmūd, son of Sultan Ibrāhīm, son of Mas'ūd, son of Sultan Maḥmūd of Ghaznī, on the capture of the castle—

> "The fort of Agra appeared in the midst of the dust
> Like a mountain, and its battlements like peaks."[2]

When Sikandar Lodī designed to take Gwalior he came to Agra from Delhi, which was the capital of the Sultans of India, and settled down there. From that date the population and prosperity of Agra increased, and it became the capital of the Sultans of Delhi. When God Almighty bestowed the rule of India on this illustrious family, the late king, Bābar, after the defeat of Ibrāhīm, the son of Sikandar Lodī, and his being killed, and after his victory over Rānā Sāngā, who was the chief of the Rajas of Hindustan, established on the east side of the Jumna, on improved land, a garden (*chārbāgh*) which few places equal in beauty. He gave it the name of Gul-afshān

[1] The Sanskrit Kalinda.

[2] The couplet appears in Mas'ūd's divan, B.M. MS. Egerton, 701, p. 142*a*, line 4. The preceding lines show that the dust (*gard*) referred to in the first line means the dust caused by the invading army. I take the words *barū bārhāī* to mean the battlements or pinnacles of the fortress, the *ī* at the end of *bārhā* being intensive.

(Flower-scatterer), and erected in it a small building of cut red stone, and having completed a mosque on one side of it he intended to make a lofty building, but time failed him and his design was never carried into execution.

In these Memoirs, whenever *Ṣāḥib qirānī* is written it refers to Amīr Tīmūr Gūrgān; and whenever *Firdūs-makānī* is mentioned, to Bābar Pādshāh; when *Jannat-āshyānī* is used, to Humāyūn Pādshāh; and when *'Arsh-āshyānī* is employed, to my revered father, Jalālu-d-dīn Muḥammad Akbar Pādshāh Ghāzī.

Melons, mangoes, and other fruits grow well in Agra and its neighbourhood. Of all fruits I am very fond of mangoes. In the reign of my father (*'Arsh-āshyānī*) many fruits of other countries, which till then were not to be had in India, were obtained there. Several sorts of grapes, such as the *ṣāḥibī* and the *ḥabshī* [1] and the *kishmishī*, became common in several towns; for instance, in the bazars of Lahore every kind and variety that may be desired can be had in the grape season. Among fruits, one which they call *ananās* (pineapple), which is grown in the Frank ports,[2] is of excessive fragrance and fine flavour. Many thousands are produced every year now in the Gul-afshān garden at Agra.

From the excellencies of its sweet-scented flowers one may prefer the fragrances of India to those of the flowers of the whole world. It has many such that nothing in the whole world can be compared to them. The first is the *champa* (*Michelia champaca*), which is a flower of exceedingly sweet fragrance; it has the shape of the saffron-flower, but is yellow inclining to white. The tree is very symmetrical

[1] Erskine's manuscript translation of the Tūzuk-i-Jahāngīrī, B.M. MS. Add. 26,611, and the B.M. MS. have *chīnī*, not *ḥabshī*. But I.O. MS. No. 181 and the R.A.S. MS. have *ḥusainī*, and this seems right. See Memoirs, Leyden & Erskine, p. 326, and the Haidarabad Turkī text, p. 284. The *kishmishī* is a small grape like that of which currants are made.

[2] Cf. *infra* the account of the 11th year, p. 173.

and large, full of branches and leaves, and is shady. When in flower one tree will perfume a garden. Surpassing this is the *keoṛā*[1] flower (*Pandanus odoratissimus*). Its shape and appearance are singular, and its scent is so strong and penetrating that it does not yield to the odour of musk. Another is the *rāe bel*,[2] which in scent resembles white jessamine. Its flowers are double and treble (?). Another is the *mūlsarī*[3] (*Mimusops Elengi*). This tree, too, is very graceful and symmetrical, and is shady. The scent of its flowers is very pleasant. Another is the *ketakī*[4] (*Pandanus* ?), which is of the nature of the *keoṛā*, but the latter is thorny, whereas the *ketkī* has no thorns. Moreover, the *ketkī* is yellowish, whereas the *keoṛā* is white. From these two flowers and also from the *chambelī*[5] (*Jasminum grandiflorum*), which is the white jessamine of *wilāyat* (Persia or Afghanistan), they extract sweet-scented oils. There are other flowers too numerous to mention. Of trees there are the cypress (*sarw*), the pine

[1] See Memoirs, L. & E., p. 330.

[2] The name *rāe bel* is not given in Clarke's Roxburgh, but perhaps it is one of the jessamines, and may be the *bela* of Clarke (p. 30). The *rāe bel* is described by Abu-l-faẓl (Blochmann, pp. 76 and 82). The statement about its flowers being double and treble is obscure. Erskine renders the passage "The leaves are generally two and three fold." The Persian word is *ṭabaqa*, which apparently is equivalent to the *tūī* or fold of the Āyīn-i-Akbarī, Persian text, i, 96. The reference may be to the flowers growing in umbels.

[3] This is the *bokul* of Indian gardens (Clarke, p. 313), and well deserves Jahāngīr's praise. It is probably the *bholsārī* mentioned in the Āyīn (Blochmann, No. 10, p. 83). Blochmann gives *bholsirī* (p. 70) as the name of a fruit-tree, and the *bholsārī* of p. 83 may be a mistake for *mūlsarī*.

[4] The text has *sewtī*, but the *sewtī* seems to be the *Rosa glandulifera* of Roxburgh (Clarke, p. 407) and has no resemblance to the *Pandanus*. See also the description of the *sewtī*, Blochmann, p. 82. (Perhaps there are two *sewtīs*, one famous for fragrance, the other for beauty. See l.c., pp. 76 and 82.) What is meant in the text is evidently a *Pandanus* and the *ketkī* of Blochmann, p. 83. I have followed, therefore, I.O. MS. 181, and have substituted *ketkī* for *sewtī*. The *ketkī* may be *Pandanus inermis*, which has no thorns (Clarke, p. 708). Erskine also has *ketkī*.

[5] L.c., p. 33 et seq.

(*sanūbar*), the *chanār* (*Platanus orientalis*), the white poplar (*safīdār, Populus alba*), and the *bīd mūllā* (willow), which they had formerly never thought of in Hindustan, but are now plentiful. The sandal-tree, which once was peculiar to the islands (i.e., Java, Sumatra, etc.), also flourishes in the gardens.

The inhabitants of Agra exert themselves greatly in the acquirement of crafts and the search after learning. Various professors of every religion and creed have taken up their abode in the city.

After my accession, the first order that I gave was for the fastening up of the Chain of Justice, so that if those engaged in the administration of justice should delay or practise hypocrisy in the matter of those seeking justice, the oppressed might come to this chain and shake it so that its noise might attract attention. Its fashion was this: I ordered them to make a chain of pure gold,[1] 30 *gaz* in length and containing 60 bells. Its weight was 4 Indian maunds, equal to 42 'Irāqī maunds. One end of it they made fast to the battlements of the Shāh Burj of the fort at Agra and the other to a stone post fixed on the bank of the river. I also gave twelve orders to be observed as rules of conduct (*dastūru-l-'amal*) in all my dominions—

(1) Forbidding the levy of cesses under the names of *tamghā* and *mīr baḥrī* (river tolls), and other burdens which the *jāgīrdārs* of every province and district had imposed for their own profit.

(2) On roads where thefts and robberies took place, which roads might be at a little distance from habitations, the

[1] Du Jarric, who got his information from missionary reports, seems to imply that the chain was of silver, and says that Jahāngīr was following the idea of an old Persian king. It is mentioned in the Siyar al-muta'akhkhirīn (reprint, i, 230) that Muḥammad Shāh in 1721 revived this, and hung a long chain with a bell attached to it from the octagon tower which looked towards the river.

jāgīrdārs of the neighbourhood should build *sarā'īs* (public rest-houses), mosques, and dig wells, which might stimulate population, and people might settle down in those *sarā'īs*. If these should be near a *khāliṣa* estate (under direct State management), the administrator (*mutaṣaddī*) of that place should execute the work.

[1] (3) The bales of merchants should not be opened on the roads without informing them and obtaining their leave.

(4) In my dominions if anyone, whether unbeliever or Musalman, should die, his property and effects should be left for his heirs, and no one should interfere with them. If he should have no heir, they should appoint inspectors and separate guardians to guard the property, so that its value might be expended in lawful expenditure, such as the building of mosques and *sarā'īs*, the repair of broken bridges, and the digging of tanks and wells.

(5) They should not make wine or rice-spirit (*darbahra*)[2] or any kind of intoxicating drug, or sell them; although I myself drink wine, and from the age of 18 years up till now, when I am 38, have persisted in it. When I first took a liking to drinking I sometimes took as much as twenty cups of double-distilled spirit; when by degrees it acquired a great influence over me I endeavoured to lessen the quantity, and in the period of seven years I have brought myself from fifteen cups to five or six. My times for drinking were varied; sometimes when three or four sidereal hours of the day remained I would begin to drink, and sometimes at night and partly by day. This went on till I was 30 years old. After that I took to drinking always at night. Now I drink only to digest my food.

[3] (6) They should not take possession of any person's house.

[1] In text this is wrongly made part of regulation 2.

[2] Gladwin and the MSS. have *dilbahra* (exhilarating drink), and this is probably correct. Jahāngīr would know little about rice-spirit.

[3] This regulation is more fully expounded in Price, p. 7.

(7) I forbade the cutting off the nose or ears of any person, and I myself made a vow by the throne of God that I would not blemish anyone by this punishment.

(8) I gave an order that the officials of the Crown lands and the *jāgīrdārs* should not forcibly take the ryots' lands and cultivate them on their own account.

(9) A government collector or a *jāgīrdār* should not without permission intermarry with the people of the *pargana* in which he might be.

(10) They should found hospitals in the great cities, and appoint physicians for the healing of the sick; whatever the expenditure might be, should be given from the *khāliṣa* establishment.

(11) In accordance with the regulations of my revered father, I ordered that each year from the 18th[1] of Rabī'u-l-awwal, which is my birthday, for a number of days corresponding to the years of my life, they should not slaughter animals (for food). Two days in each week were also forbidden, one of them Thursday, the day of my accession, and the other Sunday, the day of my father's birth. He held this day in great esteem on this account, and because it was dedicated to the Sun, and also because it was the day on which the Creation began. Therefore it was one of the days on which there was no killing in his dominions.[2]

(12) I gave a general order that the offices and *jāgīrs* of my father's servants should remain as they were. Later, the *manṣabs* (ranks or offices) were increased according to

[1] It is curious that Jahāngīr should give the 18th Rabī'u-l-awwal as his birthday, while the authorities give it as the 17th. Probably the mistake has arisen from Jahāngīr's writing Rabī'u-l-awwal instead of Shahrīwar. His birthday was Rashn the 18th day of Shahrīwar (see Akbarnāma, ii, 344), but it was the 17th Rabī'u-l-awwal. See Muḥammad Hādī's preface, p. 2, and Beale, and Jahāngīr's own statement a few lines above. Possibly Jahāngīr wished to make out that he was born on the 18th Rabī'u-l-awwal and a Thursday, because he regarded Thursday as a blessed day (*mubārak shamba*), whilst he regarded Wednesday as peculiarly unlucky, and called it *kam*, or *gam*, *shamba*.

[2] Cf. Elliot's translation, vi, 513, and note 2.

each one's circumstances by not less than 20 per cent. to 300 or 400 per cent. The subsistence money of the *aḥadīs* was increased by 50 per cent., and I raised the pay of all domestics by 20 per cent. I increased the allowances of all the veiled ladies of my father's harem from 20 per cent. to 100 per cent., according to their condition and relationship. By one stroke of the pen I confirmed the subsistence lands [1] of the holders of *aimas* (charity lands) within the dominions, who form the army of prayer, according to the deeds in their possession. I gave an order to Mīrān Ṣadr Jahān, who is one of the genuine Sayyids of India, and who for a long time held the high office of *ṣadr* (ecclesiastical officer) under my father, that he should every day produce before me deserving people (worthy of charity). [2] I released all criminals who had been confined and imprisoned for a long time in the forts and prisons.[3]

At a propitious hour I ordered that they should coin gold and silver of different weights. To each coin I gave a separate name, viz., to the *muhr* of 100 *tola*, that of *nūr-s̲h̲āhī*; to that of 50 *tola*, that of *nūr-sulṭānī*; to that of 20 *tola*, *nūr-daulat*; to that of 10 *tola*, *nūr-karam*; to that of 5 *tola*, *nūr-mihr*; and to that of 1 *tola*,

[1] The MSS. have "the subsistence lands of people in general (*ahālī*) and the *aimas*."

[2] In the text and in Elliot, vi, 515, this is made a separate order, but it is not so in the MSS. If it were, we should have thirteen instead of twelve regulations. This is avoided in text and in Elliot by putting the 6th and 7th regulations into one ordinance. With regard to the regulation about releasing the prisoners, Sir Henry Elliot is somewhat unjust to Jahāngīr in his commentary at p. 515. It was only those who had been *long* imprisoned whom Jahāngīr released, and his proceedings at Ranthambhor in the 13th year (Tūzuk, p. 256) show that he exercised discrimination in releasing prisoners. The account in Price, p. 10, may also be consulted. There Jahāngīr says he released 7,000 men from Gwalior alone. It may be remembered that most of these were political offenders. Private criminals were for the most part put to death, or mutilated, or fined. There were no regular jails.

[3] The above translation of the Institutes should be compared with Sir Henry Elliot's translation and his commentary: History of India, E. & D., vol. vi, Appendix, p. 493.

nūr-jahānī. The half of this I called *nūrānī*, and the quarter, *rawājī*. With regard to the silver coins (*sikkas*), I gave to the coin of 100 *tola* the name of *kaukab-i-ṭāli‘* (star of horoscope); to that of 50 *tola*, the name of *kaukab-i-iqbāl* (star of fortune); to that of 20 *tola*, the name of *kaukab-i-murād* (star of desire); to that of 10 *tola*, the name of *kaukab-i-bakht* (star of good luck); to that of 5 *tola*, the name of *kaukab-i-sa‘d* (star of auspiciousness); to that of 1 *tola*, the name of *jahāngīrī*. The half *jahāngīrī* I called *sulṭānī*; the quarter, *niṣārī*[1] (showering money); the dime, *khair-i-qabūl* (the acceptable). Copper, also, I coined in the same proportions, and gave each division a particular name. I ordered that on the gold *muhr* of 100, 50, 20, and 10 *tola* the following verse by Āṣaf Khān[2] should be impressed—namely, on the obverse was this couplet:—

> "Fate's pen wrote on the coin in letters of light,
> The Shāh Nūru-d-dīn Jahāngīr";

and between the lines of the verse the Creed (*Kalima*) was impressed. On the reverse was this couplet, in which the date of coinage was signified:—

> "Through this coin is the world brightened as by the sun,
> And the date thereof is 'Sun of Dominion' (Āftāb-i-Mamlakat)."[3]

Between the lines of the verse, the mint, the Hijra year, and the regnal year were impressed. On the *nūr-jahānī*, which is in the place of the ordinary gold *muhr* and exceeds it in weight by 20 per cent. (as 12 to 10), is impressed this couplet of the Amīru-l-umarā:—

> "Shāh Nūru-d-dīn Jahāngīr ibn Akbar Pādshāh
> Made gold's face bright with the sheen of sun and moon."

[1] Erskine's MS. has *iṣārī* for *niṣārī*, and *akhtar-i-qabūl* instead of *khair-i-qabūl*.

[2] This is Blochmann's Āṣaf Khān No. iii, viz. Mīrzā Ja‘far Beg. See pp. 368 and 411.

[3] The words Āftāb-i-Mamlakat yield, according to the numeration by *abjad*, the date 1014 A.H. (1605).

Accordingly, a hemistich was impressed on each face, and also the mint, and the Hijra and regnal year. The *jahāngīrī sikka*, also, which is greater in weight by 20 per cent., was reckoned as equal to a rupee, its weight being fixed in the same manner as that of the *nūr-jahānī* (each was a *tola* in weight, but one was in gold and the other was in silver). The weight of a *tola* is 2½ *misqāls* of Persia and Tūrān.[1]

It would not be good to give all the versified chronograms which were made for my accession. I therefore content myself with the one which Maktūb Khān, the superintendent of the library and picture gallery, and one of my old servants, composed—

"The second lord of conjunction, Shāhinshāh Jahāngīr,
With justice and equity sat on the throne of happiness.
Prosperity, Good Fortune, Wealth, Dignity, and Victory,
With loins girt in his service, stood rejoicing before him.
It became the date of the accession when Prosperity
Placed his head at the feet of the Ṣāḥib-Qirān-i-Ṣānī."[2]

To my son Khusrau a lakh of rupees was presented that he might build up for himself the house of Mun'im Khān,[3] the (former) Khānkhānān, outside the fort. The administration and government of the Panjab was bestowed on

[1] Page 4 of the text is followed by engravings of the coins of Jahāngīr and the inscriptions thereon, for which the editor, Saiyid Aḥmad, says he is indebted to Mr. Thornhill, the Judge of Meerut. They do not show the lines of poetry. There is an interesting article on the couplets on Jahāngīr's coins by Mr. C. J. Rodgers, J.A.S.B. for 1888, p. 18.

[2] The chronogram is ingenious. The words Ṣāḥib-Qirān-i-Ṣānī yield only 1013 according to *abjad*, and this is a year too little. But the verse states that Prosperity (or Fortune), Iqbāl, laid his head at the second lord of conjunction's feet, and the head of Iqbāl, according to the parlance of chronogram-composers, is the first letter of the word, that is, alif, which stands for one (ا) in *abjad*, and so the date 1014 is made up. Ṣāḥib-Qirān-i-Ṣānī means 'the second lord of conjunction,' and is a title generally applied to Shāh Jahān; the first lord of conjunction (i.e. the conjunction of Jupiter and Venus) was Tīmūr.

[3] A great officer under Humāyūn and Akbar. See Āyīn, Blochmann, p. 317.

Sa'īd Khān,[1] who was one of the confidential nobles and connected with my father by marriage. His origin was from the Moghul tribe, and his ancestors were in the service of my forefathers. At the time of his taking leave, as it was said that his eunuchs oppressed and tyrannized over the weak and the poor, I sent a message to him that my justice would not put up with oppression from anyone, and that in the scales of equity neither smallness nor greatness was regarded. If after this any cruelty or harshness should be observed on the part of his people, he would receive punishment without favour.[2]

Again, having previously bestowed on Shaikh Farīd Bukhārī, who had been *Mīr Bakhshī* in my father's service, a dress of honour, a jewelled sword, a jewelled inkstand and pen, I confirmed him in the same post, and in order to exalt him I said to him, "I regard thee as *Ṣāḥibu-s-saif-wa-l-qalam*" ("Captain Sword and Captain Pen"). Muqīm,[3] to whom my father had given at the end of his reign the title of Wazīr Khān and the viziership of his dominions, I selected for the same title, rank, and service. I also gave Khwājagī Fatḥu-llah a dress of honour, and made him a bakhshi, as formerly. 'Abdu-r-Razzāq Ma'mūrī, although when I was prince he had left my service without cause or reason and had gone over to my father, I made bakhshi as formerly, and I gave him a dress of honour. To Amīnu-d-daula, who when I was prince had the post of bakhshi, and without my leave had run away and taken service with my revered father, not looking to his offences I gave the office

[1] Blochmann, p. 331. He had 1,200 eunuchs. He is generally styled Sa'īd Chaghatai. The exact nature of his relationship does not appear. It is not mentioned in his biography in the Ma'āṣir, ii, 403. Perhaps the word (*nisbat*) does not here mean affinity by marriage.

[2] According to the account in Price, p. 16, and in the Ma'āṣir, ii, 405, Sa'īd Khān gave a bond that if his people were oppressive he would forfeit his head.

[3] He does not seem to have had any real power, and he was soon superseded. See Ma'āṣir, iii, 932.

of *Ātish-i-begī*[1] (Head of the Artillery), which he had held under my father. I left all those who were in possession of posts, both inside and outside, in the positions which they had with my father. Sharīf Khān[2] had lived with me from his early years. When I was prince I had given him the title of *khān*, and when I left Allahabad to wait upon my honoured father I presented him with a drum and the *tūmān-togh* (standard of *yāk* tails). I had also promoted him to the rank of 2,500 and given him the government of the province of Bihar. I gave him complete control over the province, and sent him off there. On the 4th of Rajab, being fifteen days after my accession, he waited upon me. I was exceedingly pleased at his coming, for his connection with me is such that I look upon him as a brother, a son, a friend, and a companion. As I had perfect confidence in his friendship, intelligence, learning, and acquaintance with affairs, having made him Grand Vizier, I promoted him to the rank of 5,000 with 5,000 horse and the lofty title of *Amīru-l-umarā*, to which no title of my servants is superior. Though his position might have warranted a higher rank, he himself represented to me that until some notable service on his part had become perceptible to me he would not accept a higher grade than that mentioned (5,000).

As the reality of the loyalty of my father's servants had not yet become apparent, and certain faults and errors and unbecoming intentions which were not approved at the throne of the Creator or pleasing to His creatures had

[1] It appears from Erskine and from I.O. MS. that this is a mistake for Yātish-begī, 'Captain of the Watch,' and that the name is Amīnu-d-dīn, and not Amīnu-d-daula. See Akbarnāma, iii, 474, etc.

[2] Sharīf Khān had been sent by Akbar to recall Jahāngīr to his duty, but instead of coming back he stayed on. He did not accompany Jahāngīr when the latter went off the second time to wait upon his father. Probably he was afraid to do so. Jahāngīr appointed him to Bihar before he left Allahabad to visit his father for the second time. Jahāngīr says Sharīf waited upon him fifteen days after his accession, and on

shown themselves, they of themselves became ashamed. Though on the day of my accession I had forgiven all offences and determined with myself that I would exact no retribution for past deeds, yet on account of the suspicion that had been aroused in my mind about them I considered the Amīru-l-umarā my guardian and protector; although God Almighty is the guardian of all His servants, and is especially so of kings, because their existence is the cause of the contentment of the world. His father, 'Abdu-ṣ-Ṣamad, who in the art of painting had no equal in the age, had obtained from the late king (*Jannat-āshyānī*) Humāyūn the title of *Shīrīn-qalam* (Sweet pen), and in his council had attained a great dignity and was on intimate terms with him (the king). He was one of the chief men of Shīrāz. My honoured father, on account of his former services, paid him great honour and reverence. I made Raja Mān Singh—who was one of the greatest and most trusted noblemen of my father, and had obtained alliances with this illustrious family, inasmuch as his aunt had been in my father's house (i.e. was his wife),[1] and I had married his sister, and Khusrau and his sister Sulṭānu-n-nisā Begam, the latter of whom is my eldest child, were born of her—as before, ruler of the province of Bengal. Though as in consequence of certain of his acts he had no expectation of this favour towards himself, I dignified him with a *chārqab* (vest without sleeves) as a robe of honour, a jewelled sword, and

4th Rajab. This is another proof, if proof were needed, that the copyists have misread the opening sentence of the Tūzuk and have written *hashtam* instead of *bistam*, for 4th Rajab is fifteen days after 20th Jumādā-l-ākhir. The Pādshāhnāma and Khāfī Khān have 20th, and Price and Price's original say that Sharīf arrived sixteen days after the accession.

[1] I.O. MS. 181 and Muḥammad Hādī have Sulṭān Niṣār Begam. Khāfī Khān, i, 245, has Sulṭān Begam, and says she was born in 994. Price's Jahāngīr, p. 20, says she was born a year before Khusrau. She built a tomb for herself in the Khusrau Bāgh, Allahabad, but she is not buried there (see J.R.A.S. for July, 1907, p. 607). She died on 4th Sha'bān, 1056 (5th September, 1646), and was at her own request buried in her grandfather's tomb at Sikandra (Pādshāhnāma, ii, 603–4).

one of my own horses, and sent him off to his province, which is a place of (or can keep up) 50,000 horse. His father was Raja Bhagwān Dās. His grandfather, Raja Bihārī Mal, was the first of the Kachwāha Rājpūts to have the honour of entering my father's service, and he excelled his tribe in truth and sincerity of friendship, and in the quality of valour. After my accession, when all the nobles with their retinues presented themselves at my palace, it came into my mind that I should send this body of retainers under my son, Sultan Parwīz, to make a holy war against the Rānā, who was one of evil deeds, and a foul infidel of the country of Hindustan, and in my father's time had had troops sent constantly against him, but had not been driven off. In a fortunate hour I invested my said son with gorgeous robes of honour, a jewelled waist-sword, a jewelled waist-dagger, and a rosary of pearls intermixed with rubies of great price of the value of 72,000 rupees, 'Irāq and Turkmān horses and famous elephants, and dismissed him. About 20,000 horsemen with nobles and chief leaders were appointed to this service. The first was Āṣaf K͟hān, who in my father's time was one of his confidential servants, and for a long time had been confirmed in the post of bakhshi and afterwards became *dīwān ba istiqlāl* (Chancellor with full powers); him I advanced from the rank of an Amīr to that of Vizier, and promoting him from the command of 2,500 horse to that of 5,000 made him guardian to Parwīz. Having honoured him with a robe of honour, jewelled waist-sword, a horse and an elephant, I ordered that all the *manṣabdārs* (commanders), small and great, should not depart from such orders as he thought proper to give them. I made 'Abdu-r-Razzāq Ma'mūrī his bakhshi and Muk͟htār Beg, Āṣaf K͟hān's paternal uncle, diwan to Parwīz. I also presented to Raja Jagannāth, son of Raja Bihārī Mal, who had the rank of 5,000, a robe of honour and a jewelled waist-sword.

Again, I gave Rānā S͟hankar, cousin of the Rānā—to

whom my father had given the title of Rānā, proposing to send him with Khusrau against the Rānā, but at that time he (Akbar) became a *shanqar* (a falcon, i.e. he died)—a robe of honour and a jewelled sword, and sent him with him.

I presented Mādho Singh, brother's son of Raja Mān Singh, and Rāwal Sāl Darbārī with flags, from this consideration, that they were always present at Court and belonged to the Sekhāwaṭ[1] Rājpūts, and were confidential servants of my father. Each received also the rank of 3,000.

I promoted Shaikh Ruknu-d-dīn the Afghan, to whom when I was prince I had given the title of Shīr Khān, from the grade of 500 to that of 3,500. Shīr Khān is the head of his clan and a very valiant man. He lost his arm by the sword in service against the Uzbegs.[2] 'Abdu-r-Raḥman, son of Shaikh Abu-l-faẓl, Mahā Singh, grandson of Rāja Mān Singh, Zāhid Khān, son of Ṣādiq Khān, Wazīr Jamīl, and Qarā Khān Turkmān were exalted to the rank of 2,000; all these obtained robes of honour and horses, and were dismissed. Manohar also obtained leave to join the expedition. He is of the tribe of the Sekhāwaṭ Kachhwāhas, and on him in his young days my father bestowed many favours. He had learned the Persian language, and, although from him up to Adam the power of understanding cannot be attributed to any one of his tribe, he is not without intelligence. He makes Persian verses, and the following is one of his couplets:—

> "The object of shade in Creation is this:
> That no one place his foot on the light of my Lord, the Sun."[3]

[1] Should be Shaikhāwaṭ.

[2] The R.A.S. and I.O. MSS. have here Umrā instead of Uzbegs. Umrā here stands, I think, for Umr Singh, the Rānā of Udaipūr, and the meaning is that Shīr Khān lost his arm in service against the Rānā.

[3] The point of the verse seems to be that light is regarded as something spread like a carpet on the ground, and that to place the foot upon

If the details were to be described of all the commanders and servants appointed by me, with the conditions and connections and rank of each, it would be a long business. Many of my immediate attendants and personal followers and nobles' sons, house-born ones (*k͟hānazādān*) and zealous Rajputs, petitioned to accompany this expedition. A thousand ahadis, the meaning of which is single ones (Blochmann, p. 20), were also appointed. In short, a force was collected together such that if reliance on the Friend (God) were vouchsafed, it could have embarked on enmity and conflict with any one of the monarchs of power.

> "Soldiers came up from all sides,
> Seizing life from heroes of the world in battle;
> They had no fear of death from the sharp sword,
> No terror of water [1] and no flight from fire;
> In valour singular, in vigour a crowd,
> Anvils in endurance, rocks in attack."

When I was prince I had entrusted, in consequence of my extreme confidence [2] in him, my own *ūzuk* seal [3] to the Amīru-l-umarā (S͟harīf), but when he was sent off to the province of Bihar I made it over to Parwīz. Now that Parwīz went off against the Rānā, I made it over, according to the former arrangement, to the Amīru-l-umarā.

Parwīz was born of Ṣāḥib-Jamāl (Mistress of Beauty),

it is to insult the sun. Compare Price, p. 33; but Manohar's verse is wrongly translated there owing to a badly written MS. For Manohar see Akbarnāma, iii, 221, and Badayūnī, iii, 201, also Blochmann, p. 494, and his article in *Calcutta Review* for April, 1871, also the Dabistān, translation, ii, 53.

[1] Probably here *āb* means both water and the water of the sword. These lines are not in the R.A.S. or I.O. MSS.

[2] Text, *iḥtiyāṭ* (caution); the MSS. have *i'tiqād* (confidence), and I adopt this reading.

[3] Blochmann, p. 52. It was a small round seal. *Ūzūk* or *ūzuk* is a Tartar word meaning a ring, i.e. a signet-ring.

the cousin[1] of Zain Khān Koka, who, in point of affinity, was on the same footing[2] as Mīrzā 'Azīz Koka, in the 34th year of my father's reign, in the city of Kabul, two years and two months after the birth of Khusrau. After several other children had been born to me and had been received into God's mercy, a daughter was born of Karamsī,[3] who belonged to the Rāṭhor clan, and the child received the name of Bihār Bānū Begam. To Jagat Gosā'īn,[4] daughter of the Mota Raja (the fat raja), was born Sulṭān Khurram, in the 36th year of my father's reign, corresponding to A.H. 999,[5] in the city of Lahore. His advent made the world joyous (*khurram*),[6]

[1] Text, *ṣabiyya* (daughter), and this led Blochmann (p. 477, note 2) to say that if Sayyid Aḥmad's text was correct Jahāngīr must have forgotten, in the number of his wives, which of them was the mother of Parwīz. As a fact, Sayyid Aḥmad's text is not correct, though the R.A.S. MS. agrees with it. The two excellent I.O. MSS. have *khwīsh* (relative), which is here equivalent to cousin. So also has the B.M. MS. used by Erskine. According to Muḥammad Hādī's preface Parwīz's mother was the daughter of Khwāja Ḥasan, the paternal uncle of Zain Khān Koka. His birth was in Muḥarram, 998, or 19th Ābān (November, 1589). See also Akbarnāma, iii, 568.

[2] I.e., both were Akbar's foster-brothers.

[3] Price, p. 20, has Karmitty, and says the daughter only lived two months. Karamsī appears twice in the Akbarnāma as the name of a man; see Akbarnāma, ii, 261, and iii, 201. The name may mean 'composed of kindness.' The statement in Price is wrong. Bihār Bānū was married to Ṭahmuraṣ s. Prince Dāniyāl in his 20th year (see Tūzuk, M. Hādī's continuation, p. 400). According to M. Hādī's preface, Karamsī was the daughter of Rāja Kesho Dās Rāṭhor, and her daughter Bihār Bānū was born on 23rd Shahrīwar, 998 (September, 1590). Kesho Dās Rāṭhor is probably the Kesho Dās Mārū of the Tūzuk.

[4] Best known as Jodh Bāī (Blochmann, p. 619).

[5] It is extraordinary that Jahāngīr should have put Shāh-Jahān's birth into A.H. 999. The I.O. MSS. support the text, but the R.A.S. MS. has A.H. 1000, which is without doubt right. Cf. Akbarnāma, Bib. Ind., iii, 603. Later on, a great point was made of his having been born in a millennium. The date is 5th January, 1592.

[6] Muḥammad Hādī says in his preface, p. 6, that Shāh-Jahān's grandfather Akbar gave him the name of Sultan Khurram, 'Prince Joy,' because his birth made the world glad. It was noted that the child was born in the first millennium, and also that, like his father, he was born in the same month as the Prophet.

and gradually, as his years increased, so did his excellencies, and he was more attentive to my father than all (my) other children, who was exceedingly pleased with and grateful for his services, and always recommended him to me and frequently told me there was no comparison between him and my other children. He recognised him as his real child.

After that (Khurram's birth) some other children were born who died in infancy, and then within one month two sons were borne by concubines. One of these I called Jahāndār and the other Shahryār.[1]

About this time there came a petition from Sa'īd Khān with regard to granting leave to Mīrzā Ghāzī, who was a son of the ruler of the province of Thathah (Tattah in Sind).[2] I said that as my father had betrothed his sister to my son Khusrau, please God, when this alliance came into force, I would give him leave to return to Sind.

A year before I became king I had determined that I would drink no wine on Friday eve, and I hope at the throne of God that He will keep me firm in this resolve as long as I live.

Twenty thousand rupees were given to Mīrzā Muḥammad Riẓā Sabzwārī to divide amongst the faqirs and the needy of Delhi. The viziership of my dominions I gave in the proportions of half and half to Khān Beg,[3] to whom when I was prince I had given the title of Wazīru-l-mulk, and to Wazīr Khān [4] (Muqīm), and I gave to Shaikh Farīd Bukhārī, who held the rank of 4,000, that of 5,000.

[1] Gladwin says they were twins, but this seems a mistake. They were both born about the time of Akbar's death.

[2] In MS. No. 310 of Ethé's Cat. of I.O. MSS. Sa'īd Khān is described as giving as his reason for asking for M. Ghāzī that he had adopted him as his son. Price's Jahāngīr, p. 21, says the same thing.

[3] This should be Jān, and is so in I.O. MS. 181.

[4] See Ma'āṣiru-l-umarā, iii, 932. The meaning of the half and half is that the two men were made coadjutors.

I promoted Rām Dās Kachhwāha, whom my father had favoured, and who held the rank of 2,000, to that of 3,000. I sent dresses of honour to Mīrzā Rustam, son of Mīrzā Sulṭān Ḥusain and grandson of S͟hāh Ismā'īl, the ruler of Qandahar, and to 'Abdu-r-Raḥīm K͟hānk͟hānān, son of Bairām K͟hān, and to Īraj and Dārāb, his sons, and to other nobles attached to the Deccan (command). Bark͟hūrdār, son of 'Abdu-r-Raḥmān, son of Mu'ayyid Beg, as he had come to court without a summons, I ordered back to his jagir. [1] It is not according to good manners to go to the king's banquet without a summons, otherwise there would be no forbidding of the doors and walls to the foot of desire.

A month had elapsed after my auspicious accession when Lāla Beg, who while I was prince had obtained the title of Bāz Bahādur, obtained the blessing of waiting on me. His rank, which had been 1,500, was raised to 4,000. I promoted him to the Subah of Bihar and gave him 2,000 rupees. Bāz Bahādur is of the lineage of the special attendants of our family; his father's name was Niẓām, and he was librarian to Humāyūn. Kesho Dās Mārū, who is a Rājpūt of the province of Mairtha and is greater in loyalty than his contemporaries, I promoted to the rank of 1,500. I directed the *'ulamā* and the learned men of Islam to collect those of the distinctive appellations of God which were easy to remember, in order that I might make them into my rosary [2] (*ward*). On Friday eves [3] I associate with learned and pious men, and with dervishes and recluses. When Qilīj K͟hān, who was one of the old retainers of the State in my revered father's reign, was appointed to the government of the province of Gujarat, I presented him with a lakh of rupees for his expenses. I raised Mīrān

[1] In R.A.S. and I.O. MSS. the following passage is a verse. See also Mr. Lowe's translation, p. 16.

[2] *Wird* means 'daily practice,' and may be the word intended here.

[3] Cf. this with the fuller details in Price, p. 22. Following Blochmann, I take S͟hab-i-jum'a to mean Thursday and not Friday night.

Ṣadr Jahān from the rank of 2,000 to that of 4,000. I knew him in my childhood when I read the "Forty Sayings" with Shaikh 'Abdu-n-Nabī,[1] whose history is given in detail in the Akbarnāma. From these early days till now Mīrān Ṣadr Jahān has acted towards me with single-minded loyalty, and I regard him as my preceptor in religious matters (*khalīfa*). Whilst I was prince and before my revered father's illness, and during that time, when the ministers (pillars of the State) and the high nobles had become agitated, and each had conceived some idea of gain for himself and wished to become the originator of some act which could only bring ruin on the State, he had not failed in the activity of his service and devotedness. Having made 'Ināyat Beg,[2] who for a long period in the reign of my father had been Master of Works (*Dīwān-i-buyūtāt*) and held the rank of 700, half-vizier of my dominions in the place of Wazīr Khān, I gave him the high title of I'timādu-d-daula with the rank of 1,500, and I appointed Wazīr Khān to the *Dīwānī* of the province of Bengal, and assigned to him the settlement of the revenues thereof. To Patr Dās, who in the time of my father had the title of Rāy Rāyān, I gave the title of Raja Bikramājīt. The latter was one of the great Rajas of India, and it was in his reign that astronomical observatories were established in India. I made Patr Dās Master of Ordnance, and ordered that he should always have light artillery [3] in the

[1] The text has 'Abdu-l-Ghanī, but this, as the MSS. show and Blochmann has pointed out, is a mistake for 'Abdu-n-Nabī. 'Abdu-n-Nabī was strangled, and the common report is that this was done by Abu-l-fazl. If this be true it is rather surprising that Jahāngīr does not mention it as an excuse for killing Abu-l-fazl. Cf. the account of Mīrān Ṣadr Jahān in Price, p. 24. The "Forty Sayings" is a book by Jāmī. See Rieu, Cat. i, 17, and also Dr. Herbelot s.v. *Arbain*.

[2] This should be Ghiyāṣ Beg. He was father of Nūrjahān. According to the Ma'āṣiru-l-umarā (i, 129), he was commander of 1,000 under Akbar.

[3] *Topkhāna-i-rikāb*, lit. stirrup-arsenal. It means light artillery that could accompany royal progresses. See Bernier, and Irvine, A. of M., 134.

arsenal, 50,000 light guns[1] and 3,000 gun-carriages, ready and in efficient order. He was a *khatrī* by caste, and rose in my father's service from being accountant of the elephants' stables to be diwan and an amir. He is not wanting in military qualities and in administrative skill. I made Khurram, the son of Khān A'ẓam ('Azīz Koka), who had had the rank of 2,000, an officer of 2,500.

As it was my desire that many of the Akbarī and Jahāngīrī officers should obtain the fruition of their wishes, I informed the bakhshis that whoever wished to have his birthplace made into his jagir should make a representation to that effect, so that in accordance with the Chingīz canon (*tūra*) the estate might be conveyed to him by *āl tamghā* and become his property, and he might be secured from apprehension of change. Our ancestors and forefathers were in the habit of granting jagirs to everyone under proprietary title, and adorned the farmans for these with the *āl tamghā* seal, which is an impressed seal made in vermilion (i.e. red ink). I ordered that they should cover the place for the seal with gold-leaf (*ṭilāposh*) and impress the seal thereon, and I called this the *altūn*[2] *tamghā*.

[1] Text, *topchī*, which seems properly to mean a gunner, but the number is preposterous. Cf. Blochmann, p. 470, and Price, p. 28. Price's original has 6,000 *topchī* mounted on camels, and has *pāytakht*, i.e. the capital. Erskine has "To have always in readiness in the arsenal arms and accoutrements for 50,000 matchlock men." This seems reasonable, for even if Jahāngīr ordered 50,000 musketeers, he would not have required them to be kept in the arsenal. It seems to me that though *chī* in Turki is the sign of the agent (*nomen agentis*) it is occasionally used by Indian writers as a diminutive. Thus *topchī* here probably means a small gun or a musket, and in Hindustani we are familiar with the word *chilamchī*, which means a small basin. At p. 301 of the Tūzuk, four lines from foot, we have the word *īlchī*, which commonly means an ambassador—an agent of a people—used certainly not in this sense, and apparently to mean a number of horses. It is, however, doubtful if *īlchī* here be the true reading.

[2] Text, *aknūn* (now), which is a mistake for *altūn* (gold). See Elliot and Dowson, vi, 288. *Āl* is vermilion in Turkī and *altūn* gold. Jahāngīr means that he changed the name from *āl tamghā* to *altūn tamghā*.

I had selected from the other sons of Shāhrukh, Mīrzā Sulṭān,[1] son of Mīrzā Shāhrukh the grandson of Mīrzā Sulaimān, who was a descendant (great-grandson) of Mīrzā Sulṭān Abū Sa'īd and for a long time ruler of Badakhshan, and with consent of my[2] revered father brought him into my service. I count him as a son, and have promoted him to the rank of 1,000. I also promoted Bhāo Singh, son of Raja Mān Singh and the most capable of his sons, from his original rank to that of 1,500. I raised Zamāna Beg,[3] son of Ghayūr Beg of Kabul, who has served me personally from his childhood, and who, when I was prince, rose from the grade of an ahadi to that of 500, giving him the title of Mahābat Khān and the rank of 1,500. He was confirmed as bakhshi of my private establishment (*shāgird-pīsha*).

I promoted Raja Bīr Singh Deo, a Bandela Rajput, who had obtained my favour, and who excels his equals and relatives in valour, personal goodness, and simple-heartedness, to the rank of 3,000. The reason for his advancement and for the regard shown to him was that near the end of my revered father's time, Shaikh Abu-l-faẓl, who excelled the Shaikhzādas of Hindustan in wisdom and learning, had adorned himself outwardly with the jewel of sincerity, and sold it to my father at a heavy price. He had been summoned from the Deccan, and, since his feelings towards me were not honest, he both publicly and privately spoke against me. At this period when, through strife-exciting intriguers, the august feelings of my royal father were entirely embittered against me, it was certain that if he obtained the honour of waiting on him (Akbar) it would be the cause of more confusion, and would preclude me

[1] Mīrzā Sulṭān was great-grandson of Sulaimān.

[2] Perhaps the reference is to the boy's own father. He was alive at this time, and Akbar was not.

[3] This is the man who afterwards rebelled and made Jahāngīr his prisoner.

from the favour of union with him (my father). It became necessary to prevent him from coming to Court. As Bīr Singh Deo's country was exactly on his route and he was then a rebel, I sent him a message that if he would stop that sedition-monger and kill him he would receive every kindness from me. By God's grace, when S͟haik͟h Abu-l-faẓl was passing through Bīr Singh Deo's country, the Raja blocked his road, and after a little contest scattered his men and killed him. He sent his head to me in Allahabad. Although this event was a cause of anger in the mind of the late king (Akbar), in the end it enabled me to proceed without disturbance of mind to kiss the threshold of my father's palace, and by degrees the resentment of the king was cleared away.

I made Mīr Ẓiyā'u-d-dīn of Qazwīn, who had done me service in the days of my princehood and had shown loyalty, commander of 1,000 and accountant of the stables. An order was given that every day thirty horses should be produced before me for the purpose of making presents. I honoured Mīrzā 'Alī Akbars͟hāhī, who is one of the distinguished braves of this family,[1] with the rank of 4,000, and gave him the sarkar of Sambhal as his jagir.

One day the Amīru-l-umarā (S͟harīf K͟hān) greatly pleased me by an incidental remark. It was this: "Honesty and dishonesty are not confined to matters of cash and goods; to represent qualities as existing in acquaintances which

[1] Text, *ulūs-i-Dihli.* Blochmann (p. 482 n.) points out that this is a very doubtful term, as Mīrzā 'Alī came from Badakhshan. On examining three MSS. of the Tūzuk-i-Jahāngīrī I find no word *Dihli*, but the words *īn ulūs*, 'this tribe or family,' and I think this must be the correct reading, and refers to the Timurides. The same phrase occurs at text, p. 173. Blochmann suggests to read *Dūldāy* for *Dihli*, but I think it more probable that the word *Dihli* should be *'ālī.* Mīrzā 'Alī was styled *Akbars͟hāhī*, and no doubt this is why Jahāngīr writes *īn ulūs* or *ulūs-i-'ālī.* Mīrzā 'Alī is often mentioned in the Akbarnāma in connection with the wars in the Deccan, and is generally called Akbars͟hāhī, e.g. at p. 702. For an account of his pathetic death see Blochmann, l.c., the Ma'āṣiru-l-umarā, iii, 357, and the text, p. 163.

do not exist, and to conceal the meritorious qualities of strangers, is dishonesty. In truth, honesty of speech consists in making no distinction between intimates and strangers and in describing each man as he really is."

When I sent off Parwīz I had said to him, "If the Rana himself, and his eldest son who is called Karan, should come to wait upon you and proffer service and obedience, you should not do any injury to his territory." My intention in this recommendation was of two kinds; one, that inasmuch as the conquest of Transoxiana was always in the pure mind of my revered father, though every time he determined on it things occurred to prevent it, if this business could be settled, and this danger dismissed from my mind, I would leave Parwīz in Hindustan, and in reliance on Allah, myself start for my hereditary territories, especially as at this time there was no permanent ruler in that region. Bāqī K͟hān, who, after 'Abdu-llah K͟hān and 'Abdu-l-Mu'mīn K͟hān, his son, had acquired complete independence, had died, and the affairs of Walī Muḥammad K͟hān, his brother, who is now the ruler of that region, had not as yet been brought into proper order. Secondly, to bring about the termination of the war in the Deccan, of which a part in the time of my revered father had been acquired, so that it might come into possession, and be incorporated with the Imperial dominions. My hope is that through the favour of Allah both these undertakings will be accomplished.

> "Though a king should seize the seven climes,[1]
> He still would labour to take others."

I promoted Mīrzā S͟hāhruk͟h,[2] grandson of Mīrzā Sulaimān, (once) the ruler of Badakhshan, who was nearly related to

[1] The MSS. have a different reading, "If a king seize country and climes," etc.

[2] S͟hāhruk͟h was married to Jahāngīr's half-sister, S͟hakaru-n-nisā. He was a Timurid.

my family, and held the rank of 5,000 in my father's service, to the rank of 7,000. The Mīrzā is a true Turk in disposition and simple-minded. My father conferred great honour on him, and whenever he bade his own sons sit he gratified him also with this distinction. Notwithstanding the mischievous propensities of the people of Badakhshan, the Mīrzā in this familiarity never left the right road, or undertook anything that might lead to unpleasantness. I confirmed him in the Subah of Malwa just as my father had kindly conferred it on him.

I conferred on Khwāja 'Abdu-llah, who is of the Naqshbandī family, and in the commencement of his service was an ahadi, and who had risen by degrees to the command of 1,000, but without reason had gone into my father's service, the rank and jagir my father had conferred on him. Although I considered it best for my own prosperity that my attendants and people should go into his (Akbar's) service, yet this had occurred without my leave, and I was rather annoyed at it. But the fact is that he is a manly and zealous man; if he had not committed this fault he would have been a faultless hero (*jawān*).

Abū-n-nabī,[1] the Ūzbeg, who is one of the distinguished inhabitants of Māwarā'a-n-nahr and in the time of 'Abdu-l-Mu'mīn Khān was governor of Mashhad, obtained the rank of 1,500.

Shaikh Ḥasan is the son of Shaikh Bahā.[2] From the days of his childhood to this day he has always been in my service and in attendance on me, and when I was prince was distinguished by the title of Muqarrab Khān. He was very active and alert in his service, and in hunting would often traverse long distances by my side. He is

[1] The MSS. have Abū-l-walī, and this seems more likely.

[2] The MSS. have Bhīnā, and Price's original seems also to have Bhīnā. Muqarrab did not return for about seven months, as this entry could not have been made till then. See p. 35 of Persian text of Tūzuk.

skilful with the arrow and the gun, and in surgery is the most skilful of his time. His ancestors also had been well practised in this profession. After my accession, in consequence of the perfect confidence I had in him, I sent him to Burhanpur to bring the children and dependants of my brother Dāniyāl to wait on me, and sent a message to the Khānkhānān in low and high words[1] and profitable admonitions. Muqarrab Khān performed this service correctly and in a short time, and, clearing off the suspicions which had entered the minds of the Khānkhānān and the nobles of that place, brought those who had been left behind by my brother in safety and security, together with his establishment and property and effects, to Lahore, and there presented them before me.

I promoted Naqīb Khān,[2] who is one of the genuine Sayyids of Qazwīn and is called Ghiyāṣu-d-dīn ʻAlī, to the rank of 1,500. My father had distinguished him with the title of Naqīb Khān, and in his service he had complete intimacy and consideration. Shortly after his accession he (Akbar) had discussed several matters with him, and from this familiarity he called him *ākhūnd*. He has no equal or rival in the science of history and in biographies. There is in this day no chronologist like him in the inhabited world. From the beginning of Creation till the present time, he has by heart the tale of the four quarters of the world. Has Allah granted to any other person such faculty of memory?

[1] Text, *Sukhunān-i-past u buland*. Cf. Steingass, s.v. *past*. Words gentle and severe seem meant.

[2] See Blochmann, p. 447. He is mentioned by Du Jarric as disputing with the Catholic priests before Jahāngīr (see J.A.S.B. for 1896, p. 77). According to Badayūnī, iii, 98, it was Naqīb's father, ʻAbdu-l-Laṭīf, with whom Akbar read (see Akbarnāma, ii, 19). ʻAbdu-l-Laṭīf and his family arrived in 963 (1556). Erskine understands Jahāngīr's remark to mean that Naqīb was his (Jahāngīr's) teacher, but probably Jahāngīr means that it was Naqīb's father who taught Akbar, or he has confounded the father and son. As Naqīb lived till 1023 (1614), he would probably be too young in 1556 to have been Akbar's teacher.

Shaikh Kabīr, who was of the family of the venerable Shaikh Salīm, I had honoured with the title of Shajā'at Khān when I was prince, on account of his manliness and bravery. I now selected him for the rank of 1,000.

On Sha'bān 27th (28th December, 1605) a strange thing was done by the sons of Akhayrāj, son of Bhagwān Dās, the paternal uncle [1] of Raja Mān Singh. These unlucky ones, who bore the names of Abhay Rām, Bijay Rām, and Shyām Rām, were exceedingly immoderate. Notwithstanding that the aforesaid Abhay Rām had done improper (disproportioned) acts, I had winked at his faults. When at this date it was represented to me that this wretch was desirous of despatching his wives and children without leave to his own country and afterwards of himself running away to the Rāna, who is not loyal to this family, I referred to Rām Dās and other Rajput nobles, and said to them that if any one of them would become security for them, I would confirm the rank and jagir of those wretches, and passing over their offences would forgive them. In consequence of their excessive turbulence and bad disposition no one became security. I told the Amīru-l-umarā that as no one would be bound for them, they must be handed over to the charge of one of the servants of the Court until security was forthcoming. The Amīru-l-umarā gave them over to Ibrāhīm Khān Kākar, who was afterwards dignified with the title of Dilāwar Khān, and Ḥātim,[2] second son of Manglī, who held the title of Shāhnawāz Khān.[3] When these wished to disarm these foolish people, they refused, and, not observing the dues of good manners, began, together with their servants, to quarrel and fight. The Amīru-l-umarā reported the circumstance to me, and I ordered them to be

[1] Mān Singh was the adopted son of Bhagwān Dās, and it would appear from this passage that he was his nephew also.

[2] The MSS. have Ḥātim s. Bābūī Manglī, and this is right. See Blochmann, p. 370, n. i, and p. 473.

[3] The MSS. have Shāhwār.

punished according to their deeds. He betook himself to driving them off, and I sent Shaikh Farīd also after him. One Rajput armed with a sword, and another with a dagger stood up to the Amīru-l-umarā. One of his attendants named Quṭb engaged the man with the dagger and was killed. The Rajput also was cut to pieces. One of the Afghan attendants of the Amīru-l-umarā attacked the one who had the sword and killed him. Dilāwar Khān drew his dagger and turned towards Abhay Rām, who with two others was holding his ground, and after wounding one of these fell down after receiving wounds from the three. Some of the ahadis and the men of the Amīru-l-umarā opposed and slew these doomed men. A Rajput drew his sword and turned to Shaikh Farīd; he was met by a Ḥabshī slave, who brought him down. This disturbance took place in the courtyard of the public palace. That punishment served as a warning to many who had not looked to consequences. Abū-n-nabī[1] represented that if such a deed had been done in the Ūzbeg country the whole family and connections of that band of men would have been destroyed. I replied that as these people had been treated kindly and educated by my revered father I carried on the same benevolence to them, and justice demands that many shall not be chastised for the fault of one.

Shaikh Ḥusain Jāmī, who now sits on the cushion of *darwīshī* and is one of the disciples of the dervish of Shiraz,[2] had written to me from Lahore six months before my accession that he had seen in a dream that saints and pious men had delivered over the affairs of the kingdom to that

[1] I.O. MSS. have Abū-l-walī. He was an Ūzbeg, and received the title of Bahādur Khān. See Ma'āṣiru-l-umarā, i, 400, and Akbarnāma, iii, 820 and 839, where he is called Abū-l-Baqā. The real name seems to be Abūl Be or Bey, and this is how Erskine writes the name.

[2] The text seems corrupt. The I.O. MSS. say nothing about Shiraz, but merely that Ḥusain Jāmī was a disciple who had a dervish character (*sīrat*); nor does the R.A.S. MS. mention Shiraz.

chosen one of the Court of Allah (Jahāngīr), and that, rejoicing in this good news, he should await the event, and that he hoped that when it had occurred, the faults of Khwāja Zakariyyā, who was one of the Aḥrāriyya,[1] would be pardoned.[2]

I conferred on Tāsh Beg Furjī,[3] who was one of the old servants of the State, and whom my father had honoured with the title of Tāj Khān, and who had the rank of 2,000, that of 3,000, and I raised Tukhta[4] Beg Kābulī from the rank of 2,500 to that of 3,000. He is a brave and active man, and was greatly trusted in the service of my uncle, Mīrzā Muḥammad Ḥakīm. I promoted Abū-l-Qāsim Tamkīn,[5] who was one of my father's old servants, to the rank of 1,500. There are few men such as he for abundance of children; he has thirty sons, and if his daughters do not number so many they must be half that number. I dignified Shaikh 'Alā'u-d-dīn, grandson of Shaikh Salīm, who had strong connections with me, with the title of Islām Khān, and promoted him to the rank of

[1] That is, descended from the famous Central Asian saint Khwāja Aḥrār.

[2] Something seems to have fallen out of the text and MSS., for this passage is obscure and not connected with the context. It is clearer in Price's version, where it is brought in as part of Jahāngīr's statements about promotions, and where (p. 40) we read as follows:—"I shall now return to the more grateful subject of recording rewards and advancements . . . . On Khwāja Zakariyyā, the son of Khwāja Muḥammad Yaḥyā, although in disgrace, I conferred the rank of 500. This I was induced to do on the recommendation of the venerated Shaikh Ḥusain Jāmī. Six months previous to my accession," etc. Evidently the statement about Zakariyyā's promotion has been omitted accidentally from the Tūzuk. There is a reference to the Shaikh's dream in Muḥammad Hādī's preface to the Tūzuk (p. 15). He says there that it was the saint Bahā'u-l-ḥaqq who appeared in a dream to Ḥusain Jāmī and told him that Sulṭān Salīm would soon be king.

[3] I.e. of Furj or Furg in Persia. But Furjī is a mistake for Qūrchī (belonging to the body-guard). He was a Mogul. See Blochmann, p. 457.

[4] Text has wrongly Pakhta. See Blochmann, p. 469. He received the title of Sardār Khān.

[5] Should be Namakīn. See Blochmann, p. 199.

2,000. He had grown up with me from his childhood, and may be a year younger than I. He is a brave and well-dispositioned youth, and is distinguished in every way above his family. Till now he has never drunk intoxicating drinks, and his sincerity towards me is such that I have honoured him with the title of son.

I have bestowed on 'Alī Aṣghar Bārha, who has not a rival in bravery and zeal, and is the son of Sayyid Maḥmūd K͟hān Bārha, one of my father's old nobles, the title of Saif K͟hān, and thus distinguished him amongst his equals and connections. He is evidently a brave youth. He was always one of the confidential men who went with me to hunt and to other places. He has never in his life drunk anything intoxicating, and as he has abstained in his youth he probably will attain high dignities. I granted him the rank of 3,000.

I promoted Farīdūn, son of Muḥammad Qulī K͟hān Barlās, who held the rank of 1,000, to that of 2,000. Farīdūn is one of the tribe of Chag͟hatāy, and is not devoid of manliness and courage.

I promoted S͟haik͟h Bāyazīd, grandson of S͟haik͟h Salīm, who held the rank of 2,000, to that of 3,000. The first person who gave me milk, but for not more than a day, was the mother of S͟haik͟h Bāyazīd.

[1]One day I observed to the Pandits, that is, the wise men of the Hindus, "If the doctrines of your religion are based on the incarnation of the Holy Person of God Almighty in ten different forms by the process of metempsychosis, they are virtually rejected by the intelligent. This pernicious idea requires that the Sublime Cause, who is void of all limitations, should be possessed of length, breadth, and thickness. If the purpose is the manifestation of the Light of God in these bodies, that of itself is existent equally in

[1] This passage has been translated by Elliot (vi, 289). See also Price (p. 44), where the discussion is fuller.

all created things, and is not peculiar to these ten forms. If the idea is to establish some one of God's attributes, even then there is no right notion, for in every faith and code there are masters of wonders and miracles distinguished beyond the other men of their age for wisdom and eloquence."[1] After much argument and endless controversy, they acknowledged a God of Gods, devoid of a body or accidents,[2] and said, "As our imagination fails to conceive a formless personality (*z̤āt-i-mujarrad*), we do not find any way to know Him without the aid of a form. We have therefore made these ten forms the means of conceiving of and knowing Him." Then said I, "How can these forms be a means of your approaching the Deity?"

My father always associated with the learned of every creed and religion, especially with Pandits and the learned of India, and although he was illiterate, so much became clear to him through constant intercourse with the learned and wise, in his conversations with them, that no one knew him to be illiterate, and he was so acquainted with the niceties of verse and prose compositions that his deficiency was not thought of.

In his august personal appearance he was of middle height, but inclining to be tall; he was of the hue of wheat; his eyes and eyebrows were black, and his complexion rather dark than fair; he was lion-bodied,[3] with a broad chest, and his hands and arms long. On the left side of his nose he had a fleshy mole, very agreeable in appearance, of the size

[1] Jahāngīr's idea is somewhat vaguely expressed, but his meaning seems to be that the ten incarnations do not illustrate any attribute of God, for there have been men who performed similar wonders. The corresponding passage in the text used by Major Price is differently rendered by him, but his version is avowedly a paraphrase, and it appears incorrect in this passage.

[2] Literally, "of the How and the Why."

[3] Text, *s̲h̲īr-andām*, 'tiger-shaped,' which I think means thin in the flank (see Steingass, s.v.). I have taken the translation of the words *malāḥat* and *ṣabāḥat* from Elliot. See his note vi, 376, where the two words seem wrongly spelt.

of half a pea. Those skilled in the science of physiognomy considered this mole a sign of great prosperity and exceeding good fortune. His august voice was very loud, and in speaking and explaining had a peculiar richness. In his actions and movements he was not like the people of the world, and the glory of God manifested itself in him.

> "Greatness in his manner, kingship in his lineage,
> As if Solomon would have put the ring on his finger." [1]

Three months after my birth my sister, Shāhzāda Khānam, was born to one of the royal concubines; they gave her over to his (Akbar's) mother, Maryam Makānī. After her a son was born to one of the concubines, and received the name of Shāh Murād. As his birth occurred in the hill country of Fatḥpūr, he was nicknamed *Pahārī.* When my revered father sent him to conquer the Deccan, he had taken to excessive drinking through associating with unworthy persons, so that he died in his 30th year, in the neighbourhood of Jālnāpūr, in the province of Berar. His personal appearance was fresh-coloured; he was thin in body and tall of stature. Dignity and authority were evident in his movements, and manliness and bravery manifested themselves in his ways. On the night of Jumādā-l-awwal 10th, A.H. 979 (September, 1572), another son was born to one of the concubines. As his birth took place at Ajmīr in the house of one of the attendants of the blessed shrine of the reverend Khwāja Mu'īnu-d-dīn Chishtī, whose name was Shaikh Dāniyāl, this child was called Dāniyāl.

After the death of my brother Shāh Murād, he (Akbar), towards the end of his reign, sent Dāniyāl to conquer the Deccan and followed him himself. When my revered father was besieging Āsīr (Āsīrgarh) he, with a large body of nobles such as the Khānkhānān and his sons, and Mīrzā Yūsuf Khān, invested the fort of Ahmadnagar, and it came

[1] Erskine has "Let Sulaimān place his ring on his finger."

into the possession of the victorious officers about the time that Āsīr was taken. After my father 'Arsh-āshyānī had returned in prosperity and victory from Burhanpur towards his capital, he gave the province to Dāniyāl and left him in possession of that territory. Dāniyāl took to improper ways, like his brother Shāh Murād, and soon died from excessive drinking, in the 33rd year of his age. His death occurred in a peculiar way. He was very fond of guns and of hunting with the gun. He named one of his guns *yaka u janāza*, 'the same as the bier,' and himself composed this couplet and had it engraved on the gun :—

> "From the joy of the chase with thee, life is fresh and new ;
> To everyone whom thy dart strikes, 'tis the same as his bier." [1]

When his drinking of wine was carried to excess, and the circumstance was reported to my father, farmans of reproach were sent to the Khānkhānān. Of course he forbade it, and placed cautious people to look after him properly. When the road to bring wine was completely closed, he began to weep and to importune some of his servants, and said : "Let them bring me wine in any possible way." He said to Murshid Qulī Khān, a musketeer who was in his immediate service : "Pour some wine into this *yaka u janāza*, and bring it to me." That wretch, in hope of favour, undertook to do this, and poured double-distilled spirit into the gun, which had long been nourished on gunpowder and the scent thereof, and brought it. The rust of the iron was dissolved by the strength of the spirit and mingled with it, and the prince no sooner drank of it than he fell down.

> "No one should draw a bad omen : [2]
> If he does, he draws it for himself."

[1] Price translates—
"In pleasure of the chase with thee, my soul breathes fresh and clear ;
But who receives thy fatal dart, sinks lifeless on his bier."

[2] Perhaps referring to the name which Dāniyāl gave to his gun, and which recoiled on himself, but the MSS. and text have *nagīrad*, and not *bagīrad*.

Dāniyāl was of pleasing figure, of exceedingly agreeable manners and appearance; he was very fond of elephants and horses. It was impossible for him to hear of anyone as having a good horse or elephant and not take it from him. He was fond of Hindi songs, and would occasionally compose verses with correct idiom in the language of the people of India, which were not bad.

After the birth of Dāniyāl a daughter was born to Bībī Daulat-Shād whom they named Shakaru-n-nisā Begam.[1] As she was brought up in the skirt of my revered father's care, she turned out very well. She is of good disposition and naturally compassionate towards all people. From infancy and childhood she has been extremely fond of me, and there can be few such relationships between brother and sister. The first time when, according to the custom of pressing the breast of a child and a drop of milk is perceptible, they pressed my sister's breast and milk appeared, my revered father said to me: "Bābā! drink this milk, that in truth this sister may be to thee as a mother." God, the knower of secrets, knows that from that day forward, after I drank that drop of milk, I have felt love for my sister such as children have for their mothers.

After some time another girl was born to this same Bībī Daulat-Shād, and he (Akbar) called her Ārām Bānū Begam.[2] Her disposition was on the whole inclined to excitement and heat. My father was very fond of her, so much so that he described her impolitenesses as politenesses, and in his august sight they, from his great love, did not appear bad. Repeatedly he honoured me by addressing me, and said: "Bābā! for my sake be as kind as I am, after me, to this sister, who in Hindi phrase is my darling

[1] The MSS. have Shakar-niṣār, 'sugar-sprinkling.' She lived into Shāh-Jahān's reign.

[2] She died unmarried in Jahāngīr's reign.

(that is, dearly cherished). Be affectionate to her and pass over her little impolitenesses and impudences."

The good qualities of my revered father are beyond the limit of approval and the bounds of praise. If books were composed with regard to his commendable dispositions, without suspicion of extravagance, and he be not looked at as a father would be by his son, even then but a little out of much could be said.

Notwithstanding his kingship and his treasures and his buried wealth, which were beyond the scope of counting and imagination, his fighting elephants and Arab horses, he never by a hair's breadth placed his foot beyond the base of humility before the throne of God, but considered himself the lowest of created beings, and never for one moment forgot God.

> "Always, everywhere, with everyone, and in every circumstance,
> Keep the eye of thy heart secretly fixed on the Beloved."

The professors of various faiths had room in the broad expanse of his incomparable sway. This was different from the practice in other realms, for in Persia [1] there is room for Shias only, and in Turkey, India, and Tūrān there is room for Sunnis only.

As in the wide expanse of the Divine compassion there is room for all classes and the followers of all creeds, so, on the principle that the Shadow [2] must have the same properties as the Light, in his dominions, which on all sides were limited only by the salt sea, there was room for the professors of opposite religions, and for beliefs good and bad, and the road to altercation was closed. Sunnis and Shias met in one mosque, and Franks and Jews in one church, and observed their own forms of worship.

[1] This must, I think, be the meaning, though according to the wording the statement would seem to be that there is no room for Shias except in Persia. Erskine has "None but Shias are tolerated in Persia, Sunnis in Rūm and Tūrān, and Hindus in Hindustan."

[2] Kings are regarded as shadows of God.

He associated with the good of every race and creed and persuasion, and was gracious to all in accordance with their condition and understanding. He passed his nights in wakefulness, and slept little in the day; the length of his sleep during a whole night and day (*nycthemeron*) was not more than a watch and a half. He counted his wakefulness at night as so much added to his life. His courage and boldness were such that he could mount raging, rutting elephants, and subdue to obedience murderous elephants which would not allow their own females near them—although even when an elephant is bad-tempered he does no harm to the female or his driver—and which were in a state in which they might have killed their drivers or the females, or not have allowed their approach. He would place himself on a wall or tree near which an elephant was passing that had killed its mahout and broken loose from restraint, and, putting his trust in God's favour, would throw himself on its back and thus, by merely mounting, would bring it under control and tame it. This was repeatedly seen.

He ascended the throne in his 14th year. Hemū, the infidel whom the Afghan ruler had raised to high station, collected a wonderful force after King Humāyūn's death, with a stud of elephants such as no ruler of Hindustan had at that time, and he went towards Delhi. Humāyūn had appointed Akbar to drive off some of the Afghans from the foot-hills of the Panjab, but just then he exemplified the hemistich which is a description of the accident and the chronogram of his death—

> "The august monarch (Humāyūn) fell from the roof. The news (of the death) was conveyed to my father by Naẓar-jīvī."[1]

Bairām Khān, who was then his tutor, having collected the nobles who were in the province, chose an auspicious

[1] The chronogram is one year short, yielding 962 instead of 963.

hour and seated him on the throne of rule in pargana Kalānūr, near Lahore.

When Hemū reached the neighbourhood of Delhi, Tardī Beg Khān and a large force that was in the city drew up to oppose him. When the preparations for the combat had been made the armies attacked one another, and, after considerable endeavours and strife, defeat fell on Tardī Beg Khān and the Moguls, and the army of darkness overcame the army of light.

> "All things and battles and fights are of God,
> He knows whose will be the victory.
> From the blood of the brave and the dust of the troops,
> The earth grew red and the heavens black."

Tardī Beg Khān and the other defeated ones took the road to my revered father's camp. As Bairām Khān disliked Tardī Beg, he made this defeat an excuse to put him to death.

A second time, through the pride engendered in the mind of this accursed infidel by his victory, he came out of Delhi with his force and elephants and advanced, while the glorious standards of His Majesty (Akbar) proceeded from Kalānūr for the purpose of driving him away. The armies of darkness and light met in the neighbourhood of Panipat, and on Thursday, Muḥarram 2nd, A.H. 964 (November 5th, 1556), a fight took place. In the army of Hemū were 30,000 brave fighting horsemen, while the *ghāzīs* of the victorious army were not more than 4,000 or 5,000. On that day Hemū was riding an elephant named Hawā'ī. Suddenly an arrow struck the eye of that infidel and came out at the back of his head. His army, on seeing this, took to flight. By chance Shāh Qulī Khān Maḥram with a few brave men came up to the elephant on which was the wounded Hemū, and would have shot an arrow at the driver, but he cried "Do not kill me; Hemū is on this elephant." A number of men immediately conveyed Hemū as he was to the king (Akbar). Bairām Khān represented that it would be proper if the king with his own hand should strike the infidel with a sword, so that obtaining the reward of a ghāzī (warrior of the Faith) he might use this title on the imperial farmans. The king answered, "I have cut him in pieces before this," and explained: "One day, in Kabul, I was copying a picture in presence of Khwāja 'Abdu-ṣ-Ṣamad Shīrīn Qalam, when a form appeared from my brush, the parts of which were separate and divided from each other. One of those near asked, 'Whose picture is this?' It came to my tongue to say that it was the likeness of Hemū." Not defiling his hand with his (Hemū's) blood, he told one of his servants to cut off his head. Those killed in the defeated army numbered 5,000 in addition to those who fell in various places round about.

Another of the well-known deeds of Akbar was the victorious expedition against Gujarat, and his rapid march there, at the time when Mīrzā Ibrāhīm Ḥusain, Muḥammad Ḥusain Mīrzā, and Shāh Mīrzā revolted from this State and went towards Gujarat, and all the nobles of that province, combining with the turbulent of those parts, besieged the fort of Ahmadabad in which was Mīrzā 'Azīz Koka with the royal army. His Majesty, in consequence of the distracted state of Jījī Angā, the mother of the last-named Mīrzā, started for Gujarat with a body of royal troops without delay from the capital of Fathpur. Having covered in the space of nine days the long road which it should take two months to accomplish, sometimes on horseback, sometimes on a camel or in a bullock-cart, he arrived at Sarnāl.

When, on 5th Jumādā-l-awwal, 980 (September 15th, 1572), he reached the neighbourhood of the enemy's camp, he consulted with those who were loyal to him Some said he should make a night attack on the camp. His Majesty, however, said that a night attack was the resort of the faint-hearted and the way of the deceitful, and immediately gave orders to beat the drums and set the horsemen at them. When the river Sābar Mahī (Sābarmatī) was reached, he ordered his men to cross it in order. Muḥammad Ḥusain Mīrzā was agitated by the noise of the army of victory, and himself came forward to reconnoitre. Subḥān Qulī Turk, also with a troop of brave men, went to the river's bank to enquire into the enemy's position. The Mīrzā asked what troops these were. Subḥān Qulī replied that they were of the army of King Jalālu-d-dīn Akbar. That ill-fated one would not believe this, and said his spies had seen the king fourteen days before in Fathpur, and that it was clear Subḥān Qulī was lying. To this Subḥān Qulī rejoined, "Nine days ago the king with this expedition started from Fathpur." "How could elephants have come?" [1] asked the Mīrzā. "What need was there of elephants?" answered Subḥān Qulī. "Young men and heroes who cleave rocks, and are better than famous and raging elephants, have come; the difference between loyalty and sedition will now become known." The Mīrzā, after this conversation, turned aside and began to marshal his troops. The king waited until his advanced guard sent word that the enemy had put on their armour. He then moved forward, and although he sent several times to order the Khān A'ẓam to advance, the latter stood still. It was said to Akbar that, as the enemy was in force, it would be well to remain on his side of the river until the army of Gujarat arrived from within the fort. His Majesty answered: "Always, and especially in this affair, I have put my trust in God. If I had considered routine, I should not have come in this rapid manner. Now that our foe is ready for the fight, we ought not to delay." With these words, and with his innate reliance on God as his shield, he put his horse into the river with a few chosen men whom he had appointed to ride with him. Though it was not supposed

[1] According to the Ṭabaqāt, Elliot, v, 366, what the Mīrzā said was "Where are the elephants?"

that there was a ford, he crossed in safety. He had called for his helmet, but in the agitation of bringing it his armour-bearer dropped the face-guard (*buffe*). His comrades did not regard this as a good omen, but he said at once, "It is an excellent omen, for it has revealed my face."[1] Meantime the wretched Mīrzā arrayed his ranks to fight his benefactor.

> "If thou come out (to fight) with thy benefactor,
> If thou wert the sphere, thou wouldest be reversed."

The Khān A'ẓam had had no idea that the king would cast the shadow of his compassion on these regions with such speed and eagerness, and he believed no one who gave him news of that arrival, until convinced by visible proof. Then, arraying the army of Gujarat, he prepared to march. Meanwhile Āṣaf Khān also sent news to him. Before his army issued from the fort the enemy had appeared from amongst the trees. The king, taking the Divine aid as the security of his courage, started off. Muḥammad Qulī Khān Turk and Tardī Khān Dīwāna came forward with a band of brave followers, and after a little fighting turned rein. On this His Majesty said to Bhagwān Dās, "The enemy are unnumbered and we are few; we must attack with one face and one heart; for a clenched fist is more useful than an open hand." With these words he drew his sword, and with shout of *Allahu-akbar* and *Yā Mu'īn*[2] charged with those devoted to him.

> "The sense of the age evaporated with the clamour,
> The ear of the heavens was split with the shouts."

The royal right and left wings and a band of brave men in the centre fought with valour. Stars (*kaukabā'ī*), which are a kind of firework, were lighted by the enemy; they

[1] The word for 'face-guard' is *pīsh-rūy* (front-face), and Jahāngīr makes his father pun upon the word, saying, "It has loosed (opened) my front-face." Cf. Price, p. 54.

[2] 'The helper.' This is an allusion to Akbar's patron saint, Mu'īnu-d-dīn Chishtī, whose name he adopted as his battle-cry.

twisted about among the thorn-bushes, and created such confusion that a noted elephant of the enemy began to move and threw their troops into disarray. With this the royal centre came up and dispersed Muḥammad Ḥusain and his force. Mān Singh Darbārī overcame his foe under the king's eyes, and Rāgho Dās Kachhwāha sacrificed his life. Muḥammad Wafā, who was of the house-born of the State, behaving very bravely, fell wounded from his horse. By the favour of the Creator who cherishes His servants, and simply through the courage and good fortune of the exalted king, the enemy were scattered and defeated. In gratitude for this great victory the king turned his face in supplication to the throne of his merciful Maker, and poured forth his thanks.

One of the kalāwants (musicians) represented to His Majesty that Saif K͟hān Kokaltās͟h had offered the coin of his life in loyalty to the State, and on enquiry it appeared that when Muḥammad Ḥusain Mīrzā with some of his riffraff was attacking the centre Saif K͟hān met him and fighting valiantly became a martyr. The Mīrzā himself was wounded by the hands of the brave men of the main body. The Kokaltās͟h mentioned is the elder brother of Zain K͟hān Koka.

A strange circumstance was this: on the day before the battle, when the king was eating, he asked Hazāra, who was learned in the science of looking at the shoulder-blades (a kind of divination), to see on whose side the victory would be. Hazāra said: "The victory will be on your side, but one of the chiefs of your army will become a martyr." Whereupon Saif K͟hān Koka said, "Would that this blessing might fall to my lot!"

> "Many an omen that we have treated as jest[1]
> Became true when the star passed by."

[1] The reading in the lithograph seems wrong; the MSS. have *az bāzīcha*, 'in jest.'

In short, Mīrzā Muḥammad Ḥusain turned his reins, but his horse's feet became entangled in the thorn-brake and he fell. An ahadi of the king, Gadā 'Alī by name, found him, and having mounted him before him on his horse took him to the king. As two or three claimed a share in his capture, His Majesty asked who had made him prisoner. "The king's salt," he answered. The king ordered his hands, that had been fastened behind him, to be tied in front. Meanwhile he asked for water. Farḥat K͟hān, who was one of the confidential slaves, struck him on the head, but the king, disapproving of this, sent for his private drinking water and satisfied his thirst. Up to this time Mīrzā 'Azīz Koka and the garrison of the fort had not come out. After the capture of the Mīrzā, His Majesty was proceeding slowly towards Ahmadabad. He had delivered the Mīrzā to Rāy Rāy Singh Rāṭhor, one of the Rajput chiefs, to be put on an elephant and brought with him. Meanwhile Ik͟htiyāru-l-mulk, who was one of the influential Gujarati leaders, made his appearance with an army of nearly 5,000 men. Complete confusion fell upon the royal troops. The king, as his natural valour and lofty disposition required, ordered the drums to be beaten, and Shajā'at K͟hān, Rāja Bhagwān Dās, and some others charged on in front to fight this force. Fearing that the enemy might get possession of Mīrzā Muḥammad Ḥusain, Rāy Rāy Singh's men, by the advice and plan of the aforesaid Raja (Bhagwān Dās), cut off his head. My father did not want to kill him. The forces of Ik͟htiyāru-l-mulk also were dispersed, and he was thrown from his horse into the thorn thicket. Suhrāb Beg Turkmān cut off his head and brought it in. It was only by the grace and power of God that such a victory was won by a small number of men.

In the same way are beyond all reckoning the conquest of the province of Bengal, the capture of well-known and celebrated forts in Hindustan such as Chitor and Rantambhor, the subjection of the province of Khandesh, and the taking of the fort of Āsīr and of other provinces which by the exertions of the royal armies came into the possession of the servants of the State. If these were related in detail it would be a long story.

In the fight at Chitor, the king with his own hand killed Jitmal, the leader of the men in the fort. He had no rival in shooting with a gun, and with the one with which he killed Jitmal, and which was called Sangrām, he killed some 3,000 or 4,000 birds and beasts.[1] I may be reckoned a true pupil of his. Of all sports I am most disposed to that with the gun, and in one day have shot eighteen deer.

Of the austerities practised by my revered father, one was the not eating the flesh of animals. During three months of the year he ate meat, and for the remaining nine contented himself with Ṣūfī food, and was no way pleased with the slaughter of animals. On many days and in many months this was forbidden to the people. The days and months on which he did not eat flesh are detailed in the Akbarnāma.

On the day I made I'timādu-l-mulk diwan, I put Mu'izzu-l-mulk in charge of the *dīwānī-i-buyūtāt* (care of buildings). The latter is a Sayyid of Bākharz,[2] and under my revered father was accountant of the *kurkarāq* department.[3]

On one of my accession days, a hundred of the Akbarī and Jahāngīrī servants were promoted to higher rank and jagirs. At the commencement of the Ramaẓān 'Īd, as it was the first after my accession, I came down to the 'Īdgāh from my auspicious throne. There was a great crowd, and having performed the dues of thanksgiving and praise

[1] Abū-l-faẓl is more moderate; he says (Blochmann, p. 116) that Akbar killed 1,019 animals with Sangrām.

[2] Blochmann says, of Mashhad, p. 381.

[3] The furriery. See Blochmann, pp. 87 n. and 616. *Kurk* means 'fur' in Turki.

I returned to the palace, where according to the verse "From the table of kings favours come to beggars," I commanded a sum of money to be spent in alms and charity. Some lakhs of dāms of this were entrusted to Dūst Muḥammad (afterwards Khwāja Jahān), who divided them amongst faqirs and those who were in want, and a lakh of dāms each was given to Jamālu-d-dīn Ḥusain Anjū (the lexicographer), Mīrzā Ṣadr Jahān, and Mīr Muḥammad Riẓā Sabzawārī to dispose of in charity in different quarters of the city. I sent 5,000 rupees to the dervishes of Shaikh Muḥammad Ḥusain Jāmī, and gave directions that each day one of the officers of the watch[1] should give 50,000 dāms to faqirs. I sent a jewelled sword to the Khānkhānān, and promoted Jamālu-d-dīn Anjū to the rank of 3,000. The office of *Ṣadr* was entrusted to Mīrān Ṣadr Jahān, and I ordered Ḥājī Koka, who was one of my father's foster-sisters,[2] to bring before me in the palace such women as were worthy to be presented with land and money. I promoted Zāhid Khān, son of Muḥammad Ṣādiq Khān, from the rank of 1,500 to that of 2,000.

It had been the custom[3] that when the gift of an elephant or horse was made to anyone, the naqibs and the Masters of the Horse (*Mīr Ākhūrān*) took from him a sum of money as *jilawāna* (bridle-money). I gave orders that this money should be paid by the government, so that people might be freed from the importunities and demands of that set of men.

At this time Sālbāhan arrived from Burhanpur and produced before me the horses and elephants of my deceased brother Dāniyāl. Of the elephants, one male named Mast

[1] The word *yātish* is omitted in text, but occurs in the MSS.

[2] Ḥājī Koka was sister of Sa'ādat Yār Koka (Akbar-nāma, iii, 656). According to Price this passage refers to a widows' fund.

[3] This was one of Akbar's regulations (Blochmann, p. 142). The amount was ten dams on each muhr of the horse's value, calculated on an increase of 50 per cent. See also Price, p. 61.

Alast appeared to me the best, and I gave him the name of Nūr Gaj. A wonderful thing showed itself in this elephant; on the sides of his ears small lumps had grown about the size of melons, and from them came fluid such as drops from an elephant in the rutting season; moreover, the top of his forehead was more prominent than in other elephants. It was a splendid and imposing animal.[1]

I gave to my son Khurram (Shāh-Jahān) a rosary of jewels, with the hope that he might obtain fulfilment of all his desires, both in visible and in spiritual things.

As I had remitted in my dominions customs duties amounting to krors, I abolished also all the transit dues (*sā'ir-jihāt*) in Kabul, which is one of the noted towns on the road to Hindustan. These brought in 1 kror and 23 lakhs of dams. From the provinces of Kabul and Qandahar large sums used to be derived every year from customs (*zakā't*), which were in fact the chief revenue of those places. I remitted these ancient dues, a proceeding that greatly benefited the people of Iran and Turan.

Āṣaf Khān's jagir in the subah of Bihār had been given to Bāz Bahādur; I therefore ordered that a jagir in the Panjab should be given to him. As it was represented to me that a large sum was in arrears in his jagir, and now that the order for exchange had been given its collection would be difficult, I directed that a lakh of rupees should be given to him from the Treasury and the arrears recovered from Bāz Bahādur for the royal revenues.

I promoted Sharīf Āmulī to the rank of 2,500, original and increase. He is a pure-hearted, lively-spirited man. Though he has no tincture of current sciences, lofty words and exalted knowledge often manifest themselves in him. In the dress of a faqir he made many journeys, and he

[1] This passage is not clear, but the peculiarity to which attention is drawn seems rather the prominent forehead than the oozing fluid. Price (p. 62) has a fuller account of this elephant.

has friendship with many saints and recites the maxims of those who profess mysticism. This is his conversation, not his practice (*qāli-ū ast na ḥālī*). In the time of my revered father he relinquished the garments of poverty and asceticism, and attained to amirship and chiefship. His utterance is exceedingly powerful, and his conversation is remarkably eloquent and pure, although he is without Arabic. His compositions also are not devoid of verve.[1]

A garden in Agra had been left by S͟hāh Qulī K͟hān Maḥram, and as he had no heirs I handed it over to Ruqayya Sulṭān Begam, the daughter of Hindāl Mīrzā, who had been the honoured wife of my father.[2] My father had given my son K͟hurram into her charge, and she loved him a thousand times more than if he had been her own.

THE GREAT FEAST OF NAURŪZ.

On the night of Tuesday, Ẕī-l-qa'da 11th, A.H. 1014 (March 11th or 12th, 1606), in the morning, which is the time of the blessing of light, his Eminence the Great Luminary passed from the constellation of the Fish to the House of Honour in the constellation of the Ram. As this was the first New Year's Day after my auspicious accession I ordered them to decorate the porticoes of the private and public halls of the palace, as in the time of my revered father, with delicate stuffs, and to adorn them handsomely. From the first day of the Naurūz to the 19th degree of the Ram (Aries), which is the day of culmination, the people gave themselves over to enjoyment and happiness. Players and singers of all bands and castes were gathered together. Dancing lulis and charmers of India whose caresses would

[1] See Blochmann, pp. 176, 452, and the very full account of him in the Ma'āṣir, iii, 285. Amul is an old city south of the Caspian and west of Astrabad.

[2] She was Akbar's first and principal wife, but bore him no children. She long survived him.

captivate the hearts of angels kept up the excitement of the assemblies. I gave orders that whoever might wish for intoxicating drinks and exhilarating drugs should not be debarred from using them.

> "Cupbearer! brighten my cup with the light of wine;
> Sing, minstrel, for the world has ordered itself as I desire."[1]

In my father's time it had become established that one of the great nobles should prepare an entertainment on each of the 17 or 18 days of the festival, and should present His Majesty the king with choice gifts of all kinds of jewels and jewelled things, precious stuffs, and elephants and horses, and should invite him to take the trouble to come to his assembly. By way of exalting his servants, he would deign to be present, and having looked at the presents would take what he approved of and bestow the remainder on the giver of the entertainment. As my mind was inclined to the comfort and ease of the army and subjects, I this year let them off their gifts with the exception of a few from my immediate retainers, which I accepted in order to gratify them. In those same days many servants of the State obtained higher rank. Amongst them I raised Dilāwar Khān Afghān to 1,500, and I raised Rāja Bāso, who was a landholder of the hill country of the Panjab, and who from the time I was prince till now has kept the way of service and sincerity towards me and held the rank of 1,500, to 3,500. Shāh Beg Khān, the governor of Qandahar, I promoted to 5,000, and Rāy Rāy Singh, a Rājpūt noble, obtained the same rank. I gave 12,000 rupees for expenses to Rānā Shankar.

At the beginning of my reign, a son of that Muẓaffar Gujarātī who claimed to be descended from the rulers of that country lifted up the head of disturbance and attacked and plundered the environs of the city of Ahmadabad.

[1] These are the opening lines of an ode of Ḥāfiẓ.

Some sardars such as Pīm[1] Bahādur Ūzbeg and Rāy 'Alī Bhatī, who were amongst the distinguished and brave men there, became martyrs in that outbreak. At length Rāja Bikramājīt and many mansabdars were provided by me with 6,000 or 7,000 horse, and appointed to assist the army of Gujarat. It was decided that when things had quieted down, by the driving off of those seditious people, Rāja Bikramājīt should be Subahdar of Gujarat. Qilīj Khān, who had been previously nominated to this office, should come to Court. After the arrival of the royal troops the thread of the rebels' union was severed; they took refuge in different jungles, and the country was reduced to order. The news of this victory reached the ear of my state and dignity in the most acceptable of hours (New Year time).

About this time there came a representation from my son Parwīz that the Rānā had left *thāna* Mandal, which is about 30[2] or 40 *kos* from Ajmīr, and had run away, and that a force had been appointed to pursue him; and that it was to be hoped the good fortune of Jahāngīr would cause him to become non-existent.

On the last day of the feast of the New Year, many servants of the State were honoured with favours and increase of rank. Pīshrau Khān was an old retainer and had come from Persia (*wilāyat*) with Humāyūn; indeed, he was one of the men whom Shāh Ṭahmāsp had sent with Humāyūn. His name was Mihtar Sa'ādat. As under my father he was superintendent (*dārogha*) and head (*mihtar*) of the *farrāsh-khāna* (store department), and had no equal in this service, he had given him the title of Pīshrau Khān (the active Khān). Though he was a subordinate (?) servant and had an artificer's disposition (*qalaqchī mashrab*),

[1] Ma'āṣiru-l-umarā, *Yatīm* instead of Pīm or Bīm. See Blochmann, p. 470. Erskine has Saīn Bahādur.

[2] MS. 181 has 34.

I looked to his claims of service and gave him the rank of 2,000.[1]

THE FLIGHT OF KHUSRAU IN THE MIDDLE OF THE FIRST YEAR OF MY REIGN.

Futile[2] ideas had entered the mind of Khusrau in consequence of his youth and the pride youths have, and the lack of experience and the lack of foresight of worthless companions, especially at the time of my revered father's illness. Some of these short-sighted ones, through the multitude of their crimes and offences, had become hopeless of pardon and indulgence, and imagined that by making Khusrau a tool they might conduct the affairs of State through him. They overlooked the truth that acts of sovereignty and world rule are not things to be arranged by the worthless endeavours of defective intellects. The just Creator bestows them on him whom he considers fit for this glorious and exalted duty, and on such a person doth He fit the robe of honour.

> "He who is seized of Fortune cannot be deprived of it;
> Throne and diadem are not things of purchase;
> It is not right to wrest crown and dominion
> From the head which God, the Crown-cherisher, has indicated."

As the futile imaginations of the seditious and short-sighted had no result but disgrace and regret, the affairs of the kingdom were confirmed in the hands of this suppliant

[1] I think Jahāngīr means that though the Khān was an excellent servant in his own line, he was hardly fit for the command of 2,000 or for the title of Khān. Cf. his praise of him at p. 71 (Blochmann, p. 498). He was called Pīshrau probably from his going on ahead with the advance camp, as being in charge of the carpets, etc., as well as because of his personal activity.

[2] In Price's Jahāngīr, p. 15, Jahāngīr states that he had imprisoned Khusrau in the upper part of the royal tower in the castle of Agra. It was from this confinement that Khusrau escaped.

at the throne of Allah. I invariably found Khusrau pre-occupied and distracted. However much, in favour and affection for him, I wished to drive from his mind some of his fears and alarms, nothing was gained until, at last, by the advice of those whose fortune was reversed, on the night of Sunday, Ẕī-l-ḥijja 8th, of the year mentioned (April 6th, 1605), when two gharis had passed, he made a pretence[1] of going to visit the tomb of His Majesty (Akbar), and went off with 350 horsemen, who were his adherents, from within the fort of Agra. Shortly after, one of the lamp attendants who was acquainted with the Wazīru-l-mulk gave him the news of Khusrau's flight. The Vizier took him to the Amīru-l-umarā, who, as the news seemed true, came in a distracted state of mind to the door of the private apartments and said to one of the eunuchs, "Take in my request and say that I have a necessary representation to make, and let the king honour me by coming out." As such an affair had not entered my thoughts, I supposed that news had come from the Deccan or Gujarat. When I came out and heard what the news was, I asked, "What must be done? Shall I mount myself, or shall I send Khurram?" The Amīru-l-umarā submitted that he would go if I ordered it. "Let it be so," I said. Afterwards he said, "If he will not turn back on my advice, and takes up arms, what must be done?" Then I said, "If he will go in no way on the right road, do not consider a crime anything that results from your action. Kingship regards neither son nor son-in-law. No one is a relation to a king."

When I had said these words and other things, and had dismissed him, it occurred to me that Khusrau was very much annoyed with him, and that in consequence of the

[1] Du Jarric says it was in this way that he was allowed to pass the sentinels. Du Jarric gives the date of Khusrau's flight as 15th April, 1606 (this would be New Style). By Sunday night is meant Saturday evening. Sunday was Akbar's birthday.

dignity and nearness (to me) which he (the Amīr) enjoyed, he was an object of envy to his equals and contemporaries.[1] Perhaps they might devise treachery and destroy him. I therefore ordered Mu'izzu-l-mulk to recall him, and selecting in his place Shaikh Farīd Bakhshī-begī commanded him to start off at once, and to take with him the mansabdars and ahadis who were on guard. Ihtimām Khān the *kotwāl* was made scout and intelligence officer. I determined, God willing, to start off myself when it was day. Mu'izzu-l-mulk brought back the Amīru-l-umarā.

About this time, Aḥmad Beg Khān and Dūst Muḥammad Khān had been sent off to Kabul,[2] and had got as far as Sikandra, which was on Khusrau's route. On his arrival they came out of their tents with some of their people, and returned and waited on me with the news that Khusrau had taken the Panjab road and was hastening on. It occurred to me that he might change his route and go somewhere else. As his maternal uncle, Mān Singh, was in Bengal, it occurred to many of the servants of the State that he might go in that direction. I sent out on every side, and ascertained that he was making for the Panjab. Meantime day dawned, and in reliance on the grace and favour of God Almighty, and with clear resolve, I mounted, withheld by nothing and no one.

> "In truth, he who is pursued by sorrow
> Knows not how the road is or how he may travel it.
> This he knows, that horror drives him on:
> He knows not with whom he goes nor whom he leaves behind."

1 Elliot (vii, 292) makes the Amīru-l-umarā envious of his peers, and Jahāngīr apprehensive lest he should destroy Khusrau, but he had just told him that nothing he did against Khusrau would be wrong. Clearly Jahāngīr's fear was that his favourite should be destroyed by Khusrau, or perhaps by the Amīr's treacherous associates.

2 The text has a curious mistake here: instead of *ba Kābul* it has *bakāwal* ('superintendent of the kitchen') as part of Dūst Muḥammad's name. Dūst was not *bakāwal*, but held higher office, and was later put in charge of the fort of Agra and given the title of Khwāja Jahān.

When I reached the venerable mausoleum of my revered father, which is three kos from the city, I begged for aid to my courage from the spirit of that honoured one. About this time they captured and brought in [1] Mīrzā Ḥasan, son of Mīrzā Shāhrukh, who had proposed to accompany Khusrau. He could not deny it when I questioned him, and I ordered them to tie his hands and mount him on an elephant.[2] This was the first good omen manifested through the kindness and blessing of that venerable one. At midday, as it had become exceedingly hot, having rested awhile under the shade of a tree, I said to the Khān A'ẓam that we, with all our composure, were in such a state that we had not taken till now our regular allowance of opium, which it was the practice to take the first thing in the morning, and no one had reminded us of the omission. We might imagine from this what was now the condition of that graceless one (Khusrau).[3]

My trouble was this, that my son without any cause or reason should become an opponent and an enemy. If I should make no endeavour to capture him, the fractious or rebellious would have an instrument, or else he would take his own way and go for an asylum to the Ūzbegs or the Persians, and contempt would fall upon my government. On this account, having made a special point of capturing him, I went on after a short rest two or three kos beyond pargana Mathura, which is 20 kos from Agra, and I alighted at one of the villages of that pargana where there is a tank.

When Khusrau arrived at Mathura, he met Ḥusain Beg Badakhshī, who was of those who had received favours from my revered father and was coming from

[1] Price, p. 6, note.

[2] According to Khāfī Khān (i, 250) he was put to death, unless the expression "claws of death" is merely rhetorical. The Ma'āṣir (iii, 334) says he was imprisoned.

[3] The above obscure passage is explained in Price, p. 69.

Kabul to wait on me. As it is the temperament of the Badakhshīs to be seditious and turbulent, Khusrau regarded[1] this meeting as a godsend, and made Ḥusain Beg the captain and guide of 200 or 300 Badakhshan Aimāqs, who were with him.

Anyone whom they met, they plundered of horses and goods. Merchants and conveyers of goods were plundered by these rascals, and wheresoever they went men's wives and children were not safe from the calamity of these wretches. With his own eyes Khusrau was witnessing the oppression practised in the hereditary dominions of his ancestors, and after being a witness of the improper deeds of these rascals he a thousand times every moment wished death for himself. Finally, he had no remedy but to temporize with and support those dogs. If good luck and fortune had assisted him in his affairs, he would have made repentance and regret his voucher, and come without any deceit to wait on me. God, who knows the world of secrets, knows that I should have passed over his offences entirely and shown him such favour and affection that to the extent of a hair's point no estrangement or fear would have remained upon his mind. Inasmuch as during the lifetime of the late king (Akbar) an intention of joining in the sedition of some of the rebels had manifested itself in his mind, and he knew that this had come to my knowledge, he placed no reliance on my kindness and affection. His mother, while I was prince, in grief at his ways and behaviour and the misconduct of her brother Mādho Singh,[2] killed herself by swallowing opium (*tiryāq*).[3] What shall I write of her excellences and goodness? She had perfect intelligence, and her devotion to me was such that she would have

[1] Elliot (vi, 293) observes that this is a very involved and obscure passage.

[2] Blochmann, p. 418.

[3] The word *tiryāq* means both opium and antidote.

sacrificed a thousand sons and brothers for one hair of mine. She constantly wrote to Khusrau and urged him to be sincere and affectionate to me. When she saw that it was of no use and that it was unknown how far he would be led away, she from the indignation and high spirit which are inherent in the Rajput character determined upon death. Her mind was several times disturbed, for such feelings were hereditary, and her ancestors and her brothers had occasionally showed signs of madness, but after a time had recovered. At a time when I had gone hunting, on Ẕī-l-ḥijja 26th, 1013[1] (May 6th, 1605), she in her agitation swallowed a quantity of opium, and quickly passed away. It was as if she had foreseen this behaviour of her unworthy son.

My first marriage and that at the commencement of my adolescence was with her. After Khusrau's birth I gave her the title of Shāh Begam. When she could not endure the bad conduct of her son and brother towards me she became disgusted with life and died, thereby escaping the present grief and sorrow. In consequence of her death, from the attachment I had for her, I passed some days without any kind of pleasure in life or existence, and for four days, which amount to 32 watches, I took nothing in the shape of food or drink. When this tale was told to my revered father, a letter of condolence of excessive kindness and affection reached this devoted disciple, and he sent me a robe of honour and the auspicious turban tied just as he had taken it off his head. This favour threw water on the flame of my grief and afforded complete quiet and repose to my unquietude and disturbance. My intention in relating these circumstances is to point out that no evil fortune is greater than when a son, through the impropriety

[1] Blochmann, relying on Khāfī Khān, puts her death in 1011, and the Akbar-nāma (iii, 826) puts it in 1012. The chronogram in the Khusrau Bāgh yields 1012. See J.R.A.S. for July, 1907, p. 604.

of his conduct and his unapproved methods of behaviour, causes the death of his mother and becomes contumacious and rebellious to his father, without cause or reason, but simply through his own imaginations and futile ideas, and chooses to avoid the blessing of waiting upon him. Inasmuch as the Almighty Avenger lays a proper punishment on each action, of necessity his condition finally came to this, that he was caught under the worst circumstances, and falling from a position of trust became captive to perpetual incarceration.

> "When the man of sense behaves as if drunk,
> He puts his foot in a snare, his head in a noose."

To sum up, on Tuesday, Z̲ī-l-ḥijja 10th, I alighted at the station of Hoḍal.[1] S̲h̲aik̲h̲ Farīd Bak̲h̲s̲h̲ī and a band of valiant men were chosen to pursue K̲h̲usrau and became the vanguard of the victorious army. I sent back Dūst Muḥammad, who was in attendance on me, on account of his previous service and his white beard, to take charge of the fort of Agra and of the zanāna and the treasuries. When leaving Agra, I had placed the city in the charge of I'timādu-d-daula and Wazīru-l-mulk. I now said to Dūst Muḥammad, "As we are going to the Panjab, and that province is in the diwani of I'timādu-d-daula, you will despatch him to us, and will imprison and keep watch over the sons[2] of Mīrzā Muḥammad Ḥakīm who are in Agra; as when such proceedings manifest themselves in the son of one's loins what may one expect from nephews and cousins?" After the dispatch of Dūst Muḥammad, Mu'izzu-l-mulk became bakhshi.

On Wednesday I alighted at Palwal, and on Thursday at Farīdābād; on Friday, the 13th, I reached Delhi.

[1] Where Lord Bellomont died in 1656. See Manucci (Irvine), i, 71.

[2] Probably this means the grandsons. At p. 329 it is mentioned that the grandsons had been confined in Gwalior up to the 16th year.

From the dust of the road (i.e. immediately) I hastened to the venerated tomb of Humāyūn, and there besought help in my purpose, and with my own hand distributed money to poor persons and dervishes. Thence turning to the shrine of the venerable saint Shaikh Niẓāmu-d-dīn Auliyā, I performed the dues of pilgrimage. After this I gave a portion[1] of money to Jamālu-d-dīn Ḥusain Anjū and another portion to Ḥakīm Muẓaffar that they might divide it amongst the poor and dervishes. On Saturday the 14th I stayed in Sarāy Narela.[2] This rest-house (*sarāy*) Khusrau had burned as he went.

The rank of Āqā Mullā, brother of Āṣaf Khān, who had been exalted by becoming my servant, was fixed in original and increase at 1,000 with 300 horse. He was in close attendance during this journey. Considering that some of the Aimāqs attached to the royal army were in league with Khusrau, and fearing that consequently some fraud or sedition might enter their minds, 2,000 rupees were given to their leaders to distribute amongst their men and make them hopeful of the Jahāngīrī favour. I gave money to Shaikh Faẓlu-llah and Rāja Dhīrdhar to distribute to faqirs and brahmans on the road. I gave orders that to Rānā Shankar in Ajmir should be given 30,000 rupees by way of assistance for his expenditure.

On Monday, the 16th, I reached the pargana of Pānīpat.[3] This station and place used to be very propitious to my gracious father and honoured ancestors, and two great victories had been gained in it. One was the defeat of Ibrāhīm Lodī, which was won by the might of the victorious hosts of His Majesty Firdūs-makānī. The story of this has been written in the histories of the time.

[1] *Pāra*, qu. 'a heap'?

[2] Narela is said to be 15½ miles north-west of Delhi. William Finch, in his itinerary, mentions the stage as Nalera, a name that corresponds with Jahāngīr's.

[3] 53 miles north of Delhi.

The second victory was over the wicked Hemū, and was manifested from the world of fortune in the beginning of the reign of my revered father, as has been described by me in detail.

At the time that Khusrau had left Delhi and was proceeding to Panipat, it happened that Dilāwar Khān had arrived there. When shortly before Khusrau's arrival he heard of this affair, he sent his children across the Jumna and bravely determined to hasten on and throw himself into the fort of Lahore before Khusrau should arrive. About this time 'Abdu-r-Raḥīm also reached Panipat from Lahore, and Dilāwar Khān suggested to him that he too should send his children across the river, and should stand aside and await the victorious standards of Jahāngīr. As he was lethargic and timid, he could not make up his mind to do this, and delayed so much that Khusrau arrived. He went out and waited on him, and either voluntarily or in a state of agitation agreed to accompany him. He obtained the title of Malik Anwar and the position of vizier. Dilāwar Khān, like a brave man, turned towards Lahore, and on his road informed everyone and everybody of the servants of the court and the *karoriyān*, and the merchants whom he came across, of the exodus of Khusrau. Some he took with him, and others he told to stand aside out of the way. After that, the servants of God were relieved of the plundering by robbers and oppressors. Most probably, if Sayyid Kamāl in Delhi, and Dilāwar Khān at Panipat, had shown courage and determination, and had blocked Khusrau's path, his disorderly force would not have been able to resist and would have scattered, and he himself would have been captured. The fact is that their talents (*himmat*) were not equal to this, but afterwards each made amends for his fault, viz., Dilāwar Khān, by his rapid march, entered the fort of Lahore before Khusrau reached it, and by this notable service made amends for his earlier shortcoming, and Sayyid Kamāl manfully exerted himself in the engagement with Khusrau, as will be described in its own place.

On Ẕī-l-ḥijja 17th the royal standards were set up in the pargana of Karnāl. Here I raised ʻĀbidīn Khwāja, son of Khwāja Kalān Jūybārī and *pīrzāda* (spiritual adviser), son of ʻAbdu-llah Khān Ūzbeg, who had come in the time of my revered father, to the rank of 1,000. Shaikh Niẓām Thaneswarī, who was one of the notorious impostors (*shayyādān*) of the age, waited on Khusrau, and having gratified him with pleasant news, again[1] led him out of the (right) path, and then came to wait on me. As I had heard of these transactions, I gave him his road expenses and told him to depart for the auspicious place of pilgrimage (Mecca). On the 19th the halt was in pargana Shāhābād. Here there was very little water, but it happened that heavy rain fell, so that all were rejoiced.

I promoted Shaikh Aḥmad Lāhorī, who from my princehood had filled the relationship of service and discipleship and the position of a house-born one (*khānazāda*) to the office of Mīr-i-ʻAdl (Chief Justice). Disciples[2] and sincere followers were presented on his introduction, and to each it was necessary to give the token[3] and the likeness (*shast*

[1] Instead of *tāza* the MSS. have *pāra*, and the meaning seems to be that he accompanied Khusrau for some distance. In Price's Jahāngīr (p. 81) it is said that Niẓām received 6,000 rupees.

[2] This is an interesting passage, because it is Jahāngīr's account of his father's 'Divine Faith.' But it is obscure, and copyists seem to have made mistakes. It is explained somewhat by the MS. used by Price (trans., pp. 82, 83), where more details are given than in the text. It is there stated that Aḥmad was Mīr-i-ʻAdl of Jahāngīr before the latter's accession.

[3] The text has *dast u sīna* (hand and bosom), but the correct words, as is shown in the I.O. MS., No. 181, are *shast u shabiha* or *shabah*, and these refer to the ring or token and the portrait given by Akbar to the followers of the 'Divine Faith.' See Blochmann, pp. 166 n. and 203; and Badayūnī, ii, 338. Aḥmad appears to be the Aḥmad *Sūfī* of Blochmann, pp. 208, 209, and of Badayūnī, ii, 404, and Lowe, p. 418. He was a member of the 'Divine Faith.'

u shabah). They were given on his recommendation (?). At the time of initiation some words of advice were given to the disciple: he must not confuse or darken his years with sectarian quarrels, but must follow the rule of universal peace with regard to religions; he must not kill any living creature with his own hand, and must not flay anything. The only exceptions are in battle and the chase.

> "Be not the practiser of making lifeless any living thing,
> Save in the battlefield or in the time of hunting."

Honour the luminaries (the Sun, Moon, etc.), which are manifesters of God's light, according to the degree of each, and recognize the power and existence of Almighty God at all times and seasons. Be careful indeed that whether in private or in public you never for a moment forget Him.

> "Lame or low[1] or crooked or unrefined,
> Be amorous of Him and seek after Him."

My revered father became possessed of these principles, and was rarely void of such thoughts.

At the stage of Alūwa (?)[2] I appointed Abū-n-nabī (?)[3] Ūzbeg with fifty-seven other mansabdars to assist Shaikh Farīd, and gave the force 40,000 rupees for its expenses. To Jamīl Beg were given 7,000 rupees to divide among the Aimāqs (cavalry). I also presented Mīr Sharīf Āmulī[4] with 2,000 rupees.

On Tuesday the 24th of the same month they captured five of the attendants and comrades of Khusrau. Two of

[1] Text, *pūj* or *pūch*, but the manuscript reading *lūk* is preferable. Erskine's MS. has *lūj*, naked.

[2] Price (p. 83) has Anand or Anwand. Apparently Alūwa is right; it is a place 18 miles north-west of Umballa. Cf. "India under Aurangzib," by J. N. Sarkar.

[3] Abū-l-Bey, the Abū-l-Baqā of Akbar-nāma, iii, 820.

[4] A member of the 'Divine Faith' (Blochmann, p. 452, etc.).

these, who confessed to his service, I ordered to be thrown under the feet of elephants, and three who denied were placed in custody that enquiry might be made. On Farwardīn 12th of the first year of my reign, Mīrzā Ḥusain and Nūru-d-dīn Qulī the *kotwāl* entered Lahore, and on the 24th of the same month a messenger of Dilāwar Khān arrived (there) with news that Khusrau was moving on Lahore and that they should be on their guard. On the same day the city gates were guarded and strengthened, and two days later Dilāwar Khān entered the fort with a few men and began to strengthen the towers and walls. Wherever these were broken and thrown down he repaired them, and, placing cannon and swivel guns on the citadel, he prepared for battle. Assembling the small number of the royal servants who were in the fort, they were assigned their several duties, and the people of the city also with loyalty gave their assistance. Two days later, and when all was ready, Khusrau arrived, and, having fixed a place for his camp, gave orders to invest[1] the city and to prepare for battle, and to burn one of the gates on any side where one could be got at. "After taking the fort," he said to his wicked crew, "I will give orders to plunder the city for seven days and to make captive the women and children."

This doomed lot set fire to a gate, and Dilāwar Beg Khān, Ḥusain Beg the dīwān, and Nūru-d-dīn Qulī the kotwal built a wall inside opposite the gateway.

Meantime Sa'īd Khān, who was one of those appointed to Kashmir and was now encamped on the Chenāb, having heard the news, started rapidly for Lahore. When he reached the Ravi he sent word to the garrison of the fort that he came with a loyal intention and that they should admit him. They sent someone at night and conducted him and some of his men inside. When the siege had

[1] The text has *qatl* by mistake for *qabl*.

lasted nine days, news of the approach of the royal army came repeatedly to K͟husrau and his adherents. They became helpless (*bī pā*), and made up their minds that they must face the victorious army.

As Lahore is one of the greatest places in Hindustan, a great number of people gathered in six or seven days. It was reported on good authority that 10,000 or 12,000 horse were collected, and had left the city with the view of making a night attack on the royal vanguard. This news was brought to me at the *sarāy* of Qāẓī 'Alī on the night of Thursday the 16th. Although it rained heavily in the night I beat the drum of march and mounted. Arriving in Sulṭānpūr at dawn I remained there till noon. By chance, at this place and hour the victorious army encountered that ill-fated band. Mu'izzu-l-mulk had brought a dish of roast meat,[1] and I was turning towards it with zest when the news of the battle was brought to me. Though I had a longing to eat the roast meat, I immediately took a mouthful by way of augury and mounted, and without waiting for the coming up of men and without regard to the smallness of my force I went off in all haste. However much I demanded my *chiltah* (wadded coat), they did not produce it. My only arms were a spear and sword, but I committed myself to the favour of God and started off without hesitation. At first my escort did not number more than fifty horsemen; no one had expected a fight that day. In fine, when I reached the head of the bridge of Gobindwāl,[2] 400 or 500 horse, good and bad, had come together. When I had crossed the bridge the news of a victory was brought to me. The bearer of the good news was S͟hamsī, *tūs͟hakchī* (wardrobe man), and for his good news he obtained the title of

[1] *Biryānī*. See Blochmann, p. 60.

[2] The Gundvāl of Tiefenthaler, i, 113. Cunningham, in his history of the Sikhs, spells it Goīndwāl. It is on the Beas.

K͟hūs͟h-k͟habar K͟hān. Mīr Jamālu-d-dīn Ḥusain, whom I had sent previously to advise K͟husrau, came up at the same time and said such things about the number and bravery of K͟husrau's men as frightened his hearers. Though news of the victory came continuously, this simple-minded Sayyid would not believe it, and expressed incredulity that such an army as he had seen could be defeated by S͟haik͟h Farīd's force, which was small and not properly equipped. When they brought K͟husrau's litter[1] with two of his eunuchs, the Mīr admitted what had happened. Then, alighting from his horse, he placed his head at my feet and professed every kind of humility and submission, and said that there could be no higher or more lofty fortune than this.

In this command S͟haik͟h Farīd behaved with sincerity and devotion. The Sayyids of Bārha, who are of the brave ones of the age, and who have held this place in every fight in which they have been, formed the van. Saif K͟hān, son of Sayyid Maḥmūd K͟hān Bārha, the head of the tribe, had shown great bravery and had received seventeen wounds. Sayyid Jalāl, also of the brethren of this band, received an arrow in his temple and died a few days later. At the time when the Sayyids of Bārha, who were not more than fifty or sixty in number, having received wounds from 1,500 Badak͟hs͟hī horsemen, had been cut to pieces, Sayyid Kamāl, who, with his brothers, had been appointed to support the van, came up on the flank and fought with wondrous bravery and manliness. After that the men of the right wing raised the cry of *Pāds͟hāh salāmat* ("Long live the King") and charged, and the rebels hearing the words, gave up and scattered abroad to various hiding-places. About 400 Aimāqs became crushed on the plain of anger and overcome by the

[1] The text has *singhāsan* instead of *sukhāsan*. Kāmgār Ḥusainī has *sukhpāl*.

victorious army. Khusrau's box of jewels and precious things which he had always with him, fell into our hands.

> "Who thought that this boy of few years
> Would behave so badly to his sire?
> At the first taste of the cup he brings up the lees.
> He melts away my glory and his own modesty.
> He sets on fire[1] the throne of Khūrshīd,
> He longs for the place of Jamshīd."

Short-sighted men in Allahabad had urged me also to rebel against my father. Their words were extremely unacceptable and disapproved by me. I know what sort of endurance a kingdom would have, the foundations of which were laid on hostility to a father, and was not moved by the evil counsels of such worthless men, but acting according to the dictates of reason and knowledge I waited on my father, my guide, my *qibla*,[2] and my visible God, and as a result of this good purpose it went well with me.

In the evening of the day of Khusrau's flight I gave Rāja Bāso, who is a trusty zamindar of the hill-country of Lahore, leave to go to that frontier, and, wherever he heard news or trace of Khusrau, to make every effort to capture him. I also appointed Mahābat Khān and Mīrzā 'Alī Akbarshāhī to a large force, which was to pursue Khusrau in whatever direction he might go. I resolved with myself that if Khusrau went to Kabul, I would follow him and not turn back till he was captured. If not delaying in Kabul he should go on to Badakhshan and those regions, I would leave Mahābat Khān in Kabul and return myself (to India). My reason for not going to Badakhshan was that that wretch would (in that case) certainly ally himself with the Ūzbegs, and the disgrace would attach to this State.

[1] Instead of the *basūzānād* of the text, the MSS. have *bashūrānad*, he defiles. In the last line they have *jāy* instead of *takht*.

[2] I.e. the place to which to turn in prayer.

On the day on which the royal troops were ordered to pursue Khusrau, 15,000 rupees were given to Mahābat Khān and 20,000 to the ahadis, and 10,000 more were sent with the army to be given to whom it might be necessary to give it on the way.

On Saturday, the 28th, the victorious camp was pitched at Jaipāl,[1] which lies seven kos from Lahore. On the same day Khusrau arrived with a few men on the bank of the Chenāb. The brief account of what had happened is that after his defeat those who had escaped with him from the battle became divided in opinion. The Afghans and Indians, who were mostly his old retainers, wished to double back like foxes into Hindustan, and to become a source of rebellion and trouble there. Ḥusain Beg, whose people and family and treasure were in the direction of Kabul, suggested going to Kabul. In the end, as action was taken according to the wish of Ḥusain Beg, the Hindustanis and the Afghans decided to separate themselves from him. On arriving at the Chenāb, he proposed to cross at the ferry of Shāhpūr, which is one of the recognized crossings, but as he could find no boats there he made for the ferry of Sodharah, where his people got one boat without boatmen and another full of firewood and grass.

The ferries over the rivers had been stopped because before Khusrau's defeat orders had been given to all the jagirdars and the superintendents of roads and crossings in the subah of the Panjab that as this kind of dispute had arisen they must all be on the alert. Ḥusain Beg wished to transfer the men from the boat with firewood and grass to the other, so that they might convey Khusrau across. At this juncture arrived Kīlan,[2] son-in-law of Kamāl

[1] Elliot (vi, 299) has Jahān, and the word in the MSS. does not look like Jaipāl.

[2] This word appears to be a mistake; it is not in the MSS.

Chaudharī of Sodharah, and saw a body of men about to cross in the night. He cried out to the boatmen that there was an order from the king Jahāngīr forbidding unknown men from crossing in the night, and that they must be careful. Owing to the noise and uproar, the people of the neighbourhood gathered together, and Kamāl's son-in-law took from the boatmen the pole with which they propel the boat, and which in Hindustani is called *ballī*, and thus made the boat unmanageable. Although money was offered to the boatmen, not one would ferry them over. News went to Abū-l-Qāsim Namakīn, who was at Gujarat, near the Chenāb, that a body of men were wanting to cross the river by night, and he at once came to the ferry in the night with his sons and some horsemen. Things went to such a length that Ḥusain Beg shot arrows at the boatmen,[1] and Kamāl's son-in-law also took to shooting arrows from the river-bank. For four kos the boat took its own way down the river, until at the end of the night it grounded, and try as they would they could not get it off. Meantime it became day. Abū-l-Qāsim and Khwāja Khiẓr Khān, who by the efforts of Hilāl Khān had assembled on this (? the west) side of the river, fortified its west bank, and the zamindars fortified it on the east.

Before this affair of Khusrau's, I had sent Hilāl Khān as *sazāwal* to the army appointed for Kashmīr under Sa'īd Khān, and by chance he arrived in the neighbourhood (of the ferry) that same night; he came in the nick of time, and his efforts had great effect in bringing together Abū-l-Qāsim Khān Namakīn, and Khwāja Khiẓr Khān in the capture of Khusrau.

On the morning of Sunday, the 24th of the aforesaid month, people on elephants and in boats captured Khusrau, and on Monday, the last day of the month, news of this

[1] When the boat stuck, the boatmen swam ashore, and it was probably then that Ḥusain shot at them. See Blochmann, p. 414, n. 2.

reached me in the garden of Mīrzā Kāmrān. I immediately ordered the Amīru-l-umarā to go to Gujarat and to bring Khusrau to wait on me.

In counsels on State affairs and government it often happens that I act according to my own judgment and prefer my own counsel to that of others. In the first instance I had elected to wait on my revered father from Allahabad in opposition to the advice of my faithful servants, and I obtained the blessing of serving him, and this was for my spiritual and temporal good. By the same course of conduct I had become king. The second instance was the pursuit of Khusrau, from which I was not held back by taking time to ascertain the (auspicious) hour, etc., and from which I took no rest until I captured him. It is a strange thing that after I had started I asked Ḥakīm 'Alī, who is learned in mathematics, how the hour of my departure had been (i.e. whether propitious or not), and he replied that in order to obtain my object if I had wished to select an hour, there could not have been for years one selected better than that in which I mounted.

On Thursday, Muḥarram 3rd, 1015, in Mīrzā Kāmrān's garden, they brought Khusrau before me with his hands tied and chains on his legs from the left side[1] after the manner and custom of Chingīz Khān. They made Ḥusain Beg stand on his right hand and 'Abdu-r-Raḥīm on his left. Khusrau stood weeping and trembling between them. Ḥusain Beg, with the idea that it might profit him, began to speak wildly. When his purport became apparent to me I did not allow him to continue talking, but handed over Khusrau in chains, and ordered these two villains to be put in the skins of an ox and an ass, and that they

[1] "With a chain fastened from his left hand to his left foot, according to the law of Chingīz Khān" (Gladwin's Jahāngīr, quoted by Elliot, vi, 507). But apparently what is meant is that Khusrau was led up from the left side of the emperor.

should be mounted on asses with their faces to the tail[1] and thus taken round the city. As the ox-hide dried more quickly than that of the ass, Ḥusain Beg remained alive for four watches and died from suffocation. 'Abdu-r-Raḥīm, who was in the ass's skin and to whom they gave some refreshment from outside, remained alive.

From Monday, the last day of Ẕī-l-ḥijja, until the 9th of Muḥarram of the aforesaid year, I remained in Mīrzā Kāmrān's garden because the time was unpropitious.[2] I bestowed Bhairawal,[3] where the battle had taken place, on Shaikh Farīd, and rewarded him with the high title of Murtaẓā Khān. For the sake of good government I ordered posts to be set up on both sides of the road from the garden to the city, and ordered them to hang up and impale the seditious Aimāqs and others who had taken part in the rebellion. Thus each one of them received an extraordinary punishment. I gave headship to those landholders who had shown loyalty, and to every one of the Chaudharīs between the Jhelam and the Chenāb I gave lands for their support.

Of Ḥusain Beg's property there were obtained from the house of Mīr Muḥammad Bāqī nearly seven lakhs of rupees. This was exclusive of what he had made over to other places and of what he had with him. After this, whenever his name is mentioned, the words[4] *gāwān u kharān*

[1] Du Jarric, in his history of the Jesuit Missions, gives some details about the punishment. The bullock and ass were slaughtered on the spot and their skins were sewed on the bodies of the unhappy men. Horns and ears were left on the skins.

[2] Perhaps the meaning is that the weather was bad.

[3] The proper form seems to be Bhaironwāl, the Bhyrowal of the maps. It is on the right bank of the Bīāh (Beas) on the road from Jalandhar to Amritsar. See Blochmann, p. 414, note.

[4] The words are omitted in the text. Erskine read in his MS. *gāu jizwan,* which I do not understand. The I.O. MSS. and B.M. MS. Or 3276 have *gāwān u kharān.* Ḥusain Beg, whose proper name was Ḥasan, was a brave soldier, and did good service under Akbar. See his biography in Blochmann, p. 454.

(bullocks and asses) will be used. When he came to this Court in company with Mīrzā Shāhrukh he had one horse. By degrees his affairs flourished so that he became possessed of treasure both visible and buried, and projects of this kind entered his mind.

While Khusrau's affair was still in the will of God, as there was no actual governor between Afghanistan and Agra, which is a source of sedition and mischief, and, fearing that Khusrau's affair might be prolonged, I ordered my son Parwīz to leave some of the sardars to look after the Rānā and to come to Agra with Āṣaf Khān and a body of those nearly connected with him in the service. He was to consider the protection and management of that region his special charge. But by the blessed favour of Allah, Khusrau's affair was settled before Parwīz arrived in Agra; I accordingly ordered my aforesaid son to come and wait on me.

On Wednesday, Muḥarram 8th, I auspiciously entered the fort of Lahore. A number of loyalists represented to me that my return to Agra would be for the good of the State at this time when much was going amiss in Gujarat, in the Deccan, and in Bengal. This counsel did not meet with my approval, for the reports of Shāh Beg Khān, the governor of Qandahar, showed that the officers of the Persian border were meditating an attack on that fortress. They had been moved thereto by the machinations of the residuum of the Mirzas of Qandahar's army, which was always shaking the chain of contention. The Persian officers had written letters to these malcontents, and there was likelihood of a disturbance. It occurred to me that the death of His Majesty Akbar and the unreasonable outbreak of Khusrau might put an edge on their design, and that they might attack Qandahar. What had occurred to my mind became a realized fact. The governor of Farāh, the Malik of Sīstan, and the jagirdars of that neighbourhood, with the assistance of Ḥusain Khān, the governor of Herat, invaded Qandahar. Praise is due to the manliness and courage of Shāh Beg Khān, who planted his foot firmly like a man, and strengthened the fort, and seated himself on the top of the third (?) citadel of the aforesaid fort in such a manner that outsiders could see his entertainments. During the siege he girded not his loins, but with bare head and feet arranged parties of pleasure; yet no day passed that he did not send a force from the fort to meet the foe and did not make manly efforts. This went on as long as he was in the fort. The Qizilbāsh army had invested on three sides. When news of this reached Lahore it was clearly advisable to remain in that neighbourhood. A large force was immediately appointed under the leadership of Mīrzā Ghāzī, who was accompanied by a number of men of rank and servants of the Court, such as Qarā Beg and Tukhta Beg, who had been promoted with the titles of Qarā Khān and Sardār Khān. I appointed Mīrzā Ghāzī to a mansab of 5,000 personal, and horsemen, and bestowed drums on him. Mīrzā Ghāzī was the son of Mīrzā Jānī Tarkhān, king of Thathah (Sind), and by the efforts of 'Abdu-r-Raḥīm Khānkhānān that country had been conquered in the reign of the late king. The country of Thathah was included in his jagir, and he held the rank with personality and horsemen of 5,000. After his death his son Mīrzā Ghāzī was raised to his rank and service. Their ancestors were among the amirs of Sulṭān Ḥusain Mirza Bāy-qarā, the ruler of Khurasan, and they were originally descended from the amirs of Tīmūr (*Ṣāḥib-qirānī*). Khwāja 'Āqil was appointed bakhshi of this army; 43,000 rupees were given to Qarā Khān for road expenses, and 15,000 to Naqdī Beg and Qilīj Beg, who were to accompany Mīrzā Ghāzī. I determined to stay at Lahore in order to settle this matter and with the intention of a tour to Kabul. About this time the rank of Ḥakīm Fatḥu-llah was fixed, original and increased, at 1,000 personality and 300 horse. As Shaikh Ḥusain Jāmī had

had dreams about me which had come true, I gave him twenty lakhs of dams, equivalent to 30,000 or 40,000 rupees, for the expenses of himself and his monastery and the dervishes who were with him. On the 22nd I promoted ʻAbdu-llah Khān to the rank of 2,500 personal and 500 horse, original and increased. I ordered to be given to the ahadis two lakhs of rupees to be paid in advance and deducted by degrees from their monthly pay. I bestowed 6,000 rupees on Qāsim Beg Khān, the son-in-law of Shāh Beg Khān, and 3,000 rupees on Sayyid Bahādur Khān.

In Gobindwāl, which is on the river Bīyāh (Beas), there was a Hindu named Arjun,[1] in the garments of sainthood and sanctity, so much so that he had captured many of the simple-hearted of the Hindus, and even of the ignorant and foolish followers of Islam, by his ways and manners, and they had loudly sounded the drum of his holiness. They called him *Gūrū,* and from all sides stupid people crowded to worship and manifest complete faith in him. For three or four generations (of spiritual successors) they had kept this shop warm. Many times it occurred to me to put a stop to this vain affair or to bring him into the assembly of the people of Islam.

At last when Khusrau passed along this road this insignificant fellow proposed to wait upon him. Khusrau happened to halt at the place where he was, and he came out and did homage to him. He behaved to Khusrau in certain special ways, and made on his forehead a finger-mark in saffron, which the Indians (Hinduwān) call *qashqa,*[2] and is considered propitious. When this came to my ears and I clearly understood his folly, I ordered them

[1] The fifth Gūrū of the Sikhs and the compiler of the Granth. He was the father of Har Govind. See Sayyid Muḥammad Laṭīf's history of the Panjāb, p. 253. Arjun's tomb is in Lahore.

[2] But *qashqa* is a Turkish word. The Hindi phrase seems to be *ṭīkā.*

to produce him and handed over his houses, dwelling-places, and children to Murtaẓā Khān, and having confiscated his property commanded that he should be put to death.

There were two men named Rājū and Ambā, who, under the shadow of the protection of the eunuch Daulat Khān, made their livelihood by oppression and tyranny, and had done many acts of oppression in the few days that Khusrau was before Lahore. I ordered Rājū to the gallows and a fine to be taken from Ambā, who was reputed to be wealthy. In short, 15,000 rupees were collected from him, which sum I ordered them to expend on *bulghur-khānas* (refectories) and in charity.

Sa'du-llah Khān, son of Sa'd Khān, was promoted to the rank of 2,000 personal and 1,000 horse.

In his great desire to wait upon me, Parwīz traversed long distances in a short time, in the rainy season and incessant rain, and on Thursday, the 29th, when two watches and three *gharī* of day had passed, obtained the blessing of seeing me. With exceeding kindness and affection, I took him into the embrace of favour and kissed his forehead.

When this disgraceful conduct showed itself in Khusrau, I had resolved not to delay in any place till I had captured him. There was a probability that he might turn back towards Hindustan, so it appeared impolitic to leave Agra empty, as it was the centre of the State, the abode of the ladies of the holy harem, and the depository of the world's treasures. On these accounts I had written when leaving Agra to Parwīz, saying that his loyalty had had this result, that Khusrau had fled and that Fortune had turned her face toward himself; that I had started in pursuit of Khusrau, and that he should consequently dispose of the affairs of the Rānā in some way according to the necessity of the time, and for the benefit of the kingdom should himself come quickly to

Agra. I had delivered into his charge the capital and treasury, which was equal to the wealth of Qārūn,[1] and I had commended him to the God of power. Before this letter reached Parwīz, the Rānā had been so humbled that he had sent to Āṣaf Khān to say that as by his own acts he had come to shame and disgrace, he hoped that he would intercede for him in such a way that the prince would be content with his sending Bāgha,[2] who was one of his sons. Parwīz had not agreed to this, and said that either the Rānā himself should come or that he should send Karan. Meantime the news of Khusrau's disturbance arrived, and on its account Āṣaf Khān and other loyalists agreed to the coming of Bāgha, who obtained the blessing of waiting on the prince near Manḍalgaṛh.

Parwīz, leaving Rāja Jagannāth and most of the chiefs of his army, started for Agra with Āṣaf Khān and some of those near to him and his own attendants, and with him brought Bāgha to the Court. When he came near Agra he heard the news of the victory over Khusrau and his capture, and after resting two days an order reached him that as matters appeared settled in all quarters he should betake himself to me, in order that on the prescribed date he might obtain the good fortune of waiting on me. I bestowed on him the parasol (*āftāb-gīr*),[3] which is one of the signs of royalty, and I gave him the rank of 10,000 and sent an order to the officials to grant him a *tankhwāh* jagir. At this time I sent Mīrzā 'Alī Beg to Kashmir; 10,000 rupees were delivered to Qāẓī 'Izzatu-llah to divide amongst faqirs and the poor of Kabul. Aḥmad Beg Khān was promoted to the rank of 2,000 personal and 1,250 horse, original and extra. At the same time Muqarrab Khān, who had been sent to Burhanpur to bring the children of Dāniyāl, returned after an absence of 6 months

[1] The cousin of Moses, famous for his wealth; the Korah of the Bible.
[2] Gladwin has Nāgh.
[3] Blochmann, p. 50.

22 days and had the honour of an audience, and related in detail what had occurred in those regions.

Saif Khān was promoted to the rank of 2,000 personal and 1,000 horse. Shaikh 'Abdu-l-Wahhāb[1] of the Bukhara sayyids, who was governor of Delhi under the late king, was dismissed from the post (by me) for certain ill-deeds done by his men, and was entered amongst the holders of subsistence lands and the *arbāb-i-sa'ādat.*

In the whole of the hereditary dominions, both the crown lands and the jagirs, I ordered the preparation of *bulghur-khānas* (free eating-houses), where cooked food might be provided for the poor according to their condition, and so that residents and travellers both might reap the benefit.

Amba[2] Khān Kashmīrī, who was of the stock of the rulers of Kashmir, was selected for the rank of 1,000 personal and 300 horse. On Monday, Rabī'u-l-ākhir 9th, I gave Parwīz a special sword; and jewelled swords were presented also to Quṭbu-d-dīn Khān Koka and the Amīru-l-umarā. I saw Dāniyāl's children, whom Muqarrab Khān had brought; there were three sons and four daughters. The boys bore the names Ṭahmūraṣ,[3] Bāysunghar, and Hūshang. Such kindness and affection were shown by me to these children as no one thought possible. I resolved that Ṭahmūraṣ, who was the eldest, should always be in waiting on me, and the others were handed over to the charge of my own sisters.

A special dress of honour was sent to Rāja Mān Singh in Bengal. I ordered a reward of 30 lakhs of dams to Mīrzā Ghāzī. I bestowed on Shaikh Ibrāhīm, son of

[1] Akbar-nāma, iii, 748, and Blochmann, p. 546. He was a man of piety and learning, and Jahāngīr means that he restored him to his former quiet life. The *arbāb-i-sa'ādat*, or auspicious persons, were those who offered up prayers for the king's prosperity and other blessings.

[2] Amba was killed later by Nūr-Jahān's husband, Shīr Afgan (Tūzuk, pp. 54, 55).

[3] Blochmann, p. 310.

Quṭbu-d-dīn Khān Koka, the rank of 1,000 personal and 300 horse, and dignified him with the title of Kishwar Khān.

As when I started in pursuit of Khusrau I had left my son Khurram in charge of the palaces and treasury, I now, when that affair had been settled, ordered the said son to attend upon Haẓrat Maryam-zamānī and the other ladies, and to escort them to me. When they reached the neighbourhood of Lahore, on Friday the 12th of the month mentioned, I embarked in a boat and went to a village named Dahr to meet my mother, and I had the good fortune to be received by her. After the performance of obeisance and prostration and greeting which is due from the young to the old according to the custom of Chingīz, the rules of Tīmūr and common usage, and after worship of the King of the World (God), and after finishing this business, I obtained leave to return, and re-entered the fort of Lahore.

On the 17th, having appointed Mu'izzu-l-mulk bakhshi of the army against the Rānā, I dismissed him to it. As news had come of the rebellion of Rāy Rāy Singh and his son, Dulīp, in the neighbourhood of Nāgor, I ordered Rāja Jagannāth to proceed against them with others of the servants of the State and Mu'izzu-l-mulk, and to put a stop to this disturbance. I gave 50,000 rupees to Sardār Khān, who had been appointed to the place of Shāh Beg Khān as Governor of Qandahar, and I promoted him to the rank of 3,000 personal and 2,500 horse. To Khiẓr Khān, the late ruler of Khandesh, were given 3,000 rupees, and to his brother, Aḥmad Khān,[1] who is one of the khānazādas of the State. Hāshim Khān, son of Qāsim Khān, who is one of the house-born of the State, and

[1] These words are not in the MSS., and they seem to have crept into the text by mistake and to be a premature entry of words relating to Hāshim, etc. The brother of the former ruler (or king) of Khandesh could hardly be a *khānazād*.

worthy of advancement, I promoted to the rank of 2,500 personal and 1,500 horse. I gave him also one of my own horses. I sent robes of honour to eight individuals amongst the nobles of the army of the Deccan.[1] Five thousand rupees were given to Niẓām of Shiraz, the story-teller. Three thousand rupees were given for the expenses of the *bulghūr-khāna* of Kashmir to the *wakīl* of Mīrzā ʻAlī Beg, the governor of that place, to send to Srinagar. I presented a jewelled dagger of the value of 6,000 rupees to Quṭbu-d-dīn Khān.

News reached me that Shaikh Ibrāhīm Bābā, the Afghan, had opened a religious establishment (lit. one of being a shaikh and having disciples) in one of the parganas[2] of Lahore, and as his doings were disreputable and foolish a considerable number of Afghans had collected round him. I ordered him to be brought and handed over to Parwīz to be kept in the fort of Chunar; so this vain disturbance was put an end to.

On Sunday, 7th Jumādā-l-awwal, many of the mansabdars and ahadis were promoted: Mahābat Khān obtained the rank of 2,000 personal and 1,300 horse, Dilāwar Khān 2,000 personal and 1,400 horse, Wazīru-l-mulk 1,300 personal and 550 horse, Qayyām Khān 1,000 personal and horse, Shyām Singh 1,500 personal and 1,200 horse; in the same way forty-two mansabdars were promoted. On most days the same observances occur. I presented Parwīz with a ruby of the value of 25,000 rupees. On Wednesday the 9th of the aforesaid month, the 21st of Shahrīwar,[3] after three watches and four gharis, the feast for my solar weighing, which is the commencement of the 38th year of my age, took place. According to custom they got ready

[1] This should be, according to the MSS., "army against the Rānā," not army of the Deccan.

[2] The MSS. have "in the neighbourhood of Lahore." Parwīz had then charge of Bihar.

[3] Text, wrongly, Bahman. Jahāngīr was born on the 21st of Shahrīwar.

the weighing apparatus and the scales in the house of Maryam-zamānī (his mother). At the moment appointed blessings were invoked and I sate in the scales. Each suspending rope was held by an elderly person who offered up prayers. The first time the weight in gold came to three Hindustani maunds and ten seers. After this I was weighed against several metals, perfumes, and essences, up to twelve weighings, the details of which will be given hereafter. Twice a year I weigh myself against gold and silver and other metals, and against all sorts of silks and cloths, and various grains, etc., once at the beginning of the solar year and once at that of the lunar. The weight of the money of the two weighings I hand over to the different treasurers for faqirs and those in want. On the same auspicious day I promoted Quṯbu-d-dīn Khān Koka, who for many years had expected such a day,[1] with various favours. First, I gave him the rank of 5,000 personal and horse, and with this a special robe of honour, a jewelled sword, and one of my own horses, with a jewelled saddle, and I gave him leave to go to the subahdarship of the province of Bengal and Orissa, which is a place for 50,000 horse. As a mark of honour he set off accompanied by a large force, and two lakhs of rupees were given him as a sumptuary allowance. My connection with his mother is such that as in my childhood I was under her guardianship and care, I have not so much affection for my own mother as for her. She is to me my gracious mother, and I do not hold him less dear than my own brothers and children. Quṯbu-d-dīn is the foster-brother who is most fit for fosterage. I gave 300,000 rupees to his auxiliaries. On this day I sent 130,000 as a marriage present (*sāchiq*) for the daughter of Pahārī (his brother Murād), who had been betrothed to Parwīz.

[1] Apparently, had long looked forward to the happy day when Jahāngīr should be weighed as a king.

On the 22nd, Bāz Bahādur Qalmāq, who had long been guilty of evil practices in Bengal, by the guidance of fortune obtained the honour of kissing my threshold. I gave him a jewelled dagger, 8,000 rupees, and promoted him to the rank of 1,000 personal and horse. One lakh of rupees and cash and jewels were bestowed on Parwīz. Kesho Dās Mārū was promoted to the grade of 1,500 personal and horse. Abū-l-ḥasan, who had been the diwan and factotum of my brother Dāniyāl, together with his children,[1] had the honour of an audience, and was raised to the rank of 1,000 personal and 500 horse. On the 1st of the second Jumādā Shaikh Bāyazīd,[2] who was one of the shaikhzādas of Sīkrī, well known for brilliance of understanding and knowledge, and the connection of old service,[3] was honoured with the title of Mu'aẕẕam Khān, and to him I gave the government of Delhi. On the 21st of the same month I presented Parwīz with a necklace composed of four rubies and one hundred pearls. The rank of Ḥakīm Muẓaffar was fixed at 3,000 personal and 1,000 horse, original and extra. I gave 5,000 rupees to Nathu Māl (?), Rāja of Manjholi.[4]

A remarkable occurrence was the discovery of a letter from Mīrzā 'Azīz Koka to 'Alī Khān, the ruler of Khandesh. I had had an impression that he had a particular enmity to me on Khusrau's account, who was his son-in-law. From the discovery of this writing it became clear that he had never given up his innate treachery, and had adopted this unbecoming attitude towards my revered father also. In short, this letter which he had written at some time to Rāja 'Alī Khān

[1] Perhaps the meaning is that he was introduced along with Dāniyāl's children.

[2] Blochmann, p. 492.

[3] This refers to his parentage.

[4] In the MSS. this name seems to be Bhīm Mal. Manjholi is written Manjholah in Blochmann, p. 175.

was from beginning to end full of abuse and disapprobation, and said things which no enemy even could have written and such as could not be attributed to anyone, and far less to one like His Majesty, *'Arsh-āshyānī*, a king and an appreciative sovereign, who from childhood had educated him and brought him up because of what was due for services rendered by his mother, and raised the standard of reliance on him to such a high degree as no other person possessed. This letter fell into the hands of Khwāja Abū-l-ḥasan in Burhanpur amongst the property of Rāja 'Alī Khān. He brought and laid it before me. In reading and seeing it the hair on my limbs stood on end. But for the consideration and due recognition of the fact that his mother had given her milk to my father I could have killed him with my own hand. Having procured his attendance I gave the letter into his hand and told him to read it with a loud voice to those present. When he saw the letter I thought his body would have parted from his soul, but with shamelessness and impudence he read it as though he had not written it and was reading it by order. Those present in that paradise-like assembly of the servants of Akbar and Jahāngīr and heard the letter read, loosened the tongue of reproach and of curses and abuse. I put the question to him, "Leaving aside the treacheries which in reliance on your worthless self you contrived against *my* fortune, what was done to you by my father, who raised you and your family from the dust of the road to such wealth and dignity as to make you the envy of your contemporaries, that you should write these things to the enemies of his Empire? Why did you enrol yourself amongst the wicked and disloyal? Truly, what can one make of an original nature and innate disposition? Since your temperament has been nourished by the water of treachery, what else can spring up but such actions? Passing over what you did to myself, I gave you the rank you had held before, thinking that your treachery was directed against me only. Since it has become known that you behaved in a similar way to your benefactor and visible Deity, I leave you to the thoughts and actions which you formerly had and still have." After these remarks his lips closed, and he was unable to make any reply. What could he have said in the presence of such disgrace? I gave an order to deprive him of his jagir. Although what this ingrate had done was unpardonable, yet in the end, from certain considerations, I passed it over.

On Sunday the 26th of the above-mentioned month was held the marriage feast of Parwīz and the daughter of Prince Murād. The ceremony was performed in the house of Her Highness Maryam-zamānī. The entertainment was arranged in the house of Parwīz, and all who were present were exalted with all kinds of honour and civilities. Nine thousand rupees were handed over to S͟harif Āmulī and other nobles, to be given in alms to faqirs and other poor people.

On Sunday the 10th Rajab I left the city to hunt in Girjhak and Nandana,[1] and took up my quarters in the garden of Rām Dās, where I remained four days.

On Wednesday the 13th the solar weighing of Parwīz took place. They weighed him twelve times against various metals and other things, and each weighing came to two maunds and eighteen seers. I ordered the whole to be distributed amongst faqirs. At this time the rank of S͟hajā'at K͟hān was fixed at 1,500 personal and 700 horse, original and extra.

After the march of Mīrzā G͟hāzī and his force it occurred to me to send a second contingent after him. Having bestowed on Bahādur[2] K͟hān Qūrbegī the rank of 1,500 personal and 800 horse, original and extra, I started off

[1] ? Nandanpur. These places are in Sindsagār, near Multān.

[2] MS. 181 has Bahār, and it has 600 instead of 800 horse.

a body of cavalry,[1] which came to about 3,000, with him under the leadership of Shāh Beg and Muḥammad Amīn. For the expenses of this force 200,000 rupees were given and 1,000 musketeers were also appointed.

I left Āṣaf Khān to guard Khusrau and defend Lahore. The Amīru-l-umarā was deprived of the honour of waiting on me, as he had a severe illness and remained in the city. 'Abdu-r-Razzāq Ma'mūrī, who had been summoned from the Rānā's country, was promoted to be bakhshi at headquarters, and it was ordered that in company with 'Abū-l-ḥasan he should perform this service permanently. Following my father's rule, I appoint two men in association in the discharge of the chief offices, not from want of confidence in them, but because, as they are mortal and no man is safe from accidents or illness, if any confusion or obstacle should present itself to one the other is there so that the affairs of the servants of God may not come to ruin.

At this time also news came that at the Dasahrā, which is one of the fixed feast days of the Hindus, 'Abdu-llah Khān had made an incursion from Kālpī, which is his jagir, into the province of Bandīlah, and displaying great valour made prisoner Rām Chand, son of Madhūkar, who for a long time had made a centre of disturbance in that difficult country and taken him to Kālpī. For this service he was presented with a standard and raised to 3,000 personal and 2,000 horse.

Petitions from the subah of Bihar represented that Jahāngīr Qulī Khān had had a battle with Sangrām, one of the chief zamindars of Bihar, who had about 4,000 horse and innumerable foot, on account of certain opposition and

[1] Text, *Ūymāq pūrī* (?). MS. 181 has *būrī*, and 305 seems to have the same. Can it mean 'red cavalry'? As Blochmann has pointed out, 371, n. 2, the word Ūymāq does not always mean the tribe, but was used to denote a superior kind of cavalry.

disloyalty on rough land, and that on the field the aforesaid Khān had exerted himself manfully. In the end Sangrām died of a gunshot wound; many of his men fell in the battle, and those saved from the sword took to flight. Since this distinguished affair had been brought about by Jahāngīr Qulī Khān, I promoted him to the rank of 4,500 personal and 3,500 horse.

Three months and six days passed by in hunting; 581 animals were captured with the gun, hunting leopards and nets, and a *qamargāh*; of these 158 were killed by my own gun. The qamargah was held twice; on one occasion in Girjhāk, when the ladies were present, 155 animals were killed; and the second time, in Nandīna, 110.[1] The details of the animals killed are as follows: mountain sheep, 180; mountain goats, 29; wild asses, 10; Nilgai, 9; antelope, etc., 348.

On Wednesday the 16th Shawwāl I returned safe from my hunting, and when one watch and six gharis of day had passed I entered Lahore on the day named. During this hunting a strange affair was witnessed At Chandwālah, where a minaret had been erected, I had wounded in the belly a black antelope. When wounded, a sound proceeded from him such as I have never heard from any antelope, except in the rutting season. Old hunters and those with me were astonished, and said they never remembered nor had they heard from their fathers that such a voice issued from an antelope except at rutting time. This has been written down because it is not void of strangeness. I found the flesh of the mountain goat more delicious than that of all wild animals, although its skin is exceedingly ill-odoured, so much so that even when tanned the scent is not destroyed. I ordered one of the largest of the he-goats to be weighed; it was 2 maunds and 24 seers, equal to 21 foreign maunds

[1] The *qamargāh* or ring-hunt produced 265 head of game; the rest were shot at other times; the total of the list should be apparently 576.

(Persian). I ordered a large ram to be weighed, and it came to 2 maunds and 3 seers *Akbarī*, equal to 17 Persian (*wilāyatī*) maunds. The largest and strongest of the wild asses weighed 9 maunds and 16 seers, equal to 76 Persian (wilayati) maunds. I have frequently heard from hunters and those fond of the chase that at a certain regular time a worm develops in the horns of the mountain ram, and that this worm causes an irritation which induces the ram to fight with his hind, and that if he finds no rival he strikes his head against a tree or a rock to allay the irritation. After enquiry it seems that the same worm appears in the horn of the female sheep, and since the female does not fight the statement is clearly untrue. Though the flesh of the wild ass is lawful food and most men like to eat it, it was in no way suited to my taste.

Inasmuch as before this time the punishment of Dulīp and of his father, Rāy Rāy Singh, had been ordered, there now came news that Zāhid Khān, the son of Ṣādiq Khān, and 'Abdu-r-Raḥīm, son of Shaikh Abū-l-faẓl, and Rānā Sankar and Mu'izzu-l-mulk, with another force of mansabdars and followers of the Court, had heard news of Dulīp in the neighbourhood of Nāgor, which is in the subah of Ajmir, and having moved against him had found him. As he could find no way of escape, of necessity he planted a firm foot and came to blows with the royal army. After a short encounter he was badly beaten and gave over many to slaughter, and himself, taking with him his own effects, fled into the vale of ruin.

"With broken arms and loosened belt,
No power to fight and no care for head."

In spite of his old age, I continued Qilīj Khān in his mansab because of his service under my father, and I ordered that he should get a jagir in the sarkar of Kālpī.

In the month Ẕī-l-qa'da the mother of Quṭbu-d-dīn Khān Koka, who had given me her milk and was as a mother to me or even kinder than my own kind mother, and in whose lap I had been brought up from infancy, was committed to the mercy of God. I placed the feet of her corpse on my shoulders and carried her a part of the way (to her grave). Through extreme grief and sorrow I had no inclination for some days to eat, and I did not change my clothes.

Feast of the Second New Year.

On Wednesday the 22nd Z̲ī-l-qa'da, 1015 (10th March, 1607), when 3½ gharis of the day had passed, the sun rose to his House of Honour. They decorated the palace after the usual fashion : a great entertainment was prepared, and having seated myself at an auspicious hour on the throne of accession I exalted the nobles and courtiers with kindness and favour. On this same auspicious day it was learned from the reports sent from Qandahar that the army sent under Mīrzā G̲h̲āzī, son of Mīrzā Jānī, to succour (which had been appointed to assist) S̲h̲āh Beg K̲h̲ān, had entered the city of Qandahar on the 12th of Shawwāl. When the Persians heard of the arrival of the victorious army at the last stage before the aforesaid city,[1] they became surprised and wretched and repentant, and did not draw rein until they had reached the Helmand, fifty or sixty kos distant.

In the second place it became known that the governor of Farāh and a number of the officers of that neighbourhood had taken it into their heads, after the death of the late king, that in this confusion Qandahar might easily fall into their hands, and without waiting for an order from S̲h̲āh 'Abbās had collected together and won over the Chief of Sewistān (Sīstān). Sending someone to

[1] The MSS. have the 6th stage instead of "last."

Ḥusain Khān, the governor of Herat, they asked for support from him. He also sent a force. After that they turned to attack Qandahar. Shāh Beg Khān, the governor of that place, seeing that battle has two heads, and that if (which God forbid!) he should be defeated he would lose possession of Qandahar, thought that to confine himself in a fort would be better than to fight. He therefore determined to hold the fort, and sent quick messengers to the Court. It happened that at this time the royal standards had started from Agra in pursuit of Khusrau, and had arrived at Lahore. Immediately on hearing this news (from Shāh Beg Khān), a large force was sent off of amirs and mansabdars under Mīrzā Ghāzī. Before the Mīrzā reached Qandahar the news had been carried to the Shāh (of Persia) that the governor of Farāh, with some of the jagirdars of that neighbourhood, had proceeded towards the province of Qandahar. Considering this an improper proceeding, he sent Ḥusain Beg, a well-known man and one of his own intimates, to make enquiries. He also sent a farman in their names that they should move away from the vicinity of Qandahar and go to their own places and abodes, because the friendship and amity of his ancestors with the dignified family of Jahāngīr Pādshāh were of old standing. That body, before the arrival of Ḥusain Beg and the King's order, not being able to oppose the royal army, considered the opportunity of returning a favourable one. The said Ḥusain Beg censured the men and started off to wait on me, which he had the honour to do at Lahore. He explained that the ill-fated army which had attacked Qandahar had acted without the order of Shāh 'Abbās. God forbid (he said) that in consequence of this any unpleasantness should remain in my mind. In short, after the victorious troops reached Qandahar, they, according to orders, delivered the fort over to Sardār Khān, and Shāh Beg Khān returned to Court with the relieving force.

On the 27th Ẕī-l-qaʻda, ʻAbdu-llah Khān, having brought Rām Chand Bandīlah into captivity and chains, brought him before me. I ordered them to take the fetters from his legs, and bestowed on him a robe of honour, and handed him over to Rāja Bāso that he might take security and release him and a number of his relations who had been captured with him. This through my clemency and kindness came to pass. He had never imagined such clemency and kindness as I showed to him.

On the 2nd Ẕī-l-ḥijja I gave my son Khurram a *tūmān u tūgh*, a flag and drums, and bestowed on him the rank of 8,000 personal and 5,000 horse, and gave an order for a jagir. On the same day, having exalted Pīr Khān,[1] son of Daulat Khān Lodī, who had come from Khandesh with the children of Dāniyāl, with the title of Ṣalābat Khān and honoured him with the rank of 3,000 personal and 1,500 horse, and presented him with a standard and drums, I promoted him to the distinction of sonship (*farzandī*) beyond his fellows and equals. The ancestors and uncles of Ṣalābat Khān's grandfather had been great and honourable among the tribe of Lodī. An earlier Daulat Khān, uncle of Ṣalābat Khān's grandfather, when Ibrāhīm after his father Sikandar's death, began to behave ill to his father's amirs and destroyed many, became apprehensive, and sent his younger son, Dilāwar Khān, to wait upon H.M. Bābar in Kabul, and suggested to him the acquisition of Hindustan. As Bābar also had this enterprise in mind, he at once proceeded in that direction, and did not turn his rein till he reached the neighbourhood of Lahore. Daulat Khān with his followers obtained the good fortune to wait upon him, and performed loyal service. As he was an old man, adorned with inward and outward excellencies, he did much good service. He (Bābar) generally called him "father," and entrusting to him as

[1] This is the famous Khān Jahān Lodī of Shāh Jahān's reign.

before[1] the government of the Panjab placed its amirs and jagirdars under his jurisdiction. Taking Dilāwar Khān with him he (Bābar) returned to Kabul. When he (Bābar) came a second time into the Panjab with intent to invade Hindustan, Daulat Khān waited on him, and about the same time died. Dilāwar Khān was honoured with the title of Khānkhānān, and was with Bābar in the battle he had with Ibrāhīm. In the same way he was permanently in waiting on the late king Humāyūn. In the *thānā* of Mungir, at the time of his (Humāyūn's) return from Bengal, he fought bravely against Shīr Khān Afghān, and was made prisoner on the field of battle. Although Shīr Khān urged him to take service with him, he refused and said, "Thy ancestors were always the servants of mine: how, then, could I do this?" Shīr Khān was enraged, and ordered him to be shut up in a wall.[2]

'Umar Khān, the grandfather of Ṣalābat Khān Farzand, who was cousin of Dilāwar Khān, had been treated with respect in the time of Salīm Khān. After Salīm Khān's death and the slaughter of Fīrūz, his son, at the hand of Muḥammad Khān, 'Umar Khān and his brethren became suspicious of Muḥammad Khān and went to Gujarat, where 'Umar Khān died. Daulat Khān, his son, who was a brave young man of pleasant appearance, and good at all things, chose the companionship of 'Abdu-r-Raḥīm, son of Bairām Khān, who had been dignified with the title of Khānkhānān in the reign of Akbar, and performed excellent service. The Khānkhānān regarded him as his own brother, or even a thousand times better than his brother, and dearer. Most of the Khānkhānān's victories were gained through Daulat Khān's valour and manliness.[3] When my

[1] Text, *ba dastūr*.

[2] I.e. built him up in it.

[3] Jahāngīr did not like the Khānkhānān, and so here belittles his services.

revered father, having taken the province of Khandesh and the fort of Āsīr, returned to Agra, he left Dāniyāl in charge of that province and of all the provinces acquired from the rulers of the Deccan. At this time Dāniyāl had separated Daulat Khān from the Khānkhānān, and was keeping him in attendance on himself and handing over to him for disposal all the business of the State. He showed him much favour and perfect affection until he died in his service. He left two sons, one Muḥammad Khān, and the other Pīr Khān; Muḥammad Khān, who was the elder, died a short time after his father. Dāniyāl, too, wore himself out with drinking. After my accession I summoned Pīr Khān to Court. As I discovered in him a good disposition and natural abilities, I raised the pedestal of regard for him to the point that has been described. To-day there is not in my government any person of greater influence than he, so much so that on his representation I pass over faults which are not pardoned at the intercession of any of the other servants of the Court. In short, he is a young man of good disposition, brave, and worthy of favour, and what I have done for him has been done rightly, and he will be exalted by further favours.[1]

As I had made up my exalted mind to the conquest of Māwarā'a-n-nahr (Transoxiana), which was the hereditary kingdom of my ancestors, I desired to free the face of Hindustan from the rubbish of the factious and rebellious, and leaving one of my sons in that country, to go myself with a valiant army in due array, with elephants of mountainous dignity and of lightning speed, and taking ample treasure with me, to undertake the conquest of my ancestral dominions. In accordance with this idea, I despatched Parwīz to drive back the Rānā, and intended to go myself to the Deccan, when just at that moment the

[1] During Shāh Jahān's reign, Khān Jahān Lodī fled from Court, was pursued, and killed.

improper action of Khusrau took place, and it became necessary to pursue him and put an end to that disturbance. For the same reason, the undertaking of Parwīz did not assume a promising appearance, and regarding the exigency of the time he gave a respite to the Rānā. Bringing with him one of the Rānā's sons, he came to wait on me, and had the bliss of attending me in Lahore. When I was at ease about Khusrau's disturbance, and the repulse of the Qizilbāshes, who had invested Qandahar, had been brought about in a facile way, it came into my mind to make a hunting tour to Kabul, which is like my native land. After that I would return to Hindustan, when the purposes of my mind would pass from design to action. In pursuance of these steps, on the 7th Ẕī-l-ḥijja, at an auspicious hour, I left the fort of Lahore and took up my quarters in the Dil-āmīz Garden, which is on the other side of the Ravi, and stayed there four days. Sunday, the 19th Farwardīn, which is the culmination of His Majesty the Sun, I passed in the garden, and some of the servants of the Court were favourably and kindly honoured with increased rank. Ten thousand rupees were bestowed on Ḥasan Beg, the envoy of the ruler of Persia (Shāh 'Abbās). Leaving Qilīj Khān, Mīrān Ṣadr Jahān, and Mīr Sharīf Āmulī in Lahore, I ordered them to settle in consultation any matters that might present themselves. On Monday I marched from the garden mentioned, and encamped at the village of Harhar, 3½ kos distant from the city. On Tuesday the royal standards alighted at Jahāngīrpūr, which is one of my fixed hunting-places. In this neighbourhood had been erected by my order a *manār* at the head of the grave of an antelope called Mansarāj,[1] which was without equal in fights with tame

[1] Perhaps the antelope's name was Rāj, and the syllable *man* the pronoun 'my,' when the translation would be 'my antelope Rāj.' See Elliot, vi, 302, and R.A.S. MS., No. 124.

antelopes and in hunting wild ones. On a stone of that manar was carved this prose composition, written by Mullā Muḥammad Ḥusain of Kashmir, who was the chief of the elegant writers of the day: "In this enchanting place an antelope came into the world-holding (*jahān-gīrī*) net of the God-knowing ruler Nūru-d-dīn Jahāngīr Pādshāh. In the space of one month, having overcome his desert fierceness, he became the head of the special antelopes." On account of the rare quality of this antelope, I commanded that no person should hunt the deer of this plain, and that their flesh should be to Hindus and Muhammadans as is the flesh of cows and pigs. They made the gravestone in the shape of an antelope. I ordered Sikandar Mu'īn, the jagirdar of the aforesaid pargana, to build a strong fort in the village of Jahangirpur.

On Thursday, the 14th, I encamped in the pargana of Chandāla.[1] Thence on Saturday, the 16th, making one stage in the middle, I came to Ḥāfiẓābād.[2] I stayed in the station which had been erected by the exertions of the *karorī* of that place, Mīr Qiyāmu-d-dīn. Having reached the Chenāb in two marches on Thursday, the 21st Ẕī-l-ḥijja, I crossed the river by a bridge which had been built there, and my camp was pitched in the neighbourhood of the pargana of Gujrat. At the time when His Majesty Akbar went to Kashmir, a fort had been built on that bank of the river. Having brought to this fort a body of Gujars who had passed their time in the neighbourhood in thieving and highway robbery, he established them here. As it had become the abode of Gujars, he made it a separate pargana, and gave it the name of Gujrat. They call Gujars a caste which does little manual work and subsists on milk and curds. On Friday I pitched at K͟hawāṣṣpūr, five kos from Gujrat, founded by K͟hawāṣṣ

[1] Perhaps the Jandiāla of the Indian Gazetteer, vii, 137.
[2] Indian Gazetteer, v, 239.

K͟hān, a slave of S͟hīr K͟hān Afg͟hān. Thence, with two halts in the middle, I pitched on the bank of the Bihaṭ (Jhelam). On that night a great wind blew and a black cloud hid the face of the sky. The rain was of such violence that old men remembered none such. It turned to hail, and every hailstone was the size of a hen's egg. From the flooding of the river and the force of the wind and rain, the bridge broke. I, with the inmates of the harem, crossed in a boat. As there were few boats, I ordered the men not[1] to cross in these, but to rebuild the bridge. It was finished in a week, and the whole army crossed with ease. The source of the Bihaṭ is a spring in Kashmir called the Vīr-nāg; in the language of India a snake is *vīr-nāg*. Clearly there had been a large snake at that place. I went twice to the spring in my father's lifetime; it is 20 kos from the city of Kashmir. It is an octagonal reservoir about 20 yards by 20. Near it are the remains of a place of worship for recluses; cells cut out of the rock and numerous caves. The water is exceedingly pure. Although I could not guess its depth, a grain of poppy-seed is visible until it touches the bottom. There were many fish to be seen in it. As I had heard that it was unfathomable, I ordered them to throw in a cord with a stone attached, and when this cord was measured in *gaz* it became evident that the depth was not more than once and a half the height of a man. After my accession I ordered them to build the sides of the spring round with stone, and they made a garden round it with a canal; and built halls and houses about it, and made a place such that travellers over the world can point out few like it. When the river reaches the village of Pāmpūr, at a distance of ten kos from the city, it increases, and all the saffron of Kashmir is obtained in this village. I do not know if there is so much saffron in any other place in the world.

[1] Text omits the negative.

The annual crop is 500 maunds by Hindustan weight, equal to 5,000 *wilāyat* (Persian) maunds. In attendance on my revered father, I went to this place at the season when the saffron was in flower. On other plants of the world, first the branches (stems) shoot out and then the leaves and flowers. On the contrary, when the saffron stem is four fingers breadth from the dry ground, its flowers shoot out, of the colour of the iris,[1] with four petals, and in the middle are four threads (*rīsha*) of an orange colour like that of the flower, and of the length of a finger-joint. This is the saffron. The land is not ploughed[2] or irrigated, the plant springs up amongst the clods. In some places its cultivation extends for a kos, and in others for half a kos. It looks better from a distance. At the time of plucking, all my attendants got headache from its sharp scent. Though I drank wine and took a cup, I too got headache. I asked the animal-like Kashmiris, who were employed in picking the flowers, how they felt. I ascertained that they had never experienced headache in their lives.

The waters from the spring Vīr-nāg and of other streams and nullahs that join from right and left form the river Bihat, which passes through the heart of the city. Its breadth in most places is not more than a bowshot.[3] No one drinks its water, because of its heaviness and indigestibility. All the people of Kashmir drink the water of a lake that is near the city, and is called Dall. The river Bihat enters this lake and flows through to the Panjab by the Bārāmūla Pass, Paklī, and Dantūr.

[1] Text, *sūsanī*; apparently a blue iris.

[2] The text has *shumār* wrongly for *shiyār*, and it seems that the negative of the text is wrong, since it does not occur in the MSS. Abū-l-fażl gives the number of petals and stamens more correctly than Jahāngīr.

[3] *Az tikka andāzī*; perhaps 'the cast of a javelin.'

In Kashmir there is plenty of water from streams and springs. By far the best is that of the Lār valley, which joins the Bihat in the village of Shihābu-d-dīn-pūr. This village is one of the celebrated places of Kashmir, and is on the Bihat. About a hundred plane-trees (*chanār*) of graceful form clustered[1] together on one plot of ground, pleasant and green, join each other so as to shade the whole plot, and the whole surface of the ground is grass and trefoil[2]; so much so that to lay a carpet on it would be superfluous and in bad taste. The village was founded by Sulṭān Zainu-l-'ābidīn, who for 52 years ruled Kashmir with absolute sway. They speak of him as the great Pādshāh. They tell many strange customs of his. There are many remains and traces of buildings of his in Kashmir. One of these is in the midst of a lake called Wulūr, and of which the length and breadth are more than three or four kos. It is called Zain-lankā, and in making it they have exerted themselves greatly. The springs of this lake are very deep. The first time they brought a large quantity of stone in boats and poured it on the place where now the building stands it had no result. At last they sank some thousands of boats with stones, and with great labour recovered a piece of ground 100 gaz by 100 gaz out of the water, and made a terrace, and on one side thereof the Sultan erected a temple for the worship of his supreme God. Than this there is no finer place.[3] He often came to the spot by boat and engaged in worship of the King of Wisdom. They say he spent many "forty days" in that place. One day a wicked son of his came to that place to kill him, and finding him alone, drew a sword and went in. When his eye fell on the Sultan,

[1] Lit. 'have joined hands.'

[2] *Sih-barga*; but this reading seems doubtful; perhaps it is *sīr-i-barga*, full of leaves. Jahāngīr says that to lay a carpet on the grass would be *bī-dardī*, unfeeling, unsympathetic, and *kam salīqagī*.

[3] The text has *naqsh bar jāy*, but the true reading seems to be *nafīẓtar*.

however, on account of his venerable dignity and the might of his virtues, he became confused and bewildered and turned away. The Sultan shortly after came out and seated himself in the boat with this same son, and started for the city. On the way he said to his son, "I have forgotten my rosary; get into a canoe and fetch it for me." The son having gone into the temple sees his father in the same place, and the graceless man with complete shame of face falls at his father's feet and asks pardon for his fault. They have told many tales of such miracles as this of him, and they say also that he had well practised the science of *khala'*.[1] When, from the ways and methods of his sons, he perceived in them signs of haste in seeking for rule and government, he would say to them, "To me it is very easy to abandon rule, and even to pass away from life, but when I am gone you will do nothing, and the time of your prosperity will not endure long, but in a short time you will obtain the recompense of your evil deeds and your own dispositions." Having spoken thus, he gave up eating and drinking, and passed forty days in this manner. He made not his eye acquainted with sleep, and employed himself after the manner of men of piety and austerity in the worship of God Almighty. On the fortieth day he gave up the deposit of his existence, and entered into the mercy of God. He left three sons—Ādam Khān, Ḥājī Khān, and Bahrām Khān. They quarrelled with each other, and all three were ruined. The government of Kashmir was transferred to the tribe of the Chaks, who belonged to the class of the common soldiers of the country. During their dynasty three of the rulers constructed buildings on three sides of the terrace formed by Zainu-l-'ābidīn in the Wulur Lake, but none of these is as strong as his.

[1] *'Ilm-i-khala'-i-badan*, 'withdrawal of the soul from the body' (Erskine).

Autumn and Spring in Kashmir are things worthy to be seen. I witnessed the Autumn season, and it appeared to me to be better than what I had heard of it. I have never seen Spring in that province, but hope to do so some day. On Saturday the 1st of Muḥarram (18th April, 1607) I left the bank of the Bihat, and with one day between reached the fort of Rohtās, which was built by S͟hīr K͟hān Afg͟hān. This fort was founded in a cleft of the ground, and the strength of it cannot be imagined. As the place is near the Ghakhar territory, and they are a proud and rebellious people, he had looked to this fort specially as a means of punishing and defeating them. When a little of the building had been done S͟hīr K͟hān died and his son, Salīm K͟hān, obtained the grace to complete it. On each of the gates[1] they have carved on a stone the cost of erecting the fort; 16 krors, 10 lakhs of dams, and more were expended, equal in Hindustan reckoning to 4,025,000 rupees, and according to the currency of Iran to 120,000 *tūman*, and in the currency of Turan to 1 *arb*, 21 lakhs and 75,000 *k͟hānī*, that are now current.[2]

On Tuesday the 4th of the month, having travelled four kos and three-quarters, I encamped at Tīla.[3] Thence I came down to the village of Bhakra. In the Ghakhar

[1] So in text, but the MSS. and Elliot, vi, 307, have "on one of the gates."

[2] The figures seem wrong, and the MSS. differ. See Elliot, vi, 307. Apparently the correct sum in rupees is 34 lakhs 25,000. At p. 61 the khani of Turan is reckoned at one-third of a rupee. If the dam be taken at its ordinary value of one-fortieth of a rupee, the number of rupees should be 40 lakhs 25,000, and if the khani of Turan be one-third of a rupee we should read one kror instead of one arb. Probably Jahāngīr has used arb as meaning kror, and not 100 krors. There is a valuable note on his expedition through the Ghakkar country in Blochmann, p. 486. Blochmann takes the figures for the rupees to be four krors, but probably this is due to wrong pointing.

[3] The MSS. and text have Pila or Pīla. I adopt Tīla from Blochmann, p. 487, note. Elliot has Tillah, vi, 307, and note.

tongue *bhakra*[1] is a jungle. The jungle was composed of clusters of flowers, white and scentless. I came the whole way from Tīla to Bhakra in the middle of the river-bed,[2] which had running water in it, with oleander flowers of the colour of peach-blossom. In Hindustan this plant is always in full bloom (*purbār*). There was much of it on the banks of this river. The horsemen and men on foot who were with me were told to put bunches of the flower on their heads, and whoever did not do so had his turban taken off; a wonderful flower-bed was produced.

On Thursday the 6th of the month the halting-place was at Hatyā. On this road many palās-trees (*Butea frondosa*) were in blossom. This flower, too, is peculiar to the jungles of Hindustan; it has no scent, but its colour is flaming orange. The base of the flower is black; the flower itself is as big as a red rose. It is so beautiful that one cannot take one's eyes off it. As the air was very sweet and clouds had hidden the sun, and rain was gently sprinkled about, I felt an inclination to drink wine. In short this road was traversed with great enjoyment and pleasure. They call the place Hatyā because it was founded by a Ghakkar named Hāthi (elephant). From Mārgala to Hatyā the country is called Pothūwār.[3] In these regions there are few crows. From Rohtās to Hatyā is the place and abode of the Bhūgyāls,[4] who are related to and of the same ancestry as the Ghakkars.

Marching on Friday the 7th, I travelled 4½ kos and alighted at the station of Pakka.[5] This place is called

[1] In Tolbort's account of Lūdhiyāna, J.A.S.B. for 1869, p. 86, *bhakhra* is given as the name of a creeping plant (*Pedalium murex*).

[2] *Rūd-khāna*; this, according to Blochmann, should be the river Kahan, *khāna* being a mistake for Kahan. See p. 487 note. But all the MSS. have *khāna*.

[3] See Elliot, vi, 309 note.

[4] Būgyāls; Elliot, vi, 309. They are descendants of Sulṭān Būgā.

[5] Paka is mentioned in Tiefenthaler, i, 114.

Pakka because the *sarāy* is of burnt brick, and in the Hindi language what is ripe (that is, not raw material) is called *pakka*. The station was strangely full of dust and earth. The carts reached it with great difficulty owing to the badness of the road. They had brought from Kabul to this place *rīwāj* (rhubarb), which was mostly spoiled.

On Saturday the 8th we marched 4½ kos and encamped at the village of Khar.[1] *Khar* in the Ghakkar language is a rent and breakage. There are few trees in this country. On Sunday the 9th I halted beyond Rāwalpindī. This place was founded by a Hindu named Rāwal, and *pindī* in the Ghakkar tongue means a village. In the valley near this station there was a stream flowing, the waters of which were collected in a pool. As this halting-place was not devoid of freshness I alighted there for a time, and I asked the Ghakkars the depth of the pool. They gave me no precise answer, but said they had heard from their fathers that there were alligators in the pool which wounded animals that came there, and on that account no one had the boldness to go in. I ordered them to throw in a sheep. It swam across the pool and came out. I then ordered a *farrāsh* to go in, and he also came out safe. It thus became clear that there was no foundation for what the Ghakkars had said. The pool was an arrow's flight in width.

On Monday the 10th the village of Kharbūza[2] was our stage. The Ghakkars in earlier times had built a dome here and taken tolls from travellers. As the dome was shaped like a melon it became known by that name. On Tuesday the 11th I halted at Kāla-pānī, which in Hindi means black water. There is a mountain pass (*kotal*) at this place called Mārgalla; in Hindi *mār* means

[1] Khor; Elliot, vi, 309 note. Near the Mānikyāla tope.

[2] Kharbūza Sarāy is marked on Elphinstone's map.

to beat and *galla* is a caravan, the name therefore means the place of the plundering of the caravan. The boundary of the Ghakkar country is here. This tribe are wonderfully like animals; they are always squabbling and fighting with one another. Although I wished to put an end to this fighting, I was unable to do so.

"The soul of the fool is doomed to trouble."[1]

On Wednesday the 12th the camp was at Bābā Ḥasan Abdāl. One kos to the east of this station there is a waterfall over which the stream rushes with great force. There is no fall like it on the way to Kabul. On the road to Kashmir there are two or three like it.[2]

In the middle of the basin, in which is the source of the stream, Rāja Mān Singh has erected a small building. There are many fish in the basin of the length of half a gaz and a quarter gaz. I halted three days at this enchanting place, drinking wine with those who were intimate with me and employing myself in catching fish. Until now I had never thrown a *sufra* net, which is a famous kind of net, and which in Hindi they call *bhanwar*[3] *jāl*. It is not easy to throw. I threw it with my own hand and caught twelve fish, and putting pearls into their noses,[4] let them loose in the water. I enquired

[1] Mr. Rogers has "The soul of the fool thou canst purchase for little." Perhaps the sense is "God grants life to the fool on hard terms." Erskine has "To serve a fool is hard indeed." Possibly the literal meaning is "You buy the soul of the fool at a high price," that is, it costs a great deal to win him over. Elliot had what is probably the best rendering, "Barbarous characters should be treated with severity"; though in Elliot, vi, 310, the translation is, "The life of fools is held very cheap in troublous times."

[2] Apparently this remark must have been written after Jahāngīr's visit to Kashmir by the Bāramūla route in the fourteenth year.

[3] *Bhanwar,* as Mr. Lowe has pointed out, means in Hindi an eddy or whirlpool.

[4] William Finch says that at Ḥasan Abdāl there were many fish with gold rings in their noses hung by Akbar, and that the water is so clear that you may see a penny in the bottom. Jahāngīr's informants were

into the story of Bābā Ḥasan from the story-tellers and from the inhabitants of the place, but no one could tell me any particulars. The celebrated place at that station is a spring which flows from the foot of a little hill, exceedingly clear, sweet, and nice, as witness this couplet of Amīr Khusrau :—

> "In the bottom of the water, from its clearness, a blind man
> Can count the sand-grains in the heart of the night."

Khwāja Shamsu-d-dīn Muḥammad Khwāfī, who was for long employed as Vizier by my revered father, had made a platform and a reservoir there, into which is led the water from the spring, and thence is used in cultivation and in gardens. On the edge of this terrace he had built a dome for his own burial. By chance his destiny was not there, and (the bodies of) Ḥakīm Abū-l-fatḥ Gīlānī and his brother Ḥakīm Humām, who were close to the person and had the complete confidence of my revered father, were placed in that dome in accordance with his order.

On the 15th the halt was at Amrohī.[1] It is a wonderfully green place, in which no ups and downs were visible. In this village and its neighbourhood there are 7,000 or 8,000 households of Khaturs and Dalāzāks. All kinds of mischief and oppression and highway robbery take place through this tribe. I ordered the government of this region and Attock to be given to Ẓafar Khān, son of Zain Khān Koka, and that by the time of the return of the royal standards from Kabul they should march all the Dalāzāks to Lahore and capture the head men of the Khaturs and keep them in prison.

apparently not versed in hagiography. Bābā Ḥasan Abdāl is apparently the saint who was an ancestor of Ma'ṣūm Bhakarī, and is buried at Qandahar. See Beale, and Jarrett's translation of the Āyīn, ii, 324 note. The Sikhs identify the place with their Bābā Nānak. It is not a wife of Akbar who is buried at Ḥasan Abdāl, but Ḥakīm Abū-l-fatḥ and his brother.

[1] Elliot has Amardī, but the MSS. have Amrohī. The Ma'āṣir, ii, 755, has Āhrū'ī. See Blochmann, p. 522.

On Monday, the 17th, a march was made, and, with one stage in between, the royal standards alighted near the fort of Attock on the bank of the river Nīlāb (Indus). At this stage Mahābat Khān was promoted to the rank of 2,500. This fort was built by the late king Akbar, and was completed by the labours of Khwāja Shamsu-d-dīn Khwāfī. It is a strong fort. At this time the water of the Nīlāb was low,[1] and accordingly a bridge had been made with eighteen boats, and the people crossed over easily. I left the Amīru-l-umarā at Attock on account of weakness of body and illness. An order was given to the bakhshis that, as the province of Kabul could not support a large army, they should only allow the immediate attendants of the Court to cross the river, and until the return of the royal standards the royal camp should remain at Attock. On Wednesday, the 19th, with the princes and some of the private servants, having mounted on to a raft (with inflated skins underneath), and having crossed the river Nīlāb safely, I alighted on the bank of the river Kāma. The Kāma is a river that flows by the *qaṣba* (fortified town) of Jalālābād. The *jāla* is a structure they make of bamboos and grass and place underneath it skins full of air. In this province they call them *shāl* (or *sāl*). In rivers and streams in which there are rocks they are safer than boats. 12,000 rupees were given to Mīr Sharīf Āmulī and to a number of men, who had been appointed to perform services at Lahore, to divide amongst the faqirs. An order was given to ʻAbdu-r-Razzāq Maʻmūri[2] and to Bihārī Dās, bakhshi of the Ahadis, to complete the force that had been appointed

[1] *Az ṭaghyān farūd āmada.* Perhaps the meaning is exactly the opposite, viz. 'had come down in violence.' But if so, could a bridge have been made, and with eighteen boats? The time was the 4th or 5th May. Elliot has "the Nīlāb was very full."

[2] According to the Ma'āṣiru-l-umarā, iii, 376, Maʻmūr is a village in Arabia.

to accompany Ẓafar K͟hān and send them away. With one stage in between, the camp halted at the saray of Bāra. On the other side of the river Kāma there is a fort which Zain K͟hān Koka built at the time when he was appointed to subjugate the Yūsufza'e Afghans, and called Naus͟hahr (Newcastle). About 50,000 rupees were spent upon it. They say that Humāyūn used to hunt rhinoceros in this region. I also heard from my father that he had twice or thrice witnessed such a hunt in the company of his father. On Thursday, the 25th, I alighted at the saray of Daulatābād. Aḥmad Beg of Kabul, jagirdar of Peshawar, with the Maliks of the Yūsufza'es and the G͟horiya-khel, came and waited on me. As the service of Aḥmad Beg was not approved, I transferred him from that territory (wilāyat) and conferred it on S͟hīr K͟hān, the Afghan. On Wednesday, the 26th, I encamped in the garden of Sardār K͟hān, which he had made in the neighbourhood of Peshawar. I walked round Ghorkhatrī, which is the worshipping-place of the jogīs in this neighbourhood, with the idea that I might see some faqirs from association with whom I might obtain grace. But that was like looking for the phœnix or the philosopher's stone. A herd without any religious knowledge came to my view, from seeing whom I derived nothing but obscurity of mind. On Thursday, the 27th, I arrived at the halting-place of Jamrūd, and on Friday, 28th, at the K͟haibar Kotal (Khyber Pass) and encamped at 'Alī Masjid, and on Saturday I traversed the tortuous (*mārpīch*, i.e. snake-twisting) Pass, and alighted at G͟harīb-k͟hāna. At this stage Abū-l-qāsim Namakīn, Jagirdar of Jalālābād, brought an apricot, which was not inferior in beauty to good Kashmir apricots. At the stage of Daka they brought from Kabul *gīlās* (cherries), which my revered father had entitled *S͟hāh-ālū*. As I was much inclined to eat them, inasmuch as I had not (hitherto ?) obtained them, I ate them with great zest as a relish to wine. On Tuesday,

2nd Ṣafar, I encamped at Basāwal, which is on the bank of the river. On the other side of the river there is a mountain which has no trees or grass on it, and on that account they call this mountain the hill of Bīdaulat (unfortunate). I heard from my father that in mountains like this there are mines of gold. On the mountain of Āla Būghān, at the time when my revered father went to Kabul, I had had a *qamargāh* hunt, and killed several[1] red deer. As I had handed over the administration of all civil affairs to the Amīru-l-umarā, and his illness increased greatly, and forgetfulness came over his faculties to such an extent that what was settled in one hour he forgot in the next, and his forgetfulness was increasing day by day, on Wednesday, the 3rd Ṣafar, I entrusted the duties of the viziership to Āṣaf Khān, presenting him with a special robe of honour, and inkstand and a jewelled pen. It was a remarkable coincidence that twenty-eight years previously to this, at the same halting-place, my revered father had promoted him[2] to the rank of Mīr Bakhshī (chief paymaster). A ruby which his brother[3] Abū-l-qāsim had bought for 40,000 rupees and sent him, he presented as an offering on obtaining the viziership. He petitioned that Khwāja Abū-l-ḥasan, who held the offices of bakhshi and the *Qūr*, etc., might go with him. Jalālābād was transferred from Abū-l-qāsim Namakīn to 'Arab Khān. A white rock was present in the river-bed; I ordered them to carve it in the form of an elephant

[1] The MSS. have *ṣad* instead of *chand*, i.e. 100.

[2] This Āṣaf Khān is Qawāmu-d-dīn Ja'far Beg and the No. iii of Blochmann, p. 411. Apparently his appointment as Mir Bakhshi was made in 989 (1581), in which year Akbar went to Kabul. Blochmann says Āṣaf Khān was made Mir Bakhshi in the room of Qāẓī 'Alī, and we find at p. 372 of A.N., iii, that Qāẓī 'Alī Bakhshī was appointed in that year to the Panjab. Twenty-eight years before 1016 (to the beginning of which Jahāngīr is referring) yields 988. Basāwal is on right bank of Kabul River below Jalālābād.

[3] Text *baulī*, but the MSS. have *lūlī*, i.e. dancing-girl.

and cut upon its breast this hemistich, which agrees with the date of the Hijra year: "The white stone elephant of Jahāngīr Pādshāh," that is, 1016.

On the same day Kalyān, son of Rāja Bikramājīt, came from Gujarat. Certain extraordinary proceedings on the part of this rebellious rascal had been reported to me. Amongst these was this. He had kept a Musulmān *lūlī* woman in his house, and for fear this affair should become known had killed her father and mother and buried them in his house. I ordered that he should be imprisoned until I could enquire into his proceedings, and after ascertaining the truth I ordered first that they should cut out his tongue and place him in perpetual confinement, and that he should eat his food with dog-keepers and outcasts. On Wednesday I encamped at Surkhāb. Thence I alighted at Jagdalak. At this stage I saw many *ballūṭ*[1]-trees (oak or chestnut), which are the best wood for burning. Although this stage had neither passes nor declivities there were plenty of rocks. On Friday, the 12th, I encamped at Āb-i-bārīk, and Saturday, the 13th, at Yūrt-i-pādshāh. On Sunday, the 14th, I alighted at Khūrd Kābul (little Kabul). At this stage I entrusted the Chief Justiceship and Qaziship of the city of Kabul to Qāẓī 'Ārif, son of Mullā Ṣādiq Ḥalwā'ī. They brought some ripe *shāh-ālū* (cherries) from the village of Gulbahār to this place; of these I ate with much enjoyment nearly a hundred. Daulat, the head of the village of Jigrī[2] (?), brought some uncommon flowers, such as I had never seen in my life. Thence I alighted at Bikrāmī. At this place they brought to show me a piebald[3] animal, like the flying (i.e. jumping) mouse, which in the Hindi tongue they call *galahrī* (squirrel), and said that mice would not

[1] Generally spelt *ballūṭ*, either the oak or the chestnut. Cf. Erskine's Baber, p. 145. Sir Alexander Burnes calls the *ballūṭ* the holly.

[2] See below, p. 52, where the *Ra'īs* or headman of Chikrī is mentioned.

[3] Cf. Erskine's Baber, p. 145.

frequent any house in which this animal was. On this account they call this animal the master of mice. As I had never seen one before, I ordered my painters to draw a likeness of it. It is larger than a mongoose. On the whole it is very like a civet cat. Having appointed Aḥmad Beg Khān to punish the Afghans of Bangash, I ordered 'Abdu-r-Razzāq Ma'mūrī, who was in Attock, to take 2,000,000 rupees under the charge of Mohan Dās, son of Rāja Bikramājīt, with him, and divide it among the auxiliaries of the aforesaid army. One thousand musketeers were also ordered to accompany this army.

Shaikh 'Abdu-r-Raḥmān, son of Shaikh Abū-l-faẓl, was promoted to the rank of 2,000 personal and 1,500 horse, and obtained the title of Afẓal Khān. 15,000 rupees were presented to 'Arab Khān, and 20,000 rupees more for the repair of the fort of Pesh Bulāgh.[1] I bestowed Sarkār Khānpūr[2] in fief on Dilāwar Khān Afghān. On Thursday, the 17th, from the Mastān bridge as far as the Shahr-ārā garden, which was the encamping place for the royal standards, scattering rupees, half-rupees, and quarter-rupees to faqirs and indigent persons on both sides of the road, I entered the aforesaid garden. It appeared to be very green and fresh. As it was a Thursday I gave a wine entertainment to my intimates, and on account of hilarity and excitement ordered those who were of equal age to myself and had been my playfellows to jump over the stream that flowed through the middle of the garden and was about four gaz in width. Most of them could not jump it, and fell on the bank or into the stream. Although I jumped it, yet now that I was 40 years of age I could not jump it with the

[1] The fort of Pesh Bulāq is mentioned in the third volume of the Akbar-nāma, p. 512. It is marked on the map of Afghanistan between Daka and Jalālābād.

[2] *Sic* in text, but should be Jaunpūr as in the MSS.

activity that I had shown in the presence of my revered father when I was 30. On this day I perambulated seven of the famous gardens of Kabul. I do not think that I ever walked so far before.

First of all I walked round the Shahr-ārā (city-adorning), then the Mahtāb (moonlight) garden, then the garden that Bīka Begam, grandmother of my father, had made, then passed through the Ūrta-bāgh (middle garden), then a garden that Maryam-makānī, my own grandmother, had prepared, then the Ṣūrat-khāna garden, which has a large *chanār*-tree, the like of which there is not in the other gardens of Kabul. Then, having seen the Chārbāgh, which is the largest of the city gardens, I returned to my own abode. There were abundance of cherries on the trees, each of which looked as it were a round ruby, hanging like globes on the branches. The Shahr-ārā garden was made by Shahr-bānū[1] Begam, daughter of Mīrzā Abū Sa'īd, who was own aunt to the late king Bābar. From time to time it has been added to, and there is not a garden like it for sweetness in Kabul. It has all sorts of fruits and grapes, and its softness is such that to put one's sandalled[2] feet on it would be far from propriety or good manners. In the neighbourhood of this garden an excellent plot of land came to view, which I ordered to be bought from the owners. I ordered a stream that flows from the *guzargāh* (ferry, also bleaching green) to be diverted into the middle of the ground so that a garden might be made such that in beauty and sweetness there should not be in the inhabited world another like it. I gave it the name of Jahān-ārā (world-adorning). Whilst I was at Kabul I had several entertainments in the Shahr-ārā garden,

[1] There was also a Shahr-bānū who was Bābar's sister. Bīka Begam was Bābar's widow and the lady who carried his bones to Kabul.

[2] *Bakafsh-pāy*, which Erskine renders 'with slippers on' and Elliot 'with his shoes on.'

sometimes with my intimates and courtiers and sometimes with the ladies of the harem. At nights I ordered the learned and the students of Kabul to hold the cooking entertainment,[1] *bughra,* and the throwing of bughra, together with *arghushtak* dances.

To each of the band of *Bughrā'iyān* I gave a dress of honour, and also gave 1,000 rupees to divide amongst themselves. To twelve of the trustworthy courtiers I ordered 12,000 rupees to be given, to be bestowed every Thursday, as long as I was in Kabul, on the poor and needy. I gave an order that between two plane-trees that were on the canal bank in the middle of the garden—to one of which I had given the name of Faraḥ-bakhsh (joy-giver) and the other Sāya-bakhsh (shade-giver)—they should set up a piece of white stone (marble ?) one gaz in length and three-quarters of a gaz in breadth, and engrave my name thereon (and those of my ancestors) up to Tīmūr. It was set forth on the other side that I had done away with the whole of the customs dues and charges of Kabul, and whichever of my

[1] Bāyazīd Biyāt describes Humāyūn as holding a cooking festival in Badakhshān. See A.N., i, translation, p. 496, n. 2. They cooked *bughra,* which appears to be macaroni. The text wrongly has *raqẓ az 'ishq* (love-dances). The real word, as the MSS. show, is *arghushtaq,* which is a kind of dance (not a child's game as in Johnson). It is described in Vullers, s.v., in accordance with the account in the Burhān-i-qāṭi'. It is a dance by girls or young men, and is accompanied with singing and with clapping of hands, etc. Probably it is the dance described by Elphinstone in his account of Kabûl, i, 311, where he says: "The great delight of all the western Afghans is to dance the Attun or Ghoomboor. From ten to twenty men or women stand up in a circle (in summer before their houses and tents, and in winter round a fire); a person stands within the circle to sing and play on some instrument. The dancers go through a number of attitudes and figures; shouting, clapping their hands, and snapping their fingers. Every now and then they join hands, and move slow or fast according to the music, all joining in chorus. When I was showed this, a love-song was sung to an extremely pretty tune, very simple, and not unlike a Scottish air." Erskine's translation is: "Custards and confections were presented, and the amusements of dancing girls and arghustak were introduced."

descendants and successors should do anything contrary to this would be involved in the wrath and displeasure of God. Up to the time of my accession these were fixed and settled, and every year they took large sums on this account from the servants of God (the Muhammadan people in general). The abolition of this oppression was brought about during my reign. On this journey to Kabul complete relief and contentment were brought about in the circumstances of my subjects and the people of that place. The good and leading men of Ghaznīn and that neighbourhood were presented with robes of honour and dealt kindly with, and had their desires excellently gratified.

It is a strange coincidence that (the words) *rūz-i-panjshanba hīzhdaham-i-Ṣafar*,[1] Thursday, 18th Ṣafar, which is the date of my entry into Kabul, give the Hijra date thereof.

I ordered them to inscribe this date on the stone. Near a seat (*takht*) on the slope of a hill to the south of the city of Kabul, and which is known as Takht-i-shāh, they have made a stone terrace where Firdūs-makānī (Bābar) used to sit and drink wine. In one corner of this rock they have excavated a round basin which could contain about two Hindustani maunds of wine. He caused his own blessed name with the date to be carved on the wall of the terrace which is next to the hill. The wording is, "The seat of the king, the asylum of the world, Ẓahīru-d-dīn Muḥammad Bābar, son of 'Umar Shaikh Gūrgān, may God perpetuate his kingdom, 914 (1508–9)." I also ordered them to cut out of stone another throne parallel

[1] The words seem to me to yield 1066, but if we read *pajshanba* instead of *panjshanba* we get 1016, which is the Hijra date of Jahāngīr's entry into Kabul and corresponds to 4th June, 1607. A marginal note on I.O.M. 305 makes the chronogram clear by writing *rūz-i-panchanba hizhdah-i-Ṣafar*, thereby getting rid of the *mīm* and the *yā* of *hīzhdaham* and bringing out the figures 1016.

to this, and dig another basin of the same fashion on its side, and engrave my name there, together with that of Ṣāḥib-qirānī (Tīmūr). Every day that I sat on that throne I ordered them to fill both of the basins with wine and give it to the servants who were present there. One of the poets of Ghaznin found the date of my coming to Kabul in this chronogram—"The king of the cities of the seven climes" (1016). I gave him a dress of honour and a present, and ordered them to engrave this date on the wall near the aforesaid seat. Fifty thousand rupees were given to Parwīz; Wazīr-al-mulk was made Mir Bakhshi. A firman was sent to Qilīj Khān to despatch 170,000 rupees from the Lahore treasury for expenses of the army at Qandahar. After visiting the Khiyābān (avenue) of Kabul and the Bībī Māh-rū, I ordered the governor of that city to plant other trees in the place of those cut down by Ḥusain Beg Rū-siyāh (the black-faced). I also visited the Ūlang-yūrt of Chālāk and found it a very pleasant place. The Ra'is of Chikrī (Jigrī ?) shot with an arrow a *rang*[1] and brought it to me. Up to this time I had never seen a rang. It is like a mountain goat, and there is a difference only in its horns. The horns of the rang are bent, and those of the goat are straight and convoluted.

In connection with the account of Kabul the commentaries of Bābar[2] passed in view before me. These were in his own handwriting, except four sections (*juz'*[3]) that I wrote myself. At the end of the said sections a sentence was written by me also in the Turkī character, so that it might be known that these four sections were written by me in my own hand. Notwithstanding that I grew up in Hindustan, I am not ignorant of Turkī

[1] Evidently a kind of sheep.

[2] This is a reference to Bābar's Memoirs.

[3] A *juz'* is said to consist of eight leaves or sixteen pages. Does Jahāngīr mean that he wrote sixty-four pages?

speech and writing.[1] On the 25th Ṣafar I with the people of the harem visited the *julgāh* (plain) of Safīd-sang, a very bright and enjoyable place. On Friday, the 26th, I enjoyed the blessing of a pilgrimage to (the tomb of) H.M. Firdūs-makānī (Bābar). I ordered much money and food, bread, and sweetmeats for the souls of the departed to be distributed to faqirs. Ruqayya Sulṭān Begam, daughter of Mīrzā Hindāl, had not performed a pilgrimage to her father's tomb, and on that day had the honour to do so. On Thursday, 3rd Rabī'u-l-awwal, I ordered them to bring my racehorses (*āspān-i-dawanda*) to the K͟hiyābān (avenue). The princes and the Amirs raced them. A bay Arab horse, which 'Ādil K͟hān, the ruler of the Deccan, had sent to me, ran better than all the other horses. At this time the son of Mīrzā Sanjar Hazāra and the son of Mīrzā Mās͟hī, who were the chief leaders of the Hazāras, came to wait on me. The Hazāras of the village of

[1] Probably the sections which Jahāngīr wrote were those printed in the Ilminsky edition and which bring the narrative down to Bābar's death. They seem to have been in great measure copied from the Akbar-nāma. Jahāngīr does not say if he wrote them when he was in Kabul or previously. According to Blochmann, J.A.S.B. for 1869, p. 134, one *juz'* = two sheets of paper. The passage is translated in Elliot, vi, 315. Though Jahāngīr does not say when he wrote the four sections, I think that his language implies that these additions were in the manuscript when he was looking at it in Kabul. Perhaps he made them when he was a student in India, and for the sake of practice in Turkī. He may have translated the sections from the Akbar-nāma. All, I think, he did in Kabul was to put the Turkī note, stating that the sections were his. But possibly even this was done before. Elliot, vi, 315, has the words "to complete the work," but these words do not occur in the MSS. that I have seen. The translation in Elliot, seems to represent Jahāngīr's words as meaning that the work was complete, but that the four sections were not, like the rest, in Bābar's handwriting, and so Jahāngīr re-copied them. But it does not appear that there could be any object in his doing this. There is a valuable article in the Zeitschrift d. Deutschen Morgenl. Gesellsch. for 1883, p. 141, by Dr. Teufel, entitled "Bâbur und Abû'l-faẓl," in which the fragments in Ilminsky are discussed. But the passage in the Tūzuk-i-Jahāngīrī is not referred to.

Mīrdād produced before me two rangs[1] that they had killed with arrows. I had never seen a rang of this size; it was larger by 20 per cent. than a large *mārkhūr* (?).

News came that Shāh Beg Khān, the governor of Qandahar, had reached the parganah of Shor,[2] which is his jagir. I determined to give Kabul to him and return to Hindustan. A petition came from Rāja Bīrsing-deo that he had made a prisoner of his nephew, who had been creating a disturbance and had killed many of his men. I ordered him to send him to the fort of Gwalior to be imprisoned there. The parganah of Gujrāt[3] in the Panjab Sarkār I bestowed on Shīr Khān, the Afghan. I promoted Chīn Qilīj, son of Qilīj Khān, to the rank of 800 personal and 500 horse. On the 12th I sent for Khusrau and ordered them to take the chains off his legs that he might walk in the Shahr-ārā garden. My fatherly affection would not permit me to exclude him from walking in the aforesaid garden. I transferred the fort of Attock and that neighbourhood from Aḥmad Beg to Ẓafar Khān. To Tāj Khān, who was nominated to beat back the Afghans of Bangash, I gave 50,000 rupees. On the 14th I gave 'Alī Khān Kaṛorī,[4] who was one of my revered father's old servants and was the *dārogha* of the Naqārakhāna (drum-house), the title of Naubat Khān, and promoted him to the rank of 500 personal and 200 horse. I made Rām Dās *ātālīq* to Mahā Singh, grandson of Rāja Mān Singh, who had also been nominated to drive back the rebels of Bangash. On Friday, the 18th, the *wazn-i-qamarī* (the weighing according to the lunar year) for my 40th year took place. On that day the

[1] The text mentions a horse, but the MSS. have not this, and it seems to be a mistake.

[2] Apparently the Shorkot of I.G., xii, 424. In the Rechnau Dūāb (Jarrett, ii, 321). It is north of Multan and in the Jhang district.

[3] I.G. v, 188.

[4] Perhaps the 'Alī Dūst Khān of Blochmann, p. 533.

assembly was held when two watches of the day had passed. I gave 10,000 rupees of the money of the weighing to ten of my confidential servants to divide amongst those who deserved it and the needy. On this day a petition came from Sardār Khān, governor of Qandahar, by way of Hazāra and Ghaznīn, in twelve days; its purport was that the ambassador of Shāh 'Abbās, who had started for the Court, had entered the Hazāra [1] (country). The Shah had written to his own people: "What seeker of occasion and raiser of strife has come against Qandahar without my order? Perhaps he does not know what is our connection with H.M. Sulṭān Tīmūr, and especially with Humāyūn and his glorious descendants. If they by chance should have taken the country into their possession they should hand it to the friends and servants of my brother Jahāngīr Pādshāh and return to their own abodes." I determined to tell Shāh Beg Khān to secure the Ghaznin road in such a way that travellers from Qandahar might reach Kabul with ease. At the same time I appointed Qāẓī Nūru-d-dīn to the Ṣadārat of the province of Malwah and Ujjain. The son of Mīrzā Shādmān Hazāra and grandson of Qarācha Khān, who was one of the influential Amirs of Humāyūn, waited on me. Qarācha Khān had married a woman from the Hazāra tribe, and this son [2] had been born by her. On Saturday, the 19th, Rānā Shankar, son of Rānā Ūday Singh, was promoted to the rank of 2,500 personal and 1,000 horse. An order was given for the rank of 1,000 personal and 600 horse for Rāy Manohar. The Shinwārī Afghans brought a mountain ram the two horns of which had become one and had become like a rang's horns. The same Afghans killed and brought

[1] The MSS. have Herat, and this is probably correct.

[2] That is, apparently, Mīrzā Shādmān, but perhaps the meaning is that Qarācha had sought a wife for his son among the Hazāras, and not that he had himself married an Hazāra woman.

a *mārkhūr* (Erskine translates this 'a serpent-eating goat'), the like of which I had never seen or imagined. I ordered my artists to paint him. He weighed four Hindustani maunds; the length of his horns was 1½ gaz.[1] On Sunday, the 27th, I gave the rank of 1,500 personal and 1,000 horse to Shajā'at Khān, and the *ḥawīlī* (district surrounding) of Gwalior was placed in the jagir of I'tibār Khān. I appointed Qāẓī 'Izzatu-llah with his brothers to the Bangash duty. At the end of the same day a petition came to me from Islām Khān from Agra, together with a letter which Jahāngīr Qulī Khān had written to him from Bihar. Its purport was that on the 3rd Ṣafar (30th May, 1607), after the first watch, 'Alī Qulī Istājlū had wounded Quṭbu-d-dīn Khān at Bardwan, in the province of Bengal, and that he had died when two watches of the same night had passed. The details of this matter are that the aforesaid 'Alī Qulī was *sufrachī* (table servant) to Shāh Ismā'īl (the 2nd), ruler of Iran; after his death he took to flight through his natural wickedness and habit of making mischief, and came to Qandahar, and having met at Multan the Khānkhānān, who had been appointed to the charge of the province of Tulamba,[2] started with him for that province. The Khānkhānān in the field[3] placed him among the servants of the late king (Akbar), and he having performed services in that campaign was promoted to a rank in accordance with his condition, and was a long time in the service of my revered father. At the time when he (Akbar) went in prosperity to the provinces of the Deccan, and I was ordered against the Rānā, he came and became servant to me. I gave him the title of Shīr-

[1] The MSS. have "less than 1½ gaz by ⅛ (*nīm-pāo*)."

[2] Should, I think, be Tattah, i.e. Sind.

[3] *Ghaibāna*, 'secretly.' But the phrase merely means that the appointment was not made in the Emperor's presence.

afgan (tiger-throwing). When I came from Allahabad to wait on my revered father, on account of the unfriendliness that was shown me, most of my attendants and people were scattered abroad, and he also at that time chose to leave my service. After my accession, out of generosity I overlooked his offences, and gave an order for a jagir for him in the Subah of Bengal. Thence came news that it was not right to leave such mischievous persons there, and an order went to Quṭbu-d-dīn Khān to send him to Court, and if he showed any futile, seditious ideas, to punish him. The aforesaid Khān had reason to know him (his character), and with the men he had present, immediately the order arrived, went hastily to Bardwan, which was his jagir. When he (Shīr-afgan) became aware of the arrival of Quṭbu-d-dīn Khān, he went out to receive him alone with two grooms. After he arrived and entered into the midst of his army (his camp) the aforesaid Khān surrounded him. When from this proceeding on the part of Quṭbu-d-dīn Khān a doubt arose in his mind, he by way of deceiving him said: "What proceeding is this of thine?"[1] The aforesaid Khān, keeping back his own men, joined him alone in order to explain the purport of the order to him. Seeing his opportunity he immediately drew his sword and inflicted two or three severe wounds upon him. Amba Khān Kashmīrī, who was descended from the rulers of Kashmir and was connected (by marriage?) with the aforesaid Khān, and had a great regard for him by way of loyalty and manliness, rushed forward and struck a heavy blow on 'Alī Qulī's head, and that vicious fellow inflicted a severe wound on Amba Khān with the point of his sword.[2] When they saw Quṭbu-d-dīn Khān in this

[1] Text *bargasht*, 'he turned round.' But the MSS. have *chi rawish-i-tūzukast*, "What kind of arrangement is this?"

[2] *Shamshīr-i-sīkhakī*, 'pointed sword, poniard'?

state, his men attacked him (Shīr-afgan), and cut him in pieces and sent him to hell. It is to be hoped that the place of this black-faced scoundrel will always be there. Amba Khān obtained martyrdom on the spot, and Quṭbu-d-dīn Khān Koka after four watches attained the mercy of God in his quarters. What can I write of this unpleasantness? How grieved and troubled I became! Quṭbu-d-dīn Khān Koka was to me in the place of a dear son, a kind brother, and a congenial friend. What can one do with the decrees of God? Bowing to destiny I adopted an attitude of resignation. After the departure of the late King and the death of that honoured one, no two misfortunes had happened to me like the death of the mother of Quṭbu-d-dīn Khān Koka and his own martyrdom.

On Friday, the 6th Rabīʻu-l-ākhir, I came to the quarters of Khurram (Shāh-Jahān), which had been made in the Ūrta Garden. In truth, the building is a delightful and well-proportioned one. Whereas it was the rule of my father to have himself weighed twice every year, (once) according to the solar and (once according to the) lunar year, and to have the princes weighed according to the solar year, and moreover in this year, which was the commencement of my son Khurram's 16th lunar year, the astrologers and astronomers [1] represented that a most important epoch according to his horoscope would occur, as the prince's health [2] had not been good, I gave an order that they should weigh him according to the prescribed rule, against gold, silver, and other metals, which should be divided among faqirs and the needy. The whole of that day was passed in enjoyment and pleasure in the house of Bābā Khurram, and many of his presents were approved.

[1] The meaning of two words being used probably is that both Hindu and Persian astrologers are referred to. Blochmann, p. 311, says that Shāh-Jahān's birthday was 30th Rabīʻu-l-awwal.

[2] Lit., "His disposition had changed from equability."

As I had experienced the excellencies of Kabul, and had eaten most of its fruits, in consequence of important considerations and the distance from the capital, on Sunday, the 4th Jumādā-l-awwal, I gave an order that they should send out the advance camp in the direction of Hindustan. After some days I left the city, and the royal standards proceeded to the meadow of Safīd-sang. Although the grapes were not yet fully ripe, I had often before this eaten Kabul grapes. There are many good sorts of grapes, especially the Ṣāḥibī and Kishmishī. The cherry also is a fruit of pleasant flavour, and one can eat more of it than of other fruits; I have in a day eaten up to 150 of them. The term *shāh-ālū* means *gīlās*[1] (cherry), which are obtainable in most places of the country, but since *gīlās* is like *gīlās*, which is one of the names of the *chalpāsa* (lizard), my revered father called it *shāh-ālū*. The *zard-ālū paywandī*[2] is good, and is abundant. There is especially a tree in the Shahr-ārā garden, that Mīrzā Muḥammad Ḥakīm, my uncle, planted, and is known as the Mīrzā'ī. The apricots of this tree are quite unlike the apricots of other trees. The peaches also are very delicious and plentiful. They had brought some peaches from Istālif. I had them weighed in my presence, and they came exactly in weight to 25 rupees, which is 68 current *misqāl*. Notwithstanding the sweetness of the Kabul fruits, not one of them has, to my taste, the flavour of the mango. The parganah of Mahāban was given as jagir to Mahābat Khān. 'Abdu-r-Raḥīm, paymaster of the Ahadis, was promoted to the rank of 700 personal

[1] *Gīlās* is a cherry in Kashmiri. See Blochmann's Āyīn, p. 616. Abū-l-faẓl mentions in the Āyīn (Blochmann, p. 66) that Akbar called *gīlās shāh-ālū*.

[2] *Paywandī* means 'to graft,' and possibly this is the meaning here, but Steingass gives *paywandī* as part of the name of a plum. The text seems to be corrupt, and perhaps what Jahāngīr wrote was "the *zard-ālū* resembles the *khūbānī*."

and 200 horse. Mubārak Khān Sarwānī was appointed to the faujdarship of the sarkar of Ḥiṣār. I ordered that Mīrzā Farīdūn Barlās should have a jagir in the Subah of Allahabad. On the 14th of the aforesaid month I gave Irādat Khān, brother of Āṣaf Khān, the rank of 1,000 personal and 500 horse, and presenting him with a special robe of honour and a horse, bestowed on him the paymastership of the Subah of Patna and Ḥājīpūr. As he was my *qūrbegī*, I sent by his hand a jewelled sword for my son (*farzand*) Islām Khān, the governor of the aforesaid Subah. As we were going along I saw near 'Alī Masjid and Gharīb-khāna a large spider of the size of a crab that had seized by the throat a snake of one and a half gaz in length and half strangled it. I delayed a minute to look on at this, and after a moment it died (the snake).

I heard at Kabul that in the time of Maḥmūd of Ghazni a person of the name of Khwāja Tābūt[1] had died in the neighbourhood of Ẓuḥāk and Bāmiyān, and was buried in a cave, whose limbs had not yet rotted asunder. This appeared very strange, and I sent one of my confidential record writers with a surgeon to go to the cave and, having seen the state of affairs as they were, to make a special report. He represented that half of the body which was next the ground had most

[1] Text has Yāqūt, but it is clear from the Iqbāl-nāma, p. 25, and from I.O. MS. 181 that the name is Khwāja Tābūt, 'the coffin Khwāja.' The author of the Iqbāl-nāma was the person sent to make the inquiry, and he gives a long account of what he saw. A surgeon was sent with him, as the Khwāja was said to have been martyred, and it was necessary to report on the wounds. The coffin story is mentioned in the Āyīn, i, 194. See Jarrett, ii, 409–10, but the translation is not quite accurate, I think. The punctuation of the text seems to me to be correct. It is characteristic of Jahāngīr and the author of the Iqbāl-nāma that they take no notice of the colossal figures at Bāmiyān, though Abū-l-faẓl does. See Jarrett's note. It is stated in the Iqbāl-nāma that Khwāja Tābūt was said to have been killed in the time of Chingīz Khān. If so, the Sulṭān Maḥmūd mentioned by Jahāngīr must be Sulṭān Maḥmūd Ghorī.

of it come asunder, and the other half which had not touched the ground remained in its own condition. The nails of the hands and feet and the hair of the head had not been shed, but the hair of the beard and moustache as far as one side of the nose had been shed. From the date that had been engraved on the door of the cave it appeared that his death had occurred before the time of Sulṭān Maḥmūd. No one knows the exact state of the case.

On Thursday, the 15th Arslān Bī, governor of the fort of Kāhmard, who was one of the servants of middle rank (?) of Walī Muḥammad Khān, ruler of Tūrān, came and waited on me.[1] I had always heard that Mīrzā Ḥusain, son of Shāhrukh Mīrzā, had been killed by the Ūzbegs. At this time a certain person came and presented a petition in his name, and brought a ruby of the colour of an onion, which was worth 100 rupees, as an offering. He prayed that an army might be appointed to assist him, so that he might take Badakhshan out of the Ūzbegs' hands. A jewelled dagger-belt was sent him, and an order given that, as the royal standards had alighted in those regions, if he really was Mīrzā Ḥusain, son of Mīrzā Shāhrukh, he should first hasten into my presence, so that having examined his petitions and claims I might send him to Badakhshan. Two hundred thousand rupees were sent for the army that had been sent with Mahā Singh and Rām Dās against the rebels of Bangash.

On Thursday, the 22nd, having gone to the Bālā Ḥiṣār, I inspected the buildings in that place. As the place was not fit for me I ordered them to destroy these buildings and to prepare a palace and a royal hall of audience. On the same day they brought a peach from Istālif, *barābar sar-i-buh bakalānī*, "as big as an owl's

[1] He was appointed governor of Sehwān (Iqbāl-nāma, p. 27).

head" (?).[1] I had not seen a peach of such a size, and ordered it to be weighed, and it came to 63 Akbari rupees, or 60 tolas. When I cut it in half its stone also came into two pieces, and its substance was sweet. I had in Kabul never eaten better fruit from any tree. On the 25th news came from Malwa that Mīrzā Shāhrukh had bid farewell to this transitory world, and God Almighty had submerged him in His mercy. From the day on which he entered the service of my revered father till the time of his departure, from no act of his could dust be brought into the royal mind. He always did his duty with sincerity. The aforesaid Mīrzā apparently had four sons: Ḥasan and Ḥusain were born of the same womb (i.e. they were twins). Ḥusain fled from Burhanpur and went by sea to Iraq, and thence to Badakhshan, where they say he now is, as has been written about his message and his sending some one to me. No one knows for certain whether it is the same Mīrzā Ḥusain, or the people of Badakhshan have raised up this one like other false Mīrzās and given him the name of Mīrzā Ḥusain. From the time when Mīrzā Shāhrukh came from Badakhshan and had the good fortune to wait on my father until now, nearly 25 years have passed. For some time the people of Badakhshan, on account of the oppression and injury they have to undergo from the Ūzbegs, have given notoriety to a Badakhshan boy, who had on his face the marks of nobility, as really the son of Mīrzā Shāhrukh and of the race of Mīrzā Sulaimān. A large number of the scattered Ūymāqs, and the hill-people of Badakhshan,

[1] The MSS. merely have "of a size that I had never seen before." Probably the text is corrupt, and the meaning may be "as big as a head." *Bih* is a quince, and perhaps this is what is meant here. Or the meaning may be "equal to the biggest for size." Or *sar* may be a mistake for *sih* and the meaning be "equal in size to three (ordinary peaches)."

whom they call Gharchal (Georgians ?), collected round him, and showing enmity and disputing with the Ūzbegs, took some of the districts of Badakhshan out of their possession. The Ūzbegs attacked that false Mīrzā and captured him, and placing his head on a spear sent it round to the whole country of Badakhshan. Again the seditious people of Badakhshan quickly produced another Mīrzā. Up to now several Mīrzās have been killed. It appears to me that as long as there is any trace of the people of Badakhshan they will keep up this disturbance. The third son of the Mīrzā is Mīrzā Sulṭān, who excels in appearance and disposition all the other sons of the Mīrzā. I begged him from his revered father, and have kept him in my own service, and having taken great pains with him reckon him as my own child. In disposition and manners he has no likeness to his brothers. After my accession I gave him the rank of 2,000 personal and 1,000 horse, and sent him to the Subah of Malwa, which was his father's place. The fourth son is Badī'u-z-zamān, whom he always had in attendance on himself; he obtained the rank of 1,000 personal and 500 horse.

While I was at Kabul, no *qamargāh* hunt had taken place. As the time for returning to Hindustan had come near, and I was very desirous of hunting red deer, I ordered them to go forward as soon as possible and surround the hill Faraq,[1] which is seven kos from Kabul. On Tuesday, the 4th Jumādā-l-awwal, I went to hunt. Nearly 100 deer had come into the enclosure (qamargah). About a half of these were taken, and a very hot hunt took place. I gave 5,000 rupees in rewards to the ryots who were present at the hunt. On the same day an increase of 500 horse was ordered to the rank of Shaikh

[1] I.O. MS. 181 has Qarqara mountains. There is also the reading Kharaq.

'Abdu-r-Raḥmān, son of S̲h̲aik̲h̲ Abū-l-faẓl, so as to bring it to 2,000 personal and (2,000) horse. On Thursday, the 6th, I went to the throne-place of the late king Bābar. As I was to leave Kabul on the next day I looked on that day as a feast day, and ordered them to arrange a wine-party on the spot, and fill with wine the little reservoir they had cut in the rock. Cups were given to all the courtiers and servants who were present, and few days have passed in such enjoyment and pleasure. On Friday, the 7th, when a watch of day had passed, leaving the city auspiciously and with pleasure, a halt was made at the *julgāh* (meadow) of the Safīd-sang. From the S̲h̲ahr-ārā as far as the julgah I scattered to faqirs and poor people *darb* and *charan*, that is, half and quarter rupees.[1] On that day, when I mounted my elephant for the purpose of leaving Kabul, the news arrived of the recovery of the Amīru-l-umarā and S̲h̲āh Beg K̲h̲ān. The news of the good health of these two chief servants of mine I took as an auspicious omen for myself. From the julgah of the Safīd-sang, marching one kos on Tuesday, the 11th, I halted at Bikrām. I left Tās̲h̲ Beg K̲h̲ān at Kabul to take proper care of Kabul and neighbourhood until the coming of S̲h̲āh Beg K̲h̲ān. On Tuesday, the 18th, I marched two and a half kos from the halting-place of Būtk̲h̲āk by the road Dū'āba,[2] and encamped at a spring on the bank of which there are four plane-trees. No one till now had looked to the preparation of this halting-place, and they were ignorant of its condition and suitability. It is in truth a most excellent spot, and one fit to have a building erected in it. At this halting-place another qamargah hunt took place, when about 112 deer, etc., were taken. Twenty-four rang antelope and 50 red antelope and 16 mountain goats were

[1] Blochmann, p. 31.

[2] Dū'āba is mentioned as a stage by W. Finch.

taken. I had never till now seen a rang antelope alive.[1] It is in truth a wonderful animal of a beautiful shape. Although the black buck of Hindustan looks very finely made, the shape and fashion and appearance of this antelope is quite a different thing. They weighed a ram and a rang; the ram came to a maund and 33 seers and the rang to two maunds and 10 seers. The rang, although of this size, ran so that ten or twelve swift dogs were worn out and seized it with a hundred thousand difficulties. The flesh of the sheep of the Barbary goat in flavour does not surpass that of the rang. In the same village kulangs (demoiselle crane) were also caught.

Although Khusrau had repeatedly done evil actions and deserved a thousand kinds of punishment, my fatherly affection did not permit me to take his life. Although in the laws of government and the ways of empire one should take notice of such disapproved deeds, I averted my eyes from his faults, and kept him in excessive comfort and ease. It became known that he was in the habit of sending men to scoundrels who did not consider consequences, and of inciting them to give trouble and attempt my life, and making them hopeful with promises. A band of these ill-fated ones of little foresight having joined together, desired to attack me in the hunts that took place in Kabul and those parts. As the grace and protection of God Almighty are the guardians and keepers of this sublime dynasty, they did not attain to their end. On the day when the halt was at the Surkhāb, one of that band went at the risk of his life to Khwāja Waisī, the Dīwān of my son Khurram, and revealed that nearly 500 men at Khusrau's instigation had conspired with Fatḥu-llah, son of Ḥakīm Abū-l-fatḥ, Nūru-d-dīn, son of Ghiyāṣu-d-dīn 'Alī Āṣaf-khān, and Sharīf, son of I'timādu-d-daulah (Nūr-Jahān's father), and were awaiting an opportunity

[1] The text omits the word *zinda*, 'alive.'

to carry out the designs of the enemies and evil-wishers of the king. Khwāja Waisī told this to Khurram, and he in great perturbation immediately told me. I gave Khurram the blessing of felicity, and prepared to get hold of the whole set of those short-sighted ones and punish them with various kinds of punishment. Again, it came to my mind, as I was on the march, and the seizure of these people would create a disturbance and confusion in the camp,[1] to order the leaders of the disturbance and mischief to be apprehended. I handed over Fatḥu-llah in confinement to certain trusty men, and ordered capital punishment for the other two wretches, with three or four of the chief among the black-faced (conspirators). I had dignified Qāsim 'Alī, who was one of the servants of the late king Akbar, after my accession with the title of Dayānat Khān. He always accused Fatḥu-llah of a want of loyalty, and said things about him. One day he said to Fatḥu-llah: "At the time when Khusrau fled and the king pursued him, you said to me: 'The Panjab should be given to Khusrau and this quarrel cut short.'" Fatḥu-llah denied this, and both resorted to oaths and curses (on themselves). Ten or fifteen days had not passed after this altercation when that hypocritical wretch was arrested, and his false oath did its business.

On Saturday, the 22nd Jumādā-l-awwal, the news came of the death of the Ḥakīm Jalālu-d-dīn Muẓaffar Ardistānī, who was of a family of skill and medicine and claimed to be a descendant of Galen. At all events he was an unequalled healer. His experience added to his knowledge.[2] As he was very handsome and well-made

[1] The *urdū* or camp was probably not with Jahāngīr then, and he thought that if he sent to it for the capture of 500 there would be confusion. He therefore contented himself at the time with arresting the ringleaders. There is a full account of the conspiracy in the Iqbāl-nāma, p. 27, etc.

[2] Possibly the meaning is "his experience was greater than his skill."

in the days of his youth (*sāda-rū'īhā*)[1] he frequented the assemblies of S͟hāh Ṭahmāsp, and the king recited this hemistich about him:—

"We have a pleasant physician: come, let us all be ill."

Ḥakīm 'Alī, who was his contemporary, exceeded him in skill. In short, in medical skill and auspiciousness and rectitude and purity of method and disposition he was perfect. Other physicians of the age could not compare with him. In addition to his medical skill he had many excellencies. He had perfect loyalty towards me. He built at Lahore a house of great pleasantness and purity, and repeatedly asked me to honour it (with my presence). As I was very fond of pleasing him I consented. In short, the aforesaid Ḥakīm, from his connection with me and being my physician, had great skill in the management of affairs and business of the world, so that for some time at Allahabad I made him Diwan of my establishment. On account of his great honesty he was very exacting in important business, and people were vexed at this method of proceeding. For about twenty years he had ulcerated lungs, and by his wisdom preserved in some measure his health. When he was talking he mostly coughed so much that his cheek and eyes became red, and by degrees his colour became blue. I often said to him: "Thou art a learned physician: why dost thou not cure thy own wounds?" He represented that wounds in the lungs were not of such a nature that they could be cured. During his illness one of his confidential servants put poison into some medicine he was in the habit of taking every day and gave it to him. When he perceived this he took remedies for it. He objected very much to be bled, although this was necessary. It happened that he was going to the privy when his cough overcame him and

[1] Lit., when he was smooth-faced, i.e. beardless.

opened the wounds in his lungs. So much blood poured out of his mouth and brain that he became insensible and fell, and made a fearful cry. An *āftābachī* (ewer-bearer) becoming aware of this, came into the assembly-room, and seeing him smeared with blood cried out: "They have killed the ḥakīm." After examining him it was seen that there was no sign of wounds on his body, and that it was the same wound in the lungs that had begun to flow. They informed Qilīj Khān, who was the Governor of Lahore, and he, having ascertained the true state of the affair, buried him. He left no capable son.

On the 24th, between the garden of Wafā and Nīmlah, a hunt took place, and nearly forty red antelope were killed. A female panther (*yūz*) fell into our hands in this hunt. The zamindars of that place, Laghmānīs, Shālī, and Afghans, came and said that they did not remember nor had they heard from their fathers that a panther had been seen in that region for 120 years. A halt was made on the 2nd Jumādā-l-ākhir, at the Wafā Garden, and the assembly for the solar weighing was held. On the same day Arslān Bī, an Ūzbeg who was one of the Sardars and nobles of ʻAbdu-l-Mūmin Khān, and was at that time governor of the fort of Kāhmard, having left his fort, had the blessing of waiting on me. As he had come from friendship and sincerity, I exalted him with a special robe of honour. He is a simple Ūzbeg, and is fit to be educated and honoured. On the 4th of the month an order was given that ʻIzzat Khān, the governor[1] of Jalālābād, should make the hunting-ground of the Arzina plain into a qamargah (ring-hunting ground). Nearly 300 animals were captured,

[1] The I.O. MSS. do not call him governor, and the names of the animals captured differ in the MSS. from those given in the text. The latter are obviously wrong, and I have discarded them. The Iqbāl-nāma, p. 30, has Arzana as the name of the hunting-ground. Erskine has Arzina.

namely, 35 *qūch* (rams ?), 25 *qūshqī* (?), 90 *arghalī* (wild sheep), 55 *tūghlī* (yaks ?), 95 antelope (*safīda*).

As it was the middle of the day when I arrived at the hunting-place and the air was very hot, the (*tāzī*) Arabian dogs had been exhausted.[1] The time for running dogs is in the morning or at the end of the day. On Saturday, the 12th, the halt was at Akūra Saray (?). At this stage Shāh Beg Khān,[2] with a good force, came and waited on me. He was one who had been brought up by my father, the late king Akbar. In himself he is a very brave man and energetic, so much so that constantly in the time of my father he fought several single combats, and in my own reign defended the fort of Qandahar from the hosts of the ruler of Iran. It was besieged for a year before the royal army arrived to his assistance. His manners towards his soldiers are those of an Amir (nobleman, *umarāyāna*), and not according to discipline (*qudrat*), especially towards those who have helped him in battles or are with him in campaigns. He jokes much with his servants, and this gives him an undignified appearance.[3] I have repeatedly warned him about this, but as it is in his nature my remonstrances have had no effect.

On Monday, the 14th, I promoted Hāshim Khān, who is one of the household, born ones of our dynasty, to

[1] Erskine has "many of the hounds were destroyed." *Sagān-i-tāzī* probably means greyhounds, whether bred in Arabia or elsewhere.

[2] Blochmann, p. 377, and Ma'āṣiru-l-umarā, ii, 642. He was an Arghūn.

[3] The passage is obscure and the text is corrupt. Erskine's translation is: "His manners towards the soldiers is frank and gallant, but not according to the rules of discipline, especially towards those who have been or are in the wars with him. He is much flattered by his servants, which gives him a light appearance." Evidently Erskine read *nāzī* or *nāz* instead of *bāz* as in the text, and the MSS. support his reading. I think, however, that *nāz kashīdan* means 'to jest.' Instead of the *tā bamāndand* of text the MSS. have *yā namāyand*, the meaning being those soldiers who have served him well, or are doing so. We learn from Blochmann, p. 378, that Shāh Beg was "a frank Turk."

the rank of 3,000 with 2,000 horse, and I made him governor of the province of Orissa. On the same day news came that Badī'u-z-zamān, son of Mīrzā Shāhrukh, who was in the province of Malwa, through folly and youth had started with a body of rebels to go to the province of the Rānā and join him. 'Abdu-llah Khān, the governor of that place, being informed of this event went after him, and having made him prisoner on the way, slew several of the wretches who had joined with him. An order was given that Ihtimām Khān should start from Agra and bring the Mīrzā to the court. On the 25th of the aforesaid month news came that Imām Qulī Khān, nephew of Walī Khan, ruler of Māwarā'a-n-nahr, had killed him who was called Mīrzā Ḥusain, who had been reported to be the son of Mīrzā Shāhrukh. In truth, the killing of the sons of Mīrzā Shāhrukh is like the killing of the demons, as they say that from every drop of their blood demons are produced. In the station of Dhaka, Shīr Khān, the Afghan, whom when I left I had placed at Peshawar to guard the Khaibar Pass, came and waited on me. He had made no default in preserving and guarding the road. Ẓafar Khān, son of Zain Khān Koka, had been appointed to move on the Dalāzāk Afghans and the tribe of Khatur, who had perpetrated all kinds of misdeeds in the neighbourhood of Attock and the Beas and that vicinity. After performing that service and the conquest of those rebels, who numbered about 100,000 houses, and sending them off towards Lahore, he came and waited upon me at the same halting-place, and it was evident that he had performed that service as it ought to have been done. As the month of Rajab, corresponding with the Ilāhī month of Ābān, had arrived,[1] and it was known that this

[1] The peculiarity of this year was that the lunar month and the solar month of Akbar's birth, viz. Rajab and Ābān, coincided, so that there was a double celebration.

was one of the months fixed for the lunar weighing (*wazn-i-qamarī*) of my father, I determined that the value of all the articles which he used to order for his own weighing in the solar and lunar years should be estimated, and that what this came to should be sent to the large cities for the repose of the soul of that enlightened one, and be divided amongst the necessitous and the faqirs. The total came to 100,000 rupees, equal to 300 Irāq tumāns, and 300,000 of the currency of the people of Māwarā'a-n-nahr.

Trustworthy men divided that sum among the twelve chief cities, such as Agra, Delhi, Lahore, Gujarat (Ahmadabad), etc. On Thursday, the 3rd Rajab, I favoured with the title of Khān-jahān my son (*farzand*) Ṣalābat Khān, who is not less to me than my own sons, and ordered that they should in all firmans and orders write of him as Khān-jahān. A special robe of honour and a jewelled sword were also given him. Also, having entitled Shāh Beg Khān Khān-daurān, I presented him with a jewelled waist-dagger, a male elephant, and a special horse. The whole of the sarkars of Tīrah, Kabul, Bangash, and the province of Sawād (Swat) Bajaur, with the (task of) beating back the Afghans of those regions, and a jagir and the faujdarship were confirmed to him. He took leave from Bābā Ḥasan Abdāl. I also ordered Rām Dās Kachhwāha to receive a jagir in this province and to be enrolled among the auxiliaries of this Subah. I conferred on Kishan Chand, son of the Mota (fat) Rāja, the rank of 1,000 personal and 500 horse. A firman was written to Murtaẓā Khān (Sayyid Farīd), governor of Gujarat, that as the good conduct and excellence and abstemiousness of the son of Miyān Wajīhu-d-dīn [1] had been reported to me, he should hand over to him from me a sum of money, and that he should write and send me some of

[1] Wajīhu-d-dīn was a famous Gujarat saint. He died in 998.

the names of God which had been tested. If the grace of God should be with me I would continually repeat[1] them. Before this I had given leave to Ẕafar K͟hān to go to Bābā Ḥasan Abdāl to collect together game for sport. He had made a *s͟hāk͟hband* (literally a tying together of horns or branches). Twenty-seven red deer and 68 white ones came into the *s͟hāk͟hband.* I myself struck with arrows 29 antelope, and Parwīz and K͟hurram also killed some others with arrows. Afterwards orders were given to the servants and courtiers to shoot. K͟hān Jahān was the best shot, and in every case of his striking an antelope the arrow penetrated through and through.[2] Again, on the 14th of the month of Rajab, Ẕafar K͟hān had arranged a qamargah at Rawalpindi. I struck with an arrow a red deer at a long distance, and was highly delighted at the arrow striking him and his falling down. Thirty-four red deer and 35 *qarā-qūyrūg͟h* (black-tailed) antelope, which in the Hindi language they call *chikāra,* and two pigs were also killed. On the 21st another qamargah had been arranged within three kos of the fort of Rohtas by the efforts and exertions of Hilāl K͟hān. I had taken with me to this hunt those who were screened by the curtains of honour (the members of the zanānah). The hunt was a good one and came off with great *éclat.* Two hundred red and white antelope were killed. Passing on from Rohtas, the hills of which contain these antelope, there are in no place in the whole of Hindustan, with the exception of Girjhāk and Nandanah, red deer of this description. I ordered them

[1] The word used by Jahāngīr, and which has been translated 'repeat continually,' is *mudāwamat,* and Erskine understood it to mean that Jahāngīr hoped to prolong his life by this exercise.

[2] *Har ahū'ī kih zad bar sar-i-tīr raft.* The literal rendering apparently is: "whenever an antelope was struck by him the arrow entered up to its (the arrow's) head." Perhaps the meaning simply is every arrow (or bullet) that he shot went home.

to catch and keep some of them alive, in order that possibly some of them might reach Hindustan for breeding purposes. On the 25th another hunt took place in the neighbourhood of Rohtas. In this hunt also my sisters and the other ladies were with me, and nearly 100 red deer were killed. It was told me that Shams Khān, uncle of Jalāl Khān [1] Gakkhar, who was in that neighbourhood, notwithstanding his great age took much delight in hunting, such that young men had not so much enjoyment in it. When I heard that he was well-disposed towards faqirs and dervishes I went to his house, and his disposition and manners pleased me. I bestowed on him 2,000 rupees, and the same sum on his wives and children, with five other villages with large receipts by way of livelihood for them, that they might pass their days in comfort and contentment. On the 6th Sha'ban, at the halting-place of Chandālah, the Amīru-l-umarā came and waited on me. I was greatly pleased at obtaining his society again, for all the physicians, Hindu and Musulman, had made up their minds that he would die. Almighty God in His grace and mercy granted him the honour of recovery, in order that it might be known to such as do not recognize His will that for every difficult ill, which those who look on the outside of causes only may have given up as hopeless, there is One who is powerful to provide a cure and remedy out of His own kindness and compassion. On the same day Rāy Rāy Singh,[2] one of the most considerable of the Rajput Amirs, ashamed on account of the fault he had committed in the matter of Khusrau, and who was living at his home, came, and under the patronage of the Amīru-l-umarā obtained the good

[1] Jalāl Khān was a grandson of Sulṭān Ādam (Blochmann, pp. 455 and 486).

[2] See *infra* for another notice of him in the chapter on Gujrat.

fortune of waiting on me; his offences were pardoned. At the time that I left Agra in pursuit of Khusrau I had in full confidence left him in charge of Agra, so that when the ladies (*maḥalhā*)[1] should be sent for he might come with them. After the ladies were sent for he went for two or three stages with them, and in the village of Mathura, on merely hearing foolish tales, separated from them, and went to his native place (Bikanir). He thought that as a commotion had arisen he would see where the right road was. The merciful God, who cherishes His servants, in a short time having arranged that affair broke the rope of the alliance of those rebels, and this betrayal of his salt remained a burden on his neck. In order to please the Amīru-l-umarā I ordered the rank which he formerly held to be confirmed to him, and his jagir to remain as it was. I promoted Sulaimān Beg, who was one of my attendants from the time when I was prince, to the title of Fidā'ī Khān. On Monday, the 12th, a halt was made at the garden of Dil-āmīz, which is on the bank of the river Ravi. I waited on my mother in this garden. Mīrzā Ghāzī, who had done approved service in command of the army at Qandahar, waited on me, and I bestowed great favour on him.

On Tuesday, the 13th, I auspiciously entered Lahore. The next day Mīr Khalīlu-llah, son of Ghiyāṣu-d-dīn Muḥammad, Mīrmīrān, who was of the descendants of Shāh Ni'matu-llah Walī, paid his respects.[2] In the reign of Shāh Ṭahmāsp there was no family of such greatness in the whole country, for the sister of the Shah, by name Jānish Begam, was in the house of (married to) Mīr Ni'matu-llah, the father of the Mīrmīrān.

[1] One of Jahāngīr's wives was a daughter of Rāy Rāy Singh (of Bikanir). See Blochmann, p. 310.

[2] See Rieu, Cat. ii, p. 634.

A daughter who was born to them, the Shah gave in marriage to his own son Isma'īl Mīrzā, and making the sons of that Mīrmīrān sons-in-law, gave his younger daughter to his eldest son, who had the same name as his grandfather, and connected (in marriage) the daughter of Isma'īl Mīrzā, who was born of the niece of the Shah, to another son, Mīr Khalīlu-llah. After the death of the Shah, by degrees the family went to decay, until in the reign of Shāh 'Abbās they became all at once extirpated, and they lost the property and effects that they had and could no longer remain in their own place. Mīr Khalīlu-llah came to wait upon me. As he had undergone trouble on the road, and the signs of sincerity were apparent from his circumstances, having made him a sharer of my unstinted favours I gave him 12,000 rupees in cash, and promoted him to the rank of 1,000 personal and 200 horse, and gave an order for a jagir.

An order was given to the civil department (*dīwāniyān*) to confer the rank of 8,000 personal and 5,000 horse on my son Khurram, and to provide a jagir for him in the neighbourhood of Ujjain, and to assign the Sarkar of Ḥiṣār Fīrūza to him. On Thursday, the 22nd, on the invitation of Āṣaf Khān, I went with my ladies to his house and passed the night there. The next day he presented before me his own offerings, of the value of ten lacs of rupees, in jewels and jewelled things, robes, elephants, and horses. Some single rubies and jacinths and some pearls, also silk cloths with some pieces of porcelain from China and Tartary, were accepted, and I made a present of the rest to him. Murtaẓā Khān from Gujarat sent by way of offering a ring made of a single ruby of good colour, substance, and water, the stone, the socket, and the ring being all of one piece. They weighed 1½ tanks and one surkh, which is equal to one misqal and 15 surkh. This was sent to me and much approved. Till that day no one had ever heard of such a ring having come to the hands of any sovereign. A single ruby weighing six surkhs or two tanks and 15 surkhs,[1] and of which the value was stated to be £25,000, was also sent. The ring was valued at the same figure.

On the same day the envoy of the Sharif of Mecca came to wait on me with a letter and the curtain of the door of the Ka'bah. He showed great friendship towards me. The said envoy had bestowed on him 500,000 *dām*, equal to 7,000 or 8,000 rupees, and I resolved to send the Sharif the equivalent of 100,000 rupees of the precious things of Hindustan. On Thursday, the 10th of the month, a piece of the Subah of Multan was added to the jagir of Mīrzā Ghāzī, though the whole of the province of Thattah had been given to him in jagir. He was also promoted to the rank of 5,000 personalty and 5,000 horse. The government of Qandahar and the protection of that region, which is the frontier of Hindustan, were assigned to his excellent administration. Conferring on him a robe of honour and a jewelled sword I gave him his leave. In fine, Mīrzā Ghāzī possessed perfection,[2] and he made also good verses. He used Waqārī as his *takhalluṣ*, or poetic name (Rūz-i-rūshan, Bhopal 1297, p. 455; also Ma'āṣiru-l-umarā, vol. iii, p. 347). This is one of his couplets:—

> "If my weeping should cause her to smile, what wonder?
> Though the cloud weep, the cheek of the rose-bush smiles."

[1] There is evidently something wrong in the text, for a ruby weighing 6 surkhs could not weigh 2 tanks and 15 surkhs. I.O. MS. 181 has *barja* instead of *surkh*, but I do not know what this means. Perhaps *shash-gūsha*, 'hexagonal,' was intended. This view is confirmed by the Iqbāl-nāma, p. 31, which has *shash pahlū*, 'six-sided.' Erskine's MS. also had 'six-sided,' and he translates "a six-sided ruby which weighed two *tangs* fifteen *surkhs*." I.O. MS. 305 has *shash pārcha*, and it is evident that this word, as also the *barja* of No. 181, is the *pārche* of Steingass, which means a segment or facet.

[2] This remark about Mīrzā Ghāzī, and also the quotation, do not occur in the two I.O. MSS.

On the 15th the offering of the Khankhanan was presented to me: 40 elephants, some jewelled and decorated vessels, some Persian robes, and cloth that they make in the Deccan and those parts, had been sent by him, altogether of the value of 150,000 rupees. Mīrzā Rustam and most of the office-holders of that Subah had also sent good offerings. Some of the elephants were approved. News of the death of Rāy Durgā,[1] who was one of those who had been brought up by my revered father, arrived on the 18th of the month. He had been in attendance for forty years and more in the position of an Amir on my revered father, until, by degrees, he had risen in rank to 4,000. Before he obtained the good fortune of waiting on my father, he was one of the trusted servants of Rānā Ūday Singh. He died on the 29th. He was a good military man. Sulṭān Shāh, the Afghan, whose disposition was turbulent and mischievous, passed his time in the service of Khusrau, and had his complete intimacy, so much so that this rebel was the cause of the running away of that unfortunate one. After the defeat and capture of Khusrau he went off alone (?)[2] into the skirts of the hills of Khiẓrābād and that region. At last he was made prisoner by Mīr Mughal, the *karorī* of that place. As he had been the cause of the destruction and ruin of such a son, I ordered them to shoot him with arrows on the plain of Lahore. The aforesaid karori was promoted to higher rank, and was dignified with a grand dress of honour. On the 29th Shīr Khān, the Afghan, who was one of my old servants, died. One might say that he took his own life, because he was continually drinking wine, to the extent that in every watch he used to drink four brimming cups of arrack of double strength. He had broken the fast of the Ramaẓān of the past year,

[1] Blochmann, p. 417.

[2] *Bayaktā*, but the I.O. MSS. have *batagpāy*, 'rapidly.'

and took it into his head this year that he would fast in the month of Sha'bān on account of his having broken the fast of Ramaẓān, and would fast for two months together. In abandoning his usual custom, which is a second nature, he became weak and his appetite left him, and becoming very weak he passed away in his 57th year. Patronising his children and brothers according to their circumstances, I bestowed on them a portion of his rank and jagir.

On the 1st of the month of Shawwāl I went to visit Maulānā Muḥammad Amīn, who was one of the disciples of Shaikh Maḥmūd Kamāngar (the bow-maker). The Shaikh Maḥmūd[1] mentioned was one of the great men of his age, and H.M. Humāyūn had entire reliance on him, so much so that he once poured water on his hands. The aforesaid Maulānā is a man of good disposition, and is free, notwithstanding the attachments and accidents (of the world), a faqir in manner and ways, and acquainted with brokenness of spirit. His company pleased me exceedingly. I explained to him some of the griefs that had entangled themselves in my mind and heard from him good advice and agreeable words, and found myself greatly consoled at heart. Having presented him with 1,000 *bīghā* and 1,000 rupees in cash by way of maintenance, I took leave. One watch of day had passed on Sunday when I left Lahore on my way to the capital of Agra. Having made Qilij Khān governor, Mīr Qawāmu-d-dīn diwan, Shaikh Yūsuf bakhshi, and Jamālu-d-dīn kotwal, and presented each according to his circumstances with dresses of honour, I turned towards my desired way. On the 25th, having passed over the river at Sultanpur, I proceeded two kos and halted at Nakodar. My revered father had given

[1] Properly Zainu-d-dīn Maḥmūd. See the story in Badayūnī, Ranking, p. 589; also Akbar-nāma translation, i, 611, and Blochmann, p. 539 and note.

Shaikh Abū-l-fazl[1] gold of the weight of 20,000 rupees to build an embankment between these two parganahs and prepare a waterfall, and in truth I found a halting-place exceedingly pleasant and fresh. I ordered Mu'izzu-l-mulk, the jagirdar of Nakodar, to erect a building and prepare a garden on one side of this embankment, so that wayfarers seeing it might be pleased. On Saturday, 10th Zī-l-qa'da, Wazīru-l-mulk, who before my ascension had the good fortune to serve me, and was Diwan of my establishment, died of diarrhœa. At the end of his life a son of evil fortune (lit. footsteps) had been born in his house, who in the space of forty days ruined[2] (Erskine has 'ate') both his father and mother, and who himself died when he was two or three years old. It occurred to me that the house of Wazīru-l-mulk must not all at once be ruined, and patronising Manṣūr, his brother's son, I gave him rank. Indeed,[3] he showed no love to me (the scent of love did not come from him). On Monday, the 14th, I heard on the road that between Panipat and Karnal there were two tigers that were giving much trouble to wayfarers. I collected the elephants and sent them off. When I arrived at their (the tigers') place I mounted a female elephant, and ordered them to place the elephants round them after the manner of a qamargah (enclosure), and by the favour of Allah killed both with a gun, and thus got rid of the raging tigers that had closed the road to the servants of God. On Thursday,

[1] I do not know if this is the author. There appears to be no mention of the construction in the Akbar-nāma. Nakodar is in the Jalandhar district (I.G., x, 180, and Jarrett, ii, 317). Perhaps the two tombs at Nakodar mentioned in I.G. as of Jahāngīr's time are those of Muqīm the Wazīru-l-mulk and his wife. See Tūzuk, pp. 6 and 64.

[2] *Khwurd*, lit. 'devoured.' Apparently he refers to the fact of the birth as a misfortune. I.O. MS. 181 has *sar-i-mādar u pidar rā khwurd*, and the A.S. 124 has *shīr-i-mādar u pidar-i-khūd*, 'the milk of his own mother and father'!

[3] This is given as a quotation in No. 181.

the 18th,[1] I halted at Delhi and alighted at the residence which Salīm Khān, the Afghan, had made in the days of his rule in the middle of the river Jumna and called Salīmgaḍh. My revered father had given the place to Murtaẓā Khan, who was originally an inhabitant of Delhi. The aforesaid Khan had built on the margin of the river a terrace of stone excessively pleasant and bright. Below that building[2] near the water there was made a square *chaukandī* with glazed tiles by the order of H.M. Humāyūn, and there are few places with such air. In the days when the late king Humāyūn honoured Delhi with his presence, he often sat there with his intimates, and associated with the members of his assemblies. I passed four days in that place, and with my courtiers and intimates enjoyed myself with wine parties. Mu'aẕẕam Khān, who was governor of Delhi, presented offerings. The jagirdars and citizens also made offerings and presents, each according to his circumstances. I was desirous to employ some days in a qamargah hunt in the parganah of Pālam, which is one of the places near the aforesaid city and one of the fixed hunting-grounds. As it was represented to me that the (fortunate) hour for approaching Agra had come very near, and another proper hour was not to be obtained at all near that time, I gave up the intention, and embarking on board a boat went on by water. On the 20th of the month of Ẕī-l-qa'da four boys and three girls, children of Mīrzā Shāhrukh, whom he had not mentioned to my father, were brought. I placed the boys among my confidential servants, and made over the girls to the attendants of the ladies of the harem in order that they might look after them. On the 21st of the same month Rājā Mān Singh came and waited on me

[1] This should be the 17th if Monday was the 14th.

[2] The MSS. seem to have *mutaṣṣil-i-māb-i-chaukandī*, 'in shape like a chaukandī (?).' It was from the roof of this building that Humāyūn fell.

from the fort of Rohtas, which is in the province of Patna and Behar, after orders had been sent to him six or seven times. He also, like Khān A'ẓam, is one of the hypocrites and old wolves of this State. What they have done to me, and what has happened to them from me, God the knower of secrets knows; possibly no one could mention such another case (?). The aforesaid Raja produced as offerings 100 elephants, male and female, not one of which was fit to be included among my private elephants. As he was one of those who had been favoured by my father, I did not parade his offences before his face, but with royal condescension promoted him.

On this day they brought a talking *jal* (lark) which distinctly said "Miyān Ṭūṭī." It was very strange and wonderful. In Turki they call this bird *turghai*.[1]

The Third New Year's Feast from my Accession.

On Thursday, the 2nd Ẕī-l-ḥijja, corresponding with the 1st Farwardīn (19th March, 1608), the Sun, which enlightens and heats the world with its splendour, changed from the constellation of Pisces to the joyful mansion of Aries, the abode of pleasure and rejoicing. It gave the world fresh brightness, and being aided by the Spring clothed those who had been plundered by the cold season, and tyrannised over by the Autumn, with the robes of honour of the New Year and the garments of emerald green, and gave them compensation and recuperation.

> "Again to Not-Being came the world's lord's order,
> 'Restore what thou hast devoured.'"

[1] *Turghai* or *turghei* is a thrush according to Vambéry, and was the name of Timur's father. Perhaps the bird was the large *mainā*, the Bhīmrāj or Bhringraj (?) of the Āyīn, Jarrett, ii, p. 125 and note. In Scully's Glossary, *turghai* is said to be the lark. The text arranges the words differently from the MSS. They have *mushakhkhaṣ Miyān Ṭūṭī gufta*, and Erskine translates 'which said clearly Miyān Tuti.' But possibly Jahāngīr meant that it spoke clearly like a parrot.

The feast of the New Year was held in the village of Rankatta,[1] which is five kos off (from Agra), and at the time of transit (of the sun) I seated myself on the throne with glory and gladness. The nobles and courtiers and all the servants came forward with their congratulations. In the same assembly I bestowed on Khānjahān the rank of 5,000 personal and horse. I selected Khwāja Jahān for the post of bakhshi. Dismissing Wazīr Khān from the Viziership of the province of Bengal, I sent in his place Abū-l-ḥasan Shihābkhānī; and Nūru-d-dīn Qulī became kotwal of Agra. As the glorious mausoleum of the late king Akbar was on the road, it entered my mind that if in passing by I should have the good fortune of a pilgrimage to it, it might occur to those who were short-sighted that I visited it because it was the place where my road crossed. I accordingly had determined that this time I would enter Agra, and after that would go on foot on this pilgrimage to the shrine, which is two and a half kos off, in the same way that the Ḥaẓrat (my father), on account of my birth, had gone from Agra to Ajmir. Would that I might also traverse the same on my head! When two watches of day had passed of Saturday, the 5th[2] of the month, at an auspicious hour, I returned towards Agra, and scattering with two hands 5000 rupees in small coins on the way, entered the august palace which was inside the fort. On this day Rāja Bīr Singh Deo brought a white cheeta to show me. Although other sorts

[1] Blochmann, p. 332. Sikandra, Akbar's tomb, lies half-way between Rankattah and Agra. Tiefenthaler, i, 206, gives the name as Runcta, and says it is a famous place, as Rām there took the figure of Paras Rām. Jarrett, ii, 180, has Rangtah, and it is there described as a village on the Jumna, near the city, and a much frequented place of worship. The Agra volume of the N.W.P. Gazetteer, p. 764, spells it Runkutta, and says it is 9 miles north-west of Agra. See also Ma'āṣir, ii, 407, art. Sa'īd Khān, where mention is made of Rankatta and Hilālābād, and Blochmann, p. 332.

[2] If Thursday was the 2nd, Saturday would be the 4th. He went first to Agra from Rangta, apparently.

of creatures, both birds and beasts, have white varieties, which they call *ṭūyghān*,[1] I had never seen a white cheeta. Its spots, which are (usually) black, were of a blue colour, and the whiteness of the body was also inclined to bluishness. Of the albino animals that I have seen there are falcons, sparrow-hawks, hawks (*shikara*) that they call *bīgū* [2] in the Persian language, sparrows, crows, partridges, florican, *podna* [3] (*Sylvia olivacea*), and peacocks. Many hawks in aviaries are albinos. I have also seen white flying mice (flying squirrels) and some albinos among the black antelope, which is a species found only in Hindustan. Among the *chikāra* (gazelle), which they call *safīda* in Persia, I have frequently seen albinos. At this time Ratan, son of Bhoj-hāra, who is one of the chief Rajput nobles, came to the camp and waited on me, bringing three elephants as an offering. One of these was much approved, and they valued it in the office at 15,000 rupees. It was entered among my private elephants, and I gave it the name of Ratangaj. The value of elephants of the former great Rajas of India was not more than 25,000 rupees, but they have now become very dear. I dignified Ratan with the title of Sarbuland Rāy. I promoted Mīrān Ṣadr Jahān to the rank of 5,000 personal and 1,500 horse and Mu'aẓẓam Khān to 4,000 personal and 2,000 horse. 'Abdu-llah Khān was promoted to 3,000 and 500 horse. Muẓaffar Khān and Bhāo Singh each obtained the rank of 2,000 personal and 1,000 horse. Abū-l-ḥasan diwan had 1,000 and 500 horse. I'timādu-d-daulah that of 1,000 personal and 250 horse. On the 25th Rāja Sūraj Singh, the maternal uncle of my son Khurram, came and paid his respects to me. He brought with him Shyām, the cousin of the turbulent

[1] *Ṭūyghun* or *ṭūyghūn* is given in Zenker as Turkī for the white falcon. See Elliot, vi, 317.

[2] *Bīghū*, which is given in Zenker, is Turkī. The text has *līfū*. The I.O. MSS. have *bīgū*.

[3] Should be *būdana*, 'quail.'

Umrā. In truth he possesses some skill and understands well how to ride elephants. Rāja Sūraj Singh had brought with him a poet who wrote verse in the Hindi tongue. He laid before me a poem in my praise to the purport that if the Sun had a son it would be always day and never would be night, because after his setting that son would sit in his place and keep the world in light. Praise and thanksgiving to God that God gave your father such a son that after his death men should not wear mourning which is like the night. The Sun had envy on this account, saying, "Would I might also have a son who, taking my place, should not allow night to approach the world, for from the light of your rising and the illumination of your justice, notwithstanding such a misfortune, the spheres are so bright that one might say 'night had neither name nor sign.'" Few Hindi verses of such freshness of purport have ever reached my ear. As a reward for this eulogy I gave him an elephant. The Rajputs call a poet Chāran (name of a caste who are many of them poets). One of the poets of the age has turned [1] these sentiments into (Persian) verse—

"If the world-illuminator had a son,
There would be no night; it would be always day;
For when his gold-crowned head was hidden
His son would display his tiara peak.
Thanks that after such a father
Such a son sits in his place.
For from the demise of that king
No one made black robes for mourning."

On Thursday, the 8th Muḥarram, 1017 [2] (24th April, 1608), Jalālu-d-dīn Mas'ūd, who held the rank of 400 personal and was not wanting in bravery, and who in several battles had done great deeds, died at about the age of 50 or 60 years of diarrhœa. He was an opium-eater, and used to eat opium after breaking it in pieces, like

[1] Apparently this is a translation from the Hindi.
[2] Text wrongly has 1014.

cheese, and it is notorious that he frequently ate opium from the hand of his own mother. When his disease became violent and there was a prospect of his death, his mother from excessive love for him ate more opium than was right out of that which she used to give her son, and two or three hours after his death she also died. I have never heard of such affection on the part of a mother for her son. It is the custom among the Hindus that after the death of their husbands women burn themselves, whether from love, or to save the honour of their fathers, or from being ashamed before their sons-in-law, but nothing like this was ever manifested on the part of mothers, Musulman or Hindu. On the 15th of the same month I presented my best horse by way of favour to Rāja Mān Singh. Shāh ʻAbbās had sent this horse with some other horses and fitting gifts by Minūchihr, one of his confidential slaves, to the late king Akbar. From being presented with this horse the Raja was so delighted that if I had given him a kingdom I do not think he would have shown such joy. At the time they brought the horse it was three or four years old. It grew up in Hindustan. The whole of the servants of the Court, Moghul and Rajput together, represented that no horse like this had ever come from Iraq to Hindustan. When my revered father gave the province of Khandesh and the Subah of the Deccan to my brother Dāniyāl, and was returning to Agra, he by way of kindness told Dāniyāl to ask of him whatever he desired. Seizing the opportunity, he asked for this horse, and he accordingly gave it to him. On Tuesday, the 20th, a report came from Islām Khān with the news of the death of Jahāngīr Qulī Khān, the governor of the Subah of Bengal, who was my special slave. On account of his natural excellence and innate merit he had been enrolled in the list of the great Amirs. I was much grieved at his death. I bestowed the rule of Bengal and the tutorship

rekhtabooks.com

TAX INVOICE

Sold By:

REKHTA FOUNDATION
Gyan Avenue 12 Pragati Market
Ashok Vihar Phase-II, New Delhi
North West Delhi 110052
Delhi
India
State Code : 07
Ph: 9899492060
GSTIN No.: 09AABTR9771N1ZK

Invoice No. : RMP202085806
Invoice Date : 23/09/2025
Order No. : 85403-C
Order Date : 23/09/2025

Delivered To:

Batul Mukhtiar
A-1301, Valencia, Raheja Exotica, Madh Island
Madh Marve Road, Malad West
Mumbai 400061
Maharashtra
India
State Code : 27

Payment Method : prepaid
Shipped By : Ekart Surface 2kg
AWB No. : SRSP8566776248
eWaybill No. :

Description	HSN	Qty	Unit Price	Unit Disc.	Taxable Value	IGST	Total
Jahangiri Or Memoirs of Jahangir - Paperback SKU : 43990934946029		1	1534.50	93.53	1440.97	0.00	1440.97
THE AKBAR NAMA OF ABU-L-FAZL: HISTORY OF THE REIGN OF AKBAR INCLUDING AND ACCOUNT OF HIS PREDECESSORS Volume 3rd - Paperback SKU : 43957591769325		1	2557.50	155.87	2401.63	0.00	2401.63
Net Total		**2**					**3842.60**

All disputes are subject to Delhi jurisdiction only. Goods once sold will only be taken back or exchanged as per the store's exchange/return policy.

Authorised Signature for
REKHTA FOUNDATION

Whether tax is payable under reverse charge:No

to Prince Jahāndār on my *farzand*[1] Islām Khān, and in his place gave the government of the Subah of Behar to Afẓal Khān (son of Abū-l-faẓl). The son of Ḥakīm 'Alī, whom I had sent on some duties to Burhanpur, came and brought with him some Karnatic jugglers who had no rivals or equals; for instance, one of them played with ten balls, each of which was equal to an orange and one to a citron, and one to a *surkh*,[2] in such a way that notwithstanding some were small and some large he never missed one, and did so many kinds of tricks that one's wits became bewildered. At the same time a dervish from Ceylon came and brought a strange animal called a *deonak*[3] (or *devang*). Its face was exactly like a large bat, and the whole shape was like that of a monkey, but it had no tail. Its movements were like those of the black tailless monkey which they call *ban mānush* (jungle man) in the Hindi language. Its body was like that of a young monkey two or three months old. It had been with the dervish for five years.[4] It appeared that the animal would never grow larger. Its food is milk and it also eats plantains. As the creature appeared very strange, I ordered the artists to take a likeness of it in various kinds of movement. It looked very ugly.

On the same day Mīrzā Farīdūn Barlās was promoted to the rank of 1,500 personal and 1,300 horse. An order was given that Pāyanda[5] Khān Moghul, as he had reached old age after exerting himself as a soldier, should receive a jagir equal to 2,000 personal. Ilf Khān was promoted to the rank of 700 personal and 500 horse. The rank of Islām Khān, my son (*farzand*),

[1] Jahāngīr calls Islām *farzand* because he was the son of his foster-brother. Jahāngīr Qulī means 'slave of Jahāngīr.'

[2] The seed of *Abrus precatorius*.

[3] Or *devtaq*. Qu. *devanāyak*? The MSS. have *yūnk* and *wabūnk*. The text is corrupt and has converted the word for 'bat' into a 'lamb.'

[4] The text is corrupt.

[5] Blochmann, p. 387.

the governor of the Subah of Bengal, was fixed at 4,000 personal and 3,000 horse. The guardianship of the fort of Rohtas was bestowed on Kishwar Khān, son of Quṭbu-d-dīn Khān Koka. Ihtimām Khān was raised to the rank of 1,000 personal and 300 horse, and made *mīr baḥr* (admiral) and was appointed to the charge of the *nawāra* (fleet) of Bengal. On the 1st Ṣafar Shamsu-d-dīn Khān, son of Khān A'ẓam, made an offering of ten elephants, and, receiving the rank of 2,000 personal and 1,500 horse, was selected for the title of Jahāngīr Qulī Khān, and Ẓafar Khān received the rank of 2,000 personal and 1,000 horse. As I had demanded in marriage the daughter of Jagat Singh, eldest son of Rāja Mān Singh, I on the 16th sent 80,000 rupees for the *sāchaq* (a marriage present) to the house of the aforesaid Raja in order to dignify him. Muqarrab Khān sent from the port of Cambay a European curtain (tapestry), the like of which in beauty no other work of the Frank painters had ever been seen. On the same day my aunt, Najību-n-nisā Begam,[1] died in the 61st year of her age of the disease of consumption and hectic fever. I promoted her son, Mīrzā Wālī, to the rank of 1,000 personal and 200 horse. A man of Māwarā'a-n-nahr, of the name of Aqam Ḥājī, who for a long time had been in Turkey and was not without reasonableness and religious knowledge, and who called himself the ambassador of the Turkish Emperor, waited upon me at Agra. He had an unknown writing (? illegible letter). Looking to his circumstances and his proceedings none of the servants of the Court believed in his being an ambassador. When Tīmūr conquered Turkey, and Yildirīm Bāyazīd, the ruler

[1] Sister of Mīrzā Ḥakīm, also known as Fakhru-n-nisā (Blochmann, p. 322). The MSS. have Bakhtu-n-nisā, and it would seem that the Najību-n-nisā of the text is a wrong reading. See Gulbadan Begam's Memoirs, p. 214.

of that place, fell alive into his hands, he, after levying tribute and taking one year's revenue, determined to hand back into his possession the whole of the country of Turkey. Just at that time Yildirīm Bāyazīd died, and (Tīmūr), having handed over the kingdom to his son Mūsā Chelebī, returned. From that time until now, notwithstanding such favours, no one had come on the part of the emperors, nor has any ambassador been sent: how, then, can it now be believed that this person from Māwarā'a-n-nahr should have been sent by the emperor? I could in no way understand the affair, and no one could bear witness to the accuracy of his claim: I therefore told him to go wherever he might wish. On the 4th Rabī'u-l-awwal the daughter of Jagat Singh entered the harem, and the marriage ceremony was performed in the house of Her Highness Maryam-zamānī. Amongst the things sent with her by Rāja Mān Singh were 60 elephants.

As I had determined to conquer the Rānā, it occurred to me that I should send Mahābat Khān. I appointed 12,000 fully armed cavalry under able officers to go with him, and in addition 500 ahadis, 2,000 musketeers on foot, with artillery made up of 70 to 80 guns mounted on elephants and camels; 60 elephants were appointed to this duty. Two million rupees of treasure were ordered to be sent with this army. On the 16th of the said month Mīr Khalīlu-llah, grandson of Mīr Ni'matu-llah Yazdī, the whole of whose circumstances and family history has already been written, died of diarrhœa. In his appearance the traces of sincerity and dervishhood were manifest. If he had lived and passed a long time in my service he would have risen to high rank. The bakhshi of Burhanpur had sent some mangoes, one of which I ordered to be weighed; it came to 52½ tolas. On Wednesday, the 18th, in the house of Maryam-zamānī, the feast of the lunar weighing of my 40th year was held. I ordered the money used in weighing to be divided amongst women and needy persons. On Thursday, the 4th Rabī'u-l-āk͟hir, Ṭāhir Beg, the bakhshi of the Ahadis, was given the title of Muk͟hliṣ K͟hān, and Mullā-i-Taqiyyā S͟hūstarī,[1] who was adorned with excellencies and perfections, and was well acquainted with the science of history and genealogy, that of Mu'arrik͟h K͟hān. On the 10th of the same month, having given Bark͟hūrdār, the brother of 'Abdu-llah K͟hān, the title of Bahādur K͟hān, I dignified him among his fellows. Mūnis K͟hān, son of Mihtar K͟hān, presented me with a jug of jasper (jade), which had been made in the reign of Mīrzā Ulugh Beg Gūrgān, in the honoured name of that prince. It was a very delicate rarity and of a beautiful shape. Its stone was exceedingly white and pure. Around the neck of the jar they had carved the auspicious name of the Mīrzā and the Hijra year in *riqā'*[2] characters. I ordered them to inscribe my name and the auspicious name of Akbar on the edge of the lip of the jar. Mihtar[3] K͟hān was one of the ancient slaves of this State. He had the honour of serving the late king Humāyūn, and during the reign of my revered father had attained the rank of nobility. He regarded him as one of his confidential servants. On the 16th a firman was issued that the country of Sangrām,[4] which had been given for a year by way of reward to my son (*farzand*) Islām K͟hān, should be handed over for the same purpose for a year to Afẓal K͟hān, the governor of the Subah of Behar. On this day I promoted Mahābat K͟hān to the rank of 3,000 personal and 2,500 horse, and Yūsuf K͟hān, son of Ḥusain K͟hān Tukriyah, obtained that of 2,000

[1] Text wrongly has S͟hams͟hīrī. The MSS. have S͟hūstarī, and this is right. See Blochmann, pp. 208, 209, and 518.

[2] *Riqā'* is a kind of writing (Blochmann, pp. 99, 100).

[3] Blochmann, p. 417. His name was Anīsu-d-dīn.

[4] This must be Rāja Sangrām of K͟harakpur, who had been a rebel. See Blochmann, p. 446 and note.

personal and 800 horse. On the 24th I gave leave to Mahābat Khān and the Amirs and men who had been appointed to subdue the Rānā. The aforesaid Khan was honoured with a robe of honour, a horse, a special elephant, and a jewelled sword. Ẓafar Khān, having been honoured with a standard, was presented with a private robe of honour and a jewelled dagger. Shajā'at Khān also was presented with a standard, and I gave him a robe of honour and a special elephant. Rāja Bīr Singh Deo received a robe of honour and a special horse, and Manglī Khān a horse and jewelled dagger. Narāyan Dās Kachhwāhah, 'Alī Qulī Darman, and Hizabr Khān Tahamtan obtained leave. On Bahādur Khān and Mu'izzu-l-mulk the bakhshi jewelled daggers were conferred, and in the same manner all the Amirs and leaders, each one according to his degree, were honoured with royal gifts. A watch of the day had passed when the Khankhanan, who had been selected for the high honour of my Ātālīq (guardian), came from Burhanpur and waited on me. Delight and happiness had so overpowered him that he did not know whether he came on his head or his feet. He threw himself bewildered at my feet. By way of favour and kindness I lifted up his head and held it in an embrace of kindliness and affection, and kissed his face. He brought me as offerings two strings of pearls and some rubies and emeralds. The value of the jewels was 300,000 rupees. Besides these he laid before me many valuable things. On the 17th Jumādā-l-awwal Wazīr Khān, the Diwan of Bengal, came and waited on me, and offered 60 elephants, male and female, and one Egyptian[1] ruby. As he was one of the old servants and he performed every duty, I ordered him to remain in attendance on me. As Qāsim Khān and his elder brother, Islām Khān, could in no way

[1] Text Quṭbī, but I think the word is Qibṭī, 'Egyptian.'

keep the peace together, I had sent for the former to my own presence; and he yesterday came and waited on me. On the 22nd, Āṣaf Khān, made me an offering of a ruby of the weight of seven *ṭānk*, which Abū-l-qāsim, his brother, had bought in the port of Cambay for 75,000 rupees. It is of a beautiful colour and well-shaped, but to my belief is not worth more than 60,000 rupees. Great faults had been committed by Dulīp Rāy, son of Rāy Rāy Singh, but as he took refuge with my *farzand* Khān Jāhān his offences were pardoned, and I knowingly and purposely passed over his delinquencies. On the 24th the sons of Khānkhānān, who had followed after him, arrived and waited on me and produced as an offering the sum of 25,000 rupees. On the same day the said Khan offered 90 elephants. On Thursday, the 1st Jumādā-ṣ-ṣānī, the feast of my solar year was celebrated in the house of Maryam-zamānī. Some of the money I divided among the women, and an order was given that the balance should be distributed to the poor of the hereditary kingdoms. On the 4th of the month I ordered the Diwans to give a jagir, according to his rank, of 7,000 rupees to Khān A'ẓam.

On this day a female antelope in milk was brought that allowed itself to be milked with ease, and gave every day four seers of milk. I had never seen or heard of anything of the kind before. The milk of the antelope, of the cow, and the buffalo in no way differs. They say it is of great use in asthma. On the 11th of the month Rāja Mān Singh asked for leave to complete the army of the Deccan to which he had been appointed, as well as to visit Amber, his native place. I gave him a male elephant of my own called Hushyār-mast, and gave him leave. On Monday, the 12th, as it was the anniversary of the death of the late king Akbar, in addition to the expenses of that entertainment, which are fixed separately, I sent 4,000 rupees more to be divided among the faqirs and dervishes who are present in the enlightened mausoleum of the venerated one. On that day I exalted 'Abdu-llah, the son of Khān A'zam, with the title of Sarfarāz Khān, and 'Abdu-r-Raḥīm, son of Qāsim Khān, with that of Tarbiyat Khān. On Tuesday, the 13th, I sent for Khusrau's daughter, and saw a child so like her father as no one can remember to have seen. The astrologers used to say that her advent would not be auspicious to her father, but would be auspicious to me. At last it became known that they had augured rightly. They said that I should see her after three years. I saw her when she had passed this age. On the 21st of the month Khānkhānān determined to clear out the province of the Niẓāmu-l-mulk, into which, after the death of the late king Akbar, some disturbances had found their way, and stated in writing that "If I do not complete this service in the course of two years, I shall be guilty (of a faulṭ), on the condition that in addition to the force that had been allotted to that Subah 12,000 more horse with 1,000,000 rupees should be sent with me." I ordered that materials for the army and the treasure should be quickly prepared, and he should be despatched. On the 26th Mukhliṣ Khān, bakhshi of the ahadis, was appointed bakhshi of the Subah of the Deccan, and I bestowed his place on Ibrāhīm Ḥusain Khān, the Mīr Baḥr. On the 1st Rajab, Pīshrau Khān and Kamāl Khān, who belonged to the servants who were in constant attendance on me (*rū-shināṣ*), died. Shāh Ṭahmāsp had given Pīshrau Khān as a slave to my grandfather, and he was called Sa'ādat. When he was promoted in the service of the late king Akbar to the daroghahship and superintendence of the *farrāshkhāna* (carpet department), he obtained the title of Pīshrau. He was so well acquainted with this service that one might say it was a garment they had sewn on the stature of his capacity. When he was 90 years old he was quicker than lads of 14. He had the good fortune to serve my grandfather, my father, and me. Until he breathed his last he was never for a moment without the intoxication of wine.

> "Besmeared with wine Fighānī[1] went to the dust.
> Alas! if the angels[2] smelt his fresh shroud!"

He left 1,500,000 rupees. He has one very stupid son, called Ri'āyat. On account of his father's claims for services performed, I gave the superintendence of half the farrashkhana to him and the other half to Tukhmāq Khān. Kamāl Khān was one of the slaves sincerely devoted to my service; he is of the caste of the Kalāls of Delhi. On account of the great honesty and trustworthiness that he had shown I made him *bakāwal-begī* (chief of the kitchen). Few such servants are ever met with. He had two sons, to both of whom I showed great kindness, but where are there others like him? On the 2nd of the said month La'l[3] Kalāwant, who from his childhood had grown up in my father's service, who had taught him every breathing and sound that appertains to the Hindi language, died in the 65th or 70th year of his age. One of his girls (concubines) ate opium on this event and killed herself. Few women among the Musulmans have ever shown such fidelity.

In Hindustan, especially in the province of Sylhet,[4] which is a dependency of Bengal, it was the custom for the people of those parts to make eunuchs of some of their sons and give them to the governor in place of revenue (*māl-wājibī*). This custom by degrees has been adopted in other provinces, and every year some children are thus

[1] Fighānī was a famous poet and also a drunkard. See Rieu, ii, p. 651, and Sprenger, Oude Cat., p. 403. *Fighānī* also means lamentation, and there is a play in the couplet on the double meaning.

[2] In the Elliot MSS., B.M., the second line is translated "Alas! if the angels made his shroud of another kind of odour!" The angels meant are Nakīr and Munkar.

[3] Blochmann, p. 612.

[4] Cf. Jarrett, ii, p. 122.

ruined and cut off from procreation. This practice has become common. At this time I issued an order that hereafter no one should follow this abominable custom, and that the traffic in young eunuchs should be completely done away with. Islām K͟hān and the other governors of the Subah of Bengal received firmans that whoever should commit such acts should be capitally punished, and that they should seize eunuchs of tender years who might be in anyone's possession. No one of the former kings had obtained this success. Please Almighty God, in a short time this objectionable practice will be completely done away with, and the traffic in eunuchs being forbidden, no one shall venture on this unpleasant and unprofitable proceeding. I presented the K͟hānk͟hānān with a bay horse out of those sent me by S͟hāh 'Abbās; it was the head of the stable of my private horses. He was so rejoiced over it that it would be difficult to describe. In truth a horse of this great size and beauty has hardly come to Hindustan. I also gave him the elephant Futūḥ, that is unrivalled in fighting, with twenty other elephants. As Kis͟han Singh, who was accompanying Mahābat K͟hān, performed laudable service, and was wounded in the leg by a spear in the fight with the Rānā's men, so that about twenty noblemen of his were killed and about 3,000 made captive, he was promoted to the rank of 2,000 personal and 1,000 horse. On the 14th of the same month I gave an order for Mīrzā G͟hāzī to betake himself to Qandahar. A strange occurrence was that as soon as the aforesaid Mīrzā started from Bakhar for that province the news of the death of Sardār K͟hān, the governor of that place, came. Sardār K͟hān was one of the permanent and intimate attendants of my uncle Muḥammad Ḥakīm, and was known as Tuk͟hta[1] Beg. I gave half his rank (the pay of it) to his sons. On Monday, the 17th, I went on

[1] Blochmann, p. 469.

foot on my pilgrimage to the enlightened mausoleum of the late king. If it had been possible, I would have traversed this road with my eyelashes and head. My revered father, on account of my birth, had gone on foot on a pilgrimage to the shrine of Khwāja Mu'īnu-d-dīn Sanjarī Chishtī, from Fatḥpūr to Ajmir, a distance of 120 kos: if I should traverse this road with my head and eyes, what should I have done? When I was dignified with the good fortune of making this pilgrimage, I saw the building that had been erected in the cemetery. It did not come up to my idea of what it ought to be, for that would be approved which the wayfarers of the world should point to as one the like of which was not in the inhabited world. Inasmuch as at the time of erecting the aforesaid building the affair of the ill-starred Khusrau took place, I started for Lahore, and the architects had built it after a design of their own. At last a certain expenditure was made until a large sum was expended, and work went on for three or four years. I ordered that experienced architects should again lay the foundations, in agreement with men of experience, in several places, on a settled plan. By degrees a lofty building was erected, and a very bright garden was arranged round the building of the shrine, and a large and lofty gateway with minarets of white stone was built. On the whole they told me the cost of this lofty edifice was 1,500,000 rupees, equivalent to 50,000 current tumans of Persia and 4,500,000 khanis, according to the currency of Tūrān.

On Sunday, the 23rd, I went with a band of courtiers who had not seen it to look at the reservoir in the house of Ḥakīm 'Alī, like one that had been made at Lahore in the time of my father. The reservoir is 6 gaz by 6 gaz. At its side has been erected a well-lighted room, the entrance to which is through the water, but the water does not get into it. Ten or twelve people could meet in it. He made an offering of some of the cash and jewels that had accumulated[1] in his time. After looking at the room, and the entering of a number of courtiers therein, I raised him to the rank of 2,000, and returned to the palace. On Sunday, the 14th S̲h̲aʻbān, the K̲h̲ānk̲h̲ānān was honoured with a jewelled sword for the waist, a robe of honour, and a special elephant, and was given leave to go to his duty in the Deccan. Rāja Sūraj Singh, who was attached to him in that service, was raised to the rank of 3,000 personal and 2,000 horse. As it was again represented to me that oppression was being committed by the brethren and attendants of Murtaẓā K̲h̲ān on the ryots and people of Ahmadabad in Gujarat, and that he was unable properly to restrain his relations and people about him, I transferred the Subah from him and gave it to Aʻẓam K̲h̲ān, and it was settled that the latter should attend at court, and that his eldest son Jahāngīr Qulī K̲h̲ān should go to Gujarat as his deputy. The rank of Jahāngīr Qulī K̲h̲ān was fixed at 3,000 personal and 2,500 horse. An order was given that in company with Mohan Dās dīwān and Masʻūd Beg Hamaẕānī bak̲h̲s̲h̲ī he should carry on the business of the province. Mohan Dās was promoted to the rank of 800 with 500 horse, and Masʻūd Beg to 300 with 150 horse. Tarbiyat K̲h̲ān, one of the personal servants, was given the rank of 700 with 400 horse, and Naṣru-llah the same. Mihtar K̲h̲ān, whose circumstances have been related, died at this time, and I promoted his son Mūnis K̲h̲ān to the rank of 500 personal and 130 horse. On Wednesday, the 4th Ẕī-l-ḥijja, K̲h̲usrau had a son born to him by the daughter of the K̲h̲ān Aʻẓam, and I gave him the name of Buland-ak̲h̲tar. On the 6th of the same month Muqarrab K̲h̲ān sent a picture (with a report) that the

[1] "What money and articles he could produce at the time" (Elliot, vi, 320).

belief of the Franks was this, that the picture was that of Tīmūr. At the time when Yildirīm Bāyazīd was taken prisoner by his victorious army, a Nazarene, who at that time was ruler[1] of Constantinople, had sent an ambassador with gifts and presents in token of submission and service, and an artist who had been sent with the ambassador took his likeness and brought it away. If this story were true, no better gift could be presented to me. But as the picture had no resemblance to any of his descendants I was not satisfied of the truth of the statement.

The Fourth New Year's Feast after the auspicious Accession.

The passing of the great star that illumines the world into the constellation of Aries took place on the night of Saturday, the 14th Z̤ī-l-ḥijja, in Hijra 1017 (21st March, 1609), and New Year's Day that made brilliant the world began with good auspices and rejoicing. On Friday, the 5th Muḥarram, in the year 1018, Ḥakīm 'Alī died. He was an unrivalled physician; he had derived much profit from Arabic sciences. He had written a commentary on the Canon (of Avicenna) in the time of my revered father. He had greater diligence than understanding, just as his appearance was better than his disposition, and his acquirements better than his talents; on the whole he was bad-hearted, and of an evil spirit. On the 20th Ṣafar I dignified Mīrzā Bark͟hūrdār with the title of K͟hān 'Ālam. They brought from the neighbourhood of Fatḥpūr a water-melon, greater than any I had ever seen. I ordered them to weigh it, and it came to 33 seers. On Monday, the 19th Rabī'u-l-awwal, the feast of my annual lunar weighing

[1] Apparently the person spoken of as a Nazarene (Christian) was the Emperor of Constantinople. Can this picture be the original of that prefixed to White & Davey's translation of Tīmūr's Institutes?

was arranged in the palace of my revered mother; a part of the money was divided among the women who had assembled there on that day.

As it had been evident that in order to carry on the affairs of the State in the Subah of the Deccan it was necessary to send one of the princes there, it came into my mind to send my son Parwīz there. I ordered them to send his equipments and fix the hour for his departure. I summoned to Court Mahābat Khān, who had been nominated to the command of the army against the rebel Rānā to arrange certain matters at headquarters, and appointed in his place 'Abdu-llah Khān, whom I exalted with the title of Fīrūz-jang. I sent 'Abdu-r-Razzāq bakhshī to carry an order to all the mansabdars of that army not to depart from the orders of the aforesaid Khān, and to pay every heed to his thanks and blame. On the 4th Jumādā-l-awwal one of the goatherds, who are a particular tribe, brought before me a gelded goat that had teats like a female, and gave every day sufficient milk to take with a cup of coffee.[1] As milk is one of the favours of Allah, and the source which nourishes many animals, I looked on this strange affair as an omen for good. On the 6th of the same month, having given him the rank of 2,000 personal and 1,500 horse, I sent Khurram, son of Khān A'ẓam, to the government of the province of Sorath, which is known as Jūnagaḍh (in Kaṭhiyawāḍ). I honoured[2] Ḥakīm Ṣadrā with the title of Masīḥu-z-zamān, and gave him the rank of 500 personal and 30 horse. On the 16th a jewelled waist-sword was sent to Rāja Mān Singh. On the 22nd, having handed over 2,000,000 rupees for the expenses of the army of the Deccan, which had been ordered for Parwīz, to a separate treasurer, 500,000 rupees more were given for

[1] Perhaps the meaning is enough milk to fill a coffee-cup.

[2] According to the contemporary, but anonymous, author quoted in Elliot, vi, 448, this was in reward for restoring the sight of Khusrau.

the private expenses of Parwīz. On the 25th, Wednesday, Jahāndār (his son), who previously to this had been appointed, together with Quṭbu-d-dīn Khān Koka, to Bengal, came and waited on me. In reality it became known to me that he was a born devotee.[1] As my mind was taken up with the preparations for the Deccan, on the 1st Jumādā-l-ākhir I nominated the Amīru-l-umarā as well to that duty. He was honoured with the favour of a robe of honour and a horse. Having promoted Karam Chand, son of Jagannāth, to the rank of 2,000 personal and 1,500 horse, I sent him in company with Parwīz. On the 4th of the month 370 ahadi horse were appointed with 'Abdu-llah Khān to the assistance of the army employed against the Rānā. One hundred horses were also despatched from the government stables to be given as he thought proper to the mansabdars and ahadis. On the 17th I gave a ruby of the value of 60,000 rupees to Parwīz, and another ruby with two single pearls, worth about 40,000 rupees, to Khurram. On Monday, the 28th, Jagannāth was promoted to the rank of 5,000 personal and 3,000 horse, and on the 8th of Rajab, Rāy Jāy Singh was promoted to that of 4,000 personal and 3,000 horse, and was dismissed for service in the Deccan. On Thursday, the 9th, Prince Shahriyār from Gujarat came and waited on me. On Tuesday, the 4th, I despatched my son Parwīz on the service of conquering the country of the Deccan. He was presented with a robe of honour, a special horse, a special elephant, a sword, and a jewelled dagger. The Sardars and Amirs who were appointed with him each according to his condition received and were made happy with the favour of a horse, a robe of honour, an elephant, a sword, and a jewelled dagger. I appointed 1,000 ahadis to be in

[1] *Majẕūb-i-mādar-zād.* Probably the meaning is that he was a born idiot.

attendance on Parwīz for the service of the Deccan. On the same day a representation came from 'Abdu-llah Khān that having pursued the rebel Rānā into the hill country into rough places, he had captured several of his elephants and horses. When night came on he had escaped with difficulty with his life. As he had made things go hard with him, he would soon be taken prisoner or killed. I promoted the said Khān to the rank of 5,000 personal, and a rosary of pearls, worth 10,000 rupees, was given to Parwīz. As I had given the province of Khandesh and Berar to the said son, I also conferred on him the fort of Āsīr, and 300 horses were sent with him to be given to ahadis, mansabdars, and whomever else he might consider worthy of favour. On the 26th, Saif Khān Bārha was given the rank of 2,500 personal and 1,350 horse, and appointed to the faujdarship of the Sarkar of Hisar. On Monday, the 4th Sha'bān, an elephant was given to Wazīr Khān. On Friday, the 22nd, I gave an order that as *bang* and *būza* (rice spirit) were injurious, they should not be sold in the bazars, and that gambling should be abolished, and on this subject I issued stringent orders. On the 25th they brought a tiger from my private menagerie to fight with a bull. Many people gathered together to see the show, and a band of Jogis (religious mendicants) with them. One of the Jogis was naked, and the tiger, by way of sport, and not with the idea of rage, turned towards him. It threw him on the ground and began to behave to him as it would to its own female. The next day and on several occasions the same thing took place. As no such thing had ever been seen before and was exceedingly strange, this has been recorded.[1] On the 2nd of the month of Ramaẓān, at the request of Islām

[1] The story is also told in the Iqbāl-nāma, p. 37, where it is said that the tiger was one brought by a calendar as a present. It had the name of La'l Khān and was very tame. It is added that the tiger did no injury to the jogi with his claws or teeth.

Khān, Ghiyās[1] Khān was promoted to the rank of 1,500 personal and 800 horse. Farīdūn Khān Barlās was promoted to the rank of 2,500 with 2,000 horse. One thousand *tolcha* of gold and silver and 1,000 rupees were given in alms on the day of the procession of the sun into the constellation of the Scorpion, which, according to the general acceptation of the Hindoos, is called the Sankrānt. On the 10th of that month an elephant was presented to Shāh Beg Yūzī[2] (? the panther-keeper), and Salāmu-llah, the Arab, who is a distinguished young man and a relative (son-in-law ?) of Mubārak, the ruler of Darful.[3] On account of some suspicion that Shāh 'Abbās had entertained against him, he came to wait upon me. I patronised him, and gave him the rank of 400 personal and 200 horse. Again, another force, containing 193 mansabdars and 46 ahadis, I sent after Parwīz for service in the Deccan. Fifty horses were also entrusted to one of the servants of the Court to convoy to Parwīz.

On Friday, the 13th, a certain idea came into my mind, and this rhymed *ghazal* was produced :—

"What shall I do, for the arrow of loss of thee has pierced my liver !
So that the (evil) eye not reaching me again may reach another ?
Thou movest as if frenzied, and the world is frenzied for thee.
I burn rue lest thy eye should reach me.

[1] The MSS. have 'Ināyat.

[2] I.O. MS. No. 181, Shāh Beg Khān.

[3] Salāmu-llah is mentioned later on (p. 78), and is described as brother's son of Mubārak, who held the country of Jotra (?) and Darful. He is also mentioned in the Iqbāl-nāma, p. 38, where Mubārak is described as ruler (*ḥākim*) of Jūyza and Safūl (?). But a MS. of the Iqbāl-nāma in my possession only mentions Jūyza or Jūyna. I think Jūyza must be Juina or Juanny, which, according to Sir William Jones, is one of the names of the island of Johanna or Hinzuan (one of the Comorro Islands), and that Safūl must be Sofala, a town on the east coast of Africa. Sir W. Jones was landed on Johanna, and has a long account of the island (see his works). The Iqbāl-nāma says that Salāmu-llah killed himself with drink. There is a short notice of him in the Ma'āṣir, ii, 641, where he is called by his title of Shajā'at Khān.

I am frenzied at union with my friend, and in despair at her absence.
Alas for the grief that has o'erwhelmed me !
I've grown mad that I may rush on the pathway of meeting :
Woe for the time that brought me the news !
Jahāngīr, the time for humility and prayer is every morning,[1]
I hope that some spark of light may take effect."

On Sunday, the 15th, I sent 50,000 rupees as *sāchaq* to the house of the daughter of Muẓaffar Ḥusain Mīrzā, son of Sulṭān Ḥusain Mīrzā, son of Bahrām Mīrzā, son of Shāh Isma'īl Ṣafawī, who had been demanded in marriage for my son Khurram. On the 17th of the month Mubārak Khān Sarwānī was honoured with the rank of 1,000 personal and 300 horse. Five thousand rupees were also given to him, and 4,000 rupees to Ḥājī Bī Ūzbeg. On the 22nd a ruby and a pearl were given to Shahriyār. One hundred thousand rupees were given for the subsistence of the Ūymāqs (special cavalry) who had been appointed for service in the Deccan. Two thousand rupees were given to Farrukh Beg, the painter, who is unrivalled in the age. Four thousand rupees were sent for expenditure on Bābā Ḥasan Abdāl. One thousand rupees were handed to Mullā 'Alī Aḥmad Muhrkan (engraver) and Mullā Rūzbihān Shīrāzī to expend on the anniversary festival of Ḥaẓrat Shaikh Salīm at his mausoleum. An elephant was given to Muḥammad Ḥusain, the writer, and 1,000 rupees to Khwāja 'Abdu-l-Ḥaqq Anṣārī. I gave orders to the Diwans that having raised the rank of Murtaẓā Khān to 5,000 personal and horse they should give him a jagir. I ordered Bihārī Chand Qānūngū, of the Sarkar of Agra, to take 1,000 footmen and equipment from the Zamindars of Agra, and, fixing their monthly pay, to send them to Parwīz in the Deccan, and 500,000 rupees more were fixed for the expenses of Parwīz. On Thursday, the 4th Shawwāl,

[1] The I.O. MSS. have a different reading here. Instead of 'every morning' they have 'renew (humility).' The word *nūr*, 'light,' in the last line probably refers to Jahāngīr's name of Nūru-d-dīn.

Islām Khān was promoted to the rank of 5,000 personal and 5,000 horse, Abū-l-walī Beg Ūzbeg to that of 1,500 and Ẓafar Khān to that of 2,500. Two thousand rupees were given to Badīʻu-z-zamān, son of Mīrzā Shāhrukh, and 1,000 rupees to Pathān Miṣr. I ordered that drums should be given to all of them as their rank had been raised to 3,000 and higher. Five thousand rupees more of the money from my weighing were entrusted for the construction of a bridge at Bābā Ḥasan Abdāl and the building that is there to Abū-l-wafā, son of Ḥakīm Abū-l-fatḥ, in order that he might exert himself and put the bridge and the aforesaid building in perfect order. On Saturday, the 13th, when four gharis of day were left, the moon began to be eclipsed. By degrees the whole of its body was obscured, and it continued till five gharis of night had passed. In order to avert the bad omen of this I had myself weighed against gold, silver, cloth, and grain, and gave away in alms all kinds of animals, such as elephants, horses, etc., the cost of all of which was 15,000 rupees. I ordered them to be distributed among the deserving and the poor. On the 25th, at the request of her father, I took the daughter of Rām Chand Bandīlah into my service (i.e. married her). I gave an elephant to Mīr Fāẓil, nephew of Mīr Sharīf, who had been appointed to the faujdarship of Qabūlah and those regions. ʻInāyat-ullah was dignified with the title of ʻInāyat Khān. On Wednesday, the 1st Ẕī-l-qaʻda, Bihārī Chand was granted the rank of 500 personal and 300 horse. A *khapwa* (dagger), adorned with jewels, was given to my son Bābā Khurram. Mullā Ḥayātī, by whom I had sent a message to the Khānkhānān, with a verbal message containing (expressions of) all kinds of condescension and affection, came and brought before me a ruby and two pearls of the value of about 20,000 rupees, which the Khānkhānān had sent by him. Mīr Jamālu-d-dīn Ḥusain, who was in Burhanpur and whom

I had sent for, came and waited on me. I presented Shajā'at Khān Dakhanī with 2,000 rupees. On the 6th of the aforesaid month, before Parwīz arrived at Burhanpur, a petition came from the Khankhanan and the Amirs that the Dakhanis had assembled together and were making disturbances. When I discovered that, notwithstanding the nomination of Parwīz and the army that had proceeded with him and been appointed to his service, they were still in need of support and assistance, it occurred to me that I should go myself, and by Allah's favour satisfy myself with regard to that affair. In the meanwhile a petition came also from Āṣaf Khān that my coming there would be for the advantage of the daily-increasing State. A petition from 'Ādil Khān, from Bijapur, also came, that if one of the trusted ones of the Court could be appointed there to whom he could tell his desires and claims, so that the envoy might convey them to me, he hoped that it might become the means of affording profit to these slaves (i.e. himself). On this account I consulted with the Amirs and loyal men, and told them to represent whatever entered into anyone's mind. My son Khān Jahān represented that inasmuch as so many Amirs had been despatched for the conquest of the Deccan, it was not necessary for me to go in person. If he were ordered, he himself would go and attend on the prince and would, please God, perform this duty while serving him. Those words were approved of by all those who were loyal. I had never contemplated separation from him, but as the affair was an important one I necessarily gave him permission, and ordered that as soon as matters had been arranged he should return without delay, and should not remain more than a year in those regions. On Tuesday, the 17th Ẕī-l-qa'da, he was free to go. I presented him with a special gold-embroidered robe of honour, a special horse with a jewelled saddle, a jewelled sword, and a special elephant.

I also gave him a yak-tail standard (*tūmān ṭūgh*). I appointed Fidā Khān, who was one of my faithful servants, and to whom I gave a robe of honour and a horse and his expenses, promoting him to the rank of 1,000 personal and 400 horse, original and extra, to go with Khān Jahān, in order that if it were necessary to send anyone to 'Ādil Khān according to his request, he might despatch him. Lankū Pandit, who in the time of the late king Akbar had come with offerings from 'Ādil Khān, I also gave leave to go with Khān Jahān, bestowing on him a horse, a robe of honour, and money. Of the Amirs and soldiers who had been appointed with 'Abdu-llah Khān to the duty of beating back the Rānā, men such as Rāja Bīr Singh Deo, Shajā'at Khān, Rāja Bikramājīt, and others, with 4,000 or 5,000 horse, were nominated to support Khān Jahān. I sent Mu'tamad Khān with the announcement that I had made him a *sazāwal* (i.e. one who urges on others), and that he was to act along with Khān Jahān in Ujjain. Out of the men of the palace, I sent 6,000 or 7,000 horse with him, such as Saif Khān Bārha, Ḥājī Bī Ūzbeg, Salāmu-llah 'Arab, brother's son of Mubārak 'Arab, who had in his possession the province of Jūtra (?)[1] and Darfūl (?) and that neighbourhood, and other mansabdars and courtiers. At the time of giving them leave I gave each one an increase of rank and robe of honour and money for their expenses. Making Muḥammad Beg pay-master of the army, I provided him with 1,000,000 rupees to take with him. I sent to Parwīz a special horse, and to the Khankhanan and other Amirs and officers who were appointed to that Subah dresses of honour.

After carrying out these matters I left the city for the purpose of hunting. One thousand rupees were given to

[1] See note above. Jūtra or Jotra is probably a mistake for the island of Johanna, i.e. Hinzuan. Darfūl is Dazfūl in I.O. MS. No. 181.

Mīr ʻAlī Akbar. As the Rabīʻ Faṣl (Spring season) had arrived, for fear any damage should happen to the cultivation of the ryots from the passage of the army, and notwithstanding that I had appointed a *qūrīsāwul* [1] (Erskine has Kor, the Yasawal) (probably a kind of provost marshal) with the band of ahadis for the purpose of guarding the fields, I ordered certain men to see what damage had been done to the crops from stage to stage and pay compensation to the ryots. I gave 10,000 rupees to the daughter of the Khankhanan, the wife of Dāniyāl, 1,000 rupees to ʻAbdu-r-Raḥīm K͟har (i.e. ass) for expenses, and 1,000 to Qāchā the Dakhani. On the 12th, K͟hānjar K͟hān, brother of ʻAbdu-llah K͟hān, received the rank of 1,000 personal and 500 horse, original and extra, and Bahādur K͟hān, another brother, that of 600 personal and 300 horse. On this day two antelopes with horns and one doe were taken. On the 13th I bestowed on and sent to K͟hān Jahān a special horse. Having promoted Badīʻu-z-zamān, son of Mīrzā S͟hāhruk͟h, to the rank of 1,000 and 500 horse, I gave him 5,000 rupees for expenses, and he was sent off with K͟hān Jahān for service in the Deccan. On this day two male and three female antelope were killed. On Wednesday, the 10th, I killed a female *nīlgāw* and a black antelope with a gun, and on the 15th a female nilgaw and a *chikāra* (gazelle). On the 17th of the month two rubies and a pearl were brought to me by Jahāngīr Qulī K͟hān from Gujarat, as well as a jewelled opium box, which Muqarrab K͟hān had sent from the port of Cambay. On the 20th I killed with a gun a tigress and a nilgaw. There were two cubs with the tigress, but they disappeared from view in consequence of the thickness of the jungle and the number of trees. An order was given that they should search for and bring them. When I reached the

[1] Possibly *Qūr Yasāwul* is right, but most probably it was a *yasāwul* attached to the *Qūr*, for which see Blochmann, p. 50.

halting-place my son Khurram brought me one of the cubs, and the next day Mahābat Khān caught the other and brought it. On the 22nd, when I had got within shot of a nilgaw, suddenly a groom (*jilaudār*) and two *kahār* (bearers) appeared, and the nilgaw escaped. In a great rage I ordered them to kill the groom on the spot, and to hamstring[1] the kahars and mount them on asses and parade them through the camp, so that no one should again have the boldness to do such a thing. After this I mounted a horse and continued hunting with hawks and falcons, and came to the halting-place.

Next day, under the guidance of Iskandar Mu'īn, I shot a large nilgaw, and promoted him to the rank of 600 personal and 500 horse. On Friday, the 24th, Ṣafdar Khān, who had come from the Subah of Behar, had the good fortune to perform his obeisance to me. He presented as offerings a hundred muhrs, a sword, and five female and one male elephant. The male elephant was accepted. On the same day Yādgār Khwāja of Samarkand came from Balkh and paid his respects. He made offerings of an album, some horses, and other presents, and was dignified with a robe of honour. On Wednesday, 6th Ẕī-l-ḥijja, Mu'izzu-l-mulk, who had been removed from the paymastership of the army against the rebel Rānā, ill and miserable, waited on me. On the 14th of the said month, having pardoned all the faults of 'Abdu-r-Raḥīm Khar,[2] I promoted him to the rank of *yūzbāshī* (centurion) and 20 horse, and ordered him to go to Kashmir, and in

[1] Jahāngīr's conduct was sufficiently brutal, but the text has made it worse than it was by omitting the word *pay* before *pāy*. The back tendons of the bearers' feet were cut. Their feet were not cut off. Erskine translates the passage rightly, and the I.O. MSS. agree with him.

[2] This was the same 'Abdu-r-Raḥīm who was a companion of Khusrau, and after his capture was sweated in a skin. As he had life left in him he escaped from that destruction, and, on being released, became one of the personal servants, and served His Majesty till by degrees the latter became gracious to him. (Note of Sayyid Aḥmad.)

company with the bakhshi of that place hold a muster of the troops of Qilīj K͟hān and all the jagirdars and Uymaks in the service or not, and to bring the list. Kis͟hwar K͟hān, son of Quṭbu-d-dīn K͟hān, came from the fort of Rohtas and had the good fortune to pay his respects to me.

The Fifth New Year's Feast from the Auspicious Accession.

On Sunday, the 24th Ẕī-l-ḥijja (20th March, 1610), after two watches and three gharis the sun entered into the constellation of Aries, which is the house of honour and good fortune, and at this auspicious hour the New Year's feast was arranged at Bāk Bhal, one of the villages of the parganah of Bārī, and according to the rules of my revered father I mounted the throne. On that morning, which was the New Year's Day that lighted up the world, and coincided with the 1st of Farwardīn of the 5th year from my accession, I held a public reception, and all the nobles and servants of the Court had the good fortune to pay their respects. Some of the nobles' offerings were laid before me. K͟hān A'ẓam gave a pearl worth 4,000 rupees; Mīrān Ṣadr Jahān, twenty-eight hawks and falcons, and other gifts; Mahābat K͟hān, two European boxes, the sides of which were made with slabs of glass, so that whatever was placed inside could be seen from outside in a way that you might say there was nothing between them; Kis͟hwar K͟hān, twenty-two male and female elephants. In the same way each of the servants of the Court laid before me the presents and offerings that they had. Naṣru-llah, son of Faṭhu-llah s͟harbatchī (in charge of the *s͟harbat*), was placed in charge of the offerings. By Sārang Deo, who had been appointed to carry orders to the victorious army of the Deccan, I sent souvenirs (*tabarruk*) to

Parwīz and to each of the officers. I presented Ḥusāmu-d-dīn, son of Ghāzī Khān[1] Badakhshī, who had taken to the ways of a dervish and seclusion, with 1,000 rupees and a *farjī* shawl. The day after the New Year's Day I mounted and started for a tiger-hunt. Two males and a female were killed. I gave rewards to the ahadis who had shown bravery and gone in to the tigers, and increased their monthly pay. On the 26th of the same month I went and busied myself mostly with hunting nilgaw. As the air was hot and the (propitious) hour for re-entering Agra had nearly arrived, I went to Rūpbās, and hunted antelope in that neighbourhood for some days. On Saturday, the 1st Muḥarram, 1019, Rūp Khawāṣṣ, who was the founder of Rūpbās, presented the offering that he had prepared. That which pleased was accepted and what remained was given him back as a reward. At the same time Bāyazīd Mankalī and his brothers, who had come from the Subah of Bengal, were honoured with paying their respects. Sayyid Ādam, son of Sayyid Qāsim Bārha, who had come from Ahmadabad, also had the same good fortune. He presented an elephant as an offering. The faujdarship of the Subah of Multan was given to Walī Bī Ūzbeg in place of Tāj Khān.

On Monday, the 3rd Muḥarram of the 5th year, I halted at the Mandākar Garden, which is in the neighbourhood of the city. On the morning on which was the auspicious hour of entry into the city, after a watch and two gharis had passed I mounted and rode on a horse to the beginning of the inhabited part, and when I came to the immediate neighbourhood mounted on an elephant, so that the people from far and near might see, and scattering money on both sides of the road, at the hour

[1] Ghāzī Khān was one of the famous officers of Akbar. Ḥusām his son was married to Abū-l-faẓl's sister. See Blochmann, p. 440.

that the astrologers had chosen, after midday had passed, entered with congratulation and happiness the royal palace. In accordance with the usual custom of the New Year I had ordered them to decorate the palace, which is like the courts of heaven. After seeing the decorations, Khwāja Jahān laid before me the offering that he had prepared. Having accepted out of the ornaments and jewels, dresses and goods, whatever I approved of, I gave the rest as a reward to him. I had ordered the clerks of the hunting department to write out (a list of) all the animals that had been killed from the time of my leaving until I re-entered the city. At this time they represented that in 56 days 1,362 animals, quadrupeds, and birds had been killed; the tigers were 7 in number; nilgaw, male and female, 70; black buck, 51; does and mountain goats and antelope (*rojh*), etc., 82; *kulang* (cranes), peacocks, *surkhāb*,[1] and other birds, 129; fish, 1,023. On Friday, the 7th, Muqarrab Khān came from the ports of Cambay and Surat, and had the honour of waiting on me. He had brought jewels and jewelled things, and vessels of gold and silver made in Europe, and other beautiful and uncommon presents, male and female Abyssinian slaves, Arab horses, and things of all kinds that came into his mind. Thus his presents were laid before me for two and a half months, and most of them were pleasing to me. On this day Ṣafdar Khān, who held the rank of 1,000 personal and 500 horse, had an increase of 500 personal and 200 horse, and was presented with a standard, and given leave to return to his former jagir. Standards were also given to Kishwar Khān and Farīdūn[2] Khān Barlās. A fighting elephant for Afẓal Khān (Abū-l-faẓl's son) was handed over to his son Bishūtan, to take to his father. I bestowed

[1] Brahmini ducks.

[2] A son of Akbar's officer, Muḥammad Qulī Barlās (Blochmann, pp. 342 and 478).

1,000 rupees on K͟hwāja Ḥusain, a descendant of K͟hwāja Mu'īnu-d-dīn Chis͟htī, as was usual for the half-year. The Khankhanan had sent as an offering a "Yūsuf and Zulaik͟hā" in the handwriting of Mullā Mīr 'Alī,[1] with illustrations and in a beautiful gilt binding, worth 1,000 muhrs. This Ma'ṣūm, his Wakil, brought and submitted. Up to the day of culmination, which is the conclusion of the New Year's feast, every day many offerings were laid before me by the Amirs and servants of the Court. Whichever of the rarities was approved of by me I accepted, and gave back what was left. On Thursday, the 13th, corresponding to the 19th Farwardīn, which is the day of culmination of the sun and of gladness and pleasure, I ordered them to prepare an entertainment of different kinds of intoxicating drinks, and an order was given to the Amirs and servants of the Court that everyone might choose the kind of drink he affected. Many took wine and some *mufarriḥ* (exhilarating drinks), whilst some ate what they wished of the preparations of opium. The assembly was successfully held. Jahāngīr Qulī K͟hān from Gujarat had sent as an offering a throne of silver, inlaid and painted, of a new fashion and shape, which was presented to me. A standard was also conferred on Mahā Singh. In the commencement of my reign I had repeatedly given orders that no one should make eunuchs or buy or sell them, and whoever did so would be answerable as a criminal. At this time Afẓal K͟hān sent some of these evildoers to Court from the Subah of Behar, who were continually perpetrating this vile offence. I ordered these unthinking ones (*bī-'āqibatān*) to be imprisoned for life.

[1] Mīr 'Alī was a famous calligrapher. See Rieu, Cat., ii, 531. Can the copy mentioned by Jahāngīr be that in the Bodleian Library, which Sir W. Jones praised so highly? A writer in the Journal of the Moslem Institute for January–March, 1907, p. 186, suggests that the copy is in the Bankipur Library.

On the night of the 12th an uncommon and strange event took place. Some Delhi singers (*Qawwālān*, see Jarrett, ii, 236) were singing songs in my presence, and Sayyidī [1] Shāh was, by way of buffoonery, mimicking a religious dance. This verse of Amīr Khusrau was the refrain (*miyān-khāna*) of the song—

> "Each nation has its right road of faith and its shrine (*qibla-gāhī*).
> I've set up my shrine (*qibla*) on the path of him with the cocked cap."

I asked what was the real meaning of the (last) hemistich. Mullā 'Alī Aḥmad,[2] the seal engraver, who in his own craft was one of the first of the age, and had the title of Khalīfa, and was an old servant, and with whose father I had learned when I was little, came forward and said, "I have heard from my father that one day Shaikh Nizāmu-d-dīn Auliyā had put his cap on the side of his head, and was sitting on a terraced roof by the bank of the Jumna and watching the devotions [3] of the Hindus. Just then Amīr Khusrau appeared, and the Shaikh turned to him and said, 'Do you see this crowd,' and then he recited this line:—

> 'Each race has its right road of faith and its shrine' (qibla-gāhī).

The Amīr, without hesitating, respectfully did homage to the Shaikh, and addressing him said—

> 'I've set up my shrine in the direction of him with the cocked cap.'" [4]

The aforesaid Mullā, when these words were uttered, and the last words of the second hemistich passed over his tongue, became senseless and fell down. Conceiving

[1] The Iqbāl-nāma, p. 41, has Shayyādī, 'a dervish, a hypocrite,' and the R.A.S. MS. has Sayyidī Shayyād. Shayyād is used at p. 60 to mean an impostor. Here, perhaps, it would mean a buffoon.

[2] 'Alī Aḥmad's father was Shaikh Ḥusain. See Blochmann, p. 53.

[3] It was the bathing of the Hindus that the saint was watching.

[4] The point of Amīr Khusrau's hemistich is that *kaj-kulāh* literally means 'the awry cap,' and so refers to the saint, who had his cap on his ear or on the side of his head. But it also means one who is presumptuous, and has left the true path of religion. It also means, according to Steingass, a beloved person.

a great fear from his falling down, I went to his head. Most of those who were present doubted whether he had not had an epileptic fit. The physicians who were present distractedly made inquiry and felt his pulse and brought medicine. However much they beat their hands and feet and exerted themselves, he did not come to. Immediately he fell he had delivered his soul to the Creator. As his body was quite warm, they thought that possibly some life might be left in him. After a short time it became evident that the thing was all over and he was dead. They carried him away dead to his own house. I had never seen this kind of death, and sent money to his sons for his shroud and burial, and the next morning they sent him to Delhi and buried him in the burial-place of his ancestors.

On Friday, the 21st, Kis̲h̲war K̲h̲ān, who held the rank of 1,500, was promoted to 2,000 personal and horse, and, having been presented with an Iraq horse out of my private stable, a robe of honour and a private elephant, named Bak̲h̲t-jīt,[1] and the Faujdarship of the country of Uch, was dismissed with a view to the punishment of the rebels of that region. Bāyazīd Mankalī, having been honoured with a robe and a horse, was sent off together with his brothers in the company of Kis̲h̲war K̲h̲ān. An elephant from my private stud, by name 'Ālam-gumān, was entrusted to Ḥabību-llah for Rāja Mān Singh and sent. A special horse was sent to Bengal for Kes̲h̲o Dās Mārū,[2] and a female elephant was now given to 'Arab K̲h̲ān, the jagirdar of Jalalabad. At this time Iftik̲h̲ār K̲h̲ān had sent an offering of a rare elephant from Bengal. As I approved of it, it was entered among my private elephants. I raised the rank of Aḥmad[3] Beg K̲h̲ān, who

[1] I.O. MS. 181 has *Tak̲h̲t-i-bak̲h̲t* (Throne of fortune).

[2] Kes̲h̲o Dās was perhaps the father of Karamsī, one of Akbar's wives. See Blochmann, p. 310.

[3] Blochmann, p. 465.

had been nominated to the command of the army of Bangash on account of his good service and that of his sons, from his original rank of 2,000 personal and 1,500 horse by 500 more personal. I sent a gold throne [1] of jewelled work for Parwīz, and a *sarpīch,* which was of rubies and pearls, and made at a cost of 2,000 rupees, was sent for Khān Jahān by the hand of Ḥabīb, son of Sarbarāh Khān, to Burhanpur. At this time it became known that Kaukab, son of Qamar Khān, had become intimate with a Sanyasi, and by degrees his words, which were all blasphemous and impious, made an impression on that foolish fellow. He had made 'Abdu-l-Laṭīf, son of Naqīb Khān, and Sharīf, his cousins, partners in that error. When this affair was discovered, with only a slight frightening they revealed certain circumstances with regard to themselves, the relation of which would be extremely disgusting. Considering their punishment advisable, I imprisoned Kaukab [2] and Sharīf after giving them a whipping, and ordered 'Abdu-l-Laṭīf a hundred lashes in my presence. This special chastisement (was given) for the purpose of carrying out the Divine law in order that other ignorant persons might not be disposed towards the same actions. On Monday, the 24th, Mu'aẓẓam Khān was despatched to Delhi to punish the rebels and disaffected of that neighbourhood. Two thousand rupees were given to Shajā'at Khān Dakhanī. I had ordered Shaikh Ḥusain Darshanī to proceed with certain firmans to Bengal and presents to each of the Amirs of that Subah. I now gave him his orders and despatched him. With an eye on his actions and his approved services, I promoted Islām Khān to the rank of 5,000 personal and horse, and bestowed on him a special dress of honour.

[1] *Takhtī*, qu. a signet?

[2] Kaukab is mentioned again at the end of the twelfth year. For notice of his father see Blochmann, p. 485.

I gave a special dress of honour also to Kishwar Khān, and presented Rāja Kalyān with an Iraq horse, and similarly to the other Amirs there were given robes of honour or horses. Farīdūn Barlās, who held the rank of 1,500 personal and 1,300 horse, I promoted to 2,000 personal and 1,500 horse.

On the night of Monday, the 1st Ṣafar, through the carelessness of the servants, a great fire occurred in the house of Khwāja Abū-l-ḥasan, and before they became aware of it and the fire could be put out many of his properties were burnt. In order to afford consolation to the mind of the Khwāja and to make up for the loss he had sustained, I gave him 40,000 rupees. On Saif Khān Bārha, who had been cherished and brought up by me, I bestowed a standard. I increased the rank of Mu'izzu-l-mulk, who had been appointed to the Diwanship of Kabul, from his original of 1,000 personal and 225 horse by 200 personal and 275 horse, and dismissed him. The next day I sent a *phūl-kaṭāra* (dagger) studded with valuable jewels to Burhanpur to Khān Jahān.

A widow woman complained that Muqarrab Khān had taken her daughter by force in the port of Cambay, and after some while, during which he had kept her in his own house, when she enquired for the girl had said that she had died by an unavoidable death. I ordered an enquiry to be made into the affair. After much search I discovered that one of his attendants had been guilty of this outrage, and had him put to death, and reduced Muqarrab Khāṇ's mansab by one half, and made an allowance to the woman who had been thus injured.

As on Sunday, the 7th of the month, a *qirān-i-naḥsīn* (an unlucky conjunction) had occurred, I gave alms of gold and silver and other metals, and different kinds of cereals, to faqirs and indigent people to be divided in most parts of the dominion. On the night of Monday, the 8th, having sent for Shaikh Ḥusain Sirhindī and

Shaikh Muṣṭafā, who were celebrated for the adoption of the ways of dervishdom and the state of poverty, a party was held, and by degrees the assembly engaged warmly in *samā'* and *wajd* (dervish dancing and ecstasy). Hilarity and frenzy were not wanting. After the meeting was over I gave money to each and gave him leave. As Mīrzā Ghāzī Beg Tarkhān repeatedly made representations with regard to provisions for Qandahar and the monthly pay of the musketeers of the said fort, I ordered 200,000 rupees to be sent there from the treasury of Lahore.[1]

On the 19th Urdibihisht, in the fifth year of my reign, corresponding with the 4th Ṣafar, there occurred a strange affair at Patna, which is the seat of government of the province of Behar. Afẓal Khān, the governor of the Subah, went off to the jagir to which he had just been appointed, and which was at a distance of 60 kos from Patna, and handed over the fort and the city to the charge of Shaikh Banārasī and Ghiyāṣ Zain-khānī, the Diwan of the Subah, and to a number of other mansabdars. With the idea that there were no enemies in that region he did not satisfy himself as he should have with regard to the protection of the fort and city. By chance, at that time an unknown man of the name of Quṭb belonging to the people of Uch, who was a mischievous and seditious fellow, came to the province of Ujjainiyya,[2] which is in the neighbourhood of Patna, with the look of a dervish and the clothes of a beggar, and having made acquaintance with men of that part, who were always seditious, represented to them that he was Khusrau, who had escaped from prison and conveyed himself there; saying that if they would accompany and assist him, after the affair had been completed they would be the ministers of his State. In

[1] Elliot, vi, 321.

[2] Ujjainiyya here means Bhojpūr.

short, deceiving those simpletons with foolish words he brought them over to him and persuaded them that he was Khusrau. He showed those deceived ones the parts about his eyes, where at some time he had produced scars, of which the marks were still apparent, and told them that in the prison they had fastened cups (*kaṭorī*) on them and those were the marks.[1] Through these falsehoods and deceit a number of foot- and horsemen had collected round him, and had obtained information that Afẓal Khān was not at Patna. Considering this a great opportunity, they made a raid, and when two or three hours of the day had passed on Sunday came to the city, and being hindered by nothing went for the fort. Shaikh Banārasī, who was in the fort, obtaining news of this, went in a disturbed state to the gate of the fort. The enemy, who came on with speed, did not give him time to close the gate of the fort. Together with Ghiyāṡ, he betook himself to the side of the river by a wicket gate, and procuring a boat proposed to go to Afẓal Khān. Those rebels came with ease into the fort and took possession of Afẓal Khān's property and the royal treasury; and some of those wretched creatures who wait on events, who were in the city and its neighbourhood,

[1] Apparently we may infer from this that Jahāngīr did blind or attempt to blind his son Khusrau, though he says nothing about it. Else why should this impostor pretend that he had marks of the blinding? Tavernier says Khusrau was blinded. Du Jarric also tells us that Jahāngīr blinded Khusrau on his way back from Kabul, when he came to the place where Khusrau had fought the battle. He was blinded by some juice of a plant being poured into his eyes. The juice resembled milk (qu. *Euphorbia*). One of his captains, who was also a judge, was likewise blinded there along with his son. W. Finch, too, speaks of this outbreak. He also says that Khusrau was reported to have been blinded on the battlefield with a glass. Another story was that Jahāngīr merely caused a handkerchief to be tied over his eyes and had it sealed with his own seal. It is mentioned in Whiteway's "Rise of the Portuguese Power in India," p. 165, note, that fifteen relatives of the King of Ormuz had been blinded by red-hot bowls having been passed close to their eyes.

joined them. This news reached Afẓal Kẖān at Gorakhpur (Kẖarakpūr),[1] and Shaikẖ Banārasī and Gẖiyāṣ also came to him there by way of the river. Letters came from the city that this wretch, who called himself Kẖusrau, was in reality not Kẖusrau. Afẓal Kẖān, placing his trust on the grace and mercy of Allah, and through my good fortune, started without delay against those rebels. In five days he reached the neighbourhood of Patna. When the news of Afẓal Kẖān's coming reached those scoundrels, they entrusted the fort to one of those whom they had confidence in, and the horse and foot arraying themselves went out for four kos to meet Afẓal Kẖān. A fight took place on the bank of the river Pūn Pūn, and after a slight skirmish the array of those ill-fated ones was broken and they became scattered. In great bewilderment a second time that wretch was coming into the fort with a few men. Afẓal Kẖān followed him, and did not allow them to close the gate of the fort. Going to Afẓal Kẖān's house in a state of confusion, they fortified the house and remained there for three watches, and fought. They wounded about thirty people with arrows. After his companions had gone to *jahannam* (hell) he himself became helpless, and asked for quarter, and waited upon Afẓal Kẖān. In order to put a stop to this affair, Afẓal Kẖān executed him on the same day, and imprisoned some of his companions who had fallen alive into his hand. These items of news one after another reached the royal ear. I summoned to Agra Shaikẖ Banārasī and Gẖiyāṣ Zain-kẖānī and the other mansabdars who had made default in holding the fort and protecting the city, and ordered their hair and beards

[1] Kẖarakpūr. The word is written Gorakẖpur in some MSS., but I think it is clear that Kẖarakpūr is the place meant, for 'Abdu-r-Raḥmān had lately got Sangrām's estate of Kẖarakpūr in jagir. The fact, too, that he fought with the impostor at the Pūn Pūn to the east of Patna shows that he was coming back from down the Ganges.

to be cut off, and that they should be clothed in women's clothes, seated on asses, and paraded round the city of Agra and in the bazars, as a warning and example to others.

At this time representations succeeded each other from Parwīz and the Amirs appointed to the Deccan and those who were well-wishers of the State, that 'Ādil Khān Bījāpūrī prayed that they would send to him Mīr Jamālu-d-dīn Ḥusain Injū, on whose words and acts all the rulers of the Deccan had great reliance, that he might associate himself with them and dispel the fear in their minds, and the affairs of that place might be arranged as it might seem proper to 'Ādil Khān, who had chosen the way of loyalty and service. In any case, he might drive out of their minds the fear that was in them, and soothing them might give him hopes of the royal favour. In order to obtain this end, on the 16th of the same month I despatched the above-mentioned Mīr, giving him a present of 10,000 rupees. I increased the former rank of Qāsim Khān, which was 1,000 personal and 500 horse, by 500 personal and horse, in order that he might go to the support of his brother Islām Khān in Bengal. At the same time, in order to punish Bikramājīt, Zamindar of the province Bāndhū,[1] who had withdrawn his foot from the circle of obedience and service, I appointed Mahā Singh, grandson of Rāja Mān Singh, to proceed to put down the disaffection in that region and at the same time administer the estate of the jagir of the Raja, which was in that neighbourhood.

On the 20th of the month I gave an elephant to Shajā'at Khān Dakhanī. As the governor of Jalalabad had written and represented the ruinous state of the fort of that place, I ordered what might be required for the repair of the said fort to be taken from the treasury of

[1] Text wrongly has Māndhū.

Lahore. Iftikhār Khān had done approved service in Bengal. On the request of the governor of that Subah I increased his original rank, which was 1,500, by 500. On the 28th a representation came from 'Abdu-llah Khān Fīrūz-jang, containing recommendations in favour of some of the zealous servants who had been sent with him to subdue the rebel Rana. As Ghaznīn Khān Jālwarī had shown the greatest zeal of all in this service, I increased by 500 personal and 400 horse his former rank, which was 1,500 personal and 300 horse. In the same manner each one of those persons was promoted according to his services.

Daulat Khān, who had been sent to Allahabad to bring the throne of black stone, came on Wednesday, the 4th of the month of Mihr (15th September, 1610), and had an audience and brought the stone safe and sound. In truth it was a wonderful slab, very black and shining. Many say it is of a species of touchstone; in length it was one-eighth less than four cubits, and in breadth 2½ cubits and one *tasū*,[1] whilst its thickness may be three *tasū*. I ordered stone-cutters to carve suitable couplets on the sides of it. They had attached feet to it of the same kind of stone. I often sat on that throne.

As the brothers of Khān 'Ālam became security for him, I brought out of prison 'Abdu-s-Subḥān Khān, who was in confinement for certain offences, and promoted him to the rank of 1,000 personal and 400 horse, and appointed him to the faujdarship of the Subah of Allahabad, and gave him the jagir of Qāsim Khān, the brother of Islām

[1] A *tasū*, or *ṭasū*, is said in Wilson's Glossary to be the 24th part of a gaz or about a third of an inch. I.O. MS. makes the breadth 3½ cubits 1 tasu. The slab is described in Keene's Guide and in the N.W.P. Gazetteer, Agra volume. One inscription has the date 1011, or 1602. Archæological Report, lv, pp. 132–5, says it is 10 ft. 7½ ins. long, 9 ft. 10 ins. broad, and 6 inches thick. It is supported on octagonal pedestals. See also Beale's Miftāḥu-t-tawārīkh, pp. 300, 301, where a representation of the stone and copies of the inscriptions are given.

Khān. I sent Tarbiyat Khān to the faujdarship of the Sarkar of Alwar. On the 12th of the same month a representation arrived from Khān Jahān that the Khankhanan, according to my order, had started for the Court in company with Mahābat Khān, and that Mīr Jamālu-d-dīn Ḥusain, who had been nominated by the Court to go to Bijapur, had also gone from Burhanpur, together with the wakils of 'Ādil Khān, to Bijapur. On the 21st of the same month I promoted Murtaẓā Khān to the subadarship of the Panjab, which is one of the largest charges in my dominions, and gave him a special shawl. Having appointed Tāj Khān, who was in the Subah of Multan, to the governorship of Kabul, I added 500 horse to the rank of 3,000 personal and 1,500 horse already held by him. At the request of 'Abdu-llah Khān Fīrūz-jang, the son of Rānā Shankar was also promoted in rank. When Mahābat Khān, who had been sent to Burhanpur to ascertain the numbers of the forces of the Amirs appointed to the Deccan, and to bring the Khankhanan, arrived in the neighbourhood of Agra, he left the Khankhanan some stages off the city and came on in front himself, and was honoured with the good fortune of paying his respects and kissing the threshold. After a few days, on the 12th Ābān, the Khankhanan came and waited on me. As many of those who were loyal had represented the state of his affairs, whether true or false, according to their ideas, and I was displeased with him, because the degree of favour and regard that I previously had observed in his case and that I had seen in my revered father had not produced its effect, I did justice in the matter, for previously to this a letter of appointment to the service of the Deccan for a certain time had been given to him, and he had proceeded there in attendance on Sulṭān Parwīz with other nobles for that important matter. After he arrived at Burhanpur he had not looked to the opportuneness of the time, and at an improper season for moving, and when forage and other necessaries had not been laid in, he had taken Sulṭān Parwīz and his forces above the Ghats, and by degrees, in consequence of want of concert among the Sardars and his treachery, and of conflicting opinions, things had come to such a pass that grain was obtained with difficulty, and not a *mān* was to be got for large sums of money. The affairs of the army became so confused that nothing went on properly, and horses, camels, and other four-footed beasts died. In consequence of the exigency of the time he had patched up a kind of peace with the enemy and withdrawn Sulṭān Parwīz and the army to Burhanpur. As this business did not turn out well, all the well-wishers of the State knew that this division (of counsels) and confusion had arisen from treachery and want of arrangement of the Khankhanan, and represented this to the Court. Although this appeared altogether incredible, at last this impression was left upon my mind, and a representation came from Khān Jahān to the effect that all this mischief and confusion had arisen through the treachery of the Khankhanan; either this service should be left entirely in his control, or, summoning him to Court, I should appoint to this duty this man whom I had myself cherished and brought up, and appoint 30,000 horse to support this slave (Khān Jahān himself), in order that in the space of two years, having freed the whole of the royal province, now in the possession of the enemy, and having brought the fort of Qandahar[1] and other forts on the border into the occupation of the servants of the Court, he should include in the royal dominions the province of Bijapur. If he did not complete this service in that time, he might be debarred from the good fortune of paying his respects (to me) and would not show his face to the servants of

[1] A fort in the Deccan "sixty miles north of Bidar" (Elliot, vi, 70).

the Court. When the relations between the Sardars and the Khankhanan reached this point, I did not consider it advisable for him to be there any longer, and handed over the command to Khān Jahān and sent for him to Court. In reality the cause of my disinclination and want of favour to him was this. The degree of inclination and disinclination towards him in future will be in accordance with whatever may become clear.

I favoured and promoted Sayyid 'Alī Bārha, who is one of our distinguished young men, with an increase of 500 personal and 200 horse beyond his previous rank, which was 1,000 personal and 500 horse, and gave Dārāb Khān, son of the Khankhanan, the rank of 1,000 personal and 500 horse, with the Sarkar of Ghazipur as his jagir. Previously to this I had had the daughter of Mīrzā Muzaffar Ḥusain, son of Sulṭān Ḥusain Mīrzā Ṣafawī, ruler of Qandahar, betrothed to my son Sulṭān Khurram, and on this date, the 17th Ābān, as the marriage meeting had been arranged, I went to the house of Bābā Khurram and passed the night there. I presented most of the Amirs with robes of honour. Some of those confined in the fort of Gwalior I released, and especially Ḥājī Mīrak. Islām Khān had collected 100,000 rupees from the *khāliṣa* (directly managed) parganahs. As he was at the head of the army and the service, I handed this over to him as a present. Giving a little gold and silver and some of every kind of jewellery and grain to trustworthy men, I determined that they should distribute them to the poor of Agra. On the same day a report came from Khān Jahān that Īraj, the son of the Khankhanan, had obtained leave from the prince, and according to orders he had despatched him to Court. With regard to what had been ordered in the case of Abū-l-fatḥ, of Bijapur, as the above-mentioned was an experienced man, and his being sent would cause despair to the other Sardars of the Deccan to whom promises had been made, he had (therefore) kept him under surveillance.[1] An order had been sent that as Kes͟ho Dās, the son of Rāy Kalah (?), was in the service of Parwīz, if any impediment should occur in sending him, he (K͟hān Jahān) should despatch him whether he wished it or not. Immediately on this becoming known to Parwīz, he gave him leave and said to K͟hān Jahān: "These few words from my mouth thou wilt represent, that as I would give my existence and life for the service of my visible God (Jahāngīr), what is there in the being or annihilation of Kes͟ho Dās[2] that I should show any resistance in sending him? When they (i.e. the king) send for my confidential servants for any reason it produces a feeling of hopelessness and disquietude of mind in the rest, and becoming known in these regions gives an idea of disfavour on the part of our lord and Qibla (place looked towards in worship). As for the rest, it is His Majesty's order." From the date on which the fort of Ahmadnagar, by the efforts of my deceased brother Dāniyāl, came into the possession of the heads of the victorious State, up till now, the guardianship and preservation of that place had been entrusted to K͟hwāja Beg Mīrzā Ṣafawī, who was a relative of the asylum of pardon S͟hāh Ṭahmāsp. After the disturbance of the rebel Deccanis went to a great length, and they besieged the said fort, he had committed no fault in the duties of devotedness and holding of the fort. When the Khankhanan and the Amirs and other leaders who had assembled at Burhanpur in waiting on Parwīz devoted themselves to the driving back and defeat of the rebels, and from the differences of opinion and quarrels of the Amirs, and the absence of provision of forage and grain,

[1] So in MSS. Apparently K͟hān Jahān's meaning was that if this Deccani man were sent to Agra (as if to be punished) the other Deccani leaders would be discouraged.

[2] The text seems corrupt. Apparently I.O. MS. has Sargala, and this may have been Kes͟ho Dās's title.

those who looked after matters of importance brought this large army into improper roads and among hills and difficult passes, they in a short space of time rendered it wretched and impotent, and matters had come to such a pass and the difficulty with regard to grain was such that they were giving a life for a loaf. They then turned back helplessly with their objects unfulfilled. The garrison of the fort, who were expecting aid from this army, on hearing this news, lost heart and stability, and tumultuously wished to vacate the fort at once. When Khwāja Beg Mīrzā became aware of this he endeavoured to soothe and quiet the men, but though he did his best it had no good result. At last, under an agreement, he vacated the fort, and proceeded to Burhanpur, and on the day mentioned waited on the prince. Representations with regard to his coming reached me, and, as it was clear that he had not been wanting in bravery and loyalty, I ordered his rank of 5,000 personal and horse to be confirmed and a jagir to be given him. On the 9th a petition came from some of the Amirs in the Deccan that on the 22nd Sha'bān Mīr Jamālu-d-dīn Ḥusain had gone to Bijapur. 'Ādil Khān sent his wakil forward for 20 kos, and himself received him at a distance of 3 kos, and took the Mīr by the same road to his own residence.

As the desire to hunt overcame me, at a propitious hour determined by the astrologers, when a watch and six gharis had passed on the night of Friday, the 15th Ramaẓān, corresponding with the 10th Āẕar in the 5th year (of my reign), I started to hunt, and made my first halt in the Dahrah Garden, which is near the city. At this stage I gave Mīr 'Alī Akbar leave to go into the city after bestowing on him 2,000 rupees and a special warm wrapper (*fargul*). In order that the grain and cultivation should not be trodden down by my men I ordered that all should remain in the city but the men who were actually wanted and my personal servants.

Having entrusted the charge of the city to Khwāja Jahān I gave him his leave. On the 14th Sa'du-llah Khān, son of Sa'īd Khān, was given an elephant. On the 28th, corresponding with the 21st Ramazān, forty-four elephants, which Hāshim Khān, son of Qāsim Khān, had sent as an offering from Orissa, were produced before me. Of these one was very good and tame; this one I put in my private stud. On the 28th an eclipse (of the sun, *kusūf*) took place, in order to do away with the unluckiness of which I weighed myself against gold and silver; it came to 1,800 tolas of gold and 4,900 rupees. This, along with several kinds of vegetables and sorts of animals such as elephants and horses and cattle, I ordered to be divided among deserving people who were unprovided for and helpless poor of the city of Agra and other cities in the neighbourhood.

As the affairs of the army which had been nominated for the subjugation of the Deccan under the command of Parwīz, and leadership of the Khankhanan and other high Amirs such as Rāja Mān Singh, Khān Jahān, Āṣaf Khān, the Amīru-l-umarā, and other mansabdars, and other leaders of every tribe and condition, had ended in this, that they had turned back from half-way and returned to Burhanpur, and all the confidential servants and news-writers who spoke the truth had sent in reports to the Court, that although there were many causes for the ruin of this army, yet the chief reason was the disagreement of the Amirs, especially the treachery of the Khankhanan, it came into my mind that I must send Khān A'ẓam with another fresh and powerful army to make amends for and set to rights some of the improper proceedings that had arisen from the disagreement of the Amirs that has been described. On the 11th of Day he (Khān A'ẓam) was honoured with the charge of this duty, and an order was given to the Diwans to make preparations and send him off quickly. I appointed Khān 'Ālam, Farīdūn Khān

Barlās, Yūsuf Khān, son of Ḥusain Khān Tukriyah, 'Alī Khān Niyāzī, Bāz Bahādur Qalmāq, and other mansabdars, near to the number of 10,000 horse, to accompany him. It was settled that in addition to the ahadis who were appointed to this duty 2,000 others should accompany him, making altogether 12,000 horse. Having sent with him thirty lakhs of rupees and several elephants, I gave him his leave and presented him with a magnificent dress of honour, a jewelled sword-belt, a horse with a jewelled saddle, a private elephant, and 500,000 rupees for expenses. An order was given that the chiefs of the civil department should recover this from his jagir. The Amirs who were under his orders were honoured with robes of honour, horses, and presents. I increased by 500 more horse the rank held by Mahābat Khān, of 4,000 personal and 3,000 horse, and ordered him to conduct Khān A'ẓam and this army to Burhanpur, and having enquired into (the circumstances of) the destruction of the army, should give the order of the appointment of the Khān A'ẓam to the Amirs of those regions and make them of one purpose and counsel with him. He was to see the state of preparation of the army of those parts, and after arranging all matters should bring the Khankhanan with him to Court. On Sunday, the 4th Shawwal, when near the end of the day, I engaged in a cheetah hunt. I had determined that on this day and Thursdays no animals should be killed and I would eat no meat, on Sunday especially because of the respect my revered father had for that day in not being inclined to eat flesh on it, and in forbidding the killing of any animals for the reason that on the night of Sunday his own honoured birth had taken place. He used to say it was better on that day that all animals should be free from the calamity of those of a butcherly disposition. Thursday is the day of my accession. On that day also I ordered that animals should not be killed, so that whilst sporting

I should not shoot an arrow or a gun at wild animals. In hunting with cheetahs Anūp Rāy, who is one of my close attendants, was heading the men who were with him in the hunt at a little distance [1] from me and came to a tree on which some kites were sitting. When his sight fell on those kites he took a bow and some pointless arrows (*tukkā*) and went towards them. By chance in the neighbourhood of that tree he saw a half-eaten bullock. Near it a huge, powerful tiger got up out of a clump that was near and went off. Though not more than two gharis of day remained, as he knew my liking for tiger-hunting, he and some of those who were with him surrounded the tiger and sent some one to me to give me the news. When it reached me I rode there at once in a state of excitement and at full speed, and Bābā K͟hurram, Rām Dās, I'timād Rāy, Ḥayāt K͟hān, and one or two others went with me. On arriving I saw the tiger standing in the shade of a tree, and wished to fire at him from horseback, but found that my horse was unsteady, and dismounted and aimed and fired my gun. As I was standing on a height and the tiger below, I did not know whether it had struck him or not. In a moment of excitement I fired the gun again, and I think that this time I hit him. The tiger rose and charged, and wounding the chief huntsman, who had a falcon on his wrist and happened to be in front of him, sat down again in his own place. In this state of affairs, placing another gun on a tripod,[2] I took aim (*majrā* [3]

[1] *Pāra dūrtar*, but it would seem from the Ma'āṣir, ii, 231, five lines from foot, that *pāra*, or *bāra*, is a word meaning a body of men. Perhaps it is *bārah*, 'twelve.'

[2] At p. 256 we have the phrase *majrā gīrand* applied to the directing of cannon against the buildings of Fort Ranthambhor. I confess that I do not know whether Jahāngīr fired the gun that was on the stand or the one that Kamāl loaded.

[3] *Majrā giriftam* seems rather to mean here 'adjusted the tripod,' for from what follows it appears that the gun was not then loaded. The Iqbāl-nāma, p. 47, has *māsha rā zīr kard*, 'applied the match' (?).

giriftam). Anūp Rāy stood holding the rest, and had a sword in his belt and a baton (*kutaka*) in his hand. Bābā Khurram was a short distance off to my left, and Rām Dās and other servants behind him. Kamāl the huntsman (*qarāwul*) loaded the gun and placed it in my hand. When I was about to fire, the tiger came roaring towards us and charged. I immediately fired. The ball passed through the tiger's mouth and teeth. The noise of the gun made him very savage, and the servants who had crowded together could not stand his charge and fell over one another, so that I, through their pushing and shock, was moved a couple of paces from my place and fell down. In fact, I am sure that two or three of them placed their feet on my chest and passed over me. I'timād Rāy and the huntsman Kamāl assisting me, I stood up. At this moment the tiger made for those who were on the left-hand side. Anūp Rāy let the rest slip out of his hand and turned towards the tiger. The tiger, with the same activity with which he had charged, turned on him, and he manfully faced him, and struck him twice with both hands on the head with the stick he had in his hand. The tiger, opening his mouth, seized both of Anūp Rāy's arms with it, and bit them so that his teeth passed through both, but the stick and the bracelets on his arms were helpful, and did not allow his arms to be destroyed. From the attack and pushing of the tiger Anūp Rāy fell down between the tiger's fore-feet, so that his head and face were opposite the tiger's chest. At this moment Bābā Khurram and Rām Dās came up to the assistance of Anūp Rāy. The prince struck the tiger on the loins with his sword, and Rām Dās also struck him twice with his sword, once on the shoulder-blade. On the whole it was very warm work, and Ḥayāt Khān struck the tiger several blows over the head with a stick he had in his hand. Anūp Rāy with force dragged his arms out of the tiger's mouth and struck him two or three times on the cheek with his fist, and rolling over on his side stood up by the force of his knees. At the time of withdrawing his arms from the tiger's mouth, as his teeth had passed through them, they were partly torn, and both his paws passed over his shoulders. When he stood up, the tiger also stood up and wounded him on the chest with his claws, so that those wounds troubled him for some days. As the ground was uneven, they rolled over each other, holding on like two wrestlers. In the place where I was standing the ground was quite level. Anūp Rāy says that God Almighty gave him so much intelligence that he bore the tiger over deliberately to [1] one side (in the original, that side), and that he knew no more. At this time the tiger left him and was making off. He in that state of bewilderment raised up his sword and followed him and struck him on the head. When the tiger turned his face round, he struck him another blow on the face, so that both his eyes were cut, and the skin of the eyebrows, which had been severed by the sword, fell over his eyes. In this state of affairs, a lamp-man of the name of Ṣāliḥ, as it was time to light the lamps, came in a hurry and by a blind chance [2] came across the tiger. The tiger struck him one blow with his paw and knocked him down. To fall and give up his life were the same thing. Other people came in and finished the tiger's business. As Anūp Rāy had done this service to me and I had witnessed the way in which he offered his life, after he had recovered from the pain of his wounds and had the honour of waiting on me, I bestowed on him the title of Anīrā'ī

[1] Apparently the meaning is that he rolled the tiger over to the side furthest from Jahāngīr.

[2] *Kūragī.* The Iqbāl-nāma, p. 48, says the night was dark, and so the lamplighter blindly (*az kūragī*) fell upon the tiger and was killed. This tiger hunt and Jahāngīr's danger, etc., are described by William Finch (Purchas, i, 430).

Singh-dalan. Anīrā'ī[1] they call in the Hindi language the leader of an army, and the meaning of Singh-dalan is a tiger-slayer. Giving him a special sword of my own, I increased his mansab. I gave Khurram, son of Khān A'ẓam, who had been appointed to the governorship of the province of Junagadh, the title of Kāmil Khān. On Sunday, the 3rd Zī-l-qa'da, I employed myself in fishing, and 766 fish were caught; these were divided in my presence among the Amirs, *Ibachkiān* (?),[2] and most of the servants. I eat no fish but those that have scales, but not because the professors of the Shiah faith look on those without scales as unlawful, but the cause of my aversion is this, that I have heard from old men, and it has become known to me by experience as well, that fish without scales eat the flesh of dead animals and fish with scales do not eat it. From this cause, to eat them is contrary to my disposition. The Shiahs know[3] why they do not eat them and for what reason they consider them unlawful. One of my home-bred camels that was with me in the hunt carried five nilgaws that weighed 42 Hindustani maunds. I had before this sent for Naẓīrī of Nīshāpūr, who excelled other men in the art of poetry, and passed his time in Gujarat as a merchant. At this time he came and waited on me, and imitating a poem of Anwarī,

"Again, what youth and beauty this is for the world!"

laid before me a poem that he had composed on me. I presented him with 1,000 rupees, a horse, and a robe of honour as a gift for this poem. I had also sent for Ḥakīm Ḥamīd Gujarātī, whom Murtaẓā Khān greatly

[1] Anīkini means an army in Sanskrit and Rai is a title meaning leadership.

[2] Text, *Zangchiyān* (?). I.O. 181 has *Ibachkiyān*, i.e. people of the *Ibachkī-khāna* or closet. See Āyīn, Persian text, i, 42, and Blochmann, i, 46.

[3] This is said ironically.

praised, and he came and waited on me. His good qualities and purity were better than his doctoring. He waited on me for some time. When it became known that there was no physician but himself in Gujarat, and I found he himself desired leave to go, I gave him and his sons 1,000 rupees and some shawls, and set aside a whole village for his maintenance; he went off to his native place quite happy. Yūsuf K͟hān, son of Ḥusain K͟hān Tukriyah, came from his jagir and waited on me. On Thursday, the 10th Z̤ī-l-ḥijja, was the festival of the Qurbān (the sacrifice of Ishmael). As it is forbidden to take life on that day (Thursday), I ordered that on the Friday they should kill the sacrificial animals. Having sacrificed three sheep with my own hand, I mounted to go hunting, and returned when six gharis of night had passed. On this day was killed a nilgaw (commonly called blue bull) of the weight of 9 maunds and 35 seers. The story of this nilgaw is written because it is not devoid of strangeness. In the two past years, during which I had come to this same place to wander about and hunt, I had shot at him each time with a gun. As the wounds were not in a fatal place, he had not fallen, but gone off. This time again I saw that nilgaw in the hunting-ground (*s͟hikārgāh*), and the watchman recognized that in the two previous years he had gone away wounded. In short, I fired at him again three times on that day. It was in vain. I pursued him rapidly on foot for three kos, but however much I exerted myself I could not catch him. At last I made a vow that if this nilgaw fell I would have his flesh cooked, and for the soul of K͟hwāja Mu'īnu-d-dīn would give it to eat to poor people. I also vowed a muhr and one rupee to my revered father. Soon after this the nilgaw became worn out with moving, and I ran to his head and ordered them to make it lawful (cut its throat in the name of Allah) on the spot, and having brought it to the camp I fulfilled my vow as I had proposed. They cooked the nilgaw, and expending the muhr and rupee on sweets, I assembled poor and hungry people and divided them among them in my own presence. Two or three days afterwards I saw another nilgaw. However much I exerted myself and wished he would stand still in one place, so that I might fire at him, I could get no chance. With my gun on my shoulder I followed him till near evening until it was sunset, and despaired of killing him. Suddenly it came across my tongue, "Khwāja, this nilgaw also is vowed to you." My speaking and his sitting down were at one and the same moment. I fired at and hit him, and ordered him, like the first nilgaw, to be cooked and given to the poor to eat. On Saturday, the 19th Ẕī-l-ḥijja, I fished again. This time about 330 fish were caught. On the night of Wednesday, the 28th[1] of the same month, I encamped at Rūpbās. As this was one of my fixed hunting-places and there was an order that no one should hunt in the neighbourhood, a great number of antelope had come together in the desert there, so much so that they came into the inhabited parts and were not subject to any kind of molestation. I hunted for two or three days in those desert plains, and shot, and hunted with cheetahs many antelopes. As the hour for entering the city was near, making two halts on the way, I alighted on the night of Thursday, the 2nd Muḥarram, in the year 1020 (17th March, 1611), at the garden of ʻAbdu-r-Razzāq Maʻmūrī, which is near, in fact close to, the city. On this night many of the servants of the Court, such as Khwāja Jahān, Daulat Khān, and a number who had remained in the city, came and waited on me. Īraj also, whom I had sent for from the Subah of the Deccan, had the honour of kissing the threshold. I stayed in that garden also on the Friday. On that day ʻAbdu-r-Razzāq presented his own offerings. As this was the last day for hunting, an order was given

[1] The text has 14th night, but I follow the I.O. MS. 181.

that the duration of the hunt and the number of animals killed should be counted up to me. The time of the hunt was from the 9th of the month of Āẕar to the 29th Isfandārmuẕ of the 5th year, or three months and twenty days. In this time tigers 12, deer (*gāwzan*) 1, *chikārah* (gazelle) 44, *kūtāh-pācha* (hog-deer) 1 head, fawns 2 head, black buck 68 head, does 31 head, foxes 4, *kūrāra* deer 8, *pātal* (?) 1, bears 5, hyænas 3, hares 6, nilgaw 108, fish 1,096, eagle 1, bustard 1, peafowl 5, herons 5, partridges 5, brahminī ducks (*surkhāb*) 1, *sāras* 5, *dhīk* (?) 1; total, 1,414.

On Saturday, the 29th Isfandārmuẕ, corresponding to the 4th Muḥarram, I mounted an elephant and went to the city. From the garden of 'Abdu-r-Razzāq to the palace the distance is a kos and 20 *ṭanāb*. I scattered 1,500 rupees to the crowd. At the fixed hour I entered the palace. The bazars had been decorated with cloths after the manner of the New Year's feast. As at the hunting-time an order had been given to Khwāja Jahān to prepare in the *Maḥall* (Zenanah) a building fit for me to sit in, the said Khwāja had in the space of three months prepared and brought to perfection this kind of lofty building, and with folded hands (in humility) had done exceedingly active work. Coming off the dust of the road I entered that Paradise-like building and went to look round that abode, and it was very much to my taste. Khwāja Jahān was dignified with much praise and commendation. The offerings he had prepared were displayed to me in the same building. Some of these were approved and accepted and the remainder presented to him.

THE SIXTH NEW YEAR'S FEAST AFTER MY AUSPICIOUS ACCESSION.

Two gharis and forty seconds of day had passed on the Monday when the sun (lit. his honour the greatest star) entered his tower of honour, which is in the constellation of

Aries. That day was the 1st Farwardīn, corresponding with the 6th Muḥarram[1] (21st March, 1611). The feast of the New Year having been prepared, I seated myself on the throne of good fortune. The Amirs and all the servants of the Court enjoyed the good fortune of waiting on me, and gave their congratulations. The offerings of the servants of the Court, Mīrān Ṣadr Jahān, 'Abdu-llah K͟hān Fīrūz-jang, and Jahāngīr Qulī K͟hān, were laid before me. On Wednesday, the 8th Muḥarram, the offering of Rāja Kalyān, who had sent it from Bengal, was laid before me. On Thursday, the 9th of the same month, S͟hajā'at K͟hān and some of the mansabdars, who had come on summons from the Deccan, waited on me. I gave a jewelled waist-dagger to Razzāq-wirdī Ūzbeg. On the same day the New Year's offering of Murtaẓā K͟hān was laid before me. He had prepared all kinds of things. Having inspected all these, I took what I approved in the shape of valuable jewels, fine cloths, elephants, and horses, and gave back the rest. I presented a jewelled dagger to Abū-l-fatḥ Dakhanī, 3,000 rupees to Mīr 'Abdu-llah, and an Iraq horse to Muqīm K͟hān. I increased the rank of S͟hajā'at K͟hān, which was 1,500 personal and 100 horse, by 500 personal and horse. I had summoned him from the Deccan for the purpose of sending him to Bengal to Islām K͟hān, in reality to take his place permanently, and I entrusted him with the charge of that Subah. K͟hwāja Abū-l-ḥasan laid before me (as offerings) two rubies, one royal pearl, and ten rings. I gave Īraj, the son of K͟hānk͟hānān, a jewelled dagger. The rank of K͟hurram was 8,000 personal and 5,000 horse; I increased his personal allowance by 2,000, and

[1] Jahāngīr does not mention that it was in this year that he married Nūr-Jahān. He saw her on New Year's Day (Iqbāl-nāma, p. 56), and it appears from a note of Jahāngīr on p. 132 of B.M. MS. Or. 3276 that he married her on 14th K͟hurdād (end of May, 1611). It was in the 11th year that she got the title of Nūr-Jahān. Before that she was known as Nūr-Maḥall. It would seem that Jahāngīr married Nūr-Jahān four years and a few days after her first husband's death.

increased that of Khwāja Jahān, which was 1,500 personal, 1,000 horse by 500 personal, 200 horse. On 24th Muḥarram, 18th Farwardīn, the day of the ascendant, Yādgār 'Alī Sulṭān, ambassador of Shāh 'Abbās, ruler of Persia, who had come on a visit of condolence on the death of the late king and with congratulations on my accession, had the honour of waiting on me, and laid before me the gifts Shāh 'Abbās, my brother, had sent. He had brought good horses, cloth stuffs, and every kind of fitting present. After he had presented the gifts, on the same day I gave him a superb robe of honour and 30,000 rupees, which were equivalent to 1,000 Persian tumans. He handed me a letter in which were mingled congratulations and condolences for the death of my revered father. As in the letter of congratulation he expressed the greatest friendship, and omitted no point of regard and concord, it has pleased me to enter here an exact copy of it.

Copy of the letter of Shāh 'Abbās.

"May the sprinklings of the cloud of the grace of God and the dropping of the favour of the Almighty impart freshness to the gardens of wonderful men and inventors (of new things)! May the flower-bed of sovereignty and rule and the mead of magnificence and exalted happiness of his Honour of heavenly dignity, of sun-like grandeur, the king whose fortune is young, of Saturn-like majesty, the renowned prince, possessing the authority of the spheres, the Khedive, the world-gripper (Jahāngīr) and country-conquering sovereign, the prince of the exaltedness of Sikandar, with the banner of Darius, he who sits on the throne of the pavilion of greatness and glory, the possessor of the (seven) climes, the increaser of the joys of good fortune and prosperity, adorner of the gardens of happiness, decorator of the rose-parterre, lord of the happy conjunction (of the planets), the opener of the countenance, the perfection of kinghood, expounder of the mysteries of the sky, the adornment of the face of learning and insight, index of the book of creation, compendium of human perfections, mirror of the glory of God, elĕvator of the lofty soul, increaser of good fortune and of the beneficent ascension, sun of the grandeur of the skies, the shadow of the benignity of the Creator, he who has the dignity of Jamshīd among the stars of the host of heaven, lord of conjunction, refuge of the world, river of the favours of Allah, and fountain of unending mercy, verdure of the plain of purity, may his land (lit. surface) be guarded from the calamity of the evil eye; may his fountain of perfection be preserved in truth, his desire and love; the tale of his good qualities and benevolence cannot be written.

"'The pen has not the tongue to express the secret of love.'

Although outwardly the distance (between us) prevents my attaining to the *kaʿbah* of desire, yet he is the *qiblah* of my keen longing for spiritual intercourse. Thank God that by virtue of essential oneness this humble supplicant and that pure nursling of glory have in reality been united to one another. The distance of space and outward separation of the body not having prevented nearness of soul and spiritual union, my face is still towards friendship, and accordingly the dust of sorrow has not settled on the sunlike mirror of my mind, but it has received the reflection of the beauty of that exhibitor of perfection, and the olfactory of my soul has been ever scented with the sweet savour of friendship and love and the ambergris-perfumed breezes of affection and concord, and spiritual fellowship and perpetual union have rubbed off the rust from friendship.

"'I sit beside thee in thought, and my heart is at ease,
For this is an union not followed by separation's pain.'

"Praise be given to the most mighty and pure God that the plant of the desire of true friends hath borne the fruit of fruition. Success (*maqṣūd*), that beauty who for years was hidden behind the veil, has by dint of humility and supplication at the throne of the Almighty, come forth and manifested herself from the hidden bridal chamber, and a ray of perfection has been thrown on the plain of the hopes of the expectants; she has ascended the auspicious throne and seated herself beside the king who adorns the assembly and enhances the glory of the tribune of the king of kings. The world-opening standard of the Caliphate and rule, and the sky-scraping umbrella of justice and world-sway of that creator of the diadem and throne, and that opener of the knots of knowledge and wisdom have cast the shade of equity and sovereignty and mercy over the heads of the inhabitants of the world. My hope is that the chief of desire-granters may make the auspicious ascension of that blessed rising of fortune brighten the crown and illuminate the throne, making it of good omen and prosperous to all, and may the things that appertain to kingship and rule of the world and the causes of dignity and prosperity be ever on the increase! For long past the customs of amity and the ways of intimacy, which have been in existence between our ancestors, and now freshly have been re-established between this one who is bent on friendship and him who is intent on equity, demanded that when the good news of the accession of him who sits on the Gūrgānī throne and is the heir of the crown of Tīmūr reached this country, one of the confidants of the royal palace should be quickly nominated to convey congratulations, but inasmuch as the business of Āẕarbījān and the conquest of the province of S̲h̲irwān just then occurred, and until my loving mind was satisfied as to the affairs of that province, I could not return to my capital, some delay took place in the accomplishment of this important duty. Although outward ceremonial observances and politenesses have not much weight with people of knowledge and discernment, yet the observance of them is the observance of the dues of friendship. Of necessity, therefore, at this auspicious time when the attention of the servants of holy angels (?) has been withdrawn from the affairs of that province, which have been arranged in accordance with the desires of my well-wishers, and I am at ease in that quarter, I have returned and settled down in my capital of Isfahan, which is the permanent seat of rule. Therefore I have despatched Kamālu-d-dīn Yādgār 'Alī, who possesses the attributes of nobility, is perfect in sincerity and fully reliable, who is moreover of the number of devoted servants and Ṣūfīs of pure design of our family, to the most exalted Court, that after he has obtained the good fortune to salute you, to condole with you, and kissed the carpet of honour, and performed the dues of inquiry (after health, etc.) and congratulations, he may obtain leave to return, and may convey to the sincere mind of your well-wisher the good tidings of the safety of your angelic person and the health of your temperament that is of the brightness of the sun and increases joy. It is hoped that the tree of hereditary friendship and assiduousness, and the garden of intimacy and regard, both apparent and spiritual, which by the irrigation of the rivers of affection and the brooks of sincere regard acquire great splendour and greenness, not casting their leaves, may set in motion the cord of intimacy and drive away the misfortune of estrangement by the arrival of correspondence, which is the communication of the soul, and may connect by spiritual chains our visible friendship, and may favour the course and accomplishment of business.

"May God Almighty give the assistance of the secret powers to that living family of dignity and glory and that household of grandeur and good fortune."

Up to this is the copy of the letter of my brother S͟hāh 'Abbās.

My brothers Sulṭān Murād and Dāniyāl, who had died in the lifetime of my revered father, people had called by several names. I ordered that one of them should be called S͟hāhzāda mag͟hfūr (the pardoned prince), and the other S͟hāhzāda marḥūm (the prince admitted to mercy). I promoted I'timādu-d-daulah and 'Abdu-r-Razzāq Ma'mūrī, who each held the rank of 1,500, to that of 1,800, and increased the horse-rank of Qāsim K͟hān, brother of Islām Kkankhanan, by 250. I dignified Īraj, eldest son of the Khankhanan, with the title of S͟hāh-nawāz K͟hān, and Sa'du-llah, son of Sa'īd K͟hān, with the appellation of Nawāzis͟h K͟hān.

At the time of my accession I had increased weights and measures (lit. *gaz*), viz. to the extent of three ratis (small weight equal to eight barleycorns), in the weight of muhrs and rupees. At this time it was represented to me that in mercantile transactions it would be for the convenience of the people that muhrs and rupees should be of the same weight as previously. As in all affairs the contentment and ease of the people are to be looked to, I gave an order that from the present day, that is, the 11th Urdībihis͟ht in the 6th year of my reign, they should strike muhrs and rupees of the former weight in all the mints of my dominions. As before this, on Saturday, the 2nd of the month of Ṣafar, in the year 1020, the evil-dispositioned Aḥdād had heard that Kabul was deprived of an eminent leader, that K͟hān Daurān[1] was in the interior, and only Mu'izzu-l-mulk with a few servants of the aforesaid was in Kabul, thinking it a good opportunity he (Aḥdād) betook himself unexpectedly to Kabul with a large number of horsemen and foot-soldiers. Mu'izzu-l-mulk, according to the measure of his ability, displayed activity, and the Kabulis and other inhabitants, especially the Farmulī[2] tribe, barricaded up the streets and fortified their houses. The Afghans with some guns came in to the streets and bazars

[1] K͟hān Daurān was away in the district of Ningnahar (Iqbāl-nāma, p. 53).

[2] Text wrongly has Qizilbāshes.

from different directions. The people from the shelter of their terraces and houses killed many of these wretches with arrows and guns, and Bargī,[1] one of the confidential leaders of Aḥdād, was killed. From the occurrence of this affair, for fear that the people from all sides and quarters should assemble and block the road for them to get out, giving up their hearts and feet (in a state of distraction), in fear and confusion they turned back. About 800 of those dogs went to jahannam (hell), and 200, having caught horses, hastily escaped with their lives from that deadly place. Nād 'Alī Maidānī, who was in Lahūgar, at last on the same day arrived there, and pursued them for a short distance. As the distance (between them) was too great and his band small, he turned back. For the energy he had shown in coming quickly, and for the activity displayed by Mu'izzu-l-mulk, they were both promoted in rank; Nād 'Alī, who held that of 1,000 personal to that of 1,500, and Mu'izzu-l-mulk, who held the rank of 1,500, to 1,800. As it transpired that K͟hān Daurān and the Kabulis were in the habit of passing their days in carelessness, and the repelling of the evil disposition of Aḥdād had taken a long time, it occurred to me that as the Khankhanan was without employment I might appoint him and his sons to this duty. Soon after this idea occurred Qilīj K͟hān, to summon whom a firman had already been issued, came from the Panjab and obtained the honour of an audience. It became evident from the forehead of his circumstances (his manner) that he was annoyed at the duty of driving back the ill-dispositioned Aḥdād being assigned to K͟hānk͟hānān. As he faithfully promised to take up this duty, it was settled that the governorship of the Subah of the Panjab should belong to Murtaẓā K͟hān, and that the Khankhanan should remain at home, and that Qilīj K͟hān should be promoted to the rank of 6,000 personal and 5,000 horse, and be appointed

[1] Or Bārkī.

to Kabul to drive back Aḥdād and the up-country robbers. I ordered the Khankhanan to have a jagir in the Subah of Agra in the Sarkars of Qanauj and Kalpi, that he might inflict condign punishment on the rebels of that region and exterminate them (pull them out by the roots). When I dismissed them I gave each of them special robes of honour and horses and elephants, and having received the robes of exaltation they started of. At the same time, on account of the sincerity of his friendship and his old services, I bestowed on I'timādu-d-daulah the rank of 2,000 personal and 500 horse, and presented him with a sum of 5,000 rupees by way of gift. Mahābat K͟hān, whom I had sent to make the necessary preparations for war for the victorious army of the Deccan and point out to the Amirs the desirability of concord and unanimity, paid his respects to me at the capital of Agra on the 12th of the month of Tīr, the 21st of Rabī'u-ṣ-ṣānī. It was brought to notice in a letter from Islām K͟hān that 'Ināyat K͟hān had performed approved service in the Subah of Bengal; on this account I increased by 500 personal the rank he already held of 2,000. I also increased by 500 personal and 300 horse, so as to make it up altogether to 1,500 personal and 800 horse, the rank of Rāja Kalyān, who was one of the officials of that Subah. I appointed Hās͟him K͟hān,[1] who was in Orissa, to the government of Kashmir, and sent his uncle, K͟hwāja Muḥammad Ḥusain, there to look after the affairs of that country until his arrival. In the time of my revered father his father, Muḥammad Qāsim, had conquered Kashmir. Chīn Qilīj, who was the eldest son of Qilīj K͟hān, came from the Subah of Kabul and waited on me. As in addition to his natural excellence he was a *k͟hānazād* (houseborn one), he was honoured with the title of Khan, and according

[1] The text has here the word *g͟hāyatan*, which does not seem to have much meaning. Erskine has 'without his knowledge,' so he probably had *g͟hā'ibāna* in his MS.

to the prayer of his father, and on condition of his undertaking service in Tīrah, I increased his rank by 500 personal and 300 horse. On the 14th Amardād, on account of the previous service and great sincerity and ability of I'timādu-d-daulah, I bestowed on him the high rank of the viziership of the kingdom, and on the same day presented a belt with a jewelled dagger to Yādgār 'Alī, ambassador of the ruler of Iran. As 'Abdu-llah Khān, who had been appointed to command the army against the rebel Rānā, promised to enter the province of the Deccan from the direction of Gujarat, I promoted him to be Subahdar of that province, and at his request appointed Rāja Bāso to the command of the army against the Rānā, increasing his rank by 500 horse. In place of Gujarat I conferred the Subah of Malwa on Khān A'ẓam and sent 400,000 rupees to provide for the army and warlike materials for the force that had been appointed to accompany 'Abdu-llah Khān by way of Nāsik, which is near the province of the Deccan. Ṣafdar Khān, with his brothers, came from the Subah of Behar, and had the honour of kissing the threshold.

One of the royal slaves who was serving in the seal-cutting departments prepared and laid before me a design such as I had never seen or heard of before. As it is exceedingly strange, a detailed[1] description of it is given. In the shell of a filbert four compartments had been carved out of ivory. The first compartment was one of wrestlers, in which two men were engaged in wrestling, a third was standing with a spear in his hand, a fourth with a hard stone.[2] Another was sitting with his hands placed on the ground, while in front of him were laid a piece of wood, a bow and a pot. In the second a throne had been made

[1] Compare Elliot, vi, 324.

[2] *Sang-i-durushtī*. Elliot had the same reading and translates 'a heavy stone.' But both MSS. have *sang u rasanī*, 'a stone and a cord,' query a sling, and this is certainly the right reading. See Iqbāl-nāma, p. 57.

above which a *shamiyāna* (a tent-fly or canopy) was depicted, and a man of wealth (a prince) was seated on the throne with one leg placed over the other and a pillow at his back. Five servants were standing around and before him, and tree-boughs threw a shade over the throne. In the third compartment is a company of rope-dancers, who have raised upright a pole with three ropes fastened to it. A rope-dancer upon it (qu. on the ropes ?[1]) has taken hold of his own right foot with his left hand behind his head, and standing on one foot has placed a goat on the top of the pole. Another person has thrown a drum on his neck and is beating it, whilst another man is standing with his hands lifted up and looking at the rope-dancer. Five other men are also standing, of whom one has a stick in his hand. In the fourth compartment there is a tree, below which the figure of the revered (*ḥaẓrat*) Jesus is shown. One person has placed his head at Jesus' feet, and an old man is conversing with Jesus and four others are standing by.[2] As he had made such a masterpiece, I honoured him with a present and with increased salary.

On the 30th Shahrīwar, Mīrzā Sulṭān, who had been sent for from the Deccan, came and waited on me. Ṣafdar Khān had an increase of rank conferred on him, and was appointed to go to the assistance of the army against the rebel Rānā. As 'Abdu-llah Khān Bahādur Fīrūz-jang had proposed to enter the neighbouring province of the Deccan by way of Nāsik, it occurred to me to appoint Rām Dās Kachhwāha, who was one of the sincere servants of my

[1] Text *bar pāy*, but the I.O. MS. and Iqbāl-nāma, p. 58, have *bar bāzī* ('on the rope'? or perhaps 'is doing gymnastics').

[2] Note of Sayyid Aḥmad (to the fourth compartment).—"Evidently this masterpiece was not the work of a slave in the seal department, for no reason appears why the portrait of Jesus should be introduced into the fourth compartment. Probably this masterpiece was the work of Frank artists and had fallen into the hands of the slave, and he had ascribed it to his own workmanship. (Perhaps the scene depicted was the Transfiguration.)"

revered father, to accompany him in order that he might in every place look after him, and not allow him to be too rash and hasty. For this purpose I bestowed on him great favours, as well as the title of Raja, which he had not thought of for himself. I also gave him drums and the fort of Ranthanbūr, which is one of the noted castles in Hindustan, and honouring him with a superb robe of honour and an elephant and horse I dismissed him. I appointed Khwāja Abū-l-ḥasan, who had been transferred from the chief Diwanship, to the duty of the Subahdarship of the Deccan, as he had been for a long time in those regions in the service of my deceased brother (Dāniyāl). I honoured Abū-l-ḥasan, son of I'timādu-d-daulah, with the title of I'tiqād Khān, and having promoted the sons of Mu'aẓẓam Khān to fitting ranks sent them to Bengal to Islām Khān. At the request of Islām Khān, Rāja Kalyān was appointed to the government of the Sarkar of Orissa and had an increase in rank of 200 personal and horse. I presented Shajā'at Khān Dakhanī with 4,000 rupees. On the 7th Ābān Badī'u-z-zamān, son of Mīrzā Shāhrukh, came from the Deccan and waited on me.

About this time, in consequence of the disturbances that had occurred in the country of Māwarā'a-n-nahr, many of the Amirs and Ūzbeg soldiers, such as Ḥusain Bī, Pahluwān Bābā, and Nauras Bī Darman, and Baram Bī and others came to Court and waited on me. They were all honoured with robes of honour, horses, cash, mansabs, and jagirs. On the 2nd Āẕar Hāshim Khān came from Bengal and had the honour of kissing my threshold. I sent 500,000 rupees for the expenses of the victorious army of the Deccan, of which the leader was 'Abdu-llah Khān, to Ahmadabad in Gujarat by the hands of Rūp Khawāṣṣ and Shaikh Anbiyā. On the 1st day I went to the village of Samonagar, which is one of my fixed hunting-places, to hunt. Twenty-two antelope were killed, of which I myself killed sixteen and Khurram the other six. Remaining there two days and two nights, on the night of Sunday I returned to the city in health and safety, and one night this couplet threw its brilliance on my mind:—

> "As long as there's in heaven light for the sun,
> Be not the reflection far from the Shah's umbrella."

I ordered the lamplighters and the relators of stories that at the time of their salutations and telling stories they should commence with this couplet, and it is still in use. On Saturday, the 3rd day, a letter came from Khān A'ẓam that 'Ādil Khān Bījāpūrī had given up his evil ways and become penitent, and in the rank of servants was now more loyal than ever. On the 14th day, corresponding with the last day of Shawwāl, leave was given to Hāshim Khān to go to Kashmir. I gave a special wrapper[1] (*fargal*) to Yādgār 'Alī, ambassador of Persia. I presented I'tiqād Khān with one of my special swords called Sar-andāz (thrower of heads). Having honoured Shādmān, son of Khān A'ẓam, with the title of Shādmān Khān, I increased his rank to 1,700 personal and 500 horse. He was also honoured with a standard. Sardār Khān, brother of 'Abdu-llah Khān Fīrūz-jang, and Arslān Bī Ūzbeg, who had been appointed to the charge of Sīvistān,[2] were also presented with standards. I ordered that *jā'i-namāz* (prayer carpets) should be made of the skins of the antelopes I had myself killed, and be kept in the public audience hall for people to use in saying their prayers. By way of special respect to the Law I ordered that the Mīr-i-'Adl and Qāẓī, who are the pivot of affairs of the divine law, should not kiss the ground (before me), which is a kind of *sijda*. On Thursday, the 22nd day, I went again to Samonagar to hunt. As many antelope had collected together in that neighbourhood I had this time sent off Khwāja Jahān to prepare a qamargah and drive in the antelope into a broad place from all sides, to place canvas-

[1] See Blochmann, p. 89, note. It came from Europe.

[2] In Scinde; it is the same as Sahwan, and is on the Indus.

walls (*sarā-parda*) and a *gulāl-bāṛ*[1] round it. They enclosed a kos and half of ground with sarapardas. When news came that the hunting-place had been prepared and a great deal of game had been confined, I went there and began to hunt on the Friday. Until the next Thursday I went every day to the qamargah with the ladies and hunted as much as I liked. Some of the deer were taken alive and some killed with arrows and guns. On the Sunday and Thursday, on which I do not fire guns at animals, they took them alive in nets. In these seven days 917 head, male and female, were caught, and of these 641 deer were caught alive. Four hundred and four head were sent to Fathpur to be let loose on the plain there, and with regard to 84 I ordered them to put silver rings in their noses and set them free in the same place. The 276 other antelope that had been killed with guns and arrows and by cheetahs were divided from day to day among the Begams and the slaves of the palace, and Amirs and servants of the palace. As I became very tired (*dilgīr*) of hunting, I gave orders to the Amirs to go to the *shikārgāh* (hunting-place) and hunt all that were left over, and myself returned in safety to the city. On the 1st Bahman, corresponding with the 17th Zī-l-qa'da, I ordered that in the large cities of my dominions, like Ahmadabad, Allahabad, Lahore, Delhi, Agra, etc., they should arrange bulghur-khanas (places for the distribution of cooked food) for the poor; thirty mahalls (districts) had been ordered. Six had already been established, and twenty-four other districts were now ordered. On the 4th Bahman I increased the rank of Rāja Bīr Singh Deo by 1,000 personal; it was previously 4,000 personal and 2,000 horse: I gave him a jewelled sword. Another sword out of my special ones, that was called Shāh-bacha (king's child), was presented to Shāh-nawāz Khān. On the 16th Isfandārmuz, Badī'u-z-zamān, son of Mīrzā Shāhrukh,

[1] Blochmann, p. 45.

was appointed to the army against the rebel Rānā and a sword sent by his hand for Rāja Bāso. Having again heard that the Amirs on the borders interfere with authority in matters that do not concern them, and do not observe laws and regulations, I ordered [1] that the Bakhshis should circulate orders, to be obeyed amongst the Amirs of the borders, that hereafter they should not interfere in such things, which are the private affair of kings. The first thing is this, that they should not sit in the *jharokha* (private window), and should not trouble their officers and captains of the auxiliaries with keeping guard or saluting them, and should not have elephant fights, and should not inflict the punishment of blinding, and should not cut off ears and noses, and should not force Islam on anyone, and should not confer titles on their servants, and should not order the royal servants to do *kūrnish* or prostration, and should not force singers to remain on duty in the manner customary in (royal) darbars, and should not beat drums when they go out, and when they give a horse or elephant to anyone, whether to the king's attendants or to their own servants, they should not place reins or elephant's goads on their backs and make them perform obeisance. In going in procession they should not take with them on foot in their retinue the royal attendants. If they write anything to them they should not put a seal on it.[2] The regulations which have been styled the rules of Jahāngīr (Āyīn-i-Jahāngīrī) are now in force.[3]

[1] Elliot, vi, 325.

[2] Both MSS. have *bar rū* instead of *bar ū*, 'in front' or 'in the face' of the letter, and this is no doubt the correct reading. See Iqbāl-nāma, p. 59. See Blochmann, p. 263, for the different places where seals are to be put. Jahāngīr's order apparently was that the provincial governors were not to impress their seals on the face of their letters or other documents.

[3] The reference seems to be, not to these subsidiary regulations, but to the code of twelve rules promulgated by him at the commencement of his reign.

THE SEVENTH NEW YEAR'S FESTIVAL AFTER THE AUSPICIOUS ACCESSION.

On Tuesday, the 1st Farwardīn of the seventh year from my accession on the 16th Muḥarram u-l-ḥarām (19th March, 1612) in the year 1021, the New Year's assembly that illuminates the world, and the festival that brings joy, were held in the capital of Agra. After four gharis of the night had passed on Thursday, the 3rd of the aforesaid month, the hour that the astrologers had chosen, I sat on the throne. I had ordered that, according to annual custom, the bazars should be decorated and the assembly should be kept up until the day of culmination (*rūz-i-sharaf*). Khusrau Bī Ūzbeg, who was known among the Uzbegs as Khusrau *Qimchī*,[1] came on these days and had the honour of waiting on me. As he was one of the influential men of Māwarā'a-n-nahr, I bestowed many favours on him, and gave him a fine robe of honour. I gave 15,000 rupees to Yādgār 'Alī, ambassador of the ruler of Iran, for his expenses. On the same day the offering of Afẓal Khān, which he had sent from the Subah of Behar, was laid before me. There were 30 elephants and 18 ponies (*gūnṭh*), and pieces of Bengal cloth, sandalwood, some pods of musk, aloes-wood (*Agallochum*), and all kinds of things. The offering of Khān Daurān was also produced before me. He had sent 45 head of horse and two strings of camels, porcelain from China, dressing-gowns (*pūstīnhā* [2]) of sable (*sammūr*), and other valuable presents procurable in Kabul and its neighbourhood. The officers of the palace had taken trouble about their offerings, and according to the yearly custom from day to day of the festival the offerings of the servants were laid before me. Having looked at them

[1] *Qūruqchī* in I.O. MS. and in Iqbāl-nāma, p. 60. Steingass gives it as meaning one who looks after the king's game, and as a sentinel.

[2] Text has *pūsthā*, skins, but I.O. MS. has *pūstīnhā*.

in detail, I took what I approved and gave them the remainder. On the 13th Farwardīn, corresponding with the 29th Muḥarram, a representation from Islām K͟hān arrived to the effect that through the blessing of Allah's favour and through the benign influence of the royal grace, Bengal had been freed from the disturbance of 'Uṣmān, the Afghan. Before the circumstances of this war are written down, some particulars with regard to Bengal will be recorded.[1] Bengal is a country of great extent, and in the second clime its length, from the port of Chittagong to Garī, is 450 kos; and its breadth, from the Northern hills to the boundary of Sarkar Madāran, 220 kos. Its revenue is about 60 krores of dams.[2] The former rulers of this place always had 20,000 horse, a lakh of foot-soldiers, 1,000 elephants, and 4,000 or 5,000 war-boats. From the time of S͟hīr K͟hān and his son Salīm K͟hān, this country was in the possession of the Afghans. When the throne of sovereignty of Hindustan in the hands of my revered father acquired beauty and splendour, he ordered the victorious forces (of the empire) into it, and for a long time made the conquest of it his object, until the aforesaid province, through the great efforts of the chiefs of the victorious State, passed from the possession of Dā'ūd Karānī, who was the last of its rulers. That wretch was killed in the fight with K͟hān Jahān, and his army became scattered and in desperate condition. From that date until now the province is in the possession of the servants of the State. In the end a few of the remaining Afghans had remained in the corners and sides of the country, and kept a few distant places in their possession, until, by degrees, most of that body became despised and helpless,

[1] Copied from Āyīn. See Jarrett, ii, 115. See also Elliot, vi, 326.

[2] This is equal to one krore, fifty lakhs of rupees. The Sarkar of Orissa was included in Bengal, and its revenue is included in this. (Note of Sayyid Aḥmad.)

and were captured by the chiefs of the State in the places of which they had still possession. When the arrangement of the affairs of rule and empire, simply through the grace of God, became entrusted to this humble servant of the throne of Allah, in the first year after my accession I sent for Rāja Mān Singh, who had been appointed to the rule and government of that place, to Court, and sent Quṭbu-d-dīn Khān, who, out of all the officials, was distinguished as my foster-brother, in his place. As he entered the province he attained to martyrdom at the hand of one of those mischievous ones who had been appointed to that country, and that man, who had not thought of the consequences, also obtained the reward of his deeds, and was slain. I promoted Jahāngīr Qulī Khān, who was governor and a Jagirdar in the province of Behar, on account of his nearness to that neighbourhood, to the rank of 5,000 personal and horse, and ordered him to go to Bengal and take possession of the province. I sent an order to Islām Khān, who was at the capital of Agra, to go to Behar and consider that province his jagir. When a short time had passed under the rule of Jahāngīr Qulī Khān, he contracted a severe illness, in consequence of the bad water and air of that place, and by degrees the power of the disease and his weakness became so great as to end in his destruction. When the news of his death came to my hearing at Lahore, an order was issued in the name of Islām Khān to proceed as soon as possible to Bengal. When I appointed him to this important duty, most of the servants of the State made remarks on his youth and want of experience. As the excellence of his disposition and his natural capacity had been noticed by my judicious eye, I myself chose him for this duty. As it happened, the affairs of this province were carried on by him in such a manner as from the time when it first entered into the possession of the Chiefs of the everlasting State until this day has never been attained to by any of the servants of the Court. One of his noteworthy deeds was the driving away of the rebel 'Uṣmān, the Afghan. He frequently in the time of the late king encountered the royal forces, but his expulsion was not accomplished. When Islām Khān made Dhaka (Dacca) his place of abode and made the subjection of the Zamindars of that neighbourhood his chief object, it occurred to him that he should send an army against the rebel 'Uṣmān and his province. If he agreed to serve loyally, well and good, but if not, they should punish and annihilate him like other seditious people. At that time Shajā'at Khān[1] joined Islām Khan, and the lot of leading in this service[2] fell on his name. Several others of the State servants were also appointed to go with him, such as Kishwar Khān, Iftikhār Khān, Sayyid Ādam Bārha, Shaikh Achhay,[3] nephew of Muqarrab Khān, Mu'tamad Khān, the sons of Mu'aẓẓam Khān, Ihtimām Khān, and others. He took with him also some of his own men. At the hour when Mushtarī (Jupiter) was propitious, he started off this band, and appointed Mīr Qāsim, son of Mīrzā Murād, its chief paymaster and news-writer. He took also some of the Zamindars with him to show the road. The victorious armies started. When they reached the neighbourhood of 'Uṣmān's fort and land, they sent some eloquent men to admonish him and point out to him the way of loyalty, and bring him back from the road of rebellion to the right path. As much pride had seated itself in his brain-cup, and he had in his head a desire to seize the country, beside other fancies, he turned a deaf ear to their words and

[1] Also called Shaikh Kabīr Chishtī (Blochmann, p. 519; Ma'āṣiru-l-umarā, ii, 630).

[2]. Perhaps this is only rhetoric, but Abū-l-faẓl describes how lots were cast between him and Rāja Bīrbal as to who should go on the Yūsufzai expedition.

[3] *Ichī* means a hawk, but the meaning may be a Shaikh of Uch. *Acha* is given in Zenker as meaning a father in Turki. The Iqbāl-nāma has Ajha.

prepared himself for conflict and fight. The battlefield happened to be on the bank of a nullah in a place which was a complete bog. On Sunday (12th March, 1612), the 9th Muḥarram, Shajā'at Khān, choosing the hour for the fight, arrayed the victorious forces, so that everyone should go to his place and be prepared for the battle. 'Usmān had not settled the battle for that day with himself. When he heard that the royal army had come prepared for battle, having no remedy he himself mounted and came to the bank of the nullah, and arrayed his own horse and foot opposite the victorious army. When the affair grew hot, and the two forces opposed each other, that foolish, obstinate man at the first onset threw his own fighting raging elephant against the advanced guard. After much fighting many of the leaders of the advanced guard, as Sayyid Ādam[1] Bārha and Shaikh Achhay, attained the dignity of martyrdom. Iftikhār Khān, the leader of the right wing, was in no way remiss in attacking, and sacrificed his own life. The band that was with him fought to such a degree that they were all cut to pieces. In the same way Kishwar[2] Khān and his band of the left wing bravely sacrificed themselves in the affair of their master, but many of the enemy (lit. those of dark fortune) were also wounded and killed. That evil one ('Usmān) took account of the combatants and ascertained that the leaders of the advanced guard and right and left wings were killed. The centre alone remained. He took no account of the killed and wounded on his own side, but attacked the centre (of the royal army) with the same energy. On this side the son and brothers and sons-in-law of Shajā'at Khān, as well as other officers, stopped the advance of those lost ones, and attacked them like tigers and leopards armed with claws and teeth. Some of them attained the dignity of

[1] Text wrongly has A'ẓam. See Blochmann, p. 521, note.

[2] Kishwar was the son of Jahāngīr's foster-brother Quṭbu-d-dīn, who was killed by Shīr-afgan.

martyrdom, and those that remained alive bore away fatal wounds. At this time ('Uṣmān) drove a raging elephant of the name of Gajpat,[1] which was his premier elephant, at Shajā'at Khān, who laid hold of his spear and struck the elephant. What does a raging elephant care for a javelin! He then seized his sword and struck him two blows one after another. How did he regard these either! He then drew his dagger and struck him twice with it, but for this, too, he did not turn back, but overthrew Shajā'at Khān with his horse. Immediately he was separated from his horse; calling out "Jahāngīr Shāh," he leapt up, and his equerry struck the elephant on both front legs a blow with a two-handed sword. As the elephant fell on his knees, the equerry pulled the elephant driver down off the elephant, and Shajā'at with the dagger he had in his hand, and while on foot, struck such blows on the trunk and forehead of the elephant that the elephant roared out at the pain and turned round. As he was severely wounded, he went to his own army and fell down. Shajā'at Khān's horse got up safely. As he was mounting his horse those vile ones drove another elephant at his standard-bearer, and overthrew his horse and standard. Shajā'at Khān gave a manly shout and roused the standard-bearer, saying: "Be bold: I'm alive and the standard is at my feet (?)."[2] At this critical moment all the servants of the State who were present seized their arrows and daggers and swords, and smote the elephant. Shajā'at himself came up and shouted to the standard-bearer to rise, and got another horse for the standard-bearer and mounted him on it. The standard-bearer unfurled the standard and maintained his ground. At the time of this struggle

[1] The Iqbāl-nāma and the B.M. MSS. call it Bakhla.

[2] These last words seem to be part of Shajā'at's speech, but see Iqbāl-nāma, p. 63. See also Elliot, vi, 329, and the translation of the Iqbāl-nāmā account in Appendix L, Stewart's Cat. of Tippo Sultan's MSS., p. 275. The Iqbāl-nāma says that 'Uṣmān's corpulence compelled him to ride on an elephant.

a (ball from a) gun struck that rebel on his forehead. However much they enquired for the man who fired it, he could not be found. When this struck him, he recognized that he was a dead man. Yet for two watches, notwithstanding this fatal wound, he urged on his men to the fight, and the battlefield was still deadly and the struggle warm. Afterwards the enemy turned their faces, and the victorious army pursued them, and continually striking them drove back those vile ones into the place where they had encamped. With arrows and guns those wretches would not allow the royal troops to enter the place where they were. When Walī, the brother of ʻUṣmān, and Mamrez, his (ʻUṣmān's) son and other relations and followers became aware of ʻUṣmān's wound, they made up their minds that he would not recover from it, and that if they, defeated and put to flight, should go towards their fort none would reach it alive. They thought it best to remain for the night in the place where they had encamped, and towards the end of the night seek an opportunity and get to their fort. Two watches of night had passed when ʻUṣmān went to hell. In the third watch they raised his lifeless body, and leaving his tent and the things they had with them in the camp, proceeded to their fortress. The scouts of the victorious army, having obtained news of this, informed S͟hajāʻat K͟hān. On the morning of Monday the loyalists assembled and decided to follow them, and not allow breathing-time to those of dark fortune. In the end, in consequence of the tired state of the soldiers, and in order to bury the martyrs and out of sympathy for the wounded, they were perplexed in their minds as to going or settling down (where they were). Just at this time ʻAbdu-s-Salām, son of Muʻaẓẓam K͟hān, arrived with a body of servants of the State, altogether 300 horse and 400 musketeers (*tūpchī*). When this fresh body of men arrived it was determined to pursue, and they accordingly went on.

When Walī, who after 'Uṣmān was the stock of the disturbance, learned that Shajā'at Khān with the victorious army had come together with another fresh force, he saw no resource for himself but to go to Shajā'at Khān on the straight line of faith and loyalty. In the end he sent a message that he who had been the cause of the disturbance had gone, and that the body of those who were left were servants and Musulmans. If he would give his word they would wait upon him and would agree to serve the State, giving their elephants as an offering. Shajā'at Khān and Mu'taqid Khān, who had arrived on the day of the battle and had done approved service, and all those who were loyal, in accordance with the necessity of the time and with what was best for the State, gave their word and encouraged them. On the next day, Walī and the sons, brothers, and sons-in-law of 'Uṣmān all came and waited upon Shajā'at Khān and the other servants of the State. They brought forty-nine elephants as an offering. After the completion of this work Shajā'at Khān, leaving some of the royal servants in Adhār[1] and the neighbourhood which was in the

[1] The text has *dar adhār u ṭarf kih dar taṣarruf-i-ān tīra-rūzgār būd.* I do not know if *adhār* is the name of a place or what its meaning is. The I.O. MSS., Nos. 181 and 305, have *arhād.* Blochmann, p. 520, on the authority of the Makhzan-i-Afghānī, says the fight took place 100 kos from Dacca and in a place called Nek Ujyāl, and he points out in a note that there are several Ujyāls in Eastern Bengal. Possibly Adhār is Udhār or Uzār, and a corruption of Ujyāl. The 'hills of Dacca,' referred to by Blochmann, might be Ran Bhawal or the Madhūpūr jungle. The Riyāẓu-s-salāṭīn does not mention the site of the battle, and the translator, Maulawī 'Abdu-s-Salām, has in his note at p. 175 confounded two 'Īsā Khāns, and so drawn groundless inferences. Blochmann points out, p. 520, that the Ma'āṣiru-l-umarā says the prisoners were afterwards put to death. The passage is at vol. ii, p. 632. It says they were put to death by Jahāngīr's orders by 'Abdu-llah (who certainly was brute enough for anything). Jahāngīr, Tūzuk, p. 112, mentions the arrival of 'Uṣmān's sons and brothers at Court, so that Blochmann's statement at p. 520 about their being executed on the road is not correct. It appears, too, they came to Court after Shajā'at's death. Jahāngīr says (Tūzuk, p. 112) he made over the prisoners to responsible servants of government. 'Abdu-llah may have been one of these, and

possession of that one of evil fortune, took with him Walī and the other Afghans, and on Monday, the 6th of the month of Ṣafar, came to Jahāngīrnagar (Dacca) and joined Islām Khān. When the joyful news reached in Agra this supplicant at the throne of Allah, he performed the prostrations of gratitude, and recognized that the driving away of this description of enemy was brought about simply through the unstinted mercy of the Almighty Giver. As a reward for this good service I promoted Islām Khān to the rank of 6,000 personal, and honoured Shajā'at Khān with the title of "Rustam of the age" (Rustam-zamān), as well as increased his rank by 1,000 personal and horse. I also increased the rank of other servants according to the measure of their services, and they were selected for other honours.

When this news first came of the killing of 'Uṣmān it appeared to be a joke, but by way of ascertaining the truth or falsehood of the words I took an omen from the divān of the tongue of the unseen world, Khwāja Ḥāfiẓ of Shiraz, and this ghazal[1] turned up:—

"I make my eyes red and throw patience to the wilds,
And in such a case throw my heart into the sea.
I'm wounded by the shaft of heaven:
Give wine, so that intoxicated I may cast a knot in the girdle of the Twins."

have got rid of his prisoners by killing them. It would appear that the battle with 'Uṣmān took place to the east or south-east of Dacca, and not near Orissa, as Stewart supposed.

[1] The lines occur in Ḥāfiẓ' divān, under the letter M, Brockhaus' ed., No. 396, but Jahāngīr has missed out two lines in his quotation. An Indian lithograph has *rakht* in the first line instead of *ṣabr*, but the latter reading occurs in Brockhaus. In the fourth line *nargis* is a mistake for *tīrkash*. *Tīr-i-falak*, 'the arrow of the spheres,' is also a name for the planet Mercury. *Tīrkash-i-Jauzā* means both a particular constellation in the sign Gemini, which is supposed to resemble a quiver in appearance, and also the strings of a musical instrument. The meaning of the lines seems to be, "I have been wounded by the shaft of heaven: give me wine that I may become intoxicated and be able to tie a knot in the quiver-girdle of the Gemini." The appositeness of the *fāl* is not very apparent, but the mention of an arrow was taken to be an allusion to the death of 'Uṣmān by a shot from an unknown hand.

As this couplet was very appropriate to the occasion, I drew an omen from it. After some days news came again that the arrow of Fate, or rather of God, had struck 'Uṣmān, for however much they enquired for him, he who fired the shot was not made manifest. This has been recorded on account of its strange nature.

On the 16th Farwardīn, Muqarrab Khān, who is one of my chief retainers and the old confidants of the Jahangiri service, who had attained the rank of 3,000 personal and 2,000 horse, came from the fort of Cambay and had the honour of waiting on me. I had ordered him, on account of certain business, to go to the port of Goa[1] and buy for the private use of the government certain rareties procurable there. According to orders he went with diligence to Goa, and remaining there for some time, took at the price the Franks asked for them the rareties he met with at that port, without looking at the face of the money at all (i.e. regardless of cost). When he returned from the aforesaid port to the Court, he produced before me one by one the things and rareties he had brought. Among these were some animals that were very strange and wonderful, such as I had never seen, and up to this time no one had known their names. Although King Bābar has described in his Memoirs the appearance and shapes of several animals, he had never ordered the painters to make pictures of them. As these animals appeared to me to be very strange, I both described them and ordered that painters should draw them in the Jahāngīr-nāma, so that the amazement that arose from hearing of them might be increased. One of these animals in body is larger than a peahen and smaller than a peacock.[2] When

[1] Elliot, vi, 331.

[2] They call this in the English language a turkey, and the people of India call it *pīrū*; Persian-knowing Indians call it in Persian *fīlmurgh*. They are now plentiful in India. (Note of Sayyid Aḥmad.)

it is in heat and displays itself, it spreads out its feathers like the peacock and dances about. Its beak and legs are like those of a cock. Its head and neck and the part under the throat are every minute of a different colour. When it is in heat it is quite red—one might say it had adorned itself with red coral—and after a while it becomes white in the same places, and looks like cotton. It sometimes looks of a turquoise colour. Like a chameleon it constantly changes colour. Two pieces of flesh it has on its head look like the comb of a cock. A strange thing is this, that when it is in heat the aforesaid piece of flesh hangs down to the length of a span from the top of its head like an elephant's trunk, and again when he raises it up it appears on its head like the horn of a rhinoceros, to the extent of two finger-breadths. Round its eyes it is always of a turquoise colour, and does not change. Its feathers appear to be of various colours, differing from the colours of the peacock's feathers. He also brought a monkey of a strange and wonderful form. Its hands, feet, ears, and head are like those of a monkey, and its face like that of a fox. The colour of its eyes is like that of a hawk's eye, but the eyes are larger than those of a hawk. From its head to the end of its tail it is an ordinary cubit in length. It is lower than a monkey and taller than a fox. Its hair is like the wool of a sheep and its colour like that of ashes. From the lobe of its ear to its chin it is red and of the colour of wine. Its tail is two or three finger-breadths longer than half a cubit, quite different from that of other monkeys. The tail of this animal hangs down like the tail of a cat. Sometimes it makes a sound like a young antelope. On the whole it is a very strange beast. Of the wild birds which they call *tadrū* (pheasant) till now it has never been heard that they breed in captivity. In the time of my revered father they made great efforts to obtain eggs and young ones but it was not managed. I ordered them to keep some of them, male and female, in one place, and by degrees they bred. I ordered them to place the eggs under hens, and in a space of two years sixty or seventy young were produced and fifty or sixty grew up. Whoever heard of this matter was astonished. It was said that in the Wilāyat (Persia ?) the people there had made great efforts, but no eggs were produced and no young were obtained.

In these days I increased the mansab of Mahābat K̲h̲ān by 1,000 personal and 500 horse, which thus became 4,000 personal and 3,500 horse. The mansab of I'timādu-d-daulah, original and increased, was fixed at 4,000 personal and 1,000 horse. To the mansab of Mahā Singh also an increase of 500 personal and horse was given: it was originally and with increase 3,000 personal and 2,000 horse. The mansab of I'tiqād K̲h̲ān was increased by 500 personal and 200 horse, and made up to 1,000 personal and 300 horse. K̲h̲wāja Abū-l-ḥasan in these days came from the Deccan and waited on me. Daulat K̲h̲ān, who had been appointed to the faujdarship of Allahabad and of the Sarkar of Jaunpur, came and paid his respects: an increase of 500 was made to his mansab, which was 1,000. On the day of culmination (*rūz-i-s̲h̲araf*), which was the 19th Farwardīn, I raised the mansab of Sulṭān K̲h̲urram, which was 10,000, to 12,000, and made that of I'tibār K̲h̲ān, which was 3,000 personal and 1,000 horse, up to 4,000. I raised the mansab of Muqarrab K̲h̲ān from 2,000 personal and 1,000 horse by 500 personal and horse; and increased that of K̲h̲wāja Jahān, which was 2,000 personal and 1,200 horse, by 500. As these were the days of the New Year, many of the servants (of the State) obtained an increase of their mansabs. On the same day Dulīp came from the Deccan and waited on me. As his father Rāy Rāy Singh had died, I honoured him with the title of Rāy and clothed him in a dress of honour. Rāy Rāy Singh had another son, by name Sūraj Singh. Although Dulīp was his *ṭīkā* (marked with the *ṭīkā*) son, he wished Sūraj Singh to succeed him, in consequence of the love that he bore to his mother. When the circumstances of his death were reported to me, Sūraj Singh, in consequence of his want of intelligence and tender years, represented to me: "My father has made me his successor and given me the *ṭīkā*." This remark was not to my liking, and I said: "If thy father has given the *ṭīkā* to thee, we shall give it to Dulīp." Then marking the *ṭīkā* with my own hand, I presented the latter with his father's jagir and hereditary possessions. I bestowed on I'timādu-d-daulah an inkstand and jewelled pen. Rūdar, the father of Lakhmī Chand, Raja of Kumaon, who is one of the considerable Rajas of the hill country, had come in the time of the late King Akbar,[1] and when he came had petitioned[2] that the son of Rāja Ṭoḍar Mal might take him by the hand and bring him to wait on him. In consequence, the Raja's (Ṭoḍar Mal's) son had been appointed to bring him. Lakhmī Chand now similarly asked that the son of I'timādu-d-daulah might bring him to pay his respects. I sent Shāpūr[3] to bring him to wait on me. He laid before me rare things from his own hill country, such as *gūnṭh* ponies, and birds of prey, such as hawks, *jurra* (falcons), royal falcons, *qaṭās* (yaks), navels of musk, and skins of the musk antelope with the musk-bags on them, swords which in their language they call *khānḍā*, and daggers which they call *kaṭār*, and all kinds of things. Amongst the Rajas of this hill country this Raja is well known for the large quantities of gold he has. They say there is a gold-mine in his territory.[4]

[1] Akbar-nāma, iii, 533. It was in the 33rd year.

[2] He asked Ṭoḍar Mal's protection, but the son was sent (Akbar-nāma, iii, 533).

[3] This name is not in all the MSS. It is another name for I'tiqād, son of I'timādu-d-daulah.

[4] Blochmann, p. 508.

In order to lay the foundation of a palace at Lahore, I sent there Khwāja Jahān Khwāja Dūst Muḥammad, who is well skilled in this kind of business.

As the affairs of the Deccan, in consequence of the disagreements among the Sardars and the carelessness of Khān A'ẓam, did not look well, and the defeat of 'Abdu-llah Khān had taken place, I had sent for Khwāja Abu-l-ḥasan to make enquiries into the real state of these quarrels. After much enquiry and investigation it became clear that the defeat of 'Abdu-llah Khān had been caused by his pride and his sharp temper, and not listening to words (of advice), and partly by the quarrels and want of agreement between the Amirs. Briefly, it had been determined that 'Abdu-llah Khān should start from the direction of Nāsik and Trimbak with the Gujarat army and the Amirs who had been appointed to accompany him. This army had been brought into proper order by trustworthy leaders and zealous Amirs, such as Rāja Rām Dās, Khān A'lam, Saif Khān, 'Alī Mardān Bahādur, Ẓafar Khān, and other servants of the State. The number of the army had passed 10,000 and come up to near 14,000. On the side of Berar it was settled that Rāja Mān Singh, Khān Jahān, the Amīru-l-umarā, and many other leaders should proceed. These two armies should be aware of each other's marches and halts, so that on an appointed day they might catch the enemy between the two. If this rule had been observed and their hearts had been in unison, and self-interest had not come between, it is most probable that Almighty God would have given them the victory of the day. When 'Abdu-llah Khān passed the Ghats and entered the enemy's country, he did not take care to send runners (*qāṣidān*) to bring intelligence from the other army, nor did he, in accordance with the arrangements, make his movements harmonise with theirs, so that on an appointed day they might take the enemy between two armies. Rather he relied on his own strength, and considered that if he could gain the victory alone it would be better. This idea fixed itself in his mind, and however much Rām Dās desired him to promise to go forward with due deliberation, it was of no use. The enemy, who were observing him closely, had sent a large number of leaders and Bargīs (Mahrattas) against him, and encounters took place with them every day. They did not fail to throw rockets and different fireworks at night. At last the enemy drew near, and yet he obtained no intelligence about the other army, though he had approached Daulatabad, which was the place of assembly of the Dakhanis. 'Ambar, the black-faced, had raised to sovereignty a child who, in his opinion, bore relationship to the family of Niẕāmu-l-mulk. In order that men might fully accept his (the child's) sovereignty, he raised him up and took him by the hand, and made himself the Peshwa and leader. He sent men again and again (against 'Abdu-llah), and the number of the enemy was continually increasing till at last they made an attack, and by throwing rockets and other fireworks made matters hot for him.[1] At length the loyalists thought it best, as no assistance had come to them from the other army and all the Dakhanis had turned against them, to retreat at once and try some other arrangement. All agreed, and with one consent started off before dawn. The Dakhanis followed them to the boundaries of their own country, and the two armies, meeting every day, did not fail in fighting. In these days several of the ambitious and zealous young men were killed. 'Alī Mardān K͟hān Bahādur, behaving like a brave man, carried away terrible wounds and fell into the hands of the enemy, and showed his companions an example of fidelity to his salt and of life-sacrifice. Ẕū-l-faqār Beg also displayed manly actions, and a rocket struck him on

[1] Elliot, vi, 333.

the leg, and two days afterwards he died. When they entered the country of Rāja Bharjū,[1] who was one of those loyal to the throne, that body (the enemy) turned back, and 'Abdu-llah Khān proceeded towards Gujarat. The real truth is this, that if in going he had drawn his rein (gone slowly) and allowed the other army to have come up to him, the matter would have turned out according to the wish of the chief men of the victorious State.[2] As soon as the news of the retreat of 'Abdu-llah Khān reached the leaders of the army that was advancing from Berar, not seeing any advantage from further stay, they also retired, and joined the camp of Parwīz at 'Ādilābād in the neighbourhood of Burhanpur. When this intelligence reached me at Agra I was greatly agitated, and proposed to go there myself and destroy root and branch those servants who had become masters. The Amirs and other devoted ones would in no way consent to this. Khwāja Abū-l-ḥasan represented that as no one understood the business of that region as the Khankhanan did I ought to send him, and that he should again arrange matters that had fallen into disorder, and according to the exigencies of the time should compose differences so that affairs might return to their original condition. Other well-wishers being consulted, all their opinions were at one in this, that the Khankhanan must be sent and that Khwāja Abū-l-ḥasan should accompany him. Agreeing with this determination, those who had charge of the affairs of the Khankhanan and his companions obtained leave to go on Sunday, the 17th Urdībihisht, in the 7th year. Shāh-nawāz Khān, Khwāja Abū-l-ḥasan, Razzāq-birdī Ūzbeg, and several others of his associates paid their parting salutations on the same day. The Khankhanan was promoted to the rank of 6,000 personal, Shāh-nawāz Khān

[1] Raja of Baglāna.

[2] A periphrasis for Jahāngīr himself.

to that of 3,000 and horse, that of Dārāb Khān increased by 500 personal and 300 horse (altogether 2,000 personal and 1,500 horse), and to Raḥman-dād, his (the Khankhanan's) younger son, I also gave a fitting mansab. I presented the Khankhanan with a grand dress of honour, a jewelled dagger, a special elephant with *talāyir* (accoutrements), and an Iraq horse. In the same way I bestowed on his sons and companions dresses of honour and horses. In the same month Mu'izzu-l-mulk came from Kabul with his sons, and had the good fortune to kiss the threshold. Shyām Singh and Rāy Mangat Bhadauriya, who belonged to the army of Bangash, according to the request of Qilīj Khān, were promoted to higher mansabs. Shyām Singh had 1,500 personal and was increased by 500, and Rāy Mangat was also raised to a higher rank.

For a long time past news had come of the illness of Āṣaf Khān; sometimes the disease was got under and sometimes recurred, until he died at Burhanpur in the 63rd year of his age. His understanding and capacity were very good. He was very quick-witted. He also wrote poetry. He composed "Khusrau and Shīrīn," dedicating it to me, and called it the "Nūr-nāma" (the writing of light).[1] He had been ennobled in the time of my revered father and made Vizier. In the days when I was a prince he had several times done foolish things, and most men, and indeed Khusrau himself, were of opinion that after my accession I would do unpleasant things (with regard to him). In a manner contrary to what had entered the minds of himself and others, I favoured him and promoted him to the rank of 5,000 personal and horse, and after he had for some time been Vizier with full authority, neglected no point in increasing favour towards him. After his death I gave mansabs to his sons and bestowed kindnesses on them. At last

[1] The history of Nūr, i.e. the history of Nūru-d-dīn Jahāngīr.

it was clear that his disposition and sincerity were not as they should be, and, considering his own evil deeds, he had always been suspicious with regard to me. They say he was aware of the conspiracy and disturbance that took place on the Kabul expedition, and had given support to the wretches. Indeed, I had no confidence that notwithstanding my favour and kindness to him he was not disloyal and of perverse fortune.

After a short space of time, on the 25th of the same month of Urdībihisht, the news of Mīrzā Ghāzī's death arrived. The said Mīrzā was of the ruling family of Thatta (Tatta), of the tribe of Tarkhānī. His father, Mīrzā Jānī, in the time of my revered father became loyal, and with the Khankhanan, who had been appointed to his province, he had the good fortune to have the honour of waiting on Akbar near Lahore. By the royal favour he was given his own province, and, choosing himself to serve at Court, he sent his men to the charge and administration of Thatta, and remained in the service while he lived. At last he died at Burhanpur. Mīrzā Ghāzī Khān, his son, who was at Thatta, in accordance with the firman of the late king obtained the government of that country. Sa'īd Khān, who was at Bhakar (Bukkur), received an order to console him and bring him to Court. The aforesaid Khan sent men to him to recommend loyalty to him. At last, having brought him to Agra, he procured him the honour of kissing the feet of my revered father. He was at Agra when my father died and I ascended the throne. After I arrived at Lahore for the pursuit of Khusrau news came that the Amirs on the borders of Khurasan had assembled together and proceeded against Qandahar, and that Shāh Beg, the governor of that place, was shut up in the fort and looking out for assistance. Of necessity an army was appointed for the relief of Qandahar under the leadership of Mīrzā Ghāzī and other Amirs and generals. When this army reached the neighbourhood of Qandahar, the army of Khurasan, not seeing in themselves the power to await it, returned. Mīrzā Ghāzī, having entered Qandahar, handed over the country and the fort to Sardār Khān, who had been appointed to the government of the place, and Shāh Beg went to his own jagir. Mīrzā Ghāzī started for Lahore by way of Bhakar. Sardār Khān was only a short time at Qandahar before he died, and that province was again in need of a leader and master. This time I added Qandahar to Thatta and handed it over to Mīrzā Ghāzī. From that time till his death he remained there continuously in performance of the duties of its protection and government. His conduct towards the disaffected was excellent. As it was necessary to send a leader to Qandahar in the place of Mīrzā Ghāzī, I appointed Abū-l-bī Ūzbeg,[1] who was at Multan and in that neighbourhood, to that post. I promoted him in rank from 1,500 personal and 1,000 horse to 3,000 personal and horse, and honoured him with the title of Bahādur Khān and a standard. The governorship of Delhi and the protection and administration of that province was conferred on Muqarrab Khān. I dignified Rūp Khawāṣṣ, who was one of the personal servants of my revered father, with the title of Khawāṣṣ Khān, and, giving him the rank of 1,000 personal and 500 horse, bestowed on him the faujdarship of the Sarkar of Qanuj. As I had sought the daughter[2] of I'tiqād Khān, son of I'timādu-d-daulah, in marriage for Khurram, and the marriage

[1] Should be Abū-n-nabī. See *infra*.

[2] This was Arjumand Bānū or Mumtāz-maḥall, the favourite wife of Shāh Jahān and the mother of fourteen of his children. She was the niece of Nūr-Jahān, her father being Nūr-Jahān's brother, the Āṣaf Khān IV and Abū-l-ḥasan of Beale, who also had the names of I'tiqād Khān and Yamīnu-d-daulah. There is an account of the betrothal and wedding in the Pādshāh-nāma, i, 388. It seems that the betrothal took place five years and three months before the marriage, and when Shāh Jahān was 15 years old. At the time of the marriage Shāh Jahān was

festival had been arranged for, I went on Thursday, 18th Khūrdād, to his house, and stayed there one day and one night. He (Khurram) presented offerings (to me) and he gave jewels[1] to the Begams, and to his mothers (including stepmothers) and to the female servants of the harem, and dresses of honour to the Amirs.

I sent 'Abdu-r-Razzāq, the bakhshi of the palace (*darkhāna*), to settle the country of Thatta (Sind) until a Sardar should be appointed who could conciliate the soldiery and the cultivators, and so bring the province into order. I increased his rank and presented him with an elephant and a shawl (*parmnarm*), and sent him off. I made Mu'izzu-l-mulk bakhshi in his room. Khwāja Jahān, who had been sent to inspect the buildings in Lahore and to arrange about them, came in the end of this month and waited on me. Mīrzā 'Īsā Tarkhān, one of the relations of Mīrzā Ghāzī, had been appointed to the army of the Deccan. I sent for him to arrange about the business of Thatta, and on the same day he had the good fortune to pay his respects. As he was deserving of favour, he was given the rank of 1,000 personal and 500 horse. The disease

20 years and 3 months old and Arjumand Bānū was 19 years and 1 month. 18th Khūrdād, 1021, would correspond to about the end of May, 1612, but the Pādshāh-nāma gives the eve of Friday, 9th Rabī'u-l-awwal of 1021, corresponding to 22nd Urdībihisht, as the day of the marriage. This would correspond to 30th April, 1612, so that apparently Jahāngīr's visit to the house (apparently I'timādu-d-daulah's, but possibly Shāh Jahān's) took place about a month after the marriage. Arjumand Bānū died in childbed at Burhanpur in 1040, or July, 1631, the chronogram being one word, viz. *gham*, 'grief.' She must have been born in 1591, and was in her 40th year when she died. She was not Shāh Jahān's first wife, for he was married to the daughter of Muẓaffar Ḥusain Ṣafawī, a descendant of Shāh Isma'īl of Persia, in September, 1610 (Rajab, 1019), but the betrothal to Arjumand was earlier than this. It was in Arjumand's honour that the Tāj was built.

[1] *Tūrhā.* The corresponding passage in the Iqbāl-nāma, p. 67, last line, shows that jewels are meant. The text omits the preposition *ba* before *Begamān.*

of *khūn-pāra* [1] had affected my health. By the advice of the physicians on Wednesday, the (date not given) of the said month, I drew about a sir (*āṣār*) [2] of blood from my left arm. As great lightness resulted, it occurred to me that if they were to call blood-letting 'lightening' it would be well. Nowadays this expression is made use of. To Muqarrab Khān, who had bled me, I gave a jewelled *khapwa* (dagger). Kishan Dās, accountant of the elephant department and stable, who from the time of the late king until now has been the clerk in charge of two departments, and for ages had been hopeful of the title of Raja and the rank of 1,000 personal, and before this had been gratified with a title, now had the rank of 1,000 conferred on him. Mīrzā Rustam, son of Sulṭān Ḥusain Mīrzā Ṣafawī, who had been appointed to the army of the Deccan, I sent for at his request. On Saturday, the 9th of the month of Tīr, he came with his sons and waited on me. He made an offering of a ruby and forty-six royal pearls. I increased the rank of Tāj Khān, the governor of Bhakar, who was one of the old Amirs of this State, by 500 personal and horse.

The tale of the death of Shajā'at Khān is a very strange affair. After he had performed such services and Islām Khān had given him leave to go to the Sarkar of Orissa, one night on the road he was riding on a female elephant *chaukandī-dār* [3] (?in a square howdah or four-pillared canopy), and had given a young eunuch a place behind him. When he left his camp they had

[1] *Khūn-pāra*, 'congestion of blood'; *pāra* or *bāra* is used to mean a collection or gathering. See Ma'āṣiru-l-umarā, ii, 221, where we have *bāra ya'nī jam'ī*. Erskine, in spite of his MS., reads *chūn pāra* and translates 'as quicksilver.'

[2] *Āṣār*, which, according to Forbes, is a sir weight.

[3] Perhaps it was only what is called a *chār-jāma* and not an enclosed howdah.

fastened up an elephant that was in heat on the road. From the noise of the horses' hoofs and the movement of the horsemen he attempted to break his chain. On this account a great noise and confusion took place. When this noise reached the ear of the eunuch, he in a state of bewilderment awoke Shajā'at Khān, who was asleep or in the insensibility of wine, and said: "An elephant in heat has got loose and is coming in this direction." As soon as he heard this he became confused and threw himself down from the front of the chaukandi. When he threw himself off his toe struck against a stone and was torn open, and he died in two or three days of that same wound. In short, from hearing this affair I was completely bewildered. That a brave man on the mere hearing of a cry or a word coming from a child should become so confused and throw himself down without control from the top of an elephant is in truth a matter of amazement. The news of this event reached me on the 19th of the month of Tīr. I consoled his sons with kindnesses and the conferring of offices. If this accident had not happened to him, as he had done notable service, he would have obtained exaltation with greater favours and kindnesses.

"One cannot strive against destiny."

Islām Khān had sent 160 male and female elephants from Bengal; they were brought before me and placed in my private elephant stables. Rāja Tekchand, the Raja of Kumaon, asked for leave to depart. As in the time of my father there had been given to his father 100 horses, I gave him the same number as well as an elephant, and while he was at Court bestowed on him dresses of honour and a jewelled dagger. Also to his brothers I gave dresses of honour and horses. I presented him with his territory according to previous arrangements, and he went back to his home happy and successful.

It happened incidentally that this verse of the Amīru-l-umarā was quoted :—

"Pass, O Messiah, o'er the heads of us slain by love;
Thy restoring one life is worth a hundred murders." [1]

As I have a poetical disposition I sometimes intentionally and sometimes involuntarily compose couplets and quatrains. So the following couplet came into my head :—

"Turn not thy cheek, without thee I cannot live a moment;
For thee to break one heart is equal a hundred murders."

When I had recited this, everyone who had a poetical vein composed a couplet in the same mode. Mullā 'Alī Aḥmad,[2] the seal-engraver, of whom an account has been given previously, had not said badly—

"O Censor, fear the weeping of the old vintner;
Thy breaking one jar is equal to a hundred murders."

Abū-l-fatḥ Dakhanī,[3] who was one of the most considerable of 'Ādil K̲h̲ān's Amirs, and had two years previously taken to being loyal and had entered himself among the leaders of the victorious army, on the 10th

[1] The reference is to the Messiah as the restorer to life by His breath. For *baguzar*, 'pass by,' Erskine had in his MS. *maguzar*, 'pass not.' Apparently the verse means that it is more meritorious for the Messiah to restore one man to life than it is for another to slay a hundred infidels.

[2] 'Alī Aḥmad died suddenly two years before this, unless indeed the passage at p. 169 refers to the mimic and not to 'Alī Aḥmad. Probably the meaning is that 'Alī Aḥmad had made this couplet on some previous occasion, and that one of the courtiers now quoted it. His verse about the hundred murders may contain a play on the word *k̲h̲ūn*, 'blood,' and refer to the spilling of the blood-like wine. It is difficult to understand how Jahāngīr came to introduce the verse into his Memoirs here. It does not seem to have any connection with the account of the Raja of Kumaon. Jahāngīr says it was quoted 'incidentally,' *bā taqarrubī*. Perhaps the word here means 'by way of parody,' or 'by way of paraphrase.' In the MS. used by Erskine the words of the first line seem to be *Maguzar Masīḥ bar sar-i-mā*, and so Erskine translates "Pass not, O Messiah, over the heads of us victims of love." Perhaps *maguzar* means 'do not pass by.'

[3] This is the Dakhanī chief mentioned previously at p. 192.

of Amurdād waited on me, and being accepted by my grace and favour had bestowed on him a special sword and a robe of honour, and after some days I also gave him a special horse. Kh̲wājagī Muḥammad Ḥusain,[1] who had gone to Kashmir as the deputy for his brother's son, when he was satisfied in his mind with the state of affairs of that place, came on the same day and waited on me. As a Sardar was needed to be sent for the governorship of Patna and the rule of that place, it occurred to me to send Mīrzā Rustam. Having raised his rank from 5,000 personal and 1,500 horse to 5,000 personal and horse, on the 26th Jumādā-ṣ-ṣānī, corresponding to the 2nd S̲h̲ahrīwar, I gave him the government of Patna, and bestowing on him a special elephant, a horse with a jewelled saddle, a jewelled sword, and a superb dress of honour, I dismissed him. His sons and the sons of his brother Muẓaffar Ḥusain K̲h̲ān Mīrzā'ī were exalted with increased rank, elephants, horses, and dresses of honour, and sent off with him. I appointed Rāy Dulīp to support Mīrzā Rustam. As his residence was near that place, he collected a good body of men for that service. I increased his rank by 500 personal and horse, so that it became 2,000 with 1,000 horse, and also gave him an elephant. Abū-l-fatḥ Dakhanī had obtained a jagir in the Sarkar of Nagpur and that neighbourhood. He was dismissed in order that he might administer his jagir and look to the guarding and government of that country as well. K̲h̲usrau Bī Ūzbeg was appointed to the faujdarship of the Sarkar of Mewar. His rank of 800 personal and 300 horse was now increased to 1,000 personal and 500 horse, and I also presented him with a horse. As I had my eye on the old service of Muqarrab K̲h̲ān, it occurred to me that I must not pass by the desire of his heart. I had

[1] Blochmann, p. 485. He acted in Kashmir for his brother Hās̲h̲im.

increased his rank and he had obtained good jagirs, but he longed for a standard and drums, and he was now honoured with these as well. Ṣāliḥ, the adopted son of Khwāja Beg-Mīrzā Ṣafawī, was a youth of great bravery and zeal. I gave him the title of Khanjar Khān, and made him eager in the service.

On Thursday, the 22nd Shahrīwar, corresponding with 17th Rajab, 1021, the feast of my solar weighing took place in the house of Maryam-zamānī. It is an approved custom with me to weigh myself in this manner. The late king Akbar, who was the place of manifestation of kindness and grace, also approved of the custom, and twice in every year weighed himself against several sorts of metals, gold, silver, and many precious articles, once according to the solar and once according to the lunar year, and divided their total value, which was worth about a lakh of rupees, among faqirs and needy people. I also observe this annual custom and weigh myself in the same manner, and give those valuables to faqirs. Mu'taqid Khān, Diwan of Bengal, who had been relieved from that service, produced before me the sons and brothers and some of the servants of 'Uṣmān, whom Islām Khān had sent with him to the Court. The charge of each one of the Afghans was entrusted to a responsible servant. Then he (Mu'taqid) produced his own offering, which consisted of twenty-five elephants, two rubies, a jewelled *phūl kaṭāra*[1] (a kind of dagger), trustworthy eunuchs, Bengal stuffs, etc. Mīr Mīrān, son of Sulṭān Khwāja, who was in the Deccan army, obtained the honour of kissing the threshold and gave a ruby as an offering. As between Qilīj Khān, leader of the army of Bangash

[1] The *kaṭāra* was a long, narrow dagger. See Blochmann's Āyīn, pl. xli, fig. 9. But the word *phūl* (flower) is obscure. Perhaps it means the knot or crochet of jewels called by Chardin, iv, 164, ed. Rouen, "une enseigne ronde de pierreries," and which, he says, the Persians called 'rose de Poignard.'

on the borders of Kabul, and the Amirs of that Subah, who had been sent as companions to him under his leadership, there were quarrels, especially with K͟hān Daurān, I sent K͟hwāja Jahān to make enquiry as to which side was in fault. On the 11th of the month of Mihr, Mu'taqid K͟hān was appointed to the high dignity of bakhshi, and his mansab was raised to 1,000 personal and 300 horse. Raising for the second time the mansabs of Muqarrab K͟hān a little, I made it 2,500 personal and 1,500 horse by an increase of 500. On the representation of the Khankhanan, Farīdūn K͟hān Barlās was raised to the mansab, original and increase, of 2,500 personal and 2,000 horse. Rāy Manohar received that of 1,000 personal and 800 horse, and Rāja Bīr Singh Deo that of 4,000 personal and 2,200 horse. Bhārat, grandson of Rāmchand Bandīlah, I, after the latter's death, honoured with the title of Raja. On the 28th Ābān, Ẓafar K͟hān, having come according to summons from the Subah of Gujarat, waited on me. He brought as offerings a ruby and three pearls. On the 6th Āẕar, corresponding with the 3rd S͟hawwāl, news came from Burhanpur that the Amīru-l-umarā had died on Sunday, the 27th Ābān, in the parganah of Nihālpūr. After the illness he had at Lahore his intelligence appeared to be less, and a great loss of memory happened to him. He was very sincere. It is sad that he left no son capable of patronage and favour. Chīn Qilīj K͟hān came from his father, who was at Peshawar, on the 20th Āẕar, and offered (on his father's behalf) 100 muhrs and 100 rupees, and also presented the offerings he had of his own in the shape of a horse and cloth stuffs and other things. To the government of Behar I promoted Ẓafar K͟hān, who is one of the trustworthy house-born ones and foster-children, and increasing his mansab by 500 personal and horse, I made it up to 3,000 personal and 2,000 horse, and also honouring his brothers with robes of honour and horses, allowed them to go off to that province. He had always hoped that he might obtain some separate service in order that he might show his natural ability. I also desired to prove him and make this service the touchstone by which to try him. As it was the season for travelling and hunting, on Tuesday, the 2nd Z̤ī-l-qa'da (25th December, 1612), corresponding with the 4th Day, I left Agra with the intention of hunting and encamped in the Dahrah garden, remaining there four days.[1] On the 10th of the same month the news came of the death of Salīma Sulṭān Begam, who had been ill in the city. Her mother was Gul-rukh Begam, daughter of King Bābar, and her father Mīrzā Nūru-d-dīn Muḥammad, of the Naqshbandī Khwājas. She was adorned with all good qualities. In women this degree of skill and capacity is seldom found. H.M. Humāyūn, by way of kindness (to Bairām), had betrothed her who was his sister's daughter to Bairām Khān. After his death, in the beginning of the reign of the late king Akbar, the marriage took place. After the said Khan had been killed, my revered father married her himself. She received mercy (died) in the 60th year of her age.[2] On the same day I marched from the Dahrah garden and sent I'timādu-d-daulah to bury her (lit. lift her up), and ordered him to place her in the building in the Mandākar

[1] He must have remained more than four days, for he got the news of Salīma's death while in the garden. See *infra*. Perhaps the date 10th refers to Day and not to Z̤ī-l-qa'da. The Dahrah garden was in the environs of Agra.

[2] This statement is wrong. Salīma was 76 when she died, she having been born on 4th Shawwāl, 945, or 23rd February, 1539. She died on or about 10th Z̤ī-l-qa'da, 1021 (2nd January, 1613), so that she was 73 solar years old. See note in B.M. MS. Or. 171, Rieu, 257*a*, and an article in J.A.S.B. for 1906. The note is by the author of the Tārīkh-i-Muḥammadī and is at 72*a* of the B.M. MS. Or. 171, and the corresponding passage appears in MS. Or. 182, on p. 140. The chronogram of Salīma's birth was *Khūsh-ḥāl*, which yields 945. She was about 3½ years older than Akbar.

garden which she herself had made. On the 17th of the month of Day, Mīrzā 'Alī Beg Akbarshāhī came from the army of the Deccan and waited on me. Khwāja Jahān, whom I had despatched to the Subah of Kabul, returned on the 21st of the same month and waited on me. The time for his going and coming had extended to three months and eleven days. He brought twelve muhrs and twelve rupees as an offering. On the same day Rāja Rām Dās also came from the victorious army of the Deccan and paid his respects, and made an offering of 101 muhrs. As robes of honour for the winter season had not been sent to the Amirs of the Deccan, they were forwarded by the hand of Ḥayāt Khān. As the port of Surat had been assigned in jagir to Qilīj Khān, he prayed that Chīn Qilīj (his son) might be despatched for its guardianship and administration. On the 27th Day he had a dress of honour, and being honoured with a dress of honour and the title of Khān, and a standard, obtained leave to go. For the purpose of advising the Amirs of Kabul, and on account of the disagreements that had sprung up between them and Qilīj Khān, I sent Rāja Rām Dās, and bestowed on him a horse and robe of honour and 30,000 rupees for expenses. On the 6th Bahman, when my camp was in the parganah of Bārī, there came the news of the death of Khwājagī Muḥammad Ḥusain, who was of the ancient servants of this State. His elder brother, Muḥammad Qāsim Khān, in the time of my revered father, found great favour, and Khwāja Muḥammad Ḥusain as well was one of his confidential servants, and held employments such as that of superintendent of the kitchen (*bakāwul*) and such like. He left no son and was beardless, and not a single hair of moustache or whiskers appeared on him. At the time of speaking he spoke very shrilly, and was looked upon as an eunuch. Shāh-nawāz Khān, whom the Khankhanan had sent from Burhanpur to make certain representations, came on the 15th of the same month and waited on me. He presented 100 muhrs and 100 rupees. As the affairs of the Deccan, in consequence of the hasty proceedings of 'Abdu-llah Khān and the treachery of the Amirs, did not present a good prospect, the Dakhanis obtained an opportunity for speaking and began to talk of peace to the Amirs and well-wishers there. 'Ādil Khān embraced the robe of loyalty, and prayed that if the affairs of the Deccan were entrusted to him he would so arrange that some of the districts which had been taken out of the possession of the officers of the State should be restored. The loyal ones, looking to the necessities of the time, represented this, and a settlement of some kind was arrived at, and the Khankhanan undertook to settle matters. The Khān A'ẓam was also desirous of putting down the rebel Rānā, and begged for this service by way of obtaining merit (as a *ghāzī*). He was ordered to go to Malwa, which was his jagir, and after arranging matters there to take up this duty. The mansab of Abū-l-bī Ūzbeg[1] was increased by 1,000 personal and 500 horse to 4,000 personal and 3,500 horse. My hunting went on for 2 months and 20 days, and during that time I went out every day to hunt. As not more than 50 or 60 days remained before the world-illumining New Year, I returned, and on the 24th Isfandiyār encamped in the Daḥrah garden. The courtiers and some of the mansabdars, who by order had remained in the city, came on that day and waited on me. Muqarrab Khān presented a decorated jar, Frank hats, and a jewelled sparrow (?). I remained three days in the garden, and on the 27th Isfandiyār entered the city. During this time[2] 223 head of deer, etc., 95 nilgaw, 2 boars, 36 cranes (or herons), etc., and 1,457 fish were killed.

[1] The real name appears to be Abū-n-nabī. He had the title of Bahādur Khān. See Ma'āṣiru-l-umarā, i, 400. In the Akbar-nāma, iii, 820 and 839, he is called Abū-l-baqā.

[2] This must refer to the 2 months and 20 days of hunting.

The Eighth New Year after the auspicious Accession.

The eighth year after my accession, corresponding with Muḥarram, 1022. On the night of Thursday, the 27th Muḥarram, corresponding with the 1st Farwardīn in the eighth year after my accession, after 3½ gharis of day had elapsed, his honour the sun passed from the constellation of Pisces to that of Aries, which is his abode of rejoicing and victory. Early in the morning of the New Year's Day the feast was prepared and adorned after the custom of every year. At the end of that day I sat on the throne of State, and the Amirs and ministers of the State and the courtiers of the palace came to salute and congratulate me. On these days of happy augury I sat the whole day in the public audience hall. Those who had anything to ask or claim presented their petitions, and the offerings of the servants of the palace were laid before me. Abū-l-bī, governor of Qandahar, had sent for an offering Iraq horses and hunting dogs, and they were brought before me. On the 9th of the same month Afẓal K͟hān came from the Subah of Behar, and in waiting on me presented 100 muhrs and 100 rupees, as well as an elephant. On the 12th the offering of I'timādu-d-daulah was laid before me, consisting of jewels, cloths, and other things. That which pleased me attained to the dignity of acceptance. Of the elephants of Afẓal K͟hān's offering ten others were inspected on this day. On the 13th the offerings of Tarbiyat K͟hān were laid before me. Mu'taqid K͟hān bought a house at Agra, and passed some days in that place. Misfortunes happened to him one after another. We have heard that prosperity and bad luck depend on four things: first, upon your wife; second, upon your slave; third, upon your house; fourth, upon your horse. In order to know the prosperity or ill-luck of a house a rule has been established, indeed they say it is infallible. One must clear a small piece of the site from earth, and again strew the earth upon the same ground. If it cover it, one may call it middling good fortune for that house, neither prosperity nor misfortune; if it become less (i.e. does not cover it exactly) it points to ill-luck, and if it does more (than cover it) it is fortunate and auspicious. On the 14th the mansab of I'tibār Khān was raised from 1,000 and 300 horse to 2,000 personal and 500 horse. I increased the mansab of Tarbiyat Khān by 500 personal and 50 horse, so that it became 2,000 personal and 850 horse. Hūshang, son of Islām Khān, who was in Bengal with his father, came at this time and paid his respects. He brought with him some Maghs, whose country is near Pegu and Arracan, and the country is still in their possession. I made some enquiries as to their customs and religion. Briefly they are animals in the form of men. They eat everything there is either on land or in the sea, and nothing is forbidden by their religion. They eat with anyone. They take into their possession (marry) their sisters by another mother. In face they are like the Qarā Qalmāqs, but their language is that of Tibet and quite unlike Turkī. There is a range of mountains, one end of which touches the province of Kāshghar and the other the country of Pegu. They have no proper religion or any customs that can be interpreted as religion. They are far from the Musulman faith and separated from that of the Hindus.

Two or three days before the Sharaf (the sun's highest point) my son Khurram desired me to go to his house that he might present his New Year's offerings from that place. I agreed to his request, and remained for one day and one night at his house. He presented his offerings. I took what I approved of and gave him back the rest. The next day Murtaẓā Khān presented his offerings. Every day until the day of culmination (*rūz-i-sharaf*) the offerings of one or of two or three of the Amirs were laid before me.

On Monday, the 19th Farwardīn, the assembly of the Sharaf was held. On that auspicious day I sat on the throne of State, and an order was given that they should produce all sorts of intoxicating things, such as wine, etc., so that every one according to his desire might take what he liked. Many took wine. The offerings of Mahābat Khān were on this day brought to me. I gave one gold muhr of 1,000 tolas, which is called the star of destiny (*kaukab-i-ṭāliʻ*), to Yādgār ʻAlī Khān, the ambassador of the ruler of Iran. The feast went off well. After the assembly broke up I ordered that they might carry off the furniture and decorations. The offering of the Muqarrab Khān had not been arranged on New Year's Day. All sorts of rareties and excellent presents were now produced which he had collected together. Amongst others, twelve Iraq and Arab horses that had been brought in a ship, and jewelled saddles of Frank workmanship [1] were produced before me. To the mansab of Nawāzish Khān 500 horse were added so as to make it one of 2,000 personal and horse. An elephant called Bansībadan, which Islām Khān had sent from Bengal, was brought to me and put among my special elephants. On the 3rd Urdībihisht, Khwāja Yādgār, brother of ʻAbdu-llah Khān, came from Gujarat and waited on me; he offered 100 Jahāngīrī muhrs. After he had been in attendance a few days he was honoured with the title of Sardār Khān. As a competent bakhshi had to be sent to the army of Bangash and those regions, I chose Muʻtaqid Khān for this duty, and increased his mansab by 300 personal and 50 horse so that it became 1,500 with 350 horse, and dismissed him. It was settled that he must go quickly. I sent off Muḥammad Ḥusain Chelebī, who understood the purchase of jewels and collecting curiosities, with money to go by

[1] *Zīn-i-muraṣṣaʻ kārī-i-Farangī.* The MSS. in the B.M. seem to have *zaram* instead of *zīn.*

way of Iraq to Constantinople and buy and bring for the Sarkar curiosities and rareties. For this purpose it was necessary that he should pay his respects to the ruler of Iran. I had given him a letter and a memorandum (of what he was to procure). Briefly, he saw my brother, Shāh 'Abbās, in Mashhad, and the king enquired from him what kind of things should be brought for his master's Sarkar. As he was urgent, Chelebī showed the list he had brought with him. In that list there were entered good turquoise and *mūmīyā* (bitumen) from the mine of Ispahan. He told him that these two articles were not to be bought, but he would send them for me. He authorized Uwaisī Tūpchī (gunner), who was one of his private servants, to hand over to him six bags (*ambāncha*) of turquoise earth holding about 30 seers, with 14 tolas of mumiya and four Iraq horses, one of which was a piebald, and he wrote a letter containing many, many expressions of friendship. With regard to the inferior quality of the turquoise dust (*khāka*) and the small quantity of mumiya he made many apologies. The khaka appeared very inferior. Although the jewellers and makers of rings made every endeavour, no stone that was fit to be made into a finger ring could be produced. Probably in these days turquoise dust is not procurable from the mines such as it was in the time of the late king Ṭahmāsp. He mentioned all this in the letter. With regard to the effect of mumiya I had heard much from scientists, but when I tried it no result was apparent. I do not know whether physicians have exaggerated its effect, or whether its efficacy had been lessened by its being stale. At any rate, I gave it to a fowl with a broken leg to drink in larger quantity than they said and in the manner laid down by the physicians, and rubbed some on the place where it was broken, and kept it there for three days, though it was said to be sufficient to keep it from morning till evening. But after I had examined it, no effect was produced, and the broken place remained as it was.[1] In a separate letter the Shah had written a recommendation of Salāmu-llah, the Arab. I immediately increased his mansab and his jagir.

I sent one of my private elephants with trappings to 'Abdu-llah Khān and gave another to Qilīj Khān. I ordered that assignments (*tankhwāh*) should be made to 12,000 horse on the establishment[2] of 'Abdu-llah Khān at the rate of three horses and two horses for each trooper. As previously with a view to service in Junagarh I had increased the mansab of his brother Sardār Khān by 500 personal and 300 horse, and had afterwards assigned the duty to Kāmil Khān, I ordered that he should retain his increase and that it should be counted (permanently) in his mansab. I increased the rank of Sarfarāz Khān, which was that of 1,500 personal and 500 horse, by 200 horse more. On the 27th Urdībihisht, corresponding with the 26th Rabī'u-l-awwal, in the eighth year of my reign, in the year 1022 of the Hijra era, on Thursday, the meeting for my lunar weighing took place in the house of Maryam-zamānī (his mother). Some of the money that was weighed I ordered to be given to the women and the deserving ones who had assembled in my mother's house. On the same day I increased by 1,000 the mansab of Murtaẓā Khān, so that it came to 6,000 personal and 5,000

[1] Jahāngīr's words seem to imply that he caused the fowl's leg to be broken in order to try the experiment. Manucci, i, 55, has a good deal to say about *mūmīyā*, though he admits that he had not himself witnessed its effects. I do not find that Hājī Bābā descants on its virtues, though at the end of the first chapter he says that his mother gave him an unguent which she said would cure all fractures. The Persian translator, no doubt rightly, has rendered the word 'unguent' by *mūmīyā*. With regard to the derivation of the word, may it not be connected with *mom*, 'wax'? Vullers has a long article on the word.

[2] The text has *birādārī*, 'brotherhood,' but the true reading, as shown by the B.M. MSS., is *bar āwardī*, برآوردی, and this means either the establishment of 'Abdu-llah or a list submitted by him. Perhaps 'list' is a better translation, the word *āwardī* being connected with the *āwarda-nawīs* of Wilson's Glossary.

horse. Khusrau Beg, a slave of Mīrzā Khān, came from Patna in the company of 'Abdu-r-Razzāq Ma'mūrī and waited on me, and Sardār Khān, brother of 'Abdu-llah Khān, obtained leave to go to Ahmadabad. An Afghan had brought from the Carnatic two goats that had *pāzahar* (bezoar stones, an antidote against poison). I had always heard that an animal that has pazahar is very thin and miserable, but these goats were very fat and fresh. I ordered them to kill one of them, which was a female. Four pazahar stones became apparent, and this caused great astonishment.

It is an established fact that cheetahs in unaccustomed places do not pair off with a female, for my revered father once collected together 1,000 cheetahs. He was very desirous that they should pair, but this in no way came off. He had many times coupled male and female cheetahs together in gardens, but there, too, it did not come off. At this time a male cheetah, having slipped its collar, went to a female and paired with it, and after two and a half months three young ones were born and grew up. This has been recorded because it appeared strange. As cheetahs did not pair with cheetahs, (still less) had it ever been heard in former times (?) that tigers mated in captivity. As in the time of my reign wild beasts have abandoned their savagery, tigers have become so tame that troops of them without chains or restraint go about amongst the people, and they neither harm men nor have any wildness or alarm. It happened that a tigress became pregnant and after three months bore three cubs; it had never happened that a wild tiger after its capture had paired. It had been heard from philosophers that the milk of a tigress was of great use for brightening eyes. Although we made every effort that the moisture of milk should appear in her breasts, we could not accomplish it. It occurs to me that as it is a raging creature, and milk appears in the breasts of mothers by reason of the affection they have for their young, as milk[1] comes into their breasts in connection with their young ones drinking and sucking at the time of their taking (the milk), their (the mothers') rage increases and the milk in their breasts is dried up.

At the end of Urdībihisht, Khwāja Qāsim, brother of Khwāja 'Abdu-l-'Azīz, who is of the Naqshbandī Khwājas, came from Māwarā'a-n-nahr and waited on me. After a few days 12,000 rupees were given to him as a present. As Khwāja Jahān had made a melon-bed in the neighbourhood of the city, when two watches of day had passed on Thursday, the 10th Khūrdād, I got into a boat and went to inspect the melon-bed, and took the ladies with me. We reached there when two or three gharis of day were left, and passed the evening in walking among the beds. A wonderfully sharp wind and whirlwind sprang up, so that the tents and screens fell down. I got into the boat and passed the night in it. I also passed part of the Friday in walking about the melon-bed, and returned to the city. Afẓal Khān, who for a long time had been afflicted with boils and other sores, died on the 10th Khūrdād. I transferred the jagir and hereditary land of Rāja Jagman, who had failed in his service in the Deccan, to Mahābat Khān. Shaikh Pīr, who is one of the emancipated ones who hold aloof from the attachments of the age, and who on account of the pure friendship that he bears towards me has chosen to be my companion and servant, had before this founded a mosque in the parganah of Mairtha, which is his native place. At this time he took occasion to mention the circumstance. As I found his mind bent on the completion of this building I gave him 4,000 rupees, so that he himself might go and expend it, and also gave him a valuable

[1] The sentence is very obscure. MS. No. 181 I.O. has *khūn*, 'blood,' instead of *chūn*, 'as,' and perhaps the meaning is blood in the breasts turns to milk on account of love for their cubs, and then the sucking by the latter increases the mother's natural ferocity and the milk dries up.

shawl and dismissed him. In the public audience hall there were two railings (*maḥjar*) of wood. Inside the first, Amirs, ambassadors, and people of honour sat, and no one entered this circle without an order. Within the second railing, which is broader than the first, the mansabdars of inferior rank,[1] ahadis, and those who had work to do are admitted. Outside this railing stand the servants of the Amirs and all the people who may enter the Diwankhana. As there was no difference between the first and second railings, it occurred to me that I should decorate the first with silver. I ordered this railing and the staircase that led from this railing to the balcony of the Jharokha, as well as the two elephants placed on the two sides of the seat of the Jharokha, which skilful people had made of wood, to be decorated with silver. After this was completed it was reported to me that 125 maunds of silver in Hindustani weight, equal to 880 maunds of Persia, had been used up; indeed, it now assumed a worthy appearance.

On the 3rd of the month of Tīr, Muẓaffar K͟hān came from Thatta[2] and waited on me. He made an offering of twelve muhrs and a Koran with a jewelled cover, and two jewelled roses (?) (*dū gul*). On the 14th of the same month Ṣafdar K͟hān came from the Subah of Behar and waited on me, offering 101 muhrs. After Muẓaffar K͟hān had been some days in attendance, I increased his former mansab by 500 personal, and giving him a standard and a private shawl dismissed him to Thatta.[3]

I knew that every animal or living thing bitten by a mad dog died, but this had not been ascertained in

[1] In the B.M. MSS. the words are *manṣabdārān-i-rīzā-manṣab*. These last two words are wanting in the text.

[2] Text Patna, but B.M. MSS. have Thatta.

[3] Text has Patna.

the case of an elephant. In my time it so happened that one night a mad dog came into the place where was tied one of my private elephants, Gajpatī[1] by name, and bit the foot of a female elephant that was with mine. She at once cried out. The elephant-keepers at once ran in, and the dog fled away into a thorn-brake that is there. After a little while it came in again and bit my private elephant's fore-foot as well. The elephant killed it. When a month and five days had passed after this event, one day when it was cloudy the growling of thunder came to the ear of the female elephant, that was in the act of eating, and it of a sudden raised a cry and its limbs began to tremble. It threw itself on the ground, but rose again. For seven days water ran out of its mouth, then suddenly it uttered a cry and showed distress. The remedies the drivers gave it had no effect, and on the eighth day it fell and died. A month after the death of the female elephant they took the large elephant to the edge of the river in the plain. It was cloudy and thundery in the same way. The said elephant in the height of excitement all at once began to tremble and sat down on the ground. With a thousand difficulties the drivers took it to its own place. After the same interval and in the same way that had happened to the female elephant this elephant also died. Great amazement was caused by this affair, and in truth it is a matter to be wondered at that an animal of such size and bulk should be so much affected by a little wound inflicted on it by such a weak creature.

As K͟hānk͟hānān had repeatedly begged for leave to be given to his son S͟hāh-nawāz K͟hān, on the 4th Amurdād I gave him a horse and a robe of honour and dismissed him to the Deccan. I promoted Ya'qūb Badak͟hs͟hī, whose

[1] Text Kachhī, but it is Gajpatī in B.M. MSS.

mansab was 150, to 1,500 personal and 1,000 horse, on account of the bravery he had displayed, and gave him the title of Khan as well as a standard.

The Hindus are in four divisions, and each of these acts according to its own rules and ways. In every year they keep a fixed day. The first is the caste of the Brahmans,[1] that is, those who know the Incomparable God. Their duties are of six kinds—(1) to acquire religious knowledge, (2) to give instructions to others, (3) to worship fire, (4) to lead men to the worship of fire, (5) giving something to the needy, (6) taking gifts. There is for this caste an appointed day, and that is the last day of the month of Sāwan, the second month of the rainy season.[2] They consider this an auspicious day, and the worshippers go on that day to the banks of rivers and tanks, and recite enchantments, breathe upon cords and coloured threads; on another day, which is the first of the New Year, they fasten them on the hands of the Rajas and great men of the time, and look on them as (good) omens. They call this thread *rākhī*,[3] that is, preservation (*nigāh-dāsht*). This day occurs in the month of Tīr, when the world-heating sun is in the constellation of Cancer. The second caste is that of the Chhatrī, which is known as Khatrī. Their duty is to protect the oppressed from the evil of the oppressors. The customs of this caste are three

[1] This seems taken from Abū-l-faẓl. See Jarrett, iii, 115. The third duty, which Jahāngīr calls "worshipping fire," is by Abū-l-faẓl termed Yāg, i.e. sacrifice.

[2] It is the day of the full moon in Sāwan that is holy.

[3] Blochmann, p. 184, and Wilson's Glossary. Badayūnī (Lowe, p. 269) speaks of Akbar's wearing the *rākhī* on the 8th day of Virgo. I do not know why Jahāngīr calls the day after the last day of Sāwan the first day of the New Year. Perhaps *rūz-i-duyam* here means 'another day,' and not 'the next day'; but then, if so, why is it the rakhi day, for that is in Sāwan? The Hindu New Year begins in Baisākh (April). It will be observed from Jarrett, ii, 17, that Sāwan is also the name of a month of a particular length. Perhaps Jahāngīr has confused the two things.

things—(1) that they study religious science themselves but do not teach others; (2) that they worship fire, but do not teach others to do so; (3) that they give to the needy, but although they are needy take nothing themselves. The day of this caste is the *Bijay dasamīn*, 'the victorious tenth.'[1] On this day with them it is lucky to mount and go against one's enemy with an army. Rām Chand, whom they worship as their god, leading his army on that day against his enemy won a victory, and they consider this a great day, and, decorating their elephants and horses, perform worship. This day falls in the month of Shahrīwar,[2] when the Sun is in the mansion of Virgo, and on it they give presents to those who look after their horses and elephants. The third caste is that of Baish (Vaishya). Its custom is this, that they serve the other two castes of which mention has been made. They practise agriculture and buying and selling, and are employed in the business of profit and interest. This caste has also a fixed day which they call the Dewālī; this day occurs in the month of Mihr when the sun is in the constellation of Libra, the 28th day of the lunar month. On the night of that day they light lamps, and friends and those who are dear assemble in each other's houses and pass their time busily in gambling. As the eyes of this caste are on profit and interest, they consider carrying over and opening new accounts on that day auspicious. The fourth caste is the Sudras, who are the lowest caste of the Hindus. They are the servants of all, and derive no profit from those things which are the specialities of every (other) caste. Thursday is the Holī, which in their belief is the last day of the year. This day occurs in the month of Isfandārmuz, when the sun is in the constellation of Pisces. On the night of

[1] It is the 10th of Aswīn (September).

[2] The text wrongly has *dar har māh* instead of only *dar māh*.

this day they light fires at the head of the streets and ways, and when it becomes day they for one watch scatter the ashes on each other's heads and faces, and make a wonderful noise and disturbance, and after this wash themselves, put on their apparel, and walk about in the gardens and on the plains. As it is an established custom of the Hindus to burn the dead, to light fires on this night, which is the last night of the year that has passed, signifies that they burn the last year, which has gone to the abode of the dead. In the time of my revered father the Hindu Amirs and others in imitation of them performed the ceremony of rakhi in adorning him, making strings of rubies and royal pearls and flowers jewelled with gems of great value and binding them on his auspicious arms. This custom was carried on for some years. As they carried this extravagance to excess, and he disliked it, he forbade it. The brahmans by way of auguries used to tie these strings and (pieces of) silk according to their custom. I also in this year carried out this laudable religious practice, and ordered that the Hindu Amirs and the heads of the caste [1] should fasten rakhis on my arms. On the day of the rakhi, which was the 9th Amurdād, they performed the same rites, and other castes by way of imitation did not give up this bigotry; this year I agreed to it, and ordered that the brahmans should bind strings (of cotton) and silk after the ancient manner. On this day by chance fell the anniversary of the death of the late king.[2] The commemoration of such an anniversary is one of the standing rules and customs in Hindustan. Every year on the day of the death of their fathers and those who

[1] The negative in text is wrong apparently. It does not occur in MS. No. 181 I.O. nor in the B.M. MSS., which have *ba* instead of *na*.

[2] That is, 9th Amurdād corresponded with the Ḥijra date of Akbar's death, viz. 13th Jumādā-ṣ-ṣānī, which this year, 1022, occurred in July. According to the solar calendar Akbar's death was in October.

are dear to them, each according to his circumstances and ability prepares food and all kinds of perfumes, and the learned men, the respectable and other men assemble, and these assemblies sometimes last a week. On this day I sent Bābā Khurram to the venerated tomb to arrange the assemblage, and 10,000 rupees were given to ten trustworthy servants to divide among fakirs and those who were in want.

On the 15th of the month of Amurdād the offering of Islām Khān was laid before me. He had sent 28 elephants, 40 horses of that part of the country which are known as *ṭānghan*, 50 eunuchs, 500 *pargāla nafīs sitārkānī*.[1]

It had been made a rule that the events of the Subahs should be reported according to the boundaries of each, and news-writers from the Court had been appointed for this duty. This being the rule that my revered father had laid down, I also observe it, and much gain and great advantage are to be brought about by it, and information is acquired about the world and its inhabitants. If the advantages of this were to be written down it would become a long affair. At this time the news-writer of Lahore reported that at the end of the month of Tīr ten men had gone from the city to Amānābād, which lies at a distance of 12 kos. As the air was very hot, they took shelter under a tree. Soon afterwards wind and a dust-storm (*chakrī*) sprang up, and when it blew on that band of men they trembled, and nine of them died under the tree, and only one remained alive; he was ill for a long time, and recovered with great difficulty. In that neighbourhood such bad

[1] *Pargālas* seem to be clothes of some sort. Perhaps the word is another form of the *fargūl* of Blochmann, p. 89. The text has *sitārkāni*. *Sitār* means a veil, but probably we should read *Sonargāoni*, 'of Sonargaon.' Both the MSS. give the number of elephants as 68 instead of 28 as in text.

air was created that numerous birds who had their nests in that tree all fell down and died, and that the wild beasts (beasts of the plain, perhaps cattle) came and threw themselves on to the cultivated fields, and, rolling about on the grass, gave up their lives. In short, many animals perished. On Thursday, the 13th Amurdād, having said my prayers (lit. counted my rosary), I embarked on board a boat for the purpose of hunting in the village of Samonagar, which is one of my fixed hunting-places. On the 3rd Shahrīwar, Khān 'Ālam, whom I had sent for from the Deccan in order to despatch him to Iraq in company with the ambassador of the ruler of Iran, came and waited on me at this place. He offered 100 muhrs. As Samonagar was in Mahābat Khān's jagir, he had prepared a delightful halting-place there on the bank of the river, and it pleased me greatly. He presented offerings of an elephant and an emerald ring. The former was put into my private stud. Up to the 6th Shahrīwar I was employed in hunting. In these few days 47 head of antelope, male and female, and other animals were killed. At this time Dilāwar Khān sent as an offering a ruby, which was accepted. I sent a special sword for Islām Khān. I increased the mansab of Ḥasan 'Alī Turkumān, which was 1,000 personal and 700 horse, by 500 personal and 100 horse. At the end of Thursday, the 20th of the same month, in the house of Maryam-zamānī, my solar weighing took place. I weighed myself according to the usual custom against metals and other things. I had this year attained to the age of 44 solar years. On the same day Yādgār 'Alī, ambassador of the ruler of Iran, and Khān 'Ālam, who had been nominated to accompany him from this side, received their leave to go. On Yādgār 'Alī there were bestowed a horse with a jewelled saddle, a jewelled sword, a vest without sleeves with gold embroidery, an aigrette with feathers and a *jīgha* (turban ornament), and 30,000 rupees in cash, altogether 40,000 rupees, and on Khān 'Ālam a jewelled *khapwa* or *phūl kaṭāra* (a sort of dagger) with a pendant of royal pearls. On the 22nd of the same month I visited the venerated mausoleum of my revered father at Bihishtābād, riding on an elephant. On the way 5,000 rupees in small coin were scattered round, and I gave other 5,000 rupees to Khwāja Jahān to divide among the dervishes. Having said my evening prayers, I went back to the city in a boat. As the house of I'timādu-d-daulah was on the bank of the river Jumna, I alighted there until the end of the next day. Having accepted what pleased me of his offerings, I went towards the palace; I'tiqād Khān's house was also on the bank of the river Jumna; at his request I disembarked there with the ladies, and walked round the houses he had lately built there. This delightful place pleased me greatly. He had produced suitable offerings of cloth stuffs and jewels and other things; these were all laid before me and most of them were approved. When it was near evening I entered the auspicious palace. As the astrologers had fixed an hour in this night for starting for Ajmir, when seven gharis of the night of Monday, the 2nd Sha'bān, corresponding with the 24th Shahrīwar, had passed, I started in happiness and prosperity with intent to go there from the capital of Agra. In this undertaking two things were agreeable to me, one a pilgrimage to the splendid mausoleum of Khwāja Mu'īnu-d-dīn Chishtī, from the blessing of whose illustrious soul great advantages had been derived by this dignified family, and whose venerable shrine I had not visited after my accession to the throne. The second was the defeat and beating back of the rebel Rānā Amar Singh, who is one of the most considerable of the Zamindars and Rajas of Hindustan, and whose headship and leadership and those of his ancestors all the Rajas and Rays of this province agree to. The administration has for long been in the hands of this family, and they have long borne rule towards the East, that is the Pūrab. They became in that time well known under the title of Rajas. After this they fell on the Deccan[1] and took possession of many of the countries of that region. In the place of Raja they have taken the title of Rāwal. After this they came into the hill country of Mewāt, and by degrees got into their possession the fort of Chitor. From that date until this day, which is in the eighth year after my accession, 1,471 years have passed.[2]

There are twenty-six others of this caste who have ruled for 1,010 years. They have the title of Rāwal, and from the Rāwal who was first known as Rāwal down to Rānā Amar Singh, the present Rānā, there are twenty-six individuals who have ruled for the space of 461 years. During this long time they have never bent their necks in obedience to any of the kings of the country of Hindustan, and have for most of the time been rebellious and troublesome, so much so that in the reign of the late king Bābar, Rānā Sāngā collected together all the Rajas, Rays, and Zamindars of this province, and fought a battle in the neighbourhood of Biyāna with 180,000 horse and several lakhs of foot-soldiers. By the aid of Almighty God and the assistance of fortune the victorious army of Islām prevailed against the infidel forces, and a great defeat happened to them. The details of this battle have been given in the Memoirs of King Bābar. My revered father (may his bright tomb be the abode of unending Grace) exerted himself greatly

[1] See Jarrett, ii, 268, where it is said that an ancestor of Bāppa came to Berar.

[2] According to Tod, Bāppa, the ancestor of the Rānā, acquired Chitor in A.D. 728. Jahāngīr makes twenty-six princes rule for 1,010 years and twenty-six others only reign for 461 years ! Tod says the legendary ancestor Kenek Sen, the sixty-third from Loh, the son of Rām, emigrated from the Panjab to Gujarat in 145 A.D. Perhaps the Mewāt of the Tūzuk is a mistake for Mewār.

to put down these rebels, and several times sent armies against them. In the twelfth year after his accession he set himself to capture the fort of Chitor, which is one of the strongest forts of the inhabited world, and to overthrow the kingdom of the Rānā, and after four months and ten days of siege took it by force from the men of Amar Singh's father, after much fighting, and returned after destroying the fort. Every time the victorious forces pressed him hard in order to capture him or make him a fugitive, but it so happened that this was not effected. In the end of his reign, on the same day and hour that he proceeded to the conquest of the Deccan, he sent me with a large army and reliable Sardars against the Rānā. By chance these two affairs, for reasons which it would take too long to recount, did not succeed. At last I came to the throne, and as this matter was only half done, the first army I sent to the borders was this one. Making my son Parwīz its leader, the leading nobles who were at the capital were appointed to this duty. I sent abundant treasure and artillery with him. As every matter depends on its own season, at this juncture the unhappy affair of Khusrau occurred, and I had to pursue him to the Panjab. The province and the capital of Agra remained void. I had necessarily to write that Parwīz should return with some of the Amirs and take charge of Agra and the neighbourhood. In short, this time again the matter of the Rānā did not go off as it should. When by the favour of Allah my mind was at rest from Khusrau's disturbance, and Agra became again the alighting place of the royal standards, a victorious army was appointed under the leadership of Mahābat Khān, 'Abdu-llah Khān, and other leaders, and from that date up to the time when the royal standards started for Ajmir his country was trodden under foot by the victorious forces. As finally the affair did not assume an approved form, it occurred to me that, as I had nothing to do at Agra, and I was convinced that until I myself went there the affair would not be set to rights, I left the fort of Agra and alighted at the Dahrah garden. On the next day the festival of the Dasahrā took place. According to the usual custom they decorated the elephants and horses, and I had them before me. As the mothers and sisters of Khusrau repeatedly represented to me that he was very repentant of his deeds, the feelings (lit. sweat) of fatherly affection having come into movement, I sent for him and determined that he should come every day to pay his respects to me. I remained for eight days in that garden. On the 28th news arrived that Rāja Rām Dās, who was doing service in Bangash and the neighbourhood of Kabul with Qilīj Khān, had died. On the 1st of the month of Mihr I marched from the garden, and dismissed Khwāja Jahān to look after the capital of Agra and guard the treasure and the palace, and gave him an elephant and a special robe (*fargul*). On the 2nd Mihr news arrived that Rāja Bāso had died in the thanah of Shahabad,[1] which is on the border of the territory of Amar. On the 10th of the same month I halted at Rūp Bās, which has now been named Amānābād. Formerly this district had been given as jagir to Rūp Khawāṣṣ. Afterwards, bestowing it on Amānu-llah, son of Mahābat Khān, I ordered it to be called by his name. Eleven days were passed at this halting-place. As it is a fixed hunting-place, I every day mounted to go hunting, and in these few days 158 antelopes, male and female, and other animals were killed. On the 25th of the month I marched from Amānābād. On the 31st, corresponding with the 8th Ramaẕān, Khwāja Abū-l-ḥasan, whom I had sent for from Burhanpur, came and waited on me,

[1] Probably the town of that name in the Rajputana State of Jhalāwar. See "Rajputana Gazetteer," ii, 211.

and presented as offerings 50 muhrs, 15 jewelled vessels, and an elephant, which I placed in my private stud. On the 2nd Ābān, corresponding with the 10th Ramaẓān, news came of the death of Qilīj Khān. He was one of the ancient servants of the State, and obtained the mercy of God in the 80th year of his age. He was employed at Peshawar in the duty of keeping in order the Afghans full of darkness.[1] His rank was 6,000 personal and 5,000 horse. Murtaẓā Khān Dakhanī was unrivalled in the art of *pūlta-bāzī,* which in the language of the Dakhanis they call *yagānagī,* and the Moguls *shamshīr-bāzī,* 'sword-play' (fencing). For some time I studied it with him. At this time I exalted him with the title of Warzish Khān (Exercise-Khān). I had established a custom that deserving people and dervishes should be brought before me every night, so that I might bestow on them, after personal enquiry into their condition, land, or gold, or clothes. Amongst these was a man who represented to me that the name Jahāngīr, according to the science of *abjad* (numerals reckoned by letters), corresponded to the great name "Allah Akbar."[2] Considering this a good omen, I gave him who discovered (this coincidence) land, a horse, cash, and clothing. On Monday, the 5th Shawwāl, corresponding to the 26th Ābān, the hour for entering Ajmir was fixed. On the morning of the said day I went towards it. When the fort and the buildings of the shrine of the revered Khwāja appeared in sight, I traversed on foot the remainder of the road, about a kos. I placed trustworthy men on both sides of the road, who went along giving money to fakirs and the necessitous. When four gharis of day had passed, I entered the city and its inhabited portion, and in the fifth ghari had the honour of visiting the venerated mausoleum. After visiting it I proceeded to

[1] The Raushanīs, called by their enemies the Tārīkīs.
[2] Both Jahāngīr and Allah Akbar yield 288.

the auspicious palace, and the next day ordered all those present in this honoured resting-place, both small and great, belonging to the city, and travellers, to be brought before me, that they might be made happy with numerous gifts according to their real circumstances. On the 7th Āẕar I went to see and shoot on the tank of Pushkar, which is one of the established praying-places of the Hindus, with regard to the perfection of which they give (excellent) accounts that are incredible to any intelligence, and which is situated at a distance of three kos from Ajmir. For two or three days I shot water-fowl on that tank, and returned to Ajmir. Old and new temples which, in the language of the infidels, they call Deohara [1] are to be seen around this tank. Among them Rānā Shankar, who is the uncle of the rebel Amar, and in my kingdom is among the high nobles, had built a Deohara of great magnificence, on which 100,000 rupees had been spent. I went to see that temple. I found a form cut out of black stone, which from the neck above was in the shape of a pig's head, and the rest of the body was like that of a man. The worthless religion of the Hindus is this, that once on a time for some particular object the Supreme Ruler thought it necessary to show himself in this shape; on this account they hold it dear and worship it.[2] I ordered them to break that hideous form and throw it into the tank. After looking at this building there appeared a white dome on the top of a hill, to which men were coming from all quarters. When I asked about this they said that a Jogī lived there, and when the simpletons come to see him he places in their hands a handful [3] of flour, which they put into their mouths and imitate the cry

[1] Sanskrit Devaharā, 'an idol temple.'

[2] "Rajputana Gazetteer," ii, 69.

[3] Instead of *kaff ārdi*, 'a handful of flour,' the R.A.S. MS. has *kaf az way*, 'his spittle,' and this seems more likely.

of an animal which these fools have at some time injured, in order that by this act their sins may be blotted out. I ordered them to break down that place and turn the Jogī out of it, as well as to destroy the form of an idol there was in the dome. Another belief they have is that there is no bottom to this tank. After enquiry it appeared that it is nowhere deeper than 12 cubits. I also measured it round and it was about 1½ kos.

On the 16th Āẕar news came that the watchmen had marked down a tigress. I immediately went there and killed it with a gun and returned. After a few days a nilgaw (blue bull) was killed, of which I ordered them to take off the skin in my presence and cook it as food for the poor. Over 200 people assembled and ate it, and I gave money with my own hand to each of them. In the same month news came that the Franks of Goa had, contrary to treaty, plundered four cargo vessels[1] that frequented the port of Surat in the neighbourhood of that port: and, making prisoners a large number of Musulmans, had taken possession of the goods and chattels that were in those ships. This being very disagreeable to my mind, I despatched Muqarrab Khān, who is in charge of the port, on the 18th Āẕar, giving him a horse and elephant and a dress of honour, to obtain compensation for this affair. On account of the great activity and good services of Yūsuf Khān and Bahāduru-l-mulk in the Subah of the Deccan, I sent standards for them.

It has been written that my chief object, after my visit to the Khwāja, was to put a stop to the affair of the rebel Rānā. On this account I determined to remain myself at

[1] Text *ajnabī*, 'foreign' or 'strange,' and Dowson had the same reading, for at vi, 337, we have the translation 'ships engaged in the foreign trade of Surat.' But I adopt the reading of I.O. MS. 181, which is *ajnāsī*, as it does not seem likely that Jahāngīr would interest himself about 'foreign' ships.

Ajmir and send on Bābā Khurram, my fortunate son. This idea was a very good one, and on this account, on the 6th of Day, at the hour fixed upon, I despatched him in happiness and triumph. I presented him with a *qabā* (outer coat) of gold brocade with jewelled flowers and pearls round the flowers, a brocaded turban with strings of pearls, a gold woven sash with chains of pearls, one of my private elephants called Fatḥ Gaj, with trappings, a special horse, a jewelled sword, and a jewelled *khapwa*, with a *phūl kaṭāra*. In addition to the men first appointed to this duty under the leadership of Khān A'ẓam, I sent 12,000 more horse with my son, and honoured their leaders, each according to his condition, with special horses and elephants and robes of honour, and dismissed them. Fidā'ī Khān was nominated to the paymastership of this army. At the same time Ṣafdar Khān was despatched to the government of Kashmir in place of Hāshim Khān. He received a horse and robe of honour. On Wednesday, the 11th, Khwāja Abū-l-ḥasan was made general paymaster (*bakhshī-kul*), and received a dress of honour. I had ordered them to make a large caldron[1] at Agra for the revered mausoleum of the Khwāja. On this day it was brought, and I ordered them to cook food for the poor in that pot, and collect together the poor of Ajmir to feed them whilst I was there. Five thousand people assembled, and all ate of this food to their fill. After the food I gave money to each of the dervishes with my own hand. At this time Islām Khān, governor of Bengal, was promoted to the mansab of 6,000 personal and horse, and a flag was given to Mukarram Khān, son of Mu'āẓẓam Khān.

On the 1st of Isfandārmuẕ, corresponding with the 10th Muḥarram, 1023 (20th February, 1614), I left

[1] "Rajputana Gazetteer," ii, 63. There are now two large caldrons (*dīg*) inside the *dargāh* enclosure.

Ajmir to hunt nilgaw, and returned on the 9th. I halted at the fountain of Ḥāfiẓ Jamāl,[1] two kos from the city, and passed the night of Friday[2] there. At the end of the day I entered the city. In these twenty days ten nilgaw had been killed. As the good service of Khwāja Jahān and the smallness of his force for the defence and government of Agra and that neighbourhood were brought to my notice, I increased his mansab by 500 personal and 100 horse. On the same day Abū-l-fatḥ Dakhanī came from his jagir and waited on me. On the 3rd of the same month news came of the death of Islām Khān; he had died on Thursday, the 5th Rajab, in the year 1022 (21st August, 1613). In one day, without any previous illness, this inevitable event occurred. He was one of those born and brought up in the house (house-born). The naturally good disposition and knowledge of affairs that showed themselves in him were seen in no one else. He ruled Bengal with entire authority, and brought within the civil jurisdiction of the province countries that had never previously come under the sway of any of the jagirdars or into the possession of any of the Chiefs of the State. If death had not overtaken him he would have done perfect service.

The Khān A'ẓam had himself prayed that the illustrious prince should be appointed to the campaign against the Rānā, yet, notwithstanding all kinds of encouragement and gratification on the part of my son (Shāh Jahān), he would not apply himself to the task, but proceeded to act in his own unworthy manner. When this was heard by me, I sent Ibrāhīm Ḥusain, who was one of my most trusty attendants, to him, and sent affectionate

[1] Ḥāfiẓ Jamāl was the name of the saint Mu'īnu-d-dīn's daughter ("Rajputāna Gazetteer," ii, 62). It lies at the back of the Taragarh hill, and is now commonly called Nūr-chashma. The fountains, etc., are in a ruined state. Sir Thomas Roe visited this place (id., p. 123).

[2] *Shab-i-jum'a*, which is Friday eve according to Blochmann.

messages to him to say that when he was at Burhanpur he had daily begged this duty of me, as he considered it equivalent to the happiness of both worlds, and had said in meetings and assemblies that if he should be killed in this enterprise he would be a martyr, and if he prevailed, a ghāzī. I had given him whatever support and assistance of artillery he had asked for. After this he had written that without the movement of the royal standards to those regions the completion of the affair was not free of difficulty. By his counsel I had come to Ajmir, and this neighbourhood had been thus honoured and dignified. Now that he had himself prayed for the prince, and everything had been carried out according to his counsel, why did he withdraw his foot from the field of battle and enter the place of disagreement? To Bābā Khurram, from whom up till now I had never parted, and whom I sent in pure reliance on his (Khān A'ẓam's) knowledge of affairs, he should show loyalty and approved good-will, and never be neglectful day or night of his duty to my son. If, contrariwise, he should draw back his foot from what he had agreed to, he must know that there would be mischief. Ibrāhīm Ḥusain went, and impressed these words on his mind in the same detailed way. It was of no avail, as he would not go back from his folly and determination. When Bābā Khurram saw that his being in the affair was a cause of disturbance, he kept him under observation and represented that his being there was in no way fitting, and he was acting thus and spoiling matters simply on account of the connection he had with Khusrau.[1] I then ordered Mahābat Khān to go and bring him from Udaipur, and told Muḥammad Taqī, the diwan of buildings, to go to Mandesūr and bring his children and dependants to Ajmir.

On the 11th of the month news came that Dulīp, son

[1] Khusrau was married to his daughter.

of Rāy Singh, who was of a seditious and rebellious disposition, had been heavily defeated by his younger brother, Rāo Sūraj Singh, who had been sent against him, and that he was making disturbance in one of the districts of the Sarkar of Ḥiṣṣar. About this time Hāshim of Khost, the faujdar, and the jagirdars of that neighbourhood seized him, and sent him as a prisoner to Court. As he had misbehaved repeatedly, he was capitally punished, and this was a warning to many of the seditious. In reward for this service an increase of 500 personal and 200 horse was made to the mansab of Rāo Sūraj Singh. On the 14th of the month a representation came from my son Bābā Khurram that the elephant 'Ālam-gumān, of which the Rānā was very fond, together with seventeen other elephants, had fallen into the hands of the warriors of the victorious army, and that his master would also soon be captured.

The Ninth New Year's Feast after my auspicious Accession.

The commencement of the ninth year after my auspicious accession, corresponding with the Hijra year 1023 (1614).

Two watches and one ghari had passed on the night of Friday, the 9th Ṣafar (21st March, 1614), when the world-warming sun shed his rays on the constellation of Aries, which is his house of dignity and honour; it was the first morning of the month of Farwardīn. The assembly for the New Year's festival took place in the pleasant regions of Ajmir, and at the time of entry (of the sun into Aries), which was the propitious hour, I seated myself on the throne of good fortune. They had in the usual manner decorated the palace with rare cloth-stuffs and jewels and gem-decked things. At this auspicious moment the elephant 'Ālam-gumān,[1] which was fit to be entered in the private stud, with the seventeen other male and female elephants which my son Bābā Khurram had sent of the Rānā's elephants, were presented before me, and the hearts of the loyal rejoiced. On the 2nd day of the New Year, knowing it to be propitious for a ride, I mounted it and scattered about much money. On the 3rd I conferred on I'tiqād Khān a mansab of 3,000 personal and 1,000 horse, increasing thus that which he had already, which was of 2,000 personal and 500 horse, and I distinguished him with the title of Āṣaf Khān, with which title two of his family had been previously honoured. I also increased the mansab of Dayānat Khān by 500 personal and 200 horse. At the same time I promoted I'timādu-d-daulah to the mansab of 5,000 personal and 2,000 horse. At the request of Bābā Khurram I increased the mansab of Saif Khān Bārha by 500 personal and 200 horse, that of Dilāwar Khān by the same number, that of Kishan Singh by 500 horse, and that of Sarfarāz Khān by 500 personal and 300 horse. On Sunday, the 10th, the offering of Āṣaf Khān was produced before me, and on the 14th I'timādu-d-daulah produced his own offering. From these two offerings I took what pleased me and gave back the rest. Chīn Qilīj Khān, with his brothers, relations, and the army and retinue of his father, came from Kabul[2] and waited on me. Ibrāhīm Khān, who had a mansab of 700 personal and 300 horse, having been promoted to that of 1,500 personal and 600 horse, was appointed jointly with Khwāja Abū-l-ḥasan to the exalted dignity of paymaster of the household. On the 15th of this month Mahābat Khān, who had been appointed to bring Khān A'ẓam and his son 'Abdu-llah, came and waited

[1] The "Arrogant of the Earth" (Tod).

[2] Perhaps this means Peshawar, for apparently Qilīj was there when he died.

on me. On the 19th the assembly of honour was held. On that day the offering of Mahābat Khān was laid before me, and I sent a private elephant called Rūp Sundar for my son Parwīz. When that day had passed I ordered them to deliver Khān A'ẓam into the charge of Āṣaf Khān, that he might keep him in the fort of Gwalior. As my object in sending him to the fort was in case some disagreement and disturbance should occur in the matter of the Rānā in consequence of the attachment that he had to Khusrau, I ordered him not to be kept in the fort like a prisoner, but that they should provide everything necessary for his comfort and convenience in the way of eating and clothing. On the same day I promoted Chīn Qilīj Khān to a mansab of 2,500 personal and 700 horse. To the rank of Tāj Khān, who had been appointed to the charge of the province of Bhakar, I added 500 personal and horse. On the 18th Urdībihisht I forbade Khusrau to pay his respects. The reason was this, that through the affection and fatherly love (I bore him) and the prayers of his mother and sisters, I had ordered again that he should come every day to pay his respects (*kūrnish*). As his appearance showed no signs of openness and happiness, and he was always mournful and dejected in mind, I accordingly ordered that he should not come to pay his respects. In the time of my revered father, Muẓaffar Ḥusain Mīrzā and Rustam Mīrzā, sons of Sulṭān Ḥusain Mīrzā, nephews of Shāh Ṭahmāsp Ṣafawī, who had in their possession Qandahar and Zamīndāwar and that neighbourhood, sent petitions to the effect that in consequence of the nearness to Khurasan and the coming of 'Abdu-llah Khān Ūzbeg to that country, they could not leave the charge of looking after the country and come (to pay their respects), but that if he (Akbar) would send one of the servants of the palace they would hand over the country to him, and themselves come to pay their respects.

As they repeatedly made this request, he sent Shāh Beg Khān, who is now honoured with the title of Khān Daurān, to the governorship of Qandahar and Zamīn-dāwar and that neighbourhood, and wrote firmans full of favour to the Mīrzās summoning them to the Court. After their arrival favours appropriate to the case of each were bestowed on them, and he gave them a territory equal to two or three times the collections of Qandahar. In the end, the management expected from them was not achieved, and by degrees the territory deteriorated. Muẓaffar Ḥusain Mīrzā died during the lifetime of my revered father, and he sent Mīrzā Rustam with the Khankhanan to the Subah of the Deccan, where he had a small jagir. When the throne was honoured by my succession, I sent for him from the Deccan with the intention of showing him favour and sending him to one of the border territories. About the time he came Mīrzā Ghāzī Tarkhān, who held the governorship of Thatta and Qandahar and that neighbourhood, died. It occurred to me to send him to Thatta, so that he might show there his natural good qualities and administer that country in an approved manner. I promoted him to a mansab of 5,000 personal and horse, 200,000 rupees were given to him for expenses, and I despatched him to the Subah of Thatta. My belief was that he would do good service[1] on those borders. In opposition to my expectation he did no service, and committed so much oppression that many people complained of his wickedness. Such news of him was heard that it was considered necessary to recall him.

[1] According to the Ma'āṣir, iii, 486, in the biography of 'Īsā Khān, Rustam was sent to put down the Tarkhāns, and succeeded in doing so. See also ibid., p. 438, in the biography of Rustam, where it is said that Jahāngīr told him to send away the Arghuns. Perhaps the passage in Ma'āṣir, p. 438, which according to Blochmann, p. 314, means that Rustam ill-treated the Arghuns, rather means that he intrigued with them but oppressed the peasantry.

One of the servants of the Court was appointed to summon him, and I sent for him to Court. On the 26th Urdībihisht they brought him. As he had committed great oppression on the people of God, and inquiry into this was due according to the requirements of justice, I handed him over to Anīrā'ī Singh-dalan that he might enquire into the facts, and that if guilty he might receive prompt punishment and be a warning to others. In those days the news also came of the defeat of Aḥdād, the Afghan. The facts are that Mu'taqid Khān came to Pūlam[1] Guzar (ferry ?), in the district of Peshawar, with an army, and Khān Daurān with another force in Afghanistan and blocked the path of that rascal (lit. black-faced one). Meanwhile a letter came to Mu'taqid Khān from Pish Bulagh that Aḥdād had gone to Koṭ Tīrāh, which is 8 kos from Jalalabad, with a large number of horse and foot, and had killed a few of those who had chosen to be loyal and obey, and made prisoners of others, and was about to send them to Tīrāh, and intended to make a raid on Jalalabad and Pish Bulagh. Immediately on hearing this news Mu'taqid Khān started in great haste with the troops he had with him. When he arrived at Pish Bulagh he sent out spies to ascertain about the enemy. On the morning of Wednesday, the 6th, news reached him that Aḥdād was in the same place. Placing his trust on the favour of God, which is on the side of this suppliant at the throne of Allah, he divided the royal army into two, and went towards the enemy, who, with 4,000 or 5,000 experienced men, had seated themselves haughtily in complete carelessness,

[1] Though the text has Pūlam, the real word seems to be Īlam or Ailam. Ailam Guzar appears to be a pass in a range of hills. It may, however, be a ferry on the Kabul River. That river seems to be also known as the Shāh 'Ālam, and there is a ferry on it of that name. The text speaks of Koṭ Tīrāh as 8 kos from Jalalabad, but Tīrāh is much further away. The B.M. MSS. have *Kotal-i-Tīrāh*, 'the Tīrāh defile.'

and did not suspect that besides Khān Daurān's there was an army in the neighbourhood that could oppose itself to them. When news came that the royal forces were coming against that ill-fortuned man, and the signs of an army were becoming manifest, in a state of bewilderment he distributed his men into four bodies, and seating himself on an eminence a gunshot away, to get to which was a difficult matter, he sent his men to fight. The musketeers of the victorious army assailed the rebel with bullets, and sent a large number to hell. Mu'taqid Khān took the centre of his army to his advanced guard, and, not giving the enemy more than time to shoot off their arrows two or three times, swept them clean away, and pursuing them for 3 or 4 kos, killed nearly 1,500 of them, horse and foot. Those left of the sword took to flight, most of them wounded and with their arms thrown away. The victorious army remained for the night in the same place on the battlefield, and in the morning proceeded with 600 decapitated heads[1] towards Peshawar and made pillars of the heads there. Five hundred horses and innumerable cattle and property and many weapons fell into their hands. The prisoners of Tīrāh were released, and on this side no well-known men were killed. On the night of Thursday, the 1st of Khūrdād, I proceeded towards Pushkar to shoot tigers, and on Friday killed two of them with a gun. On the same day it was represented to me that Naqīb Khān had died. The aforesaid Khān was one of the Saifī Sayyids, and was originally from Qazwin. The tomb of his father, Mīr 'Abdu-l-Laṭīf, is at Ajmir. Two months before his death his wife,[2] between whom and her husband there was

[1] Compare Price's Jahāngīr, p. 94. It appears from that account that Mu'taqid *alias* Lashkar Khān was originally called Abū-l-ḥusain. According to the account there, the prisoners were brought to Jahāngīr with the decapitated heads of 17,000 (!) suspended from their necks !

[2] She was a daughter of Mīr Maḥmūd, Akbar's secretary (Blochmann, p. 449).

a great affection, and who for twelve days was ill with fever, drank the unpleasant draught of death. I ordered them to bury him by the side of his wife, whom they had placed in the Khwāja's venerated mausoleum. As Mu'taqid Khān had done approved service in the fight with Aḥdād, in reward he was exalted with the title of Lashkar Khān. Dayānat Khān, who had been sent to Udaipur in the service of Bābā Khurram and to convey certain orders, came on the 7th Khūrdād and gave good account of the rules and regulations made by Bābā Khurram. Fidā'ī Khān, who in the days of my princehood was my servant, and whom after my accession I had made bakhshi in this army, and who had obtained favour, gave up the deposit of his life on the 12th of the same month. Mīrzā Rustam, as he showed signs of repentance and regret for his misdeeds, and generosity demanded that his faults should be pardoned, was, in the end of the month, summoned to my presence, and I satisfied his mind, and having given him a dress of honour, ordered him to pay his respects to me. On the night of Sunday, the 11th of the month of Tīr, a female elephant in the private elephant stud gave birth to a young one in my presence. I had repeatedly ordered them to ascertain the period of their gestation; at last it became evident that for a female young one it was 18 months and for a male 19 months. In opposition to the birth of a human being, which is in most cases by a head delivery, young elephants are born with their feet first. When the young one was born, the mother scattered dust upon it with her foot, and began to be kind and to pet it. The young one for an instant remained fallen, and then rising, made towards its mother's breasts. On the 14th the assembly of Gulāb-pāshī (sprinkling of rose-water) took place; from former times this has been known as *āb-pāshī* (water-sprinkling), and has become established from amongst customs of former days. On the 5th Amurdād (middle July, 1614) came news of the death of Rāja Mān Singh.[1] The aforesaid Raja was one of the chief officers of my revered father. As I had sent many servants of the State to serve in the Deccan, I also appointed him. After his death in that service, I sent for Mīrzā Bhāo Singh, who was his legitimate heir. As from the time when I was prince he had done much service with me, although the chiefship and headship of their family, according to the Hindu custom, should go to Mahā Singh, son[2] of Jagat Singh, the Raja's eldest son, who had died in the latter's lifetime, I did not accept him, but I dignified Bhāo Singh with the title of Mīrzā Rāja, and raised him to the mansab of 4,000 personal and 3,000 horse. I also gave him Amber, the native place of his ancestors, and, soothing and consoling the mind of Mahā Singh, increased his former mansab by 500, and gave him as an *in'ām* the territory of Garha.[3] I also sent him a jewelled dagger belt, a horse, and dress of honour. On the 8th of this month of Amurdād I found a change in my health, and by degrees was seized with fever and headache. For fear that some injury might occur to the country and the servants of God, I kept this secret from most of those familiar with and near to me, and did not inform the physicians and hakims. A few days passed in this manner, and I only imparted this to Nūr-Jahān Begam, than whom I did not think anyone was fonder of me; I abstained from eating heavy foods, and, contenting myself with a little light food, went every day, according to my rule, to the public Dīwān-khāna (hall of audience), and entered the Jharokha and *ghusal-khāna* (parlour)

[1] Mān Singh died in the Deccan in 1614, and apparently in the month of June.

[2] Text *pidar* by mistake for *pisar*.

[3] Garha, described as Bāndhū in Ma'āṣir, ii, 175. It is Garha-Katanga, i.e. Jabalpur.

in my usual manner, until signs of weakness showed themselves in my skin.[1] Some of the nobles[2] became aware of this, and informed one or two of my physicians who were trustworthy, such as Ḥakīm Masīḥu-z-zamān, Ḥakīm Abū-l-qāsim, and Ḥakīm 'Abdu-sh-Shakūr. As the fever did not change, and for three nights I took my usual wine, it brought on greater weakness. In the time of disquietude, and when weakness prevailed over me, I went to the mausoleum of the revered Khwāja, and in that blessed abode prayed to God Almighty for recovery, and agreed to give alms and charity. God Almighty, in His pure grace and mercy, bestowed on me the robe of honour of health, and by degrees I recovered. The headache, which had been very severe, subsided under the remedies of Ḥakīm 'Abdu-sh-Shakūr, and in the space of twenty-two days my state returned to what it was before. The servants of the palace, and indeed the whole of the people, made offerings for this great bounty. I accepted the alms of no one, and ordered that everyone in his own house should distribute what he wished among the poor. On the 10th Shahrīwar news came that Tāj Khān, the Afghan, governor of Thatta,[3] had died; he was one of the old nobles of the State.

During my illness it had occurred to me that when I completely recovered, inasmuch as I was inwardly an ear-bored slave of the Khwāja (Mu'īnu-d-dīn) and was indebted to him for my existence, I should openly make holes in my ears and be enrolled among his ear-marked slaves. On Thursday, 12th Shahrīwar,[4] corresponding to the month of Rajab, I made holes in my ears and drew into each a shining pearl. When the servants of the palace and my loyal friends saw this, both those who

[1] Perhaps the meaning is that there was an eruption.

[2] *Buzurgān*, which perhaps here means elder ladies of the harem.

[3] This is Tāsh Beg (Blochmann, p. 457). The text wrongly has Patna.

[4] Jahāngīr was born in this month, which then corresponded to Rajab.

were in the presence and some who were in the distant borders diligently and eagerly made holes in their ears, and adorned the beauty of sincerity with pearls and rubies which were in the private treasury, and were bestowed on them, until by degrees the infection caught the Ahadis and others. At the end of the day of Thursday, the 22nd of the said month, corresponding with the 10th Sha'bān, the meeting for my solar weighing was arranged in my private audience hall, and the usual observances were carried out. On the same day Mīrzā Rāja Bhāo Singh, gratified and prosperous, returned to his native country with the promise that he would not delay (there) more than two or three months. On the 27th of the month of Mihr news came that Farīdūn Khān Barlās had died at Udaipur. In the clan of Barlās no leader remained but he. As his tribe had many claims on this State and endless connection with it, I patronised his son Mihr 'Alī, and raised him to the mansab of 1,000 personal and horse. On account of the approved services of Khān Daurān, I increased by 1,000 his mansab, which became 6,000 personal and 5,000 horse, original and increase. On the 6th Ābān the *qarāwuls* (*shikārīs*) reported that three tigers had been met at a distance of 6 kos. Starting after midday, I killed all three of them with a gun. On the 8th of the month the festival of the Dewālī came on. I ordered the attendants of the palace to have games with each other for two or three nights in my presence; winnings and losings took place. On the 8th of this month they brought to Ajmir the body of Sikandar Mu'īn Qarāwul (Shikārī), who was one of my old attendants and had done much service for me when I was prince, from Udaipur, which was the place where my son Sulṭān Khurram was staying. I ordered the qarawuls and his fellow-tribesmen to take his body and bury it on the bank of Rānā Shankar's tank. He was a good servant to me. On the 12th Āẕar two daughters whom

Islām Khān in his lifetime had taken from the Zamindar of Kūch (Behar), whose country is on the boundary of the eastern provinces, together with his son and 94 elephants, were brought before me. Some of the elephants were placed in my private stud. On the same day, Hūshang, Islām Khān's son, came from Bengal, and had the good fortune to kiss the threshold, and presented as offerings two elephants, 100 muhrs, and 100 rupees. On one particular night in Day I dreamt that the late king (Akbar) said to me: "Bābā, forgive for my sake the fault of 'Azīz Khān, who is the Khān A'ẓam." After this dream, I decided to summon him from the fort (of Gwalior).

There is a ravine in the neighbourhood of Ajmir that is very beautiful. At the end of this ravine a spring appears which is collected in a long and broad tank, and is the best water in Ajmir. This valley and spring are well known as Ḥāfiẓ Jamāl. When I crossed over to this place I ordered a suitable building to be made there, as the place was good and fit for developing. In the course of a year a house and grounds were made there, the like of which those[1] who travel round the world cannot point out. They made a basin 40 gaz by 40, and made the water of the spring rise up in the basin by a fountain. The fountain leaps up 10 or 12 gaz. Buildings are laid on the edge of this basin, and in the same way above, where the tank and fountain are, they have made agreeable places and enchanting halls and resting-rooms pleasant to the senses. These have been constructed and finished off in a masterly style by skilled painters and clever artists. As I desired that it should be called by a name

[1] Is this an allusion to some complimentary remark of Sir Thomas Roe? Sir Thomas did not come to Ajmir till December, 1615, but Jahāngīr is here apparently writing of what happened a year after his visit to Ḥāfiẓ Jamāl. The chronogram was 1024 (1615).

connected with my august name, I gave it the name of Chashma-i-Nūr, or 'the fountain of light.' In short, the one fault it has is this, that it ought to have been in a large city, or at a place by which men frequently pass. From the day on which it was completed I have often passed Thursdays and Fridays there. I ordered that they should think out a chronogram for its completion. Sa'īdā Gīlānī, the head of the goldsmiths, discovered it in this clever hemistich:—

"The palace[1] of Shāh Nūru-d-dīn Jahāngīr" (1024).

I ordered them to put a stone with this carved upon it on the top of the portico of the building.

In the beginning of the month of Day, merchants came from Persia and brought pomegranates of Yazd and melons from Kārīz, which are the best of Khurasan melons, so many that all the servants of the Court and the Amirs of the frontiers obtained a portion of them and were very grateful to the True Giver (God) for them. I had never had such melons and pomegranates. It seemed as if I had never had a pomegranate or a melon before. Every year I had had melons from Badakhshan and pomegranates from Kabul, but they bore no comparison with the Yazd pomegranates and the Kārīz melons. As my revered father (may God's light be his witness!) had a great liking for fruit, I was very grieved that such fruits had not come to Hindustan from Persia in his victorious time, that he might have enjoyed and profited by them. I have the same regret for the *Jahāngīrī 'iṭr* (so-called otto of roses), that his nostrils were not gratified with such essences. This 'itr is a discovery which was made during my reign through the efforts of the mother of Nūr-Jahān Begam. When she was making rose-water

[1] Maḥall-i-Shāh Nūru-d-dīn Jahāngīr, 1024 (1615). See Proceedings A.S.B. for August, 1873, pp. 159–60.

a scum formed on the surface of the dishes into which the hot rose-water was poured from the jugs. She collected this scum little by little; when much rose-water was obtained a sensible portion of the scum was collected. It is of such strength in perfume that if one drop be rubbed on the palm of the hand it scents a whole assembly, and it appears as if many red rosebuds had bloomed at once. There is no other scent of equal excellence to it. It restores hearts that have gone and brings back withered souls. In reward for that invention I presented a string of pearls to the inventress. Salīma[1] Sulṭān Begam (may the lights of God be on her tomb) was present, and she gave this oil the name of '‘itr-i-Jahangiri.'

Great difference appeared in the climates of India. In this month of Day, in Lahore, which is between Persia and Hindustan, the mulberry-tree bore fruit of as much sweetness and fine flavour as in its ordinary season. For some days people were delighted by eating it. The news-writers of that place wrote this. In the same days Ba<u>kh</u>tar <u>Kh</u>ān Kalāwant, who was closely connected with ‘Ādil <u>Kh</u>ān, inasmuch as he (‘Ādil) married his own brother's daughter to him, and made him his preceptor in singing and *durpat*[2] *guftan*, appeared in the habit of a dervish. Summoning him and enquiring into his circumstances, I endeavoured to honour him. In the first assembly I gave him 10,000 rupees in cash and 50 pieces of cloth of all sorts and a string of pearls, and having made him a guest of Āṣaf <u>Kh</u>ān, ordered him to enquire into his circumstances. It did not appear whether he had come without ‘Ādil <u>Kh</u>ān's permission, or the latter

[1] Salīma died in the 7th year, so that the discovery must have occurred some time before this mention of it.

[2] Hindustani, *dhurpad*, "petit poëme ordinairement composé de cinq hémistiches sur une même rime." "It was invented by Rāja Mān of Gwalior" (Garçin de Tassy, Hist. Litt. Hindouie, i, 12).

had sent him in this guise in order that he might find out the designs of this Court and bring him news about them. Considering his relationship to 'Ādil Khān, it is most probable that he has not come without 'Ādil Khān's knowledge. A report by Mīr Jamālu-d-dīn Ḥusain, who at this time was (our) ambassador at Bijapur, corroborates this idea, for he writes that 'Ādil Khān has, on account of the kindness which has been shown by H.M. (Jahāngīr) to Bakhtar Khān, been very gracious to him (Jamālu-d-dīn). Every day he has shown him more and more favour, keeps him beside him at nights, and recites to him durpats, which he ('Ādil Khān) has composed, and which he calls *nauras*[1] (Juvenilia). "The remainder of the facts will be written on the day when I get my dismissal."

In these days they brought a bird from the country of Zīrbād (Sumatra, etc., Blochmann, p. 616) which was coloured like a parrot, but had a smaller body. One of its peculiarities is that it lays hold with its feet of the branch or perch on which they may have placed it and then makes a somersault, and remains in this position all night and whispers to itself. When day comes it seats itself on the top of the branch. Though they say that animals also have worship, yet it is most likely that this practice is instinctive. It never drinks water, and water acts like poison upon it, though other birds subsist on water.

In the month[2] of Bahman there came pieces of good

[1] See Rieu, 741*b*, who calls the *nauras* a treatise on music composed by Ibrāhīm 'Ādil Shāh II. This 'Ādil Shāh was Firishta's patron, and reigned till 1626. Jamālu-d-dīn is the dictionary-maker and friend of Sir T. Roe. The sentence about reporting the remainder of the facts seems to be an extract from his report. Muḥammad Wāriṣ, in his continuation of the Pādshāh-nāma, B.M. MS. Add. 6556, p. 438, mentions, with reprobation, that 'Ādil Shāh had given his niece in marriage to a singer.

[2] Translated Elliot, vi, 339.

news one after the other. The first was that the Rānā Amar Singh had elected for obedience and service to the Court. The circumstances of this affair are these. My son of lofty fortune, Sulṭān Khurram, by dint of placing a great many posts, especially in some places where most people said it was impossible to place them on account of the badness of the air and water and the wild nature of the localities, and by dint of moving the royal forces one after another in pursuit, without regard to the heat or excessive rain, and making prisoners of the families of the inhabitants of that region, brought matters with the Rānā to such a pass that it became clear to him that if this should happen to him again he must either fly the country or be made prisoner. Being without remedy, he chose obedience and loyalty, and sent to my fortunate son his maternal uncle, Subh Karan, with Haridās Jhālā, who was one of the men in his confidence, and petitioned that if that fortunate son would ask forgiveness for his offences and tranquillise his mind, and obtain for him the auspicious sign-manual,[1] he would himself come and wait on my son, and would send his son and successor Karan to Court, or he, after the manner of other Rajas, would be enrolled amongst the servants of the Court and do service. He also begged that he himself might be excused from coming to Court on account of his old age. Accordingly my son sent them in company with his own Diwan Mullā Shukru-llah, whom after the conclusion of this business I dignified with the title of Afẓal Khān, and Sundar Dās, his major-domo, who, after this matter was settled, was honoured with the title of Rāy Rāyān, to the exalted Court, and represented the circumstances. My lofty

[1] Lit. procure for him the sign of the blessed *panja* (five fingers). The sign-manual was that of Jahāngīr. See below. See also Tod's Rajasthan, reprint, i, 411, for a representation of the *panja*; also p. 383, note id.

mind was always desirous, as far as possible, not to destroy the old families. The real point was that as Rānā Amar Singh and his fathers, proud in the strength of their hilly country and their abodes, had never seen or obeyed any of the kings of Hindustan, this should be brought about in my reign. At the request of my son I forgave the Rānā's offences, and gave a gracious farman that should satisfy him, and impressed on it the mark of my auspicious palm.[1] I also wrote a farman of kindness to my son that if he could arrange to settle the matter I should be much pleased. My son also sent them[2] with Mullā Shukru-llah and Sundar Dās to the Rānā to console him and make him hopeful of the royal favour. They gave him the gracious farman with the sign-manual of the auspicious hand, and it was settled that on Sunday, the 26th of the month of Bahman, he and his sons should come and pay their respects to my son. The second piece of good news was the death of Bahādur, who was descended from the rulers of Gujarat, and was the leaven of disturbance and mischief (there). Almighty God had annihilated him in His mercy: he died of a natural illness. The third piece of news was the defeat of the Warzā (Portuguese Viceroy), who had done his best to take the castle and port of Surat. In the roadstead[3] of the port of Surat a fight took place between the English, who had taken shelter there, and the Viceroy. Most of his ships were burnt by the English fire. Being helpless he had not

[1] *Panja mubārak* (Tod's Rajasthan, i, 383 and 411).

[2] Perhaps the uncle and Haridās, or the *īnhā*, 'them,' may mean the farman. See Elliot, vi, 340, which has 'my letters.' Tod has translated this part of the Tūzuk, i, 382.

[3] The text has *khaurmiyān*, and I.O. 181 has *khaur-i-bandar*. *Khaur* means a bay or gulf in Arabic. The battle is that between Captain Downton and the Portuguese, which took place in January, 1615, and is described in Orme's Hist., Fragments, p. 351, etc. See also Danvers' "Portuguese in India," ii, 170. The engagement was in the Swally channel.

the power to fight any more, and took to flight. He sent some one to Muqarrab Khān, who was the governor of the ports of Gujarat, and knocked at the door of peace, and said that he had come to make peace and not to make war. It was the English who had stirred up the war. Another piece of news was that some of the Rajputs, who had determined to attack and kill 'Ambar (misprinted Ghīr), had made an ambush, and finding a good opportunity had gained access to him; when a slight wound had been inflicted on him by one of them. The men who were round 'Ambar (again misprinted Ghīr) had killed the Rajputs and taken 'Ambar to his quarters. A very little[1] more would have made an end of him. In the end of this month, when I was employed in hunting in the environs of Ajmir, Muḥammad Beg,[2] an attendant on my fortunate son Sulṭān Khurram, came and brought a report from that son, and stated that the Rānā had come with his sons and paid his respects to the prince; "the details would be made known by the report." I immediately turned the face of supplication to the Divine Court, and prostrated myself in thanksgiving. I presented a horse, an elephant, and a jewelled dagger to the aforesaid Muḥammad Beg, and honoured him with the title of Ẕū-l-faqār Khān.[2] From the report it appeared that on Sunday, the 26th Bahman, the Rānā paid his respects to my fortunate son with the politeness and ritual that servants pay their respects, and produced as offerings a famous large ruby that was in his house, with some decorated articles and seven elephants, some of them fit for the private stud, and which had not fallen into

[1] Elliot, vi, 340. As Mr. Rogers remarks, the sentence is not easily intelligible. Probably the translation should be, "No one remained (all the Rajputs having been killed) who could finish off Malik 'Ambar."

[2] Probably the father or grandfather of the Muḥammad Beg Ẕū-l-faqār who was a servant of Aurangzīb (Ma'āṣiru-l-umarā, ii, 89).

our hands and were the only ones left him, and nine horses.

My son also behaved to him with perfect kindness. When the Rānā clasped his feet and asked forgiveness for his faults, he took his head and placed it on his breast, and consoled him in such a manner as to comfort him. He presented him with a superb dress of honour, a jewelled sword, a horse with a jewelled saddle, and a private elephant with silver housings, and, as there were not more than 100 men with him who were worthy of complete robes of honour (*sar u pā*), he gave 100 sarupa and 50 horses and 12 jewelled *khapwa* (daggers). As it is the custom of the Zamindars that the son who is the heir-apparent should not go with his father to pay his respects to a king or prince, the Rānā observed this custom, and did not bring with him Karan, the son who had received the *ṭīkā*. As the hour (fixed by astrology) of the departure of that son of lofty fortune from that place was the end of that same day, he gave him leave, so that, having himself gone, he might send Karan to pay his respects. After he had gone, Karan also came and did so. To him also he gave a superb dress of honour, a jewelled sword and dagger, a horse with a gold saddle, and a special elephant, and on the same day, taking Karan in attendance, he proceeded towards the illustrious Court. On the 3rd Isfandārmuz my return to Ajmir from hunting took place. From the 17th Bahman up to that date, during which I was hunting, one tigress with three cubs and thirteen nilgaw had been killed. The fortunate prince encamped on Saturday, the 10th of the same month, at the village of Devrānī, which is near the city of Ajmir, and an order was given that all the Amirs should go to meet him, and that each should present an offering according to his standing and condition, and on the next day, Sunday, the 11th, he should have the good fortune to wait upon me. The next day the prince, with great magnificence, with all the victorious forces that had been appointed to accompany him on that service, entered the public palace. The hour for him to wait on me was when two watches and two gharis of the day had passed, and he had the good fortune to pay his respects, and performed his prostrations and salutations. He presented 1,000 ashrafis and 1,000 rupees by way of offering, 1,000 muhrs and 1,000 rupees by way of charity. I called that son forward and embraced him, and having kissed his head and face, favoured him with special kindnesses and greetings. When he had finished the dues of service and had presented his offerings and charities, he petitioned that Karan might be exalted with the good fortune of prostrating himself and paying his respects. I ordered them to bring him, and the Bakhshis with the usual ceremonies of respect produced him. After prostration and salutation were completed, at the request of my son Khurram, I ordered them to place him in front on the right hand of the circle. After this I ordered Khurram to go and wait on his mothers, and gave him a special dress of honour, consisting of a jewelled *chārqab* (sleeveless vest), a coat of gold brocade, and a rosary of pearls. After he had made his salutation, there were presented to him a special dress of honour, a special horse with a jewelled saddle, and a special elephant. I also honoured Karan with a superb robe of honour and a jewelled sword, and the Amirs and mansabdars had the honour of prostrating themselves and paying their respects, and presented their offerings. Each of these, according to his service and rank, was honoured with favours. As it was necessary to win the heart of Karan, who was of a wild nature and had never seen assemblies and had lived among the hills, I every day showed him some fresh favour, so that on the second day of his attendance a jewelled dagger, and on the next day a special Iraqi horse with jewelled saddle, were given to him. On the day when he went to the darbar in the female apartments, there were given to him on the part of Nūr-Jahān Begam a rich dress of honour, a jewelled sword, a horse and saddle, and an elephant. After this I presented him with a rosary of pearls of great value. On the next day a special elephant with trappings (*talāyir*) were given. As it was in my mind to give him something of every kind, I presented him with three hawks and three falcons, a special sword, a coat of mail, a special cuirass, and two rings, one with a ruby and one with an emerald. At the end of the month I ordered that all sorts of cloth stuffs, with carpets and cushions (named *takiya*) and all kinds of perfumes, with vessels of gold, two Gujrati carts, and cloths, should be placed in a hundred trays. The Ahadis carried them in their arms and on their shoulders to the public audience hall, where they were bestowed on him.

Ṣābit Khān[1] at the paradise-resembling assemblies was always addressing unbecoming speeches and making palpable allusions to I'timādu-d-daulah and his son Āṣaf Khān. Once or twice, showing my dislike of this, I had forbidden him to do so, but this was not enough for him. As I held very dear I'timādu-d-daulah's good-will towards me, and was very closely connected with his family, this matter became very irksome to me. As one night without reason and without motive he began to speak unpleasant words to him, and said them to such an extent that signs of vexation and annoyance became evident in I'timādu-d-daulah's face, I sent him next morning, in the custody of a servant of the Court, to Āṣaf Khān to say that as on the previous evening he had spoken unpleasant words to his father, I handed him over to him, and he might shut him up either there or in the fort of Gwalior, as he pleased; until he

[1] R.A.S. MS. has Dayānat Khān, and so has I.O. MS. 181.

made amends to his father I would never forgive his fault. According to the order Āṣaf Khān sent him to Gwalior fort. In the same month Jahāngīr Qulī Khān was promoted to an increased manṣab, and was given that of 2,500 personal and 2,000 horse. Aḥmad Beg Khān, who is one of the old retainers of the State, committed some faults on the journey to the Subah of Kabul, and Qilīj Khān, who was the commander of the army, had repeatedly complained of his making himself disagreeable. Necessarily I summoned him to Court, and in order to punish him handed him over to Mahābat Khān to confine him in the fort of Ranṭambhor. Qāsim Khān, governor of Bengal, had sent two rubies as an offering, and they were laid before me. As I had made a rule that they should bring before me after two watches of the night had passed the dervishes and necessitous people who had collected in the illustrious palace, this year also after the same manner I bestowed on the dervishes with my own hand and in my own presence 55,000 rupees and 190,000 bighas of land, with fourteen entire villages, and twenty-six ploughs,[1] and 11,000 *kharwār*[2] (ass-loads) of rice; I presented as well 732 pearls, of the value of 36,000 rupees, to the servants who by way of loyalty had bored their ears.

At the end of the aforesaid month news came that when four and a half gharis of night had passed on Sunday, the 11th of the month, in the city of Burhanpur, God Almighty had bestowed on Sulṭān Parwīz a son by the daughter of Prince Murād. I gave him the name of Sulṭān Dūr-andīsh[3] (long-thoughted).

[1] *Qulba*. It does not appear that this is a land-measure.

[2] *Kharwār*. It is a weight. See Jarrett, ii, 394, where a kharwar is said to be equal to ten Hindustani maunds.

[3] Probably this was the son who died in the 14th year (Tūzuk, p. 282).

THE TENTH NEW YEAR'S FESTIVAL AFTER MY AUSPICIOUS ACCESSION.

When 55 seconds had passed on Saturday, 1st Farwardīn, in my 10th year, corresponding with the 8th[1] of the month of Ṣafar (March, 1615), 1024 Hijra, the sun from the constellation of Pisces entered the house of honour of Aries. When three gharis had passed on the night of Sunday I seated myself on the throne of State. The New Year's feast and ceremonials were prepared in the usual manner. The illustrious princes, the great Khans, the chief officers and Ministers of State made their salutations of congratulation. On the 1st of the month the mansab of I'timādu-d-daulah was increased from 5,000 personal and 2,000 horse by 1,000 personal and horse. Special horses were given to the Kunwar Karan, Jahāngīr Qulī Khān, and Rāja Bīr Singh Deo. On the 2nd the offering of Āṣaf Khān was laid before me; it was an approved offering of jewels and jewelled ornaments and things of gold, of cloth stuffs of all kinds and descriptions, and was looked over in detail. That which I approved was worth 85,000 rupees. On this day a jewelled sword with a belt and band (?) (*band u bār*) was given to Karan, and an elephant to Jahāngīr Qulī Khān. As I had made up my mind to proceed to the Deccan, I gave an order to 'Abdu-l-Karīm Ma'mūrī, to go to Mandu and prepare a new building for my private residence, and repair the buildings of the old kings. On the 3rd day the offerings of Rāja Bīr Singh Deo were laid before me, and one ruby, some pearls, and one elephant had the honour of being accepted. On the 4th day the mansab of Muṣṭafā Khān was increased by 500 personal and 200 horse to 2,000 personal

[1] Should be 18th. See Elliot, vi, 341. I.O. 181 has 20th, and this is probably correct, *bīstam* and *hashtam* being often mistaken for one another by the copyists. B.M. MS. Add. 26215 has *dūshamba*, Monday, instead of *shamba*, Saturday.

and 250 horse. On the 5th I gave a standard and drums to I'timādu-d-daulah, and an order was given him to beat his drums. The mansab of Āṣaf Khān was increased by 1,000 personal and horse to 4,000 personal and 2,000 horse, and having increased the mansab of Rāja Bīr Singh Deo by 700 horse, I dismissed him to his own country, directing that he should present himself at Court at stated periods. On the same day the offering of Ibrāhīm Khān was laid before me. Some of all the kinds of things pleased me. Kishan Chand, of the sons of the Rajas of Nagarkot, was honoured with the title of Raja. On Thursday, the 6th, the offerings of I'timādu-d-daulah were laid before me at Chashma-i-Nūr; a large meeting had been arranged, and by way of favour the whole of his offerings were inspected. Of the jewels and jewelled things and choice cloth stuffs the value of 100,000 rupees was accepted, and the remainder given back. On the 7th day I increased by 1,000 personal the mansab of Kishan Singh, which had been 2,000 personal and 1,500 horse. On this day a tiger was killed in the neighbourhood of Chashma-i-Nūr. On the 8th I gave Karan the mansab of 5,000 personal and horse, and gave him a small rosary of pearls and emeralds with a ruby in the centre, which in the language of the Hindus is called *smaran* (Sanskrit for 'remembrance'). I increased the mansab of Ibrāhīm Khān by 1,000 personal and 400 horse, so as to make it 2,000 personal and 1,000 horse, original and increase. The mansab of Ḥājī Bī Ūzbeg was increased by 300 horse, and that of Rāja Shyām Singh by 500 personal, so as to make it 2,500 personal and 1,400 horse. On Sunday, the 9th, there was an eclipse of the sun, when twelve gharis of the day had passed. It began from the west, and four out of five parts of the sun were eclipsed in the knot of the dragon. From the commencement of the seizure until it became light eight gharis elapsed.

Alms of all kinds, and things in the shape of metals, animals, and vegetables, were given to fakirs and the poor and people in need. On this day the offering of Rāja Sūraj Singh was laid before me; what was taken was of the value of 43,000 rupees. The offering of Bahādur Khān, the governor of Qandahar, was also laid before me on this day; its total value came to 14,000 rupees. Two watches of the night had passed on the night of Monday, the 29th Ṣafar (30th March, 1615), in the ascension of Sagittarius, when a boy was born to Bābā Khurram by the daughter of Āṣaf Khān; I gave him the name of Dārā Shukūh. I hope that his coming will be propitious to this State conjoined with eternity, and to his fortunate father. The mansab of Sayyid 'Alī Bārha was increased by 500 personal and 300 horse, so as to bring it to 1,500 personal and 1,000 horse. On the 10th the offering of I'tibār Khān was laid before me, and what was of the value of 40,000 rupees was accepted. On this day the mansab of Khusrau Bī Ūzbeg was raised by 300 horse, and that of Manglī Khān by 500 personal and 200 horse. On the 11th the offering of Murtaẓā Khān was laid before me. Of it seven rubies, one rosary of pearls, and 270 other pearls were accepted, and their value was 145,000 rupees. On the 12th the offerings of Mīrzā Rāja Bhāo Singh and Rāwat Shankar were laid before me. On the 13th, out of the offering of Khwāja Abū-l-ḥasan, one *quṭbī* (Egyptian ?) ruby, one diamond, one string of pearls, five rings, four pearls, and some cloths, altogether the value of 32,000 rupees, were accepted. On the 14th the mansab of Khwāja Abū-l-ḥasan, which was 3,000 personal and 700 horse, was increased by 1,000 personal and 500 horse, and that of Wafādār Khān, of 750 personal and 200 horse, by 2,000 personal and 1,200 horse. On the same day Muṣṭafā Beg, the ambassador of the ruler of Iran, had the good fortune to wait upon me. After completing the matter of Gurjistan (Georgia), my exalted brother sent him with a letter consisting of expressions of friendship and assurances of sincerity, with several horses, camels, and some stuffs from Aleppo, which had come for that fortunate brother from the direction of Rūm. Nine large European hunting dogs, for which a request had gone, were also sent by him.

Murtaẓā Khān, on this day, obtained leave to go for the capture of the fort of Kāngra, the equal of which for strength they cannot point to in the hill country of the Panjab or even all the habitable world. From the time when the sound of Islam reached the country of Hindustan up to this auspicious time when the throne of rule has been adorned by this suppliant at the throne of Allah, none of the rulers or kings has obtained possession of it. Once in the time of my revered father, the army of the Panjab was sent against this fort, and besieged it for a long time. At length they came to the conclusion that the fort was not to be taken, and the army was sent off to some more necessary business. When he was dismissed, I gave Murtaẓā Khān a private elephant with trappings. Rāja Sūraj Mal, son of Rāja Bāso, as his country was near that fort, was also appointed, and his previous mansab was increased by 500 personal and horse. Rāja Sūraj Singh also came from his place and jagir and waited on me, and presented an offering of 100 ashrafis. On the 17th the offering of Mīrzā Rustam was laid before me. Two jewelled daggers, one rosary of pearls, some pieces of cloth, an elephant, and four Iraq horses were accepted, and the rest returned; their value was 15,000 rupees. On the same date the offering of I'tiqād Khān, of the value of 18,000 rupees, was laid before me. On the 18th the offering of Jahāngīr Qulī Khān was inspected. Of jewels and cloth stuffs the value of 15,000 rupees was accepted. The mansab of I'tiqād Khān, which was 700 personal and 200 horse, I increased by 800 personal and 300 horse, so that with original and increase it came to 1,500 personal and 500 horse. Khusrau Bī Ūzbeg, who was one of the distinguished soldiers, died of the disease of dysentery. On the 8th day, which was Thursday, after two watches and four and a half gharis had passed, the *sharaf* (highest point of the sun's ascension) began. On this auspicious day I ascended the throne in happiness and prosperity, and the people saluted and congratulated me. When one watch of the day remained I went to the Chashma-i-Nūr. According to agreement the offering of Mahābat Khān was laid before me at that place. He had arranged beautiful jewels and jewellery, with cloth stuff and articles of all kinds that were pleasing to me. Among these, a jewelled khapwa (dagger), which at his request the royal artificers had made, and the like of which in value there did not exist in my private treasury, was worth 100,000 rupees. In addition to this, jewels and other things of the value of 138,000 rupees were taken. Indeed, it was a splendid offering. To Muṣṭafā Beg, the ambassador of the ruler of Iran, I gave 20,000 *darab*, or 10,000 rupees. On the 21st I sent robes of honour by the hand of 'Abdu-l-Ghafūr to fifteen of the Amirs of the Deccan. Rāja Bikramājīt obtained leave to go to his jagir, and a special shawl (*parm narm*[1]) was given to him. On the same day I gave a jewelled waist-dagger to Muṣṭafā Beg, the ambassador. I increased the mansab of Hūshang, the son of Islām Khān, which was 1,000 personal and 500 horse, by 500 personal and 200 horse. On the 23rd, Ibrāhīm Khān was promoted to the Subah of Behar. Ẓafar Khān was ordered to present himself at Court. To the mansab of Ibrāhīm Khan, which was 2,000 personal and 1,000 horse, I added 500 personal and 1,000 horse. Saif Khān on the same day was dismissed to his jagir, as well as

[1] Akbar used the word *parm narm*, 'very soft,' as a substitute for 'shawl' (Blochmann, p. 90).

Ḥājī Bī Ūzbeg, who was honoured with the title of Ūzbeg K͟hān. Bahāduru-l-mulk, who belonged to the army of the Deccan, and held the mansab of 2,500 personal and 2,100 horse, received an increase of 500 personal and 200 horse. An increase of 200 was made in the mansab of K͟hwāja Taqī, which was 800 personal and 180 horse. On the 25th an increase of 200 horse was made in the rank of Salāmu-llah, the Arab, so that it became 1,500 personal and 1,000 horse. I presented Mahābat K͟hān with the black piebald horse out of my special horses which the ruler of Iran had sent me. At the end of the day of Thursday I went to the house of Bābā K͟hurram and remained there till a watch of the night had passed. His second offering was laid before me on that day. On the first day he paid his respects he laid before me a celebrated ruby of the Rānā, which, on the day of his paying his respects, he had made an offering of to my son, and which the jewellers valued at 60,000 rupees. It was not worthy of the praise they had given it. The weight of this ruby was eight *tānk*,[1] and it was formerly in the possession of Rāy Maldeo, who was the chief of the tribe of the Rāṭhors and one of the chief rulers (or Rays) of Hindustan. From him it was transferred to his son Chandar Sen, who, in the days of his wretchedness and hopelessness, sold it to Rānā Uday Singh. From him it went to Rānā Partāp, and afterwards to this Rānā Amar Singh. As they had no more valuable gift in their family, he presented it on the day that he paid his respects to my fortunate son Bābā K͟hurram, together with the whole of his stud of elephants, which, according to the Indian idiom, they call *gheta chār*.[2]

[1] According to Gladwin, 96 tanks = one sir. Four mashas make a tank, and a masha is about 18 grains troy.

[2] Text كهيته چار, *kheta chār*. But the two B.M. MSS. which I have consulted have no *yā*, and have *khatta* or *ghatta chār*. I think that the word must be **घटा**, *ghaṭā*, which in Sanskrit means a troop.

I ordered them to engrave on the ruby that at the time of paying his respects Rānā Amar Singh had presented it as an offering to Sulṭān Khurram. On that day certain other things from among the offerings of Bābā Khurram were accepted. Among them was a little crystal box of Frank work, made with great taste, with some emeralds, three rings, four Iraq horses, and various other things, the value of which was 80,000 rupees. On the day on which I went to his house he had prepared a great offering, in fact there were laid before me things and rarities worth about four or five lakhs of rupees. Of these the equivalent of 100,000 rupees was taken away and the balance given to him.

On the 28th the mansab of Khwāja Jahān, which was 3,000 personal and 1,800 horse, was increased by 500 personal and 400 horse. In the end of the month I presented Ibrāhīm Khān with a horse, a robe of honour, a jewelled dagger, a standard and drums, and dismissed him to the province of Behar. The office of *'arẓ-mukarrir* (reviser of petitions), that belonged to Khwājagī Ḥājī Muḥammad, as he had died, I gave to Mukhliṣ Khān, who was in my confidence. Three hundred horse were increased in the mansab of Dilāwar Khān, who now had 1,000 personal and horse. As the hour of the leave-taking of Kunwar Karan was at hand, I was desirous of showing him my skill in shooting with a gun. Just at this time the *qarāwulān* (shikaris) brought in news of a tigress. Though it is an established custom of mine only to hunt male tigers, yet, in consideration that no other tiger might be obtained before his departure, I went for the tigress. I took with me Karan, and said to him that I would hit it wherever he wished me to do so. After this arrangement I went to the place where they had

of elephants assembled for war. I am not sure what the word *chār* means, but perhaps it is only an affix. According to Abū-l-faẓl a herd of (wild) elephants is called *sahn* (Blochmann, p. 122).

marked down the tiger. By chance there was a wind and disturbance in the air, and the female elephant on which I was mounted was terrified of the tigress and would not stand still. Notwithstanding these two great obstacles to shooting, I shot straight towards her eye. God Almighty did not allow me to be ashamed before that prince, and, as I had agreed, I shot her in the eye. On the same day Karan petitioned me for a special gun, and I gave him a special Turkish one.

As on the day for his departure I had not given Ibrāhīm Khān an elephant, I now gave him a special elephant, and I also sent an elephant to Bahāduru-l-mulk and one to Wafādār Khān. On the 8th Urdībihisht the assemblage for my lunar weighing was held, and I weighed myself against silver and other things, distributing them amongst the deserving and needy. Nawāzish Khān took leave to go to his jagir, which was in Malwa. On the same day I gave an elephant to Khwāja Abū-l-ḥasan. On the 9th they brought Khān A'ẓam, who had come to Agra from the fort of Gwalior, and who had been sent for. Though he had been guilty of many offences, and in all that I had done to him I was right, yet when they brought him into my presence and my eye fell on him, I perceived more shame in myself than in him. Having pardoned all his offences, I gave him the shawl I had round my waist. I gave Kunwar Karan 100,000 *darab*. On the same day Rāja Sūraj Singh brought a large elephant of the name of Ran-rāwat, which was a celebrated elephant of his, as an offering. In fact, it was such a rare elephant that I put it into my private stud. On the 10th the offering of Khwāja Jahān, which he sent me from Agra by the hand of his son, was laid before me. It was of all kinds of things, of the value of 40,000 rupees. On the 12th the offering of Khān Daurān, which consisted of forty-five[1] horse,

[1] *Panj tuqūz*, i.e. 9 by 5. The text has تاقور, *tāqūr*.

two strings of camels, Arabian dogs (greyhounds), and hunting animals (hawks ?), was brought before me. On the same day seven other elephants from Rāja Sūraj Singh were also brought to me as an offering, and were placed in my private stud. Taḥayyur Khān, after he had been in attendance on me for four months, to-day got leave to go. A message was sent to 'Ādil Khān. I impressed on him the profit and loss of friendship and enmity, and made an agreement (with Taḥayyur Khān) that all these words should be repeated to 'Ādil Khān, and he should bring him back to the path of loyalty and obedience. At the time of his taking leave I also bestowed on him certain things. On the whole, in this short time, what with the gifts bestowed on him by me privately, by the princes, and those given him by the Amirs according to order, the account mounted up to about 100,000 rupees that he had received. On the 14th the rank and reward of my son Khurram were fixed. His mansab had been one of 12,000 personal and 6,000 horse, and that of his brother (Parwīz) 15,000 personal and 8,000 horse. I ordered his mansab to be made equal with that of Parwīz, besides other rewards. I gave him a private elephant of the name of Panchī Gaj,[1] with accoutrements of the value of 12,000 rupees. On the 16th an elephant was given to Mahābat Khān. On the 17th the mansab of Rāja Sūraj Singh, which was 4,000 personal and 3,000 horse, was increased by 1,000, and it was raised to 5,000. At the request of 'Abdu-llah Khān the mansab of Khwāja 'Abdu-l-Laṭīf, which was 500 personal and 200 horse, was raised by 200, and it was ordered to be 1,000 personal and 400 horse. 'Abdu-llah, the son of Khān A'ẓam, who was imprisoned in the fort of Ranṭambhor, was sent for at the request of his father. He came to the Court, and

[1] The B.M. MSS. seem to have *panch kunjar*, 'five elephants,' i.e. equal to five elephants (?).

I took the chains off his legs and sent him to his father's house. On the 24th, Rāja Sūraj Singh presented me with another elephant, called Fauj-sangār ('ornament of the army'), by way of offering. Although this is also a good elephant, and has been placed in my private stud, it is not to be compared with the first elephant (he sent), which is one of the wonders of the age, and is worth 20,000 rupees. On the 26th, 200 personal were added to the mansab of Badī'u-z-zamān, son of Mīrzā Shāhrukh; it was 700 personal and 500 horse. On the same day Khwāja Zainu-d-dīn, who is of the Naqshbandī Khwājas, came from Māwarā'a-n-nahr and waited on me, bringing as an offering eighteen horses. Qizilbāsh Khān, who was one of the auxiliaries of the province of Gujarat, had come to Court without the leave of the governor. I ordered that an ahadi should put him into confinement, and that he be sent back to the governor of Gujarat, so that others might not desire to do the same. The mansab of Mubārak Khān Sazāwal I raised 500 personal, so that it should be 1,500 personal and 700 horse. On the 29th I gave Khān A'ẓam 100,000 rupees, and ordered that the parganahs of Ḍāsna [1] and Kāsna,[1] which are equivalent to 5,000 personal, should be made his jagir. At the end of the same month I gave leave to Jahāngīr Qulī Khān, with his brothers and other relatives, to go to Allahabad, which had been appropriated to them as jagir. At this meeting twenty horse, a *qabā* (*parm narm*) of Cashmere cloth, twelve deer, and ten Arabian dogs were given to Karan. The next day, which was the 1st Khūrdād, forty horse, the next day forty-one horse, and the third day twenty, amounting in the space of three days to 101 head, were given as a present to Kunwar Karan. In return for the elephant Fauj-sangār, an elephant worth 10,000 rupees out of

[1] In Sarkār Delhi (Jarrett, ii, 287).

my private stud was presented to Rāja Sūraj Singh. On the 5th of the month ten turbans (*chīra*), ten coats (*qaba*), and ten waist-bands were given to Karan. On the 20th I gave him another elephant.

In these days the news-writer of Kashmir had written that a Mullā of the name of Gadā'ī, a disciplined dervish, who for forty years had lived in one of the monasteries of the city, had prayed the inheritors of that monastery two years[1] before he was to deliver over the pledge of his life that he might select a corner in that monastery as a place for his burial. They said, "Let it be so." In short, he selected a place. When the time for his delivery came he informed his friends and relations and those who were dear to him that an order had reached him that, delivering over the pledge (of life) he had, he should turn towards the last world. Those who were present wondered at his words, and said that the prophets had no such information, and how could they believe such words? He said, "Such an order has been given to me." He then turned to one of his confidants, who was of the sons of the Qāẓīs of the country, and said: "You will expend the price[2] of my Koran, which is worth 700 tankas, in carrying me (to the grave). When you hear the call to Friday's prayer you will enquire for me." This conversation took place on the Thursday, and he divided all the goods in his room among his acquaintance and disciples, and went, and at end of the day bathed at the baths. The Qāẓī-zāda aforesaid came before the call for prayer, and enquired as to the health of the Mullā. When he came to the door of the cell

[1] The text does not expressly say that the dervish foretold two years before his death the period of his death, but apparently Jahāngīr means this, for he goes on to speak of the time mentioned for his delivery. See also Iqbāl-nāma, p. 81, where the dervish is called Ḥāfiẓ, and where it is added that the whole population of Srinagar followed the bier.

[2] Lit. give it, for the Koran cannot be directly sold.

he found the door closed and a servant sitting there. He asked the slave what had happened, and the servant said, "The Mullā has enjoined me that until the door of the cell open of its own accord I must not go in." Shortly after these words were said the door of the cell opened. The Qāẓī-zāda entered the cell with that servant and saw that the Mullā was on his knees with his face turned toward the qibla, and had given up his soul to God. Happy the state of the freed who can fly away from this place of the snares of dependence with such ease!

By the increase of 200 personal and 50 horse in the mansab of Karam Sen Rāṭhor, I raised it to 1,000 personal and 300 horse. On the 11th of this month the offering of Lashkar Khān, which consisted of three strings of Persian camels and twenty cups and plates from Khiṭā (China) and twenty Arabian dogs, was brought before me. On the 12th a jewelled dagger was bestowed on I'tibār Khān, and to Karan I gave a plume (*kalgī*) worth 2,000 rupees. On the 14th I gave a dress of honour to Sar-[1] buland Rāy, and gave him leave to go to the Deccan.

On the night of Friday, the 15th, a strange affair occurred. By chance on that night I was at Pushkar. To be brief, Kishan, own brother to Rāja Sūraj Singh, was in great perturbation through Gobind Dās, the Vakil of the said Raja having some time ago killed his nephew, a youth of the name of Gopāl Dās. The cause of the quarrel it would take too long to tell. Kishan Singh expected that, as Gopāl Dās was also the nephew of the Raja (Sūraj Singh), the latter would kill Gobind Dās. But the Raja, on account of the experience and ability of Gobind Dās, relinquished the idea of seeking revenge for his nephew's death. When Kishan saw this neglect on the part of the Raja, he resolved himself to take

[1] Text *pisar*, 'son of Buland Rāy,' but from the B.M. MSS. it appears that *pisar* is a mistake for Sar.

revenge for his nephew, and not allow his blood to pass away unnoticed. For a long time he kept this matter in his mind, until on that night he assembled his brothers, friends, and servants, and told them that he would go that night to take Gobind Dās's life, whatever might happen, and that he did not care what injury might happen to the Raja. The Raja was in ignorance of what was happening, and when it was near dawn Kishan came with Karan, his brother's son, and other companions. When he arrived at the gate of the Raja's dwelling he sent some of the experienced men on foot to the house of Gobind Dās, which was near the Raja's. He himself (Kishan) was on horseback, and stationed himself near the gate. The men on foot entered Gobind Dās's house, and killed some of those who were there on guard. Whilst this fight was going on Gobind Dās awoke, and seizing his sword in a state of bewilderment was coming out from one side of the house to join the outside watchmen. When the men on foot had finished killing some of the people, they came out of the tent to endeavour to find out Gobind Dās, and, meeting him, they finished his affair (killed him). Before the news of the killing of Gobind Dās reached Kishan, he, unable to bear it any more, dismounted and came inside the dwelling. Although his men protested in a disturbed state that it was not right to be on foot, he would in no way listen to them. If he had remained a little longer and the news of his enemy having been killed had reached him, it is possible that he would have escaped safe and sound, mounted as he was. As the pen of destiny had gone forth after another fashion, as soon as he alighted and went in, the Raja, who was in his *maḥall* (female apartment), awoke at the uproar among the people, and stood at the gate of his house with his sword drawn. People from all sides were aroused and came in against the men who were on foot. They saw what the number of men on foot was, and came out in great numbers and faced Kis͟han Singh's men, who were about ten in number. In short, Kis͟han Singh and his nephew Karan, when they reached the Raja's house, were attacked by these men and both of them killed. Kis͟han Singh had seven and Karan nine wounds. Altogether in this fight 66 men on the two sides were killed, on the Raja's side 30 and on Kis͟han Singh's 36. When the sun rose and illumined the world with its light, this business was revealed, and the Raja saw that his brother, his nephew, and some of his servants, whom he considered dearer than himself, were killed, and the whole of the rest had dispersed to their own places. The news reached me in Pushkar, and I ordered them to burn those who were killed, according to their rites, and inform me of the true circumstances of the affair. In the end it became clear that the affair had happened in the manner in which it has been written here, and that no further enquiry was necessary.

On the 8th Mīrān Ṣadr Jahān came from his native place and waited on me with an offering of 100 muhrs. Rāy Sūraj Singh was dismissed to his duty in the Deccan. I presented him with a couple of pearls for his ears and a special Kashmir shawl (*parm narm*). A pair of pearls were also sent to K͟hān Jahān. On the 25th I increased the mansab of I'tibār K͟hān by 600 horse, so as to bring it to 5,000 personal and 2,000 horse. On the same day Karan obtained leave to go to his jagir. He received a present of a horse, a special elephant, a dress of honour, a string of pearls of the value of 50,000 rupees, and a jewelled dagger which had been completed for 2,000 rupees. From the time of his waiting on me till he obtained leave, what he had had in the shape of cash, jewellery, jewels, and jewelled things was of the value of 200,000 rupees, with 110 horses, five elephants, in addition to what my son K͟hurram bestowed on him at various times. I gave Mubārak Khān Sazāwal a horse and an elephant, and appointed him to accompany him. I sent several verbal messages to the Rānā. Rāja Sūraj Singh also obtained leave to go to his native country, with a promise to return in two months. On the 27th, Pāyanda Khān Moghul,[1] who was one of the old Amirs of the State, gave up the deposit of his life.

At the end of this month news came that the ruler of Iran had executed his eldest son Ṣafī Mīrzā. This was a cause of great bewilderment. When I enquired into it they said that at Darash,[2] which is one of the noted cities of Gīlān, he ordered a slave of the name of Bihbūd to kill Ṣafī Mīrzā. The slave found an opportunity, early in the morning on the 5th of Muḥarram, in the year 1024 (25th January, 1615), when the Mīrzā was returning from the baths towards his house, and finished his affair for him with two wounds from a sword (*sīkhakī*).[3] After a great part of the day had passed, while his body lay between the water and the mud, Shaikh Bahā'u-d-dīn Muḥammad, who was the best known man in the country for learning and holiness, and on whom the Shah had full reliance, reported the affair, and, obtaining leave to lift him up, took his corpse and sent it to Ardabīl, where was the burial-ground of his ancestors. Although much enquiry was made of travellers from Iran, no one would say a word of this affair that satisfied my mind with regard to it. The killing of a son must have some powerful motive in order to do away with the disgrace of it.

[1] Blochmann, p. 387. Possibly he was the part author of a translation of Bābar's Commentaries.

[2] The name is wrong. The Iqbāl-nāma, p. 84, has Rasht (Rashd), which is a well-known town on the Caspian.

[3] According to the Iqbāl-nāma the true reading is *sanjakī* (see p. 84). But Olearius, who gives a full account of the murder (p. 352 of English translation, ed. 1662), says Bihbūd gave him two stabs with a *chentze*, which is a kind of poniard.

On the 1st of the month of Tīr I gave an elephant of the name of Ranjīt with its trappings to Mīrzā Rustam and another to Sayyid 'Alī Bārha. Mīrak Ḥusain, a relation of Khwāja Shamsu-d-dīn, was appointed bakhshi and news-writer of the Subah of Behar, and took leave to go. I gave Khwāja 'Abdu-l-Laṭīf Qūsh-begī (the falconer) an elephant and a dress of honour, and dismissed him to his jagir. On the 9th of the same month I gave a jewelled sword to Khān Daurān, and a jewelled dagger was sent for Allahdād, the son of Jalālā the Afghan, who had become loyal. On the 13th took place the meeting for the festival of the *Āb-pāshān*[1] (rose-water scattering), and the servants of the Court amused themselves with sprinkling rose-water over each other. On the 17th, Amānat Khān was appointed to the port of Cambay. As Muqarrab Khān proposed to come to Court, the (charge of the) aforesaid port was changed. On the same day I sent a jewelled waist-dagger to my son Parwīz. On the 18th the offering of Khānkhānān was laid before me. He had prepared all kinds of jewellery and other things, jewels with jewelled things, such as three rubies and 103 pearls, 100 rubies (*yāqūt*), two jewelled daggers and an aigrette adorned with rubies and pearls, a jewelled water-jar, a jewelled sword, a quiver bound with velvet, and a diamond ring, altogether of the value of about 100,000 rupees, in addition to jewels and jewelled things, cloth from the Deccan and Carnatic, and all kinds of gilt and plain things, with fifteen elephants and a horse whose mane reached the ground. The offering of Shāh-nawāz Khān (his son) also, consisting of five elephants, 300 pieces of all kinds of cloth, was brought before me. On the 8th I honoured Hūshang with the title of Ikrām Khān. Rūz-afzūn, who was one of the princes of the Subah of Behar, and who had

[1] A Persian festival in memory of a rain which fell on the 13th Tīr and put an end to a famine (Bahār-i-'ajam).

been from his youth one of the permanent servants of the Court, having been honoured by admission into Islam, was made Raja of the province of his father, Rāja Sangrām.[1] Though the latter had been killed in opposing the leaders of the State, I gave him an elephant and leave to go to his native place. An elephant was presented to Jahāngīr Qulī Khān. On the 24th, Jagat Singh, son of Kunwar Karan, who was in his 12th year, came and waited on me, and presented petitions from his grandfather, the Rānā Amar Singh, and from his father. The signs of nobility and high birth were evident on his face. I pleased him with a dress of honour and kindness. To the mansab of Mīrzā 'Īsā Tarkhān an addition of 200 personal was made, so that it attained to 1,200 personal and 300 horse. In the end of the month, having honoured Shaikh Ḥusain Rohīla with the title of Mubāriz Khān, I dismissed him to his jagir. Ten thousand darabs (5,000 rupees) were given to the relations of Mīrzā Sharafu-d-dīn Ḥusain Kāshgharī, who at this time had come and had the honour of kissing the threshold. On the 5th Amurdād, to the mansab of Rāja Nathmal, which was 1,500 personal and 1,100 horse, an addition of 500 personal and 100 horse was made. On the 7th, Kesho (Dās) Mārū, who had a jagir in the Sarkar of Orissa, and who had been sent for to Court on account of a complaint[2] against the governor of the Subah of that place, came and paid his respects. He produced as an offering four elephants. As I had a great desire to see my *farzand* (son) Khān Jahān (Lodī), and for the purpose of enquiring into important matters connected with the Deccan, it was necessary for him to come at once, I sent for him. On Tuesday, the 8th of the same

[1] Sangrām was Raja of Kharkpur in Behar, and was killed in battle with Jahāngīr Qulī Khān (Blochmann, p. 446, note).

[2] *Shakwā'i-ṣāḥib-i-Sūba.* I presume it means a complaint against the governor, and perhaps one made by Kesho.

month, he waited on me, and presented as an offering 1,000 muhrs, 1,000 rupees, 4 rubies, 20 pearls, 1 emerald, and a jewelled *phūl kaṭāra,* the total value being 50,000 rupees. On the night of Sunday, as it was the anniversary of the great Khwāja (Mu'īnu-d-dīn), I went to his revered mausoleum, and remained there till midnight. The attendants and Sufis exhibited ecstatic states, and I gave the fakirs and attendants money with my own hand; altogether there were expended 6,000 rupees in cash, 100 *ṣaub-kurta* (a robe down to the ankles), 70 rosaries of pearls,[1] coral and amber, etc. Mahā Singh, grandson of Rāja Mān Singh, was honoured with the title of Raja, and a standard and drums given him. On the 16th an Iraq horse out of my private stable and another horse were presented to Mahābat Khān. On the 19th an elephant was given to Khān A'ẓam. On the 20th, 200 horse were added to the mansab of Kesho (Dās) Mārū, which was 2,000 personal and 1,000 horse, and he was dignified with a dress of honour. An increase of 200 personal and horse was made to the mansab of Khwāja 'Āqil, which was 1,200 personal and 600 horse. On the 22nd, Mīrzā Rāja Bhāo Singh took leave to go to Amber, which was his ancient native place, and had given him a special Kashmir *phūp* (?) robe.[2] On the 25th, Aḥmad Beg Khān, who was imprisoned at Ranṭambhor, paid his respects to me, and his offences were pardoned on account of his former services. On the 28th, Muqarrab Khān came from the Subah of Gujarat and waited on me, and offered an aigrette and a jewelled throne.[3] An increase of 500 personal and horse was made to the mansab of Salāmu-llah, the Arab, and it was brought to 2,000 personal and 1,100 horse. On the 1st of the month of Shahrīwar the following increases were made

[1] The pearls are omitted in the MSS.
[2] It is *phūl* in MS. No. 181.
[3] *Takhtī,* qu. a signet? No. 181 has a *lāl takhtī.*

in the rank of a number of men who were going on service to the Deccan:—To Mubāriz Khān 300 horse, making 1,000 personal and horse. Nāhir Khān was also raised to 1,000 personal and horse. Dilāwar Khān was raised by 300 horse to 2,500 personal and horse. Manglī Khān's rank was increased by 200 horse to 1,500 personal and 1,000 horse. Girdhar, the son of Ray Sāl, had the rank of 800 personal and horse bestowed on him, and Ilf Khān Qiyām Khān the same mansab, original and increase. Yādgār Ḥusain was raised to 700 personal and 500 horse, and Kamālu-d-dīn, son of Shīr Khān, to the same mansab. One hundred and fifty horse were added to the rank of Sayyid 'Abdu-llah Bārha, which then came to 700 personal and 300 horse, original and increase. On the 8th of the said month I bestowed one Nūr-jahānī muhr, which is equal to 6,400 rupees, on Muṣṭafā Beg, the ambassador of the ruler of Iran, and presented five cheetahs to Qāsim Khān, governor of Bengal. Mīrzā Murād, eldest son of Mīrzā Rustam, on the 12th of the same month was honoured with the title of Iltifāt Khān. On the night of the 16th, corresponding with the *Shab-i-barāt* (consecrated to the memory of forefathers), I ordered them to light lamps on the hills round the Ānā Sāgar tank and on its banks, and went myself to look at them. The reflection of the lamps fell on the water and had a wonderful appearance. I passed the most of that night with the ladies of the mahall on the bank of that tank.

On the 17th, Mīrzā Jamālu-d-dīn Ḥusain,[1] who had gone as an ambassador to Bijapur, came and waited on me, and presented three rings, the stone of one of which was a cornelian from Yemen, of great beauty and pureness of water, the like of which is seldom seen among the cornelians of Yemen. 'Ādil Khān sent a person of the name of Sayyid Kabīr Khān on his own part with the said

[1] Sir Thomas Roe's friend.

Mir, and forwarded as offerings elephants with gold and silver fittings, Arab horses, jewels and jewelled things, and all kinds of cloth made in that country. On the 24th of this month they were brought before me with a letter he had brought. On the same day the assembly for my solar weighing was held. On the 26th, Muṣṭafā Beg, the ambassador, took his leave. In addition to what had been bestowed on him during the time of his attendance, I gave him 20,000 rupees more in cash and a dress of honour, and in answer to the letter he had brought sent a friendly letter written in the perfection of friendship. On the 4th of the month of Mihr the mansab of Mīr Jamālu-d-dīn Ḥusain, which was 2,000 personal and 500 horse, was fixed at 4,000 personal and 2,000 horse. On the 5th, Mahābat Khān, in company with Khān Jahān, who had been appointed to serve in the Deccan, at the hour that had been appointed for him, took his leave; he was honoured with a dress of honour, a jewelled dagger, a *phūl kaṭāra,* a special sword, and an elephant. On the 8th, Khān Jahān took his leave, and I presented him with a dress of honour, and a special *nādirī* (a dress), and an ambling horse with a saddle, a special elephant, and a special sword. On the same date 1,700 horse of those under the command of Mahābat Khān were ordered to have assignments (*tankhwāh*) for two or three horses given them. The whole of the men who were at this time appointed for service in the Deccan were 330 mansabdars, 3,000 ahadis, 700 horse from the Ūymaqs, and 3,000 Dalazāk Afghans. Altogether there were 30,000[1] cavalry, and 3,000,000 rupees of treasure, and an efficient artillery, and war elephants. They proceeded on this duty. The mansab of Sarbuland Rāy was increased by 500 personal and 260 horse, and came to 2,000 personal and 1,500 horse. Bāljū, nephew of Qilīj Khān, was

[1] Text wrongly has 3 instead of 30.

promoted to the mansab of 1,000 personal and 700 horse, original and increase. I also increased Rāja Kis͟han Dās's mansab by 500. At the request of K͟hān Jahān, the mansab of S͟hāhbāz K͟hān Lodī, who belonged to the Deccan force, was fixed, original and increase, at 2,000 personal and 1,000 horse; and 200 horse were added to the mansab of Wazīr K͟hān. The mansab of Suhrāb K͟hān, son of Mīrzā Rustam, was fixed at 1,000 personal and 400 horse, original and increase. On the 14th of the same month 1,000 was added to the mansab of Mīr Jamālu-d-dīn Ḥusain, and by increasing it also by 500 horse he was raised to the exalted rank of 5,000 personal and 2,500 horse. On the 19th, Rāja Sūraj Singh, with his son Gaj Singh, who had gone home, came and paid their respects, and presented as offerings 100 muhrs and 1,000 rupees. I gave Sayyid Kabīr, who had been sent by 'Ādil K͟hān, one Nūrjahānī muhr, which weighed 500 *tūlcha*. On the 23rd, ninety elephants of those which Qāsim K͟hān had acquired from the conquest of the country of Kūch (Behar), and the conquest of the Maghs and the zamindars of Orissa, were brought before me and placed in the special elephant houses. On the 26th, Irādat K͟hān was raised to the rank of Mīr-sāmānī (head butler), Mu'tamad K͟hān to that of Bakhshi of the Ahadis, Muḥammad Riẓā Jābirī to that of Bakhshi of the Subah of the Panjab and news-writer of that place. Sayyid Kabīr, who had come on the part of 'Ādil K͟hān to beg pardon for the offences of the rulers (*dunyā-dārān*) of the Deccan, and to promise the restoration of the fort of Ahmadnagar and the royal territory which had been taken out of the possession of the chiefs of the victorious State through the rebellion of certain rebels, came and waited on me, and obtained leave to go on this date; and, having received a dress of honour, an elephant, and a horse, started off. As Rāja Rāj Singh Kachhwāha had died in the Deccan, I promoted his son Rām Dās to the mansab of 1,000 personal and 400 horse. On the 4th of Ābān, drums were given to Saif K͟hān Bārha and his mansab increased by 300 horse, so as to bring it up to 3,000 personal and 2,000 horse. On the same date I released Rāja Mān, who was in confinement in the fort of Gwalior, on the security of Murtaẓā K͟hān, and, confirming his mansab, sent him to the said K͟hān for duty at the fort of Kāngra. At the request of K͟hān Daurān, an increase of 300 horse was ordered to the mansab of Ṣādiq K͟hān, raising it to 1,000 personal and horse. Mīrzā 'Īsā Tark͟hān came from the province of Sambhal, which was his jagir, and waited on me, and offered 100 muhrs. On the 16th, Rāja Sūraj Singh obtained leave to go to his duty in the Deccan, and I increased his mansab by 300 horse, so as to make it 5,000 personal and 3,300 horse; he received a dress of honour and a horse, and started. On the 18th I confirmed the mansab of Mīrzā 'Īsā, original and increase, at 1,500 personal and 800 horse, and gave him an elephant and a dress of honour, and he took leave to go to the Deccan.

On the same day the news of the death of the wretch Chīn Qilīj was received by a letter from Jahāngīr Qulī K͟hān. After the death of Qilīj K͟hān, who was one of the old servants of this State, I had made this inauspicious man an Amir, and shown him great favour, and given him in jagir such a place as Jaunpur. I also sent his other brothers and relations with him and made them his deputies. He had one brother of the name of Lahorī,[1] of a very wicked disposition. It was reported to me that the servants of God (people) were greatly oppressed by his conduct. I sent an ahadi to bring him (Lahorī) from Jaunpur. At the coming of the ahadi, suspicion without any cause prevailed over Chīn Qilīj, and it came into his mind to run away, taking

[1] Apparently because born in Lahore (see Blochmann, p. 500).

his misguided brother with him. Leaving his mansab, his government, place, and jagir, money, property, children, and people, he took a little money and gold and a few jewels and went with a small body among the ẕamindars. This news arrived a few days ago and caused great astonishment. In short, to whatever zamindar he went he took money[1] from him (?) and then let him go (?), until news came that he had entered the country of Johaṭ.[2] When this news reached Jahāngīr Qulī Khān, he sent some of his men to take and bring that thoughtless one. They took him as soon as they arrived, and were intending to take him to Jahāngīr Qulī Khān, when he at that very moment went to hell. Some of those who had accompanied him said that for some days previously he had contracted an illness and it had killed him. But this was heard of him as well, that he committed suicide, in order that they might not take him to Jahāngīr Qulī Khān in this state. In any case, they brought his body with his children and servants who were with him to Allahabad. They made away with most of the money that he had, and the zamindars took it from him. Alas, that salt (i.e. loyalty) should not have brought such black-faced wretches to condign punishment!

"Behind the duty that lies on all people is the duty to the sovereign and benefactor" (?).[3]

[1] According to I.O. MS. 181 every zamindar took some money from Chīn Qilīj and sent him out of his estate, and this seems to be the probable meaning, for we are told later on that the zamindars plundered Chīn Qilīj.

[2] Tirhut. R.A.S. MS. has "It chanced that the zamindar of this place was with Jahāngīr Qulī, and the latter sent him with some people to seize Chīn Qilīj." I.O. MS. has the same, and this seems correct. The text has "It chanced that the zamindar of that place was spending some days in that neighbourhood (?)." Perhaps a negative has been omitted before 'spending.' I.O. MS. seems to have Johirhat as the name of the zamindar's estate.

[3] Apparently the verse is quoted with reference to Jahāngīr Qulī's failure to exact retribution from the zamindars. There is an account of Chīn Qilīj in the Ma'āṣir, iii, 351.

On the 22nd, at the request of Khān Daurān, 200 horse were added to the mansab of Nād 'Alī Maidānī, one of the officers appointed to Bangash, which brought it to 1,500 personal and 1,000 horse; 100 horse were also added to the mansab of Lashkar Khān, which was 2,000 personal and 900 horse. On the 24th I confirmed the mansab of Muqarrab Khān, which was 3,000 personal and 2,000 horse, and increased it to 5,000 personal and 2,500 horse. On the same day I bestowed the title of Khan on Qiyām, son of Shāh Muḥammad Qandahārī, who was an Amīr-zāda, and was in service as a huntsman. On the 5th of the month of Āzar a jewelled dagger was given to Dārāb Khān, and by the hand of Rāja Sārang Deo dresses of honour were bestowed on the Amirs of the Deccan. As some (evil) things had been heard about Ṣafdar Khān, governor of Kashmir, I dismissed him from the government, and favouring Aḥmad Beg Khān on account of his previous services, I promoted him to be Subadar of Kashmir, and confirmed his mansab of 2,500 personal and 1,500 horse, honoured him with a jewelled waist-dagger and a dress of honour, and gave him leave. By the hand of Ihtimām Khān I sent winter dresses of honour to Qāsim Khān, governor of Bengal, and the Amirs that were attached to that province. On the 15th of the month there was laid before me the offering of Maka'ī, son of Iftikhār Khān, consisting of an elephant, *goṭ*[1] horses, and pieces of cloth. He was honoured with the title of Muruwwat Khān. At the request of I'timādu-d-daula, I had sent for Dayānat Khān, who was in the fort of Gwalior, and he had the good fortune to pay his respects; his property, which had been confiscated, was restored to him.

At this time Khwāja Hāshim, of Dahbīd, who at this day vigorously maintains in Transoxiana the profession

[1] *Gūnṭh*, a breed of small horses or ponies.

of a dervish, and in whom the people of that country have great belief, sent a letter by the hand of one of his disciples pointing out his old devotion (to the royal family) and connection and friendship of his ancestors with this illustrious family, together with a *farjī*[1] and a bow and a couplet which the late king Bābar had made for a saint of the name of Khwājagī, who also belonged to that sect of dervishes. The last hemistich is as follows:—

"We are bound to the Khwājagī and are servants to the Khwājagī."

I also with my own pen wrote some lines in the style of that writing, and sent impromptu quatrains with 1,000 Jahāngīrī muhrs to the said Khwāja—

"O thou whose kindness to me is ever more and more,
The State has remembrance of thee, O Dervish,
As from good tidings our heart is rejoiced,
We are glad that thy kindness passes all bounds."

As I ordered that whoever had the poetic temperament should recite (compose ?) this quatrain,[2] Ḥakīm Masīḥu-z-zamān said, and said very well—

"Although we have the business of kingship before us,
Every moment more and more we think on the dervishes.
If the heart of our Dervish be gladdened by us
We count that to be the profit of our kingship."

I gave the Ḥakīm 1,000 muhrs for the composition of this quatrain. On the 7th of the month of Day, when I was coming back from Pushkar and returning to Ajmir, on the way forty-two wild pigs were taken.

On the 20th, Mīr Mīrān came and waited on me. A summary of his circumstances and of his family is

[1] A *farjī* is a coat (see Blochmann, p. 89).

[2] Text *īn rubā'ī*, 'this quatrain,' which does not seem to make sense. Perhaps *īn* here should be *āyīn-i-rubā'ī*, 'the rules or the custom of a quatrain.' Similarly, *īn kitābat* five lines down may be *āyīn-i-kitābat*, 'the rules of writing.'

now written. On the side of his father[1] he is the grandson of Mīr Ghiyāṣu-d-dīn Muḥammad Mīr Mīrān, son of Shāh Ni'matu-llah Walī. During the reigns of the Ṣafawī kings the family had attained to great respect, so that Shāh Ṭahmāsp gave his own sister Jānish[2] Khānim to Shāh Ni'matu-llah, and so on account of his being a great Shaikh and of his being an instructor he was made a relative and a son-in-law (of kings). On the side of his mother he was the daughter's son of Shāh Isma'īl Khūnī (Isma'īl II, the Bloody). After the death of Shāh Ni'matu-llah, his son Ghiyāṣu-d-dīn Muḥammad Mīr Mīrān received great consideration, and the late Shāh (Ṭahmāsp) gave to his eldest son in marriage a daughter from the royal family. He gave the daughter of the above-mentioned Shāh Isma'īl to another son of his, Khalīlu-llah, to whom Mīr Mīrān was born. The aforesaid Mīr Khalīlu-llah, seven or eight years before this, had come from Persia and waited on me at Lahore. As he belonged to a high and saintly family, I was much interested in his affairs, and gave him a mansab and a jagir, and honoured and cherished him. After the seat of government was at Agra, in a short time he was attacked by bilious[3] diarrhœa from eating too many mangoes, and in ten or twelve days gave up his soul to the Creator. I was grieved at his going, and ordered what he had left in cash and jewels to be sent to his children in Persia. Meanwhile Mīr Mīrān, who was 22 years old, became a qalandar and dervish, and came to me at Ajmir in a way that nobody on the road could recognize him. I soothed all the troubles of his mind and the miseries of his inward and outward condition,

[1] His father was Khalīlu-llah, previously mentioned in the Tūzuk, and who had lately died (Iqbāl-nāma, p. 84, and Tūzuk, pp. 62 and 69). Ṭahmāsp gave Ni'matu-llah's daughter in marriage to his own son Isma'īl.

[2] Khānish Khānim in Ma'āṣir, iii, 339.

[3] *Ishāl-i-kabd.*

and gave him a mansab of 1,000 personal and 400 horse, and presented him with 30,000 darabs in cash. He is now in waiting and attendance on me.

On the 12th, Ẓafar Khān, who had been removed from the Subah of Behar, came and waited on me, and made an offering of 100 muhrs, as well as three elephants. On the 15th of Day I increased the mansab of Qāsim Khān, the Subahdar of Bengal, by 1,000 personal and horse, so as to make it 4,000 personal and horse. As the diwan and bakhshi of Bengal, Ḥusain Beg and Ṭāhir, had not done approved service, Mukhliṣ Khān, who was one of the confidential servants of the Court, was nominated to these duties. I conferred on him a mansab of 2,000 personal and 700 horse, and also gave him a standard. The duty of *'arẓ-mukarrir* (reviser of petitions) I ordered to be given to Dayānat Khān. On the 25th, Friday, the weighing of my son Khurram took place. Up to the present year, when he is 24 years old, and is married and has children, he has never defiled himself with drinking wine. On this day, when the assembly for his weighing was held, I said to him: "Bābā, thou hast become the father of children, and kings and kings' sons have drunk wine. To-day, which is the day of thy being weighed, I will give thee wine to drink, and give thee leave to drink it on feast days and at the time of the New Year, and at all great festivals. But thou must observe the path of moderation, for wise men do not consider it right to drink to such an extent as to destroy the understanding, and it is necessary that from drinking only profit should be derived." Bū 'Alī (Avicenna), who is one of the most learned of hakims and physicians, has written this quatrain—

> "Wine is a raging enemy, a prudent friend;
> A little is an antidote, but much a snake's poison.
> In much there is no little injury,
> In a little there is much profit."

With much trouble wine was given to him. I had not drunk it till I was 15[1] years old, except when in the time of my infancy two or three times my mother and wet-nurses gave it by way of infantile remedy. They asked for a little spirit from my revered father, and gave it me to the extent of a tola mixed with water and rosewater to take away a cough, designating it as medicine. At the time when the camp of my revered father had been pitched in order to put down the disturbance of Yūsufza'e Afghans at the fort of Attock, which is on the bank of the Nīlāb (Indus) River, one day I had mounted to go out to hunt. When I had moved about a good deal and the signs of weariness had set in, a gunner of the name of Ustād S̲h̲āh-qulī, a wonderful gunner out of those under my revered uncle Mīrzā Muḥammad Ḥakīm, said to me that if I would take a cup of wine it would drive away the feeling of being tired and heavy. It was in the time of my youth, and as I felt disposed towards it I ordered Maḥmūd, the Āb-dār (person in charge of drinking water, etc.), to go to the house of Ḥakīm 'Alī and bring me an intoxicating draught. He sent me[2] the amount of one and a half cups of yellow wine of a sweet taste in a little bottle. I drank

[1] Two I.O. MSS. and the R.A.S. MS. have 18 instead of 15. Elliot has "up to my fourteenth" year. Jahāngīr was born in Rabī', 977, or 31st August, 1569, and the beginning of wine-drinking to which he refers must have taken place at earliest in January, 1586. He tells us that it was after the death of Muḥammad Ḥakīm, and at the time when his father was at Attock. Now Akbar arrived there on 15th Muḥarram, 994, according to Niẓāmu-d-dīn, and on 12th Day, 994, according to Abū-l-faẓl, iii, 976, i.e. about the end of December, 1585, and at that time Jahāngīr was 17 years and 4 months of age, or in his 18th year. He continued to drink heavily for nine years, i.e. till he was 26 (17+9), then he moderated for seven years, i.e. till he was 33, and he kept to that for fifteen years more, i.e. till he was 48. These years were lunar years, and he tells that at the time of writing he was 47 years and 9 months old, according to the lunar calendar. It seems to follow that the MSS. are right, and that we should read 18.

[2] Elliot, vi, 341.

it, and found its quality agreeable. After that I took to drinking wine, and increased it from day to day until wine made from grapes ceased to intoxicate me, and I took to drinking arrack (*'araq*, spirits), and by degrees during nine years my potions rose to twenty cups of doubly distilled spirits, fourteen during the daytime and the remainder at night. The weight of this was six Hindustani sirs or one and a half maunds of Iran. The extent of my eating in those days was a fowl [1] with bread and vegetables (lit. radish).[2] In that state of matters no one had the power to forbid me, and matters went to such a length that in the crapulous state from the excessive trembling of my hand I could not drink from my own cup, but others had to give it me to drink, until I sent for Ḥakīm Humām, brother of Ḥakīm Abū-l-fatḥ, who was of the most intimate with my revered father, and informed him of my state. He, with excessive sincerity and unfeigned burning of heart, said to me without hesitation, "Lord of the world, by the way in which you drink spirits, God forbid it, but in six months matters will come to such a pass that there will be no remedy for it." As his words were said out of pure good-will, and sweet life was dear to me, they made an impression on me, and from that day I began to lessen my allowance and set myself to take *filūnīyā*.[3] In

[1] The two good I.O. MSS. have, not *murgh* or *murghī*, but *tughdarī* or *tūghdarī*, a 'bustard,' unless indeed the word be *taghaddī*, 'breakfast.' But probably the word is *tughdarī*, a bustard, and the reference is to the particular memorable day when he first drank wine. His food that day, he says, was a bustard with bread and a radish (*turb*).

[2] Blochmann. *Calcutta Review*, 1869, has 'turnips.'

[3] *Filūnīyā*. The word is not given in ordinary dictionaries, but it is explained in Dozy's Supplement. It is stated there that it is a sedative electuary, and that the word is derived from the Greek, being φιλωνια, which is the name of an antidote or drug invented by Philon of Tarsus. There is an account of Philon and a reference to his drug in Smith's Classical Dictionary. Philon lived in or before the first century after Christ, and is referred to by Galen and others. The word as given there is φιλωνειον. We are not told what it was made of. In

proportion as I diminished my liquor, I increased the amount of filuniya.

I also ordered that the arrack should be diluted with wine of the grape so that there should be two parts wine and one part arrack. Every day I diminished the quantity I took, and in the course of seven years I brought it down to six cups. The weight of each cupful was 18¼ misqals. It is now fifteen years that I have drunk at this rate, neither more nor less. And my drinking time is the night except on the day of Thursdays, as it is the day of the blessed accession. Also on the eve[1] of Friday, which is the most blessed eve of the week, and is the prelude to a blessed day (I do not drink). I drink at the end of each day with these two[2] exceptions, for it does not appear right that this eve (Thursday night) should be spent in neglect, and that there should be an omission (on Friday) of returning thanks to the True Benefactor. On the day of Thursday and on the day of Sunday I do not eat

Price's Jahāngīr, filuniya, misread there as Kelourica, is described by Jahāngīr as brother's son to *tiryāq*, i.e. theriaca (see Price, p. 6). *Tiryāk* or *ṭiryāq* is supposed to be a Greek word (see Lane), and means an antidote against poison, etc. It is so used in the verse from Avicenna quoted by Jahāngīr to his son Shāh Jahān. See D'Herbelot, s.v. *Teriak*. But it is also often used apparently as a synonym for opium. The mixing of wine with spirits was intended to dilute the potation, for hitherto Jahāngīr had been taking raw spirit. A *misqāl* is said to be 63½ grains troy, and so 18 misqals would be about 3 ounces, and the six cups would be about 1½ lb. troy. In Elliot, Jahāngīr is made to say that he does not drink on Thursdays and Fridays. But the *shab-i-jum'a*, as Blochmann has pointed out elsewhere, Āyīn translation, p. 171, n. 3, means Thursday night or Friday eve, and this is clearly the case here, for Jahāngīr speaks of the eve's being followed by a blessed day. It should be noted that there is no connection in Jahāngīr's mind between abstaining from wine and abstaining from meat. He did not eat meat on Thursdays or Sundays because he did not approve of taking life on these days, but he drank on both of them.

[1] Cf. Blochmann's translation and *Calcutta Review* for 1869.

[2] I understand the two exceptions (*dū chīz*) to be that on Thursdays he drank in the daytime, contrary to the general rule of only drinking at night, and that on Thursday evenings he did not drink.

meat. Not on Thursday, because it is the day of my auspicious accession, and not on Sunday, because it is the birthday of my revered father, and he greatly honoured and held dear the day. After some time I substituted opium for filuniya. Now that my age has arrived at 46 solar years and 4 months, I eat eight surkhs (a red berry used as a weight) of opium when five gharis of day have passed, and six surkhs after one watch of night.

I gave a jewelled dagger to 'Abdu-llah Khān by the hand of Maqṣūd 'Alī. Shaikh Mūsā, a relation of Qāsim Khān, was dignified with the title of Khān, and promoted to the mansab of 800 personal and 400 horse, and was allowed to go to Bengal. The mansab of Ẓafar Khān was increased to 500 personal and horse, and he was appointed to duty in Bangash. On the same day Muḥammad Ḥusain, brother of Khwāja Jahān, was given the faujdarship of the Sarkar of Ḥiṣṣār and dismissed, his mansab being increased by 200 horse to raise it to 500 personal and 400 horse, with the gift of an elephant. On the 5th Bahman an elephant was conferred on Mīr Mīrān. When the merchant 'Abdu-l-Karīm left Iran for Hindustan, my exalted brother Shāh 'Abbās sent me by his hand a rosary of cornelian from Yemen and a cup of Venetian workmanship, which was very fine and rare. On the 9th of the same month they were laid before me. On the 18th some offerings of many kinds of jewelled ornaments, etc., which Sulṭān Parwīz had sent to me, were laid before me. On the 7th Isfandārmuẕ, Ṣādiq, nephew of I'timādu-d-daulah, who was permanently employed as Bakhshi, was honoured with the title of Khān. I had also conferred this title on Khwāja 'Abdu-l-'Azīz. According to what was right, I called him by the title of 'Abdu-l-'Azīz Khān and Ṣādiq by that of Ṣādiq Khān. On the 10th, Jagat Singh, son of Kunwar Karan, who had obtained leave to go to his native country, when he took leave was presented with 20,000 rupees, a horse, an elephant, a dress of honour, and a special shawl. Five thousand rupees, a horse, and a dress of honour were also given to Haridās Jhālā, who was one of the confidants of the Rānā and tutor to Karan's son. By his hand I also sent a mace of gold (*shashparī*) for the Rānā.

On the 20th of the same month, Rāja Sūraj Singh, son of Rāja Bāso, who on account of the nearness of his dwelling-place to it had been sent with Murtaẓā Khān to capture the fort of Kāngra, came on my summons and waited on me. The aforesaid Khān had entertained certain suspicions with regard to him, and on this account, considering him an undesirable companion, had repeatedly sent petitions to the Court, and wrote things about him until an order was received to summon him.

On the 26th, Niẓāmu-d-dīn Khān came from Multan and waited on me. In the end of this year news of victory and prosperity came in from all sides of my dominions. In the first place, this was with regard to the disturbance of Aḥdād, the Afghan, who for a long time past had been in rebellion in the hill country of Kabul, and round whom many of the Afghans of that neighbourhood had assembled, and against whom from the time of my revered father until now, which is the 10th year after my accession, armies have always been employed. He by degrees was defeated, and, falling into a wretched state, a part of his band was dispersed and a part killed. He took refuge for some time in Charkh, which was a place on which he relied, but Khān Daurān surrounded it and closed the road for entry and exit. When there remained no grass for his beasts or means of living for men in the fortress, he at night brought down his animals from the hills and grazed them on the skirts, and accompanied them himself, in order that he might set an example to his men. At last this intelligence reached K͟hān Daurān. He then appointed a body of his leaders and experienced men to go into ambush on an appointed night in the neighbourhood of Chark͟h. That band went and hid itself at night in places of refuge, and K͟hān Daurān rode on the same day in that direction. When those ill-fated ones brought out their cattle and let them loose to graze, and the ill-conditioned Aḥdād himself passed by the places of ambush with his own band, suddenly a dust rose in front of him. When they enquired it became known that it was K͟hān Daurān. In a state of bewilderment he endeavoured to turn back, and the scouts announced to the aforesaid K͟hān that it was Aḥdād. The K͟hān gave his horse the reins and went at Aḥdād; the men who were in ambush also blocked the road and attacked him. The fight lasted till midday in consequence of the broken nature of the ground and the thickness of the jungle; at last defeat fell on the Afghans and they betook themselves to the hill: about 300 fighting men went to hell and 100 were taken prisoners. Aḥdād could not regain the stronghold and hold on there. Necessarily he turned his face towards Qandahar. The victorious troops, entering Chark͟h, burnt all the places and houses of those ill-fortuned ones, and destroyed and rooted them up from their foundations.

Another [1] piece of news was the defeat of the ill-starred 'Ambar and the destruction of his unfortunate army. Briefly, a band of the influential leaders and a body of Bargīs (Mahrattas), who are a hardy lot and who are the centre of resistance in that country, becoming angry with 'Ambar, showed an intention to be loyal, and begging for quarter from S͟hāh-nawāz K͟hān, who was in Bālāpūr with an army of royal troops, agreed to interview the said K͟hān, and being satisfied, Ādam K͟hān, Yāqūt K͟hān,

[1] Elliot, vi, 343.

and other leaders, and the Bargīs Jādo[1] Rāy and Bāpū Kāṭiyā, came and interviewed him. S̲h̲āh-nawāz K̲h̲ān gave each of them a horse, an elephant, money, and dress of honour, according to their quality and condition, made them hot in duty and loyalty, and marching from Balapur started against the rebel ʿAmbar in their company. On the road they fell in with an army of the Dakhanis, whose leaders were Maḥalldār,[2] Dānis̲h̲ (Ātas̲h̲ ?), Dilāwar, Bijlī, Fīrūz, and others, and routed it.

> "With broken arms and loosened loins,
> No strength in their feet, no sense in their heads."[3]

They reached the camp of that ill-starred one, and he from excessive pride determined to fight with the victorious troops. Having collected those rebels who were with him and ʿĀdil K̲h̲ān's army and that of Quṭbu-l-mulk together, and preparing their artillery, he started to meet the royal troops until a space of not more than 5 or 6 kos remained between. On Sunday, the 25th Bahman, the armies of light and darkness approached each other and the scouts became visible. Three watches of day had passed when cannon and rocket firing began. In the end Dārāb K̲h̲ān, who was in command of the vanguard, with other leaders and zealous men such as Rāja Bīr Singh Deo, Rāy Chand, ʿAlī K̲h̲ān the Tatar, Jahāngīr Qulī Beg Turkmān, and other lions of the forest of bravery, drew their swords and charged the vanguard of the enemy. Performing the dues of manliness and bravery, they scattered this army like the Banātu-n-naʿs̲h̲ ('Daughters of the Bier,' i.e. the Great Bear); and not stopping there they attacked

[1] The MSS. have Jādūn Rāy and Bāba Chokanth (Jīū Kanth ?). The Ma'āṣiru-l-umarā, ii, 646, has Mālūjī Kāntiya. The text has Bābū Kāntiya.

[2] The text is corrupt. The Ma'āṣir, id., has Ātas̲h̲ instead of Dānis̲h̲.

[3] The text is corrupt. In the second line of the verse the text has *guft*, which seems meaningless, and two I.O. MSS. and B.M. MS. Add. 26,215 have *jang*, 'battle.' The R.A.S. MS. has *pāy*, 'feet,' which seems to me the best reading. Possibly *guft* should be read *kift*, 'shoulder.'

the enemy's centre. Turning on the army opposed to them, such a hand-to-hand struggle took place that the onlookers remained bewildered. For nearly two gharis this combat went on. Heaps of the dead lay there, and the ill-starred 'Ambar, unable to offer further opposition, turned his face to flight. If darkness[1] and gloom had not come on at the cry of those black-fortuned ones, not one of them would have found the road to the valley of safety. The crocodiles of the river of conflict followed the fugitives for 2 or 3 kos. When horses and men could move no more and the defeated were scattered, they drew rein and returned to their places. The whole of the enemy's artillery, with 300 laden camels that carried rockets, war elephants, Arab and Persian horses, weapons and armour beyond reckoning, fell into the hands of the servants of the State, and there was no counting the slain and the fallen. A great many of the leaders fell alive into their hands. The next day the victorious troops, marching from the place of victory, proceeded to Karkī, which was the nest of those owlish ones, and seeing no trace of them they encamped there, and obtained news that they during that night and day had fallen miserably in different places. For some days the victorious army, delayed at Karkī, levelled with the dark earth the buildings and houses of the enemy, and burnt that populous place. In consequence of the occurrence of certain events, to describe which in detail would take too long here, they returned from that place and descended by the Rohan Khanḍa Pass. In reward for this service I ordered increases to be made in the mansabs of a number who had shown zeal and bravery.

The third piece of news was the conquest of the province of Khokharā[1] and the acquisition of the diamond

[1] It will be remembered that Jahāngīr has called 'Ambar's army the army of darkness, alluding perhaps to 'Ambar's being an Abyssinian.

mines, which were taken by the excellent exertions of Ibrāhīm K͟hān. This province is one of the dependencies of the Subah of Behar and Patna. There is a river there from which they procure diamonds. At the season when there is little water, there are pools and water-holes, and it has become known by experience to those who are employed in this work that above every water-hole in which there are diamonds, there are crowds of flying animals of the nature of gnats, and which in the language of India they call *jhīngā* (?).[2] Keeping the bed of the stream in sight as far as it is accessible, they make a collection of stones (*sangchīn*) round the water-holes. After this they empty the water-holes with spades and shovels to the extent of a yard or 1½ yards and dig up the area. They find among the stones and sand large and small diamonds[3] and bring them out. It occasionally happens that they find a piece of diamond worth 100,000 rupees. Briefly, this province and this river were in possession of a Hindu Zamindar of the name of Durjan Sāl, and although the governors of the Subah frequently sent armies against him and went there themselves, in consequence of the difficult roads and thickness of the jungles they contented themselves with taking two or three diamonds and left him in his former condition. When the aforesaid Subah was transferred from Ẓafar K͟hān, and Ibrāhīm K͟hān was

[1] Elliot, vi, and Blochmann, p. 479, n. 3.

[2] Perhaps it should be *phangā* or *feringha*, a grasshopper, or it may be *jhīngur*, a cockroach. Presumably the country was covered with thick jungle, and the cloud of insects indicated where water was. Erskine's MS. has *chika*. B.M. Or. 3276 has *chika* or *jika*. Possibly the word is *jhīngur*, a cockroach (see Blochmann in J.A.S.B. for 1871, vol. xl). He quotes a Hindustani Dict., which says that the *jhīngā* is what in Arabic is called the *jarādu-l-baḥr* or water-locust. The river referred to by Jahāngīr is the Sankh of I.G., xii, 222. V. Ball, Proc. A.S.B. for 1881, p. 42, suggests that the *jhīngā* may be thunder-stones !

[3] Compare Tavernier's account of the searching for diamonds in Sambhalpur (vol. ii, p. 311, of ed. of 1676).

appointed in his place, at the time of his taking leave I ordered him to go and take the province out of the possession of that unknown and insignificant individual. As soon as he arrived in the province of Behar he assembled a force and went against that Zamindar. According to former custom he sent some of his men with a promise to give some diamonds and some elephants, but the K͟hān did not agree to this and entered impetuously into the province. Before the fellow could collect his men he found guides and invaded it. Just when the zamindar received this news, the hills and vales that are his abode were beleaguered. Ibrāhīm sent men about to find him, and they got hold of him in a cave with several women, one of whom was his mother, while others were also his father's wives. They arrested him, and also one of his brothers. They searched and took from them the diamonds they had with them. Twenty-three male and female elephants also fell into Ibrāhīm's hands. In reward for this service the mansab of Ibrāhīm K͟hān, original and increase, was made up to 4,000 personal and horse, and he was exalted with the title of Fatḥ-jang. Orders were also given for an increase in the mansabs of those who accompanied him on this service and had shown bravery. That province is now in possession of the imperial servants of the State. They carry on work in the bed of the stream, and bring to Court whatever diamonds are found. A large diamond, the value of which has been estimated at 50,000 rupees, has lately been brought from there. If a little pains are taken, it is probable that good diamonds will be found and be placed in the jewel-room.

The Eleventh New Year's Feast after the auspicious Accession.

Fifteen gharis of day had passed on Sunday, the last day of Isfandārmuz̤, corresponding with the 1st Rabīʻu-l-awwal (19th March, 1616), when from the mansion of Pisces the sun cast the ray of prosperity on the palace of Aries. At this auspicious hour, having performed the dues of service and supplication at the throne of Almighty God, I ascended the throne of State in the public audience hall, the area of which was laid out with tents and canopies (*s̲h̲āmiyānahā*), and its sides adorned with European screens, painted gold brocades, and rare cloths. The princes, Amirs, the chief courtiers, the ministers of State, and all the servants of the Court performed their congratulatory salutations. As Ḥāfiẓ Nād ʻAlī, *gūyanda* (singer), was one of the ancient servants, I ordered that whatever offerings were made on the Monday by anyone in the shape of cash or goods should be given to him by way of reward. On the 2nd day (of Farwardīn) the offerings of some of the employés were laid before me. On the 4th day the offering of K̲h̲wāja Jahān, who had sent them from Agra, and which consisted of several diamonds and pearls, of jewelled things, cloth stuffs of all kinds, and an elephant, worth altogether 50,000 rupees, was brought before me. On the 5th day, Kunwar Karan, who had been given leave to go to his home, returned and waited on me. He presented as offering 100 muhrs, 1,000 rupees, an elephant with fittings, and four horses. To the mansab of Āṣaf K̲h̲ān, which was 4,000 personal and 2,000 horse, I on the 7th made an addition of 1,000 personal and 2,000 horse, and honoured him with drums and a standard. On this day the offering of Mīr Jamālu-d-dīn Ḥusain was laid before me; what he offered was approved and accepted. Among the things was a jewelled dagger which had been made under his superintendence.[1] On its hilt was a yellow ruby [2] (*yāqūt-i-zard*), exceeding clear and bright, in size equal to half a hen's egg. I had never before seen so large and beautiful a yellow ruby. Along with it were other rubies of approved colour and old emeralds. Brokers (*muqīmān*) valued it (the dagger) at 50,000 rupees. I increased the mansab of the said Mīr by 1,000 horse, which brought it to 5,000 personal and 3,500 horse. On the 8th I increased the mansab of Ṣādiq Ḥāẕiq by 300 personal and horse, and that of Irādat Khān by 300 personal and 200 horse, so as to raise each to 1,000 personal and 500 horse. On the 9th the offering of Khwāja Abū-l-ḥasan was laid before me; of jewelled ornaments and cloth stuffs, what was of the value of 40,000 rupees was accepted, and the remainder I made a present to him. The offering of Tātār Khān Bakāwul-begī, consisting of one ruby (*la'l*), one *yāqūt*, a jewelled *takhtī* (signet?), two rings, and some cloths, was accepted. On the 10th three elephants which Rāja Mahā Singh sent from the Deccan, and 100 and odd pieces of gold brocade, etc., which Murtaẕā Khān sent from Lahore, were laid before me. On this date Dayānat Khān presented his offering of two pearl rosaries, two rubies, six large pearls, and one gold tray, to the value of 28,000 rupees. At the end of Thursday, the 11th, I went to the house of I'timādu-d-daulah in order to add to his dignity. He then presented me with his offering, and I examined it in detail. Much of it was exceedingly rare. Of jewels there were two pearls worth 30,000 rupees, one *quṭbī* ruby which had been purchased for 22,000 rupees, with other pearls and rubies.

[1] Text, *khūd-hunarkārī*, 'his own workmanship,' but the MSS. have *khūd-sarkārī*. See also Iqbāl-nāma, p. 87, which says that Jamālu-d-dīn had had it made in Bījāpūr.

[2] Really a topaz. Tavernier points out that the natives call various precious stones rubies, distinguishing them by their colour.

Altogether the value was 110,000 rupees. These had the honour of acceptance, and of cloth, etc., the value of 15,000 rupees was taken. When I had finished inspecting the offering I passed nearly one watch of the night in conviviality and enjoyment. I ordered that cups (of wine) should be given to the Amirs and servants. The ladies of the *maḥall* (harem) were also with me, and a pleasant assembly was held. After the festive assembly was over I begged I'timādu-d-daulah to excuse me, and went to the hall of audience. On the same day I ordered Nūr-maḥall Begam to be called Nūr-Jahān Begam. On the 12th the offering of I'tibār K͟hān was laid before me. They had made a vessel (*ẓarf*) in the form of a fish, jewelled with beautiful gems, exceedingly well shaped and calculated to hold my allowance.[1] This, with other jewels and jewelled things and cloth stuffs, the value of which was worth 56,000 rupees, I accepted and gave back the rest. Bahādur K͟hān, governor of Qandahar, had sent seven Iraq horses and nine *tuqūz* (81 ?) of cloth stuffs. The offerings of Irādat K͟hān and Rāja Sūraj Mal, son of Rāja Bāso, were laid before me on the 13th. 'Abdu-s-Subḥān, who held a mansab of 1,200 personal and 600 horse, was promoted to 1,500 personal and 700 horse. On the 15th the Subahdarship of the province of Thatha was transferred from S͟hams͟hīr K͟hān Ūzbeg to Muẓaffar K͟hān. On the 16th the offering of I'tiqād K͟hān, son of I'timādu-d-daulah, was laid before me. Of this the equivalent of 32,000 rupees was taken, and I gave back the rest to him. On the 17th the offering of Tarbiyat K͟hān was inspected. Of jewels and cloth what was valued at 17,000 rupees was approved. On the 18th I went to the house of Āṣaf K͟hān, and his offering was presented to me there. From the palace

[1] Text, *ba-andāza-i-mu'tād-i-man*, 'of capacity corresponding to my custom.' Presumably it was a drinking-cup, and held Jahāngīr's customary potation.

to his house was a distance of about a kos. For half the distance he had laid down under foot velvet woven with gold and gold brocade and plain velvet, such that its value was represented to me as 10,000 rupees. I passed that day until midnight at his house with the ladies. The offerings he had prepared were laid before me in detail. Jewels, jewelled ornaments, and things of gold and beautiful cloth stuffs, things of the value of 114,000 rupees, four horses, and one camel were approved of. On the 19th (Farwardīn), which was the day of honour (*rūz-i-sharaf*) of the sun, a grand assembly was held in the palace. In order to observe the auspicious hour, when 2½ gharis of day were left of the aforesaid day, I seated myself on the throne. My son Bābā Khurram at this blessed hour laid before me a ruby of the purest water and brilliancy, which they pronounced to be of the value of 80,000 rupees. I fixed his mansab, which was 15,000 personal and 8,000 horse, at 20,000 personal and 10,000 horse. On the same day my lunar weighing took place. I increased the mansab of I'timādu-d-daulah, which was 6,000 personal and 3,000 horse, to 7,000 personal and 5,000 horse, and bestowed on him a *tūmān tūgh* (horse-tail standard), and ordered his drums to be beaten after those of my son Khurram. I increased the mansab of Tarbiyat Khān by 500 personal and horse, so as to bring it to 3,500 personal and 1,500 horse. The mansab of I'tiqād Khān was increased by 1,000 personal and 400 horse. Niẓāmu-d-dīn Khān was promoted to 700 personal and 300 horse, and appointed to the Subah of Behar. Salāmu-llah, the Arab, was honoured with the title of Shajā'at Khān, and, being dignified with a necklace of pearls, became one of the royal[1] servants. I promoted Mīr Jamālu-d-dīn Injū to the title of 'Aẓudu-d-daulah (Arm of the State). On the

[1] *Ḥalqa-ba-gūshān.* Apparently referring to his being one of those who bored their ears in imitation of Jahāngīr.

21st Almighty God gave Khusrau a son by the daughter of Muqīm, son of Mihtar Fāẓil Rikāb-dār (stirrup-holder). To Allah-dād, the Afghan, who, accepting my service, had separated himself from the evil-minded Aḥdād and come to Court, I gave 20,000 darabs (10,000 rupees). On the 25th came the news of the death of Rāy Manohar, who had been attached to the army of the Deccan. Giving his son a mansab of 500 personal and 300 horse, I bestowed upon him his father's place and property. On the 26th the offering of Nād 'Alī Maidānī, consisting of nine horses, several bits (? *dahāna kīsh*[1]), and four Persian camels (*wilāyatī*), was brought before me. On the 28th I presented Bahādur Khān, governor of Qandahar, Mīr Mīrān, son of Khalīlu-llah, and Sayyid Bāyazīd, governor of Bhakar, each with an elephant. On the 1st Urdībihisht, at the request of 'Abdu-llah Khān, I presented drums to his brother Sardār Khān. On the 3rd I gave Allah-dād Khān, the Afghan, a jewelled *khapwa* (dagger). On the same day news came that Qadam,[2] one of the Afrīdī Afghans who had been loyal and obedient, and to whom the *rāh-dārī* (transit dues) of the Khaibar Pass belonged, from some slight suspicion had withdrawn his feet from the circle of obedience and raised his head in sedition. He had sent a force against each of the posts (*thāna*), and wherever he and his men went, through the carelessness of those men (in the posts), had plundered and killed many of the people. Briefly, in consequence of the shameful action of this senseless Afghan, a new disturbance broke out in the hill country of Kabul. When this news arrived I ordered Hārūn, brother of Qadam, and Jalāl, his son, who were at Court, to be apprehended and handed over to Āṣaf Khān to be imprisoned in the fort of Gwalior. By the

[1] The text is corrupt. The true reading seems to be *ṣad dāna-i-kīsh*, 'one hundred pieces of muslin' (?). I.O. 181 seems to have *kabsh*, 'rams.'

[2] Here follow two unintelligible words, *Pagāna Bankāna*.

manifestation of the Divine mercy and kindness and the signs of God's favour, an affair took place at this time which is not devoid of strangeness. After the victory over the Rānā my son presented me in Ajmir with an exceedingly beautiful and clear ruby, valued at 60,000 rupees. It occurred to me that I ought to bind this ruby on my own arm. I much wanted two rare pearls of good water of one form to be a fit match for this kind of ruby. Muqarrab K͟hān had procured one grand pearl of the value of 20,000 rupees, and given it to me as a New Year's offering. It occurred to me that if I could procure a pair to it they would make a perfect bracelet. K͟hurram, who from his childhood had had the honour of waiting on my revered father, and remained in attendance on him day and night, represented to me that he had seen a pearl in an old turban (*sar-band*) of a weight and shape equal to this pearl. They produced an old *sar-pīch* (worn on the turban), containing a royal pearl of the same quality, weight, and shape, not differing in weight even by a trifle, so much so that the jewellers were astonished at the matter. It agreed in value, shape, lustre, and brilliance; one might say they had been shed from the same mould. Placing the two pearls alongside of the ruby, I bound them on my arm, and placing my head on the ground of supplication and humility, I returned thanks to the Lord that cherished His slave, and made my tongue utter His praise—

> "Who succeeds with hand and tongue?
> He who performs the dues of thanks."

On the 5th (Urdībihis͟ht) 30 Iraq and Turki horses that Murtaẓā K͟hān had sent from Lahore were brought before me, as also 63 horses, 15 camels, male and female, a bundle of crane's (*kulang*) plumes, 9 *'āqirī* (?),[1]

[1] Perhaps this should be *fag͟hfūrī*, 'porcelain.'

9 veined[1] fish-teeth, 9 pieces of china from Tartary, 3 guns, etc., from K͟hān Daurān, which he had sent from Kabul, were accepted. Muqarrab K͟hān presented an offering of a small elephant from Abyssinia which they had brought by sea in a ship. In comparison with the elephants of Hindustan it presents some peculiarities. Its ears are larger than the ears of the elephants of this place, and its trunk and tail are longer. In the time of my revered father I'timād K͟hān of Gujarat sent a young elephant[2] as an offering; by degrees it grew up and was very fiery and bad-tempered. On the 7th a jewelled dagger was given to Muẓaffar K͟hān, governor of Thatha. On the same day news came that a band of Afghans[3] had attacked 'Abdu-s-Subḥān, brother of K͟hān 'Ālam, who was stationed at one of the posts, and had laid siege to his post. 'Abdu-s-Subḥān, with certain other mansabdars and servants who had been appointed to go with him, had behaved valiantly. But at last, in accordance with the saying—

"When gnats get wings they smite the elephant,"

those dogs overcame them, and elevated 'Abdu-s-Subḥān with several of the men of the post to the dignity of martyrdom.[4] As a condolence for this affair a gracious farman and a special dress of honour were sent to K͟hān 'Ālam, who had been appointed ambassador to Iran (and was still in that country). On the 14th the offering of Mukarram K͟hān, son of Mu'aẓẓam K͟hān, came from Bengal. It consisted of jewels and articles procurable in that province, and was brought before me. I increased the mansab of some of the jagirdars of Gujarat. Of these,

[1] *Jauhar-dār,* defined by Vullers as bone or wood bearing veins, i.e. striated.

[2] See Akbar-nāma, ii, 315. It was sent before Jahāngīr was born. It, too, was an African elephant.

[3] Here the two words referred to at note 2 on p. 321 are repeated.

[4] Ma'āṣiru-l-umarā, i, 736. K͟hān 'Ālam's name was Mīrzā Bark͟hūrdār.

Sardār Khān, whose mansab was that of 1,000 personal and 500 horse, was raised to 1,500 personal and 300[1] horse, and had a standard given to him as well. Sayyid Qāsim, son of Sayyid Dilāwar Bārha, was raised to an original and increased mansab of 800 personal and 450 horse, and Yār Beg, nephew of Aḥmad Qāsim Koka, to one of 600 personal with 250 horse. On the 17th there came the news of the death of Razzāq of Merv, the Ūzbeg who belonged to the army of the Deccan. He was well skilled in war, and one of the distinguished Amirs of Māwarā'a-n-nahr. On the 21st, Allah-dād, the Afghan, was honoured with the title of Khān, and his mansab, which was 1,000 personal and 600 horse, was raised to 2,000 personal and 1,000 horse. Three hundred thousand rupees out of the treasury of Lahore were ordered as a reward and for expenses to Khān Daurān, who had greatly exerted himself in the Afghan disturbance. On the 28th, Kunwar Karan obtained leave to go home for his marriage. I conferred on him a dress of honour, a special Iraq horse with a saddle, an elephant, and a jewelled waist-dagger. On the 3rd of this month (Khūrdād) the news of the death of Murtaẓā Khān came. He was one of the ancients of this State. My revered father had brought him up and raised him to a position of consequence and trust. In my reign also he obtained the grace of noteworthy service, namely, the overthrow of Khusrau. His mansab had been raised to 6,000 personal and 5,000 horse. As he was at this time Subahdar of the Panjab, he had undertaken the capture of Kāngra, to which in strength no other fort in the hill country of that province or even in the whole inhabited world can be compared. He had obtained leave to go on this duty. I was much grieved in mind at this news; in truth, grief at the death of such

[1] This seems wrong; the number of horse would probably not be reduced.

a loyal follower is only reasonable. As he had died after spending his days in loyalty, I prayed to God for pardon for him. On the 4th Khūrdād the mansab of Sayyid Niẓām was fixed, original and increase, at 900 personal and 650 horse. I gave Nūru-d-dīn Qulī the post of entertainer to the ambassadors from all parts. On the 7th news came of the death of Saif Khān Bārha; he was a brave and ambitious young man. He had exerted himself in an exemplary way in the battle with Khusrau. He bade farewell to this perishable world in the Deccan through cholera (*haiẓa*). I conferred favours on his sons. 'Alī Muḥammad, who was the eldest and most upright of his children, was given the mansab of 300 [1] personal and 400 horse, and his ('Alī Muḥammad's) brother, by name Bahādur, that of 400 personal and 200 horse. Sayyid 'Alī, who was his nephew, received an increase in rank of 500 personal and horse. On the same day Khūb-Allah, son of Shāh-bāz Khān Kambū, received the title of Ran-bāz Khān. On the 8th [2] the mansab of Hāshim Khān, original and increase, was fixed at 2,500 personal and 1,800 horse. On this date I bestowed 20,000 *darabs* (10,000 rupees) on Allah-dād Khān, the Afghan. Bikramājīt, Raja of the province of Bāndhū, whose ancestors were considerable zamindars in Hindustan, through the patronage of my fortunate son Bābā Khurram, obtained the blessing of paying his respects to me, and his offences were pardoned. On the 9th, [3] Kalyān of Jesalmīr, to summon whom Rāja Kishan Dās had gone, came and waited on me. He presented 100 muhrs and 1,000 rupees. His elder brother Rāwal Bhīm was a person of distinction. When he died he left a son 2 months old, and he too did not live

[1] So in text, but No. 181 has 600, and this is more likely, for the number of horse is never, I think, larger than the *zāt* rank.

[2] I.O. MSS. have 18th.

[3] I.O. MSS. have 20th.

long. In the time when I was prince I had taken his daughter in marriage, and called her by the title of Malika-Jahān[1] (queen of the world). As the ancestors of this tribe had come of ancient loyal people, this alliance took place. Having summoned the aforesaid Kalyān, who was the brother of Rāwal Bhīm, I exalted[2] him with the *ṭīka* of Rāja and the title of Rāwal. News came that after the death of Murtaẓā Khān loyalty was shown by Rāja Mān, and that, after giving encouragement to the men of the fort of Kāngra, an arrangement had been made that he should bring to Court the son of the Raja of that country, who was 29 years old. In consequence of his great zeal in this service, I fixed his mansab, which was 1,000 personal and 800 horse, at 1,500 personal and 1,000 horse. Khwāja Jahān was promoted from his original and increased mansab to that of 4,000 personal and 2,500 horse. On this date[3] an event occurred such that, although I was greatly desirous of writing it down, my hand and heart have failed me. Whenever I took my pen my state became bewildered, and I helplessly ordered I'timādu-d-daulah to write it.

"An ancient sincere slave, I'timādu-d-daulah, by order writes in this auspicious volume[4] that on the 11th[5] Khūrdād the traces of fever were seen in the pure daughter[6] of Shāh Khurram of lofty fortune, for whom His Majesty showed much affection as the early fruit of

[1] The two I.O. MSS. have the following sentence here: "On this day it happened that however much I tried to write, my heart and hand would not act. Whenever I seized the pen my condition altered. At last I had to tell I'timādu-d-daulah to write."

[2] This sentence is not in the I.O. MSS.

[3] Here comes the passage which the two I.O. MSS. enter higher up.

[4] I.O. MS. 181 has "writes that on the 11th," etc.

[5] The I.O. MSS. add here "of the 11th year."

[6] Probably this is the Chimnī Begam, a daughter of Shāh Jahān, whose grave is near that of the saint Khwāja Mu'inu-d-dīn Chishtī ("Rajputana Gazetteer," ii, 62). Probably Chimnī should be Chamanī, which means 'verdant' and comes from *chaman*, a garden. Perhaps she died of smallpox. It was in the summer.

the garden of auspiciousness. After three days pustules (*ābila*) appeared, and on the 26th of the same month, corresponding with Wednesday, the 29th Jumādā-l-awwal (15th June, 1616), in the year 1025, the bird of her soul flew from her elemental cage and passed into the gardens of Paradise. From this date an order was given that Chār-shamba (Wednesday) should be called Kam-shamba (or *Gum-shamba*). What shall I write as to what happened to the pure personality of the shadow of God in consequence of this heartburning event and grief-increasing calamity? Inasmuch as it happened after this manner to that soul of the world, what must be the condition of those other [1] servants whose life was bound up with that pure personality? For two days the servants were not received in audience, and an order was given that a wall should be built in front of the house which had been the abode of that bird of paradise, so that it might not be seen. In addition to this he did not adorn the gate of the hall of audience (did not come there). On the third day he went in an agitated state to the house of the illustrious prince, and the servants had the good fortune to pay their salutations and found fresh life. On the road, however much the Ḥaẓrat (the Emperor) desired to control himself, the tears flowed from the auspicious eyes, and for a long time it was so that at the mere hearing of a word from which came a whiff of pain, the state of the Ḥaẓrat became bewildered. He remained for some days in the house of the prince of the inhabitants of the world, and on Monday [2] of Tīr, Divine month, he went to the house of Āṣaf Khān, and turned back thence to the Chashma-i-Nūr, and for two or

[1] Apparently the reference is to the parents of the child and to the grandfather, that is, the writer of this notice.

[2] I.O. MSS. have Monday, the 6th Tīr, and say that Jahāngīr went to Chashma-i-Nūr on the 9th, which they say was a Thursday. And we see later that Jahāngīr speaks of Saturday as the 11th.

three days employed himself there. But as long as he was in Ajmir he could not control himself. Whenever the word 'friendship' reached his ear, the tears would drop from his eyes unrestrained, and the hearts of his faithful followers were torn in pieces. When the departure of the cortège of fortune to the Subah of the Deccan took place, he gained a little composure."

On this date Prithī Chand, son of Rāy Manohar, obtained the title of Ray and the mansab of 500 personal and 400 horse, and a jagir in his native place. On Saturday, the 11th, I went from the Chashma-i-Nūr to the palace at Ajmir. On the eve of Sunday, the 12th, after 37 seconds had passed, at the time of the ascension of Sagittarius to the 27th degree, by the calculations of the Hindu astronomers, and the 15th degree of Capricorn, by the calculations of the Greeks, there came from the womb of the daughter of Āṣaf Khān (wife of Khurram) a precious pearl into the world of being. With joy and gladness at this great boon the drums beat loudly, and the door of pleasure and enjoyment was opened in the face of the people. Without delay or reflection the name of Shāh Shajā'at came to my tongue. I hope that his coming will be auspicious and blessed to me and to his father. On the 12th a jewelled dagger[1] and an elephant were bestowed on Rāwal Kalyān of Jesalmīr. On the same day arrived the news of the death of Khawāṣṣ Khān, whose jagir was in the Sarkar of Qanauj. I gave an elephant to Rāy Kunwar, Diwan of Gujarat. On the 22nd of the same month (Tīr) I added 500 personal and horse to the mansab of Rāja Mahā Singh, so as to make it one of 4,000 personal and 3,000 horse. The mansab of 'Alī Khān Tatārī, who before this had been exalted with the title of Nuṣrat Khān, was fixed at 2,000 personal and 500 horse, and

[1] The word 'dagger' is omitted in the text.

a standard was also conferred on him. With a view to the accomplishment of certain purposes, I had made a vow that they should place a gold railing with lattice-work at[1] the enlightened tomb of the revered Khwāja. On the 27th of this month it was completed, and I ordered them to take and affix it. It had been made at a cost of 110,000 rupees. As the command and leading of the victorious army of the Deccan had not been carried out to my satisfaction by my son Sulṭān Parwīz, it occurred to me to recall him, and send Bābā Khurram as the advanced guard of the victorious army, inasmuch as the signs of rectitude and knowledge of affairs were evident in him, and that I myself would follow him, so that this important matter would be carried through in one and the same campaign. With this object a farman had already been sent in the name of Parwīz ordering him to start for the Subah of Allahabad, which is in the centre of my dominions. Whilst I was engaged in the campaign, he would be entrusted with the guarding and administration of that region. On the 29th of the same month a letter came from Bihārī Dās, the news-writer of Burhānpūr, that the prince on the 20th had left the city safely and well and gone towards the aforesaid Subah. On the 1st Amurdād I bestowed a jewelled turban on Mīrzā Rāja Bhāo Singh. An elephant was conferred on the shrine of Kushtīgīr. On the 18th, Lashkar Khān had sent four ambling (*rāhwār*) horses, and they were brought before me. Mīr Mughal was appointed to the faujdarship of the Sarkar of Sambal in the place of Sayyid 'Abdu-l-Wāriṣ, who had obtained the governorship of the Subah of Qanauj in the place of Khawāṣṣ Khān. His mansab, in view of that duty, was fixed at 500 personal and horse. On the 21st the offering of Rāwal Kalyān of Jesalmīr was laid before

[1] I.O. MSS. have *bar daur*, 'round.'

me; it was 3,000 muhrs, 9 horses, 25 camels, and 1 elephant. The mansab of Qizil-bāsh Khān was fixed, original and increase, at 1,200 personal and 1,000 horse. On the 23rd, Shajā'at Khān obtained leave to go to his jagir that he might arrange the affairs of his servants and his territory, and present himself at the time agreed upon. In this year,[1] or rather in the 10th year after my accession, a great pestilence appeared in some places in Hindustan. The commencement of this calamity was in the parganahs of the Panjab, and by degrees the contagion spread to the city of Lahore. Many of the people, Musulmans and Hindus, died through this. After this it spread to Sirhind and the Dū'āb, until it reached Delhi and the surrounding parganahs and villages, and desolated them. At this day it had greatly diminished. It became known from men of great age and from old histories that this disease had never shown itself in this country[2] (before). Physicians and learned men were questioned as to its cause. Some said that it came because there had been drought for two years in succession and little rain fell; others said it was on account of the corruption of the air which occurred through the drought and scarcity. Some attributed it to other causes. Wisdom is of Allah, and we must submit to Allah's decrees!

"What does a slave who bows not his neck to the order?"

On 5th Shahrīwar 5,000 rupees towards her expenses were sent to the mother of Mīr Mīrān, the daughter of Shāh Isma'īl II, by merchants who were proceeding to the province of Iraq. On the 6th a letter came from 'Ābid Khān,[3] bakhshi and news-writer of Ahmadabad,

[1] Elliot, vi, 346. There is a better account of the plague in the Iqbāl-nāma, pp. 88, 89.

[2] The words are *dar wilāyat*, and may mean 'any country' or 'any foreign country.'

[3] The son of the historian Niẓāmu-d-dīn. Sir T. Roe refers to this affair.

to the purport that 'Abdu-llah Khān Bahādur Fīrūz-jang had quarrelled with him because he had recorded among (current) events certain affairs that had been unpleasing to him, and had sent a body of men against him, and had insulted him by carrying him away to his house, and had done this and that to him. This matter appeared serious to me, and I was desirous at once to cast him out of favour and ruin him. At last it occurred to me to send Dayānat Khān to Ahmadabad to enquire into this matter on the spot from disinterested people to see if it had actually occurred, and, if so, to bring 'Abdu-llah Khān with him to the Court, leaving the charge and administration of Ahmadabad to Sardār Khān, his brother. Before Dayānat Khān started, the news reached Fīrūz-jang, and he in a state of great perturbation confessed himself an offender and started for the Court on foot. Dayānat Khān met him on the road, and seeing him in a strange condition, as he had wounded his feet with walking, he put him on horseback, and taking him with him came to wait on me. Muqarrab Khān, who is one of the old servants of the Court, from the time when I was a prince had continually wanted the Subah of Gujarat. It thus occurred to me that, as this kind of action on the part of 'Abdu-llah Khān had come about, I might fulfil the hope of an ancient servant and send him to Ahmadabad in the place of the aforesaid Khān. A fortunate hour was chosen in these days, and I appointed him to be ruler of the Subah. On the 10th the mansab of Bahādur Khān, governor of Qandahar, which was 4,000 personal and 3,000 horse, was increased by 500 personal.

Shauqī, the mandolin player, is the wonder of the age. He also sings Hindi and Persian songs in a manner that clears the rust from all hearts. I delighted him with the title of Ānand Khān: Ānand in the Hindi language means pleasure and ease.

Mangoes[1] used not to be in season in the country of Hindustan after the month of Tīr (June–July), (but) Muqarrab Khān had established gardens in the parganah of Kairāna,[2] which is the native place of his ancestors, and looked after the mangoes there in such a manner as to prolong the season for more than two months, and sent them every day fresh into the special fruit storehouse. As this was altogether an unusual thing to be accomplished, it has been recorded here. On the 8th a beautiful Iraq horse of the name of La'l Bī-bahā (priceless ruby) was sent for Parwīz by the hand of Sharīf, one of his attendants.

I had ordered quick-handed stone-cutters to carve full-sized figures of the Rānā and his son Karan out of marble. On this day they were completed and submitted to me. I ordered them to be taken to Agra and placed in the garden[3] below the *jharoka* (exhibition-window). On the 26th the meeting for my solar weighing was held in the usual manner. The first weight came to 6,514 *tūlcha* of gold. I was weighed twelve times against different things; the second weighing was against quicksilver, the third against silk, the fourth against various perfumes, such as ambergris and musk, down to sandalwood, *'ūd*, *bān*, and so on, until twelve weighings were completed. Of animals, according to the number of

[1] Text *Anand*, but this makes no sense. The I.O. MSS. have *amba*, mangoes, and though the remark seems abrupt this is no doubt the correct reading. Jahāngīr was particularly fond of mangoes, and perhaps he is here playing on the similarity between the words *amba* and *anand*.

[2] In Sarkār Sahāranpur (Jarrett, ii, 292). It is now in the Muzaffarnagar district (I.G., vii, 308).

[3] "It is a pity that no trace of these is left at Agra. Had there been, they would have been the wonder of the age" (note of Sayyid Aḥmad). Perhaps they are the two figures which have generally been supposed to have been put up by Akbar and to represent Chitor heroes. The word *tarkīb* in the text may mean that they were mounted statues. But then the description of them as marble statues would be wrong.

years that I had passed, a sheep, a goat,[1] and a fowl (for each year) were given to fakirs and dervishes. This rule has been observed from the time of my revered father up to the present day in this enduring State. They divide after the weighing all these things among the fakirs and those in need to the value of about 100,000 rupees.

This day a ruby which Mahābat Khān had purchased at Burhanpur for 65,000 rupees from 'Abdu-llah Khān Fīrūz-jang was laid before me, and was approved of. It is a ruby of beautiful form. The special mansab of Khān Ā'ẓam was fixed at 7,000 personal, and an order was passed that the diwani establishment should pay an equivalent to that in a *tankhwāh jāgīr*. At the request of I'timādu-d-daulah, what had been deducted from the mansab of Dayānat on account of former proceedings was allowed to remain as before. 'Aẓudu-d-daulah, who had obtained the Subah of Malwa in jagir, took his leave, and was dignified with the gift of a horse and a dress of honour. The mansab of Rāwal Kalyān of Jesalmir was fixed at 2,000 personal and 1,000 horse,

[1] Text has *gūsfand-i-nar*, 'a ram,' but the MSS. have *gūsfand u bar*, or *buz*, and it is evident that the true reading is 'a sheep, a goat.' See Blochmann, p. 266, where goats are mentioned among the animals distributed by Akbar. The number of animals distributed corresponded with the years of Jahāngīr's age (48) multiplied by 3, and so would be 48 × 3 = 144 (see Blochmann, l.c.). The weight of Jahāngīr was 6,514 tulchas, and Blochmann (p. 267, n.) takes this to be the same as tolas, and estimates Jahāngīr's weight at 210½ lb. troy or 15 stone. Probably this is excessive, and his weight might be 82 sir or about 2 maunds, i.e. 164 lb. or 11½ stone. The perfumes against which he was weighed were ambergris, not amber (which has no scent), '*ūd*, i.e. lignum aloes, and *bān* (not *pān* as in text), which apparently is the same as *lubān*, 'frankincense' (see the chapter on perfumes in Blochmann, p. 77). I am not sure of the meaning of the phrase *ba-dast nihāda*. The MSS. have not the preposition *ba*. Perhaps the meaning is 'put them into the hands of the fakirs.' Jahāngīr was born on the 18th Shahrīwar, 977 = 31st August, 1569. The weighings described in the text took place on the 26th Shahrīwar. Perhaps this was because his birthday was on the 24th Shahrīwar according to the Jalālī year.

and it was ordered that that province (Jesalmir) should be given him as tankhwah. As the (auspicious) hour of his departure was on that same day, he took leave to depart for his province well pleased and exalted with the gift of a horse, an elephant, a jewelled sword, a jewelled *khapwa* (dagger), a robe of honour, and a special Kashmir shawl. On the 31st, Muqarrab K͟hān took leave to go to Ahmadabad, and his mansab, which was 5,000 personal and 2,500 horse, was fixed at 5,000 personal and horse, and he was honoured with a dress of honour, a *nādirī* (a kind of dress), a *takma*[1] of pearls, whilst two horses from my private stable, a special elephant, and a jewelled sword were also bestowed on him. He went off to the aforesaid Subah with delight and in a state of happiness. On the 11th of Mihr, Jagat Singh, son of Kunwar Karan, came from his native place and waited on me. On the 16th, Mīrzā 'Alī Beg Akbar-s͟hāhī came from the province of Oudh, which had been given him in jagir, and waited on me. He presented as offerings 1,000 rupees, and he produced before me an elephant which one of the zamindars of that province possessed, and which he had been ordered to take from him. On the 21st the offering of Quṭbu-l-mulk, the ruler of Golcondah, consisting of some jewelled ornaments, was inspected by me. The mansab of Sayyid Qāsim Bārha was fixed, original and increase, at 1,000 personal and 600 horse. On the eve of Friday, the 22nd, Mīrzā 'Alī Beg, whose age had passed 75 years, gave up the deposit of his life. Great[2] services had been performed by him for this State. His mansab rose by degrees to 4,000. He was one of the distinguished heroes of this

[1] Generally written *taghma*, 'a badge of honour,' 'a medal,' etc.

[2] See Tūzuk, p. 11, Blochmann, p. 482, and Ma'āṣiru-l-umarā, iii, 355. The statement at Tūzuk, p. 11, about Delhi seems a mistake, and is not in the MSS. Mīrzā 'Alī came from Badakhshan. He is frequently mentioned in vol. iii of the Akbar-nāma.

family (*jawānān-i īn ulūs*)[1] and of a noble disposition. He left neither son nor other descendants. He had the poetic temperament. As his inevitable destiny had been fulfilled[2] on the day on which he went to pay his devotions at the venerated mausoleum of K͟hwāja Mu'īnu-d-dīn, I ordered them to bury him in the same blessed place.

At the time when I gave leave to the ambassadors of 'Ādil K͟hān of Bijapur, I had requested that if in that province there were a wrestler, or a celebrated swordsman, they should tell 'Ādil K͟hān to send him to me. After some time, when the ambassadors returned, they brought a Mughal, by name S͟hīr 'Alī, who was born at Bijapur, and was a wrestler by profession and had great experience in the art, together with certain sword-players. The performances of the latter were indifferent, but I put S͟hīr 'Alī to wrestle with the wrestlers and athletes who were in attendance on me, and they could none of them compete with him. One thousand rupees, a dress of honour, and an elephant were conferred on him; he was exceedingly well made, well shaped, and powerful. I retained him in my own service, and entitled him "the athlete of the capital." A jagir and mansab were given him and great favours bestowed on him. On the 24th, Dayānat K͟hān, who had been appointed to bring 'Abdu-llah K͟hān Bahādur Fīrūz-jang, brought him and waited on me, and presented as an offering 100 muhrs. On the same date Rām Dās, the son of Rāja Rāj Singh, one of the Rajput Amirs who had died on duty in the Deccan, was promoted to a mansab of 1,000 personal and 500 horse. As 'Abdu-llah K͟hān had been guilty of faults, he made Bābā K͟hurram his intercessor, and on the 26th, in order to please him, I ordered the former

[1] This is the same phrase as, according to the MSS., occurs at p. 11. Apparently the *ulūs* referred to is the Timuride family to which Jahāngīr belonged. It is connected with Mīrzā 'Alī's title of Akbars͟hāhī.

[2] See in Blochmann, l.c., the affecting story of his death.

to pay his respects to me. He waited upon me with a face of complete shame, and presented as offerings 100 muhrs and 1,000 rupees. Before the coming of ʻĀdil K͟hān's ambassadors I had made up my mind that, having sent Bābā K͟hurram with the vanguard, I should myself proceed to the Deccan and carry out this important affair, which for some reasons had been put off. For this reason I had given an order that except the prince no one should represent to me the affairs of the rulers of the Deccan. On this day the prince brought the ambassadors and laid their representation before me. After the death of Murtaẓā K͟hān, Rāja Mān and many of the auxiliary Sardars had come to Court. On this day, at the request of Iʻtimādu-d-daulah, I appointed Rāja Mān as the leader in the attack on the fort of Kāngṛa. I appointed all the men to accompany him, and according to the condition and rank of each made him happy with a present—a horse, an elephant, a robe of honour, or money—and gave them leave. After some days I conferred on ʻAbdu-llah K͟hān, at the request of Bābā K͟hurram, a jewelled dagger, as he was exceedingly broken-hearted and grieved in mind, and an order was passed that his mansab should continue as it was before, and that he should remain in attendance on my son among those appointed for duty in the Deccan. On the 3rd Ābān I ordered the mansab of Wazīr K͟hān, who was in attendance on Bābā Parwīz, to be, original and increase, 2,000 personal and 1,000 horse. On the 4th, K͟husrau, who was in the charge, for safe keeping, of Anīrā'ī Singh-dalan, for certain considerations was handed over to Āṣaf K͟hān. I presented him with a special shawl. On the 7th (Ābān), corresponding with the 17th S͟hawwāl (28th October, 1616), a person of the name of Muḥammad Riẓā Beg, whom the ruler of Persia had sent as his representative, paid his respects. After performing the dues of prostration and salutation (*kūrnis͟h*, *sijda, taslīm*), he laid before me the letter he had brought. It was decided that he should produce before me the horses and other presents he had brought with him. The written and verbal messages sent were full of friendship, brotherhood, and sincerity. I gave the ambassador on that same day a jewelled tiara (*tāj*) and a dress of honour. As in the letter much friendliness and affection were displayed, an exact copy is recorded in the Jahāngīr-nāma.[1]

On Sunday, the 18th Shawwāl, corresponding to the 8th Ābān,[2] the camp equipage of my son Bābā Khurram left Ajmir for the purpose of the conquest of the provinces of the Deccan, and it was decided that my son aforesaid should start by way of advanced guard, followed by the glorious standards (of Jahāngīr). On Monday, the 19th, corresponding with the 9th Ābān, when three gharis of day had passed, the auspicious palace moved in the same direction in the like manner. On the 10th the mansab of Rāja Sūraj Mal, who had been appointed to accompany the prince, was made up, original and increase, to 2,000 personal and horse. On the night of the 19th Ābān, after my usual custom, I was in the *ghusul-khāna*. Some of the Amirs and attendants, and by chance Muḥammad Riẓā Beg, the ambassador of the ruler of Persia, were present. When six gharis had passed, an owl came and sat on top of a high terrace roof belonging to the palace, and was hardly visible, so that many men failed

[1] This letter being of the usual Persian style, and having nothing to do with Jahāngīr's history, is omitted. It relates to the sending of Muḥammad Ḥusain Chelebī with presents to the emperor, and to the offering his services for the purchase of jewels, etc.

[2] Text 20th Ābān, but the MSS. have 8th, and this is clearly right. By the latter part of the sentence Jahāngīr means that Shāh Jahān was to start first, and that he himself was to leave afterwards. The "auspicious palace" referred to in the next sentence is apparently Shāh Jahān's establishment. Jahāngīr did not leave for about a fortnight. Though Shāh Jahān and the establishment (*daulat-khāna-i-humāyūn*) made a start on the 8th or 9th Ābān, he did not finally leave till the 20th Ābān. See *infra*.

to distinguish it. I sent for a gun and took aim and fired in the direction that they pointed out to me. The gun, like the decree of heaven, fell on that ill-omened bird and blew it to pieces. A shout arose from those who were present, and involuntarily they opened their lips in applause and praise. On the same night I talked with the ambassador of my brother Shāh 'Abbās, and at last the conversation turned on the slaying of Ṣafī Mīrzā, his (the Shah's) eldest son. I asked him because this was a difficulty in my mind. He represented that if his slaughter had not been carried out at that time he would certainly have attempted the Shah's life. As this intention became manifest from his behaviour, the Shah was beforehand with him and ordered him to be killed. On the same day the mansab of Mīrzā Ḥasan, son of Mīrzā Rustam, was fixed, original and increase, at 1,000 personal and 300 horse. The mansab of Mu'tamad Khān,[1] who had been appointed to the post of paymaster of the army with Bābā Khurram, was settled at 1,000 personal and 250 horse. The time for the leave-taking of Bābā Khurram had been fixed as Friday, the 20th (Ābān). At the end of this day he paraded before me the pick of his men armed and ready in the public hall of audience. Of the distinguished favours bestowed on the aforesaid son one was the title of Shāh, which was made a part of his name. I ordered that thereafter he should be styled Shāh Sulṭān Khurram. I presented him with a robe of honour, a jewelled *chārqab,* the fringe and collar of which were decorated with pearls, an Iraq horse with a jewelled saddle, a Turki horse, a special elephant called Bansī-badan,[2] a carriage, according to the English fashion,[3] for him to sit and travel about

[1] Author of Iqbāl-nāma.

[2] 'Of body like Krishna, or like a flute'?

[3] According to Roe, it was not the English carriage, but a copy. Perhaps Jahāngīr had the original carriage and Shāh Jahān the copy.

in, a jewelled sword with a special *pardala* (sword-belt) that had been taken at the conquest of the fort of Ahmadnagar, and was very celebrated, and a jewelled dagger. He started with great keenness. My trust in Almighty God is that in this service he may gain renown (lit. become red-faced). On each of the Amirs and mansabdars, according to his quality and degree, a horse and an elephant were conferred. Loosening a private sword from my own waist, I gave it to 'Abdu-llah Khān Fīrūz-jang. As Dayānat Khān had been appointed to accompany the prince, I gave the duty of *'arẓ-mukarrir* (reviser of petitions) to Khwāja Qāsim Qilīj Khān. Previously[1] to this a band of thieves had carried off a certain sum of money from the royal treasury in the *kotwālī chabūtara* (Police Office). After some days seven men of that band, with their leader, of the name of Nawal, were caught, and a portion of that money was recovered. It occurred to me that as they had been guilty of such boldness I ought to punish them severely. Each was punished in exemplary fashion, and I ordered Nawal, the leader of them all, to be thrown under the feet of an elephant. He petitioned that if I would give the order he would fight the elephant. I ordered it to be so. They produced a very furious elephant. I bade them put a dagger into his hand and bring him in front of the elephant. The elephant several times threw him down, and each time that violent and fearless man, although he witnessed the punishments of his comrades, got up again and bravely and with a stout heart struck the elephant's trunk with the dagger, so that the animal refrained from attacking him. When I had witnessed this pluck and manliness, I ordered them to inquire into his history. After a short time, according to his evil nature and low disposition, he ran away in his longing

[1] Elliot, vi, 346.

for his own place and abode. This annoyed me greatly, and I ordered the jagirdars of that neighbourhood to hunt him up and apprehend him. By chance he was caught a second time, and this time I ordered that ungrateful and unappreciative one to be hanged. The saying of Shaikh Muṣliḥu-d-dīn Sa'dī accords with his case—

> "In the end a wolf's cub becomes a wolf,
> Although he be brought up with man."

On Tuesday,[1] the 1st Zī-l-qa'da (10th November, 1616), corresponding with the 21st Ābān, after two watches and five gharis of the day had passed, in good condition and with a right purpose I mounted the Frank carriage, which had four horses attached to it, and left the city of Ajmir. I ordered many of the Amirs to accompany me in carriages, and at about sunset alighted at a halting-place about 1¾ kos distant, in the village of Deo Rāy (Dorāī?).[2] It is the custom of the people of India that if the movement of kings or great men for the conquest of a country is towards the east they should ride a tusked elephant, and if the movement is towards the west on a horse of one colour; if towards the north in a palanquin or a litter (*singhāsan*), and if towards the south, that is, in the direction of the Deccan (as on this occasion), on a *rath*, which is a kind of cart (*arāba*) or *bahal* (two-wheeled car). I had stayed at Ajmir for five days less than three years.[3] They consider the city of Ajmir, which is the place of the blessed tomb of the revered Khwāja Mu'īnu-d-dīn, to be in the second clime. Its air is nearly equable. The capital of Agra is to the east of it; on the north are the townships (district) of

[1] The day was Saturday, not Tuesday, and it is Saturday in the MSS.

[2] Elliot has Deo Rānī, and it is Deo Rānī in I.O. MS. 305.

[3] Jahāngīr arrived in Ajmir on the 26th Ābān, 1022, and left it on the 21st Ābān, 1025. The Muhammadan dates are 5th Shawwāl, 1022, and 1st Zī-l-qa'da, 1025 = 18th November, 1613, and 10th November, 1616.

Delhi, and on the south the Subah of Gujarat. On the west lie Multan and Deālpūr. The soil of this province is all sandy; water is found with difficulty in the land, and the reliance for cultivation is on moist[1] soil and on the rainfall. The cold season is very equable, and the hot season is milder than in Agra. From this subah in time of war 86,000[2] horse and 304,000 Rajput foot are provided. There are two large lakes in this city; they call one of these the Bīsal[3] and the other the Ānāsāgar. The Bīsal tank is in ruins and its embankment is broken. At this time I ordered it to be repaired. The Ānāsāgar at the time that the royal standards were there was always full of water and waves. This *tāl* is 1½ kos and 5 *ṭanāb* (lit. tent-ropes) (in circumference?). Whilst at Ajmir I visited nine times the mausoleum of the revered Khwāja, and fifteen times went to look at the Pushkar lake; to the Chashma-i-Nūr I went thirty-eight times. I went out to hunt tigers, etc., fifty times. I killed 15 tigers, 1 cheetah, 1 black-ear (lynx), 53 nilgaw, 33 gazelle (*gawazn*), 90 antelope, 80 boars, and 340 water-fowl. I encamped seven times at Deo Rāy (Deo Rānī) (Dorāī?). At this halt 5 nilgaw and 12 water-fowl were killed. Marching on the 29th from Deo Rāy, my camp was pitched at the village of Dāsāwalī, 2 kos and 1½ quarters distant from Deo Rāy. On this day I gave an elephant to Mu'tamad Khān. I stayed the next day at this village. On this day a nilgaw was killed, and I sent two of my falcons to my son Khurram. I marched from this village on the

[1] Text *tar*, but MSS. have *abtar*, i.e. inferior and perhaps low land. The text seems corrupt.

[2] MSS. have 86,500 horse and 347,000 foot, and this agrees with the Āyīn (Jarrett, ii, 272).

[3] Text wrongly has Nīl. The tank in question is the Bīsalya tank of the Rajputana Gazetteer, ii, 4, which was made by Bīsal Deo Chohān about 1050 A.D. It is described in Tod's "Personal Narrative," i, 824, of Calcutta reprint. It is, or was, about 8 miles in circumference and is about a mile west of the Ānāsāgar, which was made by Bīsal Deo's grandson.

3rd Āzar, and pitched at the village of Bādhal (Māwal?), 2¼ kos distant. On the road six water-fowl, etc., were killed. On the 4th, having gone 1½ kos, Rāmsar,[1] which belongs to Nūr-Jahān Begam, became the place for the alighting of honour and glory. A halt was made at this place for eight days. In the place of Khidmat-gār Khān I here appointed Hidāyatu-llah *mīr-tūzak* (master of ceremonies). On the 5th day 7 antelope, 1 kulang (crane), and 15 fish were killed. The next day Jagat Singh, son of Kunwar Karan, received a horse and a robe of honour and took leave for his native place. A horse was also given to Kesho Dās Lālā and an elephant to Allah-dād Khān Afghān. On the same day I killed a gazelle, 3 antelope, 7 fish, and 2 water-fowl. On that day was heard the news of the death of Rāja Syām Singh, who belonged to the army of Bangash. On the 7th day 3 antelope, 5 water-fowl, and a *qashqaldāgh*[2] (coot) were killed. On Thursday and the eve of Friday, as Rāmsar belongs to the jagir of Nūr-Jahān, a feast and entertainment were prepared. Jewels, jewelled ornaments, fine cloths, sewn tapestry, and every kind of jewellery were presented as offerings. At night on all sides and in the middle of the lake, which is very broad, lamps were displayed. An excellent entertainment was arranged. In the end of the said Thursday, having also sent for the Amirs, I ordered cups for most[3] of the servants. On my journeys by land some boats are always taken along with the victorious camp; the boatmen convey them on carts. On the day after this entertainment I went to fish in these boats, and in a short time 208 large fish came into one net.

[1] About 20 miles south-east of Ajmir.

[2] This is the name of a water-bird in Turkī. It is also called *māgh* and water-crow (*zāgh-i-āb*), and in Hindī *jalkawā* (note of Sayyid Aḥmad).

[3] Probably the meaning is that he allowed those who wished to drink to do so. Many, or at least some, would be abstainers.

Half of these were of the species of *rahū*. At night I divided them among the servants in my own presence. On the 13th Āẕar I marched from Rāmsar, and hunting for 4 kos along the road, the camp was pitched at the village of Balodā.[1] Here I stayed for two days. On the 16th, moving 3¼ kos, I alighted at the village of Nihāl.[2] On the 18th the march was one of 2¼ kos. On this day I gave an elephant to Muḥammad Riẓā Beg, ambassador of the ruler of Persia. The village of Jonsā became the halting-place of the tents of greatness and prosperity. On the 20th I marched to the halting-place of Deogāon; I hunted along the road for a distance of 3 kos. I stayed at this place for two days, and at the end of the day went out to hunt. At this stage a strange affair was witnessed. Before the royal standards arrived at this halting-place, an eunuch went to the bank of a large tank there is in the village, and caught two young *sāras*, which are a kind of crane; at night, when we stopped at this halting-place, two large saras appeared making loud cries near the ghusul-khana (parlour), which they had placed on the edge of the tank, as if somebody were exercising oppression on them. They fearlessly began their cries and came forward. It occurred to me that certainly some kind of wrong had been done to them, and probably their young had been taken. After enquiry was made the eunuch who had taken the young saras brought them before me. When the saras heard the cries of these young ones, they without control threw themselves upon them, and suspecting that they had had no food, each of the two saras placed food in the mouths of the young ones, and made much lamentation. Taking the two young ones between them, and stretching out their wings and fondling them, they went off to their nest. Marching on the 23rd 3¾ kos, I alighted at the

[1] Namūda in MSS.

[2] Sahāl in MSS.

village of Bahāsū (Bhālū?). Here there was a halt of two days, and each day I rode to hunt. On the 26th the royal standards moved and the halt was outside of the village of Kākal. A halt was made after traversing 2 kos. On the 27th the mansab of Badī'u-z-zamān, son of Mīrzā Shāhrukh, original and increased, was fixed at 1,500 personal and 750 horse. Marching on the 29th 2¾ kos, a halt was made at the village of Lāsā, near parganah Boda.[1] This day corresponded with the festival of Qurbān (19th December, 1616). I ordered them to observe the ordinances of that day. From the date on which I left Ajmir up to the end of the aforesaid month, viz. the 30th Āzar, 67 nilgaw, antelope, etc., and 37 water-fowl, etc., had been killed. A march was made from Lāsā on the 2nd Day, and I marched and hunted for 3 kos 10 *jarīb*, and halted in the neighbourhood of the village of Kānṛā. On the 4th a march of 3¼ kos was made to the village of Sūraṭh. Marching 4½ kos on the 6th, a halt was made near the village of Barora (Bardaṛā?). On the 7th, when there was a halt, 50 water-fowl and 14 qashqaldagh (coot) were killed. The next day was a halt as well. On this day 27 water-fowl became a prey. On the 9th a march of 4⅛ kos was made. Hunting and overthrowing prey, I alighted at the halting-place of Khūsh Tāl. At this stage a report came from Mu'tamad Khān that when the territory of the Rānā became the halting-place of Shāh Khurram, though there had been no agreement to this effect (i.e. to the Rānā's meeting him), the fame and dignity of the victorious army had introduced a commotion into the pillars of his patience and firmness, and he had come and paid his respects to him when he halted at Dūdpūr,[2] which was on the border of his jagir,

[1] In Sarkār Marosor (Jarrett, ii, 208). It was in Malwa. But the I.O. MSS. have Nauda.

[2] Text Ūdaipūr, but this was not on the border of the Rānā's territory, and the MSS. have Dūdpūr.

and observing all the dues and ceremonies of service he had neglected not the smallest portion of them. Shāh Khurram had paid him every attention, and pleased him with the gift of a dress of honour, a *chārqab*, a jewelled sword, a jewelled khapwa, Persian and Turki horses, and an elephant, and dismissed him with every honour. He had also favoured his sons and relations with dresses of honour, and out of his offering, which consisted of five elephants, twenty-seven horses, and a tray full of jewels and jewelled ornaments, had taken three horses and given back the remainder. It was settled that his son Karan should attend on the stirrup of Bābā Khurram in this expedition with 1,500 horse. On the 10th the sons of Rāja Mahā Singh came from their jagir and native place (Amber) and waited on me in the neighbourhood of Ranṭambhor, making an offering of three elephants and nine horses. Each one of them, according to his condition, received an increase of mansab. As the neighbourhood of the said fort became a halting-place for the royal standards, I released some of the prisoners who were confined in that fort. At this place I halted for two days and each day went to hunt. Thirty-eight water-fowl and qashqaldagh (coot) were taken. On the 12th I marched, and after going 4 kos halted at the village of Koyalā. On the road I killed fourteen water-fowl and an antelope. On the 14th, having traversed 3¾ kos, I halted in the neighbourhood of the village of Ekṭorā,[1] killing on the road a blue bull, twelve herons (*karwānak*), etc. On the same day Āghā Fāẓil, who had been appointed deputy for I'timādu-d-daulah at Lahore, was dignified with the title of Fāẓil Khān. At this stage they had erected the royal lodging (*daulat-khāna*) on the bank of a tank, which was exceedingly bright and pleasant. On account of the pleasantness of the place

[1] Perhaps the Toda of Sir T. Roe.

I halted two days there, and at the end of each went to hunt water-fowl. To this place the younger son of Mahābat K͟hān, by name Bahra-war, came from the fort of Ranṭambhor, which is his father's jagir, to pay his respects to me. He had brought two elephants, both of which were included in my private stud. I promoted Ṣafī, son of Amānat K͟hān, to the title of K͟hān, and, increasing his mansab, made him bakhshi and news-writer of the Subah of Gujarat. Having travelled 4½ kos on the 17th, I halted at the village of Lasāyā.[1] During the halt I killed one water-fowl and twenty-three sand-grouse (*durrāj*). As I had sent for Las͟hkar K͟hān to Court on account of the disagreement that had occurred between him and K͟hān Daurān, I at this place appointed 'Ābid K͟hān,[2] bakhshi and news-writer, in his stead. On the 19th, having made a march of 2¼ kos, an encampment was made in the neighbourhood of the village of Kūrāka (Korān̲?),[3] which is situated on the bank of the Chambal. On account of the excellence of the place and the pleasantness of its air and water, a halt took place here for three days. Every day I sat in a boat and went to hunt water-fowl and to wander over the river. On the 22nd[4] there was a march, and having traversed 4½ kos, shooting on the road, the victorious camp was pitched at the villages of Sulṭānpūr and Chīla Mala (Chīlāmīlā ?). On this day of halt I bestowed on Mīrān Ṣadr Jahān 5,000 rupees, and gave him leave to proceed to the place assigned to him as his jagir. Another 1,000 rupees were given to S͟haik͟h Pīr. On the 25th I marched and hunted for 3½ kos and encamped at the village of Bāsūr.[5] According to fixed rules one halt and one march took place, and on the 27th I marched and hunted 4⅛ kos and encamped at the village of Chārdūha (Varadhā ?).

[1] Lyāsa in MSS. [2] Son of Niẓāmu-d-dīn the historian.

[3] Gorāna in MSS. and the distance 2¼ kos and 1 *jarīb*.

[4] 23rd in MSS. [5] Mānpūr in text.

Two days halt took place here. In this month of Day 416 animals were killed, namely, 97 sand-grouse (durraj), 192 qashqaldagh, 1 saras, 7 herons, 118 water-fowl, and 1 hare. On the 1st Bahman, corresponding with the 12th Muḥarram, 1026 (20th January, 1617), seating myself in boats with the ladies, I went forward one stage. When one ghari of day remained I arrived at the village of Rūpāheṛā, the halting-place, the distance being 4 kos and 15 jarib. I shot five sand-grouse. On the same day I sent by the hands of Kaikana winter dresses of honour to twenty-one Amirs on duty in the Deccan, and ordered him to take 10,000 [1] rupees from those Amirs as a thanksgiving for the dresses of honour. This halting-place had much verdure and pleasantness. On the 3rd a march took place. As on the previous day, I embarked in a boat, and after traversing 2⅛ kos the village of Kākhā-dās (Kākhāvās?)[2] became the encamping place of the victorious camp. As I came hunting on the way, a sand-grouse fell flying into a thicket. After much search it was marked, and I ordered one of the beaters to surround the thicket and catch it, and went towards it myself. Meanwhile another sand-grouse rose, and this I made a falcon seize. Soon afterwards the beater came and laid the sand-grouse before me. I ordered them to satisfy the falcon with this sand-grouse, and to keep the one we had caught, as it was a young bird. (But) before the order reached him the head huntsman fed the falcon with the sand-grouse (the second one, viz. that which the falcon had caught). After a while the beater represented to me that if he did not kill the sand-grouse it would die (and then could not be eaten as not properly killed). I ordered him to kill it if that was the case. As he laid his sword on its throat, it with a slight movement freed itself from the sword and flew away. After I had

[1] MSS. 2,000 rupees. [2] Perhaps Kānha Dās.

left the boat and mounted my horse, suddenly a sparrow (*kunjishk*) by the force of the wind struck the head of an arrow that one of the beaters who was in my retinue had in his hand, and immediately fell down and died. I was amazed and bewildered at the tricks of destiny; on one side it preserved the sand-grouse, whose time had not arrived, in a short time from three such dangers, and on the other hand made captive in the hand of destruction on the arrow of fate the sparrow whose hour of death had come—

> "The world-sword may move from its place,
> But it will cut no vein till God wills."

Dresses of honour for the winter had also been sent by the hand of Qarā, the *yasāwul* (usher), to the Amirs at Kabul. I halted at this place on account of the pleasantness of the spot and the excellence of the air. On this day there came the news of the death of Nād 'Alī Khān Maidānī at Kabul. I honoured his sons with mansabs, and at the request of Ibrāhīm Khān Fīrūz-jang[1] increased the mansab of Rāwat Shankar by 500 personal and 1,000 horse. On the 6th there was a march, and going for $4\frac{1}{8}$ kos by the pass known as Ghāṭe Chāndā, the royal camp was pitched at the village of Amḥār (Amjār ?). This valley is very green and pleasant and good trees are seen in it. Up to this stage, which is the limit of the country of the Subah of Ajmir, 84 kos had been traversed. It was also a pleasant stage. Nūr-Jahān Begam here shot with a gun a *qarīsha* (?), the like of which for size and beauty of colour had never been seen. I ordered them to weigh it, and it came to 19 tolas and 5 mashas. The aforesaid village is the commencement of the Subah of Malwa, which is in the second clime. The length[2] of this Subah from the extremity of the province of Gaṛha to the province of Bānswāla (Bānswaṛā ?) is 245 kos, and its

[1] Should be Fatḥ-jang as in MSS. [2] Jarrett, ii, 195.

breadth from the parganah of Chanderī to the parganah of Nandarbār is 230 kos. On the east is the province of Bāndho, and on the north the fort of Narwar, on the south the province of Baglānā, and on the west the Subahs of Gujarat and Ajmir. Malwa is a large province abounding in water and of a pleasant climate. There are five rivers in it in addition to streams, canals, and springs, namely, the Godavarī,[1] Bhīmā, Kālīsindh, Nīrā, and Narbada. Its climate is nearly equable. The land of this province is low, but part of it is high. In the district of Dhār, which is one of the noted places of Malwa, the vine gives grapes twice in the year, in the beginning of Pisces and the beginning of Leo, but the grapes of Pisces are the sweeter. Its husbandmen and artificers are not without arms. The revenue of the province is 24,700,000 dams. When needful there are obtained from it about 9,300[2] horse and four lakhs, 70,300 foot-soldiers, with 100 elephants. On the 8th, moving on 3½ kos, an encampment was made near Khairābād. On the road 14 sand-grouse and 3 herons were killed, and having traversed and shot over 3 kos the camp was pitched at the village of Sidhārā. On the 11th, while there was a halt, I mounted at the end of the day to hunt, and killed a blue bull. On the 12th, after traversing 4¼ kos, a halt was made at the village of Bachhayārī. On that day Rānā Amar Singh had sent some baskets of figs. In truth it is a fine fruit, and I had never seen such delicious figs in India. But one must eat only a few of them; it does harm to eat many. On the 14th there was a march; having traversed 4⅛ kos, I encamped at the village of Balbalī. Rāja Jānbā, who is an influential zamindar in these

[1] The name seems to be wrong. Jahāngīr is evidently copying from the Āyīn, and the rivers mentioned there (Jarrett, ii, 195) are the Narbada, Sipra, Kālīsindh, Betwa, and the Kodī (or Godī).

[2] 29,668 (Jarrett, ii, 198).

regions, had sent two elephants as an offering, and they were brought before me. At the same stage they brought many melons grown in Kārīz near Herat. Khān 'Ālam had also sent 50 camels. In former years they had never brought melons in such abundance. On one tray they brought many kinds of fruit—Kārīz melons, melons from Badakhshan and Kabul, grapes from Samarkand[1] and Badakhshan, apples from Samarkand, Kashmir, Kabul, and from Jalalabad, which is a dependency of Kabul, and pineapples, a fruit that comes from the European ports, plants of which have been set in Agra. Every year some thousands are gathered in the gardens there which appertain to the private domains (*khāliṣa-i-sharīfa*)[2]; *kaula*,[3] which are similar in form to an orange, but smaller and better in flavour. They grow very well in the Subah of Bengal. In what language can one give thanks for such favours? My revered father had a great liking for fruit, especially for melons, pomegranates, and grapes. During his time the Kārīz melons, which are the finest kind, and pomegranates from Yezd, which are celebrated throughout the world, and Samarkand grapes had not been brought to Hindustan. Whenever I see these fruits they cause me great regret. Would that such fruit had come in those days, so that he might have enjoyed them!

On the 15th, which was a halting day, news came of the death of Mīr 'Alī, son of Farīdūn Khān Barlās, who was one of the trusted *amīr-zādas* (descended from amirs) of this family (the Timurides). On the 16th a march took place. Having traversed 4⅛ kos, the camp of heavenly dignity was pitched near the village of Girī. On the road the scouts brought news that there was

[1] The MSS. also have sweet pomegranates from Yezd, and sub-acid (*may-khwush*) ones from Farāh, and pears from Badakhshan (see Elliot, vi, 348).

[2] The MSS. have *khāṣṣa-i-sharīfa*.

[3] Qu. *komla*? Instead of *qābiltar* the MSS. have *mā'iltar*.

a lion in this neighbourhood. I went to hunt him and finished him with one shot. As the braveness of the lion (*shīr babar*) has been established, I wished to look at his intestines. After they were extracted, it appeared that in a manner contrary to other animals, whose gall-bladder is outside their livers, the gall-bladder of the lion is within his liver (?). It occurred to me that the courage of the lion may be from this cause. On the 18th, after traversing 2¾ kos, the village of Amriyā was our halting-place. On the 19th, which was a halt, I went out to hunt. After going 2 kos, a village came to view exceedingly sweet and pleasant. Nearly 100 mango-trees were seen in one garden; I had seldom seen mango-trees so large and green and pleasant. In the same garden I saw a *bar*-tree (a banyan), exceedingly large. I ordered them to measure its length, breadth, and height in yards (*gaz*). Its height from the surface to the highest branch (*sar-shākh*) was 74 cubits (*zira'*). The circumference of its trunk was 44½ cubits and its breadth[1] 175½ measured by the gaz. This has been recorded as it is very unusual. On the 20th was a march, and on the road a blue bull was shot with a gun. On the 21st, which was a halt, I went out to hunt at the end of the day. After returning, I came to the house of I'timādu-d-daulah for the festival of Khwāja Khiẓr, whom they call Khiẓrī; I remained there till a watch of the night had passed, and then feeling inclined for food I went back to the royal quarters. On this day I honoured I'timādu-d-daulah as an intimate friend by directing the ladies of the harem not to veil their faces from him. By this favour I bestowed everlasting honour on him. On the 22nd an order was given to march, and after 3⅛ kos were traversed the camp was pitched at the village of Būlgharī (Nawalkheṛī ?). On the road two blue

[1] *Pahnā'ī.* Its area or shade. Perhaps the 175½ are yards, not cubits.

bulls were killed. On the 23rd day of Tīr, which was a halt, I killed a blue bull with a gun. On the 24th, traversing 5 kos, the village of Qāsim-kheṛā was the halting-place. On the road a white animal[1] was killed, which resembled the *kūtāh pāya* (hog-deer); it had four horns, two of which were opposite the extremities of its eyes, and two finger-breadths in height, and the two other horns four finger-breadths towards the nape of the neck. These were four finger-breadths in height. The people of India call this animal *dūdhādhārīt* (*dudhāriyā* ?). The male has four horns and the female none. It was said that this kind of antelope has no gall-bladder, but when they looked at its intestines the gall-bladder was apparent, and it became clear that this report has no foundation. On the 25th, which was a halt, at the end of the day I rode out to hunt and killed a female nilgaw with my gun. Bāljū, nephew of Qilīj K͟hān, who held the mansab of 1,000 personal and 850 horse, and had a jagir in Oudh, I promoted to 2,000 personal and 1,200 horse, dignified him with the title of Qilīj K͟hān, and appointed him to the Subah of Bengal. On the 26th a march took place, and after traversing 4¾ kos a halt was made at the village of Dih Qāẓiyān, which is in the neighbourhood of Ujjain. A number of mango-trees in this place had blossomed. They had pitched the

[1] Evidently the four-horned antelope, the *Tetracerus quadricornis* of Blanford, p. 520, and which has the Hindustani name of *doda*. Blanford describes its colour as dull pale brown. "The posterior horns are much larger than the anterior ones, which are situated between the orbits and are often mere knobs. It is the only Indian representative of the *duikarbok* of Africa. Another Indian name is *chausingha*. In jungle this species and the hog-deer may easily be mistaken the one for the other. It is not gregarious, and moves with a peculiar jerky action." The resemblance between the four-horned antelope and the hog-deer—the *kūtāh pāycha* or short-legged deer of Bābar and Jahāngīr—may account for Blanford's giving *doda* as a native name for the hog-deer (*Cervus porcinus*). For Bābar's description of the *kūtāh pāya* or *pāycha* see Erskine, p. 317. Gladwin in his history of Jahāngīr writes the native name as *Dirdhayan*.

tents on the bank of a lake, and had prepared an enchanting place. Pahāṛ, son of Ghaznīn[1] Khān, was capitally punished at this stage. Cherishing this unlucky one after the death of his father, I had given him the fort and province of Jālaur, which was the place of his ancestors. As he was of tender years, his mother used to forbid him certain evil practices. That eternally black-faced one with some of his companions one night came into the house and killed his own full mother with his own hand. This news reached me and I ordered them to bring him. After his crime was proved against him, I ordered them to put him to death (*kih ba biyāsā rasānīdand*). At this halting-place a tamarind[2]-tree came to view, the form and habit of which were somewhat strange. The original tree had one trunk; when it had grown to 6 gaz, it turned into two branches, one of which was 10 and the other 9½ gaz. The distance between the two branches was 4½ gaz. From the ground to the place where the branches and leaves came to an end (?), there were on the side of the large branch 16 gaz, and on the other branch 15½ gaz. From the place whence the branches and green leaves began (?) to the top (trunk ?) of the tree was 2½ gaz, and the circumference was 2¾ gaz. I ordered them to make a *chabūtara* (platform) round it of the height of 3 gaz. As the trunk was very straight and well-shaped, I told my artists to depict it in the illustrations to the Jahāngīr-nāma. A march was made on the 27th. After traversing 2⅛ kos, a halt was made

[1] Blochmann, p. 493.

[2] Text, *khurmā*, a date, but evidently the *khurmā-i-Hind* or the tamarind, i.e. 'the palm of India,' is meant (see Bābar's Mem., Erskine, p. 324). I do not understand the measurements. The word *yak*, 'one,' before the word *shākh* is not in the MSS. and is, I think, wrong. I think the 16 gaz and 15½ gaz are the lengths of the two branches, and that the measurements 2½ and 2¾ gaz refer to the length and circumference of the two branches at the place when they started from the trunk and before they put out leaves.

at the village of Hinduwāl[1]; on the road a blue bull was killed. On the 28th, after traversing 2 kos, the village of Kāliyādaha became the halting-place. Kāliyādaha is a building which was made by Nāṣiru-d-dīn, son of G͟hiyāṣu-d-dīn, son of Sulṭān Maḥmūd K͟haljī, who was ruler of Malwa. In the time of his rule he had made it in the neighbourhood of Ujjain, which is one of the most celebrated cities in the Subah of Malwa. They say that the heat overcame him so much that he passed his time in the water. He made this building in the middle of the river, and divided its waters into canals, and brought the water on all sides, as well as inside and outside, of the house, and made large and small reservoirs suited to the place. It is a very pleasant and enjoyable place, and one of the noted habitations of Hindustan. Before it was decided to halt at this place I sent architects and ordered them to clean up the place again. On account of its pleasantness I remained in this place for three days. At the same place S͟hajā'at K͟hān came from his jagir and waited on me. Ujjain is one of the old cities, and is one of the seven established places of worship of the Hindus. Rāja Bikramājīt, who introduced the observation of the heavens and stars into Hindustan, lived in this city and province. From the time of his observations until now, which is the 1026th Hijra year (1617 A.D.) and the 11th year from my accession, 1,675[2] years have passed. The deductions of the astronomers of India are all based on his observations. This city is on the bank of the River Sipra. The belief[3] of the

[1] Hindwas or Hindāwas in MSS.

[2] This is in accordance with and probably derived from Bābar's Commentaries, Erskine, p. 51, where he says that 1,584 years have elapsed from the time when Bikramājīt made his observatory. Erskine takes this to show that Bābar was writing in 934, and if we add 92 years, or the difference between 934 and 1026, we get 1,676 years (or 1,675 if we take the year to be 1025).

[3] See Jarrett, ii, 196. Abū-l-faẓl says there that the flow occurred a week before his arrival at Ujjain.

Hindus is that once in some year at an uncertain time the water of this river turns into milk. In the reign of my revered father, at the time when he had sent Abū-l-faẓl to set in order the affairs of my brother S͟hāh Murād, he sent a report from that city that a large body of Hindus and Musulmans had borne testimony that some days previously at night this river had become milk, so that people who took water from it that night found in the morning their pots full of milk.[1] As this obtained currency it has been recorded, but my intelligence will in no way agree to it. The real truth of this affair is known to Allah. On the 2nd Isfandārmuẕ I embarked in a boat from Kāliyādaha, and went to the next stage. I had frequently heard that an austere Sanyāsī[2] of the name of Jadrūp many years ago retired from the city of Ujjain to a corner of the desert and employed himself in the worship of the true God. I had a great desire for his acquaintance, and when I was at the capital of Agra I was desirous of sending for and seeing him. In the end, thinking of the trouble it would give him, I did not send for him. When I arrived in the neighbourhood of the city I alighted from the boat and went $\frac{1}{8}$ kos on foot to see him. The place he had chosen to live in was a hole on the side of a hill which had been dug out and a door made. At the entrance there is an opening in the shape of a *miḥrāb*,[3] which

[1] Cf. Jarrett, ii, 196.

[2] *Sanyāsī-i-murtāẓ.*

[3] Text, *miḥrābī-s͟hakl uftāda*, 'a place like a prayer-niche.' Possibly the true reading is *majrā bī-s͟hakl uftāda*, 'a passage without form.' However, the MSS. have *miḥrāb*. The account in the text may be compared with the Ma'āṣiru-l-umarā, i, 574, and with the Iqbāl-nāma, p. 94. The measurements of the mouth of the hole in the Ma'āṣir are taken from the Iqbāl-nāma, and differ from the account in the Tūzuk. The Ma'āṣir, following the Iqbāl-nāma, calls the ascetic Achhad or Ajhad. It also gives his subsequent history. He went to Mathura and was there cruelly beaten by Ḥākim Beg. Jahāngīr's visit to Jadrūp is referred to by Sir Thomas Roe, who mentions a report that the saint was said to be 300 years old. Jahāngīr does not say any such nonsense.

is in length (? height) 1 gaz and in breadth 10 *gira* (knots, each $\frac{1}{16}$ of a gaz), and the distance from this door to a hole which is his real abode is 2 gaz and 5 knots in length and in breadth 11¼ knots. The height from the ground to the roof is 1 gaz and 3 knots. The hole whence is the entrance to the abode is in length 5½ knots and its breadth 3½ knots. A person of weak body (thin ?) can only enter it with a hundred difficulties. The length and breadth of the hole are such. It has no mat and no straw. In this narrow and dark hole he passes his time in solitude. In the cold days of winter, though he is quite naked, with the exception of a piece of rag that he has in front and behind, he never lights a fire. The Mulla of Rūm (Jalālu-d-dīn) has put into rhyme the language of a dervish—

> "By day our clothes are the sun,
> By night our mattress and blanket the moon's rays."

He bathes twice a day in a piece of water near his abode, and once a day goes into the city of Ujjain, and nowhere but to the houses of three brahmins whom he has selected out of seven, who have wives and children and whom he believes to have religious feelings and contentment. He takes by way of alms five mouthfuls of food out of what they have prepared for their own eating, which he swallows without chewing, in order that he may not enjoy their flavour; always provided that no misfortune has happened to their three houses, that there has been no birth, and there be no menstruous woman in the house. This is his method of living, just as it is now written. He does not desire to associate with men, but as he has obtained great notoriety people go to see him. He is not devoid of knowledge, for he has thoroughly mastered the science of the Vedānta, which is the science of Sufism. I conversed with him for six gharis; he spoke well, so much so as to make a great impression on me. My society also suited him.

At the time when my revered father conquered the fort of Āsīr, in the province of Khandesh, and was returning to Agra, he saw him in the very same place, and always remembered him well.

The learned of India have established four modes of life for the caste of brahmins, which is the most honoured of the castes of Hindus, and have divided their lives into four periods. These four periods they call the four *āsram*.[1] The boy who is born in a brahmin's house they do not call brahmin till he is 7 years old, and take no trouble on the subject. After he has arrived at the age of 8 years, they have a meeting and collect the brahmins together. They make a cord of *mūnj* grass, which they call *mūnjī*, in length 2¼ gaz, and having caused prayers and incantations to be repeated over it, and having had it made into three strands, which they call *sih tan*, by one in whom they have confidence, they fasten it on his waist. Having woven a *zunnār* (girdle or thread) out of the loose threads, they hang it over his right[2] shoulder. Having given into his hand a stick of the length of a little over 1 gaz to defend himself with from hurtful things and a copper vessel for drinking-water, they hand him over to a learned brahmin that he may remain in his house for twelve years, and employ himself in reading the Vedas, which they believe in as God's book. From this day forward they call him a brahmin. During this time it is necessary that he should altogether abstain from bodily pleasures. When midday is passed he goes as a beggar to the houses of other brahmins, and bringing what is given him to his preceptor, eats it with his permission. For clothing, with the exception of a loin cloth (*lungī*) of cotton to cover his private parts, and 2 or 3 more gaz of cotton

[1] See Jarrett, iii, 271, etc. The Sanskrit word is Āsrama, or Ās̲h̲rama.

[2] Left shoulder in Āyīn.

which he throws over his back, he has nothing else. This state is called *brahmacharya*, that is, being busied with the Divine books. After this period has passed, with the leave of his preceptor and his father, he marries, and is allowed to enjoy all the pleasures of his five senses until the time when he has a son who shall have attained the age of 16 years. If he does not have a son, he passes his days till he is 48 in the social life. During this time they call him a *grihast*, that is, householder. After that time, separating himself from relatives, connections, strangers, and friends, and giving up all things of enjoyment and pleasure, he retires to a place of solitude from the place of attachment to sociality (*ta'alluq-i-ābād-i-kaṣrat*), and passes his days in the jungle. They call this condition *bānprasta*,[1] that is, abode in the jungle. As it is a maxim of the Hindus that no good deed can be thoroughly performed by men in the social state without the partnership of the presence of a wife, whom they have styled the half of a man, and as a portion of the ceremonies and worshippings is yet before him (has to be accomplished), he takes his wife with him into the jungle. If she should be pregnant, he puts off his going until she bear a child and it arrive at the age of 5 years. Then he entrusts the child to his eldest son or other relation, and carries out his intention. In the same way, if his wife be menstruous, he puts off going until she is purified. After this he has no connection with her, and does not defile himself with communication with her, and at night he sleeps apart.[2] He passes twelve years in this place, and lives on vegetables which may have sprung up of themselves in the desert and jungle. He keeps his zunnar by him and worships fire. He does not waste his time in looking

[1] Sanskrit, Vānaprastha.

[2] Text *qaṭ'ī dar miyān ālat nihāda*, but apparently this should be *ālat qaṭ' ba miyān nihāda*; that is, "membrum virile in involucris reponens."

after his nails or the hair of his head, or in trimming his beard and moustaches. When he completes this period in the manner related, he returns to his own house, and having commended his wife to his children and brothers and sons-in-law, goes to pay his respects to his spiritual guide, and burns by throwing into the fire in his presence whatever he has in the way of a zunnar, the hair of his head, etc., and says to him: "Whatever attachment (*ta'alluq*) I may have had, even to abstinence and worshipping and will, I have rooted up out of my heart." Then he closes the road to his heart and to his desires and is always employed in contemplation of God, and knows no one except the True Cause of Being (God). If he speak of science it is the science of Vedānta, the purport of which Bābā Fig͟hānī has versified in this couplet—

> "There's one lamp in this house, by whose rays
> Wherever I look there is an assembly."

They call this state *sarvabiyās*,[1] that is, giving up all. They call him who possesses it *sarvabiyāsī*.

After interviewing Jadrūp I mounted an elephant and passed through the town of Ujjain, and as I went scattered to the right and left small coins to the value of 3,500 rupees, and proceeding 1¾ kos alighted at Dā'ūd-k͟heṛā, the place where the royal camp was pitched. On the 3rd day, which was a halting day, I went, from desire for association with him, after midday, to see Jadrūp, and for six gharis enjoyed myself in his company. On this day also he uttered good words, and it was near evening when I entered my palace. On the 4th day I journeyed 3¼ kos and halted at the village of Jarāo[2]

[1] Text, *sarb biyāsī*, which may mean 'distributing everything.' The Iqbāl-nāma, p. 96, has *sarb nāsī*, 'destroying everything.'

[2] I.O. MS. No. 306 says nothing about a garden, but speaks of a village Khirwār and of halting under a mango-tree. Nor does No. 305 mention a garden.

in the Pāräniyā garden. This is also a very pleasant halting-place, full of trees. On the 6th there was a march; after proceeding for 4¾ kos I halted on the bank of the lake of Debālpūr Bheriyā. On account of the pleasantness of the place and the delights of the lake, I halted at this stage for four days, and at the end of each day, embarking in a boat, employed myself in shooting ducks (*murghābī*) and other aquatic animals. At this halting-place they brought *fakhrī* grapes from Ahmadnagar. Although they are not as large as the Kabul fakhri grapes, they do not yield to them in sweetness.

At the request of my son Bābā Khurram the mansab of Badī'u-z-zamān, son of Mīrzā Shāhrukh, was fixed at 1,500 personal and 1,000 horse. On the 11th I marched, and after proceeding for 3¼ kos halted in the parganah Daulatabad. On the 12th, which was a halt, I rode out to hunt. In the village of Shaikhūpūr, which belonged to the said parganah, I saw a very large and bulky banyan-tree, measuring round its trunk 18½ gaz, and in height from the root to the top of the branches 128¼ cubits. The branches spread a shade for 203½ cubits. The length of a branch, on which they have represented the tusks of an elephant, was 40 gaz. At the time when my revered father passed by this, he had made an impression of his hand by way of a mark at the height of 3¾ gaz from the ground. I ordered them also to make the mark of my hand 8 gaz above another root. In order that these two hand-marks might not be effaced in the course of time, they were carved on a piece of marble and fastened on to the trunk of the tree. I ordered them to place a *chabūtara* and platform round the tree.

As at the time when I was prince I had promised Mīr Ẓiyā'u-dīn Qazwīnī, who was one of the Saifī Sayyids, and whom during my reign I have honoured with the title of Muṣṭafā K͟hān, to give the parganah of Maldah, which is a famous parganah in Bengal, to him and his descendants[1] in *āl tamg͟hā* (perpetual royal grant), this great gift was bestowed in his honour at this halting-place. On the 13th a march took place. Going separately from this camp to look round the country and hunt with some of the ladies and intimates and servants, I proceeded to the village of Ḥāṣilpūr, and whilst the camp was pitched in the neighbourhood of Nālcha (Bālchha?) I halted at the village of Sāngor. What shall be written of the beauty and sweetness of this village? There were many mango-trees, and its lands were altogether green and delightful. On account of its greenness and pleasantness I halted here for three days. I gave this village to Kamāl K͟hān, the huntsman, in place of Kes͟hō Dās Mārū. An order was passed that they should hereafter call it Kamālpūr. At this same halting-place occurred the night of S͟hīvrāt (Shivrātri). Many Jogis collected. The ceremonies of this night were duly observed, and I met the learned of this body in social intercourse. In these days I shot three blue bulls. The news of the killing of Rāja Mān reached me at this place. I had appointed him to head the army that had been sent against the fort of Kāngṛā. When he arrived at Lahore he heard that Sangrām, one of the zamindars of the hill-country of the Panjab, had attacked his place and taken possession of part of his province. Considering it of the first importance to drive him out, he went against him. As Sangrām had not the power to oppose him, he left the country of which he had taken possession and took refuge in difficult hills and places. Rāja Mān pursued him there, and in his great pride, not looking to the means by which he himself could advance and retreat, came up to him with

[1] Cf. Elliot, vi, 348. The MSS. say nothing about two sons.

a small force. When Sangrām saw that he had no way to flee by, in accordance with this couplet—

> "In time of need when no (way of) flight is left,
> The hand seizes the edge of the sharp sword." [1]

A fight took place, and according to what was decreed, a bullet struck Rāja Mān and he delivered his soul to the Creator thereof. His men were defeated and a great number of them killed. The remainder, wounded, abandoned their horses and arms, and with a hundred alarms escaped half-dead.

On the 17th I marched from Sāngor, and after proceeding 3 kos came again to the village of Ḥāṣilpūr. On the road a blue bull was killed. This village is one of the noted places in the Subah of Malwa. It has many vines and mango-trees without number. It has streams flowing on all sides of it. At the time I arrived there were grapes contrary to the season in which they are in the Wilayat (Persia or Afghanistan). They were so cheap and plentiful that the lowest and meanest could get as much as they desired. The poppy had flowered and showed varied colours. In brief, there are few villages so pleasant. For three days more I halted in this village. Three blue bulls were killed with my gun. From Ḥāṣilpūr on the 21st in two marches I rejoined the big camp. On the road a blue bull was killed. On Sunday, the 22nd, marching from the neighbourhood of Nālcha (Bālchha ?), I pitched at a lake that is at the foot of the fort of Māndū. On that day the huntsmen brought news that they had marked down a tiger within 3 kos. Although it was Sunday, and on these two days, viz. Sunday and Thursday, I do not shoot, it occurred to me that as it is a noxious animal it ought to be done away with. I proceeded towards him, and when I arrived at the place it was sitting

[1] From the "Gulistān."

under the shade of a tree. Seeing its mouth, which was half open, from the back of the elephant, I fired my gun. By chance it entered its mouth and found a place in its throat and brain, and its affair was finished with that one shot. After this the people who were with me, although they looked for the place where the tiger was wounded, could not find it, for on none of its limbs was there any sign of a gunshot wound. At last I ordered them to look in its mouth. From this it was evident that the bullet had entered its mouth and that it had been killed thereby. Mīrzā Rustam had killed a male wolf and brought it. I wished to see whether its gall-bladder was in its liver like that of the tiger, or like other animals outside its liver. After examination it was clear that the gall-bladder was also inside the liver. On Monday, the 23rd, when one watch had passed in a fortunate ascension and a benign hour, I mounted an elephant and approached the fort of Māndū. When a watch and three gharis of day had passed, I entered the houses which they had prepared for the royal accommodation. I scattered 1,500 rupees on the way. From Ajmir to Māndū, 159 kos, in the space of four months and two days, in forty-six marches and seventy-eight halts, had been traversed. In these forty-six marches our halts were made on the banks of tanks or streams or large rivers in pleasant places which were full of trees and poppy-fields in flower, and no day passed that I did not hunt while halting or travelling. Riding on horseback or on an elephant I came along the whole way looking about and hunting, and none of the difficulties of travelling were experienced; one might say that there was a change from one garden to another. In these huntings there were always present with me Āṣaf K͟hān, Mīrzā Rustam, Mīr Mīrān, Anīrā'ī, Hidāyatu-llah, Rāja Sārang Deo, Sayyid Kāsū, and K͟hawāṣṣ K͟hān. As before the arrival of the royal standards in these regions I had sent 'Abdu-l-Karīm, the architect, to look to the repair of the buildings of the old rulers in Māndū, he during the time the camp halted at Ajmir had repaired some of the old buildings that were capable of repair, and had altogether rebuilt some places. In short, he had made ready a house the like of which for pleasantness and sweetness has probably not been made anywhere else. Nearly 300,000 rupees, or 2,000 Persian tumans, were expended on this. There should be such grand buildings in all great cities as might be fit for royal accommodation. This fort is on the top of a hill 10 kos in circumference; in the rainy season there is no place with the fine air and pleasantness of this fort. At nights, in the season of the *qalbu-l-asad* (Cor leonis or Regulus, the star *a* of Leo), it is so cold that one cannot do without a coverlet, and by day there is no need for a fan (*bād-zan*). They say [1] that before the time of Rāja Bikramājīt there was a Raja of the name of Jai Singh Deo. In his time a man had gone into the fields to bring grass. While he was cutting it, the sickle he had in his hand appeared to be of the colour of gold. When he saw that his sickle had been transmuted, he took it to a blacksmith of the name of Mādan [2] to be repaired. The blacksmith knew the sickle had been turned into gold. It had before this been heard that there was in this country the alchemist's stone (*sang-i-pāras*), by contact with which iron and copper became gold. He immediately took the grass-cutter with him to that place and procured the stone. After this he brought to the Raja of the time this priceless jewel. The Raja by means of this stone made gold, and spent part of it on the buildings of this fort

[1] Cf. Jarrett, ii, 197. The story is also told with many more details in Price's Jahāngīr, p. 108, etc.

[2] Text, *Mādan*. But the name is *Māndan*, as MS. No. 181 and the Āyīn-i-Akbari (Jarrett, ii, 197) show. The legend is intended to show how Māndū got its name (see also Tiefenthaler, i, 353).

and completed them in the space of twelve years. At the desire of that blacksmith he caused them to cut into the shape of an anvil most of the stones that were to be built into the wall of the fort. At the end of his life, when his heart had given up the world, he held an assembly on the bank of the Narbada, which is an object of worship among the Hindus, and, assembling brahmins, made presents to each of cash and jewels. When the turn of a brahmin came who had long been associated with him, he gave this stone into his hand. He from ignorance became angry and threw the priceless jewel into the river. After he came to know the true state of the affair he was a captive to perpetual sorrow. However much he searched, no trace of it was found. These things are not written in a book; they have been heard, but my intelligence in no way accepts this story. It appears to me to be all delusion. Māndū[1] is one of the famous Sarkars of the Subah of Malwa. Its revenue is 1,390,000 dams. It was for a long time the capital of the kings of this country. There are many buildings and traces of former kings in it, and up till now it has not fallen into ruin.

On the 24th I rode to go round and see the buildings of the old kings, and went first to the Jāmi' mosque, which is one built by Sulṭān Hūshang Ghūrī. A very lofty building came to view, all of cut stone, and although 180 years have passed since the time of its building, it is as if the builder had just withdrawn his hand from it. After this I went to the building containing the tombs of the Khaljī rulers. The grave of Naṣīru-d-dīn, son of Sulṭān Ghiyāṣu-d-dīn, whose face is blackened for ever, was also there. It is well known that that wretch advanced himself by the murder of his own father, Ghiyāṣu-d-dīn, who was in his 80th year. Twice

[1] Elliot, vi. 348.

he gave him poison, and he twice expelled it by means of a *zahr-muhra* (poison antidote, bezoar) he had on his arm. The third time he mixed poison in a cup of sherbet and gave it to his father with his own hand, saying he must drink it. As his father understood what efforts he was making in this matter, he loosened the zahr-muhra from his arm and threw it before him, and then turning his face in humility and supplication towards the throne of the Creator, who requires no supplication, said: "O Lord, my age has arrived at 80 years, and I have passed this time in prosperity and happiness such as has been attained to by no king. Now as this is my last time, I hope that Thou wilt not seize Naṣīr for my murder, and that reckoning my death as a thing decreed Thou wilt not avenge it." After he had spoken these words, he drank off that poisoned cup of sherbet at a gulp and delivered his soul to the Creator. The meaning of his preamble was that he had passed the time of his reign in enjoyment such as has not been attained to by any of the kings. When in his 48th year he came to the throne, he said to his intimates and those near him, "In the service of my revered father I have passed thirty years in warfare and have committed no fault in my activity as a soldier; now that my turn to reign has arrived, I have no intention to conquer countries, but desire to pass the remainder of my life in ease and enjoyment." They say that he had collected 15,000 women in his harem. He had a whole city of them, and had made it up of all castes, kinds, and descriptions—artificers, magistrates, qazis, kotwals, and whatever else is necessary for the administration of a town. Wherever he heard of a virgin possessed of beauty, he would not desist (lit. did not sit down from his feet) until he possessed her. He taught the girls all kinds of arts and crafts, and was much inclined to hunt. He had made a deer park and collected all kinds of animals in it.

He often used to hunt in it with his women. In brief, in the period of thirty-two years of his reign, as he had determined, he went against no enemy, and passed this time in ease and enjoyment. In the same way no one invaded his country. It is reported that when Shīr Khān, the Afghan, in the time of his rule, came to the tomb of Naṣīru-d-dīn, he, in spite of his brutish nature, on account of Naṣīru-d-dīn's shameful conduct, ordered the head of the tomb to be beaten with sticks. Also when I went to his tomb I gave it several kicks, and ordered the servants in attendance on me to kick the tomb. Not satisfied with this, I ordered the tomb to be broken open and his impure remains to be thrown into the fire. Then it occurred to me that since fire is Light, it was a pity for the Light of Allah to be polluted with burning his filthy body; also, lest there should be any diminution of torture for him in another state from being thus burnt, I ordered them to throw his crumbled bones, together with his decayed limbs, into the Narbada. During his lifetime he always passed his days in the water in consequence of the heat that had acquired a mastery over his temperament. It is well known that in a state of drunkenness he once threw himself into one of the basins at Kāliyādaha, which was very deep. Some of the attendants in the harem exerted themselves and caught his hair in their hands and drew him out of the water. After he had come to his senses they told him that this thing had happened. When he had heard that they had pulled him out by the hair of his head, he became exceedingly angry, and ordered the hands of the attendants to be cut off. Another time, when an affair of this kind took place, no one had the boldness to pull him out and he was drowned. By chance, after 110 years had passed since his death, it came to pass that his decayed limbs also became mingled with the water.

On the 28th, as a reward for the buildings of Māndū having been completed through his excellent exertions, I promoted 'Abdu-l-Karīm to the rank of 800 personal and 400 horse, and dignified him with the title of Ma'mūr Khān (the architect-Khān). On the same day that the royal standards entered the fort of Māndū, my son of lofty fortune, Sulṭān Khurram, with the victorious army, entered the city of Burhanpur, which is the seat of the governor of the province of Khandesh.

After some days, representations came from Afẓal Khān and the Rāy Rāyān, to whom at the time of leaving Ajmir my son had given leave to accompany the ambassador to 'Ādil Khān, reporting that when the news of our coming reached 'Ādil Khān he came out for 7 kos to meet the order and the litter of the prince, and performed the duties of salutation and respect which are customary at Court. He did not omit a hair's point of such ceremonies. At the same interview he professed the greatest loyalty, and promised that he would restore all those provinces that 'Ambar of dark fate had taken from the victorious State, and agreed to send to the Court with all reverence a fitting offering with his ambassadors. After saying this he brought the ambassadors in all dignity to the place that had been prepared for them. On the same day he sent some one to 'Ambar with a message of the matters it was necessary to acquaint him with. I heard this news from the reports of Afẓal Khān and the Rāy Rāyān.

From Ajmir up to Monday, the 23rd of the aforesaid[1] month, during four months, 2 tigers, 27 blue bulls, 6 *chītal* (spotted deer), 60 deer, 23 hares and foxes, and 1,200 water-fowl and other animals had been killed. On these nights I told the story of my former hunting expeditions and the liking I had for this occupation to

[1] Monday, the 23rd Isfandārmuẕ, the day on which he reached Māndū. It was about the 6th March, 1617.

those standing at the foot of the throne of the Caliphate. It occurred to me that I might make up the account of my game from the commencement of my years of discretion up to the present time. I accordingly gave orders to the news-writers, the hunt-accountants and huntsmen, and others employed in this service to make enquiries and tell me of all the animals that had been killed in hunting. It was shown that from the commencement of my 12th year, which was in 988 (1580), up to the end of this year, which is the 11th year after my accession and my 50th lunar year, 28,532 head of game had been taken in my presence. Of these, 17,167 animals I killed myself with my gun or otherwise, viz.: Quadrupeds, 3,203; viz., tigers, 86; bears, cheetahs, foxes, otters (*ūdbilāo*), and hyænas, 9; blue bulls, 889; *mhāka*, a species of antelope, in size equal to a blue bull, 35 head; of antelope, male and female, *chikāra*, *chītal*, mountain goats, etc., 1,670[1]; rams (*qūj*) and red deer, 215; wolves, 64; wild buffaloes, 36; pigs, 90; *rang*, 26; mountain sheep, 22; *arghalī*, 32; wild asses, 6; hares, 23. Birds, 13,964; viz., pigeons, 10,348; *lagar-jhagar* (a species of hawk), 3; eagles, 2; *qalīwāj* (*ghalīwāj*, kite), 23; owls (*chughd*), 39; *qauṭān* (gold-finch ?), 12; kites (*mūsh-khwur*, mice-eaters), 5; sparrows, 41; doves, 25; owls (*būm*), 30; ducks, geese, cranes, etc., 150; crows, 3,276. Aquatic animals, 10 *magar machha*, that is, crocodiles[2] (*nahang*).

[1] The MSS. have 1,672.

[2] See Elliot, vi, 351 and 362, note. Jahāngīr only gives details of the 17,167 animals killed by himself. The *mhāka* is possibly a clerical error for *mār-khwur*. The text says it is allied to the *gawazn*, but the MSS. have *gūr*, a wild ass. The details of the quadrupeds come to 3,203, the total stated by Jahāngīr. The details of the birds come to 13,954, but the 10 crocodiles bring up the figures to 13,964, and the total 3,203 + 13,964 comes to the 17,167 mentioned. It has been suggested to me that the *mhāka* of the text is the *mahā* or swamp-deer of the Terai, *Rucervus Duvaucelli*.

THE TWELFTH NEW YEAR'S FEAST AFTER MY AUSPICIOUS ACCESSION.

One ghari of day remained of Monday, the 30th of the aforesaid (Isfandiyār) month, corresponding to the 12th Rabīʻu-l-awwal, 1026 (20th March, 1617), when the sun changed from the constellation of Pisces into the pleasure-house of Aries, which is his abode of honour and good fortune. At the very time of transit, which was a fortunate hour, I sat upon the throne. I had ordered that according to the usual custom they should decorate the public audience hall with fine cloths, etc. Notwithstanding that many of the Amirs and chief men of the State were in attendance on my son Khurram, a meeting was arranged which was not inferior to those of previous years. I presented the offerings of Tuesday[1] to Ānand Khān. On the same day, which was the 1st Farwardīn of the 12th year (21st or 22nd March, 1617), a representation arrived from Shāh Khurram to the effect that the New Year's festival had been arranged for in the same manner as in previous years, but as the days of travelling and service had occurred the annual offerings of the servants would be remitted. This proceeding of my son was much approved. Remembering my dear son in my prayers, I besought for him from the throne of Allah his welfare in both worlds, and ordered that on this New Year's Day no one should present offerings.

In consequence of the disturbance that tobacco brings about in most temperaments and constitutions, I had ordered that no one should smoke it (lit. draw). My brother Shāh ʻAbbās had also become aware of the mischief arising from it, and had ordered that in Iran no one should venture to smoke. As Khān ʻĀlam

[1] The MSS. have Saturday instead of Tuesday, and this seems reasonable, for there were no offerings on Tuesday (see *infra*).

(ambassador to Persia) was without control in continual smoking of tobacco, he frequently practised it. Yādgār 'Alī Sulṭān, ambassador of the ruler of Iran, represented to Shāh 'Abbās that Khān 'Ālam could never be a moment without tobacco, and he (Shāh 'Abbās) wrote this couplet in answer—

> "The friend's envoy wishes to exhibit tobacco;
> With fidelity's lamp I light up the tobacco-market."

Khān 'Ālam in answer wrote and sent this verse—

> "I, poor wretch, was miserable at the tobacco notice;
> By the just Shah's favour the tobacco-market became brisk."

On the 3rd of the same month, Ḥusain Beg, the diwan of Bengal, had the good fortune to kiss the threshold, and made an offering of twelve elephants, male and female. Ṭāhir, bakhshi of Bengal, who had been accused of several offences, obtained the favour of paying his respects to me, and presented before me an offering of twenty-one elephants. Twelve of these were approved and the remainder I conferred on him. On this day a wine-feast was arranged, and I gave wine to most of the servants who were engaged in waiting on me, and made them all heated with the wine of loyalty. On the 4th the huntsmen sent news that they had marked down a lion in the neighbourhood of the Shakkar[1] tank, which is inside the fort and one of the famous constructions of the rulers of Malwa. I at once mounted and went towards that game. When the lion appeared he charged the ahadis and the retinue and wounded ten[2] or twelve of them. At last I finished his business with three shots[3] (lit. arrows) from my gun, and removed his evil from the servants of God. On the 8th the mansab of Mīr Mīrān, which was 1,000 personal and 400 horse, was

[1] Text, Sakar. Now locally called the Sāgan, 'sea,' tank.
[2] The MSS. only speak of twelve.
[3] The MSS. seem to have merely *ba tīr-i-bandūq*, 'with bullets.'

fixed at 1,500 personal and 500 horse. On the 9th, at the request of my son Khurram, I increased the mansab of Khān Jahān by 1,000 personal and horse, making it thus 6,000 personal and horse; that of Ya'qūb Khān, which was 1,500 personal with 1,000 horse, was made 2,000 personal and 1,500 horse; that of Bahlūl Khān Miyāna[1] was increased by 500 personal and 300 horse to 1,500 personal and 1,000 horse; and that of Mīrzā Sharafu-d-dīn Kāshgharī, by whom and his son great bravery had been shown in the Deccan, was increased to 1,500 personal and 1,000 horse. On the 10th Farwardīn, corresponding with the 22nd Rabī'u-l-awwal, 1026, my lunar weighing took place. On this day two 'Iraq horses from my private stable and a dress of honour were conferred on my son Khurram and sent to him by Bahrām Beg. I increased the mansab of I'tibār Khān to 5,000 personal and 3,000 horse. On the 11th, Ḥusain Beg, of Tabriz, whom the ruler of Iran had sent to the ruler of Golconda by way of embassy, as, in consequence of the quarrel of the Franks with the Persians, the road of the Mīr had been closed,[2] waited upon me with the ambassador of the ruler of Golconda. Offerings came from him of two horses and some *tuqūz*[3] (nine-pieces ?) of cloth from the Deccan and Gujarat. On the same day an 'Iraq horse from my private stable was bestowed on Khān Jahān. On the 15th, 1,000 personal were added to the mansab of Mīrzā Rāja Bhāo Singh, raising it to 5,000 personal and 3,000 horse. On the 17th, 500 horse were added to the mansab of Mīrzā Rustam, and I made it up to 5,000 personal and 1,000 horse; that of Ṣādiq Khān was fixed at 1,500 personal and 700 horse, original and increase; Irādat Khān in the same manner was raised to the mansab of 1,500 and

[1] Biyāna in text.

[2] That is, apparently, the journey back by sea from the Deccan. The MSS. have Ḥasan instead of Ḥusain, and say the route by Ormuz was closed. Perhaps the *ba Mīr* of text is a mistake for *bar baḥr*, 'by sea.

[3] *Tuqūz* means nine in Turkī.

600 horse. To the mansab of Anīrā'ī 500 personal and 100 horse were added, and it was made one of 1,500 personal and 500 horse. Three gharis of Saturday, the 19th, remained when the beginning of the *sharaf* (day of sun's culmination) occurred, and at the same time I again took my seat on the throne. Of the thirty-two prisoners from the army of the rebel 'Ambar who had been captured by the servants of the victorious State in the battle won by Shāh-nawāz Khān and the defeat of that disastrous man ('Ambar), I had handed one man over to I'tiqād Khān. The guards who had been appointed to keep him showed carelessness and let him escape. I was much annoyed at this, and I forbade I'tiqād Khān to come to wait on me for three months. As the said prisoner's name and condition were unknown, he was not caught again, although they showed activity in the matter. At last I ordered the captain of the guards who had been careless in keeping him to be capitally punished. I'tiqād Khān on this day, at the request of I'timādu-d-daulah, had the good fortune to pay his respects to me.

As for a long time no good had been heard of the affairs of Bengal and of the conduct of Qāsim Khān, it entered my mind to send to the Subah of Bengal Ibrāhīm Khān Fatḥ-jang, who had carried on successfully the affairs of the Subah of Behar and had brought a diamond mine into the possession of the State, and to despatch Jahāngīr Qulī Khān, who had a jagir in the Subah of Allahabad, in his place to Behar. I sent for Qāsim Khān to Court. At the same hour on the auspicious day (the day of culmination) an order was given that they should write royal farmans to the effect that *sazāwalān* (revenue collectors) should be appointed to take Jahāngīr Qulī Khān to Behar and to send Ibrāhīm Khān Fatḥ-jang to Bengal. Patronizing Sikandar,[1] the

[1] The I.O. MSS. seem to have Sakakdar or Sakakandar.

jeweller, I promoted him to the mansab of 1,000 personal and 300 horse.

On the 21st I gave leave to Muḥammad Riẓā, ambassador of the ruler of Iran, and bestowed on him 60,000 darbs, equal to 30,000 rupees, with a dress of honour. As an equivalent to the souvenir (*yād-būdī*) that my brother S̲h̲āh ʻAbbās had sent to me, I forwarded with the aforesaid ambassador certain presents of jewelled things which the rulers of the Deccan had sent, with cloths and rare things of every kind fit for presentation, of the value of 100,000 rupees. Among these was a crystal cup that Chelebī[1] had sent from ʻIraq. The Shah had seen this cup and said to the ambassador that if his brother (Jahāngīr) would drink wine out of it and send it to him it would be a great mark of affection. When the ambassador represented this, having drunk wine several times out of the cup in his presence, I ordered them to make a lid and a saucer for it and sent it along with the presents. The lid was of enamel (*mīnā-kārī*). I ordered the Munshis of mercurial writing (*ʻUṭārid-raqm*) to write in due form an answer to the letter he had brought.

On the 22nd the scouts brought in news of a tiger. Mounting immediately, I went against the tiger and with three shots I delivered the people from his wickedness, and himself from the wickedness of his vile nature. Masīḥu-z-zamān produced before me a cat, and represented that it was a hermaphrodite, and that in his house it had young ones, and that when it had connection with another cat, young were born to the latter.

On the 25th the contingent of Iʻtimādu-d-daulah passed before me in review on the plain under the jharoka. There were 2,000 cavalry well horsed, most of whom

[1] It appears from S̲h̲āh ʻAbbās's letter to Jahāngīr (Tūzuk, p. 165) that Muḥammad Ḥusain Chelebī had been employed by Jahāngīr to collect curios in Persia.

were Moghuls, 500 foot armed with bows and guns, and fourteen elephants. The bakhshis reckoned them up and reported that this force was fully equipped and according to rule. On the 26th a tigress was killed. On Thursday, the 1st Urdībihis͟ht, a diamond that Muqarrab K͟hān had sent by runners was laid before me; it weighed 23 *surkh*, and the jewellers valued it at 30,000 rupees. It was a diamond of the first water, and was much approved. I ordered them to make a ring of it. On the 3rd the mansab of Yūsuf K͟hān was, at the request of Bābā K͟hurram, fixed at 1,000 with 1,500 horse, and in the same way the mansabs of several of the Amirs and mansabdars were increased at his suggestion. On the 7th, as the huntsmen had marked down four tigers, when two watches and three gharis had passed I went out to hunt them with my ladies. When the tigers came in sight Nūr-Jahān Begam submitted that if I would order her she herself would kill the tigers with her gun. I said, "Let it be so." She shot two tigers with one shot each and knocked over the two others with four shots. In the twinkling of an eye she deprived of life the bodies of these four tigers. Until now such shooting was never seen, that from the top of an elephant and inside of a howdah (*'amārī*) six shots should be made and not one miss, so that the four beasts found no opportunity to spring or move.[1] As a reward for this good shooting I gave her a pair of bracelets[2] (*pahunchī*) of diamonds worth 100,000 rupees and scattered 1,000 ashrafis (over her). On the same day Ma'mūr K͟hān (the architect-

[1] Note by Sayyid Aḥmad. They say that a poet recited this impromptu couplet—

> "Though Nūr-Jahān be in form a woman,
> In the ranks of men she's a tiger-slayer."

The point of this couplet is that before Nūr-Jahān entered Jahāngīr's harem she was the wife of S͟hīr-afgan, the tiger-slayer. The line may also read "In battle she is a man-smiter and a tiger-slayer."

[2] The two I.O. MSS. have "a pair of pearls and a diamond."

Khan) obtained leave to go to Lahore to complete the buildings of the palace there. On the 10th the death of Sayyid Wāriṣ, who was faujdar of the Subah of Oudh, was reported. On the 12th, as Mīr Maḥmūd asked for a faujdarship, I dignified him with the title of Tahawwur Khān, and, increasing his mansab, appointed him to the faujdarship of some of the parganahs of the Subah of Multan. On the 22nd, Ṭāhir, the bakhshi of Bengal, who had been forbidden to pay his respects, waited upon me and presented his offerings. Eight elephants were also presented as the offering of Qāsim Khān, governor of Bengal, and two as that of Shaikh Modhū. On the 28th, at the request of Khān Daurān, an order was given for the increase of the mansab of 'Abdu-l-'Azīz Khān by 500. On the 5th Khurdād the duty of the Diwanship of Gujarat was given to Mīrzā Ḥusain in supercession of Kesho. I dignified him with the title of Kifāyat Khān. On the 8th, Lashkar Khān, who had been appointed bakhshi of Bangash, came and waited on me; he offered 100 muhrs and 500 rupees. Some days before this Ūstād Muḥammad Nāyī (flute-player), who was unequalled in his craft, was sent by my son Khurram at my summons. I had heard some of his musical pieces[1] (*majlis-sāz*), and he played a tune which he had composed for an ode (*ghazal*) in my name. On the 12th I ordered him to be weighed against rupees; this came to 6,300 rupees. I also gave him an elephant with a howdah,[2] and I ordered him to ride on it and, having packed[3] his rupees about him, to proceed to his lodging. Mullā Asad, the story-

[1] There is a fuller account of this flute-player in Price's Jahāngīr, p. 114. The melody which he composed in Jahāngīr's name is there called by Price Saut Jahāngīrī. (The text does not give the name Jahāngīrī.) It is there stated that Shāh Jahān brought the flute-player with him from Burhanpur and introduced him.

[2] *Ḥauẓa-dārī*, 'with a basin-shaped litter on it.'

[3] The word *pāshīda*, 'scattered,' does not occur in the I.O. MSS. But perhaps the word has two opposite meanings.

teller, one of the servants of Mīrzā Ghāzī, came on the same day from Tattah and waited on me. As he was a reciter and story-teller full of sweetness and smartness, I liked his society, and I made him happy with the title of Maḥẓūẓ Khān, and gave him 1,000 rupees, a dress of honour, a horse, an elephant, and a palanquin. After some days I ordered him to be weighed against rupees, and his weight came up to 4,400. He was raised to the mansab of 200 personal and 20 horse. I ordered him always to be present at the meetings for talk (*gap*). On the same day Lashkar Khān brought his men to the *darshan jharoka* before me. There were 500 horse, 14 elephants, and 100 musketeers. On the 24th news came that Mahā Singh, grandson of Rāja Mān Singh, who was entered among the great officers, had died from excessive wine-drinking at Bālāpūr in the province of Berar. His father also had died at the age of 32 [1] from the drinking of wine beyond measure. On the same day they had brought to my private fruit-house many mangoes from all parts of the province of the Deccan, Burhanpur, Gujarat, and the parganahs of Malwa. Although this province is well known and celebrated for the sweetness, freedom from stringiness, and size of its mangoes, and there are few mangoes that equal its mangoes—so much so that I often ordered them to be weighed in my presence, when they were shown to come to a seer or 1¼ seer or even more—yet in sweetness of water and delicious flavour and digestibility the mangoes of Chaprāmau,[2] in the province of Agra, are superior to all the mangoes of this province and of all other places in India.

On the 28th I sent for my son Bābā Khurram a special gold-embroidered *nādirī* of a fineness such as had never

[1] Father and son both died apparently at the same age.

[2] It was in Sarkar Qanauj (Jarrett, ii, 185). It is Chibrāmau of I.G., iii, 397, and is in Farrukhabad district.

been produced before in my establishment; I ordered the bearer to tell him that as this rarity had the speciality that I had worn it on the day I quitted Ajmir for the conquest of the Deccan, I had sent it to him. On the same day I placed the turban from my own head, just as it was, on the head of I'timādu-d-daulah, and honoured him with this favour. Three emeralds, a piece of jewelled *ūrbasī*,[1] and a ruby signet ring that Mahābat Khān had sent by way of offering were laid before me. They came to 7,000 rupees in value. On this day, by the mercy and favour of Allah, continued rain fell. Water in Māndū had become very scarce and the people were agitated about the matter, so that most of the servants had been ordered to go to the bank of the Narbada. There was no expectation of rain at that season. In consequence of the agitation of the people I turned by way of supplication to the throne of God, and He in His mercy and grace gave such rain that in the course of a day and a night tanks, ponds (*birkahā*), and rivers became full, and the agitation of the people was changed to complete ease. With what tongue can I render thanks for this favour? On the 1st of Tīr a standard was presented to Wazīr Khān. The offering of the Rānā, consisting of two horses, a piece of Gujarati cloth, and some jars of pickles and preserves, was laid before me. On the 3rd, Mu'azzā[2] (?) brought news of the capture of 'Abdu-l-Laṭīf, a descendant of the rulers of Gujarat, who had always been the originator of mischief and disturbance in that Subah. As his capture was a reason for the contentment of the people, praise was given to God, and I ordered Muqarrab Khān to send him to Court

[1] *Ūrvasī* is the name of an Apsara or celestial nymph. Probably it is here the name of a dress. (In Forbes's Hindustani Dictionary *ūrbasī* is said to denote a particular kind of ornament worn on the breast.)

[2] The MSS. have *maghra*, which may be connected with the Arabic *maghr*, 'travelling quickly.' It may be the name of a courier, or merely mean 'quickly.'

by one of his mansabdars. Many of the zamindars in the neighbourhood of Māndū came and waited on me, and laid offerings before me. On the 8th, Rām Dās, son of Rāja Rāj Singh Kachhwāha, was given the *ṭīka* of a Raja, and I honoured him with that title. Yādgār Beg, who was known in Māwarā'a-n-nahr (Transoxiana) as Yādgār Qūrchī, and had not been without connection and influence with the ruler of that country, came and waited on me. Of all his offerings a white china cup on a stand was the most approved. The offering of Bahādur Khān, governor of Qandahar, consisting of nine horses, nine *tuqūz* of fine cloth (81 pieces ?), two black foxes' skins, and other things, was brought before me. Also on this day the Rāja of Gadeha, Pem[1] Narāyan, had the good fortune to wait on me, and made an offering of seven elephants, male and female. On the 10th a horse and dress of honour were given to Yādgār Qūrchī. On the 13th was the feast of rose-water scattering (*gulāb-pāshān*). The rites due to that day were performed. Shaikh Maudūd Chishtī, one of the officers of Bengal, was honoured with the title of Chishtī Khān, and I presented him with a horse. On the 14th, Rāwal Samarsī (Samarsiṃha), son of Rāwal Ūday Singh, zamindar of Bānswāla, waited on me; he gave as offering 30,000 rupees, three elephants, a jewelled *pān-dān* (box for betel), and a jewelled belt. On the 15th nine diamonds which Ibrāhīm Khān Fatḥ-jang, the governor of Behar, had sent along with Muḥammad Beg from the mine, and from the collections of the zamindars of that place, were laid before me. Of these, one weighed 14½ tanks, and was of the value of 100,000 rupees. On the same day Yādgār Qūrchī was presented with 14,000 darbs,

[1] Apparently it should be Bhīm; see *infra*. Gadeha is probably Gadhī in Khandesh; see Lethbridge's "Golden Book of India," p. 138. It is the Garvī of I.G., v, 33, and is one of the Bhīl States in the Dāng Tract.

and I promoted him to the mansab of 500 personal and 300 horse. I fixed the mansab of Tātār Khān, *bakāwul-begī* (chief steward), original and increase, at 2,000 personal and 300 horse, and each of his sons was separately promoted to an increased mansab. At the request of Prince Sulṭān Parwīz, I increased the personal mansab of Wazīr Khān by 500.

On the 29th, which was the auspicious day of Thursday, Sayyid 'Abdu-llah Bārha, the envoy of my son of good fortune, Bābā Khurram, waited on me, and presented a letter from that son containing news of a victory over the provinces of the Deccan. All the chiefs, laying the head of duty in the noose of obedience, had consented to service and humility, and laid before him the keys of forts and strongholds, especially the fort of Ahmadnagar. In gratitude for this great favour and beneficence, placing the head of supplication on the throne of that God who requires no return, I opened my lips in thankfulness, and, humbling myself, ordered them to beat the drums of rejoicing. Thanks be to Allah that a territory that had passed out of hand has come back into the possession of the servants of the victorious State, and that the seditious, who had been breathing the breath of rebellion and boasting, have turned towards supplication and weakness, and become deliverers of properties and payers of tribute. As this news reached me through Nūr-Jahān Begam, I gave her the parganah of Boda (Ṭoḍā ?),[1] the revenue of which is 200,000 rupees. Please God, when the victorious forces enter the province of the Deccan and its forts, and the mind of my excellent son Khurram is satisfied with regard to their possession, he will bring with the ambassadors such an offering from

[1] There was a Bodah in Sarkār Marosor in Malwa, but its revenue was only 2½ lakhs of dams (Jarrett, ii, 208). The two I.O. MSS. and Debi Prasad's Hindi version have Ṭoḍā. Ṭoḍā was in Ajmir, Rantambhor Sarkar, and its revenue in Akbar's time was 1½ lakhs of rupees (Jarrett, ii, 275).

the Deccan as no other king of this age has received. It was ordered that he should bring with him the Amirs who were to receive jagirs in this Subah, in order that they might have the honour of waiting on me. They will thereafter get leave to depart, and the glorious royal standards will return with victory and rejoicing to the capital of Agra. Some days before the news of this victory reached me, I took one night an augury from the diwan of Khwāja Ḥāfiẓ as to what would be the end of this affair, and this ode turned up—

> "The day of absence and night of parting from the friend are o'er.
> I took this augury; the star passed and fulfilment came."[1]

When the secret tongue (*lisānu-l-ghaib*) of Ḥāfiẓ showed such an ending it gave me a strong hope, and accordingly, after twenty-five days, the news of victory arrived. In many of my desires I have resorted to the Khwāja's diwan, and (generally) the result has coincided with what I found there. It is seldom that the opposite has happened.

On the same day I added 1,000 horse to the mansab of Āṣaf Khān, and raised it to that of 5,000 personal and horse. At the end of the day I went with the ladies to look round the building of the Haft Manẓar[2] (seven storeys), and at the beginning of the evening returned to the palace. This building was founded by a former ruler of Malwa, Sulṭān Maḥmūd Khaljī. It has seven storeys, and in each storey there are four chambers (*ṣuffa*) containing four windows. The height of this tower (*mīnār*) is 54½ cubits, and its circumference 50 yards (*gaz*). There are 171 steps from the ground

[1] Ode 192 of Brockhaus' edition, p. 112, first couplet.

[2] This is the building described by William Finch. See the Journal of John Jourdain, ed. by Foster for the Hakluyt Society, App. D. Finch speaks of a high turret 170 steps high. The tower was the Tower of Victory erected by Sulṭān Maḥmūd I in 1443 to commemorate a victory over the Raja of Chitor. "The stump of it has been found." Jourdain speaks of six storeys. It was built of green stone like marble.

to the seventh storey. In going and returning I scattered 1,400 rupees.[1]

On the 31st I honoured Sayyid 'Abdu-llah with the title of Saif Khān, and having exalted him with a dress of honour, a horse, an elephant, and a jewelled dagger, gave him leave and sent him to do duty with my son of lofty fortune. I also sent by him a ruby of the value of more than 30,000 rupees for my son. I did not regard its value, but as for a long time I used to bind it on my own head, I sent it him by way of good augury, considering it lucky for him. I appointed Sulṭān Maḥmūd, a son-in-law of Khwāja Abū-l-ḥasan bakhshi, to be bakhshi and news-writer of the Subah of Behar, and when he took leave I gave him an elephant. At the end of the day of Thursday, 5th Amurdād, I went with the ladies to see the Nīl-kunḍ, which is one of the most[2] pleasant places in the fort of Mandu (Mānḍogaṛh). Shāh-budāgh Khān, who was one of my revered father's most considerable Amirs, at the time when he held this province in jagir, built in this place an exceedingly pleasing and enjoyable building. Delaying there till two or three gharis of night had passed I returned to the auspicious palace.

As several indiscretions on the part of Mukhliṣ Khān, diwan and bakhshi of the Subah of Bengal, had come to my ears, I reduced his mansab by 1,000 personal and 200 horse. On the 7th a war (*mastī*) elephant from among those sent as offerings by 'Ādil Khān, by name Gaj-rāj, was sent to Rānā Amr Singh. On the 11th, I went out to hunt, and came one stage from the fort. There was excessive rain, and the mud was such that there was hardly any moving. For the convenience of the people and the comfort of the animals I gave up

[1] Two hundred rupees per storey (?).

[2] Blochmann, p. 371, and Ma'āṣiru-l-umarā, ii, 537. Now locally called the Nīl-kanṭh, 'blue neck.'

this undertaking, and passing the day of Thursday outside, returned on Friday eve. On the same day Hidāyatu-llah, who is very well suited to carry out the rules and movements (in travelling) of the headquarters (lit. presence), was honoured with the title of Fidā'ī Khān. In this rainy season rain fell in such quantities that old men said that they did not remember such rain in any age. For nearly forty days there was nothing but cloud and rain, so that the sun only appeared occasionally. There was so much wind that many buildings, both old and new, fell down. On the first night there was [1] such rain and thunder and lightning as has seldom been heard of. Nearly twenty women and men were killed, and the foundations even of some of the stone buildings were broken up. No noise is more terrifying than this. Till the middle of the month was passed, wind and rain increased. After this they gradually became less. What can be written of the verdure and self-grown fragrant plants? They covered valley and plain and hill and desert. It is not known if in the inhabited world there exists another such place as Mandu for sweetness of air and for the pleasantness of the locality and the neighbourhood, especially in the rainy season. In this season, which lasts for months and extends up to the hot weather, one cannot sleep inside houses without coverlets, and in the day the temperature is such that there is no need for a fan or for change of place. All that could be written would still fall short of the many beauties of the place. I saw two things that I had not seen in any other place in Hindustan. One was the tree of the wild plantain that grows in most of the uncultivated places in the fort, and the other the nest of the wagtail (*mamūla*), which they call in Persian the *dum-sīcha* (tail-wagger). Up till now none of the hunters had pointed out its nest. By

[1] The text misses out a conjunction before *ṣadā*.

chance in the building I occupied there was its nest, and it brought out two young ones.

Three watches of day had passed on Thursday, the 19th, when I mounted with the ladies in order to go round and see the courts and buildings on the Shakkar tank, founded by former rulers of Malwa. As an elephant had not been conferred on I'timādu-d-daulah on account of his government of the Panjab, I gave him on the road one of my private elephants of the name of Jagjot. I remained in this enchanting place until the evening, and was much delighted with the pleasantness and greenness of the surrounding open spaces. After performing my evening prayer and counting my rosary, we returned to our fixed residence. On Friday an elephant named Ran-bādal (cloud of war ?), which Jahāngīr Qulī Khān had sent as an offering, was brought before me. Having adopted for myself certain special cloths and cloth-stuffs, I gave an order that no one should wear the same but he on whom I might bestow them. One was a *nādirī* coat that they wear over the *qabā* (a kind of outer vest). Its length is from the waist down to below the thighs, and it has no sleeves. It is fastened in front with buttons, and the people of Persia call it *kurdī* (from the country of the Kurds). I gave it the name of nadiri. Another garment is a Ṭūs shawl, which my revered father had adopted as a dress. The next was a coat (qaba) with a folded collar (*batū girībān*). The ends of the sleeves were embroidered. He had also appropriated this to himself. Another was a qaba with a border, from which the fringes of cloth were cut off and sewn round the skirt and collar and the ends of the sleeve. Another was a qaba of Gujarati satin, and another a *chīra* and waistbelt woven with silk, in which were interwoven gold and silver threads.

As the monthly pay of some of Mahābat Khān's horsemen, according to the regulation of three and two horsed men, for the performance of duty in the Deccan, had become increased and the service [1] had not been performed, I gave an order that the civil officers (*dīwāniyān*) should levy the difference from his jagir. In the end of Thursday, the 26th, corresponding with the 14th Sha'bān, which is the Shab-i-barāt, I held a meeting in one of the houses of the palace of Nūr-Jahān Begam, which was situated in the midst of large tanks, and summoning the Amirs and courtiers to the feast which had been prepared by the Begam, I ordered them to give the people cups and all kinds of intoxicating drinks according to the desire of each. Many asked for cups, and I ordered that whoever drank a cup should sit according to his mansab and condition. All sorts of roast meats, and fruits by way of relish, were ordered to be placed before everyone. It was a wonderful assembly. In the beginning of the evening they lighted lanterns and lamps all round the tanks and buildings, and a lighting up was carried out the like of which has perhaps never been arranged in any place. The lanterns and lamps cast their reflection on the water, and it appeared as if the whole surface of the tank was a plain of fire. A grand entertainment took place, and the drinkers of cups took more cups than they could carry.

"A feast was arranged that lighted up the heart,
It was of such beauty as the heart desired.
They flung over this verdant mead
A carpet broad as the field of genius.
From abundance of perfume the feast spread far,
The heavens were a musk-bag by reason of incense,
The delicate ones of the garden (the flowers) became glorious,
The face of each was lighted up like a lamp." [2]

[1] Apparently the meaning is that the standard of two and three horses had not been kept up.

[2] Some lines of this agree with the verses in the Akbar-nāma, ii, 190. The last two lines are quoted again in the account of the 15th year (p. 299 of Persian text).

After three of four gharis of night had passed, I dismissed the men and summoned the ladies, and till a watch of night (remained ?) passed the time in this delightful place, and enjoyed myself. On this day of Thursday several special things had happened. One was that it was the day of my ascension of the throne; secondly, it was the Shab-i-barāt; thirdly, it was the day of the *rākhī*, which has already been described, and with the Hindus is a special day. On account of these three pieces of good fortune I called the day Mubārak-shamba.

On the 27th, Sayyid Kāsū was dignified with the title of Parwarish Khān. Wednesday, in the same way that Mubārak-shamba had been a fortunate one for me, had fallen out exactly the opposite. On this account I gave this evil day the name of Kam-shamba, in order that this day might always fail from the world (lessen). On the next day a jewelled dagger was conferred on Yādgār Qūrchī, and I ordered that after this he should be styled Yādgār Beg. I had sent for Jay Singh, son of Rāja Mahā Singh. On this day he waited on me and presented an elephant as an offering. A watch and three gharis of Mubārak-shamba, the 2nd of Shahriyār, had passed, when I rode to look round the Nīl-kunḍ and its neighbourhood; thence I passed on to the plain of the 'Īd-gāh on the top of a mound that was very green and pleasant. Champa flowers and other sweet wild herbs of that plain had bloomed to such a degree that on all sides on which the eye fell the world looked like a world of greenery and flowers. I entered the palace when a watch of night had passed.

As it had been several times mentioned to me that a kind of sweetmeat was obtained from the wild plantain such that dervishes and other poor people made it their food, I wished to enquire into the matter. What I found was that the fruit of the wild plantain was an exceedingly hard and tasteless thing. The real fact is that in the lower part (of the trunk) there is a thing shaped like a fir-cone from which the real fruit of the plantain comes out. On this a kind of sweetmeat forms which has exactly the juiciness and taste of *pālūda*. It appears that men eat this and enjoy it.[1]

With regard to carrier pigeons (*kabūtar-i-nāma-bar*), it had been stated to me in the course of conversation that in the time of the Abbaside Caliphs they taught[2] the Baghdad pigeons who were styled 'letter-carriers' (*nāma-bar*), and were one-half larger[3] than the wild pigeon. I bade the pigeon-fanciers to teach their pigeons, and they taught some of them in such a manner that we let them fly from Mandu in the early morning, and if there was much rain they reached Burhanpur by 2½ pahars (watches) of the day, or even in 1½ pahars. If the air was very clear most of them arrived by one pahar of the day and some by four gharis (hours) of the day.

On the 3rd a letter came from Bābā Khurram, announcing the coming of Afẓal Khān and Rāy Rāyān and the arrival of the ambassadors of 'Ādil Khān, and their bringing suitable offerings of jewels, jewelled things, elephants, and horses, offerings such as had never come in any reign or time, and expressing much gratitude for the services and loyalty of the aforesaid Khān, and his faithfulness to his word and duty. He asked for a gracious royal firman bestowing on him the title of *farzand* (son) and for other favours, which had never

[1] The account is obscure. Elliot's translation is "In the root of the tree is found a lump of sweet substance which is exactly like that of Faluda. It is eaten by the poor." The text and some MSS. have *yak pārcha-i-shīrīnī*, but B.M. Or. 3276 has *yak pāra*. Roxburgh says nothing about any such growth on the wild plantain. *Fālūda* or *pālūda* is the name of a sweetmeat.

[2] It is curious that the word *amūkhta*, 'taught,' in the text, and which appears to be almost necessary for the sense, does not occur either in the two I.O. MSS. or in the R.A.S. one. Burhanpur is about 100 miles as the crow flies south-south-east of Mandu.

[3] The text has *par*, 'feathers,' instead of the sign of the comparative *tar*, but the MSS. have *kalāntar*.

yet been vouchsafed in his honour. Since it was very gratifying to me to please my son, and his request was reasonable, I ordered that the Munshis of the mercurial pen should write a farman in the name of 'Ādil Khān, conveying every kind of affection and favour, and exceeding in his praise ten or twelve times what had been previously written. They were ordered in these farmans to address him as farzand. In the body of the farman I wrote this couplet with my own hand—

> "Thou'st become, at Shāh Khurram's request,
> Renowned in the world as my son" (*farzandī*).

On the 4th day this farman was sent off with its copy, so that my son Shāh Khurram might see the copy and send off the original. On Mubārak-shamba, the 9th, I went with the ladies to the house of Āṣaf Khān. His house was situated in the valley, and was exceedingly pleasant and bright. It had several valleys round it; in some places there were flowing waterfalls, and mango and other trees exceedingly green and pleasant and shady. Nearly 200 or 300 *keora* shrubs (*gul-i-keoṛā, Pandanus odoratissimus*) grew in one valley. In fine that day passed in great enjoyment. A wine party was held and cups were presented to the Amirs and intimates, and an offering from Āṣaf Khān was laid before me. There were many rare things. I took whatever I approved, and the remainder was given to him. On the same day Khwāja Mīr, son of Sulṭān Khwāja, who had come on a summons from Bangash, waited on me, and presented as an offering a ruby, two pearls, and an elephant. Rāja Bhīm Narāyan, a zamindar of the province of Gadeha, was promoted to the mansab of 1,000 personal and 500 horse. An order was given that a jagir should be provided him out of his native country. On the 12th a letter came from my son Khurram that Rāja Sūraj Mal, son of Rāja Bāso, whose territory is near the fort of Kangra, had promised that in the course of a year he would bring that fort into the possession of the servants of the victorious State. He also sent his letter which covenanted for this. I ordered that after comprehending his desires and wishes, and satisfying himself with regard to them, he should send off the Raja to wait on me, so that he might set about the said duty. On the same day, which was Monday, the 11th, corresponding with the 1st Ramaẓān (2nd September, 1617), after four gharis and seven pals had passed, a daughter was born to my son by the mother of his other children, who was the daughter of Āṣaf K͟hān. This child was named Rūs͟hanārā Begam. As the Zamindar of Jaitpūr, which is in the jurisdiction[1] of Mandu, in consequence of wickedness had not had the felicity of kissing the threshold, I ordered Fidā'ī K͟hān to proceed against him with some mansabdars and 400 or 500 musketeers and plunder his country. On the 13th one elephant was given to Fidā'ī K͟hān and one to Mīr Qāsim, son of Sayyid Murād. On the 16th Jay Singh, son of Rāja Mahā Singh, who was 12 years old, was promoted to the mansab of 1,000 personal and horse. To Mīr Mīrān, son of Mīr K͟halīlullah, I gave an elephant which I had myself approved, and another to Mullā 'Abdu-s-Sattār.[2] Bhoj, son of Rāja Bikramājīt Bhadauriyā, after his father's death, came from the Deccan and waited on me, and presented 100 muhrs as an offering. On the 17th it was represented that Rāja Kalyān had come from the province of Orissa, and proposed to kiss my threshold. As some unpleasant stories had been told with regard to him, an order was given that they should hand him over with his son to

[1] The word is *ḥawālī*, which is sometimes translated 'neighbourhood,' and has been so translated here by Mr. Rogers. But either Jahāngīr has made a mistake or the word *ḥawālī* is capable of a wide interpretation, for Jaitpūr appears to be Jaitpūr in Kathiawar. See Jarrett, ii, 258, and I.G., vii, 192. Possibly Mandu is a mistake for Bāndhū. But there is a Jetgarh in Malwa (Jarrett, ii, 200).

[2] Probably this was the author who collaborated with Jerome Xavier. See Rieu's Catalogue, iii, 1077.

Āṣaf Khān to enquire into the truth of what had been said about him. On the 19th an elephant was given to Jay Singh. On the 20th 200 horses were added to the mansab of Kesho Dās Mārū, so that it came, original and increase, to 2,000 personal and 1,200 horse. On the 23rd, having distinguished Allah-dād, the Afghan, with the title of Rashīd Khān, I gave him a *parm-narm* (shawl). The offering of Rāja Kalyān Singh, consisting of eighteen elephants, was brought before me; sixteen elephants were included in my private elephant stud, and I presented him with two. As the news had arrived from Iraq of the death of the mother of Mīr Mīrān, daughter of Shāh Isma'īl II, of the race of the Ṣafawī kings, I sent him a dress of honour and brought him out of the robes of mourning. On the 25th Fidā'ī Khān received a dress of honour, and, in company with his brother Rūḥu-llah and other mansabdars, obtained leave to go to punish the Zamindar of Jaitpur. On the 28th, having come down from the fort with the intention of seeing the Narbada and to hunt in its neighbourhood, I took the ladies with me, and halted two stages down on the bank of the river. As there were many mosquitoes and fleas, I did not stay more than one night. Having come the next day to Tārāpūr, I returned on Friday, the 31st. On the 1st of the month of Mihr, Muḥsin Khwāja, who at this time had come from Transoxiana, received a dress of honour and 5,000 rupees. On the 2nd, after enquiry into the matters of Rāja Kalyān, with regard to which a report had been received, and which Āṣaf Khan had been appointed to investigate, as he appeared innocent, he enjoyed the good fortune to kiss the threshold, and presented as an offering 100 muhrs and 1,000 rupees. His offering of a string of pearls, consisting of eighty pearls and two rubies, with a bracelet with a ruby and two pearls, and the golden figure of a horse studded with jewels, was laid before me. A petition from Fidā'ī Khān arrived stating that when the victorious army entered the province of Jaitpur the zamindar had elected to run away. He could not oppose Fidā'ī, and his country was ravaged. He now repented of what he had done, and intended to come to the Court, which was the asylum of the world, and proffer service and obedience. A force with Rūḥu-llah was sent in pursuit of him to capture and bring him to Court, or to lay waste and ruin his domain and imprison his women and dependants, who had gone into the country of the neighbouring zamindars. On the 8th Khwāja Niẓām came and laid before me fourteen pomegranates from the port of Mukhā (Mocha), which they had brought to Surat in the space of fourteen days, and in eight days more to Mandu. The size of these was the same as that of the Thatta pomegranates. Though the pomegranates of Thatta are seedless and these have seeds,[1] yet they are delicate, and in freshness excel those of Thatta. On the 9th news came that while Rūḥu-llah was passing through the villages, he came to know that the women and dependants of the Jaitpūrī zamindar were in a certain village. He remained outside, and sent men into the village to make enquiries and to bring out the persons who were there. Whilst he was making enquiries, one of the devoted servants of the zamindar came along with the villagers. Whilst his men were scattered here and there, and Rūḥu-llah with some servants had brought out his furniture and was sitting on a carpet, that devoted servant came behind him and struck him with a spear; the blow was fatal and the spearhead came out at his breast. The pulling out of the spear and the reverting[2] to his original (dying) of Rūḥu-llah took place together. Those who were present sent that wretch to hell. All the men who had been

[1] I.O. MS. 305 has *dāna-ī-nāzikī*, 'soft (or small) seeds.'

[2] Note 181 has *wāṣil gas͟htan*, 'becoming united' (to the Deity).

scattered about put on their armour and attacked the village. Those doomed men (*khūn-giriftahā*) had the disgrace of harbouring[1] rebels and sedition-mongers, and were killed in the course of an astronomical hour. They brought into captivity their wives and daughters, and, setting fire to the village, made it so that nothing was seen but heaps of ashes. They then lifted up the body of Rūḥu-llah and went and joined Fidā'ī Khān. With regard to the bravery and zeal of Rūḥu-llah, there was no dispute; at the most, his carelessness brought about this turn of fortune. No traces of habitation remained in that region; the zamindar of that place went into the hills and jungles and concealed and obliterated himself. He then sent someone to Fidā'ī Khān and begged for pardon for his offences. An order was given that he should be allowed quarter and brought to Court.

The mansab of Muruwwat Khān was fixed, original and increase, at 2,000 personal and 1,500 horse, on condition that he should destroy Harbhān,[2] Zamindar of Chandra-koṭa, from whom travellers endured great annoyance. On the 13th Rāja Sūraj Mal, together with Taqī, the bakhshi who was in attendance on Bābā Khurram, came and waited on me. He represented all his requirements. His engagement to perform the work was approved, and at the request of my son he was honoured with a standard and drums. To Taqī, who had been appointed with him, a jewelled *khapwa* (dagger) was given, and it was arranged that he should finish his own affairs and start off quickly. The mansab of Khwāja 'Alī Beg Mīrzā, who had been appointed to the defence and

[1] *Jā dādan*, 'to give way,' the meaning apparently being that they had protected Rūḥu-llah's murderers. But I.O. MS. 305 seems to have *jāwidān*, 'eternal,' which would mean that they were killed and also eternally disgraced as rebels. The Ma'āṣiru-l-umarā, iii, 13, has a different account of the manner of Rūḥu-llah's death. He was Fidā'ī's elder brother.

[2] The I.O. MSS. have Pīr Bahār and Chandra Kona, which latter may be the place in Midnapur.

administration of Ahmadnagar, was fixed at 5,000 personal and horse. An elephant apiece was given to Nūru-d-dīn Qulī, Khwājagī Ṭāhir, Sayyid Khān Muḥammad, Murtaẓā Khān, and Walī Beg. On the 17th the mansab of Ḥākim Beg was fixed, original and increase, at 1,000 personal and 200 horse. On the same day, after presenting Rāja Sūraj Mal with a dress of honour, an elephant, and a jewelled khapwa, and Taqī with a dress of honour, I gave them leave to proceed on duty to Kangra. When those who had been sent by my son of lofty fortune, Shāh Khurram, with the ambassadors of 'Ādil Khān and his offerings, arrived at Burhanpur, and my son's mind was completely satisfied with regard to the affairs of the Deccan, he prayed for the Subahdarship of Berar, Khandesh, and Ahmadnagar for the Commander-in-Chief, the Khankhanan, and sent his son Shāh-nawāz Khān, who is really Khankhanan junior, with 12,000 cavalry to hold possession of the conquered provinces. Every place and estate were put as jagirs into the hands of reliable men, and fitting arrangements were made for the government of the province. He left, out of the troops that were with him, 30,000 horse and 7,000 musketeer infantry, and took with him the remainder, amounting to 25,000 horse and 2,000 gunners, and set off to wait on me. On Thursday (Mubārak-shamba), the 20th[1] of the month of Mihr (Divine month), in the twelfth year from my accession, corresponding with the 11th Shawwāl, 1026 Hijra (12th October, 1617), after three watches and one ghari had passed, he entered the fort of Mandu auspiciously and joyfully, and had the honour of waiting on me. The duration of our separation was 11[2] months and 11 days. After he had

[1] Text 8th, but should be 20th. See p. 196, where the next Thursday is mentioned as the 27th. See Elliot, vi, 351.

[2] Text 15 months and 11 days, but it should be 11 months. Shāh Jahān left his father at Ajmir on the last day of Shawwāl, 1025, and he rejoined him on 11th Shawwāl of the following year.

performed the dues of salutation and kissing the ground, I called him up into the jharokha, and with exceeding kindness and uncontrolled delight rose from my place and held him in the embrace of affection. In proportion as he strove to be humble and polite, I increased my favours and kindness to him and made him sit near me. He presented 1,000 ashrafis and 1,000 rupees as *nazar* and the same amount by way of alms. As the time did not allow of his presenting all his offerings, he now brought before me the elephant Sarnāk (?) (snake-head ?), that was the chief of the elephants of 'Ādil Khān's offering, with a casket of precious stones. After this the bakhshis were ordered to arrange according to their mansabs the Amirs who had come with my son to pay their respects. The first who had the honour of audience was Khān Jahān. Sending for him above, I selected him for the honour of kissing my feet. He presented 1,000 muhrs and 1,000 rupees as nazr, and a casket filled with jewels and jewelled things as an offering (*pīsh-kash*). What was accepted of his offering was worth 45,000 rupees. After this 'Abdu-llah Khān kissed the threshold, and presented 100 muhrs as nazr. Then Mahābat Khān had the honour of kissing the ground, and presented an offering of 100 muhrs and 1,000 rupees, with a parcel (*gaṭhṛī*) [1] of precious stones and jewelled vessels, the value of which was 124,000 rupees. Of these one ruby weighed 11 miskals; an European brought it last year to sell at Ajmir, and priced it at 200,000 rupees, but the jewellers valued it at 80,000 rupees. Consequently the bargain did not come off, and it was returned to him and he took it away. When he came to Burhanpur, Mahābat Khān bought it from him for 100,000 rupees. After this Rāja Bhāo Singh waited on me, presenting 1,000 rupees as nazr and some jewels and jewelled things as a *pīsh-kash*.

[1] So in text, but I.O. MSS. have *kursī*, 'a chair or stool' (l. 37).

In the same manner Dārāb K͟hān, son of the Khan-khanan, Sardār K͟hān, brother of 'Abdu-llah K͟hān, S͟hajā'at K͟hān the Arab, Dayānat K͟hān, S͟hāh-bāz K͟hān, Mu'tamad K͟hān bakhshi, Ūdā Rām,[1] who was one of the chief Amirs of Niẓāmu-l-mulk, and who came on the promise of my son S͟hāh K͟hurram and joined the ranks of the loyal, waited on me in the order of their mansabs. After this the Wakils of 'Ādil K͟hān had the honour of kissing the ground, and presented a letter from him. Before this, as a reward for the conquest of the Rānā, a mansab of 20,000 personal and 10,000 horse was conferred on my son of lofty fortune. When he had hastened to the capture of the Deccan he had obtained the title of Shah, and now, in reward for this distinguished service, I gave him a mansab of 30,000 personal and 20,000 horse, and bestowed on him the title of S͟hāh Jahān. An order was given that henceforth they should place a chair in the paradise-resembling assemblies near my throne for my son to sit upon. This was a special favour for my son, as it had never been the custom heretofore. A special dress of honour with a gold-embroidered *chārqab,* with collar, the end of the sleeves and the skirt decorated with pearls, worth 50,000 rupees, a jewelled sword with a jewelled *pardala* (belt), and a jewelled dagger were bestowed upon him. In his honour I myself came down from the jharokha and poured over his head a small tray of jewels and a tray of gold (coins).[2] Having called Sarnāk elephant to me, I saw without doubt that what had been heard in its praise and of its beauty was real. It stood all the tests in size, form, and beauty. Few elephants are to be seen of such beauty. As it appeared acceptable to me, I myself mounted (i.e. drove it) and took it into my private palace, and scattered a quantity of gold coins on its head,

[1] Text *būdand,* but Ūdā Rām is the only Dakhani officer mentioned.

[2] The MSS. have *zar-baft,* 'gold brocade.'

and ordered them to tie it up inside the royal palace. With regard to this I gave it the name of Nūr-bakht [1] (light of fortune). On Friday, the 24th, Rāja Bharjīv, Zamindar of Baglāṇa, came and waited on me. His name is Partāp; every Raja there has been of that place they call Bharjīv. He has about 1,500 horse in his pay (*mawājib-khwār*), and in time of need he can bring into the field 3,000 horse. The province of Baglāṇa lies between Gujarat, Khandesh, and the Deccan. It has two strong forts, Sāler and Māler (Muler), and as Māler is in the midst of a populous country he lives there himself. The country of Baglāṇa has pleasant springs and running waters. The mangoes of that region are very sweet and large, and are gathered for nine months from the beginning of immaturity [2] until the end. It has many grapes, but not of the best kinds. The aforesaid Raja does not drop the thread of caution and prudence in dealing with the rulers of Gujarat, the Deccan, and Khandesh. He has never gone himself to see any of them, and if any of them has wished to stretch out his hand to possess his kingdom, he has remained undisturbed through the support of the others. After the provinces of Gujarat, the Deccan, and Khandesh came into the possession of the late king (Akbar), Bharjīv came to Burhanpur and had the honour of kissing his feet, and after being enrolled among his servants was raised to the mansab of 3,000. At this time, when Shāh Jahān went to Burhanpur, he brought eleven elephants as an offering. He came to Court in attendance on my son, and in accordance with his friendship and service was dignified with royal favours, and had presented to him a jewelled sword, an elephant, a horse, and dress of honour. After some days I conferred on him three rings of jacinth (*yāqūt*), diamond, and ruby. On Mubārak-

[1] In reference to his own name of Nūru-d-dīn.
[2] *Ghūragī*, 'unripeness.'

shamba (Thursday), the 27th, Nūr-Jahān Begam prepared a feast of victory for my son Shāh Jahān, and conferred on him dresses of honour of great price, with a *nādirī* with embroidered flowers, adorned with rare pearls, a *sarpīch* (turban ornament) decorated with rare gems, a turban with a fringe of pearls, a waistbelt studded with pearls, a sword with jewelled *pardala* (belt), a *phūl kaṭāra* (dagger), a *sada* (?) of pearls, with two horses, one of which had a jewelled saddle, and a special elephant with two females. In the same way she gave his children and his ladies dresses of honour, *tūquz* (nine pieces) of cloth with all sorts of gold ornaments, and to his chief servants as presents a horse, a dress of honour, and a jewelled dagger. The cost of this entertainment was about 300,000 rupees. Presenting on the same day a horse and dress of honour to 'Abdu-llah Khān and Sardār Khān, his brother, I gave them leave to go to the Sarkar of Kalpi, which had been given them in jagir, and also dismissed Shajā'at Khān to his jagir, which was in the Subah of Gujarat, with a dress of honour and an elephant. I dismissed Sayyid Ḥājī, who was a jagirdar of Behar, with a gift of a horse.

It was frequently reported to me that Khān Daurān had become old and weak, so as to be unfit for active duty, and the Subahs of Kabul and Bangash is a land of disturbance, and to subdue the Afghans required riding and active movement. Inasmuch as caution is the condition of rule, I appointed Mahābat Khān, Subahdar of Kabul and Bangash, giving him a dress of honour, and promoted Khān Daurān to the governorship of the province of Thatta. Ibrāhīm Khān Fatḥ-jang had sent as an offering from Behar forty-nine elephants; these were submitted to me. On this day they brought some *sōna-kela* (golden plantains, bananas) for me. I had never eaten such plantains before. In size they are one finger, and are very sweet and of good flavour; they have no resemblance to plantains of other descriptions, but are somewhat indigestible, so that from the two that I ate I experienced heaviness, whilst others say they can eat as many as seven or eight. Though plantains are really unfit to eat, yet of all the kinds this is the one fit to eat. This year, up to the 23rd of the month of Mihr, Muqarrab K͟hān sent Gujarat mangoes by post (*ḍāk-chaukī*).

On this date I heard that Muḥammad Riẓā, ambassador of my brother S͟hāh 'Abbās, gave up the deposit of his life at Agra through the disease of *ishāl* (diarrhœa). I made the merchant Muḥammad Qāsim, who had come from my brother, his executor, and ordered that according to the will he should convey his goods and chattels to the Shah, so that he might grant them in his own presence to the heirs of the deceased. Elephants and dresses of honour were conferred on Sayyid Kabīr and Bak͟htar K͟hān, Wakils of 'Ādil K͟hān. On Mubārak-s͟hamba, the 13th Ābān, Jahāngīr Qulī Beg, Turkmān, who is dignified with the title of Jān-sipār K͟hān, came from the Deccan and waited on me. His father was included among the Amirs of Iran. He had come from Persia in the time of the late king Akbar, and having a mansab conferred on him was sent to the Deccan. He was brought up in that Subah. Although he had been appointed to a duty, yet as my son S͟hāh Jahān came at this time to pay his respects and represented his sincerity and devotion, I ordered that he should come post to Court and have the good fortune to wait upon me and then return. On this day I promoted Ūdā Rām [1] to the rank of 3,000 personal and 1,500 horse. He is a brahmin by caste, and was much relied on by 'Ambar. At the time when S͟hāh-nawāz K͟hān went against 'Ambar, Ādam K͟hān Ḥabs͟hī, Jādū Rāy, Bābū Rāy Kāyath, Ūdā Rām, and some other Sardārs of Niẓāmu-l-mulk

[1] The Ūdājī Rām of Ma'āṣiru-l-umarā, i, 142.

left him and came to Shāh-nawāz Khān. After 'Ambar's defeat they, by the persuasions of 'Ādil Khān and the deceit of 'Ambar, left the right road again and gave up their loyalty and service. 'Ambar took an oath on the Koran to Ādam Khān and put him off his guard, and, capturing him deceitfully, imprisoned him in the fort of Daulatabad, and at last killed him. Bābū Rāy Kāyath and Ūdā Rām came away and went to the borders of 'Ādil Khān's dominions, but he would not admit them into his territory. About that time Bābū Rāy Kāyath lost his life (lit. played away the coin of existence) by the deceit of his intimates, and 'Ambar sent a force against Ūdā Rām. He fought well and defeated 'Ambar's army. But afterwards, as he could not remain in that country, he threw himself on to the borders of the royal dominions, and, having got a promise, came with his family and dependants and entered the service of my son Shāh Jahān. That son distinguished him with favours and kindnesses of all sorts, and made him hopeful by giving him a mansab of 3,000 personal and 1,000 horse, and brought him to Court. As he was a useful servant, I increased this by 500 horse. I also increased the mansab of Shāh-bāz Khān, who had one of 2,000 personal and 1,500 horse, by 500 more horse, and gave him the faujdarship of the Sarkar of Sārangpūr and a part of the Subah of Malwa. A special horse and elephant were given to Khān Jahān. On Mubārak-shamba (Thursday), the 10th of the month, my son Shāh Jahān produced his own offerings—jewels and jewelled things and fine cloths and other rare things. These were all laid out in the courtyard of the jharokha, and arranged together with the horses and elephants adorned with gold and silver trappings. In order to please him I came down from the jharokha and looked through them in detail. Among all these there was a fine ruby they had bought for my son at the port of Goa for 200,000 rupees; its weight was 19½ tanks, or

17 miskals, and 5½ surkhs. There was no ruby in my establishment over 12 tanks, and the jewellers agreed to this valuation. Another was a sapphire, among the offerings of 'Ādil K͟hān; it weighed 6 tanks and 7 surkhs and was valued at 100,000 rupees. I never before saw a sapphire of such a size and good colour. Another was the Chamkoṛa diamond, also of 'Ādil K͟hān's; its weight was 1 tank and 6 surkhs, which they valued at 40,000 rupees. The name of Chamkoṛa is derived from this, that there is in the Deccan a plant called *sāg-i-chamkoṛa.*[1] At the time when Murtaẓā Niẓāmu-l-mulk conquered Berar he had gone one day with his ladies round to look at the garden, when one of the women found the diamond in a chamkora vegetable, and took it to Niẓāmu-l-mulk. From that day it became known as the Chamkora diamond, and came into the possession of the present Ibrāhīm 'Ādil K͟hān during the interregnum (*fatarāt*) of Ahmadnagar. Another was an emerald, also among 'Ādil K͟hān's offerings. Although it is from a new mine, it is of such a beautiful colour and delicacy as I have never before seen. Again, there were two pearls, one of the weight of 64 surkhs, or 2 miskals and 11 surkhs, and it was valued at 25,000 rupees. The other weighed 16 surkhs, and was of exceeding roundness and fineness. It was valued at 12,000 rupees. Another was a diamond from the offerings of Quṭbu-l-mulk, in weight 1 tank, and valued at 30,000 rupees. There were 150 elephants, out of which three had gold trappings, chains, etc., and nine had silver trappings. Though twenty[2] elephants were put into my private stud, five were very large and celebrated. The first, Nūr-bak͟ht, which my son presented on the day of meeting, was worth 125,000 rupees. The second, Mahīpati,[3] from the offerings of 'Ādil K͟hān, was valued

[1] *Jamkūra* is given in Forbes as the Dakhani word for a covering made of reeds or palm-leaves and used in rainy weather.

[2] The MS. has eight.

[3] In the MSS. the name seems to be Hansomat (swan-like ?).

at 100,000 rupees; I gave it the name of Durjansāl. Another, also from his offerings, was Bakht-buland, and valued at 100,000 rupees; I called it Girān-bār. Another was Qaddūs Khān, and the fifth was Imām Riẓā. They were from the offerings of Quṭbu-l-mulk. Each of the two was valued at 100,000 rupees. Again, there were 100 Arab and Iraq horses, most of which were good horses. Of these, three had jewelled saddles. If the private offerings of my son and those of the rulers of the Deccan were to be written down in detail, it would be too long a business. What I accepted of his presents was worth 2,000,000 rupees. In addition to this he gave his (step-)mother,[1] Nūr-Jahān Begam, offerings worth 200,000 rupees, and 60,000 rupees to his other mothers and the Begams. Altogether my son's offerings came to 2,260,000 rupees, or 75,000 tumans of the currency of Iran or 6,780,000 current Tūrān-khānīs. Such offerings had never been made during this dynasty. I showed him much attention and favour; in fact, he is a son who is worth grace and kindness. I am very pleased and satisfied with him. May God Almighty allow him to enjoy long life and prosperity!

As I had never in my life had any elephant-hunting, and had a great desire to see the province of Gujarat and to look on the salt sea, and my huntsmen had often gone and seen wild elephants and fixed on hunting-places, it occurred to me to travel through Ahmadabad and look on the sea, and having hunted elephants on my return, when it was hot and the season for hunting them, to go back to Agra. With this intention I despatched to Agra Ḥaẓrat Maryamu-z-zamān (his mother) and the other Begams and people of the harem with the baggage and extra establishments, and betook myself to a tour in the Subah of Gujarat to hunt, with such as were indispensable

[1] Text has *wālida-i-khūd*, 'his own mother.'

with me. On the eve of Friday in the month of Ābān (precise date not given, but apparently the 10th), I marched auspiciously and happily from Mandu, and pitched on the bank of the tank of Nālchhā. In the morning I went out to hunt and killed a blue bull with my gun. On the eve of Saturday, Mahābat Khān was presented with a special horse and an elephant, and obtained leave to go to his Subah of Kabul and Bangash. At his request I conferred on Rashīd Khān a robe of honour, a horse, an elephant, and a jewelled dagger, and appointed him to assist him. I promoted Ibrāhīm Ḥusain to the post of bakhshi in the Deccan, and Mīrak Ḥusain to that of news-writer in the same Subah. Rāja Kalyān,[1] son of Rāja Ṭoḍar Mal, had come from the Subah of Orissa; on account of some faults which had been attributed to him he had for some days been forbidden the honour of paying his respects. After enquiry his innocence appeared clear, and having given him a dress of honour and a horse, I appointed him to do duty together with Mahābat Khān in Bangash. On Monday I gave the Wakils of ʻĀdil Khān jewelled turban fringes after the fashion of the Deccan, one of the value of 5,000 rupees and the other worth 4,000 rupees. As Afẓal Khān and Rāy Rāyān had performed the duties of Wakils to my son Shāh Jahān in a becoming manner, I raised them both in mansab and honoured Rāy Rāyān with the title of Bikramājīt, which among Hindus is the highest title. In truth he is a servant worthy of patronage. On Saturday, the 12th, I went to hunt and shot two female nilgaw. As the hunting-ground was a long way from this halting-place, I on Monday marched 4½ kos[2] and pitched at the village of Kaid Ḥasan. On Tuesday, the 15th, I killed three blue bulls, the larger one of which weighed 12 maunds. On this day Mīrzā

[1] A repetition. [2] The MSS. have 3¾ kos.

Rustam escaped a great danger.[1] It seems that he had taken aim at a mark and fired his gun. Then he re-loaded, and as his bullet was very flexible, he rested the gun on his chest and put the bullet between his teeth in order that he might contract it and put it right. By chance the match reached the pan, and his chest at the place where the gun was resting was burnt to the extent of the palm of the hand, and the grains of powder got into his skin and flesh and a wound was made, and he suffered much pain.[2]

On Sunday (?), the 16th,[3] four nilgaw were killed, three females and one *būkra* [4] nilgaw. On Mubārak-shamba (Thursday) I went to look round a hill valley in which there was a waterfall near the camp. At this season it had but little water, but as for two or three days they had dammed the watercourse and, about the time of my reaching the place, let it loose, it flowed over very well. Its height might be 20 *gaz*. It separates at the top of the hill and flows down. In this way it is a great boon (*ghanīmat*) on the road. Having enjoyed the usual cups on the edge of the stream and the shade of the hill, I came back to the camp at night. On this day the Zamindar of Jaitpur, whose offences I had forgiven at the request of my son Shāh Jahān, had the good fortune of kissing the threshold. On Friday, the 18th, a large blue bull and a bukra, and on Saturday, the 19th, two females, were killed.

1 Text *khaṭa'*, 'fault,' but the MSS. show that the word is *khaṭar*, 'danger.'

2 The passage is obscure, and the MSS. do not throw much light on it. Fortunately for the Mīrzā, there was no bullet in his gun. The word which I have translated by 'flexible' is *rawān*. Perhaps the meaning is quite different. Possibly it is "he would fire a shot and then reload. As many of his bullets had been shot away, he put a pellet (*ghalulā*) into his mouth and was shaping it," etc.

3 He has just spoken of Tuesday as the 15th! And as Jahāngīr did not shoot on Sundays, Sunday must be a mistake for Wednesday. It is Wednesday in I.O. MS. 305.

4 Perhaps *būkra* here means a male nilgaw; *būkra* means also a he-goat.

As my huntsmen represented that there was much game in the parganah of Ḥāṣilpūr, I left my large camp at this halting-place, and on Sunday, the 20th, and with some of my close attendants, hastened to Ḥāṣilpūr, a distance of 3 kos. Mīr Ḥusāmu-d-dīn, son of Mīr Jamālu-d-dīn Ḥusain Injū, who has the title of ʻAẓudu-d-daulah, was promoted to the mansab, original and increase, of 1,000 personal and 400 horse. I presented Yādgār Ḥusain Qūsh-begi and Yādgār Qūrchī, who had been appointed to do duty in Bangash, with an elephant each. On this day some Ḥusainī grapes without seeds arrived from Kabul; they were very fresh. The tongue of this suppliant at the throne of God fails in gratitude for the favours by which, notwithstanding a distance of three months, grapes from Kabul arrive quite fresh in the Deccan. On Monday, the 21st, three small blue bulls, on Tuesday, the 22nd, one blue bull and three cows, and on Kam-shamba (Wednesday), the 23rd, one cow, were killed. On Mubārak-shamba, the 24th, a feast of cups was held on the bank of the tank of Ḥāṣilpūr. Cups were presented to my son Shāh Jahān and some of the great Amirs and private servants. On Yusūf Khān, son of Ḥusain Khān (Tukriyah), who was of the houseborn ones worthy of patronage, was bestowed the mansab of 3,000 personal and 1,500 horse, original and increase, and he was dismissed to the faujdarship of Gonḍwāna, dignifying him with a gift of a dress of honour and an elephant. Rāy Bihārī Dās, the diwan of the Subah of the Deccan, had the good fortune to kiss the threshold. On Friday Jān-sipār Khān was exalted with a standard, presented with a horse and a dress of honour, and despatched to the Deccan. This day I made a remarkable shot with a gun. By chance there was inside the palace a *khirnī* tree (*Mimusops Kauki*). A *qurīsha*[1] (?) came

[1] This is the same kind of bird that Nūr-Jahān is mentioned as having shot. Perhaps a green pigeon is meant.

and sat on a high branch, and I saw its breast in the midst of it. I fired at it and struck it in the middle of its breast; from where I stood to the top of the branch was 22 gaz. On Saturday, the 26th, marching about 2 kos, I pitched at the village of Kamālpūr. On this day I shot a blue bull.[1] Rustam K͟hān, who was one of the principal attendants of my son S͟hāh Jahān, and who had been appointed from Burhanpur with a body of the royal servants against the zamindars of Gonḍwāna, having taken a tribute of 110 elephants and 120,000 rupees, came this day to wait upon me. Zāhid, son of S͟hajā'at K͟hān, was given the mansab of 1,000 personal and 400 horse, original and increase. On Sunday, the 27th, I hunted with hawks and falcons. On Monday I killed a large blue bull and a bukra; the bull weighed 12½ maunds. On Tuesday, the 29th, a blue bull was killed. Bahlūl Miyāna and Allah-yār came from service in Gonḍwāna, and had the good fortune to wait upon me. Bahlūl K͟hān is the son of Ḥasan Miyāna, and Miyāna is an Afghan tribe. In the commencement of his career Ḥasan was a servant of Ṣādiq K͟hān, but a servant who recognized the king (worthy of a king's service), and was at last included among the royal servants and died on service in the Deccan. After his death his sons were granted mansabs. He had eight sons, and two of them became famous as swordsmen. The elder brother in his youth gave up the deposit of his life. Bahlūl by degrees was promoted to the mansab of 1,000. At this time my son S͟hāh Jahān arrived at Burhanpur, and, finding him worthy of patronage, made him hopeful with a mansab of 1,500 personal and 1,000 horse. As he had not yet waited on me and was very desirous to kiss the threshold, I summoned him to Court. He is in truth

[1] Text *nīla*, without the addition of *gaw*. The MSS. have *gor* or *chor*, a pheasant (?).

a good Khāna-zāda (household-born one), inasmuch as his heart is adorned with the perfection of bravery and his exterior is not wanting in good appearance. The mansab my son Shāh Jahān had bespoken for him was granted at his request, and he was honoured with the title of Sar-buland Khān. Allah-yār Koka was also a brave youth and a servant worthy of patronage. Finding him fit and suitable for service in my presence, I sent for him to Court. On Kam-shamba (Wednesday), the 1st of the month of Āẕar, I went out to hunt and shot a blue bull. On this day the Kashmir[1] reports were laid before me. One was that in the house of a certain silk-seller two girls were born with teeth, and with their backs as far as the waist joined together, but the heads, arms, and legs were separate ; they lived a short time and died. On Mubārak-shamba, the 2nd, on the bank of a tank where my tents were, a feast of cups was held. Presenting Lashkar Khān with a dress of honour and an elephant, I promoted him to the duty of diwan of the Subah of the Deccan, and gave him the mansab of 2,500 personal and 1,500 horse, original and increase. To each of the Wakils of ʻĀdil Khān two[2] *kaukab-i-ṭāliʻ* (horoscope star) muhrs, the weight of each of which was 500 ordinary muhrs, were given. I gave a horse and robe of honour to Sar-buland Khān. As fitting service and approved activity were manifest in Allah-yār Koka, I honoured him with the title of Himmat Khān and gave him a dress of honour. On Friday, the 3rd, I marched 4¼ kos and halted the royal standards in the parganah of Dikhtān.[3] On Saturday also I marched 4¼ kos and halted at the township of Dhār.

Dhār is one of the old cities, and Rāja Bhoj, who was

[1] Elliot, vi, 352.

[2] The 'two' is omitted in text.

[3] In Sarkār Māndū (Jarrett, ii, 207). Debi Prasad's Hindi version has *Daknā*.

one of the great Rajas of Hindustan, lived in it. From his time 1,000[1] years have passed, and in the time of the Sultans of Malwa it was for a long time the capital. At the time when Sulṭān Muḥammad Tughluq was proceeding to the conquest of the Deccan, he built a fort of cut stone on the top of a ridge. Outside it is very showy and handsome, but inside the fort is devoid of buildings. I ordered them to measure its length, breadth, and height. The length inside the fort was 12 *ṭanāb*, 7 gaz; the breadth, 17 tanab, 13 gaz, and the breadth of the fort wall 19½ gaz. Its height up to the battlements appeared to be 17½ gaz. The length of the outer circuit (?) of the fort was 55 tanabs. 'Amīd Shāh Ghorī, who was called Dilāwar Khān, and who in the time of Sulṭān Muḥammad, son of Sulṭān Fīrūz, king of Delhi, had complete authority over the province of Malwa, built the Jāmiʿ mosque in the inhabitable part outside the fort, and opposite the gate of the mosque fixed a quadrangular iron column. When Sulṭān Bahādur of Gujarat took the province of Malwa into his own possession, he wished to transfer this column to Gujarat. The artificers did not take proper precautions when they lowered it, and it fell and broke into two pieces, one of them of 7½ gaz and the other of 4¼ gaz. The column was 1¼ gaz round. As it was lying there useless, I ordered them to take the larger piece to Agra and put[2] it up in the courtyard of the mausoleum of H.M. Akbar, and to burn a lamp on the top of it at night. The aforesaid mosque has two gates. In front of the arch of one gate some sentences in prose have been carved on a stone tablet; their purport is that 'Amīd Shāh Ghorī founded this mosque in the

[1] The MSS. have "more than 1,000." Rāja Bhoj's date, according to Tod, is 567 A.D. (Jarrett, ii, 211).

[2] This iron pillar is not now in existence at the mausoleum of Akbar (Note of Sayyid Aḥmad). The pieces of the pillar are still lying at Dhār, outside the Lāt Musjid (I.G., new ed., xi, 295).

year 870,[1] and on the arch of the other gate a *qaṣīda* has been written, and these few couplets are from it—

"The lord of the age, the star of the sphere of glory,
Centre of the people of the earth, sun of the zenith of perfection,
Asylum and support of religious law, 'Amīd Shāh Dā'ūd,[2]
In whose excellent qualities Ghor glories,
Helper and protector of the Faith of the Prophet, Dilāwar Khān,
Who has been chosen by the most mighty Lord (God),
Founded the Jāmi' mosque in the city of Dhār,
At a fortunate, auspicious time, on a day of happy omen.
The date of eight hundred and seven[3] had passed
When the Court of hopes was completed by Fortune."

When Dilāwar Khān gave up the deposit of his life there was no king with full dominion over Hindustan, and it was a time of confusion. Hūshang, son of Dilāwar Khān, who was just and possessed of courage, seeing his opportunity, sat on the throne of sovereignty in Malwa. After his death through destiny the rule was transferred[4] to Maḥmūd Khaljī, son of Khān Jahān, who had been Vizier to Hūshang, and passed from him to his son Ghiyāṣu-d-dīn, and after him to Nāṣiru-d-dīn, son of Ghiyāṣu-d-dīn, who gave his father poison and sat on the throne of infamy. From him it passed to his son Maḥmūd. Sulṭān Bahādur of Gujarat took from Maḥmūd the province of Malwa. The succession of kings of Malwa ended with the aforesaid Maḥmūd.

On Monday, the 6th, I went to hunt and shot a female nilgaw. Presenting an elephant to Mīrzā Sharafu-d-dīn Ḥusain Kāshgharī, I dismissed him to duty in the Subah of Bangash. A present of a jewelled dagger, a muhr of 100 tolas, and 20,000 darbs was made to Ūdā Rām. On Tuesday, the 7th, I shot an alligator in the tank at Dhār. Though only the top of his snout was visible and the rest of his body was hidden in the water, I fired

[1] The MSS. have 807, and this is correct, for Dilāwar conquered Malwa in 803 = 1400.

[2] Probably this means that 'Amīd was the son of Dā'ūd.

[3] Text 70, but should be 7. 807 = 1405.

[4] A son of Hūshang, Muḥammad Shāh, intervened.

at a guess and hit him in his lungs and killed him with a single shot. An alligator is of the crocodile species and exists in most of the rivers of Hindustan, and grows very large. This one was not so very big. An alligator has been seen (by me) 8 gaz long and 1 gaz in breadth. On Sunday, marching 4½ kos, I halted at Sa'dalpūr. In this village there is a stream over which Nāṣiru-d-dīn Khaljī built a bridge and erected buildings. It is a place like Kāliyāda, and both are his works. Although his building is not worthy of praise, yet as it has been built in the river-bed and they have made rivulets and reservoirs, it is somewhat remarkable. At night I ordered them to place lamps all round the canals and streams. On Mubārak-shamba (Thursday), the 9th, a feast of cups was held. On this day I made a present to my son Shāh Jahān of a ruby of one colour, weighing 9 tanks and 5 surkh, of the value of 125,000 rupees, with two pearls. This is the ruby which had been given to my father at the time of my birth by Ḥaẓrat Maryam-makānī, mother of H.M. Akbar, by way of present when my face was shown, and was for many years in his *sarpīch* (turban ornament). After him I also happily wore it in my sarpich. Apart from its value and delicacy, as it had come down as of auspicious augury to the everlasting State, it was bestowed on my son. Having raised Mubāriz Khān to a mansab of 1,500 personal and horse, I appointed him to the faujdarship of the province of Mewāt, distinguishing him with the present of a dress of honour, a sword, and an elephant. A sword was given to Himmat Khān, son of Rustam Khān. I gave Kamāl Khān, the huntsman, who is one of the old servants and is always present with me on hunting expeditions, the title of Shikār Khān (hunting-Khān). Appointing Ūdā Rām to service in the Subah of the Deccan, I conferred on him a dress of honour, an elephant, and Iraq horses (lit. wind-footed ones), and sent with him for the

Commander-in-Chief, Khankhanan, the Ātāliq, a special gilt dagger (*zar-nis͟hān*). On Friday, the 10th, I halted. On Saturday, the 11th, I marched 3¾ kos and halted at the village of Ḥalwat.[1] On Sunday, the 12th, marching 5 kos, I halted in the parganah [2] of Badnor. This parganah from the time of my father had been in the jagir of Kes͟ho Dās Mārū,[3] and in fact had become a kind of *waṭan* (native country) to him. He had constructed gardens and buildings. Out of these one was a well (*bāolī*) (step-well probably) on the road, which appeared exceedingly pleasant and well made. It occurred to me that if a well had to be made anywhere on a roadside it should be built like this one. At least two such ought to be made.

On Monday, the 13th, I went to hunt and shot a blue bull. From the day on which the elephant Nūr-bak͟ht was put into the special elephant stables, there was an order that he should be tied up in the public palace (court). Among animals elephants have the greatest liking for water; they delight to go into the water, notwithstanding the winter and the coldness of the air, and if there should be no water into which they can go, they will take it from a water-bag (*mas͟hk*) with their trunks and pour it over their bodies. It occurred to me that however much an elephant delights in water, and it is suited to their temperament, yet in the winter the cold water must affect them. I accordingly ordered the water to be made lukewarm (as warm as milk) before they (the elephants) poured it into their trunks. On other days when they poured cold water over themselves they evidently shivered, but with warm water, on the contrary, they were delighted. This usage is entirely my own.

[1] The MSS. have Jalot (as in the Hindi version).

[2] Text, "the parganah aforesaid." But the MSS. have Badnor. See *infra*, p. 204 of text. (In this passage the Hindi version has *Madlor.*)

[3] Blochmann, p. 502.

On Tuesday, the 14th, marching 6 kos, I halted at Sīlgaṛh (Sabalgaṛh ?). On Wednesday, the 15th, crossing the Mahī River, a halt was made near Rāmgaṛh. A march of 6 kos was made on Thursday, the 16th, and a halt was made and a feast of cups held at a waterfall near the camp. Distinguishing Sar-buland Khān with a standard and giving him an elephant, I dismissed him to do duty in the Deccan. His mansab, original and increase, was fixed at 1,500 personal and 1,200 horse. Rāja Bhīm Narāyan, Zamindar of Gadeha, who had been promoted to the mansab of 1,000 horse, obtained leave to go to his jagir. Having raised Rāja Bharjīv, Zamindar of Baglāṇa, to the mansab of 4,000, I gave him leave to go to his native country, and an order was given that when he arrived there he should send to Court his eldest son, who was his successor, that he might do duty in my presence. I honoured Ḥājī Balūch, who was the chief of the huntsmen and was an active and old servant, with the title of Balūch Khān. On Friday, the 17th, marching 5 kos, I alighted at the village of Dhāvala. On Saturday, the 18th, which was the feast of Qurbān, after the Qurbān rites had been performed, marching 3¼ kos, I halted on the bank of the tank of the village of Nāgor.[1] On Sunday, the 19th, marching about 5 kos, the royal standards were erected on the bank of the tank of the village of Samriya. On Monday, the 20th, marching 4¼ kos, we alighted at the chief place of the Doḥad[2] parganah. This parganah is on the boundary between Malwa and Gujarat. Until I passed Badnor the whole country was a jungle, with an abundance of trees and stony land. On Tuesday, the 21st, I halted. On Kamshamba (Wednesday), the 22nd, marching 5¼ kos, I halted at the village of Ranyād (Renāv ?). On Thursday, the 23rd, I halted and held a feast of cups on the bank of

[1] MSS. Bākor.

[2] Daḥūt in MSS. But Doḥad seems right, as it means two boundaries.

the village tank. On Friday, the 24th, marching $2\frac{1}{2}$ kos, the royal standards were hoisted at the village of Jālot. At this halt some jugglers from the Carnatic came and showed their tricks. One of them placed one end of an iron chain, $5\frac{1}{2}$ gaz in length and weighing 1 seer and 2 dams,[1] in his throat and slowly swallowed it with the aid of water. It was for a while in his stomach; after this he brought it up. On Saturday, the 25th, there was a halt. On Sunday, the 26th, marching 5 kos, I alighted at the village of Nīmdah. On Monday, the 27th, also marching 5 kos, I pitched on the bank of a tank. On Tuesday, the 28th, marching $3\frac{3}{4}$ kos, the royal standards alighted near the township of Sahrā[2] on the edge of a tank. The flower of the lotus, which in the Hindi language they call *kumudinī,* is of three colours—white, blue, and red. I had already seen the blue and white, but had never seen the red. In this tank red flowers were seen blooming. Without doubt it is an exquisite and delightful flower, as they have said—

> "From redness and moistness it will melt away."[3]

The flower of the *kaṇwal*[4] is larger than the kumudini. Its flower is red. I have seen in Kashmir many kanwal with a hundred leaves (petals). It is certain that it opens during the day and becomes a bud at night. The kumudini, on the contrary, is a bud during the day and opens at night. The black bee, which the people of India call *bhauṇrā,* always sits on these flowers, and goes inside them to drink the juice that is in both of them. It often happens that the kanwal flower closes and

[1] The *dam* was also used as a weight, and was equal to 5 *tānk* or 1 *tola,* 8 *masha,* 7 *surkh* (Blochmann, p. 31).

[2] Apparently Sahrā is the name of a town, and does not mean an open space here.

[3] Perhaps the line refers to the bee, and means that the bee wishes to suck the moisture of the flower.

[4] The MSS. have *gul-i-kūl,* 'the flower of the tank.' It seems to be a water-lily.

the bee remains in it the whole night. In the same manner it remains in the kumudini flower. When the flower opens it comes out and flies away. As the black bee is a constant attendant on these flowers, the poets of India look on it as a lover of the flower, like the nightingale, and have put into verse sublime descriptions of it. Of these poets the chief was Tān Sen Kalāwant, who was without a rival in my father's service (in fact, there has been no singer like him in any time or age). In one of his compositions he has likened the face of a young man to the sun and the opening of his eyes to the expanding of the kanwal and the exit of the bee. In another place he has compared the side-glance of the beloved one to the motion of the kanwal when the bee alights on it.

At this place figs arrived from Ahmadabad. Although the figs of Burhanpur are sweet and well-grown, these figs are sweeter and with fewer seeds, and one may call them 5 per cent. better. On Kam-shamba, the 29th, and Mubārak-shamba, the 30th, we halted. At this stage Sar-farāz Khān came from Ahmadabad and had the good fortune to kiss the threshold. Out of his offerings a rosary of pearls, bought for 11,000 rupees, two elephants, two horses, two bullocks and a riding cart, and some pieces of Gujaratī cloth, were accepted, and the remainder presented to him. Sar-farāz Khān is a grandson of Muṣāḥib Beg, by which name he was called by Akbar after his grandfather, who was one of the Amirs of Humāyūn. In the beginning of my reign I increased his mansab and appointed him to the Subah of Gujarat. As he had an hereditary connection with the Court as a Khana-zada (one born in the house), he proved himself efficient in the Subah of Gujarat. Considering him worthy of patronage, I gave him the title of Sar-farāz Khān and raised him in the world, and his mansab has risen to 2,000 personal and 1,000 horse. On Friday, the 1st of Day, I marched $3\frac{3}{4}$ kos and halted on the bank of the tank of Jhasod.[1] At this stage Rāy Mān, captain of the Khidmatiya,[2] caught a *rohū* fish and brought it. As I am particularly partial to the flesh of fish, especially that of the rohu, which is the best kind of fish in Hindustan, and I had never, notwithstanding much enquiry, had one for eleven months from the time of crossing the pass of Ghātī Chand[3] until the present time, and now obtained it, I was greatly delighted. I presented a horse to Rāy Mān. Although the parganah of Dohad is reckoned as within the boundary of Gujarat, yet, in fact, it was from this stage that all things appeared different. The open plains and soil are of a different kind; the people are different and the language of another description. The jungle that appeared on the road has fruit-bearing trees, such as the mango and *khirnī* and tamarind, and the method of guarding the cultivated fields is with hedges of *ẓaqqūm*. The cultivators separate their fields with cactus, and leave a narrow road between them for coming and going. Since all this country has a sandy soil, when any movement takes place, so much dust rises that the faces of people are seen with difficulty, so that one should call Ahmadabad 'Gardābād'[4] (abode of dust). On Saturday, the 2nd, having marched $3\frac{3}{4}$ kos, I encamped on the bank of the Mahī. On Sunday, the 3rd, again after a march of $3\frac{3}{4}$ kos, I halted at the village of Bardala. At this stage a number of mansabdars who had been appointed to serve in Gujarat had the good fortune to kiss the threshold. Marching 5 kos on Monday, the 4th, the royal

[1] Query "the tank of Yasodā," the foster-mother of Krishna ?

[2] Blochmann, p. 252.

[3] Jahāngīr crossed the Ghātī Chand or Chānd, between Ajmere and Malwa, in the 11th year (see p. 172), but he does not speak of having had any rohu fish there. Perhaps the reference is to his halt at Rāmsar shortly before coming to Ghātī Chand. He got 104 rohu at Rāmsar. See p. 169.

[4] Elliot, vi, 353.

standards halted at Chitrasīmā, and the next day, Tuesday, after a march of 5 kos, in parganah Mondā.[1] On this day three blue bulls were killed; one was larger than the others and weighed 13 maunds and 10 seers. On Wednesday, the 6th, I marched 6 kos and halted in parganah Naryād.[2] In passing through the town I scattered 1,500 rupees. On Thursday, the 7th, marching 6½ kos, I halted in the parganah of Pitlād.[3] In the country of Gujarat there is no larger parganah than this; it has a revenue of 700,000 rupees, equal to 23,000 current tumans of Iraq. The population of the town (*qaṣba*), too, is dense. Whilst I passed through it I scattered 1,000 rupees. All my mind is bent upon this, that under any pretext the people of God may be benefited. As the chief way of riding among the people of this country is in carts, I also wished to travel in a cart. I sat for 2 kos in a cart, but was much troubled with the dust, and after this till the end of the stage rode on horseback. On the road Muqarrab K͟hān came from Ahmadabad, and had the good fortune to wait on me, and presented an offering of a pearl he had bought for 30,000 rupees. On Friday, the 8th, marching 6½ kos, the place of the descent of prosperity was on the shore of the salt sea.

Cambay[4] is one of the old ports. According to the brahmins, several thousand years have passed since its foundation. In the beginning its name was Trimbāwatī, and Rāja Tryambak Kunwar had the government of the country. It would take too long to write in detail the circumstances of the aforesaid Raja as the brahmins relate it. In brief, when the turn to the government came round

[1] Mondah of Jarrett, ii, 253.

[2] Text Nīlāo. No such parganah is mentioned in the Āyīn; the two I.O. MSS. have Naryād.

[3] Pitlād is mentioned in Bayley's Gujarat, p. 9, as having a very large revenue. It is the Patlād of Jarrett, ii, 253. Text wrongly has Nīlāb. Possibly Bhīl is the parganah meant.

[4] Elliot, vi, 353.

to Rāja Abhay Kumār,[1] who was one of his grandsons, by the decree of heaven a great calamity happened to this city. So much dust and earth were poured on it that all the houses and buildings were hidden, and the means of livelihood of many people was destroyed. Before the arrival of this calamity, an idol (*but*), which the Raja worshipped, came in a dream and announced this event. The Raja with his family embarked in a ship, and carried away the idol with them with a pillar it had behind it for a support. By chance the ship also was wrecked by a storm of misfortune. As there was left still a term of life for the Raja, that pillar bore the boat of his existence in safety to the shore, and he proposed to rebuild the city. He put up the pillar as a mark of repopulation and the coming together of the people. As in the Hindi language they call a pillar *istambh* and *khambh*, they called the city Istambhnagarī and Khambāwatī, and sometimes also Trimbāwatī, in connection with the Raja's name; Khambāwatī has by degrees and much use become Khambāyat (Cambay). This port is one of the largest ports[2] in Hindustan and is near a firth, which is one of the firths of the Sea of Oman. It has been estimated to be 7 kos in width, and nearly 40 kos in length. Ships cannot come inside the firth, but must cast anchor in the port of Gogā, which is a dependency[3] of Cambay and situated near the sea. Thence, putting their cargoes into *ghurābs*[4] (commonly called 'grabs') they bring them to the port of Cambay. In the same way, at the time of loading a ship they carry the cargo in ghurabs and put it in the ships. Before the arrival of the victorious host some ghurabs from European ports had come to Cambay to buy and sell, and were about to return. On Sunday,

[1] The I.O. MSS. have Abhay or Abhī Kār.

[2] Tiefenthaler, i, p. 380, etc., has an interesting notice of Cambay. He also gives a sketch of its bay (plate xxxii).

[3] Now so silted up that no tolerably large vessel can approach it.

[4] Abu-l-faẓl calls them *tāwarī* (Jarrett, ii, 241).

the 10th, they decorated them and showed them to me. Taking leave they went about their business. On Monday, the 11th, I myself went on board a ghurab for about a kos on the face of the water. On Tuesday, the 12th, I went out with cheetahs (*yūz*), and captured two[1] antelope. On Wednesday, the 13th, I went to see the tank of Tārangsar (Narangsar?),[2] and passed through the streets and bazaar on the way, scattering nearly 5,000 rupees. In the time of H.M. Akbar (may Allah's lights be his testimony), Kalyān Rāy, the superintendent of the port, by His Majesty's order built a wall of brick and cement round the city, and many merchants came from various quarters and settled there, and built fine houses and employed themselves in gaining their livelihood under easy circumstances. Although its market is small, it is clean and full of people. In the time of the Sultans of Gujarat the customs of this port came to a large sum. Now in my reign it is ordered that they should not take more than one in forty. In other ports, calling it a tithe, they take one in ten or one in eight, and give all kinds of trouble to merchants and travellers. In Jeddah, which is the port of Mecca, they take one in four or even more. One may imagine from this what the customs of the ports of Gujarat must have come to in the time of the former rulers. God be praised that this suppliant at the throne of God obtained the grace to remit the whole of the customs dues of his dominions, which came to a countless sum, and the very name of customs (*tamghā*) has passed away from my empire. At this time an order was given that tankas[3] of gold and silver should be coined twice the weight of ordinary muhrs and rupees. The legend

[1] I.O. MSS. have 'ten.'

[2] *Tāl tārang.* Possibly *tārang* should read *tarang* (waves), and the meaning be that Jahāngīr went to see the famous bore in the Gulf of Cambay.

[3] See Elliot, vi, 355, and note.

on the gold coin was on one side the words "Jahāngīr-shāhī, 1027" (1618), and on the reverse "Struck in Cambay in the 12th year of the reign." The legend for silver coins was on one side "Sikka, Jahāngīr-shāhī, 1027"; round it this hemistich, "King Jahāngīr of the conquering ray struck this"; and on the reverse, "Coined at Cambay in the 12th year of the reign," with this second hemistich round it—

> "When after the conquest of the Deccan he came to Gujarat from Māndū."

In no reign except mine have tankas been coined except of copper[1]; the gold and silver tankas are my invention. I ordered it to be called the Jahāngīrī coinage. On Mubārak-shamba (Thursday), the 14th, the offering of Amānat Khān, the superintendent (*mutaṣaddī*) of Cambay, was laid before me in the women's apartments. His mansab was fixed, original and increase, at 1,500 personal and 400 horse. Nūru-d-dīn Qulī was honoured with the mansab, original and increase, of 3,000 personal and 600 horse. On Friday, the 15th, mounted on the elephant Nūr-bakht, I made it run after a horse. It ran exceedingly well, and when it was stopped stood well. This is the third time that I myself have ridden it. On Saturday, the 16th, Rām Dās, son of Jay Singh, was promoted to the mansab, original and increase, of 1,500 personal and 700 horse. On Sunday, the 17th, an elephant each was given to Dārāb Khān, Amānat Khān, and Sayyid Bāyazīd Bārha. In these few days during which I was encamped on the shore of the salt sea, merchants, traders, indigent people, and other inhabitants of the port of Cambay having been summoned before me, I gave each according to his condition a dress of honour or a horse or travelling money or assistance

[1] In the text *aḥdī* occurs by mistake instead of *'ahdī*, and *man* instead of *mas*.

[2] Wrongly so in text, but *Jay Singh* should be corrected to *Rāj Singh*. The son of Jay Singh, Raja of Ajmir, was Rām Singh, who was born in Sambat, 1692.

in living. On this day, Sayyid Muḥammad, Ṣāḥib Sajjāda (Lord of the prayer carpet) of S̲h̲āh 'Ālam (a mosque near Ahmadabad), the sons of S̲h̲aik̲h̲ Muḥammad G̲h̲auṣ, S̲h̲aik̲h̲ Ḥaidar, grandson of Miyān Wajīhū-d-dīn, and other Shaikhs living at Ahmadabad came to meet me and pay their respects. As my desire was to see the sea and the flow and ebb of the water, I halted for ten days, and on Tuesday, the 19th (Day, about 30th December, 1618), the royal standards started for Ahmadabad. The best description of fish procurable in this place, the name of which is *'arbīyat*,[1] was caught and frequently brought for me by the fishermen. Without doubt these fish are, as compared with other fish of this country, more delicious and better, but they are not of the flavour of the *rohū*. One might say as nine to ten or even eight to ten. Of the food which is peculiar to the people of Gujarat there is the *khichṛī* of *bājrā* (a mixture of split peas and millet boiled together); this they also call *laẕīẕa*. It is a kind of split grain, which does not grow in any other country but Hindustan, and which in comparison with many other regions of India is more abundant in Gujarat; it is cheaper than most vegetables. As I had never eaten it, I ordered them to make some and bring it to me. It is not devoid of good flavour, and it suited me well. I ordered that on the days of abstinence, when I partake of dishes not made with flesh, they should frequently bring me this khichri. On the said Tuesday, having marched 6¼ kos, I halted at the village of Kosālā. On Wednesday, the 20th, I passed through the parganah of Bābrā[2] and halted on the bank of the river. This was a march of 6 kos. On Mubārak-s̲h̲amba, the 21st, I halted and held a feast of cups. In this river I caught many fish, and divided them among the servants who were present at the feast. On Friday, the 22nd, having moved on 4 kos, I pitched at

[1] Or *'Arabī* (Arabian ?). [2] Mātar or Nātar in I.O. MSS.

the village of Bāṛīchā. On this road, walls came in sight from 2½ to 3 *gaz* in length, and on enquiry it appeared that people had made them from the desire of spiritual reward. When a porter is tired on the road he places his burden on the wall and gains his breath a little, and lifting it up again with ease and without assistance from anyone proceeds towards his destination. This is one of the peculiar ideas of the people of Gujarat. The building of these walls pleased me greatly, and I ordered that in all large towns[1] they should make walls of this kind at the imperial expense. On Saturday, the 23rd, marching 4¾ kos, the camp was pitched at the Kānkriya tank. Quṭbu-d-dīn Muḥammad, grandson of Sulṭān Aḥmad, the founder of the city of Ahmadabad, made this tank, and placed round it steps of stone and cement. In the middle of the tank he constructed a little garden and some buildings. Between the bank of the tank and these buildings he had made a causeway, which was the way for entering and leaving, Since this occurred a long time ago, most of the buildings had become dilapidated, and there was no place left fit to sit in. At the time when the host of prosperity was about to proceed towards Ahmadabad, Ṣafī K͟hān, bakhshi of Gujarat, repaired at the expense of government what was broken down and in ruins, and clearing out the little garden erected a new building in it. Certainly it is a place exceedingly enjoyable and pleasant. Its style pleased me. On the side where the causeway is, Niẓāmu-d-dīn Aḥmad,[2] who was for a while bakhshi of Gujarat in my father's time, had made a garden on the bank of the tank. At this time a representation was made to me that 'Abdu-llah K͟hān, in consequence of a dispute that he had with 'Ābid, son of Niẓāmu-d-dīn Aḥmad, cut down the trees of this garden. I also heard that during his government

[1] I.O. MS. 181 has "in all the cities of Upper India."
[2] The historian.

he, at a wine party, signed to a slave, and cut off the head of an unfortunate man who was not wanting in fun and jesting, merely because in a state of drunkenness he had uttered some improper expressions by way of a joke. On hearing these two reports, my sense of justice was shocked, and I ordered the Diwans to change one thousand of his two-horsed and three-horsed cavalry into one-horsed, and to deduct from his jagir the difference (of pay), which came to 7,000,000 dams.

As at this stage the tomb of Shāh 'Ālam was by the roadside, I recited the *fātiḥa* in passing by it. About 100,000 rupees had been spent in building this mausoleum. Shāh 'Ālam was the son of Quṭb 'Ālam, and their family goes back to Makhdūm-i-Jahāniyān[1] (a saint). The people of this country, high and low, have a wonderful belief in him, and they say that Shāh 'Ālam used to raise the dead. After he had raised several dead men, his father became aware of this and sent him a prohibition, saying it was presumption in him to meddle with the workshop of God, and was contrary to true obedience. It happened that Shāh 'Ālam had an attendant (female) who had no children, but at Shāh 'Ālam's prayer God Almighty bestowed a son on her. When he reached his 27th[2] year he died, and that slave came weeping and wailing into his presence, saying, "My son has died, and he was my only son; since God Almighty gave him to me by your favour, I am hopeful that through your prayer he may become alive." Shāh 'Ālam fell into thought for a time and went into his cell, and the attendant went to his son, who greatly loved her, and besought him to ask the Shah to make his son alive. The son, who was of tender years, went into his cell, and used much entreaty.

[1] A saint of Multan who died in 1384. See Beale, s.v. *Shaikh Jalāl*, and Jarrett, iii, 369.

[2] So in text, but surely it should be "8th or 7th"? It appears from the Khazīnatu-l-aṣfiyā, ii, 71, that the attendant who lost the child was a female disciple, and that the child was young.

S̲h̲āh 'Ālam said, "If you are content to give up your life for him, perhaps my petition may be accepted." He represented "I am perfectly contented with what may be your wish and the desire of God." S̲h̲āh 'Ālam took his son's hands, and lifting him up from the ground turned his face towards heaven and said, "O God, take this kid in place of that one." Instantaneously the boy surrendered his soul to God, and S̲h̲āh 'Ālam laid him down on his own bed and covered his face with a sheet, and coming out of the house said to that attendant, "Go home, and get news of thy son; perhaps he may have been in a trance and not have died." When she arrived at her house she saw her son alive. In short, in the country of Gujarat they say many things of this sort of S̲h̲āh 'Ālam. I myself asked Sayyid Muḥammad, who is lord of his prayer carpet (in charge of the mausoleum), and who is not wanting in excellence and reasonableness, what was the real state of the case. He said, "I have also heard the same from my father and grandfather, and it has come down in succession, and wisdom is from Allah." Although this affair is beyond the laws of understanding, yet, as it has attained great notoriety among men, it has been recorded as a strange occurrence. His departure from this perishable mansion to the eternal world took place in 880 (1475), in the time of the reign of Sulṭān Maḥmūd Bīgara, and the buildings of this mausoleum are the memorial of Tāj K̲h̲ān Tariyānī,[1] who was one of the Amirs of Sulṭān Muẓaffar, the son of Maḥmūd.

As an hour on Monday had been chosen for my entry into the city, on Sunday, the 24th, I halted. At this place some melons came from Kārīz, which is a town dependent on Herat, and it is certain that in Khurasan there are no melons better than those of Kārīz. Although

[1] According to Bayley's Gujarat, p. 238, and Index, p. 515, the name is either Tāj K̲h̲ān Tūrpāli or Narpāli.

this is at a distance of 1,400 kos, and kafilahs (caravans) take five months to come, they arrived very ripe and fresh. They brought so many that they sufficed for all the servants. Together with these there came oranges (*kauṇlā*) from Bengal, and though that place is 1,000 kos distant most of them arrived quite fresh. As this is a very delicate and pleasant fruit, runners bring by post as much as is necessary for private consumption, and pass it from hand to hand. My tongue fails me in giving thanks to Allah for this.

"Thankfulness for Thy favours is one of Thy favours."

On this day Amānat K͟hān presented two elephants' tusks; they were very large, one of them being 3 cubits 8 *ṭassū* (finger-breadths) in length and 16 tassu in circumference; it weighed 3 maunds and 2 seers, or 24½ Iraq maunds. On Monday, the 25th, after six gharis, I turned towards the city in pleasure and prosperity at the propitious hour, and mounted the elephant Ṣūrat-gaj, a favourite elephant of mine, which is perfect in appearance and disposition. Although he was fractious (*mast*), I had confidence in my own riding and his pleasant paces (?).[1] Crowds of people, men and women, had assembled, and were waiting in the streets and bazars and at the gates and the walls. The city of Ahmadabad did not seem to me so worthy of praise as I had heard. Although they had made the main road of the bazar wide and spacious, they had not suited the shops to this breadth. Its buildings are all of wood and the pillars of the shops slender and mean (*zabūn*). The streets of the bazar were full of dust, and there was dust from the Kānkriyā tank up to the citadel, which in the dialect of the country they call Bhadar. I hastened along scattering

[1] *Suwārī-i-k͟hūd u k͟hwus͟h-jalū-i-ū*, "my own riding and his pleasant paces (?)." It does not seem likely that Jahāngīr would himself drive the elephant. The meaning here probably is that Jahāngīr trusted to his being on the elephant. *K͟hwus͟h-jalū* is used lower down about another elephant, and seems to refer to the elephant's paces. See p. 214.

money. The meaning of Bhadar is 'blessed' (*bhadra*). The houses of the Sultans of Gujarat, which were inside the Bhadar, have fallen into ruin within the last fifty or sixty years, and no trace of them is left. However, our servants who have been sent to the government of this country have erected buildings. When I was proceeding from Māndū to Ahmadabad, Muqarrab Khān had done up the old buildings and prepared other places for sitting that were necessary, such as a jharokha, a public audience hall, etc. As to-day was the auspicious day for the weighing of my son Shāh Jahān, I weighed him in the usual manner against gold and other things, and the 27th year from his blessed birth began in pleasure and enjoyment. I hope that the Giver of gifts will bestow him on this suppliant at His throne and let him enjoy life and prosperity. On the same day I gave the province of Gujarat in jagir to that son. From the fort of Māndū to the fort of Cambay, by the road we came, it is 124 kos, which were traversed in twenty-eight marches and thirty halts. I remained at Cambay for ten days; from that place to the city of Ahmadabad is 21 kos, which we traversed in five marches with two halts. Altogether, from Māndū to Cambay and from Cambay to Ahmadabad by the road we came is 145 kos, which we accomplished in two months and fifteen days; this was in thirty-three marches and forty-two halts.

On Tuesday, the 26th, I went to see the Jāmi' mosque, and gave with my own hand in alms to the fakirs who were present there about 500 rupees. This mosque was one of the memorials of Sulṭān Aḥmad, the founder of the city of Ahmadabad. It has three gates,[1] and on each side a bazar. Opposite the gate that looks towards the east is the mausoleum of the said Sulṭān Aḥmad. In that dome Sulṭān Aḥmad, his son Muḥammad, and his

[1] Or doors. The Iqbāl-nāma, 108, has "in front of each gate there is a bazar."

grandson Quṭbu-d-dīn are laid to rest. The length of the court of the mosque, excluding *maqṣūra* (the holy of holies), is 103 [1] cubits, and its breadth 89 cubits. Round this they have made an *aywān* (portico), in breadth 4¾ cubits. The flooring of the court is of trimmed bricks, and the pillars of the portico of red stone. The maqsura contains 354 [2] pillars, above which there is a dome. The length of the maqsura is 75 cubits, and its breadth 37 cubits. The flooring of the maqsura, the *mihrāb* (arch towards which the face is turned in prayer), and the pulpit are made of marble. On both sides of the main arch (*pīsh-ṭāq*) are two polished minarets of cut stone, containing three *āshyāna* (stories) beautifully shaped and decorated. On the right-hand side of the pulpit near the recess of the maqsura they have made a separate seat for the king. The space between the pillars has been covered in with a stone platform, and round this up to the roof of the maqsura they have put stone cages [3] (in which women sit so as not to be seen). The object of this was that when the king came to the Friday service or the 'Id he went up there with his intimates and courtiers, and performed his devotions. This in the dialect of the country they call the Mulūk-khāna (King's chamber). This practice and caution were on account of the crowding of the people. Truly this mosque is a very noble building.[4]

On Wednesday,[5] the 27th, I went to the monastery of Shaikh Wajīhu-d-dīn, which was near the palace, and the *fātiḥa* was read at the head of his shrine, which is in the court of the monastery. Ṣādiq Khān, who was one of the chief Amirs of my father, built this monastery.

[1] 123 in Iqbāl-nāma.

[2] 350 in I.O. MSS.

[3] *Panjara-i-sang*, presumably lattice-work in stone.

[4] See for dimensions of the mosque Bayley's Gujarat, p. 92 and note, and the authorities there quoted.

[5] Text wrongly has Sunday.

The Shaikh was a successor of Shaikh Muḥammad Ghauṣ,[1] but a successor against whom the teacher disputed. Wajīhu-d-dīn's loyalty to him is a clear proof[2] of the greatness of Shaikh Muḥammad Ghauṣ. Shaikh Wajīhu-d-dīn was adorned with visible excellencies and spiritual perfection. He died thirty years ago in this city (Ahmadabad), and after him Shaikh ʻAbdu-llah, according to his father's will, took his place. He was a very ascetic dervish. When he died his son Shaikh Asadu-llah sat in his place, and also quickly went to the eternal world. After him his brother Shaikh Ḥaidar became lord of the prayer carpet, and is now alive, and is employed at the grave of his father and grandfather in the service of dervishes and in looking after their welfare. The traces of piety are evident on the forehead of his life. As it was the anniversary festival of Shaikh Wajīhu-d-dīn, 1,500 rupees were given to Shaikh Ḥaidar for the expenses of the anniversary, and I bestowed 1,500 rupees more on the band of fakirs who were present in the monastery, with my own hand in charity, and made a present of 500 rupees to the grandson (?) of Shaikh Wajīhu-d-dīn. In the same way I gave something for expenses, and land to each of his relatives and adherents according to his merit. I ordered Shaikh Ḥaidar to bring before me the body of dervishes and deserving people who were associated with him, in order that they might ask for money for expenses and for land. On Thursday, the 28th, I went to look round the Rustam-Khān-bāṛī, and scattered 1,500 rupees on the road. They call a garden a *bāṛī* in the language of India. This is

[1] Muḥammad Ghauṣ was accused of heresy by some of the Gujarātī mullas. He was much respected by Humāyūn, and is buried at Gwalior.

[2] Jahāngīr means that Wajīhu-d-dīn was a very learned man, and that his devotion to Muḥammad Ghauṣ, who was an ignorant man (*ummī*), shows what a great personality the latter was. Cf. Iqbāl-nāma, 169, and Ma'āṣiru-l-umarā, ii, 583, where we are told that Wajīhu-d-dīn thanked God that both his Prophet and his Pīr were ignorant.

a garden that my brother Shāh Murād made in the name of his son Rustam. I made a Thursday entertainment in this garden, and gave cups to some of my private servants. At the end of the day I went to the little garden of the *ḥawālī* (mansion) of Shaikh Sikandar, which is situated in the neighbourhood of this garden, and which has exceedingly good figs. As picking the fruit with one's own hand gives it quite a different relish, and I had never before plucked figs with my own hand, their excellence in this respect was approved. Shaikh Sikandar[1] is by origin a Gujarati, and is not wanting in reasonableness, and has complete information about the Sultans of Gujarat. It is now eight or nine years since he has been employed among the servants (of the State). As my son Shāh Jahān had appointed to the government of Ahmadabad Rustam Khān, who is one of his chief officers, at his request I, in accordance with the association of his name, presented him with (the garden) Rustam-bāṛī. On this day Rāja Kalyān, zamindar of the province of Īḍar, had the good fortune to kiss my threshold, and presented an elephant and nine horses as an offering; I gave him back the elephant. He is one of the most considerable zamindars on the frontier of Gujarat, and his country is close to the hill-country of the Rānā. The Sultans of Gujarat constantly sent armies against the Raja of that place. Although some of them have professed obedience and presented offerings, for the most part none of them have come to see anyone personally. After the late king Akbar conquered Gujarat, the victorious army was sent to attack him. As he understood that his deliverance lay in obedience and submission, he agreed to serve and be loyal, and hastened to enjoy the good fortune of kissing the threshold. From that date he has been enrolled among the servants (of the

[1] He wrote a history of Gujarat—the Mirāt-i-Sikandarī. Rieu, Cat., i, 287.

State). He comes to see whoever is appointed to the government of Ahmadabad, and when work and service are necessary appears with a body of his men. On Saturday, the 1st of the month of Bahman, in the 12th year of my reign, Chandar Sen, who is one of the chief zamindars of this country, had the good fortune to kiss the threshold, and presented an offering of nine horses. On Sunday, the 2nd, I gave elephants to Rāja Kalyān, zamindar of Īḍar, to Sayyid Muṣṭafā, and Mīr Fāẓil. On Monday I went out hawking, and scattered nearly 500 rupees on the road. On this day pears came from Badakhshan. On Mubārak-shamba, the 6th, I went to see the "garden of victory" at the village of Sair-khaiz (Sarkhej), and scattered 1,500 rupees on the way. As the tomb of Shaikh Aḥmad Khaṭṭū [1] is on the road, I first went there and the *fātiḥa* was read. Khaṭṭū is the name of a town in the Sarkar of Nāgor, and was the birthplace of the Shaikh.[2] The Shaikh lived in the time of Sulṭān Aḥmad, who founded the city of Ahmadabad, and the latter had a great respect for him. The people of this country have a strange belief in him, and consider him one of the great saints. Every Friday night a great crowd of people, high and low, go to visit his shrine. Sulṭān Muḥammad, son of the aforesaid Sulṭān Aḥmad,

[1] Blochmann, 507, note.

[2] "Shaikh Aḥmad Khaṭṭū, who had the title of Jamālu-d-dīn, was born at Delhi of a noble family in 737 A.H. (1336–7). He was the disciple and successor of Bābā Isḥāq (Isaac) Maghribī. His name was Naṣīru-d-dīn. By the jugglery of the heavens he was separated from his home in a storm, and after a while entered the service of Bābā Isḥāq Maghribī. He acquired from him spiritual and secular learning, and came to Gujarat in the time of Sulṭān Aḥmad. High and low accepted him, and paid him homage. Afterwards he travelled to Arabia and Persia, and made the acquaintance of many saints. He is buried at Sarkhech, near Aḥmadabad."—*Āyīn-i-Akbarī* (vol. ii, p. 220, of Bib. Ind., ed. Jarrett, iii, 371). See Bayley's Gujarat, p. 90, note, and Khazīnatu-l-aṣfiyā, ii, 314, and Blochmann, 507, note, where the reference to the Khazīna, 957, seems wrong. The story told in the Khazīna is that Shaikh Aḥmad belonged to the royal family of Delhi, and was, as a baby, blown out of his nurse's arms into the street during a storm.

built lofty buildings in the shape of mausoleums, mosques, and monasteries at the head of his tomb, and near his mausoleum on the south side made a large tank, and surrounded it with stone and lime (masonry). This building was completed in the time of Quṭbu-d-dīn, son of the aforesaid Muḥammad. The shrines of several of the Sultans of Gujarat are on the bank of the tank by the feet of the Shaikh. In that dome there have been laid at rest Sulṭān Maḥmūd Bīgara, Sulṭān Muẓaffar, his son, and Maḥmūd, the martyr, grandson of Sulṭān Muẓaffar, and who was the last of the Sultans of Gujarat. Bīgara, in the language of the people of Gujarat, signifies 'turned-up moustache,' and Sulṭān Maḥmūd had a large turned-up moustache; on this account they call him Bīgara. Near his (S̲h̲aik̲h̲ K̲h̲aṭṭū's) tomb is the dome of his ladies.[1] Without doubt the mausoleum of the Shaikh is a very grand building and a beautiful place. It is estimated that 500,000 rupees were spent on it. God only knows what is true.

After performing this visitation I went to Fatḥ-bāg̲h̲ (garden of victory). This garden is situated on the ground on which the Commander-in-Chief, K̲h̲ānk̲h̲ānān Ātāliq, fought with and defeated Nabū (Nannū ? Nanhū ?), who gave himself the title of Muẓaffar K̲h̲ān. On this account he called it Bāg̲h̲-i-fatḥ; the people of Gujarat call it Fatḥ-bāṛī. The details of this are that when, by means of the good fortune of the late king Akbar, the country of Gujarat was conquered, and Nabū fell into his hands, I'timād K̲h̲ān represented that he was the son of a carter. As no son was left by Sulṭān Maḥmūd, and moreover there was no one of the descendants of the Sultans of Gujarat whom he could raise to the throne, he (I'timād) had accepted the most available course, and had made out that this was the son of Maḥmūd. He gave him

[1] Text *k̲h̲awānīn*, 'khans,' but evidently this is a mistake for *k̲h̲awātīn*, the plural of *k̲h̲ātūn*, 'a lady.'

the name of Sulṭān Muẓaffar, and raised him to the sovereignty. Men from necessity consented to this. As His Majesty considered the word of I'timād Khān of weight, he ignored Nabū, and for some time he did duty among the servants, and the king paid no attention to his case. In consequence of this he ran away from Fatḥpūr, and coming to Gujarat lived for some years under the protection of the zamindars. When Shihābu-d-dīn Aḥmad Khān was turned out from the government of Gujarat and I'timād Khān installed in his place, a body of the servants of Shihābu-d-dīn Khān, who were attached to Gujarat, separated from him, and remained at Ahmadabad in the hope of service with I'timād. After I'timād entered the city they had recourse to him, but had no good luck with him. They had not the face to go to Shihābu-d-dīn, and had no prospects in Ahmadabad. As they were without hope they thought their remedy lay in betaking themselves to Nabū, and in making him an excuse for disturbance. With this intent 600 or 700 horsemen from among them went to Nabū and carried him off along with Lonā Kāthī, under whose protection he was living, and proceeded to Ahmadabad. When he arrived near the city many wretched men on the look out for an occasion joined him, and nearly 1,000 horsemen, Mughals and Gujaratis, collected together. When I'timād Khān became aware of this he left his son Shīr Khān in the city, and hastened off in search of Shihāb Khān, who was proceeding towards the Court, in order that with his help he might quiet the disturbance. Many of the men had separated themselves from him, and he read on the faces of those who were left the signs of unfaithfulness, but Shihābu-d-dīn, in company with I'timād Khān, turned his rein. It happened that before their arrival Nabū had entered the fort of Ahmadabad. Those who were loyal drew up their troops near the city, and the rebels came out of the fort and hastened to the battlefield. When the army of the rebels showed itself, those of the servants of Shihāb Khān who were left took the wrong road and joined the enemy. Shihāb Khān was defeated and hastened towards Paṭan (Pātan ?), which was in the possession of the royal servants. His retinue and camp were plundered, and Nabū, bestowing mansabs and titles on the rebels, went against Quṭbu-d-dīn Muḥammad Khān, who was in Baroda. The servants of the latter, like the servants of Shihāb Khān, took the road of faithlessness and chose separation, as is related in detail in the Akbar-nāma. In the end, after giving his word to Quṭbu-d-dīn Muḥammad, he sent him to martyrdom, and his goods and property, which were equal to the treasure of his courtesy and grandeur, were plundered. Nearly 45,000 horsemen collected round Nabū.

When this state of affairs was represented to H.M. Akbar he sent against him Mīrzā Khān, son of Bairām Khān, with a force of brave warriors. On the day when Mīrzā Khān arrived near the city, he drew up the ranks of good fortune. He had about 8,000 or 9,000 horse, and Nabū met him with 30,000, and drew up his host tainted with ruin. After prolonged fighting and slaughter the breeze of victory blew on the flag of the loyal, and Nabū, being defeated, fled in wretched plight. My father, in reward for this victory, gave Mīrzā Khān a mansab of 5,000, with the title of Khānkhānān and the government of the country of Gujarat. The garden that Khān-khānān made on the field of battle is situated on the bank of the River Sābarmatī. He founded lofty buildings along that eminence on the river, and made a strong wall of stone and cement round the garden. The garden contains 120 *jarīb* of land, and is a charming resort. It may have cost 200,000 rupees. It pleased me greatly. One may say that in the whole of Gujarat there is no garden like this. Arranging a Thursday feast, I bestowed cups on my private servants, and remained there for the night. At the end of the day, on Friday, I entered the city, scattering about 1,000 rupees on the road. At this time the gardener represented that a servant of Muqarrab K͟hān had cut down some *champą̄* trees above the bench alongside the river. On hearing this I became angry, and went myself to enquire into the matter and to exact satisfaction. When it was established that this improper act had been committed by him, I ordered both his thumbs to be cut off as a warning to others. It was evident that Muqarrab K͟hān knew nothing of this affair, or otherwise he would have punished him there and then. On Tuesday, the 11th, the Kotwal of the city caught a thief and brought him. He had committed several thefts before, and each time they had cut off one of his members; once his right hand, the second time the thumb of his left hand, the third time his left ear, and fourth time they hamstringed him, and the last time his nose; with all this he did not give up his business, and yesterday entered the house of a grass-seller in order to steal. By chance the owner of the house was on the look out and seized him. The thief wounded the grass-seller several times with a knife and killed him. In the uproar and confusion his relatives attacked the thief and caught him. I ordered them to hand over the thief to the relatives of the deceased, that they might retaliate on him.

"The lines of the face show the thought of your head (?)."

On Wednesday, the 12th, 3,000 rupees were handed over to 'Aẓamat K͟hān and Mu'taqad K͟hān, that they might go the next day to the tomb of S͟haik͟h Aḥmad K͟haṭṭū, and divide it among the fakirs and indigent people who had taken up their abode there. On Thursday, the 13th, I went to the lodging of my son S͟hāh Jahān, and held a Mubārak-s͟hamba entertainment there, and distributed cups among my private servants. I gave my son the elephant Sundar Mathan,[1] which was

[1] I.O. MSS. have Sundar Sen.

superior to all my private elephants in speed and beauty and pleasant paces, and competed with horses, and was the first among the elephants, and one much liked by King Akbar. My son Shāh Jahān had a great liking for him, and frequently asked him of me, and seeing no way out of it I gave it to him with its gold belongings of chains, etc., together with a female elephant. A present of 100,000 of darbs was given to the wakils of 'Ādil Khān. At this time it was represented[1] to me that Mukarram Khān, son of Mu'azzam Khān, who was the governor of Orissa, had conquered the country of Khūrdā, and that the Raja of that place had fled and gone into the Rājmahendra. As he was a *khāna-zād* (houseborn one) and worthy of patronage, I ordered his mansab, original and increase, to be 3,000 personal and 2,000 horse, and honoured him with drums, a horse, and a dress of honour. Between the province of Orissa and Golconda there were two zamindars, one the Raja of Khūrdā and the second the Raja of Rājmahendra. The province of Khūrdā has come into the possession of the servants of the Court. After this it is the turn of the country of Rājmahendra. My hope in the grace of Allah is that the feet of my energy may advance farther. At this time a petition from Quṭbu-l-mulk reached my son Shāh Jahān to the effect that as the boundary of his territory had approached that of the King, and he owed service to this Court, he hoped an order would be issued to Mukarram Khān not to stretch out his hand, and to acquire possession of his country. It was a proof of Mukarram's valour and energy that such a one as Quṭbu-l-mulk should be apprehensive about his (Mukarram) becoming his neighbour.

On this day Ikrām Khān, son of Islām Khān, was appointed faujdar of Fatḥpūr and its neighbourhood, and presented with a dress of honour and an elephant; Chandar

[1] See Elliot, vi, 355.

Sen, the zamindar of Haloz (Halwad?),[1] was given a dress of honour, a horse, and an elephant. An elephant was also given to Lāchīn Qāqshāl. At the same time Muzaffar,[2] son of Mīrzā Bāqī Tarkhān, had the honour of kissing the threshold. His mother was the daughter of Bārha (Bhārā), the zamindar of Kachh. When Mīrzā Bāqī died and the government of Thatta went to Mīrzā Jānī, Muzaffar was apprehensive of Mīrzā Jānī, and he took refuge with the aforesaid zamindar. He had remained from his childhood until now in that country. Now that the fortunate retinue had reached Ahmadabad, he came and did homage. Though he had been reared among men of the wilds, and was unfamiliar with civilized ways and ceremonies, yet as his family had had the relations of service with our exalted dynasty from the times of Timur[3] —may God make his proof clear!—I considered it right to patronize him. For the present I gave him 2,000 rupees for expenses, and a dress of honour. A suitable rank will be given to him, and perhaps he will show himself efficient as a soldier.

On Thursday, the 20th, I went to the "Garden of Victory," and contemplated the red roses. One plot had bloomed well. There are not many red roses (*gul-i-surkh*) in this country, so it was pleasant to see so many here. The anemone[4] bed, too, was not bad, and the figs had

[1] This name is doubtful, for the MSS. have a different reading, apparently Namūd. There is a Halōd in Gujarat (Jarrett, ii, 242). See also Bayley's Gujarat, 439. Perhaps it is the Halol of the Indian Gazetteer.

[2] The existence of this son of Bāqī Tarkhān does not seem to have been known to Abū-l-fazl or to Blochmann. Nor is he mentioned in the Ma'āṣiru-l-umarā. See Jarrett, ii, 347, where only Payanda is spoken of as the son of Bāqī Khān, and Blochmann, p. 362. See also Ma'āṣiru-l-umarā, iii, 485, the biography of Mīrzā 'Īsā Tarkhān. His name appears, however, in the pedigree of his house in the Tarkhān-nāma of Jamāl Shīrāzī.

[3] The word *ṣānī* in *Ṣāḥib-qirān-i-ṣānī* in text is a mistake.

[4] *Shaqā'iq*, which perhaps means tulips. In Price's Jahangir, p. 115, there is much more said about the "Garden of Victory," and Jahāngīr's entertainment there by his wife Khairu-n-nisā, the daughter of the Khānkhānān.

ripened. I gathered some figs with my own hands, and weighed the largest one. It came to 7½ tolas. On this day there arrived 1,500 melons from Kārīz. The Khān 'Ālam had sent them as a present. I gave a thousand of them to the servants in attendance, and five hundred to the women of the harem. I spent four days in this garden in enjoyment, and on Monday eve, the 24th, I came to the city. Some of the melons were given to the Shaikhs of Ahmadabad, and they were astonished to see how inferior were the Gujarat melons. They marvelled at the goodness of the Deity.

On Thursday, the 27th, I held a wine-feast in the Nagīna[1] garden, which is inside the palace grounds, and which one of the Gujarat Sultans had planted. I made my servants happy with flowing bowls. A pergola (*takhta*) of grapes had ripened in this garden, and I bade those who had been drinking to gather the bunches with their own hands and partake of them.

On Monday, the 1st of Isfandārmuz, I left Ahmadabad and marched towards Malwa. I scattered money on the road till we reached the bank of the Kānkriyā tank, where I halted for three days. On Thursday, the 4th, the presents of Muqarrab Khān were laid before me. There was nothing rare among them, nor anything that I took a fancy to, and so I felt ashamed. I gave them to my children to take into the harem. I accepted jewellery and decorated vessels and cloths to the value of a lakh, and gave him back the rest. Also about one hundred Kachhi horses were taken, but there was none of great excellence.

On Friday, the 5th, I marched 6 kos, and encamped on the bank of the Ahmadabad River. As my son Shāh Jahān was leaving Rustam Khān, one of his chief servants, in charge of the government of Gujarat, I, at my son's request, gave him a standard, drums, a dress

[1] Bagīna in text. Debi Prasad has *Bakīnā*.

of honour, and a decorated dagger. Up till now it had not been the custom in this dynasty to give to the prince's servants standards or drums. For instance, H.M. Akbar, with all his affection and graciousness to me, did not decide upon giving to my officers a title or a standard. But my consideration for this son is so unbounded that I would do anything to please him, and, in fact, he is an excellent son, and one adorned with every grace, and in his early youth has accomplished to my satisfaction, everything that he has set his hand to.

On this day Muqarrab Khān took leave to go to his home.

As the shrine of Quṭb 'Ālam, the father of Shāh 'Ālam Bukhāri, was in the village of Batoh,[1] and on my way, I went there and gave 500 rupees to the guardians. On Saturday, the 6th, I entered a boat on the Maḥmūdābād River and went a-fishing. On the bank is the tomb of Sayyid Mubārak Bukhārī. He was one of the leading officers of Gujarat, and his son Sayyid Mīrān erected this monument to him. It is a very lofty cupola, and there is a very strong wall of stone and lime round it. It must have cost more than two lakhs of rupees. None of the tombs of the Gujarat Sultans that I saw came up to one-tenth of it. Yet they were sovereigns, and Sayyid Mīrān was only a servant. Genius and the help of God have produced this result. A thousand blessings on a son who has made such a tomb for his father:[2]

"That there may remain a memorial of him upon earth."

On Sunday I halted and fished, and caught 400 fish. One of them had no scales, and is called the *sang-māhī*,

[1] Banoh in text. See Bayley's Gujarat, p. 237; also Tiefenthaler, i, 377, who speaks of it as being 3 leagues south of Ahmadabad. See also Jarrett, ii, 240, n. 7.

[2] For Sayyid Mubārak and his son see Bayley's Gujarat. Sayyid Mubārak was the patron of the author of the Mirāt-i-Sikandarī. See loc. cit., p. 454.

'the stone-fish.' Its belly was very large and swollen, so I ordered them to cut it open in my presence. Inside was a fish with scales which it had recently swallowed and which had as yet undergone no change. I told them to weigh both fish. The stone-fish came to 6½ seers and the other to nearly 2.

On Monday, the 8th, I marched 4¼ kos, and encamped in the village of Moda (Mahāondat). The inhabitants praised the rainy season of Gujarat. It happened that on the previous night and on this day before breakfast some rain fell, and the dust was laid. As this is a sandy country, it is certain that there would not be any dust in the rainy season, nor would there be any mud. The fields would be green and cheerful. At any rate, a specimen of the rainy season has been seen by me. On Tuesday I marched 5½ kos, and halted at the village of Jarsīma (Jarīsamā).[1]

At this stage news came that Mān Singh Sewṛā had surrendered his soul to the lords of hell. The account of this in brief is that the Sewras[2] are a tribe of infidel Hindus who always go with their head and feet bare. One set of them root out their hair, their beards, and moustaches, while another set shave them. They do not wear sewn garments, and their central principle is that no living creature should be injured. The Banyans regard them as their *pīrs* and teachers, and even worship them. There are two sects of Sewras, one called Patā (Tapā) and the other Kanthal (Kartal). Mān Singh was the head of the latter, and Bāl Chand the head of the Patās.[3] Both of them used to attend upon H.M. Akbar. When he died and Khusrau fled and I pursued him, Rāy Singh Bhurṭiyā, zamindar of Bikanir, who had been made an Amīr by Akbar's kindness, asked Mān Singh what

[1] It is the Chandsuma of Bayley's map.

[2] Jarrett, iii, 210; and Akbar-nāma, translation, i, 147, n. 2.

[3] This should be Tapā. See Addenda.

would be the duration of my reign and the chances of my success. That black-tongued fellow, who pretended to be skilled in astrology and the extraction of judgments, said to him that my reign would, at most, last for two years. The doting old idiot (Rāy Singh) relied upon this, and went off without leave to his home. Afterwards, when the glorious God chose out this suppliant and I returned victorious to the capital, he came, ashamed and downcast, to Court. What happened to him in the end has been told in its proper place.[1] In fine, Mān Singh, in the course of three or four months, was struck with leprosy (*juẕām*), and his limbs fell off him till he was in such a state that death was by many degrees preferable to life. He was living at Bikanir, and now I remembered him and sent for him. On the road he, out of excessive fear, took poison, and surrendered his soul to the lords of hell. So long as the intentions of this suppliant at God's courts are just and right, it is sure that whoever devises evil against me will receive retribution according to his merits.

The sect of the Sewras exists in most of the cities of India, but is especially numerous in Gujarat. As the Banyans are the chief traders there, consequently the Sewras also are plentiful. Besides making idol-temples for them, they have built houses for them to dwell in and to worship in. In fact, these houses are the head-quarters of sedition. The Banyans send their wives and daughters to the Sewras, who have no shame or modesty. All kinds of strife and audacity are perpetrated by them. I therefore ordered that the Sewras should be expelled, and I circulated farmans to the effect that wherever there were Sewras in my empire they should be turned out.

[1] I.O. MS., instead of *k͟hātimat-i-aḥwāl-i-ū*, has *chunānchih aḥwāl*, "as has been stated in its place." This is probably correct, as Jahāngīr has already referred to his death. See also the account of the 2nd year, where he speaks of Rāy Singh's going home without leave.

On Wednesday, the 10th, I went out to hunt, and shot two nilgaw, one male and one female. On this day the son of Dilāwar Khān came from Pattan, which was his father's fief, and paid his respects. He presented a Kachhī horse. It was a very handsome animal, and pleasant to ride. Till I came to Gujarat no one had presented me with so fine a horse. Its value was 1,000 rupees.

On Thursday, the 11th, I had a wine party on the bank of the tank, and bestowed many favours on those servants who had been appointed to the province, and then dismissed them. Among the promotions was that of Shajā'at Khān, the Arab, to the rank of 2,500 personal and 2,000 horse. I also gave him drums, a horse, and a robe of honour. Himmat Khān was raised to the rank of 1,500 with 800 horse, and had a robe of honour and an elephant. Kifāyat Khān, who was made Diwan of the province, received the rank of 1,200 with 300 horse. Ṣafī Khān bakhshi received a horse and a robe of honour. Khwāja 'Āqil had the rank of 1,500 with 650 horse, and was made bakhshi of the Ahadis, and had the title of 'Āqil Khān. Thirty thousand darbs were given to the wakil of Quṭbu-l-Mulk, who had brought the tribute.

On this day my son Shāh Jahān presented pomegranates and quinces that had been sent to him from Farāh. I had never seen such large ones, and I ordered them to be weighed. The quince weighed 29 tolas 9 mashas and the pomegranate 40½ tolas. On Friday, the 12th, I went a-hunting and shot two nilgaw, a male and a female. On Saturday, the 13th, I shot three nilgaw, two males and one female. On Sunday, the 14th, I gave Shaikh Ismā'īl, the son of Shaikh Muḥammad Ghauṣ, a robe of honour and 500 rupees. On Monday, the 15th, I went a-hunting and shot two female nilgaw. On Tuesday, the 16th, I again presented the Shaikhs of Gujarat, who were in attendance, with robes of honour and maintenance-lands. To each of them I gave a book from my special library, such as the Tafsīr-i-kashshāf,[1] the Tafsīr-i-Ḥusainī,[2] and the Rauẓatu-l-aḥbāb.[3] I wrote on the back of the books the day of my arrival in Gujarat and the day of presentation of the books.

At the time that Ahmadabad was adorned by the setting up of the royal standards my employment by day and by night was the seeing of necessitous persons and the bestowing on them of money and land. I directed Shaikh Aḥmad the Ṣadr and some other tactful servants to bring before me dervishes and other needy persons. I also directed the sons of Shaikh Muḥammad Ghauṣ, the grandson of Shaikh Wajīhu-d-dīn, and other leading Shaikhs to produce whatever persons they believed to be in want. Similarly I appointed some women to do the same thing in the harem. My sole endeavour was that as I a king had come to this country after many years, no single person should be excluded. God is my witness that I did not fall short in this task, and that I never took any rest from this duty. Although I have not been delighted with my visit to Ahmadabad, yet I have this satisfaction—that my coming has been the cause of benefit to a large number of poor people.

On Tuesday, the 16th, they caught Kaukab, the son of Qamar Khān. He had in Burhanpur put on a faqir's dress and gone off into the wilds. The brief account of his case is this :—He was the grandson of Mīr 'Abdu-l-Laṭīf, who was one of the Saifī Sayyids and was attached to this Court. Kaukab had been appointed to the Deccan army, and had spent some days with it in poverty and wretchedness. When for a long time he did not get promotion he suspected that I was unfavourable to him, and foolishly took the dress of asceticism and went off to the wilderness. In the course of six months he

[1] Perhaps an explanation of Zamakhshari's Commentary.
[2] A Persian commentary on the Koran (Rieu, p. 96).
[3] A life of Muḥammad (Rieu, i, 147).

traversed the whole of the Deccan, including Daulatabad, Bidar, Bijapur, the Carnatic, and Golconda, and came to the port of Dābul.[1] From there he came by ship to the port of Gogā, and after visiting the ports of Surat, Broach, etc., he reached Ahmadabad. At this time Zāhid, a servant of Shāh Jahān, arrested him and brought him to Court. I ordered them to bring him before me heavily bound. When I saw him I said to him, "Considering the obligations of service of your father and grandfather, and your position as a houseborn one, why have you behaved in such an inauspicious manner?" He replied that he could not tell a lie in the presence of his *qibla* and real teacher, and that the truth was that he had hoped for favours, but as he was unlucky he had left outward ties and gone into the wilderness of exile. As his words bore the marks of truth they made an impression on me, and I abandoned my harsh tone and asked him if in his misfortunes he had waited upon 'Ādil Khān, or Quṭbu-l-Mulk, or 'Ambar. He replied that though he had been unsuccessful at this Court and had remained thirsty in this boundless ocean of beneficence, he had never—God forbid that he should—approached with his lips other fountains. Might his head be cut off if it had bowed at this Court and then lowered itself at another! From the time that he went into exile he had kept a diary showing what he had done, and by examining it it would be seen how he had conducted himself. These words of his increased my compassion for him, and I sent for his papers and read them. It appeared from them that he had encountered great hardship, and that he had spent much time on foot, and that he had suffered from want of food. On this account I felt kindly disposed towards him. Next day I sent for him and ordered them to remove the bonds from his arms and legs, and gave him a robe of honour, a horse,

[1] Dābhol (I.G., new ed., xi, 100).

and 1,000 rupees for his expenses. I also increased his rank by one half, and showed him such kindness as he never had imagined. He repeated this verse—

> "What I see, is it, O God, waking or in a trance?
> Do I behold myself in such comfort after such torture?"

On Wednesday, the 17th, I marched 6 kos and halted at the village of Bāṛasīnor (Bālasīnor). It has already been mentioned that the plague had appeared in Kashmir. On this day a report of the chronicler of events arrived, stating that the plague had taken firm hold of the country and that many had died. The symptoms were that the first day there was headache and fever and much bleeding at the nose. On the second day the patient died. In the house where one person died all the inmates were carried off. Whoever went near the sick person or a dead body was affected in the same way. In one instance the dead body was thrown on the grass, and it chanced that a cow came and ate some of the grass. It died, and some dogs that had eaten its flesh also all died. Things had come to such a pass that from fear of death fathers would not approach their children, and children would not go near their fathers. A strange thing was that in the ward in which the disease began, a fire broke out and nearly 3,000 houses were burnt. During the height of the plague, one morning when the people of the city and environs got up, they saw circles on their doors. There were three large circles, and on the face of these (i.e. inside them) there were two circles of middle size and one small one. There were also other circles which did not contain any whiteness[1] (i.e. there were no inner circles). These figures were found on all the houses and even on the mosques. From the day when the fire took place and these circles appeared, they say there was a diminution of the plague. This has been

[1] *Biyāẓ*. The meaning is not clear. Perhaps what is meant is that there was no writing, only the circles.

recorded as it seems a strange affair. It certainly does not agree with the canons of reason, and my intellect cannot accept it. Wisdom is with God! I trust that the Almighty will have mercy on his sinful slaves, and that they will be altogether freed from such calamity.

On Thursday, the 18th, I marched 2½ kos and halted on the bank of the Mahī. On this day the Jām zamindar[1] had the good fortune to kiss the ground. He presented 50 horses, 100 muhrs, and 100 rupees. His name is Jassā, and Jām is his title. Whoever succeeds is called Jām. He is one of the chief zamindars of Gujarat, and, indeed, he is one of the noted rajas of India. His country is close to the sea. He always maintains 5,000 or 6,000 horse, and in time of war can supply as many as 10,000 or 12,000. There are many horses in his country; Kachhī horses fetch as much as 2,000 rupees. I gave him a dress of honour.

On the same day Lachmī Narāyan, Raja of Kūch (Bihār), which adjoins Bengal, did homage and presented 500 muhrs. He received a dress of honour and an ornamented dagger.

Nawāzish Khān, son of Sa'īd Khān, who had been appointed to Jūnagaṛh, had the good fortune to pay his respects. On Friday, the 19th, I halted, and on Saturday, the 20th, I marched 3¾ kos and halted at the tank of Jhanūd. On Sunday I marched 4½ kos and halted at the tank of Badarwālā. On this day there came the news of the death of 'Aẕamat Khān Gujarātī. On account of illness he had remained in Ahmadabad. He was a servant who knew one's disposition, and did good work. As he had thorough knowledge of the Deccan and Gujarat, I was grieved at his death. In the tank above mentioned I noticed a plant which at the approach of the finger or the end of a stick contracts its leaves. After a while it opens them out again. Its leaves resemble those of

[1] Elliot, vi, 356.

the tamarind, and it is called in Arabic *Shajaru-l-ḥayā*, 'the plant of modesty.' In Hindī it is called *Lajvantī*. *Lāj* means modesty. It is certainly not void of strangeness. They also call it *naghzak*, and say that it also grows on dry land.

On Monday, the 22nd, I halted. My scouts reported that there was a tiger in the neighbourhood which vexed wayfarers, and in the forest where it was they had seen a skull and some bones lying. After midday I went out to shoot it, and killed it with one discharge. Though it was a large tiger, I had killed several that were larger. Among them was a tiger which I killed in the fort of Māndū, and which was 8½ maunds. This one weighed 7½ maunds, or 1 maund less.

On Tuesday, the 23rd, I marched over 3½ kos and alighted on the bank of the River Bāyab.[1] On Wednesday I marched nearly 6 kos and halted at the tank of Hamda.[2] On Thursday I ordered a halt and had a wine party, and gave cups to my special servants. I promoted Nawāzish Khān to the rank of 3,000 with 2,000 horse, which was an increase of 500 personal, and gave him a robe of honour and an elephant, and allowed him to go to his fief. Muḥammad Ḥusain Sabzak,[3] who had been sent to Balkh to buy horses, came to Court to-day and paid his respects. Of the horses he brought, one was piebald and was of fine shape and colour. I had never seen a piebald horse of this colour before. He had also brought other good roadsters. I therefore gave him the title of Tijāratī Khān.

On Friday, the 26th, I marched 5¼ kos and halted at the village of Jālod.[4] Rāja Lachmī Narāyan, the paternal uncle of the Raja of Kūch, to whom I had now given the territory of Kūch, was presented with a horse. On

[1] MSS. seem to have Mānīb. [2] MSS. seem to have Nīmda.
[3] The MSS. have Muḥammad Ḥusain Saudāgar (trader).
[4] The Jhallod of Bayley's map.

Saturday I marched 3 kos and halted at Boda.[1] On Sunday I marched 5 kos and set up the royal standards at Doḥad. It is on the borders of Malwa and Gujarat.

Pahluwān Bahā'u-d-dīn, the musketeer, brought a young monkey (*langūr*) with a goat, and represented that on the road one of his marksmen had seen the female langur with a young one in its arms on a tree. The cruel man had shot the mother, which on being struck had left the young one on a branch, and had herself dropped on the ground and died. Pahluwān Bahā'u-d-dīn had then come up and taken down the young one, and had put it beside the goat to be suckled. God had inspired the goat with affection for it, and it began to lick the monkey and to fondle it. In spite of difference of species she showed such love as if it had come out of her own womb. I told them to separate them, but the goat immediately began to lament, and the young langur also became much distressed. The affection of the monkey is not so remarkable, as it wanted to get milk, but the affection of the goat for it is remarkable. The langur is an animal belonging to the monkey tribe. But the hair of the monkey (*maimūn*) is yellowish and its face is red, while the hair of the langur is white and its face is black. Its tail, too, is twice as long as the maimun's. I have written these things on account of their strangeness. On Monday, the 29th, I halted and went to hunt nilgaw. I shot two, one male and one female. On Tuesday also, the 30th, I halted.

End of the twelfth year of the Emperor's reign, in the Tūzuk-i-Jahāngīrī.

[1] MSS. have Ranūd.

ERRATA AND ADDENDA.

Page 15, line 7 from foot. The figure 1 should be placed at Sulṭānu-n-nisā Begam.

p. 24, l. 5. *For* my *read* his. With reference to n. 2, p. 120, l. 13, shows that the father meant is S͟hāhruk͟h.

p. 34, l. 2 of verse. Solomon's greatness depended on the possession of a ring. When that was lost his power departed. See the story of its loss and recovery in Mīr K͟hwānd (Rehatsek's translation, pt. i, 100). Probably then the line should be rendered 'Call him the ring-wearing Solomon.'

p. 38, near foot. The words 'the news,' etc., are not a verse, and Naẓar-jīvī should be Naẓar Chūlī, i.e. the Naẓar who accompanied Humāyūn through the desert (*chūl*). See Akbar-nāma translation, i, 657, n. 3.

p. 39, l. 2. *For* near Lahore *read* a dependency of Lahore. Kalānūr is the Kalanaur of the maps, and is 15 miles west of Gurdāspūr (I.G., new ed., xiv, 297).

p. 43, note. *For* lithograph *read* text.

p. 46, l. 8. *For* Mīrzā *read* Mīrān.

p. 50, l. 1, and note 1. I.O. MSS. seem to have Tanam Bahādur. The reference to Ma'āṣiru-l-umarā is ii, 140. The name of Muẓaffar Gujarātī's son was Bahādur.

p. 54, n. 1. *For* Price, p. 6 *read* Price, p. 68. The Iqbāl-nāma and Khulāṣatu-t-tawārīk͟h say he was put in charge of Ihtimām Kotwāl.

p. 58, n. 2. It is Nīlera in I.O. MS. No. 181.

p. 60, l. 6. The meaning is that 'Ābidīn was the son of 'Abdu-llah Khān's spiritual adviser. 'Ābidīn is called 'Ābidī in Akbar-nāma, iii, 832. He came to India in 1013 (1604–5), and Akbar gave him the rank of 1,000 and 500 horse (iii, 834).

p. 65, l. 11. *For* know *read* knew.

p. 66, l. 7. The MSS. seem to have Jaihāl.

p. 66, last line. Kilīn means 'daughter-in-law' in Turkī. Perhaps Kīlan here is a synonym for 'son-in-law.'

p. 67, l. 8. The words 'which in Hindustani is called *ballī*' are not in the I.O. MSS. I do not know the word *ballī* as meaning a pole. Perhaps it is a mistake for *laggī*.

p. 76, l. 3 from foot. Omit the words 'who is one of the k͟hānazādas of the State.'

p. 79, l. 6. *For* and cash *read* in cash.

p. 81, n. 1. Delete question mark and the words 'near Multān.' Nandanpur, i.e. Nandana (I.G., xviii, 349), and Girjhāk are in the Jhelam district. The Rām Dās garden was some place near Lahore, where Jahāngīr took up his residence on the way to the hunting-ground. He spent 3½ months in hunting.

p. 84, l. 19. *For* 'Abdu-r-Raḥīm *read* 'Abdu-r-Raḥmān.

p. 87, l. 21. Firishta in his account of Bābar says the Daulat Khān of that time was descended from the Daulat Khān who in 816 A.H. (1413–14) was Sultan of Delhi. See Elliot, iv, 45.

p. 90, l. 4 from foot. Jahāngīrpūr is mentioned in account of 15th year, p. 317, last line (text). It is the Shekhopura of the maps, and is 22 miles from Ḥāfiẓābād and 18 miles west of Lahore. It was called Shaikhūpūra in allusion to Jahāngīr's pet name of Shaikhū Bābā, and also in honour of Shaikh Salīm. See Khulāṣa T. in account of Jahāngīr's reign. The I.G., xxii, 270, wrongly ascribes its origin to Dārā Shukūh. Mullā Ḥusain Kashmīrī, mentioned on p. 91, died in 1037 (1627–8), Rieu, ii, 7756. The minaret is still standing. See Eastwick's "Panjab Handbook," 200. Instead of 'the gravestone in the shape of an antelope' we should render, I think, 'a stone tomb with the figure of an antelope (engraved upon it).' The I.O. MSS. have Marrāj as the name of the antelope. Perhaps we should read Manorāj 'mind's lord.'

p. 99, l. 3 from foot. I.O. MSS. have *bahūr* بهور as the name of the net.

p. 109, n. 1. Delete note. The *rang* is the ibex.

p. 110, n. 1. See J.A.S.B. for February, 1908, p. 39.

p. 117. The Iqbāl-nāma mentions in connection with the story of the mummified saint that many Sabzawār saints lived in Bāmiyān. See also Kāmgār Ḥusainī.

p. 120, l. 1. Delete word 'Georgians.' I.O. MS. No. 181 has ghurja.

p. 122, l. 10. Insert 'and' after 'sheep.'

p. 125, l. 13. *For* garden *read* gardens.

p. 133, l. 4. *For* £ *read* rupees.

p. 134, l. 15. *For* he died on the 29th *read* he died in his ninth decade (i.e. between 80 and 90). The Ma'āṣiru-l-umarā, ii, 143, says he was 82 when he died.

p. 134, l. 13 from foot. Instead of 'he went off alone' the MSS. have 'carrying off his life' (i.e. escaping) with difficulty.

p. 136, n. 1. The opinion expressed in this note is proved to be wrong by General Cunningham's Report, Arch. S., xiv, p. 58. The tombs are those of a musician and his pupil.

p. 140, l. 8. Delete *Sylvia olivacea*.

p. 143, l. 7. Apparently there were twelve balls, or at least objects, ten being as large as an orange, another being a citron, and the twelfth a *surkh*. So instead of 'one to a citron' we should read, perhaps, 'a citron and a *surkh*.'

p. 143, l. 3 from foot. *For* Ilf *read* Alf.

p. 147, l. 4 from foot. Delete the word 'Egyptian' and also n. 1. It appears from the Ghiyāṣu-l-loghāt that a Quṭbī ruby is a broad ruby suitable for a ring (signet ?).

p. 153, l. 13 from foot. *For* Hamazānī *read* Hamadānī.

p. 156. According to Terry, Jahāndār was called Sultan Takht because born when Jahāngīr first sat on his throne.

p. 158, l. 9. Perhaps Yūzī = Yūz-bāshī, i.e. centurion. But I.O. 181 has not the word, only saying 'Shāh Beg Khān,' and No. 305 has Shāh Beg Khān Būrī (?).

p. 158, l. 10. The passage is wrongly translated. No elephant was presented to Salāmu-llah. The sentence should end on l. 9 after the word 'panther-keeper,' which word is probably a mistranslation. Then this new sentence should come, i.e. 'Salāmu-llah 'Arab, who is a young man of a distinguished Arabian family (*kih az jawānān-i-qarār-dāda-i-'Arab ast*) and related to Mubārak, the governor of Dizfūl, came to wait upon me on account of his being suspicious of the designs of S͟hāh 'Abbās (against himself).' 'I patronized him,' etc. (as on p. 158).

p. 158, n. 3, and p. 162, n. 1. Both notes are wrong. The place meant by Jahāngīr is Dizfūl, a town in the K͟hūzistān province of Persia, and Jūyza is evidently a copyist's error for K͟hūz or K͟hūza, another name for K͟hūzistān. Dizfūl is an ancient name, and according to Yāqūt, Barbier de Meynard's translation, p. 231, the proper spelling is Dizpūl, i.e. 'the Bridge of the Citadel,' the town being named after a famou bridge built over the river. For K͟hūz see B. de Meynard, 216.

p. 160, l. 12 from foot. Qabūlah was a town in the Bet Jālandhar Dū'āb.

p. 163, l. 9. It is 2,000 rupees in I.O. MSS.

p. 163, l. 12. It is not Qāchā Dakhanī in I.O. MSS., but I am not sure what the clause, as given by them, means. No. 181 seems to have *bafatāhāīgī* for 'assistance' (?). Two B.M. MSS. have apparently *bafatāhāī kapī*, but Add. 26,215 has the Arabic *ḥa*, while Or. 3276 has the ordinary *h*, so that the words possibly mean 'the young of the monkey' (*kapī*).

p. 166, l. 2. Ḥusāmu-d-dīn was married to Abū-l-faẓl's sister, Blochmann, 441.

p. 167, l. 16. The word *rojh* in brackets is wrong. The MSS. have *qarā-quyrag͟h* and *qarā-quyrāg͟h*. P. de Courteille gives *quyrūg͟h* as meaning a tail, so perhaps *qarā-qūyrūg͟h* means a black-tailed sheep or deer. See p. 129, l. 17, where the *qarā-qūyrūg͟h* is said to be the *chikāra*.

p. 168, last line. The MSS. has *ḥabs-i-mazīd*, which does not necessarily mean imprisonment for life.

p. 170, n. 2. *For* Akbar's wives *read* Jahāngīr's wives.

p. 172, l. 21 seq. Is this the story referred to by Hawkins (Purchas), about Muqarrab having taken a Banian's daughter ?

p. 177, note. *For* one-third of an inch *read* one and a third inches.

p. 183, l. 8. This is the annular eclipse entered in Dr. R. Schramm's Tables, Sewell's Indian Calendar, as having occurred on 5th December, 1610, which corresponds to 28th Ramaẓan, 1019.

p. 185, n. 3. Persian text, p. 309, l. 11, has the phrase *majrā girifta ātash dādand*, 'took aim and fired' (a cannon).

p. 188, l. 7 from foot. For Naẓīrī, see Rieu, ii, 807*b*, and Blochmann, 579. He died in 1622 (1613).

p. 191, l. 10. *For dhīk* (?) *read dhīk*, i.e. adjutant bird.

p. 191, l. 8. *Pātal* means 'red' or 'rose-coloured' in Sanskrit. Query 'red deer.'

p. 192, l. 2. Add year 1020.

p. 195, last line. The passage is rather obscure, but the meaning seems to be that though formalities are not regarded by the wise, yet weak persons (*qāwāṣir*, which apparently is a plural of *qāṣir*), regard externals as the means of paying the dues of friendship (and so we must attend to them). Hence when at this auspicious time a province which had gone out of my ('Abbās's) possession has been settled by the exertions of angelic servants in accordance with the hopes of well-wishers, I ('Abbās) have returned to the capital, and have despatched Kamālu-d-dīn, etc.

p. 197, l. 7. *For* Khankhānān *read* Khān.

p. 197, l. 12. The I.O. MSS. have a different reading here. They say nothing about three ratis. What they say is, "At this time I had made some increase in the amounts of weights and measures. For instance, I added one-fourth (*siwā'ī*) to the weight of the muhrs and rupees." The *sih ratī* of text is a mistake for *siwā'ī*.

p. 197, l. 12 from foot. I.O. MSS. have 'Sunday in Ṣafar,' but they wrongly have 1022.

p. 197, l. 9 from foot. Both I.O. MSS. have 'Neknahar' instead of 'in the interior.'

p. 198, l. 11. *Or* Lohgar.

p. 205, l. 14. I do not think that the translation 'should not force Islam on anyone,' or the version in Elliot, vi, 325, 'Not to forcibly impose Musulman burdens on anyone,' gives the full force of the words *taklīf-i-Musalmānī bar kasī nakunand.* I think the reference clearly is to circumcision, and that the words *taklīf-i-Musalmānī* should be rendered 'the Muhammadan ceremonial,' This explains why the injunction comes in immediately after the prohibitions against blinding and mutilation. It has been said, and I believe with truth, that the members of the Delhi royal family never were circumcised. Probably one reason for this was that in many instances they had Hindu mothers. As pointed out in Elliot, the passage is omitted in the Iqbāl-nāma. It also does not occur in the version given in 'Alī Muḥammad's "History of Gujarat," vol. i, p. 200 of lithograph.

p. 214, verse. *For* red *read* a river.

p. 216. See picture of a turkey in Havell's "Indian Sculpture," pp. 214–15.

p. 218, l. 10 from foot. About Shāpūr see Ma'āsiru-l-umarā, i, 180.

p. 224, n. 1. *For* infra *read* supra, pp. 27 and 30, note.

p. 229, ll. 9 and 14. *For* Patna *read* Tatta.

p. 229, note. *For* brother *read* brother's son.

p. 231, l. 14 from foot. *For* Nihālpūr *substitute* Thālner as in the MSS. The news of the death seems to have reached Agra very quickly.

p. 232, l. 1. Insert the word 'and' before 'allowed.'

p. 234, l. 2 from foot. The word translated 'cranes' is *kārwānak*, and probably means 'a little crane.' In Blochmann, 63, *karwānak* is rendered by 'stone-curlew.'

p. 234, l. 5 from foot. The word seems to be *kunjishk*, 'sparrow,' in the MSS., but probably it should be *kunjak*, 'a curiosity, a rarity.'

p. 235, l. 2. It is Thursday, the 28th, in the MSS., and instead of 'night' we should read 'eve.' The English date corresponding to 28th Muharram is 10th March, 1613.

p. 237, l. 8. It is 1,000 in the MSS., and this is probably correct, though B.M. MS. 1645 has changed the word for 1,000 into one for 100.

The ordinary *kaukab-i-ṭāli'* was 100 tolas in weight, see p. 11. At p. 406 two kaukab-i-tali's are mentioned of 500 tolas each. It is a mistake, I think, to regard the word muhr as always implying gold. The ordinary kaukab-i-tali' was of silver, and these large muhrs were no doubt also of silver. The note 1 to Elliott, vi, 355, is probably incorrect.

p. 237, l. 10. 'The feast went off well,' etc. The passage is obscure, but probably the translation should be 'There was a splendid assemblage (*majis shigufta gasht*), and after it was over I ordered that they should arrange an illumination.' The words in text, p. 116, l. 3, are *ḥukm kardam kih asbāb u āyin bār kunand.* The MSS. have *asbāb-i-āyīn rā.* No. 181 seems to have *bāz kunand,* and so has B.M. MS. 1645, but No. 305 has *bār kunand,* as in text. It may be that the meaning is that Jahāngīr told the servants they might appropriate the decorations, but I rather think the order was to make an illumination. It may also simply mean that he ordered the decorations to be taken down. *Bāz kunand* ordinarily means 'to open out,' *bār kunand* 'to load.'

p. 237, l. 12. Delete 'the' before Muqarrab.

p. 237, note. I.O. MSS. seem to have *zarīn,* 'golden' (?).

p. 241, l. 5 from foot. I.G., new ed., xvii, 309, speaks of a handsome mosque in Mairtha having been founded by Akbar, but probably it is this one of Shaikh Pīr. Perhaps Shaikh Pīr is the old beggar referred to in Roe's Journal.

p. 247, l. 5 from foot. For *chakrī* read *jhakkaṛ.* It was not necessarily a dust-storm.

p. 250, l. 6. The MSS. have Rūp instead of Rāwal, and so has Elliot, vi, 335. They have 'hill country of Mewāt,' as in text. They have Chitor, and not Jaipūr, as in Elliot, and they make (by error) Jahāngīr speak of the year as the 10th, instead of the 8th. Instead of 'have' at l. 12 we should read 'had,' and instead of 'from the Rāwal who was first known as Rāwal,' they have, as also has Elliot, 'Rahab, who was the first to take the title of Rānā.' Rahab is the Rahup of Tod, who says he came to the throne in 1201 A.D.

p. 253, ll. 10 and 11. I cannot find the word *pūlta-bāzī.* My friend, Mr. Irvine, suggests that we should read *paṭṭā bāzī. Paṭṭā* means a 'foil,' or 'wooden sword,' and *paṭṭā bāz* is given in Forbes as meaning a 'fencer.' *Paltha mārnā* occurs in Forbes as meaning a 'peculiar posture.' The *yagānagī* of l. 11 should be *yakāngagi,* meaning 'one body,' or 'one limb,' and corresponds to the *yakhāth* of Blochmann, 252, both phrases meaning apparently 'that the fencer fights with one hand,' that is, 'without using a shield.'

p. 260, l. 8. This I'tiqād is the father of Mumtāz-maḥall, the wife of Shāh Jahān. He now became Āṣaf Khān, and apparently the title of I'tiqād was transferred to his younger brother (or cousin ?) Shāhpūr, who was afterwards governor of Kashmir. See Ma'āṣir i, 180. The two previous Āṣaf Khāns of the family are Ghiyāṣu-d-dīn of Qazwīn (Blochmann, 433), and Mīrzā Ja'far Beg, who was Ghiyāṣu-d-dīn's nephew. The father of Nūr-Jahān was Ghiyāṣ Beg of Tīhran (Blochmann, 508). Blochmann, in his Table, 512, has not mentioned Shāhpūr, i.e. the I'tiqād who became governor of Kashmir.

p. 261, l. 17 from foot. *For* mother *read* mothers (i.e. stepmothers).

p. 261, l. 10 from foot. *For* nephews *read* nephew.

p. 278, l. 13. *For* named *read namad*, and it should be in italics.

p. 281, l. 2. The permission to beat his drums is explained by the Iqbāl-nāma, p. 79, where it is said that he was permitted to beat his drums in the capital, *dar pāy-i-takht*.

p. 281, l. 6 from foot. This eclipse is noted in Dr. Schram's Tables as occurring on 19th March, 1615.

p. 282, l. 10 from foot. Delete word 'Egyptian.'

p. 286, l. 6. *For* Frank *read* Venetian. *Kār-i-Wanadik*, as in MSS.

p. 288, l. 5. Chatūr, instead of Taḥayyur, in No. 305, and Bakhtar (?) in No. 181.

p. 293. According to the Iqbāl-nāma, 80, Kunwar Karan, son of Rānā Amar Singh, became an officer of Jahāngīr, receiving the rank of 5,000 personal and horse. He was the first of the direct royal line of his family to accept office.

p. 293, l. 2 from foot. No. 181 has 102 horses.

p. 294, n. 2. No. 181 has Rasht.

p. 300, l. 18. According to Vullers' Dict., i, 482, a *tūlcha* is 96 grains or about half a tola. The Ghīyāṣu-l-loghāt, however, says that *tūlcha* is merely the Persian form of the Hindustānī *tūlā*. According to the Burhān-i-qāti' a tola is only 2½ māsha in Upper India. Generally it is reckoned as 12 māsha. According to Sir Thomas Roe 2½ tolas were equal to 1 ounce.

p. 317, MS. No. 181 has A.H. date 1025.

p. 321, l. 11. *For* several bits *read* some marten skins. See Tūzuk text, p. 308, l. 3 from foot, and Vullers' Dict. ii, 6. The MS. No. 181 has *ṣad dāna-i-kīsh*, 'one hundred marten skins.'

p. 321, l. 13 from foot. *For* transit dues *read* for keeping open the Pass (*rāh-dārī*).

p. 321, n. 2. The words in I.O. MSS. seem to be *īgāna begāna*, which is perhaps a mere jingle on the word *afghāna*, but may mean 'known, unknown.' Jahāngīr puns on the name Qadam, which means 'a foot, a pace.' The words occur again at p. 323.

p. 322, last line. Probably *'āqirī* is, or is derived from, *'aqār*, which means a bird whose feathers were used for ornamentation. According to P. de Courteille, Turkī Dict., 384, *'aqār* is a heron.

p. 328, l. 13 from foot. *For* Shāh Shajā'at *read* Shāh Shujā'. He was Shāh Jahān's second son, and was born at Ajmir on the eve of Sunday, and on 11th Tīr. Apparently this corresponds to 24th June, 1616, which is the date of birth mentioned by Sir Thomas Roe. Beale's date of 12th May is wrong.

p. 332, l. 6 from foot. Here the word *tūlcha* is used again, and apparently as meaning the same thing as *tola*; 6,514 tūlchas or tolas would be about 82 sīrs, or over 2 maunds, and about 12 stone. Next year Sir Thomas Roe saw Jahāngīr weighed, and he understood that his weight was 9,000 rupees. If so, his weight would appear to have considerably increased during the twelve months. Perhaps we should read 8,514, instead of 6,514 tūlchas. *Hasht* (8) and *shash* (6) are often confounded.

p. 341, l. 8 from foot. *For* times *read* days, the word *rūz* (days) having been omitted from the text.

p. 344, n. 1. Apparently we should read Toda. The difference between it and Nauda is, in Persian writing, only one dot. Toda is mentioned by Roe as the place where he overtook Jahāngīr, and the stages given by him come to 21 kos, counting from Rāmsar, and this agrees very nearly with Jahāngīr's stages from the same place.

p. 351, l. 15 from foot. The MS. No. 181 has the word *gaz* twice, and makes the *pahnā'ī*, or width, 175½ *gaz* (yards).

p. 351, last line. *For* Būlgharī *read* Pūlkharī.

p. 352, l. 1. Delete the words 'of Tīr.' The month was Bahman, corresponding to January–February, 1617, and 23rd Bahman would be about 1st February. In Sayyid Aḥmad's edition the word *Tīr* is a mistake for *nīz*, 'also,' the meaning being that the 23rd was a halt as well as the 22nd.

p. 353, l. 2. G͟haznīn K͟hān is mentioned by Finch under the name of Gidney Khān, and he is said to have been originally a Hindu. But this seems doubtful, as his father's name is given in the Mir'āt-i-Aḥmadī as Malik K͟hānjī Afg͟hān. See also Bayley's "Gujarat," p. 15. Jālor is now in Jodhpūr. It is described by Finch.

p. 353, l. 2. This seems to be the case of matricide mentioned in Terry's "Voyage," p. 362, of ed. of 1777. His statement that it occurred at Aḥmadabad is presumably an oversight. Terry says the matricide was put to death by being bitten by two snakes. See also Irvine's "Manucci," iv, 422. Apparently the punishment recorded by Jahāngīr took place on the 4th February, for Sir Thomas Roe mentions that they reached Kāliyādaha, the next stage, on 6th February. The *bi* in *biyāsa* should be deleted. Jālaur, or Jalor, is in Jodhpūr (I.G., xiv, 29). It used to be in Ajmir. It is not quite clear if Terry was with Roe at Kāliyādaha, but if not he was with him at Ujjain. The execution may have taken place there.

p. 355, l. 16. For 'from the city of Ujjain,' etc., *read* 'to a rural spot near the city of Ujjain.'

p. 360, l. 22. *For* 128¼ cubits *read* 28¼ cubits. I.O. MS. 181 has 28¼ yards. The printed text of Sayyid Aḥmad has 128¼ cubits.

p. 362, l. 8 from foot. Delete (Bālchha ?).

p. 373, l. 11 seq. This I'tiqād was the younger brother or perhaps cousin of Āṣaf K͟hān, the brother of Nūr-Jahān. He was also known as S͟hāhpūr. See Ma'āṣiru-l-umarā, i, 180.

p. 375, n. 2. *Read* two diamonds.

p. 406, n. 3. Dīk͟htān or Daik͟htān seems right. It is so in both the I.O. MSS.

p. 406, l. 11 from foot. These muhrs were probably of silver, and were called muhrs because they were medals rather than coins. Dr. Kehr has given an account of a large muhr which is now apparently in Dresden. See also Richardson's Dict., article Sikka.

p. 407, l. 4. This is Jūna K͟hān, son of G͟hīyāṣu-d-dīn Tughluq. He ascended the throne in 1325 under the title of Muḥammad bin Tug͟hluq.

p. 407, l. 15. This is the prince known as Naṣīru-d-dīn. He ascended the throne as Muḥammad bin Fīrūz in 1387, and again in 1390.

p. 413, ll. 11 and 3 from foot. I.O. MSS. show that Sar-farāz should be Sarafrāz; apparently his present was 'seven bullock-carts' (*haft rās gāw bahal*) and not two bullocks.

p. 417, n. 2. Cancel note. Nārangsar seems right.

p. 417, l. 2 from foot. The words are *dah bīst wazn muhr u rūpiya ma'mūl.* Elliot, p. 354, renders this 'ten and twenty times heavier than the current gold muhr and rupee.'

p. 418, l. 10. See n. 2 in Elliot, vi, 355. Apparently Jahāngīr means that he was the first person to coin double muhrs and double rupees. There is an account of tankas in the Bahār-i-'Ajam, 261, col. 2, p. 421, n. 2. But it is 27 in I.O. MSS. 113, p. 423, l. 14. A *ṭassū* is more than a finger-breadth, it is the $\frac{1}{24}$ of a *gaz* or yard, and should be about $1\frac{1}{3}$ inches.

p. 437. I am indebted to my friend Dr. Hoernle for the explanation of the names of the two sects of Sewras. They should be Tapā and Kharatara. Mān Singh's name in religion was Jīn-simha. See *Epigraphia Indica*, i, 37, and *Ind. Antiquary*, xi, 250. Mān Singh died at Mairtha (in Jodhpūr) according to the Jain books, in the beginning of 1618. The head of the Tapā sect in Jahāngīr's time was Vījayasena. There is an elaborate paper on the Jains of Gujarat and Marwar by Colonel Miles in the Transactions R.A.S., iii, pp. 335–71.

p. 442, l. 8. There is no previous reference to the outbreak of plague in Kashmir, though there is one to its occurrence in the Panjab. There is an interesting account of the plague in K͟hāfī K͟hān, i, 286–8, in which the description is carried down to the time of Aurangzīb.

INDEX.

A

B

E

F

I

J

K

L

M

P

Q

W

Y

Z

THE TŪZUK-I-JAHĀNGĪRĪ

OR

MEMOIRS OF JAHĀNGĪR

VOL. II.

VOLUME SECOND

THE TŪZUK-I-JAHĀNGĪRĪ

OR

MEMOIRS OF JAHĀNGĪR

FROM THE THIRTEENTH TO THE BEGINNING OF THE NINETEENTH YEAR OF HIS REIGN

PREFACE

After an interval of about five years, the second volume of Mr. Alexander Rogers' translation of Jahangir's Memoirs has been published by the Royal Asiatic Society. It is a smaller work than the first volume, for it only extends over six years of the reign, as against the twelve years of its predecessor. Even then it does not include the whole of the reign, for that lasted twenty-two years. The two volumes, however, contain all that Jahangir wrote or supervised. It will be found, I think, that the present volume is fully as interesting as its predecessor. The accounts of the Zodiacal coinage (pp. 6 and 7), and of the comet, or new star (p. 48), the notice of the Plague in Agra (pp. 65-67), and the elaborate description of Kashmīr, under the chronicle of the 15th year, are valuable, and a word should be said for the pretty story of the King and the Gardener's daughter (p. 50), and for the allusions to painters and pictures.

If Bābur, who was the founder of the Moghul Empire in India, was the Cæsar of the East, and if the many-sided Akbar was an epitome of all the great Emperors, including Augustus, Trajan, Hadrian, Marcus Aurelius, Julian, and Justinian, Jahangir was certainly of the type of the Emperor Claudius, and so bore a close resemblance to our James I. All three were weak men, and under the influence of their favourites, and all three were literary, and at least two of them were fond of dabbling in theology. All three were in their wrong places as rulers. Had James I. (and VI. of Scotland) been, as he half wished, the Keeper of the Bodleian, and Jahangir been head of a Natural History Museum, they would have been better and happier men. Jahangir's best points were his love of nature and powers of observation, and his desire to do justice. Unfortunately, the last of these merits was vitiated by a propensity for excessive and recondite punishments. Like his father, grandfather, and great-grandfather, he was addicted to drugs and alcohol, and he shortened his life in this way. He made no addition to the imperial territories, but, on the contrary, diminished them by losing Qandahar to the Persians. But possibly his peaceful temper, or his laziness, was an advantage, for it saved much bloodshed. His greatest fault as a king was his subservience to his wife, Nūr-Jahān, and the consequent quarrel with his son, Shah Jahan, who was the ablest and best of his male children. The last years of his reign were especially melancholy, for he suffered from asthma and other diseases; and he had to endure the ignominy of being for a while a captive to one of his own servants—Mahābat Khān. He died on the borders of Kashmir, when on his way to Lahore, in October, 1627, in the fifty-ninth year of his age, and was buried at Shāhdara, near Lahore, where his widow, Nūr-Jahān, and her brother are also interred. At the time of his death his son Shah Jahan was at Junair in the Deccan, and there the news was conveyed in a wonderfully short time by a Hindu courier. Jahangir was succeeded by Shah Jahan, who lost no time in getting rid of his relatives, for, like the Turk, he bore no kinsman near the throne. Indeed, he is strongly suspected of having killed his elder brother, Khusrau, several years before.

I am indebted to Mr. Ellis, of the India Office, for revising the proofs.

NOTE.

In the Catalogue of Manuscripts in the Library of Trinity College, Dublin, p. 416, mention is made of a history of Hindustan during the reign of Jahangir, in two volumes, with paintings (Ouseley MSS.). I have recently ascertained that the MS. is only a modern copy of the Iqbāl-nāma.

H. BEVERIDGE.

CONTENTS

THE THIRTEENTH NEW YEAR'S FEAST

On the eve of Wednesday, the 23rd Rabī'u-l-awwal, 1027 (March 10, 1618), after the lapse of fourteen and a half *gharīs*, the entrance of the Sun—that is, H.M. the Great Light—the Benefactor of the Universe, into the constellation of the Ram, took place. Twelve years had now passed from the august Accession of this suppliant at the throne of God, in prosperity, and the New Year began in joy and thanksgiving. On Thursday, 2 Farwardīn, Divine month, the festival of my Lunar weighment took place, and the fifty-first * year of the age of this suppliant at God's throne began with rejoicings. I trust that my life will be spent in the doing of God's Will, and that not a breath of it will pass without remembering Him. After the weighment had been finished, a fresh feast of joy was arranged, and my domestic servants celebrated the day with brimming cups.

On this day Āṣaf K. (Nūr-Jahān's brother), who held the rank of 5,000 with 3,000 horse, was favoured by the grant of 4,000 two-horsed and three-horsed troopers, and Ṣābit K. was raised to the office of Examiner of Petitions. I bestowed the post of the Artillery on Mu'tamid K. A Kachh (Cutch) horse had been brought as an offering by the son of Dilāwar K. No horse so good as this had come into my establishment till I encamped in Gujarat, and as M. Rustam showed a great liking for it, I presented it to him. On the Jām were conferred four rings—viz., diamond, ruby, emerald, and sapphire

* Jahāngīr was born on Wednesday, 17 Rabī'u-l-awwal, 977 A.H., or August 31, 1569, and so on March 11, 1618, or 23 Rabī'u-l-awwal, 1027, he was in the beginning of his fifty-first lunar year. By solar computation he was not yet fifty, that is, he was in his fiftieth year. The text wrongly has 1017 instead of 1027.

—and two hawks. I also gave four rings—viz., ruby, cat's-eye, emerald, and sapphire—to Raja Lachmī Narāyan (of Kūch Bihār). Muruwwat K. had sent three elephants from Bengal, and two of them were included in my private stud. On the eve of Friday I ordered lamps to be placed round the tank, and this had a very good appearance. On Sunday Ḥājī Rafīq came from 'Irāq, and had the good fortune to kiss the threshold, and laid before me a letter which my brother Shāh 'Abbās had sent with him. The aforesaid person is a slave of Mīr Muḥammad Amīn K., the caravan leader, and the Mīr had brought him up from his childhood. In truth, he is an excellent servant. He frequently visited 'Irāq, and became intimate with my brother Shāh 'Abbās. This time he had brought tipchāq* horses and fine cloth-stuffs, such that of the horses some were put into the private stables. As he is a skilful slave, and a servant worthy of favour, I honoured him with the title of *Maliku-t-tujjār* (King of Merchants). On Monday I gave Raja Lachmī Narāyan a special sword, a jewelled rosary, and four pearls for ear-rings. On *Mubārak-shamba* (Thursday) I increased by 500 horse the manṣab of 5,000 personal and 1,000 horse held by Mīrzā Rustam; I'tiqād K. was promoted to a manṣab of 4,000 and 1,000 horse; Sarfarāz K. was promoted to a manṣab of 2,500 and 1,400 horse; Mu'tamid K. to the rank of 1,000 with 350 horse. On Anīrā'ī Singh-dalan and Fidā'ī K., horses worth 100 *muhars* were conferred. As the guarding and administration of the Punjab had been entrusted to I'timādu-d-daula, I, at his request, promoted to the government (ḥukūmat) of the said Ṣubah, Mīr Qāsim, the Bakhshī of the Aḥadīs, who is related to him, and bestowed on him a manṣab of 1,000 personal with 400 horse and the title of Qāsim K. Before this I had given Raja Lachmī Narāyan an 'Irāq horse. On this day I conferred on him an elephant and a Turkī horse, and gave him leave to go to Bengal. The Jām was dismissed to his native country with a present of a jewelled waist-sword,

* Text wrongly has *panchāq*. In Turki dictionaries it is spelt topchāq, and means a large or long-necked horse. See P. de Courteille Dict., etc.

a jewelled rosary, two horses, one from 'Irāq and the other a Turkī, and a dress of honour. Ṣāliḥ, brother's son of the deceased Āṣaf Khān,* was promoted to a manṣab of 1,000 with 300 horse, and allowed to go to Bengal, and a horse was conferred on him. On this date Mīr Jumla† came from Persia, and had the good fortune to pay his respects. The aforesaid is one of the respectable Sayyids of Isfahan and his family have always been held in honour in Persia, and now his brother's son, Mīr Riẓā, is in the service of my brother, Shāh 'Abbās, and has the rank of Ṣadr, and the Shah has married him to his own daughter. Mīr Jumla had left Persia fourteen years before this, and gone to Golconda to Muḥammad Qulī Quṭbu-l-mulk. His name is Muḥammad Amīn. Quṭbu-l-mulk gave him the title of Mīr Jumla. For ten years he had been his *Mudār 'Alaihi* (Centre of Affairs) and his *Ṣāḥib Sāmān* (factotum). After Quṭbu-l-mulk died, and the rule came to his brother's son, the latter did not treat the Mīr properly, and so he took leave and hastened to his native country. The Shah, on account of his connection with Mīr Riẓā, and the respect which he had for men ‡ of merit, showed much consideration for and kindness to him. He (the Mīr) also presented fitting offerings, and passed three or four years in Persia, and amassed properties (estates ?).§ As he several times represented that he wished to enter the service of this Court, I sent a farmān and invited him. Immediately the farmān arrived he severed his connections there, and set the face of loyalty towards this Court. This day he attained the

* Āṣaf K. III. of Blochmann ; his name was Ja'far Beg.

† See "Iqbāl-nāma," p. 111, etc. He is not the famous Mīr Jumla, who was Aurangzeb's general, though possibly the latter was his son. According to the "Iqbāl-nāma, he was the nephew, and not the uncle, of Mīr Riẓā, but Jahāngīr's statement agrees with the 'Ālam-ārā'ī (p. 623). Mīr Jumla's patron, Muḥammad Qulī Quṭb-Shāh, died in 1612. He himself died in 1637, while Aurangzeb's general died in 1663.

‡ Possibly what is meant is that Shāh 'Abbās was greedy after Mīr Jumla's (Sāmān) wealth. Kāmgār Ḥusainī distinctly says that 'Abbās wanted to get hold of Mīr Jumla's goods.

§ The Iqbāl-nāma says that 'Abbās only gave Mīr Jumla flattering words, and did not give him any high appointment. See also 'Ālam-ārā'ī, 623, and Ma'āṣiru-l-umarā, III. 415.

honour of kissing the carpet, and produced as offering twelve horses, nine *tuqūz** of silk cloths, and two rings. As he had come with devotion and sincerity, I conferred favours and kindness on him, and presented him with 20,000 *darbs* (Rs. 10,000) for his expenses and a dress of honour. On the same day I gave the post of Bakhshī of the Aḥadīs to 'Ināyat K. in place of Qāsim K. I honoured Khwāja 'Āqil, who is one of the old servants, with the title of 'Āqil K., and presented him with a horse. On Friday, Dilāwar K., coming from the Deccan, had the good fortune to kiss the threshold, and presented an offering of 100 *muhars* and Rs. 1,000. Bāqir K., Faujdār of Multan, was promoted to a manṣab of 800 personal and 300 horse. Tijārat K. and Bāhū'ī,† Zamindar of Multan, were honoured with the gift of elephants. On Saturday, the 11th, marching from Doḥad with the intention of hunting elephants, I pitched at the village of Kara Bāra (Garbara ?). On Sunday, the 12th, the village of Sajāra (Sajwara ?) became the place of alighting. It is 8 *koss* from this place to Doḥad, and 1½ *koss* to the hunting-ground. On the morning of Monday, the 13th, I went to hunt elephants with a body of my private servants. As the grazing-place of the elephants is in a hilly country, with elevations and depressions, a passage is obtained with difficulty by one on foot. Before this, a large body of horse and foot had surrounded the jungle after the manner of a *qamurgha*, and outside the jungle, on a tree, they had prepared a wooden platform for me. On all sides of this they had arranged seats on other trees for the Amirs. They had got ready 200 male elephants with strong nooses, and many female elephants. On each elephant there were seated two elephant-drivers of the tribe of *Jarga*,‡ whose special em-

* Tuqūz means "nine," but perhaps it is here only used to express a gift, and the pieces of cloth were perhaps only nine, and not eighty-one. See Vullers s.v., who refers to Quatremère.

† The I.O. MSS. have Māmū'ī, and the meaning may be "the maternal uncle of the Zamindar."

‡ Jariya in No. 181. It seems to be the Jareja tribe of Abū-l-Faẓl, Jarrett II. 250. Compare Blochmann's translation, p. 285 n., of the corresponding passage in the Iqbāl-nāma. The tribe is there called Jhariyah.

ployment is the hunting of elephants, and it had been arranged that they should bring the wild elephants from the jungle into my presence, that I might witness the hunt. It happened that at the time when the men from all sides entered the jungle, in consequence of the thickness of the forest and the heights and hollows, the chain was broken, and the order of the *qamurg͟ha* did not remain perfect. The wild elephants in bewilderment turned in every direction, but twelve male and female came to this side (where J. was). As the fear was that they might escape, they drove in the tame elephants and tied them (the wild elephants) up wherever they found them. Although many elephants were not caught, at least two excellent ones were captured, very handsome in shape, of good breed, and perfect marks. As there is a hill in the jungle in which the elephants were, called Rākas (Rākshas) Pahār,* or demon hill, I called these two elephants Rāvaṇ Sar and Pāvan Sar, these being the names of two demons. On Tuesday, the 14th, and Kam-s͟hamba (Wednesday), the 15th, I halted.

On the eve of Thursday, the 16th, I marched, and halted at the stage of Kara Bāra. Ḥākim Beg,† who is one of the household of the Court, was honoured with the title of Ḥākim K., and a sum of Rs. 3,000 was given to Sangrām, a Zamindar of the hill country of the Panjab. As the heat was very great, and marching by day was to be avoided, I marched by night. On Saturday, the 18th, a halt was made in the parganah of Doḥad. On Sunday, the 19th, the sun that bestows favour on the world attained the highest point in the constellation of Aries. On this day a great entertainment was held, and I sat on the throne. I promoted S͟hāh-nawāz K., who held a manṣab of 5,000, with the favour of 2,000 horse, of two and three horses. K͟hwāja Abū-l-Ḥasan, the Chief Bak͟hs͟hī, was given a mansab, original and increased, of 4,000 with 2,000 horse. As Aḥmad Beg K., of Kabul, who

* This must be Pāvāgarh, a hill fort in the Pānch Maḥāl district, which is 2,800 feet above the sea. See I.G. XX. 79, and XIX. 380.

† Son-in-law of I'tmādu-d-daula, being married to a sister of Nūr-Jahān. See Ma'āṣiru-l-umarā i. 573.

had obtained the governorship of Kashmir, had promised that he would conquer in the space of two years Tibet and Kishtwār, and the promised time had elapsed, and he had not fulfilled this service, I removed him, and promoted Dilāwar K. Kākar to the Government of Kashmir. I gave him a dress of honour and an elephant, and sent him off. He also made a promise in writing that in the course of two years he would conquer Tibet and Kishtwār. Badī'u-z-Zamān, s. Shāhrukh M. came from the jagir he held in Sulṭānpūr, and had the good fortune to kiss the threshold. Having at this time honoured Qāsim K. with a jewelled dagger and an elephant, I dismissed him to the Government of the Punjab.

On the night of Tuesday, the 21st, I marched from the stage mentioned, and turned the reins of the army of prosperity towards Aḥmadabad. As in consequence of the great heat and the corruption of the air I would have had to undergo much hardship, and would have had to traverse a long distance before reaching Agra, it occurred to me not to proceed at this hot season to the capital. As I heard much praise of the rainy season in Gujarat, and there was no report about the evil reputation of Aḥmadabad (see *infra* for account of epidemic there), I finally conceived the idea of remaining there. Inasmuch as the protection and guardianship of God (to Him be praise) was in all places and at all times extended to this suppliant, just at this crisis news arrived that signs of the plague (*wabā*) had shown themselves again at Agra, and many people were dying, my intention of not going to Agra, which had thrown its rays on my mind through Divine inspiration, was confirmed. The entertainment of Thursday, the 23rd, was held at the station of Jalod.*

Previously to this, the rule of coinage was that on one face of the metal they stamped my name, and on the reverse the name of the place, and the month and year of the reign. At this time it entered my mind that in place of the month they should substitute the figure of the constellation which belonged to that month; for instance, in the month of Far-

* Jhālod in the Doḥad ta'lūqa of the Pānch Maḥāl district, Bombay.

wardīn the figure of a ram, and in Urdībihisht the figure of a bull. Similarly, in each month that a coin was struck, the figure of the constellation was to be on one face, as if the sun were emerging from it. This usage is my own, and has never been practised until now.*

On this day I'tiqād K. was promoted to the dignity of a standard, and a standard was also conferred on Muruwwat K., who was attached to Bengal. On the night of Monday,† the 27th, the camp was pitched in the village of Badrwāla, in the parganah of Sahra.‡ At this stage was heard the voice of the koel (*koyal*). The koel is a bird of the crow tribe, but smaller. The crow's eyes are black, and those of the koel red. The female has white spots, but the male is all black. The male has a very pleasant voice, quite unlike that of the female. It is in reality the nightingale of India. Just as the nightingale is agitated and noisy in the spring, so is the cry of the koel at the approach of the rainy season, which is the spring of Hindustan. Its cry is exceedingly pleasant and penetrating, and the bird begins its exhilaration (*mastī*) when the mangoes ripen. It frequently sits on the mango-trees, and is delighted with the colour and scent of the mango. A strange thing about the koel is that it does not bring up its young from the egg, but, finding the nest of the crow unguarded at the time of laying, it breaks the crow's eggs with its beak, throws them out, and lays its own in the place of them, and flies off. The crow, thinking the eggs its own, hatches the young and brings them up. I have myself seen this strange affair at Allahabad.

On the night of *Kamshamba* (Wednesday), the 29th, the camp was on the bank of the Mahī, and the entertainment of *Mubārakshamba* was held there. Two springs appeared on the bank of the Mahī, that had very clear water, so much so that if a poppy-seed fell into them the whole of it was visible. All that day I passed with the ladies. As it was a pleasant

* The text (pp. 227, 228) has drawings of the twelve Zodiacal coins. See also Tavernier's account of their institution.

† Text wrongly has Saturday.

‡ Probably the Seyreh of Bayley's map, in the Lūnāvāda State, E. of Ahmadabad.

place to walk about in, I ordered them to build a raised seat round each of the springs. On Friday I fished in the Mahī, and large fish with scales fell into the net. I first told my son, Shāh-Jahān, to try his sword on them. After this I ordered the Amīrs to strike them with the swords they had in their belts. My son's sword cut better than all of theirs. These fish were divided among the servants who were present. On the eve of Saturday, the 1st of Urdībihisht, marching from the above-mentioned stage, I ordered* the mace-bearers (*yasāwulān*) and *tawāchiyān* to collect the widows and poor people from the villages on the road and near it, and bring them before me, so that I might bestow charity on them with my own hand, which would be an occupation, and the helpless ones might also find grace. What better occupation could there be than this? On Monday, the 3rd, Shajā'at K. 'Arab, and Himmat K., and other servants who belonged to the Deccan and Gujarat, had the good fortune to kiss the threshold. The holy men and the possessors of blessing (faqirs, etc.) who lived at Aḥmadabad paid their respects to me. On Tuesday, the 4th, the bank of the river at Maḥmūdābād became the alighting place. Rustam K., whom my son, Shāh-Jahān, had left in the Government of Gujarat, was honoured by paying his respects. The entertainment of Thursday, the 6th, was held on the bank of the Kānkriya tank. Nāhir K., according to order, came from the Deccan and raised the head of honour with the good fortune of prostrating himself before me.

A diamond ring was presented to my son, Shāh-Jahān, as part of the offering of Quṭbu-l-mulk. It was of the value of 1,000 muhars, and on it there appeared three letters of equal size and of good form, such that they made the word Lillahi (for God). This diamond had been sent, as it was reckoned one of the marvels of the world. In fact, veins and scratches are flaws in precious stones, but it was generally thought that the marks on this one were fabricated. Moreover, the diamond did not come from any celebrated mine. As my son, Shāh-Jahān, wished that it should be sent to my brother, Shāh

* Quoted by Blochmann, *Calcutta Review*, 1869, p. 128.

'Abbās, as a souvenir of the conquest of the Deccan it was sent to the Shah along with other gifts.*

On this day I presented Brikha Rāy *bād-farūsh* (panegyrist) with Rs. 1,000. He is a Gujaratī by origin, and is fully versed in the chronicles and circumstances of that country. His name was Būnṭā—that is, a sapling (*nihāl*). It seemed to me that it was anomalous to call an old man Būnṭā, especially now that he had become verdant (*sar-sabz*) and fruit-bearing through the irrigation (*saḥāb*, literally, cloud, or mirage) of our kindness. I therefore ordered that henceforth he should be called Brikha Rāy. Brikha means "tree" in Hindī. On Friday, the 7th of the aforesaid month, corresponding with the 1st Jumāda-l-awwal, at a chosen propitious hour, I entered the city of Ahmadabad with all enjoyment. At the time of mounting, my son of prosperous fortune, Shāh-Jahān, had brought 20,000 *charan*, or Rs. 5,000, for the *niṡār* (scattering), and I scattered them as I hastened to the palace. When I alighted there he laid before me by way of an offering a jewelled *ṭurra* (aigrette) of the value of Rs. 25,000, and those of his officers whom he had left in this Subah also presented offerings. They altogether amounted to nearly Rs. 40,000. As it was represented to me that Khwāja Beg Mīrzā Safawī had reached the neighbourhood of the forgiveness of God—*i.e.*, had died—at Aḥmadnagar, I promoted to a mansab of 2,000 personal and horse, original and increased, Khanjar K., whom he had adopted as his son, and, indeed, held dearer than a son of his loins, and who was in truth, an intelligent, ambitious youth, and a servant worthy of patronage, and entrusted him with the charge of the fort of Aḥmadnagar.

* The text has *dar zīr-i-ān* ("under it") in mentioning the position of the letters, but the I.O. MS. No. 181, has *dar zabar* ("above" or "on it."). The words *khaṭṭ-i-muḥarraf* might mean "inverted or slanting letters," and Mr. Rogers has taken the passage to mean that two of the letters were on a line with one another, and that the third was inverted and below the other two. But *muḥrif*, as the word may also be read, has the meaning of "handsome," and I think this is the meaning here. Possibly the meaning is that there was a letter or mark *above*—viz., the *tashdīd*. Another meaning may be that all three letters were equal in size, and in a slanting position on the stone.

In these days, in consequence of the great heat and the corruption of the air, sickness had broken out among the people, and of those in the city and the camp there were few who for two or three days had not been ill. Inflammatory fever or pains in the limbs attacked them, and in the course of two or three days they became exceedingly ill—so much so that even after recovery they remained for a long time weak and languid. They mostly at last recovered, so that but few were in danger of their lives. I heard from old men who resided in this country that thirty years before this the same kind of fever prevailed, and passed away happily. Anyhow, there appeared some deterioration in the climate of Gujarat, and I much regretted having come here. I trust that the great and glorious God, in His mercy and grace, will lift up this burden, which is a source of uneasiness to my mind, from off the people. On *Mubārak-shamba* (Thursday), the 13th, Badī'u-z-zamān, s. Mīrzā Shāhrukh, was promoted to the mansab of 1,500 personal and horse, and presented with a standard, and appointed faujdār of Sarkār Paṭan. Sayyid Niẓām, faujdār of Sarkār Lucknow, was raised to the mansab of 1,000 personal and 700 horse. The manṣab of 'Alī Qulī Darman, who was attached to the province of Qandahar, at the request of Bahādur K., the governor thereof, was ordered to be 1,000 personal and 700 horse. Sayyid Hizbar K. Bārha was dignified with the manṣab of 1,000 personal and 400 horse. I promoted Zabardast K. to the rank of 800 personal and 350 horse. On this day Qāsim Khwāja of Dihbīd* had sent from Mā-warā'a-n-nahr (Transoxiana) by the hand of one of his tribesmen by way of supplication five *tūyghūn* (white) falcons. One died on the road, and four arrived at Ujjain in safety. I ordered them to hand over the sum of Rs. 5,000 to someone among them, that he might purchase and take with him whatever things would be agreeable to the Khwāja, and gave a reward of Rs. 1,000 to himself. At this time Khān 'Alam, who had been sent as ambassador to the ruler of Persia, sent an *āshyānī* falcon (bird from the nest), which in

* Dihbīd, "the village of the willow," a well-known place in Transoxiana. It is Dihband in text.

the Persian language they call *ukna.** Outwardly one cannot distinguish between these and *bāz dāmī*† falcons by any particular mark, but after they have been flown the difference is clear. On Thursday, the 20th, Mīr Abū-ṣ-Ṣāliḥ, a relation (? son-in-law) of the deceased Mīrzā Yūsuf K., came from the Deccan by order, and enjoyed the good fortune of kissing the threshold. He presented as an offering 100 *muhars*‡ and a jewelled plume (*kalgī*). Mīrzā Yūsuf K.§ was one of the Riẓawī Sayyids of Mashhad, and his family was always held in great honour in Khurasan, and just now my brother Shāh 'Abbās has given his daughter in marriage to the younger brother of the aforesaid Abū-ṣ-Ṣāliḥ. His father, Mīrzā Atagh,|| was the head of the attendants of the mausoleum of Riẓā, the 8th Imam. Mīrzā Yūsuf Khān, by means of the patronage of H.M. (Akbar), had risen to nobility, and attained to the manṣab of 5,000. Without doubt he was a good Mīr, and held his many servants in good order. A number of relations gathered round him. He died¶ in the Deccan. Although he left many sons, who obtained favours in consideration of former services, special attention was paid to the development of his eldest son. In a short time I advanced him to the rank of nobility. Certainly there is a great difference between him and his father.

On *Mubārak-shamba* (Thursday), the 27th, I presented Ḥakīm Masīḥu-z-zamān with 20,000 *darbs* (8 anna pieces), and to Ḥakīm Rūḥu-llah 100 *muhars* and Rs. 1,000. As he had thoroughly diagnosed my constitution, he perceived that the climate of Gujarat was very inimical to it. He said : " As soon as you moderate your habit of taking wine and opium,

* *Ukna.* The word appears to be Arabic, and signifies a nest. It is commonly written *wukna.*

† *Bāz dāmī* apparently means hawks reared in captivity, or it may mean hawks brought by dealers—*dāmī*. Information about hawks may be found in Blochmann, 293, etc., and in Col. Phillott's recent articles in the J.A.S.B., May, 1907, etc.

‡ The I.O.MS. has " rupees."

§ Blochmann, 346.

|| Ulugh in MSS.

¶ Blochmann, 346. Yūsuf died in November, 1601. His eldest son was M. Lashkarī.

all these troubles of yours will disappear." Indeed, when I in one day diminished (the quantity I took of) both of them, there was a great gain on that first day. On *Mubārak-shamba* (Thursday), the 3rd Khūrdād, Qizilbāsh K. was promoted to the manṣab, original and increased, of 1,500 personal and 1,200 horse. A report was received from Gajpat K., superintendent of the elephant stables, and Balūch K., chief huntsman (*Qarāwul Beg*), that up to this time sixty-nine elephants, male and female, had been caught. Whatever took place after this would be reported. I ordered them to beware not to take old or small elephants; but with this exception they should catch all they saw, male or female. On Monday, the 14th,* the sum of Rs. 2,000 was presented for Shāh 'Ālam's anniversary, to Sayyid Muḥammad, his representative. A special Kachh horse, one of the good horses of the Jām which had been presented to me, was given to Rāja Bīr Singh Deo. I made a present of Rs. 1,000 to Balūch K., the chief huntsman, who is engaged in capturing elephants. On Tuesday, 15th, I found I had a severe headache, which at last ended in fever. At night I did not drink my usual number of cups, and after midnight crop-sickness† was added to my fever, and till morning I rolled about on my couch. On Wednesday, the 16th, at the end of the day, the fever diminished, and, after asking the advice of my doctors, I took my usual number of cups on the third night. Although they urged me to take some broth of pulse and rice, I could not make up my mind to do so. Since I arrived at the age of discretion, I never remember having taken *būghān*‡ broth, and hope that I may not want it in future. When they brought food for me this day, I had no inclination for it. In short, for three days and two

* The MSS. have 24th and 25th for the following day, but 14th and 15th seem right.

† The passage is translated in Elliot, vi. 357, but the mention of Saturday and of Multan doctors there is a mistake. Text has *afzūdam*, "I increased my intoxication," but this seems wrong. The MSS. have *afzūd*. Jahāngir means that the stoppage of his wine increased crapulousness. See Elliot, vi. 357.

‡ Apparently this should be *yūghān*, which is a Turki word meaning "*thick*."

nights I remained fasting. Though I had fever for a day and a night, and my weakness was such that it appeared as if I had been confined to bed for a long time, I had no appetite left, and had no inclination towards food.

I* am amazed to think what pleasure or goodness the founder of this city could have seen in a spot so devoid of the favour (of God) as to build a city on it. After him, others, too, have passed their lives in precious trouble in this dust-bin. Its air is poisonous, and its soil has little water, and is of sand and dust, as has already† been described. Its water is very bad and unpalatable, and the river, which is by the side of the city, is always dry except in the rainy season. Its wells are mostly salt and bitter, and the tanks in the neighbourhood of the city have become like buttermilk from washermen's soap. The upper classes who have some property have made reservoirs in their houses, which they fill with rainwater in the rainy season, and they drink that water until the next year. The evils of water to which the air never penetrates, and which has no way for the vapour to come out by, are evident. Outside the city, in place of green grass and flowers, all is an open plain full of thorn-brakes (*zaqqūm*), and as for the breeze that blows off the thorns, its excellence is known :

> "‡ O thou, compendium of goodness, by which of thy names shall I call thee ?
> I had already called Aḥmādābād Gardābād (the abode of dust)."

Now, I do not know whether to call it *Samūmistān* (the place of the samūm or simoom) or Bīmāristān (abode of sickness), or Zaqqūm-zār (the thorn-bed), or Jahannamābād (the house of Hell), for it contains all these varieties. If the rainy season had not prevented me, I would not have delayed one day in this abode of trouble, but, like Solomon, would have seated myself on the throne of the wind, and hastened out, and released the people of God from this pain and trouble. As the men of this city are exceedingly weak-hearted and wretched, in order to guard against any of the men from the camp entering their houses with a view to oppress them, or

* Elliot, vi. 358. † See Vol. I., p. 414.

‡ The Iqbāl-nāma, 115, has a different reading of this line.

interfering with the affairs of the poor and miserable: and lest the Qāẓī and Mīr 'Adl (judge) should, from fear of the face of men (*rū-dīdagī*), temporize and not stop such oppression, I, from the date on which I entered the city, notwithstanding the heat of the air, every day, after completing the midday prayer, went and sat in the *Jharoka*. It was towards the river, and had no impediment in the shape of gate, or wall, or watchmen (*yasāwul*), or *chobdārs* (mace-bearers). For the sake of administering justice, I sate there for two or three sidereal hours and listened to the cries for redress, and ordered punishments on the oppressors according to their faults and crimes. Even in the time of weakness I have gone every day to the *jharoka*, though in great pain and sorrow, according to my fixed custom, and have looked on ease of body as something unlawful* (*ḥarām*) for me.

> "For the care of the people of God
> At night I make not mine eyes acquainted with sleep;
> For the ease of the bodies of all
> I approve of pain for my own body."

By the grace of Allah, it has become my habit not to surrender the nycthemeron, for more than two or three sidereal hours of the coin of Time, to the plundering of sleep. In this there are two advantages—one, the knowledge of the kingdom; the other, wakefulness of heart in calling God to mind. God forbid that this life of a few days should pass in carelessness. As a heavy sleep is in front, I must reckon as a gain this time of my wakefulness, which I shall not see again in sleep, and must not be careless of recollecting God for a single wink. "Be wakeful, for a wondrous† sleep is ahead." On the same day that I contracted fever, my son Shāh-Jahān, who is close to my heart, also contracted it. His attack lasted a long time, and for ten days he could not come to pay his respects. He came on Thursday, the 24th, and waited on me, and appeared very weak and powerless, so much so that if anyone had not explained the matter, one might have supposed he had been ill for a month or more. I am grateful that at last all ended

* It should be recorded to Jahāngīr's credit that he has a reputation even at the present day for his love of justice.

† '*ajabī*. The MSS. have '*ajsī*, "lasting," which seems better.

well. On Thursday, the 31st, Mīr Jumla, who had come from Īrān—a summary of what had happened to him has been already written—was honoured with the mansab of 1,500 personal and 200 horse. On this day, in consequence of the weakness I suffered from, I bestowed as alms on deserving people an elephant, a horse, and varieties of quadrupeds, with a quantity of gold and silver and other valuable things. Most of my servants also brought alms according to their means. I told them that if their object was to parade their loyalty, their proceeding was not acceptable, and if they were acting from genuine piety there was no need for bringing their alms into the Presence; they could secretly and personally distribute them to the poor and needy. On *Mubārak-shamba* (Thursday), the 7th Tīr, Divine month, Ṣādiq K. Bakhshī was promoted to the mansab of 2,000 personal and horse, original and increased; Irādat K., the Mīr Sāmān, to that of 2,000 and 1,000 horse, Mīr Abū Ṣāliḥ Riẓawī to the mansab of 2,000 and 1,000 horse, with the title of Riẓawī Khān, and, being honoured with a standard and an elephant, he took leave for the Deccan.

At this time it was represented to me that the Commander-in-Chief, the Ātālīq Khān-khānān, as a sequel to the celebrated line, "For every rose one must bear the pain of a hundred thorns," had written an ode, and that Mīrzā Rustam Ṣafawī and Mīrzā Murād, his son, had also tried their skill. An impromptu opening couplet came into my mind:

> "A cup of wine should be poured* on the cheek of the rosebed.
> There are many clouds, much wine should be poured."

Of those who were present at the entertainment who had the poetic temperament each composed an ode, and presented it. It became known that the hemistich was from Maulānā 'Abdu-r-Raḥmān Jāmī. I looked at the whole of his ode (or odes). Except this hemistich, which like a proverb has become famous over the world, he has not written anything

* Compare Elliot, vi. 359. *Rukh-i-gulzār* also means the cheek of the rosebud (*i.e.*, the beloved one). Apparently the conceit is that the cheek of the fair one is clouded over, so it should be reddened by pouring wine on it.

epigrammatic. All is very simple and smooth.* On this day arrived the news of the death of Aḥmad Beg K., governor of Kashmir. His sons, who were of the house-born ones of the Court, and on whose foreheads the signs of intelligence and zeal were manifest, obtained suitable mansabs, and were sent to do duty in the Ṣuba of Bangash and Kabul. His mansab was that of 2,500; his eldest son obtained that of 3,000 (?),† and three other sons that of 900 each. On Thursday, the 14th, Khwāja Bāqī K., who was adorned with the high qualities of dignity, honour, generosity, and valour, under whose rule was one of the thānas of the country of Berār, was promoted to the mansab of 1,500 and 1,000 horse, original and increased, and the title of Bāqī K. Rāy Kahnūr (Kunwar ?), who was formerly Dīwān of Gujarat, was chosen for the dīwānship of Mālwa.

At this time the pairing of the *sāras*, which I had never seen before, and is reported never to have been seen by man, was witnessed by me. The *sāras* is a creature of the crane genus, but somewhat larger.‡ On the top of the head it has no feathers, and the skin is drawn over the bones of the head. From the back of the eye to six finger-breadths of the neck it is red. They mostly live in pairs on the plains, but are occasionally seen in flocks. People bring a pair in from the fields, and keep them in their houses, and they become familiar with men. In fact, there was a pair of *sāras* in my establishment to which I had given the names of Lailā and Majnūn. One day a eunuch informed me that (the) two had paired in his presence. I ordered that if they showed an inclination to pair again they should inform me. At dawn he came and told me that they were about to pair again. I immediately hastened to look on. The female having straightened its legs bent down a little: the male then lifted up one of its feet from the ground and placed it on her back, and afterwards the

* *hamwār*. Perhaps it means "mediocre" here, but we have the word a little lower down, p. 240, used in a laudatory sense.

† According to the Ma'āṣir and Blochmann, 465, it was the second son who attained the highest rank.

‡ *dah duwāzdah*, "10, 12"—*i.e.*, it is one-fifth larger. The *sāras* is the Ardea Antigone of naturalists.

second foot, and, immediately seating himself on her back, paired with her. He then came down, and, stretching out his neck, put his beak to the ground, and walked once round the female. It is possible they may have an egg and produce a young one. Many strange tales of the affection of the *sāras* for its mate have been heard. The following case has been recorded because it is very strange. Qiyām K., who is one of the k͟hānazāds (houseborn ones) of this Court, and is well acquainted with the arts of hunting and scouting, informed me that one day he had gone out to hunt, and found a *sāras* sitting. When he approached, it got up and went off. From its manner of walking he perceived signs of weakness and pain. He went to the place where it had been sitting, and saw some bones and a handful of feathers on which it had been sitting. He threw a net round it, and drew himself into a corner, and it tried to go and sit in the same place. Its foot was caught in the net, and he went forward and seized it. It appeared extremely light, and when he looked minutely he saw there were no feathers on its breast and belly : its flesh and skin had separated, and there were maggots. Moreover, there was no sign of flesh left on any of its members : a handful of feathers and bone came into his hand. It was clear that its mate had died, and that it had sate there from the day it lost its companion.

> "My burning heart hath melted my body with separation's pang;
> A soul-consuming sigh burnt me, as 'twere a lamp.
> The day of my joy became black like the night of grief,
> Separation from thee hath made my day like this."

Himmat K., who is one of my best servants, and whose word is worthy of reliance, told me that in the Doḥad* pargana he had seen a pair of *sāras* on the bank of a tank. One of his gunners shot one of them, and in the same place cut off its head and stripped† it of its feathers (?). By chance we halted

* Two boundaries. The name signifies that it is on the borders of Mālwa and Gujaru, I. G. XI. 366.

† *pāk sāk͟ht*. Lit. cleaned it, which may mean also that he disembowelled it, or even that he cooked it. Probably the gunner left the body or part of it there, and it was this that the male circumambulated.

two or three days at that place, and its mate continually walked round it, and uttered cries and lamentation. "My heart," he said, "ached at its distress, but there was no remedy for it save regret." By chance, twenty-five days afterwards, he passed by the same spot, and asked the inhabitants what had become of that *sāras*. They said it died on the same day, and there were still remains of feathers and bones on the spot. He went there himself, and saw it was as they said. There are many tales of this kind among the people, which it would take too long to tell.

On Saturday, the 16th, there came the news of the death of Rāwat Shankar, who was one of those on duty in Bihār. Mān Singh, his eldest son, was raised to the manṣab of 2,000 personal and 600 horse: his other sons and connections were also raised in manṣab, and were directed to obey him. On Thursday, the 21st, the elephant Bāvan,* the pick of my catch, which had been left in the pargana of Doḥad to be tamed, was brought to Court. I ordered him to be kept near the jharoka on the river side, that he might be constantly under my eye. In the elephant-stables of H.M. Akbar the largest elephant I saw was Durjan Sāl. It was long the premier elephant. Its height was 4 yards (*dara*'†), and 3½ quarters of the *Ilāhī gaz*, which is 8 yards and 3 fingers of the ordinary *gaz*. At present, among the elephants of my establishment, the largest athlete is 'Ālam-Gajrāj, which H.M. Akbar himself had caught. It is the chief of my special elephants. Its height is 4⅛ yards, or 7 yards and 7 fingers‡ of the ordinary yard. The ordinary *gaz* has been fixed at 24 fingers' breadth of an average-sized man, and the *Ilāhī gaz* is 40 fingers' breadth.

On this day Muẓaffar K., who had been promoted to the Subadarship of Thatta (Sind), had the good fortune to kiss the threshold. He presented 100 *muhars* and Rs. 100 as

* Apparently this should be Pāvan. It was one of those caught in the elephant hunt. It is written Bāvan in the MSS.

† For meaning of *ḍara*, "yard," see text (15th year), pp. 298 and 303. For 3½ quarters (*pāo*) the text wrongly has 3½ feet (*pā*).

‡ MSS. has 17. Text has 7. According to Elliot, Supplement II., 177, the *Ilāhī gaz* was one of 41 fingers.

nazr, and the equivalent of Rs. 100,000 in jewels and jewelled things. At this time news came that God Almighty had bestowed on my son Parwīz a son* by the daughter of Shāh Murād, deceased. It is to be hoped that his coming will be of good omen to this State.

On Sunday, the 24th, Rāy Bihārī† had the good fortune to kiss the threshold : there is not a greater Zamindar than this in the country of Gujarat. His country is close to the sea. Bihārī and the Jām are from one stem. They were united ten generations ago. As far as territory and forces go, the standing of Bihārī is greater than that of the Jām. They say that he never came to see any of the Sultans of Gujarat. Sulṭān Maḥmūd had sent an army against him, but in the fight the army of Maḥmūd was defeated. At the time when Khān A'ẓam went to conquer the fort of Jūnāgaṛh in the country of Sūrat, Nannū, who was called Sulṭān Muẓaffar, and gave himself out as heir to the kingdom, was passing his days in a state of misery under the protection of the zamindars. After this the Jām was defeated in battle with the victorious (Royal) army, and Nannū took refuge with Rāy Bihārī. Khān A'ẓam demanded Nannū from Rāy Bihārī, and as he could not oppose the Royal army, he gave him up, and by this piece of loyalty was saved from the blows of the victorious army. At the time‡ when Ahmadabad was adorned by the presence of the retinue of fortune for a short time, he did not come to wait on me. His country was somewhat distant, and time did not admit of the appointing of a force (against him). When it happened that I returned there, my son Shāh-Jahān appointed Raja Bikramājīt with an army (for this purpose), and he, seeing his own safety in coming in hastened to receive the honour of kissing the threshold, giving 200 *muhars* and

* This was not the son who died in the following year. See text, p. 282. That son was the eldest son, and probably was the one born in the 9th year. See Tūzuk, p. 137.

† The Zamindar of Cutch, whose residence was at Bhūj. See Jarrett, ii. 250, where it is said that the Jām left his original country 60 years ago.

‡ Jahāngīr is referring to his visit to Gujarat in the 12th year of his reign.

Rs. 2,000 as nazr, and 100 horses. However, there was not one of his horses that I approved of. His age appeared to me to be more than eighty* years, and he himself said he was ninety. In his senses and powers there was no appearance of decay. Among his men there was an old man with white beard, moustaches, and eyebrows. He said that Rāy Bihārī remembered him when he (the old man) was a child (infant), and that he had grown up from childhood in his service.

On this day Abū-l-Ḥasan,† the painter, who has been honoured with the title of Nādiru-z-zamān, drew the picture of my accession as the frontispiece to the Jahāngīr-nāma, and brought it to me. As it was worthy of all praise, he received endless favours. His work was perfect, and his picture is one of the *chefs d'œuvre* of the age. At the present time he has no rival or equal. If at this day the masters 'Abdu-l-Ḥayy and Bihzād were alive, they would have done him justice. His father, Āqā Riẓā'ī, of Herat,‡ at the time when I was Prince, joined my service. He (Abū-l-Ḥasan) was a *khānazād* of my Court. There is, however, no comparison between his work and that of his father (*i.e.*, he is far better than his father). One cannot put them into the same category. My connection was based on my having reared him. From his earliest years up to the present time I have always looked after him, till his art has arrived at this rank. Truly he has become Nādira-i-zamān (" the wonder of the age "). Also, Ustād Manṣūr§ has become such a master in painting that he has the title of Nādiru-l-'Aṣr, and in the art of drawing is unique in his generation. In the time of my father's reign and my own these two have had no third. As regards myself, my liking for painting and my practice in judging it have arrived at such a point that when any work is brought before me, either of deceased artists or of those of the present day, without the names being told me, I say on the spur of the moment that it is the work of such and such a man. And if there be a

* MSS. have this 70 or 80.

† Elliot, vi. 359.

‡ Text " of Merv," but the MSS. have Herat.

§ Manṣūr Naqqāsh is one of the illustrators to the Bābar-nāma in the British Museum. Rieu Supplement, p. 52. There is also a Ḥusain Naqqāsh mentioned in the MS. there described.

picture containing many portraits, and each face be the work of a different master, I can discover which face is the work of each of them. If any other person has put in the eye and eyebrow of a face, I can perceive whose work the original face is, and who has painted the eye and eyebrows.

On the eve of Sunday, the 31st of the month of Tīr, heavy rain fell, and it went on raining with great violence till Tuesday, the 1st of Amurdād.* For sixteen days there were constantly clouds and (? or) rain. As this is a sandy country, and the buildings in it are weak, many houses fell, and many lives were lost. I heard from the inhabitants of the city that they remembered no rain like that of this year. Although the channel of the Sābarmatī† appears full of water, it is in most places fordable, and elephants can always cross it. If for a day there has been no rain, horses and men can ford it. The fountain head of this river is in the hill-country of the Rānā. It comes out from the ravine of Kokra(?),‡ and, having traversed 1½ *koss*, passes below Mīrpūr,§ and in this place they call it the Wākal (?). After passing 3 *koss* beyond Mīrpūr, they call it the Sābarmatī.

On Thursday, the 10th, Rāy Bihārī was exalted with the favour of a male and a female elephant, a jewelled dagger, and four rings, of red ruby and yellow ruby (topaz), sapphire, and emerald. Before this, the Ātālīq Jān-sipār (life-jeoparding), Khān-khānān ('Abdu-r-Raḥīm), Commander-in-Chief, by order, had sent a force under the leadership of his son Amru-llah‖ towards Gondwāna, in order to seize the diamond mine of Barākar¶ (?) that was in the possession of Panjū, a Zamindar of Khandesh. On this day a report came from him that the aforesaid Zamindar, knowing that opposition to the victorious army was beyond his power, had made an offering of the mine,

* Apparently there were 32 days in this Tīr.

† The Sābarmatī rises in the hills of Mewār.

‡ I cannot find this Kokra or Gogra. The Sābarmatī falls into the Gulf of Cambay. Possibly Kokra thereby means "mountains."

§ Apparently the Mairpūr of Bayley's map.

‖ Blochmann, 339.

¶ Perhaps this is the Bīrāgam of the Ā'īn A. (Jarrett, ii. 230). Panjū Zamīndār may be the Bab-jīū, Zamindar of the Gond tribe, whom Abū-l-Fazl mentions. The word Barākar is omitted in text.

and a royal superintendent had been appointed to manage it. The diamonds of that place are superior in kind and beauty to all other kinds of diamonds, and much esteemed by jewellers. They are of good shape, and larger, and superior. Of the second rank is the mine of Kokhra,* which is on the borders of Bihar; but the diamonds of that place are not obtained from the mine, but from a river which in the rainy season comes down in flood from the hills. Before that they dam it up, and when the flood has passed over the dam and there is little water, a number of men who are skilled in this art go into the river bed and bring out the diamonds. It is now three years since this country came into the possession of the State. The Zamindar of the place is in confinement. The climate of that land is excessively poisonous, and strangers cannot live there. The third place is in the province of the Karnatik (Carnatic), near the frontier of Quṭbu-l-mulk. At a distance of 50 *koss*† there are four mines. Many very fine‡ diamonds are obtained there.

On Thursday, the 10th, Nāhir K. was promoted to the manṣab of 1,500 personal and 1,000 horse, and he was presented with an elephant. Maktūb K., superintendent of the *Kutub-khāna* (library), was given the manṣab of 1,500 personal. As I had ordered that on the Shab-i-Barāt they should place lamps round the Kānkrīya tank, at the end of the day on Monday, the 14th Sha'bān, I went out to look at them. The buildings all round the tank they had arranged with lanterns of different colours and all kinds of artifices that are practicable with lamps, and fireworks. Although at this season there were continually clouds and rain, by God's favour from the beginning of the night the air had become clear, and not a trace of cloud remained, and the lights shone just as one could wish. My domestic servants were regaled with the cups of

* See Blochmann, 480 n., Elliot, vi. 344, and the Tūzuk, annals of 10th year.

† Probably the meaning is that the four mines occur within a space of 50 *koss*. Tavernier, vol. ii., may be consulted.

‡ *Puhkta* in text, but the MSS. have not this word. Instead, they have a word which seems to be *taḥsina*, "beautiful." The R.A.S. MS. also seems to have *taḥsina*.

joy. I ordered them to light lamps in the same manner on the eve of Friday, and a strange thing was that at the close of the day of Thursday, the 17th, it continually rained (*muttaṣil bārīdagī*), but at the time of lighting the lamps the rain ceased, and the show was well seen. On this day I'timādu-d-daula presented an offering of a *quṭbī* (?) sapphire exceedingly delicate, and an elephant without tusks with silver housings. As it was handsome-looking and of good shape, it was put among my private elephants. On the bank of the Kānkrīya tank a *sanyāsī*, one of the most austere sects of Hindus, had made a hut after the dervish manner, and lived as a hermit. As I was always inclined to associate with dervishes, I hastened without ceremony to interview him, and for a while enjoyed his society. He was not wanting in information and reasonableness, and was well informed according to the rules of his own faith in the doctrines of Sufism. He had conformed to the ways of people of religious poverty and mortification, and given up all desires and ambitions. One might say that a better than he of his class was never seen.

On Monday, the 21st (Amurdād), the *sāras*, the pairing of which has been related in the preceding pages, collected together some straw and rubbish in the little garden, and laid first of all one egg. On the third day (afterwards) it laid a second egg. This pair of *sāras* were caught when they were a month old,* and had been in my establishment for five years. After five and a half years they paired, and continued doing so for a month ; on the 21st of the month of Amurdād, which the Hindus call Sāwan (Srāvan) the hen laid the eggs. The female used to sit on the eggs the whole night alone, and the male stood near her on guard. It was so alert that it was impossible for any living thing to pass near her. Once a large weasel made its appearance, and he ran at it with the greatest impetuosity, and did not stop until the weasel got into a hole. When the sun illuminated the world with his rays, the male went to the female and pecked her back with his beak. The female then rose, and the male sate in her place.

* *māhagī* ? Probably it means that they were caught when a month old, and Elliot's translator so took it.

She returned, and in the same manner made him rise, and seated herself. In short, the female sits the whole night, and takes care of the eggs, and by day the male and female sit by turns. When they rise and sit down they take great precautions that no harm shall come to the eggs.

During this season, as there was still some of the hunting time left, Gajpat K., the darogha, and Balūch K., the head huntsman, had been left to hunt elephants, to catch as many as they possibly could. In the same manner the huntsmen of my son, Shāh-Jahān, had also been employed. On this day they came and waited on me. Altogether 185 elephants had been caught, male and female: of these, 73 were males and 112 females. Out of these, 47 males and 75 females, or 122, the imperial huntsmen and faujdars had secured, while the huntsmen and elephant-drivers of my son, Shāh-Jahān, had taken 26 males and 37 females, or 63 altogether.

On Thursday, the 24th, I went to see the Bāgh-i-Fatḥ,* and spent two days there in enjoyment and pleasure. At the end of the day on Saturday I returned to the palace. As Āṣaf K. had represented that his *ḥawīlī* (house) garden was exceedingly green and pleasant, and all sorts of flowers and scented plants had bloomed there, at his request I went to it on *Mubārak-shamba* (Thursday), the 31st. In truth, it was a very nice villa, and I was much pleased. His offering of jewels and jewelled things, and cloth, of the value of Rs. 35,000, was accepted. Muẓaffar K. was favoured with a dress of honour and an elephant, and, as before, was entrusted with the charge of the government of Thatta (Sind). My brother Shāh 'Abbās sent a letter with some trifling presents by 'Abdu-l-Karīm of Gīlān, who had come with merchandise from Īrān. On this day I presented him with a dress of honour and an elephant, and gave him leave to return, and sent an answer to the Shah's letter with a memorandum. Khān 'Ālam was also honoured with a gracious farman and a special dress of honour. Friday was the 1st of the month of Shahrīwar.

* This was the garden which 'Abdu-r-Raḥīm made after his victory over Muẓaffar Gujarātī. In Price's Jahāngīr, pp. 115-16, there is an account of an entertainment given there to Jahāngīr by 'Abdu-r-Raḥīm's daughter.

From Sunday, the 3rd, till the eve of Thursday (the 7th) rain fell. It is strange that on other days the pair of *sāras* sate on the eggs five or six times in turn, but during this twenty-four hours, when there was constant rain and the air was somewhat cold, the male, in order to keep the eggs warm, sate from early in the morning until midday, and from that time until the next morning the female sat without an interval, for fear that in rising and sitting again the cold air should affect them, and the eggs become wet and be spoilt. Briefly, men are led by the guidance of Reason, and animals according to the Divine wisdom implanted in them by Nature. Stranger still is it that at first they keep their eggs together underneath the breast, and after fourteen or fifteen days have passed they leave a little space between them, for fear the heat should become too great from their contact with each other. Many become addled in consequence of (too great) heat.

On Thursday, the 7th, with great joy and congratulation, the advance camp was started towards Agra. The astrologers and astronomers had already fixed the auspicious hour for the march. As excessive rain fell, the main camp could not cross the river of Maḥmūdābād (the Vātrak) and the Mahī at this hour. Out of necessity, the advanced camp was started at the appointed hour, and the 21st Shahrīwar* was fixed for the march of the main camp.

My son Shāh-Jahān took upon himself the responsibility of the conquest of the fort of Kāngra, over which the noose of victory had not been thrown by any of the Sultans of lofty dignity, and an army under the leadership of Rāja Sūraj Mal, s. Rāja Bāso, and Taqī, who was one of his attached servants, had before this been sent for that purpose. It was now clear that the conquest could not be achieved by the force that had been previously appointed. Rāja Bikramājīt,† who was one of his principal officers, with 2,000 horse who were present of his private attendants, and a force of Jahāngīrī servants, such as Shāh-bāz K. Lodī, Hardī Narāyan Hāḍa, Rāy Prithī Chand, and the sons of Rām Chand, with 200 mounted musketeers and 500 foot-musketeers (*topchī*, perhaps cannoniers),

* Or 22 Ramaẓān, 1027 = September 2, 1618. † *Cf.* Iqbāl-nāma, 117.

in addition to the force that had previously been sent, were appointed to the duty. As the hour for departure was fixed on this day, the aforesaid (Bikramājīt) presented as an offering a rosary of emeralds of the value of Rs. 10,000. He was honoured with the gift of a dress of honour and a sword, and took his leave for this duty. As he had not a jagir in that Subah, my son Shāh-Jahān asked for him as a jagir the pargana of Barhāna (?),* the revenue of which was 2,200,000 of dams, which† he himself (? Shāh-Jahān) held in in'ām.‡ Khwāja Taqī, the Dīwān-i-Buyūtāt, who had been appointed to the Dīwānī of the Deccan, was honoured with the title of Mu'taqid§ K., a dress of honour, and an elephant. I appointed Himmat K. to the faujdarship of the Sarkar of Bharūch (Broach) and that neighbourhood, with the gift of a horse and a special *parm narm* (shawl), and despatched him. The pargana of Bharūch (Broach) was also bestowed on him as jagir. Rāy Prithī Chand, who had been nominated for service at Kāngra, was promoted to the rank of 700 and 450 horse. As the anniversary of Shaikh Muḥammad Ghauṣ|| had arrived, I gave his sons 1,000 *darbs* (Rs. 500) for its expense. Muẓaffar, s. Bahāduru-l-mulk, who was attached to the Deccan, was given the manṣab of 1,000 personal and 500 horse.

As the events of twelve years of *Jahāngīr-nāma* have been recorded, I ordered¶ the clerks of my private library to make one volume of these twelve years, and to prepare a number of copies so that I might give them to my special servants, and

* In MSS. written Marhāna or Sarhāna. Perhaps Harhāna in the Bet Jalandhar Dū'āb, Jarrett, II. 317. Though the text says 22 lakhs of dams, the MSS. only say 22 lakhs, and possibly rupees are meant.

† *Khūd bi-in'ām iltimās namūd.* "As a favour to himself." It is not likely that Shāh Jahān would ask for the pargana for Bikramājīt if it was already his own. I presume the meaning is that Shāh Jahān asked that this pargana should be given to Bikramājīt as a favour to himself. But perhaps the meaning is "which he (Shāh Jahān) had asked for, for himself."

‡ In the MSS. the word *khūd* follows *in'ām* instead of preceding it. Perhaps the meaning is, "which was his own appanage," "and he requested," etc.

§ Text wrongly has Mu'tamid.

|| The saint who is buried at Gwalior. He died September 14, 1562.

¶ Elliot, VI. 360.

that they might be sent to the various cities, so that administrators (arbāb-i-daulat) and the auspicious might adopt them as their code. On Friday, the 8th,* one of the news-writers had written the whole and made a volume, which he produced to me. As it was the first copy that had been prepared, I gave it to my son S̲h̲āh-Jahān, whom I consider to be in all respects the first of my sons. On the back of it I wrote with my own hand that I had given it him on a certain day and at a certain place. I hope that the favour of the receipt of those writings which are intended for the satisfaction of the creature and for supplication to the Creator may be a cause of good fortune.

On Tuesday, the 12th, Subḥān Qulī, huntsman, was brought to punishment. The details of this are that he is the son of Ḥājī Jamāl Balūch, who was my father's best huntsman, and after his (the King's death) he entered the service of Islām K., and went with him to Bengal. Islām K̲h̲ān, on account of his (Subḥān Qulī's) connection with this Court, showed him proper consideration, and considering him trustworthy always kept him near him when travelling or hunting. 'Us̤mān, the Afghan, who for many years passed his days in that Subah in disobedience and stubbornness, and the end of whose affairs has been recorded in the preceding pages, being much troubled by Islām K̲h̲ān, sent someone to this wretch, and made proposals for his murdering Islām. He undertook the business, and associated two or three other men with himself. By chance, before the futile idea of this ungrateful fellow was carried into execution, one of them came and informed him (Islām K.). Islām K. immediately seized and imprisoned the scoundrel. After the latter's death he came to Court. As his brothers and relatives were included among the huntsmen, he was also ordered to be enrolled among them. At this time the son (Ikrām K.) of Islām K. represented in an enigmatical way that he was unworthy of service near my person. After explanation it appeared what the charge was. Notwithstanding this,

* The 8th S̲h̲ahrīwar = August 20, 1618. The departure had been fixed for the 21st, and having mentioned this, Jahāngīr goes on to describe what occurred between the 7th and the 21st.

as his brothers strenuously represented that there was only suspicion, and Balūch K., the head huntsman, became security for him, I forbore to put him to death, and ordered him to do duty with Balūch K. In spite of this grace and the gift of his life, without cause or motive he fled from the Court, and went to Agra and that neighbourhood. Balūch K., having become his security, was ordered to produce him. He sent people to inquire for him. In one of the villages of Agra, which was not wanting in sedition, and is called Jahanda,* the brother of Balūch Khān, who had gone to make inquiries, found him, and although he endeavoured to bring him by persuasion to Court, he would in no way consent, and the people rose to assist him.

Being without remedy, he (the brother) went to Khwāja Jahān at Agra, and told him the circumstances. He sent a detachment against that village to take him by force and bring him. The people of the village, seeing their own ruin in the mirror of the case, handed him over to him. This day he came to Court in chains. I gave an order for his execution. The man of wrath (the executioner) took him to the place of punishment with all haste. After a while, through the intercession of one of the courtiers, I gave him his life, and ordered his feet to be cut off, but according to his destiny (what was written on his head) before the order arrived he had been punished. Although that doomed man was deserving of punishment, yet I regretted† the circumstance, and directed that whenever an order was given for anyone's execution, notwithstanding that the command were imperative, they should wait till sunset before putting him to death. If up to that time no order for release arrived, he should without fail be capitally punished.

On Sunday there was a great commotion in the River Mahī, and very large waves were visible. Although there formerly had been (great) rains, yet such violence, or even the half of it, had never been known. From the beginning of the day the flood began to come, and at the end of the day began to

* So in text, but MSS. give Jahanda as the name of the brother of Balūch.

† Elliot, VI. 361.

decrease. Old inhabitants of this city represented that once, during the government of Murtaẓā K. (Farīd Bukhārī), a similar great flood had occurred. But with that exception they did not remember another such flood.

In these days mention was made of an ode by Mu'izzī,* the panegyrist of Sulṭān Sanjar, and his Poet-laureate. It is a very smooth and equable† composition. It begins thus :

> " O thou whose commands heaven obeys
> Ancient Saturn is the slave of thy young Fortune."

Sa'īdā,‡ the chief goldsmith, has a poetical temperament and he imitated this ode, and presented his paraphrase to me. It was very well composed. The following are some verses from it :

> " O thou, of whose threshold the nine spheres are an examplar
> Aged Time hath grown young in thy reign
> Thy heart is bounteous as the Sun, and like it needs no cause (for bounty).
> All lives are devoted to thy gracious heart
> Heaven is but a green§ orange from the garden of Power
> Tossed by thy gardener into the atmosphere,
> O God, Thy essence has shone from eternity
> The souls of all the saints receive light from Thine;
> O king, may the world ever be at thy beck,
> May thy Shāh-Jahān ever rejoice in thy shade
> O Shadow of God, may the world be filled with thy light
> May the Light of God ever be thy canopy."

---

* Text wrongly has Maghribī, who was a much later poet, for he died in 809 A.H. = 1416. Sulṭān Sanjar belonged to the sixth century of the Hijra, and Mu'izzī, who is the poet meant by Jahāngīr, died in 542 A.H. (1147-48), having been accidentally killed with an arrow by Sulṭān Sanjar. See Rieu, II. 552*b*. The ode quoted by Jahāngīr is to be found at p. 138*b* of British Museum MS. Add. 10588.

† *hamwār* used here in a favourable sense, though some pages farther back, 233 of Persian text, it seems to be used, when speaking of Jāmī, in disparagement.

‡ See Beale art. Sa'īdā-i-Gīlānī. He was styled Bī-badal. The date 1116 in Beale is manifestly wrong. He is the Mullā Shaidā of Rieu, III., 1083*e*. See also Sprenger's Catalogue, 124 ; there is a notice of him in the Ma'āṣiru-l-Umarā, I. 405. He was the artist of the Peacock-throne.

§ *Turunj*, rendered by Vullers as " citron." Probably the reference is to the colour of the sky, which is often spoken of by Orientals as green. The concluding lines play upon Jahāngīr's title of Nūru-d-dīn, on his son's title of Shāh-Jahān, and his name of Khurram.

On *Mubārak-shamba*, the 14th, in reward for this ode, I ordered Sa'īdā to be weighed against money (*zar*, perhaps gold). At the end of the day I went to walk about the garden of Rustam-bārī,* which appeared to me very green and pleasant. Sitting in a boat in the evening, I returned to the palace.

On Friday, the 15th, a Mullā of the name of Amīrī, an old man, came from Mā-warā'a-n-nahr (Transoxiana), and had the good fortune to kiss the threshold. He represented to me that he was one of the ancient (servants) of 'Abdu-llah Khān Uzbeg, and from the days of infancy† and youth was brought up by the Khān until his death. He had been included among his old servants, and had been a confidential friend.‡ After the death of the Khān until now he had passed his days respected in that country. He had left his native country with a view to visit the blessed house (Mecca), and had come to pay his respects to me. I made him free to remain or go. He asked to remain in attendance on me for some days. Rs. 1,000 for expenses and a dress of honour were given him. He is an old man of very pleasing face, and full of talk and anecdote. My son Shāh-Jahān also gave him Rs. 500 and a robe of honour.

In the middle of the garden of Khurram (Shāh-Jahān's) residence there is a bench and a reservoir. On one side§ of that bench there is a Mūlsarī-tree (*Mimusops elengi*) against which to lean the back. As in one side of its trunk there was a hollow to the extent of three-fourths of a yard, it had an ugly look. I ordered them to cut a tablet of marble and fix it firmly in that place, so that one could lean one's back on it and sit there. At this time an impromptu couplet came to my tongue, and I ordered the stone-cutters to engrave it

* *Bārī* is a Hindu word meaning garden.

† *ayyām-i-jawānī*. The MSS. have *qazzāqī*, "raids." The name of the Mullā there seems to be Asīrī.

‡ *dar khalā wa-malā maḥram būda*.

§ MS. 305. "On every side there are Būlsarī-trees." Both I.O. MSS. have Būlsarī, for which see Blochmann, 70. Apparently there was only one tree.

on that stone, that it might remain as a memento on the page of time. This is the couplet:

> " The seat of the Shāh of the seven worlds (kishwar),
> Jahāngīr, son of Akbar Shāhinshāh.

On the eve of Tuesday,* the 19th, a bazaar was arranged in the private palace. Up to this time the custom has been for the people of the bazaar and the artificers of the city in every place to bring their shops according to order into the courtyard of the palace (royal abode, whether in camp or elsewhere), and bring jewels and jewelled things and various kinds of cloth and other goods such as are sold in the bazaar. It occurred to me that if a bazaar were prepared in the night-time, and a number of lamps were arranged in front of the shops, it would look well. Undoubtedly it came off well and was unusual. Going round all the shops, whatever jewels and jewelled things pleased me I bought. I gave some present from each shop to Mullā Amīrī, and he received so many things that he was unable to hold them.

On *Mubārak-shamba* (Thursday) the 21st of the Divine month of Shahrīwar, in the thirteenth year from my accession, corresponding with the 22nd Ramaẓān (September 2, 1618), in the Hijrī year 1027, when two and a half hours of day had passed, in prosperity and happiness, the standards of purpose turned towards the capital of Agra. From the palace as far as the Kānkrīya tank, the place of alighting, I passed along in the usual manner, scattering money (*niṣār-kunān*). On the same day the feast of my solar weighment took place, and according to solar reckoning the fiftieth year of the age of his suppliant at the throne of God commenced auspiciously. According to my usual rule I weighed myself against gold and other valuables. I scattered pearls and golden roses, and looking at night at the show of lamps passed my time in the private apartments of the royal abode in enjoyment. On Friday, the 22nd, I ordered that all the Shaikhs and men of piety who lived in the city should be brought in order that they might break their fast† in attendance on me. Three

* Elliot, VI. 361.

† This was not the 'Īd, for the month was not over. It was the feasting after nightfall usual in the Ramaẓān.

nights were passed after this manner, and every night at the end of the meeting I stood up and recited with the tongue of ecstasy:

> "Thou art the mighty One, O Lord,
> Thou art the cherisher of rich and poor;
> I'm not a world-conqueror or law-giver,
> I'm one of the beggars at this gate.
> Help me in what is good and right,
> Else what good comes from me to any one?
> I'm a master* to my servants,
> To the Lord I'm a loyal servant."

All the Faqirs who as yet had not waited on me prayed for allowances. According to their merits I gave to each of them land or money for expenses, and gratified them.

On the eve of *Mubārak-s̲hamba* (Thursday) the 21st, the sāras hatched one young one, and on the eve of Monday, the 25th, a second: that is, one young one was hatched after thirty-four† days, and the other after thirty-six days. One might say that they were one-tenth‡ larger than the young of a goose, or equal to the young of the peafowl at the age of a month. Their skin was of a blue colour. On the first day they ate nothing, and from the second day the mother, taking small locusts (or grasshoppers) in her mouth, sometimes fed them like a pigeon, or sometimes like a fowl threw them before them for them to pick up of themselves. If the locust were small, it went off well, but if it were large, she sometimes made two or three pieces of it so that the young ones might eat it with ease. As I had a great liking for seeing them I ordered them to be brought before me with every precaution that no harm might happen to them. After I had seen them I ordered them to be taken back to the same little garden inside

* *k̲h̲udāwandi-gār*. For which word see Vullers and the Bahār-i-'Ajam. Perhaps it means here a locum-tenens or officiating master.

† Apparently this should be thirty-two. The egg was laid on 21 Amurdād, see p. 237, and the interval between the hatching of the two chicks was three or four days.

‡ Text *dah yāzdah*, ten to eleven. But MS. 305 has *dah pānzdah*, ten to fifteen, which is more likely. The meaning then would be that the young of the sāras were 50 per cent., or one-half larger than goslings. The common expression for one-tenth is *dah yak*.

the royal enclosure, and to be preserved with the greatest care, and that they should be brought to me again whenever they were able to walk.

On this day Ḥakīm Rūḥu-llah was exalted with the gift of Rs. 1,000. Badī'u-z-zamān, s. M. Shāhrukh, came from his jagir and waited on me. On Tuesday, the 26th, marching from the Kānkrīya tank, I halted at the village of Kaj.* On Wednesday, the 27th, I pitched my camp on the bank of the river at Maḥmūdābād called the Īzak† (now called Meshva). As the water and air of Aḥmadābād were very bad, Maḥmūd Bīgara, by the advice of his physicians, founded a city on the bank of the aforesaid river and lived there. After he conquered Chāmpāner, he made that place his capital, and until the time of Maḥmūd the martyred‡ the rulers of Gujarat chiefly lived there. This Maḥmūd was the last of the Sultans of Gujarat, and he took up his residence at Maḥmūdābād. Undoubtedly the water and air of Maḥmūdābād have no resemblance to those of Aḥmadābād. By way of testing this I ordered them to hang up a sheep on the bank of the Kānkrīya tank after taking off its skin, and at the same time one at Maḥmūdābād, that the difference of the air might be ascertained. It happened that after seven *gharīs* of day had passed in that place (Aḥmadābād) they hung up the sheep. When three *gharīs* of day remained it became so changed and putrid that it was difficult to pass near it. They hung up the sheep at Maḥmūdābād in the morning, and it was altogether unchanged until the evening, and began to be putrid when one and a half watches of night had passed. Briefly, in the neighbourhood of Aḥmadābād it became putrid in eight sidereal hours, and in Maḥmūdābād in fourteen hours.

On Thursday, the 28th, Rustam K., whom my son of prosperous fortune, Shāh-Jahān, had appointed to the charge

* Ganj in No. 181. Perhaps it should be Gajna, see I.G., 17, p. 11.

† MSS. Atrak. It is the Wātrak of Bayley's Gujarat, p. 201, and the Vātrak of I.G., XXI. 344.

‡ Sulṭān Maḥmūd III., killed by Burhān in February, 1554, Bayley's Gujarat, pp. 449 and 453. Jahāngīr calls him the last Sulṭān of Gujarat, because Aḥmad II. and Muẓaffar III. were regarded as spurious. See Āyīn-i-Akbarī, Jarrett, II. 261.

and government of Gujarat, was honoured with the gift of an elephant, a horse, and a special *parm narm* (shawl), and given leave to depart, and the Jahāngīrī officers who were attached to that Subah were presented with horses and dresses of honour according to the rank and standing of each. On Friday, 29th Shahrīwar, corresponding with 1st Shawwāl, Rāy Bihārī was honoured with the bestowal of a dress of honour, a jewelled sword and a special horse, and took leave to go to his native place. His sons were also honoured with horses and dresses of honour. On Saturday I ordered Sayyid Muḥammad, grandson* (?) of Shāh 'Ālam, to ask for whatever he desired without concealment, and I took an oath on the Qoran to this effect. He said that as I had sworn on the Qoran he would ask for a Qoran that he might always have it by him, and that the merit of reading it might accrue to His Majesty. Accordingly, I gave the Mīr a Qoran in Yāqūt's† handwriting. It was a small, elegant‡ volume, and was the wonder of the age. On the back of it I wrote with my own hand that I had made this gift on a certain day and in a certain place to Sayyid Muḥammad. The real reason for this is that the Mīr is of an exceedingly good disposition, endowed with personal nobility and acquired excellencies, of good manners and approved ways, with a very pleasing face and open forehead. I have never seen a man of this country of such a pleasing disposition as the Mīr. I told him to translate this Qoran into plain language without ornament, and that

* Probably great-grandson, for Shāh 'Ālam died in 880 (1475-76), as Jahāngīr tells us *supra*, and he says that he questioned Sayyid Muḥammad about Shāh 'Ālam's raising the dead, and that Sayyid Muḥammad said he had the story from his father and grandfather. The Ma'āṣiru-l-Umarā, III. 447, says Sayyid Muḥammad was *five* removes from Shāh 'Ālam.

† For Yāqūt, see Blochmann, 99-100. He was a famous calligrapher, and lived in the thirteenth century. It appears, however, that Yāqūtī is also the name of a particular kind of writing.

‡ *Ba-qiṭa'-i-maṭbū'a-i-mukhtaṣar*. *Maṭbū'a* is used in modern times to mean "printed," but here, I think, it means "elegant." It is so used in the annals of the 12th year, p. 208, line 18, where it is applied to a building. *Qiṭa'* probably refers to the shape of the volume, and *mukhtaṣar* to its small size, or to the minuteness of the writing.

without occupying himself with explanations or fine language he* should translate the Qoran in simple language (*lughāt-i-rīkhta*) word by word into Persian, and should not add one letter to its exact purport. After he had completed it he should send it by his son Jalālu-d-dīn Sayyid to the Court. The Mīr's son is also a young man of external and internal intelligence. The signs of piety and blessedness are distinct on his forehead. The Mīr is proud of his son, and in truth he is worthy, as he is an excellent youth. As I had repeatedly shown kindness to the holy men of Gujarat, according to their merits, I again bestowed on each cash and jewels, and dismissed them to their homes.

As the climate† of this country was not suited to my temperament, the physicians thought it right that I should decrease somewhat my usual number of cups. According to their advice I began to decrease their number, and in the course of a week reduced them by the weight of one cup. At first it was six cups every evening, each cup being 7½ *tola*, or altogether 45 *tolas*. The wine was usually mixed with water. Now I drank six cups, each of which was 6 *tolas* and 3 *māshas*,‡ altogether 37½ *tolas*.

Sixteen or seventeen years ago I had vowed with my God at Allahabad that when I reached fifty I would give up shooting with gun and bullet, and would injure no living thing with my own hand. Muqarrab K., who was one of my confidants, knew of my determination. At this date I have reached the commencement of my fiftieth year, and one day, in consequence of excessive fever (*dūd u bukhār*) my breath was short and I was very unwell. While in this condition the compact I had

* Sayyid Muḥammad, the Mīr referred to by Jahāngīr, lived into Shāh-Jahān's reign, not dying till 1045 (1635-36). See Pādshāh-nāma, I., Part II., p. 329. But we do not hear anything more of his translation. Perhaps his ill-health prevented him. It is also the fact that orthodox Muḥammadans object to translations of the Qoran, regarding it as an impossible task. The Mīr's son became chief ecclesiastical officer (Ṣadr) under Shāh-Jahān. See Ma'āṣiru-l-Umarā, III. 447, and Pādshāh-nāma, I., Part II., p. 328.

† Elliot, V. 361.

‡ There were twelve māshas in a tola; the six cups, then, of 6 tolas and a quarter came to 37½ tolas.

made with my God came, by Divine inspiration, into my mind, and I resolved that when my fiftieth year was completed and the period of fulfilling my vow had arrived, I would, on the day* on which I visited my father's tomb—may the light of God be his testimony—by God's help, seek the confirmation of my resolve from my father's holy elements, and renounce the practice (of shooting). As soon as this thought occurred to me, my illness and trouble disappeared. I revived, and opened my mouth to praise God, and tasted the joy of thanksgiving for His mercies. I hope that I shall be sustained.

> " How well said Firdūsī of pure nature
> May mercy rest on that (his) pure tomb.
>
> " Ah ! spare yon emmet† rich in hoarded grain ;
> He lives with pleasure, and he dies with pain."

On Thursday, the 4th of the Divine month, Sayyid Kabīr and Ba<u>kh</u>tar K., the Wakils of 'Ādil K., who had brought his offering to the exalted Court, obtained leave to return. Sayyid Kabīr was honoured with a dress of honour, a horse, and a jewelled dagger, and Ba<u>kh</u>tar K. with a horse, a dress of honour, and a jewelled *ūrbasī*,‡ which the people of that country (the Deccan ?) wear round their necks, and a present of 6,000 *darbs* was given to each of them for expenses.

As 'Ādil K. was constantly asking for a likeness of myself through my prosperous son <u>Sh</u>āh-Jahān, I sent him one with a ruby of great value and a special elephant. A gracious

* Jahāngīr visited his father's tomb in the following year (the 14th). The passage describing the renunciation of shooting (not of hunting) is translated in Elliot, VI. 362.

† The version of the last two lines is by Sir William Jones, and is given by him in his Tenth Anniversary Discourse, delivered on February 28, 1793. As my friend Mr. Whinfield has pointed out to me, the quotation comes from the story of <u>Sh</u>iblī and the ant in the second chapter of the Būstān. It occurs in the sixth story of the second book and p. 161 of Graf's edition. Sir William Jones's remark is : " Nor shall I ever forget the couplet of Firdausi, for which Sadi, who cites it with applause, pours blessings on his departed spirit." The quotation from Firdūsī occurs on p. 67 of Vol. I. in Macan's edition of the <u>Sh</u>āh-nāma.

‡ Ūrvasī is the name of a celestial nymph. It is also stated by Forbes to be the name of an ornament worn on the breast.

farman was issued that he should be presented with whatever territory of Niẓāmu-l-mulk or Quṭbu-l-mulk he might get into his possession, and whenever he should require any support and assistance, Shāh-nawāz K. should prepare an army and appoint it to assist him. In former days Niẓāmu-l-mulk was the largest of the rulers of the Deccan, a superior whom all acknowledged, and whom they considered as their eldest brother. At this period 'Ādil K. did approved service, and was honoured with the exalted title of "son." I appointed him the head and leader of the whole country of the Deccan, and wrote this quatrain on the portrait with my own hand :

"O thou towards whom is always (turned) the eye of my kindness
Repose at ease under the shadow of my fortune,
I have sent thee my own portrait,
That thou mayest see me spiritually from my picture."

My son Shāh-Jahān sent Ḥakīm Khūsh-ḥāl, son of Ḥakīm Humām, who was one of the excellent house-born ones of this Court, and from his early years had been in my son's service, in company with the Wakils of 'Ādil K. to convey to him the good news of the Jahāngīrī favour towards him. On the same day Mīr Jumla was honoured with the duty of *'Arẓ-mukarrir.* As Kifāyat K., the Diwan of Gujarat, at the time when he was employed in the Diwani of Bengal, in consequence of certain accidents, had lost property (*az sāmān uftāda*), a sum of Rs. 15,000 was presented to him.

At this time two copies of the Jahāngīr-nāma that had been prepared were laid before me. One of these I had some days previously given to the *Madāru-l-mulk* (centre of the kingdom), I'timādu-d-daula, and the other I on this day bestowed on (my adopted) son (*farzandī*), Āṣaf K. On Friday, the 5th, Bahrām, son of Jahāngīr Qulī Khān, came from the province of Bihar, and had the good fortune to pay his respects. He laid before me some diamonds he had obtained from the mine of Kokra. Approved service had not been performed in that province by Jahāngīr Qulī K., and it was also frequently reported that certain of his brothers and sons-in-law had stretched out the hand of tyranny in that country, and were oppressing the servants of God (the people), and that each of them, cutting out a governorship for himself, did not regard the authority of Jahāngīr Qulī. On this account a farman written with my own hand was given to Muqarrab K., one of my confidential old servants, stating that he was appointed Governor of Bihar. I ordered that immediately on receipt of the farman he should hasten to that quarter. Some of the diamonds that Ibrāhīm Fatḥ-jang had sent to Court after the taking of the mine had been given to the Government lapidaries to cut. At this time Bahrām suddenly came to Agra, and was going on to the Court (in Gujarat). K͟hwāja Jahān (the Governor of Agra) sent along with him some diamonds that were ready. One of them is of a violet* colour, and cannot be outwardly distinguished from a sapphire. Up to this time I had not seen a diamond of this colour. It weighed several *surk͟h*,† and jewellers estimated its value at Rs. 3,000, and represented that if it had been white (*safīd*) and had had perfect marks, it would have been worth Rs. 20,000.

This year I had mangoes up to the 6th Mihr (middle of September). In this country there is abundance of lemons (*līmūn*), and they are large (*bālīda ?*). A Hindu brought some from a garden called Kākū (or Gangū), which were very pleasant and large (*bālīda*, perhaps ripe). I ordered them to weigh the largest of them, and it came to 7 *tolas*.

On Saturday, the 6th, the Dasahra festival took place. First, they decked out my horses, and paraded them before me. After that they produced the elephants, decorated in a similar way.

As the Mahī had not become fordable, so that the sublime camp could cross it, and the climate of Maḥmūdābād was quite different (*i.e.*, it was better) from that of other stages, I remained here for ten more days. On Monday, the 8th, I marched and encamped at Mūda.‡ I had already sent K͟hwāja Abū-l-Ḥasan Bak͟hs͟hī with an active body of servants,

* Text *bā naqs͟h* by mistake for *banafs͟ha*.

† I.O. MS. 181 has "thirty *surk͟h*."

‡ Perhaps the Moondah of Bayley's map, east of Maḥmūdābād.

such as boatmen, and also oars,* to make a bridge over the Mahī, with instructions not to wait till it was fordable, so that the victorious camp might cross at ease. On Tuesday, the 9th, there was a halt, and on *Kamshamba* (Wednesday), the 10th, the camp was at the village of Aina.†

At first the male *sāras* used to hold its young one by its leg upside down in his beak, and there was a fear that he might be unkind to it and it might be destroyed. I accordingly ordered them to keep the male separately, and not allow it near its young ones. I now ordered by way of experiment that it should be allowed near them, that the real degree of its unkindness and affection might be ascertained. After allowing it, he displayed much attachment and kindness, and his affection was found to be no less than that of the female; I thus knew that this performance was out of real love. On Thursday, the 11th, there was a halt, and at the end of the day I went to hunt with cheetahs, and two black buck, four does, and a *chikāra* were caught. On Sunday, the 14th, I also went to hunt with cheetahs, and caught fifteen head of male and female antelopes. I had ordered Rustam and Suhrāb‡ Khān, his son, to go out hunting and shoot as many nilgaw as they could. The father and son together killed seven head, male and female. As it was represented to me that there was a tiger in this neighbourhood, a man-killer that had taken to eating men's flesh, and the people of God were afflicted by it, I ordered my son Shāh-Jahān to save them from its wickedness. He, as ordered, shot it with his gun, and brought it to me at night. I ordered them to skin it in my presence. Although large in appearance, as it was thin, it turned out less in weight than the large tigers I had myself killed. On Monday, the 15th, and Tuesday, the 16th, I went to shoot nilgaw, and on each day shot two blue bulls. On Thursday, the 18th, on the bank of a tank at which I pitched, a feast of cups was held. Rare lotus (kanwal)

* The text has کهادا *khāda*, "an oar," but the word is perhaps *khārwa*, "a sailor." I.O. MS. 181, has *khārwa*.

† The I.O. MSS. have Albatta.

‡ The youth who was afterwards drowned in the Jhelam.

flowers had blossomed on the face of the water. My private servants enjoyed themselves greatly with cups of wine. Jahāngīr Qulī had sent twenty elephants from Bihar, and Muruwwat K. eight from Bengal, and these were brought before me. One of Jahāngīr Qulī's and two of Muruwwat's were placed in my private stud, and the rest were divided amongst my followers. Mīr K., s. Mīrzā Abū-l-Qāsim Namakīn, who was one of the khanazads of this Court, was promoted to the mansab, original and increased, of 800 personal and 600 horse. Qiyām K. was appointed to the duty of chief huntsman, and had given him the rank of 600 personal and 150 horse. 'Īzzat* K., one of the Bārha Sayyids, who was distinguished for bravery and ambition, is attached to the province of Bangash. At the request of Mahābat K., the Governor of that Subah, he was promoted to the mansab of 1,500 personal and 800 horse. Kifāyat K., Diwan of Gujarat, had an elephant given him, and was allowed to depart. I conferred a sword on Ṣafī K., Bakshi of that Subah. On Friday, the 19th, I went to hunt, and killed a blue bull. I do not remember a bullet passing through a large male nilgaw. Many have passed through females. On this day, at a distance of forty-five paces (*qadam*), it went through both skins. In the language of hunters a *qadam* means two feet (*gām*†) placed one in front of the other. On Sunday, the 21st, I enjoyed myself with hawking, and ordered Mīrzā Rustam, Dārāb K., Mīr Mīrān, and other servants to go and shoot as many nilgaw as they could. They killed nineteen head, male and female. Ten head of antelope were also caught with cheetahs. Ībrāhīm K., Bakhshi of the Deccan, was, at the request of the Commander-in-Chief, Khān Khānān, promoted to the mansab of 1,000 personal and 200 horse. On Monday, the 22nd, a march was made, and on Tuesday, the 23rd, I again marched. The huntsmen represented that there had been seen in the neighbourhood a tigress with three cubs. As it was on the road I went myself after

* I.O., No. 181, has Ghairat K.

† *gām* sometimes means a step, but here it seems to mean one foot-length. The distance mentioned by Jarrett appears to be 90 feet.

them and shot all four, and then went on to the next stage. I crossed the Mahī by the bridge that had been made. Though there were no boats on this river of which a bridge could be made, and the water was very deep and flowing rapidly, K͟hwāja Abū-l-Ḥasan, the chief Bakhshi, had built with great exertions a very strong bridge two or* three days before. Its length was 140 yards and its breadth 4 yards (*dara'*). By way of testing it I ordered the elephant Gun Sundar K͟hāṣṣ which is one of the large and strong elephants, with three females, to be sent across it. It was so firmly built that its supports did not shake with the weight of elephants of mountainous form.

From the most honoured lips of my father I heard as follows: "In early youth I had taken two or three cups (of wine), and had mounted a full-blooded (*mast*) elephant. Though I was in my senses, and the elephant in very good training, and was under my control, I pretended that I was out of my senses, and that the elephant was refractory and vicious, and that I was making him charge the people. After that, I sent for another elephant, and made the two fight. They fought, and in doing so went to the head of the bridge that had been made over the Jumna. It happened that the other elephant ran away, and as there was no other escape, he went towards the bridge. The elephant I was on pursued him, and although I had him under control, and he would have halted at the slightest signal, I thought that if I held him back from the bridge the people would regard those drunken ways (of mine) as a sham, and would believe that neither was I beside myself, nor was the elephant violent and headstrong. Such pretences on the part of kings are disapproved of, and so after imploring the aid of God—Glory be to Him—I did not restrain my elephant. Both of them went upon the bridge, and as it was made of boats, whenever an elephant put his forefeet on the edge of a boat, half of it sank, and the other half stood up. At each step there came the thought that the lashings might give way. People on seeing this were overwhelmed in the sea

* No. 181 has "in three days."

of perplexity and alarm. As the care and guardianship of the Great and Glorious God is ever and in all places the protection of this suppliant, both elephants crossed the bridge in safety." *

On Thursday, the 25th, a wine-feast was held on the banks of the Mahī, and some of my intimate servants who had admittance to such assemblies had their hearts delighted by brimming cups and ample favours. Certainly it was an entrancing halting-ground. I stayed here four days for two reasons—first, because of the beauty of the spot, and secondly in order that the people might not be confused in crossing the river.

On Sunday, the 28th, I marched from the bank of the Mahī. On Monday I marched again. On this day a strange sight was witnessed. The pair of sāras that had had young ones had been brought from Aḥmadabad on Thursday (the 25th). In the Court of the royal enclosure, which had been placed on the bank of a tank, they were walking about with their young ones. By chance both the male and female raised a cry, and a pair of wild sāras hearing it, and crying out from the other side of the tank, came flying towards them. The male with the male, and the female with the female, engaged in a fight, and although some people were standing about, the birds paid no heed to them. The eunuchs who had been told off to protect them hastened to seize them. One clung to the male and the other to the female. He who had caught the male kept hold of it after much struggling, but the one who seized the female could not hold her, and she escaped from his hand. I with my own hand put rings in his beak and on his legs, and set him free. Both went and settled in their own place.† Whenever the domestic sāras raised a cry they responded. I saw a sight of this kind in wild antelopes when I had gone to hunt in the pargana of

* Compare account in Akbar-nāma, II. 150. Akbar was then twenty years old. There is a picture of the two elephants crossing the bridge with Akbar on the elephant Hawā'ī in the Clarke MS. in the Victoria and Albert Museum, South Kensington.

† Presumably the other side of the tank; it was the wild male sāras that Jahāngīr put rings upon.

Karnāl. About thirty of my huntsmen and servants were in attendance when a black buck with some does came in sight, and we let loose the decoy-antelope* to fight him. They butted two or three times, and then the decoy came back. A second time I wanted to put a noose on its horns and to let it go, that it might capture (the wild one). Meanwhile the wild antelope, in the excess of its rage, not looking at the crowd of men, ran without regard to anything, and butting the tame buck two or three times fought with it till it fled. The wild antelope thereupon made its escape.

On this day news came of the death of 'Ināyat K. He was one of my intimate attendants. As he was addicted to opium, and when he had the chance, to drinking as well, by degrees he became maddened with wine. As he was weakly built, he took more than he could digest, and was attacked by the disease of diarrhœa, and in this weak state he two or three times fainted. By my order Ḥakīm Ruknā applied remedies, but whatever methods were resorted to gave no profit. At the same time a strange hunger came over him, and although the doctor exerted himself in order that he should not eat more than once in twenty-four hours, he could not restrain himself. He also would throw† himself like a madman on water and fire until he fell into a bad‡ state of body. At last he became dropsical, and exceedingly low and weak. Some days before this he had petitioned that he might go to Agra. I ordered him to come into my presence and obtain leave. They put him into a palanquin and brought him. He appeared so low and weak that I was astonished.

"He was skin drawn over bones."

Or rather his bones, too, had dissolved. Though painters have striven much in drawing an emaciated face, yet I have never seen anything like this, nor even approaching to it. Good God, can a son of man come to such a shape

* The hunting of deer with decoys is described in Blochmann's Āyīn, 291.

† Apparently a metaphorical expression, "fought with fire and water."

‡ *sū'u-l-qinya*, "Bad state of the body, cachexy" (Steingass).

and fashion? These two couplets of Ustād* occurred as appropriate:

> "If my shadow do not hold my leg
> I shall not be able to stand till the Resurrection
> Nor, from weakness, does my soul see a refuge
> Where it may for a while rest on my lips."

As it was a very extraordinary case I directed painters to take his portrait. In fact, I found him wonderfully changed. I said to him: "Beware; in your present state do not for a moment forget God, nor despair of His mercy! If Death grant you quarter (*amān*), regard the reprieve as a time for apologizing and for amendment. If your life has come to its close, consider every moment passed in remembrance of God as gain. Trouble not your head about those you are leaving behind. A slight claim of service is a great thing with us." As they had spoken to me about his poverty, I gave him Rs. 2,000 for road-expenses, and let him go. Next day he travelled the road of non-existence.

On Tuesday, the 30th, the bank of the River Mānab† became the halting-place for the sublime camp. The New Year's‡ feast of Thursday was prepared at this place on the 2nd of the Ilāhī month of Ābān. Amānu-llah, s. Mahābat K., at his request, was promoted to the mansab of 1,000 personal and 300§ horse, and Girdhar, s. Rāy Sāl, to that of 1,000

* I do not know of any poet with the *takhallus* Ustād. Possibly Jāmī is referred to. The lines are obscure, and I am not certain of the meaning. The I.O. MSS. omit the negatives in the first two lines.

† Not identified. I.O. MS. 305, seems to have Pānib. Can it be the Mānchan or Majham? Possibly we should read Banās.

‡ The I.O. MSS. have not the words *Nau Rūz*, "New Year," and I am not sure what New Year's day is meant. The time was October. Perhaps it was the first day of Zī-l-Qa'da that was celebrated, or it may be what is described in Richardson as the New Year's day of the Balance—viz., the entry of the Sun into the Sign of the Balance. Jahāngīr may have had special regard to that Sign as he was born under it. Perhaps all that is meant is that the feast of 1 Ābān was celebrated. Ābān was a sacred month because Akbar was born in it, and it may be that the feast was celebrated on Thursday the 2nd because the previous day, Wednesday, was regarded by Jahāngīr as unlucky, and was always spoken of as *Kam-shamba*. But most probably Nau Rūz is simply a mistake of the text.

§ I.O. MS. have 600.

personal and 800 horse. 'Ābdu-llah, son of Khān A'ẓam, obtained the mansab of 1,000 personal and 300 horse. Dilīr K., who was one of the jagirdars of Gujarat, I presented with a horse and an elephant. Ran-bāz K., s. Shāh-bāz K. Kāmbū, came by order from the Deccan, and was promoted to the post of Bakhshi and Recorder of the army of Bangash, and his mansab was fixed at 800 personal and 400 horse. I marched on Friday, the 3rd. At this stage* Prince Shujā', the beloved son (liver-corner) of my son Shāh-Jahān, who was being brought up in the chaste lap of Nūr-Jahān Begam, and towards whom I have so much affection that he is dearer to me than life, was attacked by a specially infantile disease which they call "ummu-ṣ-ṣibyān,"† and for a long time his senses left him. Although experienced people devised many remedies, they were unprofitable, and his insensibility (*bī-hūshī*) took away my senses (*hūsh*). As visible remedies were hopeless, by way of humility and submission I rubbed the head of supplication on the Court of the gracious Ruler who cherishes his slaves, and begged for the child's recovery. In this state it occurred to me that as I had made a vow‡ to my God that after I had passed my fiftieth year, this suppliant would give up hunting with bullet and gun, and would injure no creature with his own hand, if for the sake of his safety I were to give up shooting from the present date, it were possible that his life would become the means of preserving the lives of many animals, and God Almighty might give him to me. In fine, with true purpose, and sincere belief I vowed§ to God that I would thenceforward not harm any living thing with my own hand. By the grace of Allah his illness diminished. At the time when this suppliant was in his mother's womb, one day I made no movement after the manner that other children make. The attendants were

* The name of the stage is not given.

† Literally the mother of children, but explained as meaning a female demon (larva) who torments children. See Lane's Dictionary, 1650, where it is described as "flatulence."

‡ See above, p. 243 of text.

§ Apparently the vow applied only to shooting. Jahāngīr was not at that time fifty-one years of age by solar computation.

amazed, and inquiring into the cause stated the case to my father (Akbar). At that time my father was engaged in hunting with cheetahs. As that day was a Friday, for the purpose of my safety he made a vow that during his life he would not hunt with cheetahs on a Friday. Till the end of his life he remained firm in this determination, and I also in obedience to him until now have never hunted with cheetahs on a Friday. Finally, on account of the weakness of the light of my eye, Shāh Shujāʿ, for three days I halted at this stage, that God Almighty might give him his natural* life.

On Tuesday, the 7th, I marched. One day the son of Ḥakīm † ʿĀlī was praising the milk of a camel. It occurred to me that if I could continue that for some days, it was possible that it might do some good, and it might prove agreeable to me. Āṣaf Khān had a Persian camel in milk, and I took a little of it. Contrary to the milk of other camels, which is not devoid of saltness, it appeared to my taste sweet and delicious, and now for a month past I have been drinking every day a cup of it, equal in quantity to half a water-cup, and it is clearly advantageous, for it quenches my thirst. It is strange that two years ago Āṣaf K. bought this camel, but at that time it had not a young one, and had no sign of milk. At this time by chance milk flowed from its dugs. They gave it every day to drink four seers of cow's milk with five seers of wheat, one seer of black‡ sugar, and one seer of fennel (*bādyān*), to make its milk delicious, sweet, and profitable. Certainly it suited me admirably, and was to my taste. By way of testing it, I sent for some cow's and buffalo's milk, and tasted all three. There was no comparison in sweetness and flavour with the milk of this camel. I ordered them to give the same kind of food to some other female camels, that it might become clear whether the purity was in consequence of eating good food, or whether it was due to the natural sweetness of this (particular) camel's milk.§

* The natural term of life, which some Orientals regarded as being 120 years.

† The name ʿĀlī is omitted in text.

‡ *qand-i-siyāh* (? treacle).

§ We are not told what was the result of this experiment.

On Wednesday, the 8th, I marched, and halted on the 9th. The royal tent was pitched near a large tank. Shāh-Jahān presented me with a boat made after the Kashmīr fashion, the sitting-place of which they had made of silver. At the end of that day I embarked in that boat and went round the tank. On this day 'Ābid K., Bakhshi of Bangash, who had been summoned, came and had the good fortune to kiss the threshold, and was honoured with the post of Dīwān-i-buyūtāt. Sar-farāz Khan, who was one of the auxiliaries of Gujarat, received a standard, a private *tipchāq* horse, and an elephant, and, overwhelmed with honour, obtained leave to go. 'Īzzat* Khān, who was one of those attached to the army of Bangash, was exalted with the gift of a standard. Marching was ordered on Friday, the 10th. Mīr Mīrān was promoted to the mansab of 2,000 personal and 600 horse. On Saturday, the 11th, the auspicious equipage alighted in the pargana of Doḥad. On the eve of Sunday, the 12th of the Ilāhī month of Ābān, in the thirteenth year from my accession, corresponding with the fifteenth Zī-l-Qa'da of the Hijrī year 1027, in the nineteenth degree of Libra, the Giver of blessings gave my prosperous son Shāh-Jahān a precious son by the daughter of Āṣaf K. I hope that his† advent may be auspicious and blessed to this everlasting State. Halting for three days at this place, on Wednesday,‡ the 15th Ābān, the camp was pitched at the village of Ṣamarna.§ As it was necessary that the Mubārak-shamba entertainment should as far as possible be arranged for on the bank of a river and a clean place, and there was in this neighbourhood no spot which met those requirements, there was no help for it but to order a start when half of the night of Thursday (*i.e.*, Wednesday), the 16th, had passed, and when

* MSS., as before, have Ghairat instead of 'Īzzat.

† This son was Aurangzīb. See Khāfī K., I. 296. Khāfī K. has 11th instead of 15th Zī-l-Qā'da. The 11th Zī-l-Qa'da corresponds to 20th October, 1618.

‡ Text has Sunday, but Wednesday must be the correct day, for immediately after Friday is spoken of as the 17th (Ābān).

§ Perhaps the Samarnī of Jarrett, II. 207. The I.O. MSS. have Tamarna.

the sun rose the camp was pitched on the bank of the tank of Bākhūr. At the end of the day, the feast of cups was held and I presented cups to some of my private servants. On Friday, the 17th, I ordered a march. Kes͟ho Dās Mārū is a jagirdar in that neighbourhood. According to orders, he came from the Deccan, and was honoured by doing homage.

On Saturday, the 18th (Ābān), the camp was at Rām-gaṛh. For some nights before this there appeared, at three *gharīs* before sunrise, in the atmosphere, a (luminous) vapour in the shape of a pillar.* At each succeeding night it rose a *gharī* earlier. When it assumed its full form, it took the shape of a spear (*ḥarba*), thin at the two ends, and thick in the middle. It was curved like a sickle, and had its back to the south, and its face to the north. It now showed itself a watch (*pahar*) before sunrise. Astronomers took its shape and size by the astrolabe, and ascertained that with differences of appearance (?) it extended over twenty-four degrees. It moved in high heaven, but it had a movement of its own, differing from that of high heaven, for it was first in Scorpio and afterwards in Libra. Its declination (*ḥarakat-i-'arẓ* ?) was mainly southerly. Astrologers call such a phenomenon a spear (*ḥarba*) in their books, and have written that its appearance portends weakness to the kings of Arabia, and points to their enemies prevailing over them. God knows! Sixteen nights after this phenomenon, a star showed itself in the same quarter. Its head was luminous, and its tail was two or three yards long, but the tail was not luminous. It has now appeared for eight nights; when it disappears, the fact will be noticed, as well as the results of it.

I halted on Sunday, the 19th, and on Monday I alighted at the village of Sītalkhera.† On Tuesday, the 21st, there was

* I have been assisted by the translation in Elliot, VI. 363. See also Iqbāl-nāma, 117. The author there expatiates on the calamities which followed these celestial appearances. Elliot, *loc. cit.*, p. 364, has eight *years*, but the text of the Tūzuk and all the MSS. have "eight *nights*." The Iqbāl-nāma has Dai instead of Ābān, but probably Dai is a mistake for Z͟ī-l-(qā'da). Perhaps the first phenomenon was the Zodiacal Light.

† The MSS. have Sambhalkhera.

again a halt. I presented Rashīd K., the Afghan, with a robe of honour and an elephant, sending them to him by Ran-bāz K. On Wednesday, the 22nd, the camp rested in pargana Madanpūr.* On Thursday, the 23rd, I halted and had a feast of cups, and Dārāb K. had a *nādirī* dress of honour given to him. Halting on Friday, on Saturday the camp was pitched in the pargana of Nawārī.† On Sunday, the 26th, I pitched on the bank of the River Chambal, and on Monday on the bank of the River Kahnar‡ (?). On Tuesday, the 28th, the royal standards were raised in the neighbourhood of the city of Ujain. From Aḥmadabad to Ujain is a distance of ninety-eight kos. It was traversed in twenty-eight marches and forty-one halts—that is, in two months and nine days. On Wednesday, the 29th, I had an interview with Jadrūp, who is one of the austere ones of the Hindu religion, and the particulars of whose circumstances have been described in the preceding pages, and went with him to see Kāliyādaha. Certainly association with him is a great privilege.

On this day it was made known to me in the contents of a report from Bahādur K., the Governor of Qandahar, that in the Hijrī year 1026—that is, last year—the number of mice in Qandahar and the neighbourhood was so great that they destroyed all the crops and grain and cultivation and the fruits of the trees of the province, so that there had been no produce. They (the mice) cut off the ears of corn and ate them. When the cultivators gathered their crops, before they were threshed and cleaned, another§ half was destroyed, so that perhaps one-fourth of the crops only came to hand. In the same way no vestige was left of the melons (melon-beds) or garden produce. After some time the mice disappeared.

* MSS. have Badhnūr. Perhaps it is the Badhnāwar of Jarrett, II.

† Pargana Nūlā'ī in MSS., and this seems right as Nolā'ī, is mentioned in Jarrett, II. 198, as having a brick fort and as being on the Chambal.

‡ It seems to be Gambhīr in the MSS.

§ There seems to be an omission in the recital. We are not told of the first half, but evidently the meaning is that the mice (or rats) ate half the crop on the field, and half of what was brought into the threshing floor. See also Iqbāl-nāma, p. 118.

As my son Shāh-Jahān had not made a birthday entertainment for his son (Aurangzīb), he petitioned at Ujain, which is the place of his jagir, that the Thursday entertainment of the 30th should be held at his abode. Of necessity, having consented to the carrying out of his wish, the day was passed in enjoyment at his quarters. My private servants who have the *entrée* into this kind of parties and assemblies were delighted with brimming cups. My son Shāh-Jahān brought that auspicious child before me, and, presenting as offerings a tray of jewels, and jewelled ornaments, and fifty elephants, thirty male and twenty female, asked me for a name for him. Please God it will be given him in a favourable hour. Of his elephants seven were included in my private stud ; the rest were distributed among the faujdars. The value of the offerings that were accepted will be Rs. 200,000.

On this day 'Aẓudu-d-daula (Jamālu-d-dīn Ḥusain Anjū) came from his jagir, and had the good fortune to kiss the threshold. He gave eighty-one *muhars* as *nazr*, and an elephant as an offering. Qāsim K., whom I had dismissed from the government of Bengal, had been sent for, and having had the good fortune to do homage, presented 1,000 *muhars* as *nazr*. On Friday, the 1st of Āzar, I amused myself with hawking. As the retinue passed along, a field of millet (*jwār*) was met with. Though generally a stem has only one head, each of them had twelve. I was astonished. and at this time the tale of " The King and the Gardener " occurred to me.

Tale of " The King and the Gardener." *

A King came to the gate of a garden in the heat of the day. He saw an old gardener standing at the gate, and asked him if there were any pomegranates in the garden. He said : " There are." He told him to bring a cup of pomegranate juice. The gardener had a daughter adorned with grace of person, and beauty of disposition. He made a sign to her to bring the pomegranate juice. The girl went and at once

* Elliot, VI. 364.

brought a cup full of pomegranate juice, and placed some leaves upon it. The King took it from her hand and drank it. Then he asked the girl what was her reason for placing leaves on the top of the juice. She, with an eloquent tongue and a sweet voice, represented that it was not wise at once to drink off a quantity of liquid when he was bathed in perspiration, and in such a hot air. On this account she had placed the leaves on the liquid by way of precaution, so that he might drink it slowly. The King was greatly pleased with her sweet ways, and it crossed his mind to admit the girl into his Palace. After this he asked the gardener: "How much profit do you derive from this garden every year?" He answered: "Three hundred *dīnārs*." The King asked: "What do you pay the Diwan (tax-collector)?" He answered: "The King takes nothing from the trees, but takes a tenth of the cultivated crops." It came into the King's mind that there were in his dominions many gardens and countless trees. If he were to get a tenth of the garden produce as well, it would amount to a large sum, and there would be no great loss to the cultivator. Hereafter he would order a tax to be levied on garden produce. He said then: "Bring me a little more pomegranate juice." The girl went, and after a long time brought a small quantity. The King said: "The first time thou camest quickly, and broughtest more. This time thou didst stay a long time, and broughtest less." The girl said: "The first time I had filled the cup with the juice of one pomegranate, and brought it; this time I pressed out five or six pomegranates and did not get as much juice." The astonishment of the King increased. The gardener represented: "The blessing of produce depends on the goodwill of the King. It occurs to me that you must be a King. At the time when you inquired of me the income from the garden, your disposition must have changed. Consequently the blessing passed away from the fruit." The Sultan was impressed, and drove that idea out of his heart. He then said: "Bring me once more a cup of pomegranate juice." The girl went again, and quickly bringing a cup full to the brim, gave it, smiling and gladly, into the Sultan's hand. He praised the intelligence of the gardener, and explained the actual state of affairs, and begged the girl of him in marriage, and married her.

This true tale of that truth-preserving King has remained as a memento on the page of time. In truth, the manifestation of such spiritual (?)* results is the mark of good intentions, and the fruit of justice. Whenever all the energies and purposes of justice-observing Kings are devoted to the comfort of the people and the contentment of their subjects, the manifestations of well-being and the productions of fields and gardens are not far off. God be praised that in this age-enduring State no tax has ever been levied on the fruit of trees, and is not levied now. In the whole of the dominion not a *dām* nor one grain (*ḥabba*)† on this account enters the public treasury, or is collected by the State. Moreover, there is an order that whoever makes a garden on arable land, its produce is exempted. I trust that God (to whom be glory!) will always incline this suppliant towards what is good.

"When my purpose is good, do Thou grant me good."‡

On Saturday, for the second time, my desire for the company of Jadrūp increased. After performing the midday devotions, I embarked in a boat and hastened to meet him, and at the close of day I ran and enjoyed his society in the retirement of his cell. I heard many sublime words of religious duties and knowledge of divine things. Without immoderate praise, he sets forth clearly the doctrines of wholesome Sufism, and one can find delight in his society. He is sixty years old. He was twenty-two years of age, when, forsaking all external attachments, he placed the foot of determination on the highroad of asceticism, and for thirty-eight years he had lived in the garment of nakedness. When I took leave he said: "In what language can I return thanks for this gift of Allah that I am engaged in the reign of such a just King in the worship of my own Deity in ease and con-

* The word *ma'nī*, "spiritual," does not occur in the I.O. MSS., and does not appear to be wanted.

† Also a weight = two barley-grains. Blochmann, 36.

‡ The line is wanting in some MSS. In I.O. MS. 181, the conjunction *wa* is omitted (p. 145*b*).

tentment, and that the dust of discomposure from any accident settles not on the skirt of my purpose ?"

On Sunday, the 3rd, marching from Kāliyādaha, I encamped at the village of Qāsimkhera. I employed myself on the road in hawking. By chance a crane rose, and the *tūyghūn* falcon, of which I am very fond, was let fly after it. The crane sought to escape, and the falcon soared and flew so high as to disappear from sight. Although the huntsmen and the head-beaters ran after it in all directions, they found no trace of it, and it was impossible for the falcon to be caught in such a desert. Lashkar Mīr Kashmīrī, who is the head of the Kashmir huntsmen, in whose charge the falcon was, ran in a bewildered state through the desert in all directions without finding a sign or trace. Suddenly he saw a tree in the distance, and when he went up to it he found the falcon sitting on the end of a branch. Showing a domestic fowl, he called to the falcon. Three *gharīs* more had not passed when he brought it to me. This gift from the hidden world, that had entered into the thoughts of no one, increased the joy of my mind. Increasing his mansab as a reward for this service, I gave him a horse and a dress of honour.

On Monday, the 4th, Tuesday, the 5th, Wednesday, the 6th, I marched continuously, and, halting on Thursday, the 7th, I arranged a feast of pleasure on the bank of a tank. Nūr-Jahān Begam had been ill for some time, and the physicians who had the good fortune to be chosen to attend on her, Musalmans and Hindus, perceived no gain from all the medicines they gave her, and confessed their helplessness in treating her. At this time Ḥakīm Rūḥu-llah began to wait upon her, and undertook (to find) a remedy. By the aid of God (Glory be to His name !), in a short time she quite recovered. In reward for this excellent service I increased his mansab and bestowed on the Ḥakīm three villages in his native country as his private property, and an order was given that he should be weighed against silver, which should be given him as a reward. From Friday, the 8th, until Sunday,*

* So in text, but Sunday was either the 10th or the 17th. Apparently Sunday is a mistake for Wednesday, as, later on, Thursday is mentioned as the 14th.

the 13th, I made successive marches, and every day up to the end of the stage employed myself in hunting with hawks and falcons (*bāz u jurra*). Many *durrāj* (partridges) were caught. On last Sunday, Kunwar Karan, s. Rānā Amar Singh, having enjoyed the good fortune of kissing the ground, presented his congratulations on the conquest of the Deccan, offering 100 *muhars* and Rs. 1,000 by way of *nazr*, and the value of Rs. 21,000 in jewelled vessels, with some horses and elephants as *pīshkash*. The horses and elephants I returned to him, and the rest was accepted. The next day I presented him with a dress of honour. To Mīr Sharīf, Vakil of Quṭbu-l-mulk, and to Irādat K., the chief butler, an elephant each was given. Sayyid Hizabr K. was given the faujdari of Mewāt, and his mansab, original and increased, was fixed at 1,000 personal and 500 horse. Having selected Sayyid Mubārak for the charge of the fort of Rohtās, I conferred on him the mansab of 500 personal and 200 horse. On Thursday, the 14th, the camp was pitched on the bank of the tank of the village of Sandhāra, and the feast of cups was held, and chosen servants were made happy with cups of pleasure. The birds of chase, "that had been shut up in Agra to moult" (*ba-kurīz basta būdand*), were this day brought to me by Khwāja 'Abdu-l-Laṭīf, the Chief Fowler. Picking out those that were fit for my own use, the rest were given to the Amīrs and other servants.

On this day the news of the revolt and ingratitude for favours of Rāja Sūraj Mal, s. Rāja Bāso, came to my ear. Bāso had several* sons. Although the above-mentioned was the eldest, his father mostly kept him in confinement on account of his evil thoughts and mischievous tendencies, and regarded him with displeasure. After his (Bāso's) death, as this wretch was the eldest, and he had no other capable or intelligent son, I, looking to the services rendered by Rāja Bāso, for the purpose of preserving the family of a Zamindar, and the protection of his hereditary property and country, conferred on this wretch the title of Raja, with a mansab of 2,000, and gave him the position and jagir of his father,

* Iqbāl-nāma, 119, "Three sons."

which the latter had obtained by his loyalty and good service. I also gave him the sums of money and goods that his father had collected during long years. When the deceased Murtaẓā K. was sent off on the duty of conquering Kāngra, as this wretch was the chief Zamindar of that hill country, he outwardly displayed zeal in the service and loyalty, and was nominated as an auxiliary. After he reached the spot, Murtaẓā K. pressed the siege tightly against the garrison. This evil-minded fellow discovered from the appearance of things that he would soon be victorious, and began to disagree and be troublesome. He took off the veil of respect from his face, and proceeded to quarrel and be hostile to Murtaẓā K.'s men. Murtaẓā K. read the writing of misery and ruin on the page of the wretch's forehead, and reported unfavourably of him to the Court, or rather wrote plainly that the signs of rebellion and want of loyalty were clear in his conduct. As there was there such an officer as Murtaẓā K. and a large army in the hill-country, the wretch did not find the time convenient for the preparation of a disturbance. He sent a report to my son S͟hāh-Jahān that Murtaẓā K., at the instigation of interested parties, had turned against him, and desired to overthrow and ruin him, and was accusing him of wrong-doing and rebellion. He hoped that he would summon him to Court, and thus provide a means for his escape and (the prolonging of) his life. Although I had every confidence in the words of Murtaẓā K., yet as he (Sūraj Mal) begged to be sent for to Court, a doubt passed into my mind that possibly Murtaẓā K., at the instigation of seditious people, might cause a confusion, and might have accused him without due reflection. Briefly, at the request of my son S͟hāh-Jahān, passing over his offence, I summoned him (Sūraj Mal) to Court. Just at this time Murtaẓā K. died, and the conquest of the fort of Kāngra was delayed till the dispatch of another leader. When this seditious fellow arrived at Court, I, under the pressure of affairs, rapidly encompassed him with favours and sent him off to do duty with my son S͟hāh-Jahān in the conquest of the Deccan. After this, when the Deccan had come into the possession of the servants of the enduring State, he, having acquired influence in my son's service, was appointed to superintend the taking of the fort of Kāngra. Although the sending back of this ungrateful and untruthful one into that hill-country showed a want of caution and care, yet as my son had taken on himself the responsibility of the undertaking, I was obliged to give in to his wish and to leave the matter to him. My fortunate son appointed him, along with one of his own servants of the name of Taqī and a suitable army of *manṣabdārs, aḥadīs*, and royal musketeers, as has already been related summarily in these pages. When he arrived at the place, he began to show enmity and trickery toward Taqī also, and displayed his natural disposition. He continually reported unfavourably of him (Taqī), until he wrote plainly that he could not get on with him, and that Taqī could not do the work. If another general were appointed, the fort would be quickly conquered. In fine, he (Shāh-Jahān) had no choice but to summon Taqī to Court, and to appoint Rāja Bikramājīt, who was one of his chief servants, with an army of fresh men on this service. When the wretch discovered that his stratagems could no longer continue, and his deceit go no farther, he, before the arrival of Bikramājīt, gave leave to a number of the servants of the Court, on the pretence that they had been on service a long time without proper arrangements (commissariat), to hasten to their jagirs and provide themselves with their equipments before the arrival of Rāja Bikramājīt. As palpably this came to a dispersion of the forces of the loyal, and most of them left for their own jagirs, only a few experienced men remained there. Seeing his opportunity, he showed the signs of revolt and sedition. Sayyid Ṣafī Bārha, who was distinguished for his bravery, with some of his brothers and relatives, advanced the feet of courage, and tasted the wholesome draught of martyrdom, and some who were wounded with severe wounds, which are the adornment of the lions of battle, that rascal took captive from the field of strife and carried off to his own house of calamity.* Some from love† of life hastily withdrew

* Apparently the meaning is that he carried them off as prisoners.

† Text *jāda-dūstī* by mistake for *jān-dūstī*.

themselves to the corner of safety. That rascal stretched out the hand of oppression and possession over the parganas on the skirts of the hill-country (*daman-i-kūh*), which mostly belonged to the jagir of I'timādu-d-daula, and did not abate a hair's breadth from attacking and plundering. It is hoped that with the same swiftness, he will be caught with the reward of his deeds and the recompense of his actions, and that the spirit* of this State will do its work, please God!

On Sunday, the 17th, I crossed Ghāṭī Chāṇḍā. On Monday, the 18th, the Jān-sipār Ātālīq Khān-khānān, Commander-in-Chief, had the honour of kissing the threshold. As he had been absent from my presence for a long time, and the victorious retinue was passing by near the Sarkars of Khandesh and Burhānpūr, he asked to wait upon me, and an order was given that if his mind were at ease in all respects, he should come unattended and return quickly. He accordingly came with all speed, and had the good fortune to pay his respects on this day, and, having been exalted by the receipt of all kinds of royal favours and kingly benefits, he presented an offering of 1,000 *muhars* and Rs. 1,000.

As the camp had undergone great hardship in crossing the Ghāṭī, I ordered a halt for the refreshment of the people on Tuesday, the 19th. I marched on Wednesday, the 20th, and on Thursday, the 21st, halted again and held a feast of cups on the bank of a river that is known as the Sind.† I gave a special horse, of the name of Sumer, which was one of the finest horses, to the Khān-khānān. In the Hindi language they call a hill of gold Sumer (Sumeru), and he was called by this name on account of his colour and size. On Friday, the 22nd, and Saturday, the 23rd, two successive marches were made. On this day a wonderful waterfall was seen. The water is exceedingly clear, and pours down with boiling and noise from a lofty place. On all sides of it there are halting places

* *Namak*, "salt." See for a similar expression, p. 149, in the account of Chīn Qilīj. Perhaps the phrase is a reminiscence of the answer given by Muḥammad Ḥusain M. when asked who had captured him. "The king's salt," was his reply.

† The Sind is mentioned in Tieffenthaler, I. 184. See also I.G., new ed., XXII., p. 432. It is one of the chief rivers of Central India.

where one may praise God. Certainly I have not recently seen such another fine waterfall, and it is a delightful recreation-place. I was delighted with the spectacle for a while. On Sunday, the 24th, I halted, and, sitting in a boat on a tank which was in front of the royal enclosure (*ḍaulat-kh̲āna*), were shot* ducks (*murgh̲ābī*). On Monday, the 25th, Tuesday, the 26th, and Wednesday, the 27th, I marched one after the other. I bestowed on the Kh̲ān-kh̲ānān the *pūstīn* (sheep-skin coat) I had on my own person, and seven horses from my stable, on which I always rode, were also given him. On Sunday, the 2nd of the Ilāhī month of Dai, the royal standards were raised at the fort of Ranthambūr. This is one of the great forts of the Indians. In the time of Sulṭān 'Alā'u-d-dīn Kh̲aljī, Rāy Pitambar Deo was in possession of it. The Sultan besieged it for a long time, and conquered it with labour and great exertions, and in the beginning† of the reign of H.M. (Akbar)—may the light of God be his witness!—Rāy Surjan Hāḍā had it in his possession. He had always 6,000 or 7,000 horse in attendance on him. That revered one, by the aid of the glorious God, conquered it in the space of one month and twelve days, and Rāy Surjan, by the guidance of fortune, having had the good fortune to kiss the threshold, was enrolled among the number of the loyal, and became one of his respectable and trusted Amīrs. After him his son Rāy Bhoj also was included among the great Amīrs. Now his grandson, Sar-buland Rāy, is among the chief officers. On Monday,‡ the 3rd, I went to inspect the fort. There are two hills close to each other. They call one Ran, and the other Thanbūr. The fort is built on the top of Thanbūr, and, putting these two names together, they have called it Ranthanbūr. Although the fort is exceedingly strong, and has plenty of water, the hill of Ran is a specially strong fortress

* The word is *shikār*. Either the ducks were caught in nets and not shot, or the shooting was done by others, for Jahāngīr had vowed to give up shooting from the time of Sh̲ujā''s illness.

† Akbar really took it in the 14th year of his reign (March, 1569). The siege lasted a month, according to Abū-l-Faẓl. Akbar-nāma, II. 339.

‡ Elliot, VI. 366.

(in itself), and the capture of the fortress depends upon the possession of this hill. Accordingly, my revered father ordered that they should plant cannon on the top of the hill of Ran, and aim at (*majrā gīrand*) the buildings inside the fort. The first gun they fired reached the square building (*chaukandī*)* of the palace of Rāy Surjan. From the fall of that building, a trembling found its way into the foundations of his courage, and a great perplexity overpowered his heart, and thinking he would best consult his own safety in delivering up the fort, he rubbed the head of worship and humility on the throne of the king of kings, who forgave faults and accepted excuses.

I had intended to pass the night in the fort, and the next day to return to camp. As the buildings inside the fort had been built after the fashion of the Hindus, and the rooms were without air and with little space, they did not please me, nor was I disposed to stay there. I saw a bath house, which one of the servants of Dastam† Khān had built near the wall of the fort. A little garden and a lodging (*nishīman*) which overlooks (*mushrif*) the open space is not wanting in space and air, and there is no better place in the whole fort.‡ Dastam K. was one of the Amīrs of the late King (Akbar), and from his early years had been brought up in his service. His connection with him was confidential and intimate. H.M. had entrusted this fort to him from his exceeding confidence in him.

After completing my inspection of the fort and houses, I ordered that they should bring before me the criminals who were confined in the fort, so that I might look into the case of each of them and give an order in accordance with justice. In brief, with the exception of affairs of murder, and of any person through whose release disturbance or calamity might ensue in the country, I freed them all, and to each one in

* For notes about the meaning of the word *chaukandī*, "four-cornered," see Elliot, V. 347 and 503.

† Text Rustam, but it is Dastam in MS. 181, and it appears from Blochmann that Dastam or Dostam is the proper spelling. See pp. 398 and 620.

‡ Apparently Jahāngīr spent the night in this summer-house.

accordance with his circumstances gave his expenses and dresses* of honour. On the eve of Tuesday, the 4th, I returned to the royal abode after a watch and three gharis had passed. On Sunday (properly Wednesday), the 5th, having marched nearly 5 koss, I halted on Thursday, the 6th. On this day the Khān-khānān presented his offering of jewels, ornamented vessels, cloth, and an elephant. Of these I chose whatever pleased me, and returned the rest. What was accepted of his offering was of the value of Rs. 150,000. On Friday, the 7th, I marched 5 koss. I had before this captured a *sāras* with a falcon, but until now I had never seen the hunting of a *durnā*† (crane). As my son Shāh-Jahān had great pleasure in *durnā* hunting with the falcon (*shāhīn*), and his falcons were well grown, at his request I rode out early in the morning, and caught one *durnā* myself, whilst the falcon my son had on his wrist caught another. Certainly, of all good hunting amusements, this is the best. I was exceedingly pleased with it. Although the *sāras* is large, it is lazy and heavy on the wing. The chase of the *durnā* has no resemblance to it. I praise the heart and courage of the falcon that can seize such strong-bodied animals, and with the strength of his talons can subdue them. Ḥasan K., the chief hunstman of my son, was honoured with an elephant, a horse, and a dress of honour, as a reward for this exhibition of sport, and his son also received a horse and a dress of honour. On Saturday, the 8th, having marched 4¼ koss, I halted on Sunday, the 9th. On this day the Khān-khānān, the Commander-in-Chief, having raised the head of dignity through the gift of a special dress of honour, a jewelled waist-sword, and a private elephant with trappings, was reappointed to Khandesh and the Deccan. The mansab of that pillar of the kingdom, original and increase, was fixed at 7,000 personal and horse. As he did not get on with Lashkar K., at his request I assigned to 'Ābid K. the duty of Dīwān-i-

* *Khila'āt*, surely used here on account of the alliteration *kharjī u Khila'āt*. At p. 10 of Price's "Jahangir" it is stated that he released 7,000 prisoners from Gwalior Fort !

† *durnā*, or *turnā*, a crane. It is a Turki word.

buyūtāt,* and having given him the mansab of 1,000 personal and 400 horse, as well as a horse, an elephant, and a dress of honour, sent him to that Subah. On the same day Khān Daurān arrived from Kabul, and had the good fortune to pay his respects, and presented as *nazr* 1,000 muhars and Rs. 1,000, as well as an offering of a pearl rosary, fifty horses, ten Persian male and female camels, and some hawks, and china,† and porcelain (?), and other things. On Monday, the 10th, I marched 3¼ koss, and on Tuesday, the 11th, 5¾ koss. On this day the Khān Daurān arranged his men before me, and passed in review a thousand Mughal cavalry, most of whom had Turkī horses, and some 'Irāq and some Mujannas‡ horses. Though his troopers had been mostly dispersed, some going into the service of Mahābat K. and remaining in that Subah, whilst a number left him at Lahore and went into different parts of the dominion, yet he could show this body of well-mounted men. Certainly the Khān Daurān for valour and generalship is one of the unique of the ages, but alas ! I found he had become a decrepit old man, and his sight was very weak. He has two intelligent young sons, who are not wanting in reasonableness, but it will certainly be a great and difficult thing for them to show themselves his equals. On this day I gave him and his sons dresses of honour and swords. On Sunday, the 12th, traversing 3½ koss, I alighted on the bank of the tank of Māndū.§ In the middle of the

* The words *dīwān-i-buyūtāt* are repeated. It looks as if the word *buyūtāt* in the second place was a mistake, or if some word implying that Lashkar K. had been appointed director of buildings (*dīwān-i-buyūtāt*) had been omitted. Apparently 'Ābid K. went to the Deccan as Dīwān, and not as Dīwān-i-buyūtāt. Compare Iqbāl-nāma, 122.

† No. 181 has no conjunction, and makes the meaning "porcelain from Tartary."

‡ See Blochmann, 140 and 233. Abū-l-Fazl says the *mujannas* horses resemble Persian horses, and are mostly Turkī or Persian geldings.

§ So in text, but evidently Māndū, or at least Māndū in Malwa cannot be correct. The MSS. seem to have Hindaun, and possibly this is the place meant. Or it may be the place called Mandawar or Hindaun Road (see I.G., new ed., XIII. 135). The position of Hindaun agrees fairly well with Jahāngīr's itinerary, for Tieffenthaler, I., 172, says that

tank there is a stone building, and on one of the pillars the quatrain of someone had been engraved. I saw it, and was amazed. In truth, it is a fine verse :

"My congenial friends have left me :
One by one they've fallen into the hands of death.
They were poor drinkers at the banquet of life.
A moment sooner than us they became drunken."*

At this time I also heard another quatrain of the same description, which I have recorded because it was very well said :

"Alas ! that people of intelligence and wisdom have passed away.
They have been forgotten in the minds of their contemporaries.
Those who spoke with a hundred tongues
Ah ! what heard they that they became silent."

On Thursday, the 13th, I made a halt. 'Abdu-l-'Azīz K., having come from Bangash, had the good fortune to kiss the threshold. Ikrām K., who was in charge of the faujdari of Fathpūr and the neighbourhood, was honoured with waiting on me. Khwāja Ibrāhīm K., Bakhshī of the Deccan, was

---

Hindaun is 12 leagues—*i.e.*, koss—S.S.-W. from Biāna, and Jahāngīr gives the distance from Māndū or Hindaun to the neighbourhood of Bayānā as 8¼ koss. Bayānā is in the Bhartpur State, and apparently about 21 miles from Hindaun.

* The quatrain which Jahāngīr describes as that of someone (*shakhsī*) is included in 'Umar Khayyām's poems, and is thus translated by Whinfield :

"My comrades all are gone, Death, deadly foe,
Hath caught them one by one, and trampled low ;
They shared life's feast, and drank its wine with me,
But lost their heads and dropped a while ago."
(Quatrain 219, p. 148.)

Fitzgerald has it as Quatrain XXII., and his version is :

"For some we loved, the loveliest and the best
That from his Vintage rolling Time hath prest,
Have drunk their Cup a Round or two before,
And one by one crept silently to rest."

The quatrain is also quoted by Badayūnī, Lowe's translation, p. 192. The phrase *tang-sharāb* in the third line means "poor drinkers." Whinfield has *ba-yak sharāb*. But *tang-sharāb* is given in Johnson's dictionary with the meaning of being easily made drunk, unable to carry much liquor.

exalted with the title of 'Aqīdat K. Mīr Ḥājj, who is one of the auxiliaries attached to that Subah, and one of the brave young officers, was promoted to the title of Sharza (tiger-whelp) K., and received a standard. On Friday, the 14th, I marched $5\frac{1}{4}$ koss. On Saturday, the 15th, having marched 3 koss, I halted in the neighbourhood of Bayānā.* There I hastened with the ladies to see the spectacle of the top of the fort. Muḥammad, the Bakhshī of Humāyūn, who was entrusted with the charge of the fort, had built a fine house overlooking the plain, of great height and with fine air. The tomb of Shaikh Bahlūl is also in that neighbourhood, and is not wanting in excellence. The Shaikh was the elder brother of Shaikh Muḥammad Ghauṡ, and was much versed in the science of incantations by names (of God). Humāyūn had great affection for him, and the most perfect reliance on him. When he conquered the province of Bengal, he took up his abode there for some time. Mīrzā Hindāl, by his order, had remained† at Agra. A body of avaricious servants (*qulluq-chiyān*), whose character was mischievous and seditious, taking to the way of faithlessness, came from Bengal to the Mīrzā, and, working upon his base nature (shaking the chain of his vile heart), led the Mīrzā on the road of rebellion and ingratitude for favours, and of irrecognition of duty. The thoughtless Mīrzā had the *khuṭba* recited in his own name (proclaimed himself king), and openly raised the standard of rebellion and strife. When the royal ear heard what had taken place from the reports of those who were loyal, he sent Shaikh Bahlūl to admonish the Mīrzā, and to turn him back from his vain purpose, and to establish his feet on the high-road of sincerity and concord. As these wretches had made

* Bayānā (Biāna) is described in I.G., new ed., VII. 137. It is stated there that it used to have a fort with a very high tower. Bahlūl's tomb still exists. It was his brother, M. Ghauṡ, who was most known for his skill in incantations, and who wrote a book on the subject.

† The story is told in the Akbar-nāma, Vol. I. Jahāngīr is not correct in saying that Humāyūn had ordered Hindāl to remain in Agra. Hindāl went there without permission, and doubtless in order to rebel. See also Gul-badan Begam's "Memoirs," who, naturally, tries to excuse her brother.

the flavour of royalty sweet to the Mīrzā's palate, he became imbued with futile ideas, and would not be loyal. At the instigation of these seditious people he made Shaikh Bahlūl a martyr with the sword of recklessness at the Chārbāgh (garden) which H.M. Bābar had made on the bank of the Jumna. As Muḥammad Bakhshī was a disciple of the Shaikh, he carried the body into the fort of Bayānā, and buried it there.

On Sunday, the 16th, marching 4½ koss, I came to the stage of Barah.* As the garden and well which had been built by the order of Maryam-zamānī (Jahāngīr's mother) in the pargana of Jūsat was on the road, I went to inspect them. Certainly the *bā'olī* (step-well) was a grand building, and had been built exceedingly well. I ascertained from the officials that a sum of Rs. 20,000 had been expended on this well. As there was much game in this neighbourhood, I halted on Monday, the 17th.

On Tuesday, the 18th, marching 3⅛ koss, the host of prosperity halted at the village of Dāyarm'a'ū.† On Wednesday, the 19th, marching 2½ koss, the victorious standards were raised on the bank of the Lake of Fatḥpūr. As at the time when the conquest of the Deccan was meditated, the stages and distances from Ranthambūr to Ujain were recorded, it appears unnecessary to repeat them. From Ranthambūr‡ to

* This must be the Barmadh Mata mentioned by Beale (see Proceedings A.S.B. for August, 1873, p. 159). Beale says there is a place of worship of the Hindus about 1½ koss from Biana in the district of Bhartpur called Barmadh Mata. In the 7th year of Jahāngīr, 1022, 1613, Jahāngīr's mother Maryam-zamānī made a garden and a *bā'olī* (step-well) here at a cost of Rs. 20,000. The garden has disappeared, but the building which is over the *bā'olī* still exists. Beale gives the inscription. William Finch (Hakluyt Society) speaks of a place called Menhapur, near Biana, where there was a garden made by the Queen-Mother. It was a great *sarāy*. The pargana Jūsat of the text is no doubt the Chausath of Jarrett, II. 183, and of Elliot's Supp. Gloss., II., p. 83. Barah may be the Parath or Berath of Jarrett, II. 181.

† Apparently this is the Dā'ir or Dābar of Badayūnī, II. 171, and Akbar-nāma, III. 145. It is described by Badayūnī as being 4 koss from Fatḥpūr. Dā'ir may also be read Dābar in MSS., and it is Dābar in the map. It is in the Bhartpur State.

‡ So in the MSS. and the text, but must be a mistake for Aḥmadabad, which Jahāngīr left on 21 Shahrīwār or 22 Ramaẓān. See also

Fatḥpūr by the road by which I came was a distance of 234 koss, in sixty-three marches and fifty-six halts, traversed in 119 days, or, according to solar reckoning, in one day under four months, and by lunar four full months. From the date on which the army of fortune started from the capital for the conquest of the Rānā and the acquisition of the Deccan until now, when the victorious and prosperous standards have been planted again in the centre of the empire, it is five years and four months. The astrologers and astronomers chose the day of *Mubārak-s̲h̲amba* (Thursday), the 28th of the Divine month of Dai, in my thirteenth year, corresponding with the last day of the Muḥarram in the Hijrī year 1028 (January 7, 1619), as the proper time at which to enter the capital of Agra.

At this time, again, it appeared from the reports of the loyal that the disease of the plague was prevalent in Agra, so that daily about 100 people, more or less, were dying of it. Under the armpits, or in the groin, or below the throat, buboes formed, and they died. This is the third year that it has raged in the cold weather, and disappeared in the commencement of the hot season. It is a strange thing that in these three years the infection has spread to all the towns and villages in the neighbourhood of Agra, while there has been no trace of it at Fatḥpūr. It has come as far as Amānābād, which is 2½ koss from Fatḥpūr, and the people of that place (Amānābād) have forsaken their homes and gone to other villages. There being no choice, and considering the observance of caution necessary, it was decided that at this propitious* hour the victorious army should enter the inhabited part of Fatḥpūr in all joy and auspiciousness, and after the

---

Iqbāl-nāma, 117. He arrived at the environs of Fatḥpūr on 19 Dai, or about 22 Muḥarram, 1028 (end of December, 1618). Apparently he considered that he arrived at Fatḥpūr on 20 Dai. He remained on the outskirts and did not enter the town till the 28th (apparently should be 26th or 27th). The Iqbāl-nāma 122 makes Jahāngīr arrive at the outskirts of Fatḥpūr on 20 Dai, and it gives the date of his entering the town as 26 Dai or 1 Ṣafar, 1028 (January 8, 1619). See p. 123.

* Viz., the propitious hour of the 28th Dai, which had been fixed for the entry into Agra, but was now made the time for entering Fatḥpūr.

sickness and scarcity had subsided and another auspicious hour had been chosen, I should enter the capital, please the Almighty and most holy Allah!

The Thursday entertainment took place on the bank of the Lake of Fatḥpūr. As the time for entering the town (of Fatḥpūr) was fixed for the 28th, I halted eight days in this place. I ordered them to measure the circumference of the lake,* and it came to 7 koss. At this stage, with the exception of the revered Maryam-zamānī, who had become very weak, all the Begams and inhabitants of the enclosure of chastity and all the palace employés came out to meet me (istiqbāl). The daughter† of Āṣaf K., deceased, who is in the house of 'Abdu-llah K.—*i.e.*, is married to 'Abdu-llah), s. Khān Ā'ẓam, told me a strange and wonderful tale, and strongly insisted upon its truth. I write it on account of its strangeness. She said: "One day in the courtyard of the house I saw a mouse rising and falling in a distracted state. It was running about in every direction after the manner of drunkards, and did not know where to go. I said to one of my girls: 'Take it by the tail and throw it to the cat!' The cat was delighted, and jumped up from its place and seized it in its mouth, but immediately dropped it and showed disgust. By degrees an expression of pain and trouble showed itself in its face. The next day it was nearly dead, when it entered into my mind to give it a little treacle‡ (*tiryāq*, opium ?). When its mouth was opened, the palate and tongue appeared black. It passed three days in a state of misery, and on the fourth day came to its senses. After this the grain (*dāna*) of the plague (buboes) appeared in the girl, and from excess of temperature and increase of pain she had no rest. Her colour became changed—it was yellow inclining to black—and the

* The lake was to the north of the city, and is now dried up. It had been made by damming up a stream.

† Apparently this lady was relating what had occurred in Agra, for Jahāngīr has just told us that the plague did not come to Fatḥpūr. Her father was the Āṣaf K., known also as Ja'far K. The ladies seem to have come out from Agra to welcome Jahāngīr. His mother came later from Agra, *see infra*.

‡ *Tiryāq-i-Fārūq*. See Lane's Dict., p. 304, col. 3.

fever was high (*tap muḥriq gardīd*). The next day she vomited* and had motions, and died. Seven or eight people in that household died in the same way, and so many were ill that I went to the garden from that lodging. Those who were ill died in the garden, but in that place there were no buboes. In brief, in the space of eight or nine days seventeen people became travellers on the road of annihilation." She also said: "Those in whom the buboes appeared, if they called another person for water to drink or wash in, the latter also caught the infection (*sirāyat*), and at last it came to such a pass that through excessive apprehension no one would come near them."

On Saturday, the 22nd, Khwāja Jahān, who had had the charge of Agra, having had the good fortune to kiss the threshold, presented 500 *muhars* by way of *nazr*, and Rs. 400† as charity. On Monday, the 24th, a special dress of honour was conferred on him. On *Mubārak-shamba*‡ (Thursday), the 28th (? 27th), after four *gharī* § or nearly two sidereal hours (*sā'at*), had passed,

> "In an hour which agreed with two almanacs (?) (or which marked two events),"

---

* I.O. MSS. have *az bālā radd u az pāyān iṭlāq shud*, "there was vomiting from above and evacuations from below." The text misses out the words *az bālā radd*.

† 4,000 in No. 181.

‡ Certainly Thursday was the 27th according to Jahāngīr. The 28th must be a copyist's mistake here and previously.

§ Jahāngīr says four *gharī* are nearly equal to two sidereal hours. According to Abū-l-Faẓl, a *gharī* is the sixteenth part of a nychthemeron, or 360 out of the 21,600 breathings which make up a nychthemeron—*i.e.*, 24 hours. See Jarrett, III. 16 and 17, and II. 16, n. 4. According to the Bahār-i-'ajam, 2½ *gharī*=one sidereal hour, so that, correctly speaking, five *gharī*=two sidereal hours. Each *gharī* is 24 minutes (Jarrett, II. 16, n. 4). Here it should be noted that there is a mistake in the translation at p. 17, line 2, of Jarrett, vol. III., due to a faulty reading in the Bib. Ind. edition of the text. Instead of *yakī* we should read *palī*, as in two MSS. in my possession. Abū l-Faẓl's meaning then becomes clear. What he says is, a *gharī* is 360 breathings, consequently (*pas*) every *pal* (already defined as the sixtieth part of a *gharī*) is 360 divided by 60, and equal to six breathings (*nafas*). Jahāngīr's line, however, is obscure. In two I.O. MSS. we have *ba-ṭāla'ī* instead

the royal standards auspiciously and happily entered the inhabited part of Fatḥpūr. At the same hour the entertainment (of weighing) for my prosperous and noble son, Shāh-Jahān, was held. I ordered him to be weighed against gold and other things, and his twenty-eighth year according to the solar* months began auspiciously. It is hoped that he may reach the natural† limit of life. On the same day H.M. the revered Maryam-zamānī (his mother) came from Agra, and I acquired eternal good fortune from the blessing of waiting on her. I hope that the shadow of her bringing up and affection may be perennial on the head of this suppliant. As Ikrām K., s. Islām K., had performed the duties of faujdār of this neighbourhood in a proper manner, I bestowed on him the mansab of 1,500 personal and 1,000 horse, original and increased. Suhrāb‡ K., s. Mīrzā Rustam Ṣafavī, was promoted to the mansab of 1,000 personal and 300 horse.

On this day, going over in detail the buildings of the palace of the late King (Akbar), I showed them to my son, Shāh-Jahān. Inside of them a large and very clear reservoir of cut stone has been constructed, and is called the *Kapūr-talāo* (camphor tank). It is a square of 36 yards by 36,§ with

---

of *ba-sā'atī*. I think the meaning probably is that the same day which marked Jahāngīr's arrival at Fatḥpūr also marked Shāh-Jahān's birthday.

Tawallā is defined in the Bahar-i-'ajam as meaning to have friendship with anyone. It also says that it is used in the sense of *taqarrub*—*i.e.*, nearness. It may be therefore that Jahāngīr's line means "At a moment which nearly corresponded to two (hours)." *Taqwīm* would then mean established or fixed, and not a calendar. *Taqwīm kardan* is a phrase which means "to adjust, to arrange."

* Shāh Jahān was born on January 5, 1592, so that in January, 1619, he began to be in his 28th year—*i.e.*, he was 27 complete.

† That is, 120 according to Muhammadan ideas.

‡ Afterwards drowned in the Jhelam.

§ Text *dar'a*, MSS. *zirā'*. See text 298, account of fifteenth year, where a *dar'a* is defined. The *Ilāhī gaz* or *dara'* consisted of 40 digits (fingerbreadths), according to Jahāngīr. If the Kapūr tank be the one described in the Archæological Survey Reports, Vol. XVIII., for 1894, yards seem to be required here, for the tank is mentioned in the Report as being 95 feet 7 inches square. According to Jahāngīr, 34 krors odd of dams—*i.e.*, I presume, *fulūs*, in copper money, and

a depth of 4½ yards. By the order of that revered one, the officials of the public treasury had filled it with *fulūs* (copper coins) and rupees. It came to 34 krors, and 48 lakhs, and 46,000 dāms, and 1,679,400 rupees, or a total of 10,300,000 (one kror and three lakhs) according to Hindustani reckoning, and 343,000 *tūmān* according to Persian. For a long time the thirsty-lipped ones of the desert of desire were satisfied from that fountain of benignity.

On Sunday, the 1st Bahman, a reward of 1,000 *darb* (Rs. 500) was given to Ḥāfiẓ Nād 'Alī,* the reciter. For a long time past Muḥibb 'Alī, s. Budāgh† K. Chikanī, and Abū-l-Qāsim Gīlānī, whom the Ruler of Irān had blinded and driven into the desert of exile, have passed their days in ease under the refuge of this State. To each of them, according to his condition, an allowance for living had been granted. On this day they came from Agra, and had the good fortune to kiss the threshold, and each of them was presented with Rs. 1,000. The *Mubārak-shamba* entertainment was held in state in the palace, and my private servants were gladdened with cups of pleasure. Naṣru-llah, whom my son, Sulṭān

---

16 lakhs and 80,000 rupees in silver were poured into the tank, making a total of 1 kror and 3 lakhs of rupees, or 3 lakhs 43,000 *tūmāns*. Apparently the *tūmān*, which was a gold coin, was, in Jahāngīr's time, reckoned as worth 30 rupees, and Wollaston, in his Dictionary, says it was worth £3 in Shāh 'Abbās I.'s time. Jahāngīr's account of the tank should be compared with that given in the Akbar-nāma, III. 246 and 257, where the tank is called the Anūp-talāo, or the "Unequalled Tank."

In the text, difficulty has, I think, been made by the introduction of the word *kih* in p. 260, six lines from foot, and *bāshad* in the fifth line from the foot. These words make the sense to be that 34 krors odd of dams were only equal to 16 lahks odd of rupees. But this cannot be, for the dam was the fortieth part of a rupee, and so 34 krors of dams would be not far short of one kror—*i.e.*, 100 lakhs of rupees. The MSS. have not the *kih* and *bāshad* in question, and have only a conjunction after the word *dām*. Thirty-four krors odd of copper and 16 lakhs of silver were poured into the tank, making a total, in round numbers, of 1 kror, 3 lakhs of rupees. According to Abū-l-Faẓl gold was also thrown in.

* Text Yād 'Alī, but the MSS. have Nād. See also Blochmann, 508.

† This name is Bairām or Sirām in MSS. Chikanī may be a trade designation, and mean embroiderer, or worker in gold thread.

Parwīz, had sent to Court with the elephant Kūh-damān,* took his leave and returned. A copy (*jild*) of the *Jahāngīr-nāma*, together with a special tipchāq horse, were given to him to take to my son. On Sunday, the 8th, Kunwar Karan, son of Rānā Amar Singh, was presented with a horse, an elephant, a dress of honour, a jewelled *khapwa*, and a *phūl-kaṭāra*. I gave him leave to go to his jagir, and sent a horse with him for the Rānā. On the same day I went out sporting to Amānābād. As there was an order that no one should kill the antelope of that region, in the course of six years many antelope had come together, and they had grown very tame. On Thursday, the 12th, I returned to the palace, and on that day, according to custom, a feast of cups was prepared.

On the eve of Friday, the 13th (Bahman), I went to the mausoleum of the refuge of pardon, Shaikh Salīm Chishtī, a little concerning whose blessed qualities has been written in the preface† to this record of prosperity, and the *fātiḥa* was recited. Although the manifestation of miracles and wonders is not approved by the elect of the throne of God, and from humility and a feeling of their low rank (as saints) they avoid such display, yet occasionally in the excitement of ecstasy an appearance is manifested unintentionally and without control,‡ or for the sake of teaching someone the exhibition is made. Among these was this, that he before my birth gave my father the good news of the advent of this suppliant and of my two brothers. Again, one day my father incidentally asked him how old he was, and when would he depart to the abiding regions. He replied : " The glorious God knows what is secret and hidden." After much urgency he indicated this suppliant (Prince Salīm), and said : " When the Prince, by the instruction of a teacher or in any other way, shall commit something to memory and shall recite it, this will be a sign of my union with God." In consequence of this, His Majesty gave strict orders to all who were in attendance on me that no one should teach me anything in prose or verse. At length

* *Kūh-damān*, " hill-subduing."

† *dībācha*. Here meaning the early part of the Memoirs.

‡ The text has *bā* by mistake for *yā*.

when two years and seven months had passed away, it happened one day that one of the privileged* women was in the palace. She used to burn rue constantly in order to avert the evil eye, and on this pretext had access to me. She used to partake of the alms and charities. She found me alone and regardless of (or ignorant of) what had been said (by Akbar), she taught me this couplet:

> "O God, open the rosebud of hope
> Display a flower from the everlasting garden."†

I went to the Shaikh and repeated this couplet. He involuntarily rose up and hastened to wait on the King, and informed him of what had occurred. In accordance with Fate, the same night the traces of fever appeared, and the next day he sent someone to the King (with the request) to call Tān Sen Kalāwant, who was unequalled as a singer. Tān Sen, having gone to wait upon him, began to sing. After this he sent some one to call the King. When H.M. came, he said: "The promised time of union has come, and I must take leave of you." Taking his turban from his head, he placed it on mine, and said: "We have made Sulṭān Salīm our successor, and have made him over to God, the protector and preserver." Gradually his weakness increased, and the signs of passing‡ away became more evident, till he attained union with the "True Beloved."

One of the greatest monuments of my father's reign is this mosque and cemetery (*rauẓa*). Certainly they are exceedingly lofty and solid buildings. There is nothing like this mosque in any other country. It is all built of beautiful stone, and five lakhs of rupees were expended from the public treasury upon it. Quṭbu-d-dīn K. Kokaltāsh made the marble railing (*maḥjar*) round§ the cemetery, the flooring (*farsh*) of the

* *'aurāt-i-mustaḥaqqa.* Perhaps "pensioned women."

† These are the opening lines of Jāmī's Yūsuf and Zulaikhā (note by Mr. Rogers).

‡ Salīm Chishtī died on 29 Ramaẓān 979, or February 15, 1572. Jahāngīr was born on 17 Rabī' 1st, 977; and so he would be about two years and seven months old at the time of Salīm's death. See Beale and Khazīnatu-l-aṣfiyā, I. p. 435.

§ The conjunction *wa* in text, p. 262, line 16, is a mistake.

dome and portico, and these are not included in the five lakhs. The mosque has two great gateways. The one* towards the south is extremely lofty, and is very beautiful. The archway (*pīshtāq*) is 12 yards broad, 16 long, and 52 high. One must mount thirty-two steps to get to the top of it. The other gateway is smaller, and is towards the east. The length of the mosque from east to west, including the width of the walls, is 212 yards. Out of this, the *Maqṣūra* (the chancel) is 25½ yards, the middle is 15 yards by 15, the portico (*pīshtāq*) is 7 yards broad, 14 yards long, and 25 yards high. On each side of the large dome are two smaller domes 10 yards by 10. Then there is a veranda (*aiwān*) which is pillared. The breadth of the mosque from north to south is 172 yards. Round it are ninety verandas (*aiwān*) and eighty-four cells. The breadth of each cell is 4 yards,† and the length 5 yards. The verandas are 7½ yards broad. The courtyard (*ṣaḥn*) of the mosque, exclusive of the *maqṣūra*, and the verandas, and the gates, is 169 yards long and 143 yards broad. Above the verandas, the gates, and the mosque, small domes have been constructed, and on the eves of anniversaries and on holy days lamps are placed in these, and they are enveloped in coloured‡ cloths, so that they look like lamp-shades (?). Under the courtyard they have made a well, and they fill this with rainwater. As Fatḥpūr has little water, and what there is is bad, this well§ yields a sufficient supply for the

* This is the Buland Darwāza. It was built many years after the mosque. For an account of it, see Mr. Edmund Smith's Fatḥpūr Sikrī. The gateway is there said to be 134 feet high from the pavement and 176 feet from the roadway. The thirty-two steps mentioned in text must be those from the roadway to the gate. There are two flights of steps, and the total number, up to the top, is 123. The quadrangle or court is stated by Keene to be 433 feet by 366. Another statement (in the Archæological Report) is 438·9 by 359·10 feet. Salīm's tomb was erected in 1581 (988). It is 47 feet 11 inches each way.

† 4½, Iqbāl-nāma, 124.

‡ Text *aiwān*, but should be *alwān*, "coloured." See Iqbāl-nāma, 124.

§ Finch says: "Under the courtyard is a good tank of excellent water." He also speaks of the lake and of its being covered with the *singāra* (*Trapa bicornis*).

whole year for the members of the family (of Salīm Chishtī) and for the dervishes who are the *mujāwirs* (caretakers) of the mosque. Opposite the great entrance and towards the north-north-east is the tomb of the Shaikh. The middle dome is 7 yards, and round the dome is a portico of marble, and on the front side of this is a marble lattice. It is very beautiful. Opposite this tomb on the west, at a little distance, is another dome, in which are laid to rest the sons-in-law and sons of the Shaikh, such as Quṭbu-d-dīn K., Islām K., Mu'aẓẓam K.,* and others, who were all connected with this family, and rose to the position of Amirs and to lofty rank. Accordingly, the circumstances of each have been recorded in their places. At present the son of Islām K., who is distinguished by the title of Ikrām K., is the lord of the prayer-carpet. The signs of auspiciousness are manifest in him; I am much inclined to cherish him.

On Thursday, the 19th, I promoted 'Abdu-l-'Azīz K. to the mansab of 2,000 personal and 1,000 horse, and nominated him to the duty of taking the fort of Kāngṛa, and the overthrow of the ungrateful Sūraj Mal. I bestowed on him an elephant, a horse, and a dress of honour. Tursūn Bahādur was also dispatched on this duty, and his mansab was fixed at 1,200 personal and 450 horse. He was given a horse, and took his leave. As the house of I'timādu-d-daula was on the bank of a tank, and people praised it greatly as a delightful place and enchanting residence, at his request on Thursday, the 26th, an entertainment was held there. That pillar of the kingdom engaged in the dues of prostration and offerings, and prepared a grand meeting. At night, after eating food, I returned to the palace. On Thursday, the 3rd of the Divine month of Isfand-armuz, Sayyid 'Abdu-l-Wahhāb Bārha, who had done active service in Gujarat, was promoted to the mansab of 1,000 personal and 500 horse, and was honoured with the title of Dilīr K. On Saturday, the 12th, I went out to Amānābād for sport, and until Sunday, with the ladies,

* That is, Bāyazīd, a grandson of the saint. Ikrām K. is another name for Hūshang. His mother was Abū-l-Faẓl's sister. According to the Ma'āṣir, I. 120, he was a tyrant. According to local tradition, Quṭbu-d-dīn is buried in Bardwān near Shīr-afgan.

employed myself in the pleasure of hunting. On the eve of Thursday, the 27th* (17th), I returned to the palace.

By chance, on Tuesday, during the hunting, a string of pearls and rubies that Nūr-Jahān Begam had on her neck was broken, and a ruby of the value of Rs. 10,000 and a pearl worth Rs. 1,000 were lost. Although the huntsmen made every search for it on Wednesday, it did not fall into their hands. It occurred to me that as the name of the day was *Kam-s̲h̲amba*, it was impossible to find it on that day. On the contrary, as *Mubārak-s̲h̲amba* (Thursday) was always a lucky day for me, and had been blessed to me, the huntsmen on that day with but a little search found both in that trackless place (without head or foundation) and brought them to me. The best of coincidences was that on the same propitious day the entertainment for my lunar weighing and the feast of Basant-bārī (Spring festival) also took place, and the good news of the conquest of the fort of Mau and the defeat of that evil-fortuned Sūraj Mal arrived.

The particulars of this are that when Rāja Bikramājīt with the victorious army arrived in that region, the ill-fated Sūraj Mal desired to delay him for some days by trickery and babblement, but the aforesaid knew the real state of the case and did not pay attention to his words, but advanced with the foot of valour. That abandoned one, letting fall from his hand the thread of plan, neither planted the foot of intrepidity firmly for battle nor had the courage to defend the fort. After a slight struggle, and when many of his people had been slaughtered, he took to flight, and the forts of Mau† and Mahrī (?), which were the chief reliance of that ill-fated man, were both taken without difficulty. A country

* So in text, but ought to be the 17th.

† Mau was a Himalayan fort. Blochmann, 345. The text has *Mau u s̲h̲ahrī*, and so have the MSS. The Iqbāl-nāma has *Maud u Mahrī*, p. 124, and so has the Ma'āṣir U., II. 178. Evidently from what follows there were two places, unless one was the fort and the other the city. See also Tūzuk, 304, l. 10, which has pargana Maud Mahrī. In the Āyīn, Jarrett, II. 319, we have Mau and Nabah, and the next name in the list is Mahror. Gladwin has Mowd, and possibly we should translate "Mowd, a city on which he relied."

which he had held by hereditary right from his fathers was trodden under foot by the victorious troops, and he became a wanderer and a vagabond. He retired to the ravines of the hills, and cast the dust of ruin and contempt on the head of his Fortune. Rāja Bikramājīt, leaving his country behind, hastened in pursuit of him with the victorious army. When the state of affairs reached the royal ears, in reward for this becoming service I ordered drums for the Raja, and a fateful farman was issued from the Sovereign of Wrath that they should overthrow from their foundation the fort and buildings that had been erected by Sūraj Mal's father and himself, and leave not a trace of them on the face of the earth. A strange thing is that the unfortunate Sūraj Mal had a brother called Jagat Singh. When I promoted Sūraj Mal to the title of Raja, and made him an Amir, and gave him dominion, etc., without a partner or sharer, I, in order to please him, gave a small mansab to Jagat Singh, who did not get on well with him, and sent him to Bengal. This wretched one was passing his days in a poor condition far from his home, in contempt, and to the delight of his enemies, and waiting for some hidden aid, until by his good fortune this affair took place, and that unblessed one struck an axe on his own foot. Summoning Jagat Singh in all haste to Court, I honoured him with the title of Raja and the mansab of 1,000 personal and 500 horse, and bestowed 20,000 *darbs** on him out of the public treasury for his expenses. Giving him a jewelled khapwa, a robe of honour, a horse, and an elephant, I sent him to Rāja Bikramājīt, and issued a farman that if the aforesaid, by the guidance of a good destiny, should perform laudable service, and display loyalty, that country should be given over into his hand.†

As the praise of the garden of Nūr-manzil and the buildings that had been newly-erected there continually reached me, I

* The Iqbāl-nāma, 125, says Rs. 20,000 which would be 40,000 *darbs*.

† Jagat Singh afterwards became a rebel, joining Shāh-Jahān, as also did Rāja Bikramājīt, or Sundar. He rebelled also in Shāh-Jahān's reign, but was pardoned, and did good service in Kabul and Badakhshan. He died in Peshawar in 1055 (1645). See Ma'āṣir U., II. 238, and Pādishāh-nāma, II. 481.

on Monday mounted my steed, and went to the stage of Bustān-sarāy, and passed Tuesday in pleasure and at ease in that entrancing rose-garden. On the eve of Wednesday the garden of Nūr-manzil (the abode of light) was adorned by the alighting of the hosts of prosperity. This garden contains 330 *jarībs* (*bīghas*), according to the *Ilāhī gaz*. Around it there has been built a wall, lofty and broad, of bricks and cement, exceedingly strong. In the garden there is a lofty building and a residence, highly decorated. Pleasant reservoirs have been constructed, and outside the gate a large well has been made, from which thirty-two pairs of bullocks continually draw water. The canal passes through the garden, and pours water into the reservoirs. Besides this, there are other wells, the water of which is distributed to the reservoirs and plots. The beauty is increased by all kinds of fountains and cascades and there is a tank in the exact middle of the garden which is filled by rainwater. If by chance its water should fail in the extreme heat, they supplement it by water from the wells, so that it may always be full to the brim. Nearly Rs. 150,000 have been spent up to now on this garden, and it is still unfinished, and large sums will be expended in making avenues and laying down plants. It has also been settled that the middle garden shall be newly walled* round, and the channels for the coming and going of the water shall be made so strong that it may always remain full of water and the water shall not leak out in any way, and no damage accrue. It is possible that before it is complete nearly Rs. 200,000 will have been spent on it.

On Thursday, the 24th, Khwāja Jahān presented an offering of jewels, jewelled vessels, cloths, an elephant, and a horse, of the value of Rs. 150,000. Having made a selection from them, I gave him the remainder. Until Saturday I passed my time in that garden of delight in enjoyment. On the eve of Sunday, the 27th, I inclined the reins of returning towards

* It is *ḥaṣr* in text, but surely this is a mistake for *ḥafr*, and the meaning is that a new pit or well should be made in the middle of the garden. It appears to be *ḥafr* in MSS. The Nūr-manzil garden is the same as the Bāgh Dahra, and was near Agra. Blochmann, 499.

Fatḥpūr, and an order was given that the great Amirs, according to annual custom, should decorate the palace. On Monday, the 28th, I found that something had gone wrong with my eye. As it arose from too much blood, I ordered 'Alī Akbar, the surgeon, to open a vein. On the next day the benefit of this was apparent. I bestowed Rs. 1,000 on him. On Tuesday, the 29th, Muqarrab K. came from his native place, and had the good fortune to kiss the threshold, and I favoured him with many sorts of kindness.

THE FOURTEENTH NEW YEAR'S FEAST FROM THE AUSPICIOUS ACCESSION

On the morning of Thursday, the 4th of the month of Rabīʿu-l-ā<u>kh</u>ir, Hijrī 1028 (March 10, 1619), the world-enlightening sun entered his house of honour in Aries, and the fourteenth year of the reign of this suppliant commenced in all prosperity and happiness. On Thursday, the 1st of the New Year, my prosperous son, <u>Sh</u>āh-Jahān, who is the star of the forehead of accomplished desires, and the brilliancy of the brow of prosperity, prepared a grand entertainment, and presented me as offerings with a selection of the precious things of the age, and rareties and curiosities of every country. One of these is a ruby, weighing 22 *sur<u>kh</u>s,* of good colour, and water, and shape. The jewellers have valued it at Rs. 40,000. Another is a *Quṭbī** (?) ruby, in weight 3 *tānks,* and very delicate, valued at Rs. 40,000. Further, six pearls, one of them 1 *tānk* and 8 *sur<u>kh</u>s* in weight. The Vakils of my son had bought it in Gujarat for Rs. 25,000, and the five others for Rs. 33,000. Also one diamond, the price of which was Rs. 18,000. Also a jewelled *parda* (sash), a sword-hilt made in his own goldsmith's shop; most of the jewels he had himself set and cut. He had brought great dexterity to bear on the design. Its value was fixed as Rs. 50,000. The designs† were his own; no one else had up to this day thought

* Egyptian. Hitherto this has been read Quṭbī, but it really is, I think, Qibṭī, "Egyptian." Chardin, IV. 70, ed. 1723, says that the Persians state that the ruby of the East comes from Egypt. The etymology, however, is doubtful.

† Possibly the praise of <u>Sh</u>āh-Jahān's inventive powers refers to his arrangements for the orchestra. The *kuwarga* is defined in the Ain, Blochmann, 50, as a *damāma—i.e.,* a large drum. See illustra-

of them. Undoubtedly it was a fine piece of workmanship. There was also a pair of drums made of gold for playing the *mursal* (overture ?) with a whole orchestra—viz., *kuwarga, naqqāra, karanā, surnā*, etc.—whatever was required for the *naqqāra-khāna* (music-hall) of great princes, and all made of silver. At the auspicious hour at which I had seated myself on the throne of success these were all sounded. The whole of them came to a value of Rs. 65,000. Another was a seat for riding an elephant, called by moderns a howdah (*hauda*), made of gold, worth Rs. 30,000. Beside this there were two large elephants and five elephant-trappings of the offerings of Quṭbu-l-mulk, ruler of Golconda. The first elephant was named Dād-i-Ilāhī (the gift of God). As it entered the private elephant-house on New Year's Day, I gave it the name of *Nūr-i-Naurūz* (the Light of New Year's Day). In truth he is a grand elephant, and lacks nothing of size, beauty, and dignity. As he looked well to my eye, I mounted him and rode him into the courtyard of the palace. His value was fixed at Rs. 80,000, and the value of six* others at Rs. 20,000. Its golden trappings, consisting of golden chains, etc., my son had had made for the elephant Nūr-i-Naurūz, were worth Rs. 30,000. The second elephant, with silver housings, was also presented, with Rs. 10,000 more in various choice jewels. The *kurkarāqs*† of my son had also prepared and sent delicate cloths from Gujarat. If all details were to be written, it would take too long. Briefly, the whole of his offerings was of the value of Rs. 450,000. It is hoped that he will eat the fruit of long life and prosperity.

---

tion in Plate VIII. to Blochmann's Ain. The *karanā* and *surnā* are wind-instruments, and are also represented in Plate VIII. With regard to the *mursal*, Blochmann, p. 51, has : "The mursalī, which is the name of a tune played by the *mursil*." Apparently the *mursal* is the overture, or some introductory strain, and played only by a portion of the band.

* MS. No. 181 has ten instead of two as the number of elephants presented by Quṭbu-l-mulk, and this seems likely to be correct, else where do the six now mentioned come from ? But six should probably be eight.

† *Kurkarāqs.* See Blochmann, 87, *n.* 2, and p. 616. *Kurk* means fur, and *kurkarāqān* may be translated furriers.

On Friday, the 2nd, Shajā'at K. 'Arab, and Nūru-d-dīn Qulī, the kotwal, laid their offerings before me. On Saturday, the 3rd, Dārāb K., son of the Khān-khānān, and on Sunday, the 4th, Khān Jahān, prayed to be allowed to entertain me. Out of the latter's offerings I accepted one pearl, bought for Rs. 20,000, with other rareties, altogether of the value of Rs. 130,000, and presented him with the rest. On Monday, the 5th, Rāja Kishan Dās and Ḥākim K., on Tuesday, the 6th, Sardār K., and on Wednesday, the 7th, Muṣṭafā K. and Amānat K., presented their offerings. From each of these I took a trifle in order to dignify them. On Thursday, the 8th, I'timādu-d-daula, *Madār-ul-mulk* (the pivot of the country), having prepared a royal entertainment, begged to be allowed to receive me. In accepting this request his standing was raised. In fact, in decorating the assembly and the largeness of his offering, he had exceeded himself, and made many decorations, and illuminated all sides of the lake as far as the eye could reach, and decorated the streets both near and far with all kinds of lights and coloured lanterns. Among the offerings of that *Madār-us-salṭana* there was a throne of gold and silver, much ornamented and decorated, the supports of which were in the form of tigers. It had been completed with great assiduity in the space of three years, and was made at the cost of Rs. 450,000. This throne had been made by a skilful European of the name of Hunarmand (skilful), who had no rival in the arts of a goldsmith and a jeweller, and in all sorts of skill (*hunarmandī*). He had made it very well, and I gave him this name. In addition to the offerings he had brought for me, he offered the value of Rs. 100,000 in jewelled ornaments and cloths to the Begams and other ladies of the Palace. Without exaggeration, from the beginning of the reign of the late king (may the light of Allah be his testimony!) until now, which is the fourteenth year of the rule of this suppliant, not one of the great Amirs has presented such offerings. In fact, what comparison is there between him and others?

On this day Ikrām K., s. Islām K. was honoured with the mansab, original and increased, of 2,000 personal and 1,000 horse, and Anīrā'ī Singh-dalan with that of 2,000 personal and 1,600 horse, original and increased. On Friday, the 9th, I'tibār K. presented his offering, and on the same day Khān Daurān, having been presented with a horse and an elephant, took leave to go to the government of Patna.* His mansab, according to a previous rule, was fixed at 6,000 personal and 5,000 horse. On Saturday, the 10th, Fāẓil K., on Sunday, the 11th, Mīr Mīrān, on Monday, the 12th, I'tiqād K., on Tuesday, the 13th, Tātār K. and Anīrā'ī Singh-dalan, and on Wednesday, the 14th, Mīrzā Rājā Bhāo Singh, presented their offerings. Selecting from them what was delicate and new, I gave the remainder to them. On Thursday, the 15th, Āṣaf Khān prepared a grand assembly and a royal entertainment in his own house, which is a very fine and pleasant place, and begged to be allowed to receive me. At his request, giving him the dignity of acceptance, I went there with the ladies. That pillar of the kingdom looked on this as a bounty from the secret Giver, and in the increase of his offering and preparation of the entertainment displayed great magnificence. Of jewels of great price and delicate gold brocades and all sorts of gifts, that which was approved was selected, and I presented him with the remainder. Among the offerings was a ruby weighing 12½ *tānks*, which was bought for Rs. 125,000. The value of the offerings that were accepted was Rs. 167,000. On this day Khwāja Jahān was raised to the mansab of 5,000 personal and 2,500 horse.

Lashkar K., having come, by order, from the Deccan, had the honour of waiting on me. As I had determined, after the rainy season had passed and in the beginning of the good weather, to go to the perpetual spring garden of Kashmīr under the favour of Almighty God, it seemed right to me that the guardianship and administration of the fort and city of Agra and the faujdarship of the district, after the manner in which they had been held by Khān Jahān, should be entrusted to Lashkar K., and I honoured him with the good news Amānat K. was entrusted with the duty of superintendent of

* So in text, but it should be Tatta—*i.e.*, Sind. See Blochmann 378, *n.* 2, and also the Tūzuk, *infra*, p. 275.

branding (of horses) and of parading the troopers.* On Friday, the 16th, Khwāja Abū-l-Ḥasan, Chief Ba<u>khsh</u>ī, on Saturday, the 17th, Ṣādiq K. Ba<u>khsh</u>ī, on Sunday, the 18th, Irādat K., Chief Butler, and on Monday, the 19th, which was the day of the sun's culmination, 'Aẓudu-d-daula K., presented offerings, and I accepted from each of them, by way of exalting their dignity, what I approved. At this New Year the value of the accepted offerings of the servants of the Court came to Rs. 2,000,000. On the day of culmination I conferred on my auspicious son Sulṭān Parwīz† the mansab of 20,000 personal and 10,000 horse, original and increased. I'timādu-d-daula was promoted to that of 7,000 personal and horse. I selected 'Aẓudu-d-daula for the duty of tutor to the pupil of the eye of the Sultanate, <u>Sh</u>āh <u>Sh</u>ujā'. I hope that he (the latter) may endure for his natural term of life and may be one of the prosperous ones. Qāsim K. was raised to the mansab of 1,500 personal and 500 horse, and Bāqir K. to that of 1,000 personal and 400 horse. As Mahābat K. had asked for reinforcements, I appointed 500 *Aḥadī* horse to Bangash, and presented 'Izzat K., who had done approved service in that province, with a horse and a jewelled *khapwa*. At this time 'Abdu-s-Sattār‡ presented as an offering a compendium in the handwriting of the late king Humāyūn (may the lights of Allah be his testimony!), containing some prayers, an introduction to the science of astronomy, and other marvellous things, most of which he had studied and carried into practice. After reverently inspecting his auspicious handwriting, I felt a joy such as I had seldom experienced. I was exceedingly rejoiced, for, by God, no precious thing I have can be compared with this. In return I increased his mansab beyond what he had imagined possible, and gave him a present of Rs. 1,000. Hunarmand, the European who had made

* *Suwārān-i-<u>kh</u>ūd-maḥalla.* I do not know the exact force of the last two words. Possibly they are pleonastic. The word *maḥalla* is explained in Irvine A. of M. 46.

† The Iqbāl-nāma, 127, mentions that Parwīz came from Allahabad to pay his respects. See *infra*, Tūzuk, 268, and 273.

‡ Probably this is the friend of Father Jerome Xavier and the abridger of the Ẓafar-nāma. See Rieu, 177*b* and 1077*a*.

the jewelled throne, I presented with 3,000 *darb*, a horse and an elephant. I gave Rs. 1,000 to Khwāja Khāwand Maḥmūd, who is a pilgrim of the Path of the Khwājas, and is not void of dervishism and spirituality. Lashkar K. was promoted to the mansab of 3,000 personal and 2,000 horse, Ma'mūr K. to that of 900 personal and 450 horse, Khwājagī Ṭāhir to that of 800 personal and 300 horse, and Sayyid Aḥmad Qādirī to that of 800 and 60 horse. On Rāja Sārang Deo was conferred the mansab of 700 personal and 30 horse, on Mīr Khalīl-u-llah, s. 'Aẓudu-d-daula, that of 600 personal and 250 horse, on the eunuch Fīrūz K., that of 600 and 150 horse, on Khidmat Khān that of 550 and 130 horse, on Maḥram K. that of 500 and 120 horse, on 'Izzat K. that of 600 personal and 100 horse, on Rāy Newālī Dās, the accountant of the elephant department, that of 600 personal and 120 horse, on Rāy Mānī Dās, the superintendent of the Palace, that of 600 personal and 100 horse, on Nathmal and Jagmal, sons of Kishan Singh, that of 500 and 225 horse each. If the increase of mansab given to those of less than 500 were to be written in full it would be too long. Rs. 2,000 were given to Khiẓr K., who belonged* to Khandesh.

On Wednesday, the 21st, I went to Amānābād for the purpose of sport. Some days before this, in accordance with orders, Khwāja Jahān, and Qiyām K., the head huntsman, had chosen a wide plain for a *qamargha* hunt, and drawn an enclosure round it, and driven within it many antelope from the neighbouring plains. As I had vowed that I would hereafter not kill any living thing with my own hand, it occurred to me to take them all alive, and place them within the Chaugān (polo-ground) of Fathpur, so that I might both enjoy the pleasure of sport and that at the same time no harm should happen to them. I accordingly took 700 head and sent them to Fathpur. As the hour for entering the capital was near, I ordered Rāy Mān, *khidmatiyya*,† to put up a screen on two sides, like a lane, from the hunting-

* He was of the royal house of Khandesh.

† See Blochmann, 252, and *n.* 1. Jahāngīr himself saw 700 antelope taken, and Rāy Mān afterwards made a drive of 800 more.

place to the plain of Fathpur, and to drive the antelope there. About 800 antelope were sent in this way, or altogether 1,500. On the night of Wednesday, the 28th, marching from Amānābād, I halted in Būstān Sarāy, and on the eve of Thursday, the 29th, I halted at the Nūr-manzil garden.

On Friday, the 30th, the mother* of Shāh-Jahān attained the mercy of God. The next day I myself went to the house of that precious son, and having condoled with him in every way, took him with me to the palace. On Sunday, the 1st Urdībihisht, at the auspicious hour chosen by the astrologers and astronomers, I mounted a special elephant of the name of Dilīr, and in all prosperity and happiness entered the city. A great crowd of people, men and women, had collected together in the streets and bazaars, and at the gates and walls, expecting me. According to custom, I went on, scattering money on the way, to inside the palace. From the date on which the army of prosperity started for this happily terminated journey until now, when I returned in happiness and good fortune, it was five years, seven months, and nine days. At this time I ordered my son Sulṭān Parwīz that, as a long time had passed during which he had been deprived of waiting on me personally, or had been fortunate enough to pay his respects, if he were desirous of meeting me, he should come to Court. On the arrival of the gracious farmān, that son, considering the manifestation of this favour a gift from the hidden world, turned the face of his hope towards the sphere-resembling Court. At this time I gave away, as a means of livelihood, to Faqirs and deserving people 44,786 bighas of land, and two entire villages, with 320 ass-loads (*kharwār*, a weight) of grain from Kashmir, and seven ploughs† of land in Kabul. I hope that the Grace of the Bestower of desires and benevolence may be their daily lot.

* This was Jodh Bā'ī, d. the Mota (fat) Rāja. See Blochmann, 619.

† *Qulba*, ploughs. Here apparently used as a measure of land. But the expression is obscure. In Wilson's Glossary ḳulba is stated to be a measure of land in Sylhet, and equal to 1,008 cubits by 144. The corresponding Sanskrit word Sīr ("a plough") is used to mean land held by the landholder in his own possession.

One of the occurrences of this time is the revolt of Allāhdād, son of Jalāl, the Afghan. The details of this are that when Mahābat K. obtained leave to go and take possession of Bangash and overthrow the Afghans, from an idea that that wretch would do some service in return for the favours and kindness I had conferred on him, he prayed that he might take him with him. As the natural tendency of such ungrateful men, who do not recognize what is right, tends to enmity and malevolence, by way of precaution it was decided to send his son and brother to the Court that they might be as hostages. After the arrival there of his son and brother, I, by way of comforting them, did them all kinds of kindness, but, as they have said :

> "The blanket of fortune of anyone that has been woven black
> Cannot be whitened even by the waters of Zamzam and Kauṡar."

From the day on which he arrived in that country the signs of rascality and want of recognition of the right began to be apparent on the cheeks of his affairs, and Mahābat K., in order to control matters, did not loose from his hand the rope of forbearance until, at this time, he sent a force under the leadership of his son against a band of Afghans, and sent Allāhdād with him. When they reached the purposed place, from the enmity and malevolence of the aforesaid, that attack did not succceed, and they returned with their aim uncompleted. The evil-dispositioned Allāhdād, from a suspicion lest this time Mahābat K. should abandon his method of conciliation, and ascertain the real state of affairs, and that he should be caught in recompense for his evil deeds, lifted up the veil of reverence, and betrayed involuntarily the faithlessness to his salt, which he had till then concealed. When I heard from Mahābat K.'s letter the true state of affairs, I ordered them to imprison his son and brother in the fort of Gwalior. As it had happened (Jalāl Tārīkī), the father of this wretch had also fled from the service of the late king, and for years passed his time in thieving and highway robbery, until he was caught in the recompense of his own evil deeds. It is hoped that this rascal will also soon obtain the reward of his bad actions.

On Thursday, the 5th, Mān Singh, s. Rāwat Shankar, who was one of the auxiliaries of Bihar, was promoted to the mansab of 1,000 personal and 600 horse. I sent off 'Āqil K. to look after the cavalry,* and inquire into the corps of the mansabdars who had been appointed for duty in Bangash, and gave him an elephant. I sent as a gift to Mahābat K. a private dagger made after the Māzandarān fashion, along with Dūst Beg. The offering of Monday was given as a present to Maḥmūd Āb-dār, who from the time when I was a prince and the days of my childhood had served me. Mīrān (not Bīzan,† as in the printed book), son-in-law of Pāyanda K. Moghul, was promoted to the mansab of 700 personal and 450 horse. Muḥammad Ḥusain, brother of Khwāja Jahān, who was Bakhshi of Kāngra, was promoted to the mansab of 600 personal and 450 horse. On this day Tarbiyat K., who is one of the hereditary houseborn ones of this Court, and had been enrolled among the Amirs by reason‡ of his good disposition, died. He was not devoid of sluggishness (*nā-murādī*, literally want of desires) and self-indulgence (*salāmat-i-nafs*), and was a young man fond of pleasure (*'ayyāsh-ṭabī'at*). He wished to pass his whole life at ease, and was devoted to Hindu music and did not understand it badly. He was a man void of evil. Rāja Sūraj Singh was raised to the mansab of 2,000 personal and horse. To Karamu-llah, s. 'Alī Mardān K. Bahādur, Bāqir K., Faujdar of Multan, Malik Muḥibb Afghan, and Maktūb K. were given elephants. Sayyid Bāyazīd Bhakkarī, to whom was entrusted the charge of the fort of Bhakkar and the faujdarship of that region, was also honoured with an

* *Maḥalla.* Here used apparently for musters.

† Mr. Rogers corrects this to Mīrān on the authority of R.A.S., MS. It is, however, Bīzhan in I.O. MS., 181, and as Blochmann points out, Bīzan or Bīzhan is twice referred to in the Tūzuk, pp. 307, 309. He was son of Nād 'Alī Maidānī.

‡ I.O. MS. has "by favour of my rearing" (tarbiyat) and probably the words in text rather mean that he was promoted by virtue of Jahāngīr's liking for him, than that he was of good disposition. His real name was 'Abdu-r-Raḥīm. He was the son of Qā'im K., and his sister Ṣāliḥa Bānū was one of Jahāngīr's wives, and had the title of Pādishāh-Maḥall. Blochmann, 371. Before Nūr-Jahān she was the chief wife.

elephant. Amānu-llah, s. Mahābat K. was distinguished with the gift of a jewelled dagger. I gave elephants to Shaikh Aḥmad Hānsī, Shaikh 'Abdu-l-Laṭīf Sambhalī, the eunuch Firāsat K., and Rāy Kunwar Chand Mustaufī (auditor). Muḥammad Shafī' Bakhshi of the Panjāb, was raised to the mansab of 500 personal and 300 horse. The mansab of 500 personal and 150 horse was conferred on Mūnis, s. Mihtar* K. He (Mūnis) had charge of the fort of Kālinjar.

On this day arrived the news of the death of Shāh-nawāz K. s. the Commander-in-Chief Khān Khānān: It was the cause of distress of mind to me. At the time when that Ātālīq (Khān Khānān) took leave from waiting on me, it had been strictly impressed upon him that, as it had been repeatedly brought to my ear that Shāh-nawāz K. had been maddened with wine and drank immoderately, if there was truth in this it was a pity that he should destroy himself at his age. It was necessary that he should not leave him to his own way, but look after his case properly. If he could not leave his charge himself, he should write a clear report, so that, having summoned him into my presence, I might give the best order practicable under the circumstances. When he arrived at Burhanpur, having found Shāh-nawāz Khān very weak and low, he tried to make some remedy for him. After some days' confinement to bed (literally, lord of the carpet) he fell on the couch of powerlessness. Whatever remedies and plans the physicians employed were of no avail, and in the best time of his youth and prosperity, in the thirty-third year of his age, to the sorrow and grief of the world, he went to the place of the mercy and pardon of God. On hearing this unpleasant news I was greatly grieved, for in truth he was an intelligent youth and born in the house. He would have performed important services in this State, and left great traces behind him. Although this road is before all, and there is no escape for anyone out of the command of destiny, yet it appears sad to depart in this fashion. It is hoped he will be among those who are pardoned. I sent Rāja Sārang Deo, who was

* Mihtar K. was a very old servant, and died in the third year of Jahangir. Blochmann, 417.

one of my close attendants and is a tactful person, to the Ātālīq, and favoured and consoled him in every way. The mansab of 5,000 held by Shāh-nawāz I added on to those of his brothers and sons. To Dārāb, his younger brother, I gave the mansab of 5,000 personal, original and increased, and presented him with a dress of honour, an elephant, a horse, and a jewelled sword, and gave him leave to go to his father to fill, in place of Shāh-nawāz, the post of governor of Berar and Ahmadnagar. Raḥmān-dād, another brother, I promoted to the mansab of 2,000 and 800 horse. Manūchahr, s. Shāh-nawāz, was given the mansab of 2,000 personal and 1,000 horse. Ṭaghzal (Toghril ?), s. Shāh-nawāz* K. was promoted to the mansab of 1,000 personal and 500 horse. On Thursday, the 12th, Qāsim K., son-in-law of I'timādu-d-daula, was honoured with the favour of a standard. Asadu-llah, s. Sayyid Ḥājī, who had come with the intention of obtaining service, had the mansab bestowed on him of 500 personal and 100 horse. Ṣadr Jahān, son-in-law of the deceased Murtaẓā K., received that of 700 personal and 600 horse, and was appointed to the faujdarship of Sambhal, and, having had an elephant bestowed on him, I gave him leave. Bhārat Bandīla was also presented with the mansab of 600 personal and 400 horse, and had an elephant given him, and an elephant was bestowed on Sangrām, the Raja of Jammu.

In Ahmadabad I had two male *mārkhūr* goats. As I had not a female in my establishment to pair with them, it occurred to me that if I could pair them with Barbary goats, which they bring from Arabia, especially from the port of the city of Darkhar,† young of their form and qualities might be obtained. In short, I paired them with seven Barbary ewes, and after six months had elapsed each of the latter had a young one at Fathpur: there were four females and three males, very pleasing in appearance, of good shape and good colour. In their colour, those (kids) which resembled the

* Text wrongly has Shāh Nūr.

† This is the ancient Dhafur or Dofar on the south coast of Arabia now know nas Mirbāṭ. The proper spelling was Ẓafr. SeeRodhcrsc's Annotations to the History of Yemen, published by the Gibb Trust, Nos. 349, 578, and 836. See also d'Herbelot, 269, and Jarrett, III. 51.

male (*taka*, not *baka*, as in the printed copy) were dun-coloured with black stripes on their backs. Red,* indeed, appears to me a more pleasing colour than any other, and it is the mark of a better breed. Of their liveliness and laughable ways and their manner of gamboling and leaping, what can be written? Some of their ways are such that the mind derived uncontrolled pleasure from looking at them. It is notorious that painters cannot draw properly the motions of a kid. Granting that they may chance to draw the movements of an ordinary kid after a fashion, they certainly would have to acknowledge themselves at a loss how to draw the motions of these kids. When one month, or even twenty days old, they would leap up upon high places and throw themselves on to the ground in a way that if any other but a kid were to do so, not one limb would be left whole. As it pleased me, I ordered them always to be kept near me, and I gave each of them an appropriate name. I am much delighted with them, and pay great attention to bringing together mārkhūr males and well-bred she-goats. I desire to have many young ones from them, and that they may become well known among men. After their young shall have paired, most probably more delicate ones will be obtained. One of their peculiarities is that ordinary kids immediately they are born, and until they begin to suck, make a great bleating, whilst these, on the contrary, make no sound, and stand quite contented and without wailing. Perhaps their flesh would be very pleasant to the taste.

Before this, an order had been given that Muqarrab K., having been appointed to Bihar, should hasten off there. He came to Court in order to pay his respects before he repaired to his destination, and accordingly, on Thursday, the 2nd Khūrdād, an elephant with trappings, two horses, and a jewelled *khapwa* were conferred on him, and he took leave. Rs. 50,000 were given him as an advance of pay. On the same day Sardār Khān received a dress of honour, an elephant, and a horse, and obtained the Sarkar of Monghyr, which is in

* The description is rather obscure. Apparently Jahāngir regards *bamand* (dun- or bay-coloured) as equal to red (surkh).

the province of Bihar and Bengal, and took leave. Mīr Sharīf,* the Vakīl of Quṭbu-l-mulk, who was at Court, took leave. My fortunate son, Shāh-Jahān, sent with him the brother of Afẓal K., his Diwan. As Quṭbu-l-mulk had shown attachment and desire to please, and repeatedly importuned me for a portrait, I presented him, at his request, with my likeness, a jewelled *khapwa*, and a *phūl kaṭāra*. 24,000 *darb*, a jewelled dagger, a horse, and a dress of honour were also given to the aforesaid Mīr Sharīf. Fāẓil K., director of buildings, was advanced to the mansab of 1,000 personal and 500 horse, and Ḥakīm Rāgho Nāth to that of 600 personal and 60 horse. As at this time the anniversary of the late king (Akbar) occurred, Rs. 5,000 were handed over to some of my chief servants to divide among poor and deserving people. Ḥasan 'Alī K., jagirdar of the Sarkar of Monghyr, was honoured with the mansab of 2,500 personal and horse, and sent to the assistance of Ibrāhīm K. Fatḥ-jang, governor of the province of Bengal, and he was presented with a sword. As Mīrzā Sharafu-d-dīn Ḥusain Kāshgharī sacrificed his life on duty in Bangash, I promoted his son Ibrāhīm Ḥusain to the mansab of 1,000 personal and 500 horse. At this time Ibrāhīm K. constructed two boats,† which in the language of the country they call *Kosha*, one of gold and the other of silver, and sent them to me by way of offering. Undoubtedly, of their own kind they are the finest. One of these I gave to my son Shāh-Jahān. On Thursday, the 9th, Sādāt K. was granted the mansab of 1,000 personal and 60 horse. On this day 'Aẓudu-d-daula and Shajā'at K. 'Arab took leave for their jagirs. On this Thursday I presented Āṣaf K. with a jewelled *khapwa* and a *phūl kaṭāra*. As my fortunate son Sulṭān Parwīz proposed to come to Court, he asked for a special *nādirī* dress of honour, a *chīra*, and a *fota*, so that he might wear them and be distinguished on the day of meeting me and of having the good fortune to pay his respects. According to his request, I sent by the hand of his Vakil, Sharīf,

* Text has Mushrif.

† *Dū manzil kishtī* must surely mean "tray" here; or perhaps they were models. *Koshā* is a well-known Bengali name for a swift boat.

a sumptuous dress of honour with a *chīra* and a special sash. On Thursday, the 23rd, Mīrzā Wālī, son of the aunt of this suppliant, came by order from the Deccan, and had the good fortune to kiss the threshold. His father, Khwāja Ḥasan Khāldār (the freckled ?), was one of the Naqshbandī Khwājas. My uncle, Mīrzā Muḥammad Ḥakīm, gave his sister in marriage to the Khwāja. I heard much praise of the Khwāja from people: he had both good family and got on well with every one, and for a long time the management of the affairs of my uncle Mīrzā Muḥammad Ḥakīm had been in his hands, and he was on very good terms with him. Before the Mīrzā's death he had himself delivered* over the deposit of his life. Two sons survived him—viz., Mīrzā Badī'u-z-zamān and Mīrzā Wālī. M. Badī'u-z-zamān, after the death of the Mīrzā, ran away, and went to Mā-warā'a-n-nahr (Transoxania), and in that exile became a traveller on the road of non-existence. The Begam and Mīrzā Wālī came to the glorious Court, and H.M. (Akbar) behaved very kindly to the Begam. The Mīrzā also is a steady and sedate young man, not devoid of reasonableness and understanding. He is very skilled in the science of music. At this time it occurred to me to marry the daughter of the deceased Prince Dāniyāl to the Mīrzā, and my reason for sending for the Mīrzā to Court was this. This girl (Bulāqī Begam) is the offspring of the daughter of Qilīj Muḥammad K. It is hoped that the grace of striving to please and to serve, which is the means of good fortune and prosperity, may be his (M. Wālī's) lot and fortune.

On this day Sarbuland Rāy, who had been sent on duty to the Deccan, was promoted to the mansab of 2,500 personal and 1,500 horse.

At this time it was reported to me that a *Shayyād* (a loud talker, a cheat) of the name of Shaikh† Aḥmad had spread the

* Apparently Khwāja Ḥasan died in Badakhshān. Ma'āṣir, III., 459.

† This S. Aḥmad is a well-known man. He is mentioned in Beale as Aḥmad Sirhindī (Shaikh), and as having had the title of Mujaddid-i-Alf-i-Ṣānī, because he believed that he was the man of the second millenium. In other words, he claimed to be a Mahdī. He was s. 'Abdu-l-Wāḥid Fārūqī, and born in 1563. He died 29 November,

net of hypocrisy and deceit in Sirhind, and caught in it many of the apparent worshippers without spirituality, and had sent into every city and country one of his disciples, whom he called his deputy (k͟halīfa), and whom he considered more skilled than others in the adorning of shops (of deceit) and selling of religious knowledge, and in deceiving men. He had also written a number of idle tales to his disciples and his believers, and had made them into a book which he called *Maktūbāt* (letters). In that album (*Jung*) of absurdities many unprofitable things had been written that drag (people) into infidelity and impiety. Amongst these he had written in a letter as follows: "In the course of my travels I had come to the dwelling of the Two Lights (the Sun and Moon), and saw a very lofty and very splendid building. From there I passed to the abode of Discrimination (Fārūq), and from there I passed to the abode of Truth (Ṣiddīq), and to each I wrote a suitable explanation (or perhaps, of each I wrote a suitable description). From there I reached the abode of Love, and I beheld a brilliant dwelling. It had divers colours and lights and reflected glories. That is to say (God forgive us!—an exclamation of Jahāngīr's), I passed from the abode of the Vicegerents (k͟hulafā) and attained to the highest rank." There were other presumptuous expressions which it would be too long to write, and would be contrary to good manners. I according gave an order that they should bring him to the Court that is based on justice. According to order he came to pay his respects. To all that I asked him he could give no reasonable answer, and appeared to me to be extremely

1624, and is buried at Sirhind. The I.G. new edition, XXIII. 21., says there are two tombs in Sirhind known as those of the Master and the Disciple, and it may be that one of them is S. Aḥmad's, although the Gazetteer says they probably belong to the fourteenth century. There is also a reference to him in Rieu's Catalogue, III. 1058*a*., fol. 16. He belonged to the Naqs͟hbandi order, and one of his writings is called Majmū'atu-t-taṣawwuf. There is a very long account of him, and of his interviews with Jahāngīr in the K͟hazīnatu-l-Auliyā, I. 607, etc. It is said there that he was imprisoned for two years, and then released, and that he died on the last day of Ṣafar, 1035, November 20, 1625, at the age of sixty-three. Jahāngīr afterwards pardoned S. Aḥmad. See Tūzuk, 308, account of fifteenth year.

proud and self-satisfied, with all his ignorance. I considered the best thing for him would be that he should remain some time in the prison of correction until the heat of his temperament and confusion of his brain were somewhat quenched, and the excitement of the people also should subside. He was accordingly handed over to Anīrā'ī Singh-dalan to be imprisoned in Gwalior fort.

On Saturday, the 25th Khūrdād, my fortunate son Sulṭān Parwīz came from Allahabad, and with prostration at the threshold of the Khalifate illuminated the forehead of sincerity. After he had performed the ceremony of kissing the ground and been honoured with special favour, I bade him sit. He presented 2,000 muhars and 2,000 rupees by way of *nazr*, and made an offering of a diamond. As his elephants had not yet arrived, he would produce them on another occasion. He had brought with him to the Court, which is the asylum of the world, Rāja Kalyān, Zamindar of Ratanpūr, against whom this my son had by order sent an army, and had taken from him as an offering 80 elephants and Rs. 100,000. My son brought him with him, and he had the good fortune to kiss the threshold. Wazīr K., my son's Diwan who is one of the old servants of the Court, having had the good fortune to pay his respects to me, presented as offerings 28 elephants, male and female. Of these nine were accepted, and the rest bestowed on him.

As it had been represented to me that Muruwwat K., s. Iftikhār K., who was one born and bred up at this Court, had fought with a band of Maghs on the borders of Bengal and had sacrificed his life, I promoted Allāh-yār, his brother, to the mansab of 1,000 personal and 500 horse, and another brother to that of 400 personal and horse, so that those he had left behind should not be distressed. On Monday, the 3rd of the Divine month of Tīr, in the neighbourhood of the city four black bucks, a doe, and a fawn were taken. As I passed by the house of my fortunate son, Sulṭān Parwīz, he presented two tusked elephants with their trappings by way of offering; both were ordered to be placed in the private elephant-stud.

On Thursday, the 13th, Sayyid Ḥasan, the ambassador of

my happy brother, Shāh 'Abbās, ruler of Persia, having had the good fortune to kiss the threshold, produced a letter, together with a crystal drinking-cup, on the cover of which was a ruby. As it was given from excessive friendship and sincerity it was the cause of the increase of amity and good fellowship. On this day Fidā'ī K. was promoted to the mansab of 1,000 personal and 500 horse, and Naṣru-llah, s. Fatḥu-llah, in whose charge was the fort of Ambar, that of 1,500 personal and 400 horse. On Thursday, the 20th, Amānu-llah, s. Mahābat K., was promoted to the mansab of 1,500 personal and 800 horse. Having conferred on Wazīr K. the Diwanship of Bengal, I gave him a horse, a dress of honour, and a jewelled dagger. Elephants were given to Mīr Ḥusāmu-d-dīn and Zabar-dast K. On this day Ḥāfiẓ Ḥasan, a servant of Khān 'Ālam, came to Court with a precious letter from my brother Shāh 'Abbās, and a report from that pillar of the Sultanate (Khān 'Ālam). He laid before me a dagger the hilt of which was made of a fish's* tooth spotted with black, that my brother had given to Khān 'Ālam. As it was a great rarity, he (Khān 'Ālam) had sent it to me. I greatly approved of it; in fact, it is a rare present. I had never seen a spotted one until now, and I was much pleased.

On Thursday, the 27th, M. Wālī was promoted to the mansab of 2,000 personal and 1,000 horse. On the 24th, I gave 1,000 darbs as a present to Sayyid Ḥasan, the ambassador, and an elephant to 'Abdu-llah K. Bahādur Fīrūz-jang. On Thursday, the 2nd of the Divine month of Amurdād, a horse was presented to I'tibār K. 'Āqil K. was promoted to the mansab of 1,000 personal and 800 horse.

On the night of Saturday, the 4th of the Ilāhī month of Amurdād, corresponding with 15 Sha'bān, was the feast of the Shab-i-barāt. By order, they decorated and brought

* *Dandān-i-māhī*, explained in dictionary as the canine tooth of the Walrus (*Trichechus rosmarus*). But there is nothing black or piebald about walrus-teeth, and Jahāngīr would surely not admire greatly a kind of ivory which was inferior to that of the elephant. I incline to think that what is here meant is tortoise-shell. *Jauhar-dār* has two meanings—it may mean jewelled and also "striated." See Vullers, 542*a*.

before me on the river, boats with lamps and all kinds of fireworks. In truth, the lamps they had arranged appeared very pretty, and for a long time I enjoyed myself in going round and looking at them. On Tuesday, Mīrān,* s. Nād 'Alī Maidānī, who was one of the well-brought-up khanazads, was selected for the mansab of 700 personal and 500 horse, and Khwāja Zainu-d-dīn for that of 700 personal and 300 horse, and Khwāja Muḥsin for that of 700 personal and 100 horse. On Thursday, the 9th, I went to hunt at the village of Samūnagar. Passing my time pleasantly in going round and hunting on that pleasant plain until Monday, I returned on the eve of Tuesday to the palace. On Thursday, the 16th, Bishūtan, grandson of Shaikh Abū-l-Faẓl (the author), was promoted to the mansab of 700 personal and 350 horse. On this day I went round to see the garden of Gul-afshān, which is on the bank of the Jumna. On the way rain fell heavily and filled the mead with freshness and greenness. Pineapples had arrived at perfection, and I made a thorough inspection. Of the buildings that overlooked the river none† that I saw were without the charm of verdure and flowing water. These verses of Anwarī appeared appropriate to the place:

VERSE.

"'Tis a day of mirth and jollity,
A daily market of flowers and odours:
The earth-heaps are suffused with ambergris,
The zephyr sheds rose-water from his skirt,
From contact with the morning breeze the pool
Is roughened and pointed, like the edge of a file."

As this garden is in the charge of Khwāja Jahān, he presented me as offerings with some pieces of brocade of a new fashion they had lately brought for him from 'Irāq. Selecting what I approved of, I presented the remainder to him. He had arranged the garden well, and his mansab was ordered to be raised to 5,000 personal and 3,000 horse, original and increased.

* Apparently Mīrān is a mistake for Bīzhan. See *ante* and Blochmann. 508, and Tuzuk, 307. It is Bīzan in I.O. MS., 181.

† The buildings referred to are the garden-houses made by Khwāja Jahān in the Nūr-manzil garden.

A strange circumstance was that I was so much delighted with a jewelled dagger-hilt of piebald teeth which Khān 'Ālam had got from Shāh 'Abbās and sent to me (see *ante*), that I appointed several skilful men to go to Īrān and Tūrān to look for them and to be consistently searching for them, and to bring some from anywhere and any person, anyhow, and at any price. Many of my servants who knew my disposition, and dignified Amīrs in the course of their duty, engaged in the search. It happened that in this city a stupid stranger bought in the open bazaar a coloured tooth of great beauty and delicacy for a trifle; he believed that some time or other it had fallen into the fire, and that the black on it was the mark of burning! After some time he showed it to one of the carpenters on the establishment of my prosperous son Shāh-Jahān, desiring that he should take off a piece of the tooth in order to make a ring (*shast*), and pointed out that he should remove the marks of burning and the blacknesses, being ignorant that the blackness enhanced the value and price of the whiteness. Those moles and patches were what the tirewoman of destiny had given as an adornment of its beauty. The carpenter at once went to the Superintendent of his workshop, and gave him the good news that such a rare and precious thing, in search of which people were wandering and going long distances, and hastening to all corners and in all directions in various countries, had fallen for nothing into the hands of an ignorant man, who did not know its value. It could be easily and cheaply obtained from him. The Superintendent went off with him and immediately procured it, and next day produced it before my son. When my son Shāh-Jahān came to wait on me, he at first showed great delight, and after his brain had become free from the intoxication of the wine of joy, produced it, and greatly pleased me—

VERSE.

"Thy Time is happy in that thou hast made mine happy."

I invoked so many blessings on him that if one of them out of a hundred obtain acceptance, it will suffice for his spiritual and material well-being.

On this day Bahlīm K., one of the chief servants of 'Ādil K. came and waited on me. As he had chosen my service out of sincerity, I bestowed on him unstinted favours, and presented him with a dress of honour, a horse, a sword, and 10,000 darbs, with the mansab of 1,000 personal and 500 horse. At this time a petition came from Khān Daurān, stating that: "Your Majesty, from the perfection of kindness and knowledge of his worth, had appointed to the government of Thatta (Sind) an old slave, notwithstanding his great age and weak sight. As this weak old man was exceedingly bent and decrepit, and had not in him the ability to exert himself or to ride, he prays that he may be excused military service, and that he may be enrolled in the army of prayer." At his request, I ordered the chief Diwans to confirm him in the pargana of Khushāb,* with a revenue of 3,000,000 of dāms, and which he for a long time had held as a *tankhwāh* jagir, and which had become peopled and cultivated, by way of providing for his expenses, so that he might pass his time in easy circumstances. His eldest son, by name Shāh Muḥammad, was promoted to the mansab of 1,000 personal and 600 horse, his second son, Ya'qūb Beg, obtaining that of 700 personal and 350 horse. The third son, Asad Beg, was promoted to the mansab of 300 personal and 50 horse.

On Saturday, the 1st of the Divine month of Shahriwar, I sent dresses of honour for the rainy season to the Ātālīq Commander-in-Chief Khān-khānān Jān-sipār and the other great Amirs, who had been sent on duty to the Deccan, by the hand of Yazdān.†

As the purpose of visiting the eternal spring of the rose-garden of Kashmir was settled in my mind, I sent off Nūru-d-dīn Qulī to hasten on before, to repair as far as was possible the ups and downs of the Punch‡ route to it, and to prepare

* See Jarrett, II. 323; it was near the Jhelam. See also I.G., new edition, XV. 297. It is in the Shāhpūr district. The land-revenue of it was 2·4 lakhs of rupees in 1903-1904. 30 lakhs of dāms would be equal to Rs. 75,000. Khān Daurān's name was Shāh Beg K. The Ma'āṣir says his resignation was not altogether voluntary. See Blochmann, 378.

† In the MSS. the name is written Nardānī.

‡ The route from the South. See Jarrett, II. 347, *n.* 3.

it, so that the passage of laden beasts over difficult hilltops might be accomplished with ease, and that the men should not undergo labour and hardship. A large number of artificers, such as stone-cutters, carpenters, spadesmen, etc., were despatched with him, to whom an elephant was also given. On the eve of Thursday, the 13th, having gone to the garden of Nūr-manzil, I passed the time in enjoyment in that rose-garden of delight until Sunday, the 16th. Rāja Bikramājīt Baghela came from the fort of Māndpūr, which is his native place, and had the good fortune to kiss the threshold, and by way of offering presented an elephant and a jewelled plume. Maqṣūd K. was honoured with the mansab of 1,000 personal and 130 horse. On Thursday, the 20th, my son Shāh Parwīz produced two elephants as an offering, and they were ordered to be included in the private stud. On the 24th of the aforesaid month the feast of the solar weighing took place in the palace of Maryamu-z-zamānī, and my 51st year according to the solar months began in gladness and victory. It is hoped that the period of my life may be passed in obedience to God (to whom be glory !). To Sayyid Jalāl, s. Sayyid Muḥammad, the grandson (?) of Shāh 'Ālam Bukhārī, an account of whom has been written among the events of my Gujarat expedition, I gave leave to return. I gave him a female elephant for his riding, as well as his expenses. On the eve of Sunday,* the 30th, corresponding with the 14th Shawwāl, when the disk of the moon was perfect (at full moon) a moonlight feast was prepared in the buildings of the garden which overlook the River Jumna, and a very pleasant entertainment took place. On the 1st of the Divine month, out of the veined (*jauhar-dār*) spotted tooth (walrus) which my son Shāh-Jahān had given me as an offering, I ordered to be cut off sufficient for two dagger-hilts and a thumb-stall :† it came out of a beautiful colour and was very choice. I ordered the *Ustāds* (masters) Pūran and Kalyān, who had no rivals in the art of engraving,‡ to make dagger-hilts of a shape that

* I.O. MSS. have Monday.

† The word in text is *shashsat*. *Shast* is a thumbstall, but it may also mean a ring. See Blochmann, 166 and *n*. 1.

‡ *Khātam-bandī*. It also means "inlaying."

was approved at this time, and has become known as the Jahāngīrī fashion. At the same time the blade and the sheath and fastenings were given to skilful men, each of whom was unique in his age in his art. Truly, it was all carried out according to my wish. One hilt came out coloured in such a way as to create astonishment. It turned out of all the seven colours, and some of the flowers looked as if a skilful painter* had depicted them in black lines round it with a wonder-working pencil. In short, it was so delicate that I never wish it to be apart from me for a moment. Of all the gems of great price that are in the treasury I consider it the most precious. On Thursday I girded it auspiciously and with joy round my waist, and the masters who in their completion had exercised great skill and taken great pains were rewarded, Ustād Pūran with the gift of an elephant, a dress of honour, and a golden bracelet for the wrist, which the people of India call *Kara,*† and Kalyān with the title of 'Ajā'ib-dast (wondrous hand), and increased mansab, a dress of honour, and a jewelled bracelet (*pahūnchī*), and in the same way every one according to his circumstances and skill received favours.

As it had been represented to me that Amānu-llah, s. Mahābat K., having fought with the rebel Aḥdād, had defeated his army, and had made many of the Afghans—who are black-faced and black-hearted—the harvest of his blood-drinking sword, I sent him a special sword in order to dignify him.

On Saturday, the 5th, news came of the death of Rāja Sūraj Singh, who had died a natural death in the Deccan. He was the descendant of Māldeo, who was one of the principal Zamindars of Hindustan, and had a zamindari which equalled that of the Rānā, and he had even overcome him in one battle. There is a full account of him (Māldeo) in the Akbarnāma. Rāja Sūraj Singh, through the advantage of his being brought up by the late king (Akbar), and this suppliant

* *Bandu bān*. In I.O. MSS. it is *bandu bārān*. Perhaps "skilful painter" should be "the Painter of Creation."

† Should be *Karū*. See Herklots Qānūn-i-Islām, Appendix XXIV.

at the throne of God, reached high rank and great dignities. His territory surpassed that of his father or grandfather.* He had a son called Gaj Singh,† whom he entrusted with all his administrative affairs. As I knew him to be capable and worthy of favour, I promoted him to the mansab of 3,000 personal and 2,000 horse, with a standard and the title of Raja, and his younger brother to that of 500 personal and 250 horse, and gave him a jagir in his native country.

On Thursday, the 10th of Mihr, at the request of Āṣaf K., I went to his house built on the bank of the Jumna. He has erected a very fine bath-house (ḥammām), with which I was much delighted. After bathing, a feast of cups was held, and my private servants were made happy with cups of delight. Having chosen out of his offerings what I approved, I gave the remainder to him. What I took of his offering might be of the value of Rs. 30,000. Bāqir K., faujdar of Multan, was honoured with a standard.

Previously to this, according to order, they had planted trees on both sides from Agra as far as the River of Attock (the Indus), and had made an avenue, and in the same way from Agra to Bengal. I now ordered that from Agra to Lahore they should put up a pillar‡ (*mīl*) at every koss, to be the sign of a koss, and at every three koss make a well, so that wayfarers might travel in ease and contentment, and not endure hardships from thirst or the heat of the sun.

On Thursday, the 24th of Mihr, the festival of the Dasahrā was held. After the custom of India, they decorated the horses and produced them before me. After I had seen the horses they brought some of the elephants. As Mu'tamid K. on last New Year's Day had not made any offering, at this festival he presented a golden tablet (*takht*), a ruby ring, a

* *Nabīra* here cannot mean grandson, for Sūraj Singh, commonly called Sūr Singh, was fifth in descent from Maldeo (Blochmann, 359). Sūraj or Sūr was s. Rāy Rāy Singh of Bikaner. See Tod, who says Sūr Singh passed nearly all his life as an alien.

† Tod has much to say about Gaj Singh, but the account seems hardly trustworthy.

‡ The text, p. 277, has a representation of one of these milestones which was outside Delhi.

piece of coral (*bussad*), and other items. The tablet was beautifully made. The total value of the offering was Rs. 16,000. As he had brought the things from pure sincerity and loyalty, they were accepted. On this day Zabar-dast K. was promoted to the mansab of 1,000 personal and 400 horse. As the day of the Dasahrā had been fixed as the time of starting, I embarked on a boat with all happy omens and pleasure in the evening, and went on to my goal. I halted for eight days at the first stage that the men might come on, after making all preparations at leisure. Mahābat K. had sent apples from Bangash by runners (*dāk-chokī*). They arrived very fresh, and were of excellent flavour. I was greatly pleased in eating them. They cannot be compared with the *sīb-i-k͟hūb* ("the good* apples"?) of Kabul which I ate there, or with the Samarkand apples that they bring every year. For sweetness and delicacy of flavour they cannot be compared with either of the latter (*i.e.*, the Bangash apples were far better). I had until now never seen such delicate and delicious apples. They say that in Upper Bangash, near Lashkar-dara,† there is a village called Sīv Rām, in which there are three trees of this apple, and although they have made many trials, they have never found so good ones in any other place. I gave Sayyid Ḥasan, ambassador of my brother S͟hāh 'Abbās, a dish of these apples in order that he might tell me if there were any better apples in 'Irāq. He said: "In the whole of Persia the apples of Isfahan are preferred, and they are of the same quality as these."

On Thursday, the 1st of the Divine month of Ābān, I went on pilgrimage to the mausoleum of the late king (Akbar) (may the lights of Allah be his testimony!), and rubbed the head of supplication on the threshold, the abode of angels, and presented 100 muhars as nazar. All the Begams and other ladies, having sought the blessing of circulating round that shrine, which is the circling-place of angels, presented offerings. On the eve of Friday a lofty assembly was held

* Perhaps *sīb-i-k͟hūb* is the name of a kind of apple.

† I.O. MS. 181 has S͟hukr-darā and the name of the village as S͟hinwarān. The printed text has Sīwarān.

of the holy men (*Mashā'ikh*), the turbaned people (*arbāb-i-'amā'im—i.e.*, ecclesiastics, etc.), *Ḥuffāẓ* (those who recite the Qoran), and singing people, assembled in numbers, and practised ecstasies and religious dancing (*wajd* and *samā'*), to each of whom, according to the circumstances of his merit and skill, I gave a dress of honour, a *farjī*, and a shawl. The buildings of this blessed mausoleum have been made very lofty. At this time the money expended satisfied me, and was far more than it had previously been. (The MS.* here is clear, and the printed words wrong.)

On the 3rd, after four gharis of day had passed, I marched on from that stage, and having traversed 5½ koss by the river at four gharis of the day, arrived at the next stage. After midday I left the boat and caught seven partridges (*durrāj*). At the end of the day I gave Rs. 20,000 to Sayyid Ḥasan, the ambassador (of Persia), as a present, and a dress of honour of gold brocade with a jewelled *jīgha* (turban-ornament), and an elephant, and gave him leave to return, and sent for my brother with him a jewelled jug made in the shape of a cock, which could hold my usual stint of wine. It is hoped that it may reach its destination in safety. I gave leave to Lashkar K., who had been appointed to the defence and government of Agra, with a gift of a dress of honour, a horse, an elephant, drums, and a jewelled dagger. Ikrām K. was promoted to the mansab of 2,000 personal and 1,500 horse, and to the duty of faujdar of the Sarkār of Mewat. He is s. Islām K., who was the grandson of the venerable asylum of pardon Shaikh Salīm, whose excellency of person and approved disposition and connection in blessing with this illustrious family have been described in these pages with the pen of sincerity.

At this time I heard from a certain person whose words are adorned with the light of truth that at the time when I was sick and weak at Ajmir, before this evil news arrived

* Mr. Rogers here refers to the R.A.S. MS. The I.O. MSS. are not clear. Apparently what Jahāngīr says is: "On this occasion fresh items of expenditure occurred to me, and the former outlay was greatly increased." The word *taṣarrufāt* ("expenditure") is omitted in the printed copy.

in the province of Bengal, one day Islām K. was sitting in private, when he suddenly became unconscious. When he came to himself he said to one of his confidants, of the name of Bhīkan, that it had been shown him from the world of mysteries that the holy person of the Emperor had been attacked by sickness, and that the remedy for it was to sacrifice for him something that was exceedingly dear and precious to himself. It at first occurred to him to sacrifice for the head of the revered one his own son Hūshang, but as he was young in years and as yet had derived no profit from life, and not attained to the desire of his heart, he had compassion on him, and would sacrifice himself for his lord and master. He hoped that as this was from the bottom of his heart, and the sincerity of his being, it would be accepted at the throne of Allah. The arrow of prayer at once reached the target of acceptance, and he perceived himself afflicted with weakness and disease. Verily, verily, the disease increased till he reached the neighbourhood of the compassion of God (he died). The Great Physician bestowed from the hidden dispensary complete recovery on this suppliant. Although the late king (the lights of Allah be his testimony !), was much attached to the children and grandchildren of the Shaikhu-l-Islām, and bestowed favours on them all according to the capacity and aptitude of each, yet when the turn of rule came to this suppliant, they received great kindnesses in order to perform what was due to that revered one (Salīm Chishtī), and many of them attained to the high nobility, and were advanced to the posts of head of Subahs, as has been brought to record each in its own place.

As in this village the eunuch Hilāl K.,* who was one of my attendants from the time when I was prince, had built a *sarāy*, and made a garden, he made an offering to me. In order to dignify him I took a trifle from him. After marching four stages from this halting-place, the army of prosperity encamped outside Mathura. On Thursday, the 8th, I went to see Bindrāban and the idol temples of that place.

* The village must be Hilalabad, near Rankatta (Blochmann, 332).

Although* in the time of the late king the Rajput nobles had built temples after their fashion, and ornamented them highly on the outside, inside them bats and owls (*abābīl*) had made their abode to such an extent, that on account of the malodours one could not breathe.

VERSE.

"Outside, like an infidel's grave, full of cracks,†
Inside, the anger of God, the honoured and glorious."

On this day Mukhliṣ K., according to order, came from Bengal, and had the good fortune to kiss the threshold. He gave 100 muhars and 100 rupees as nazar, and by way of offering, a ruby and jewelled aigrette (ṭurra). On Friday, the 9th, Rs. 600,000 of treasure for the maintenance (*ẕakhīra*) of the fort of Asir were sent to the Commander-in-Chief, Khān-khānān.

In the foregoing pages, something has been written about Gosā'īn Jadrūp,‡ who lived as a hermit in Ujain. At this time he changed his residence to Mathura, which is one of the greatest places of worship of the Hindus, and employed himself in the worship of the true God on the bank of the Jumna. As I valued his society, I hastened to wait on him, and for a long time enjoyed his company without the presence of any stranger. In truth, his existence is a great gain to me: one can be greatly benefited and delighted.

On Saturday, the 10th, the huntsmen represented that there was in that neighbourhood a tiger that greatly troubled

* Jahāngīr says nothing about the permission that he gave to Bīr Singh Deo—as a reward for murdering Abū-l-Fazl—to build a very splendid temple at Mathura. It was destroyed by Aurangzīb. See Growse's "Mathura."

† Text *ḥalal*, which means "weakness," or *ḥulal* ("striped garments"). But according to the MSS., the true reading is *khalal*, which means "a crack" and also "corruption."

‡ The Iqbāl-nāma, 128, calls him Achadrūp, and says that the Khan A'ẓam went privately to him and begged him to use his influence with Jahāngīr for the release of Khusrau. Achadrūp spoke accordingly, and Khusrau was released and allowed to pay his respects. See *infra* for account of his release. After Jadrūp removed to Mathura, he was cruelly beaten by Ḥākim Beg. See Ma'āṣiru-l-Umarā, I. 576.

and injured the ryots and wayfarers. I immediately ordered them to bring together a number of elephants and surround the forest and at the end of the day myself rode out with my ladies. As I had vowed that I would not injure any living thing with my own hand, I told Nūr-Jahān* to shoot at him. An elephant is not at ease when it smells a tiger, and is continually in movement, and to hit with a gun from a litter (*'imārī*) is a very difficult matter, insomuch that Mīrzā Rustam, who, after me, is unequalled in shooting, has several times missed three or four shots from an elephant. Yet Nūr-Jahān B. so hit the tiger with one shot that it was immediately killed.

On Monday, the 12th, my desire to see the Gosā'īn Jadrūp again increased, and hastening to his hut, without ceremony, I enjoyed his society. Sublime words were spoken between us. God Almighty has granted him an unusual grace, a lofty understanding, an exalted nature, and sharp intellectual powers, with a God-given knowledge and a heart free from the attachments of the world, so that, putting behind his back the world and all that is in it, he sits content in the corner of solitude and without wants. He has chosen of worldly goods half a *gaz* of old cotton (*kirpās*) like a woman's veil, and a piece of earthenware from which to drink water, and in winter and summer and the rainy season lives naked and with his head and feet bare. He has made a hole in which he can turn round with a hundred difficulties and tortures, with a passage such that a suckling could hardly be put through it. These two or three couplets of Ḥakīm Sanā'ī (may God have mercy on him !) appeared appropriate :

VERSE.†

"Luqmān had a narrow hut,
Like the hollow of a flute or the bosom of a harp.
A noodle put the question to him—
'What is this house—two feet and a span ?'
Hotly and with tears the sage replied—
'Ample for him who has to die.'"

---

* Elliot, VI. 367.

† Luqmān is the Eastern Æsop, and there is much about him in D'Herbelot. In the second line the word translated "hollow" is

On Wednesday, the 14th, I again went to visit the Gosā'īn and bade him good-bye. Undoubtedly parting from him

---

gulūgāh, literally "throat place," and the word for bosom is *sīna*, the whole expression being *sīna-i-chang*. Chang is a harp or lyre, and apparently the expression refers to the narrowness of the space between the horns of a lyre (*chang*, which appears to be the Jew's harp), or the sides of a harp. The fourth line is obscure, and the version in text seems corrupt. The words *shash bidast dū pāy* seem unintelligible. They, however, occur in I.O. MS. 181, f. 161*a*, and in I.O. MS. 305, f. 225*a*. The only difference is that they have a conjunction after *bidast*. On the other hand, the Iqbāl-nāma, which inserts the lines into the record of the eleventh year, has, at p. 95, a different reading for the fourth line. The words there are *khāna yak bidast u sih pay*. *Bidast* is given in Richardson, and the Farhang-i-Rashīdī as meaning a span, so the line as given in the Iqbāl-nāma may mean 3 feet and 1 span. The author of the Iqbāl-nāma was so struck with the verse of Ḥakīm Sanā'ī and the appearance of Jadrūp's dwelling, that he composed a *maṣnavī* on the subject, which he gives at pp. 95, 96. There is a third version in Daulat Shāh's anthology, p. 97 of Professor Browne's edition. There, in the second line we, have *ḥalqa* ("ring"), or perhaps "plectrum" instead of *sīna*. We have also two lines not given in the Tūzuk or the Iqbāl-nāma, and the line containing the noodle's question is given thus : "Kīn chih jāyast yak pūst u dū pay."

"What place is this, one skin (?) and two feet."

As if the meaning was that Luqmān lived in a tent propped up by two sticks. In the first line, also, we have *wiṣāqī* instead of *kurīchī*.

The lines may be versified thus :

"Luqmān's cell was small and narrow to boot,
Like the throat of a pipe, or the breast of a lute.
A foolish one said to the grand old man—
'What house is this—three feet and six span ?'
With tears and emotion the sage made reply—
'Ample for him whose task is to die.'"

In the Nawalkishor edition of Ḥakīm Sanā'ī's poem the lines are entered as in the seventh book of the Ḥadīqa, but in two B.M. MSS. (Add. 25,329, f. 145*a*, and Or. 358, f. 172*b*), they are placed in the fifth book. Both of these MSS. have *bidast*, apparently, and Add. 25,329, has *shash* ("six"), but Or. 358 has *shass*. There is such a word, meaning hard ground. Both MSS. have *sih* ("three"). *Bidast* may properly be *bad-pusht* ("bad-backed"), or it may be *bad-past* ("bad and mean"). The reference in verse may be rather to the curvature of the *chang* (Arabic, *ṣanj*) than to its narrowness, for Jamī speaks of the back "being bent like a harp."

weighed upon my mind, that desires the truth. On Thursday the 15th, I marched and pitched near Brindāban. At this stage my fortunate son Sulṭān Parwīz took leave of me for Allahabad, and went to his jagir. I had intended that he should accompany me on this expedition, but as he had already shown symptoms of distress, I could not avoid letting him go. I presented him with a tipchāq horse, a waist dagger with a veined (*jauhar-dār*) walrus-tooth (hilt), and a sword and special shield. I hope he will come again soon, and have the good fortune of my presence. As the period of Khusrau's imprisonment had been a long one, it seemed to me that to keep him longer in confinement and deprive him of the good fortune of waiting on me, would be wanting in kindness. I accordingly sent* for him and bade him salute me. Once again the marks of his offences were washed with the pure water of forgiveness, and the dust of disgrace and humiliation was rubbed off his brow. I hope that the blessing of pleasing me, and the grace of service may be his lot.

On Friday, the 16th, I gave leave to Mukhliṣ K., whom I had sent for to take up the duties of diwan to Shāh Parwīz, and I gave him the rank he had† had in Bengal—viz., 2,000 with 700 horse. On Saturday I halted. At this stage Sayyid Niẓām s. Mīr Mīrān Ṣadr Jahān, who was faujdar of Kanauj, waited upon me, and presented two elephants, and some hawks. I accepted one elephant and a pair of hawks. On Sunday, the 18th, we marched. At this time the King of Persia had sent with Parī Beg Mīr Shikār (chief hunstman) one falcon (shunqār) of good colour. There was another which had been given to the Khān 'Ālam. This one was sent along with the Shāhī falcon (*i.e.*, the one intended for Jahāngīr), and it died on the road. The Shāhī falcon, too, got mauled by a cat owing to the carelessness of the Mīr Shikār. Though it was brought to Court, it did not live more than a week.

* Compare Price, 123.

† Ba *dustūrī* kih dar Bangāla dāsht.

I think this must mean that his men were allowed the Bengal batta, or exceptional allowance, which used to be 50 p.c. of pay elsewhere. See A.N., III. 293, the eighth reason for the rebellion.

What can I write* of the beauty and colour of this falcon? There were many beautiful black markings on each wing, and back, and sides. As it was something out of the common, I ordered Ustād Manṣūr, who has the title of *Nādiru-l-'aṣr* (wonder of the age) to paint and preserve† its likeness. I gave the Mīr Shikār Rs. 2,000 and dismissed him.

In my father's reign (the light of God be his testimony!) the weight of the seer was 30 dams.‡ About this time it came into my mind: "Why should I act contrary to his rules?" It would be better to have it still of 30 dams. One day Gosā'īn Jadrūp said that in the book of the Vedas, which the lords of his faith had written, the weight of the *sīr* was 36 dams. "As from the coincidences of the hidden world your order has fallen in with what is laid down in our book, if it be fixed at 36 dams, it will be well." It was ordered that hereafter throughout the whole territory it should be 36 dams.

On Monday, the 19th, I marched. A horse and dress of honour were given to Rāja Bhāo Singh, who had been ordered to the support of the army of the Deccan. From this day, till Wednesday, the 28th, I made successive marches. On Thursday, the 29th, Delhi, the abode of blessings, was adorned

* This passage has been translated by Colonel Phillott in the A.S.B.J. for February, 1907, p. 113. There is something wrong in the text. Khān 'Ālam certainly did not die on the road (see Blochmann, 513), for he waited upon Jahāngīr at Kalān ūr (Tūzuk, 284); nor did the Mīr Shikār, for Jahāngīr says he gave him a present and dismissed him. I presume, therefore, that the word "aforesaid" refers to Khān 'Ālam's hawk.

† *Nigāh-dārad.* Perhaps this means that the painter was afterwards to stuff the bird.

‡ This is an obscure passage, and Jadrūp's reference to the mention of *dāms* in the Vedas is curious, for *dām* is said to be derived from the Greek drachma. However, it appears from the Āyīn (Blochmann, 31), that the dam, though in value only the fortieth part of a rupee, weighed 5 *tānks* or 1 *tolā*, 8 *māshas*, 7 *surkhs*. The rupee, we are told there, weighed 11½ mashas—*i.e.*, half a masha less than a tola. Consequently the dam weighed over 20 mashas, and so was not far from being equal in weight to 2 rupees. The weight of a seer varied, and it may be 30 or 36 copper dams were reckoned as equal to a seer. By dam Jahangir probably meant *paisā*, or double *paisā*. According to Gladwin, 3½ tanks are by jeweller's weights = one tolā, and a tank is 70·112 grs. Troy.

by the alighting of the army of good fortune. At first I hastened with my children and the ladies on a visit to the enlightened shrine of Humāyūn (may the lights of God be his testimony!), and having made our offerings there, went off to circumambulate the blessed mausoleum of the king of holy men (Shaikh Nizāmu-d-dīn Chishtī), and strengthened my courage, and at the end of the day alighted at the palace, which had been got ready in Salīmgarh. On Friday, the 30th, I halted. As they had at this time preserved the hunting-place of the pargana of Pālam, according to order, it was represented that a great number of antelope had collected there. Accordingly, on the 1st of the Divine month of Āzar I started to hunt* with cheetahs. At the end of the day, during the hunt, much hail fell of the size of apples, and made the air very cold. On this day three antelope were caught. On Sunday, the 2nd, I hunted 46 antelope, and on Monday, the 3rd, 24 antelope were caught with cheetahs. My son Shāh-Jahān killed two antelope with his gun. On Tuesday, the 4th, five antelope were caught. On Wednesday, the 5th, 27 antelope were caught. On Thursday, the 6th, Sayyid Bahwa Bukhārī, who was in charge of the government of Delhi, made an offering of three elephants and eighteen horses, and other things. One elephant and other things were accepted, and I gave the rest to him. Hāshim of Khost, faujdar of some parganas in Mewāt, had the honour of kissing the threshold. I employed myself within the limits of Pālam until Thursday, the 13th, in hunting with cheetahs. In the space of twelve days 426 antelopes were caught, and I returned to Delhi. I had heard, when in attendance on my father, that it is impossible for an antelope that has escaped from the grasp of a cheetah to live, although it has not been injured by its claws. In this hunt I, in order to ascertain the fact, released several antelopes of handsome appearance and strong bodies, before they had received any wounds from teeth or claws, and ordered them to be kept in my presence, and that they should be taken the

* As stated below, the antelope which were caught all eventually died.

greatest care of. For a whole day and night they remained at ease in their natural conditions : on the second day a change was observed, and they threw about their legs as if they were drunk, without any reason, and fell down and rose up. However much *tiryāq-i-fārūqī* (preparation of opium) and other suitable medicines were administered to them, they had no effect, and when one watch had passed in this condition, they died.

On this day the bad news arrived that the eldest son of Shāh Parwīz had died at Agra. As he was somewhat grown-up,* and was very attached and affectionate towards his father, the latter was exceedingly grieved and wounded at heart at this event, and great bewilderment and weakness manifested themselves in him. In order to console and please him, I sent him gracious letters, and covered over the deadly wound of his heart with the balm of affection and kindness. I hope that God, the great and glorious, may grant him patience and resignation, for in this kind of calamities there can be no better driver away of grief than endurance and resignation.

On Friday, the 14th, at the request of Āqā† Āqāyān, I went to her house. On account of her previous service and her hereditary attachment to this illustrious family, when the late king made me a married man, he took her from my sister Shāh-zāda Khānam, and placed her in charge of my Zanana. It is 33 years from that date that she has been in my service, and I esteem her greatly, for she has served me with sincerity. In no journey or expedition had she of her own will remained absent from attendance on me. When she felt her increasing age, she requested me to order her to remain at Delhi, and to spend the remainder of her life in prayer for me, for she had no longer the power to move about, and found it a great hardship and trouble to come

* Text *gul-rang*, which seems unintelligible. No. 181 MS. has *kalānak* ("somewhat grown-up"). The child was presumably the Sultan Dūr-andīsh, born at the end of the ninth year (Tūzuk, 137), and so was now about five years old. Gul-rang occurs in B.M. MS., and may mean "ruddy."

† Text has Āghā-i-Āghāmān. The MSS. have Āqā Āqāyān ("Agha of Aghas").

and go (as she used). One of her felicities was that she was of the same age* as 'Arsh-āshyānī (Akbar). In brief, with a view to giving her rest, I ordered her to remainat Delhi, and in that place she had made for herself a garden, a saray, and a tomb, in the constructing which she has employed herself for some time past. In short, to please this ancient servitor, I went to her house, and strictly ordered Sayyid Bahwa, the governor of the city, to serve and guard her in such a manner that no dust from any road of vexation might settle on the hem of her contentment.

On this day Rāja Kishan Dās was promoted to the mansab of 2,000 personal and 300 horse, original and increased. As Sayyid Bahwa† had performed satisfactorily the duties of faujdar of Delhi, and the people of the place were much pleased with his excellent conduct, according to previous custom, the protection and administration of the city of Delhi and the faujdarship of the surrounding country were entrusted to him, and he was promoted to the mansab of 1,000 personal and 600 horse, original and increased, and he was presented with an elephant, and allowed to take leave. On Saturday, the 15th, I honoured Mīrzā Wālī with the mansab of 2,000 and 1,000 horse, and presenting him with a standard and an elephant, appointed him to the Deccan. Shaikh 'Abdu-l-Ḥaqq Dihlawī,‡ who was a pious and estimable man, had the good fortune to pay his respects to me. He had composed a book containing the biographies of the Shaikhs of India, and produced it to me. He had endured some hardships, and for a long time had lived in Delhi in seclusion, and the practice of reliance on God, and of asceticism. He is a very worthy man, and his company is not without pleasure (for me). Bestowing various kinds of kindnesses on him, I dismissed him.

On Sunday, the 16th, I marched from Delhi, and on Friday,

* Akbar was born in October, 1542, so she was now seventy-seven years old.

† Sayyid Bahwa is commonly known as Dīn-dār K. Bukhārī, and is described under that name in the Ma'āṣir, II. 23.

‡ Elliot, VI. 366, and Rieu, I. 14 and 355. The book is called Akhbāru-l-Akhyār, id.

the 21st, halted in the pargana of Kairāna.* This pargana is the native place of Muqarrab K. Its climate is equable and its soil good. Muqarrab had made buildings and gardens there. As I had often heard praise of his garden, I wished much to see it. On Saturday, the 22nd, I and my ladies were much pleased in going round it. Truly, it is a very fine and enjoyable garden. Within a masonry (*pukhta*, pucca) wall, flower-beds have been laid out to the extent of 140 bighas. In the middle of the garden he has constructed a pond, in length 220 yards, and in breadth 200 yards. In the middle of the pond is a *māh-tāb* terrace (for use in moonlight) 22 yards square. There is no kind of tree belonging to a warm or cold climate that is not to be found in it. Of fruit-bearing trees belonging to Persia I saw green pistachio-trees, and cypresses of graceful form, such as I have never seen before. I ordered the cypresses to be counted, and they came to 300. All round the pond suitable buildings have been begun and are in progress.

On Monday, the 24th, Khanjar K., in whose charge is the Fort of Ahmadnagar, was promoted to the mansab of 2,500 personal and 1,600 horse. On Wednesday, the 26th, the Giver of Bounties gave my son Shāh-Jahān a son by the daughter of Āṣaf Khān. He presented an offering of 1,000 muhars, and begged for a name for him. I gave him the name of Umīd-bakhsh (bestower of hope). I hope his advent † may be auspicious to this State. On Thursday, the 27th, I halted. In these few days I was delighted with hawking the *jarz* ‡ (bustard or florican) and *tūgh-dārī* (also a kind of bustard). I ordered the *jarz-i-būr* (the red bustard ?) to be weighed. It came to $2\frac{1}{4}$ *Jahāngīrī* sirs, and the variegated (*ablaq*) one to $2\frac{1}{8}$ sirs. The large tūgh-dārī was $\frac{1}{4}$ sir heavier than the jarz-i-būr. On Thursday, the 5th of the Divine month of Day, I left the boat at Akbarpur, and

* In Sarkār Sahāranpur. Elliot, Supp. Gloss., II. 129. I.G. new edition, XIV. 287.

† The child was born at Sirhind on Wednesday, 11 Muḥarram, 1029 (December 8, 1619), and died at Burhānpur in Rabī'u-ṣ-ṣānī, 1031 (February-March), 1622. Pādishāh-nāma, I. 392.

‡ See Erskine's Bābur, p. 321.

the victorious army then marched by land. From Agra to this halting-place, which is situated within two koss of the pargana of Buṛiya,* is by river 123 koss or 91 koss by road. I did it in 34 marches and 17 halts. In addition to this I delayed a week in leaving the city, and 12 days in sporting in Pālam : altogether (I took) 70 days. On this day Jahāngīr Qulī K. came from Bihār, and had the good fortune to pay his respects. He presented 100 muhars and Rs. 100. From the last Thursday to Wednesday, the 11th, I marched every day. On Thursday, the 12th, I was pleased with going round to see the garden of Sirhind. It is one of the old gardens, and has old trees in it. It has not the freshness it formerly had, but it is still valuable. Khwāja Waisī, who is well acquainted with agriculture and buildings, was appointed the *karorī* of Sirhind for the purpose of keeping the garden in order. I had sent him off from Agra before I marched from the capital, and he had put it somewhat in order. I strictly enjoined him again that he should remove all the old trees that had no freshness in them, and put in fresh plants, to clean up the *'irqbandī*† (it is *'irāq-bandī* in the text. The word does not occur in the B.M. MS. but is in the I.O. MS.), and repair the old buildings, and erect other buildings in the shape of baths, etc., in fitting places. On this date Dūst Beg, who was one of the auxiliaries of 'Abdullah K., was promoted to the mansab of 700 personal and 50 horse, Muẓaffar Ḥusain, s. Wazīr K., to that of 600 personal and 300 horse. Shaikh Qāsim was sent to duty in the Deccan. On Thursday, the 19th, at the request of my auspicious son Shāh-Jahān, I went to his house. On account of the birth of the son that God Almighty had bestowed on him a grand entertainment was given, and he presented offerings. Among these was a short, broad sword‡ (*shamshīr-i-nīmcha*), which

* Perhaps this is Birū'ī in Sambhal, Jarrett, II. 200. Or it may be the Mīyānī Nūriya of Jarrett, II. 317.

† To clear the roots ? Or is it to let the sap flow ? Or is *'irāq-bandī* right, meaning footpaths ? Jahāngīr's order then would be to clear out the brick footpaths.

‡ *Yak-āwīz.* Defined in Vullers as a short, broad sword, and also as a two-edged knife. See Vullers, 1519*a*. The weapon is described in text as *shamshīr-i-nīmcha-i-yak-āwīz.*

was of Venetian workmanship. The hilt and fastenings were made of a sapphire* cut in Europe: in short, it had been beautifully made. Another offering was an elephant which the Raja of Baglāna had presented to my son in Burhānpur. As that elephant was handsome and well-behaved, it was ordered to be included among the private elephants. The value of the offerings that were accepted was Rs. 130,000, and he offered about Rs. 4,000 to his mothers and benefactors. On this day Sayyid Bāyazīd Bukhārī, faujdar of Bhakkar, sent as an offering a *rang* (ibex), which he had brought from the hills when it was small and brought up in his house. It pleased me greatly. Of *mār-khūr* and hill sheep I have seen many brought up in the house, but I never saw a *rang* (tame). I ordered them to keep it with the Barbary goats, in order that they might pair and produce young ones. Without doubt, it is not allied to the mār-khūr or the quchqār. Sayyid Bāyazīd was raised to the mansab of 1,000 personal and 700 horse. On Monday, the 23rd, having honoured Muqīm K. with a robe of honour, a horse, an elephant, and jewelled *khapwa*, I appointed him to Bihār. On Sunday, the 29th, a feast was prepared for my auspicious son Shāh-Jahān on the bank of the Biya (Beas), and on the same day Rāja Bikramājīt, who was employed in the siege of Kāngra, came to Court, by order, to represent certain requirements, and had the good fortune to kiss the threshold. On Monday, the 30th, my son Shāh-Jahān took ten days' leave, and hastened to Lahore in order to see the palace buildings lately erected. Rāja Bikramājīt was presented with a special dagger, a robe of honour, and a horse, and returned to duty on the siege of Kāngra. On Wednesday, the 2nd of the Divine month of Bahman, the garden of Kalānaur was honoured by my halting there. At this place my father had ascended the throne.

When the news of the speedy arrival of Khān 'Ālam reached

* *Az nīlam-i-farang-tarāsh*. It is difficult to suppose that the hilt was a sapphire. Possibly "nīlam" is the European artist's name, or *nīlam-i-farang* may be some kind of European work or material. Query niello ?

the Court, every day I sent one of my servants to meet him. I loaded him with all kinds of favours and kindnesses, and added to his rank and dignity, and I decked the headings of the farmans sent to him with an impromptu hemistich or couplet suitable to the occasion, and so filled him with favours. Once I sent him some *Jahāngīrī* (otto of roses), and this opening verse came on my tongue:

VERSE.*

"To thee I've sent the scent of myself,
That I may bring thee the more quickly to myself."

On Thursday, the 3rd (Bahman), at the garden of Kalānaur, Khān 'Ālam was honoured by kissing the threshold. By way of nazar he brought 100 muhars and Rs. 1,000, and (stated that he) would present his offerings in due course. Zambīl Beg, the ambassador of my brother Shāh 'Abbās, was following him with the royal letter and the rarities of that country (Persia), which he had sent as presents. Of the favours and kindness conferred by my brother on Khān 'Ālam, if I were to write of them in detail, I should be accused of exaggeration. In conversation he always gave him the title of Khān 'Ālam, and never had him out of his presence. If he ever voluntarily stayed in his own quarter, he ('Abbās) would go there without ceremony, and show him more and more favour. One day there was a *qamurgha* hunt at Farrukhābād, and he ordered Khān 'Ālam to shoot with a bow. Out of good manners he brought a bow with two arrows (only). The Shah gave him 50 other arrows from his own quiver. It happened that 50 of these arrows struck the game, and two arrows missed. Then he ordered some of his attendants who had the entrée at feasts and assemblies to shoot with arrows. Most shot well. Among them Muḥammad Yūsuf (qarāwul), shot an arrow which went through two boars, and those who were standing by broke out without control into applause. At the time Khān 'Ālam took his leave, he seized him in the

* *Būy-i-khwīsh* ("my own scent"). The scent (otto of roses) was invented by Jahāngīr's mother-in-law (the mother of Nūr-Jahān). She called it after Jahāngīr's name.

embrace of honour, and showed him great affection. After he had left the city, he went to his halting-place, and made many apologies and bade him farewell. As for the beautiful and costly things that the Khān 'Ālam brought, it was indeed the assistance of his destiny that gave such rare things into his hand. Among them was the picture of the fight of Ṣāhib Qirān (Tīmūr) with Tuqtamish K., and the likenesses of him and his glorious children and the great Amirs who had the good fortune to be with him in that fight, and near each figure was written whose portrait it was. In this picture there were 240 figures. The painter had written his name as Khalīl Mīrzā Shāhrukhī (in the MS. it is Savaj and not Shāhrukhī). The work was very complete and grand, and resembled greatly the paint-brush of Ustād Bihzād. If the name of the painter had not been written, the work would have been believed to be his. As it was executed before Bihzād's date it is probable that the latter was one of Khalīl Mīrzā's pupils, and had adopted his style. This precious relic had been obtained from the illustrious library of Shāh Ismā'īl (the 1st), or had come to my brother Shāh 'Abbās from Shāh Ṭahmāsp. A person of the name of Ṣādiqī, a librarian of his, had stolen it, and sold it to someone. By chance (the painting) fell into the hands of Khān 'Ālam at Isfahan. The Shah heard that he had found such a rare prize, and asked it of him on the pretence of looking at it. Khān 'Ālam tried to evade this by artful stratagems, but when he repeatedly insisted on it, he sent it to him. The Shah recognized it immediately he saw it. He kept it by him for a day, but at last, as he knew how great was our liking for such rarities, he—God be praised—made no request* whatever for it, but told the facts of the case (about its being stolen) to Khān 'Ālam, and made the picture over to him.

At the time when I sent Khān 'Ālam to Persia, I had sent with him a painter of the name of Bishan Dās, who was unequalled in his age for taking likenesses, to take the portraits of the Shah and the chief men of his State, and bring them.

* The meaning of the clause is obscure.

He had drawn the likenesses of most of them, and especially had taken that of my brother the Shah exceedingly well, so that when I showed it to any of his servants, they said it was exceedingly well drawn.

On the same day Qāsim K., with the Bakhshi and Diwan of Lahore, had the good fortune to do homage. Bishan Dās, the painter, was honoured with the gift of an elephant. Bābā Khwāja, who was one of the auxiliaries of Qandahar, was accorded the mansab of 1,000 personal and 550 horse. On Tuesday, the 3rd, *Madāru-l-mahāmmī* (centre of important affairs) I'timādu-d-daula made ready his army. Inasmuch as the charge of the Panjab is entrusted to his agents, and he has also various jagirs in Hindustan, he held a review of 5,000 horsemen. As the area of Kashmir is not such that its produce may suffice for the expenses of the force that is always on service with the servants of the army of prosperity, and as, in consequence of the report (of the approach) of the glorious and victorious standards, the price of grains and vegetables had risen very high, an order was given, for the comfort of the public, that those servants who were in attendance on the royal stirrup should arrange their retinues, and only taking with them those who were indispensable, should send the remainder to their jagirs, and in the same way should take every precaution to reduce as far as possible the number of their beasts and followers. On Thursday, the 10th, my fortunate son, Shāh-Jahān returned from Lahore, and had the good fortune to do homage. Having honoured Jahāngīr Qulī K. with a dress of honour, a horse and an elephant, I gave him leave to proceed with his brothers and sons to the Deccan. On this day Ṭālib Āmulī received the title of *Maliku-sh-shu'arā* (king of poets), and was clothed in a dress of honour. His origin was from Āmul. For some time he was with I'timādu-d-daula. As the merits of his style surpassed that of his contemporaries, he was enrolled among the poets of the throne. The following couplets are by him :

VERSE.*

" Spring longs to rifle thy parterre,
For the flowers in thy hand are fresher than those on his branch.
I've so closed my lips from speech that you'd say
' His mouth is but a scar on his face.' "†

VERSE.

" Both first and last, Love is aye music and joy—
A pleasant wine both when fresh and when mellow."

VERSE.

" Were I glass instead of body,
I'd reveal thee to thyself without thy unveiling.
Two lips have I ; one for drinking,
And one to apologize for drunkenness."

On Monday, the 14th, Ḥusainī s. Sulṭān Qiwām produced this quatrain :

QUATRAIN.

" A speck of dust sprinkled on thee from thy skirt
Becomes Solomon's collyrium ; from the moisture of thy face‡
Were the earth at thy door examined,
The sweat of kings' brows would exude."

At this time Mu'tamid K. repeated a quatrain which greatly pleased me, and which I entered in my common-place book :

QUATRAIN.§

" You give me the poison of parting to taste, (and say) 'What matters it ?'
You shed my blood and expel me (and say), ' What matters it ?'
O, heedless of what your dividing sword can do,
Sift my dust and then you'll know."

---

* The first line is obscure and the MSS. do not help. Possibly the meaning is Spring thanks thee for robbing his garden, or it may be, Spring is exhorted to rob thy garden. The quatrain is also given in the Iqbāl-nāma, 132.

† Meaning that the lips were so closed that the mouth looked like a thin scar.

‡ The collyrium of Solomon was something which enabled one to see hidden treasures.

§ This quatrain is stated in the Iqbāl-nāma, 133, to be by Bābā Ṭālib Iṣfahānī. He is a quite different person from Ṭālib Āmulī. The same quatrain is given by Abū-l-Faẓl, and I am indebted to Mr. Blochmann, p. 607, for being able to understand it. Bābā

Ṭālib (*i.e.*, Bābā Ṭālib) is by family an Iṣfahānī. In his early youth he went to Kashmir clothed as an ascetic and calendar, and from the beauty of the place and the pleasantness of the climate set his heart on the country and settled there. After the conquest of Kashmir he joined the service of the late king (Akbar), and became enrolled among the servants of the Presence. His age is now nearly 100 years, and he is now with his sons and dependants in Kashmir, engaged in praying for the everlasting State.

As it was reported to me that in Lahore one Miyān Shaikh Muḥammad Mīr by name, who was a Darvish, a Sindī by origin, very eloquent, virtuous, austere, of auspicious temperament, a lord of ecstasy, had seated himself in the corner of reliance upon God and retirement, and was rich in his poverty and independent of the world, my truth-seeking mind was not at rest without meeting him, and my desire to see him increased. As it was impossible to go to Lahore, I wrote a note to him, and explained to him the desire of my heart, and that saint, notwithstanding his great age and weakness, took the trouble to come. I sate with him for a long time alone, and enjoyed a thorough interview with him. Truly he is a noble personage, and in this Age he is a great gain and a delightful existence. This suppliant for Grace was taken out of himself by companionship with him,* and heard from him sublime words of truth and religious knowledge. Although I desired to make him some gift, I found that his spirit was too high for this, and so did not express my wish. I left him the skin of a white antelope to pray upon, and he immediately bade me farewell and went back to Lahore.

On Wednesday, the 23rd, I pitched my camp at Daulatābād. A daughter of a gardener was brought before me

---

Ṭālib Iṣfahānī is not mentioned by Dr. Rieu. At Vol. II., 679*b*, of his Catalogue, there is an account of Ṭālib Āmulī, who, it is said, died young. Bābā Ṭālib died somewhat later, and at the age of over 100. See Iqbāl-nāma, *loc. cit.*, and Badayūnī, III. 265.

* A Muḥammad Shaikh is mentioned in Beale as the author of two books (see p. 273, col. 2). One of them was the Jām-i-Jahān-numā, and is perhaps the work mentioned in Rieu, II. 866*a*, V.

who had a moustache and a thick beard as big as the hilt of a sword. Her appearance was like that of a man. There was hair in the middle of her chest as well, but she had no breasts.* I discovered by her appearance that she ought not to have children. I told some women to take her aside and examine her, as perhaps she might be a hermaphrodite. They found she was in no way different from other women. I have recorded this in this volume on account of its strangeness.

On Thursday, the 24th, Bāqir K., having come from Multan, had the good fortune to pay his respects. In the preceding pages it has been recorded that Allāh-dād, s. Jalālā Tārīkī, had deserted from the victorious army and taken the road to ruin. He now repented, and through Bāqir K. petitioned I'timādu-d-daula for pardon. At the latter's request I ordered that if he repented of what he had done, and turned his face in hope towards the Court, his crimes would be forgiven. On this day Bāqir K. brought him to Court, and at the intercession of I'timādu-d-daula, the traces of disgrace and the dust of sorrow were washed off his forehead with the pure water of pardon. Sangrām, Zamindar of Jammu, was honoured with the title of Raja and the mansab of 1,000 personal and 500 horse, and was exalted with the gift of an elephant and a dress of honour. Ghairat K., faujdar of the Dū-āb, was promoted to the mansab of 800 personal and 500 horse. Khwāja Qāsim received the rank of 700 and 250 horse, and Taham-tan Beg, s. Qāsim Koka, received that of 500 personal and 300 horse. I gave Khān 'Ālam a private elephant with trappings. From this stage, having given Bāqir K. the mansab of 1,500 personal and 500 horse, I dismissed him again to his Subadarship.

On Monday, the 28th, I pitched in the pargana of Karohī, which is on the bank of the Bihat (Jhelam). As this hilly country is one of the established hunting-places, the huntsmen, according to order, had come on in advance and prepared a *jarga* (ring in which game is enclosed). On Wednesday, the 1st of the Divine month of Isfandārmuz, they drove

* Some unnecessary details have been omitted here.

in the game from six koss. On Thursday, the 2nd, they brought them into the enclosure, where 101 head of mountain sheep and gazelles were taken. As Mahābat K. had been prevented from the good fortune of coming before me for a long time, I ordered, at his request, that if he was satisfied with the order of affairs, and was not troubled with regard to any occurrence, he should leave his forces at their posts (*thānas*), and come to Court unattended. On this day he had the good fortune to kiss the threshold, and presented 100 muhars as nazar. K͟hān 'Ālam was promoted to the mansab of 5,000 personal and 3,000 horse. About this time a written report came from Nūru-d-dīn Qulī that he had repaired the Pūnch road, and levelled the defiles as far as possible, but that snow fell for some days and nights, and lay on the *kotāls* to the depth of three cubits. It was still falling, and if I would delay outside the hills for a month, I could cross by that route, otherwise it appeared difficult. As my intention in this undertaking was to see the spring and the sprouting of bloom, my chance of seeing this was lost by this delay, and I necessarily turned my rein, and the royal standards proceeded by the way of Paklī and Daṁtūr. On Friday, the 3rd, I crossed the River Bihat (Jhelam), although the water was waist-deep. As it was running very fast, and men crossed with great trouble, I ordered them to take 200 elephants to the fords, and cross the effects of the people over, and take across as well those who were weak and feeble, so that there might be no loss of life or goods.

On this day news arrived of the death of Khwāja Jahān. He was one of the old servants, and from the time when I was prince. Although at last he left my service, and was for some time in that of my father, yet as he had not gone to any strange place, this did not weigh heavily on my mind. Accordingly, after my accession, I did him such kindness as he had never conceived possible, and gave him the mansab of 5,000 personal and 3,000 horse. I take this opportunity to record in this volume an account of his idiosyncrasy. He became practised in great affairs and acquired a wonderful skill in business. His capabilities were the result of labour, and he was void of natural ability, and of the other qualities which are the adornment of men's nature. On this journey he suffered from heart-failure, but for some days, in spite of illness and breakdown, he kept up with the march. When his weakness increased, he was allowed to go back at Kalānaur, and went to Lahore, and there died a natural death.*

On Saturday, the 4th of the aforesaid month, the camp was pitched at the Fort of Rohtās (in the Panjab). I favoured Qāsim K. with a horse, a sword, and a special shawl (*parm-narm*, literally very soft, and Akbar's name for a shawl, see Blochmann, 90). I gave him leave to go to Lahore. There was a small garden by the roadside, and I inspected the blossoms.

At this stage *tīhū*† were obtained. The flesh of the *tīhū* is better than that of the partridge (*kabak*).

On Sunday, the 5th, M. Ḥasan s. Mīrzā Rustam, was promoted to the rank of 1,000 with 400 horse, and was appointed to the Deccan. Khwāja 'Abdu-l-Laṭīf, the chief fowler, also received the rank of 1,000 with 400 horse. At this place I saw a flower, white inside, and red outside, while some of them were red inside and yellow outside. In Persian they call it *La'la-i-bīgāna*, and in Hindī *thal kanal*. *Thal* means land, and as the lotus (kanal) is an aquatic plant, they have called this land-lotus.‡

On Thursday, the 9th, a report came from Dilāwar K., Governor of Kashmir, containing the good news of the conquest of Kishtwār. Details will be recorded by the pen of the newswriter after he (Dilāwar) comes to the foot of the throne. I sent him a gracious farman with a special dress of honour and a jewelled dagger, and granted him the revenue

* Khwāja Jahān's real name was Dūst Muḥ., and he was from Kabul. See Blochmann, 424. Jahāngīr's characterization of him is rather obscure, and I am not sure if my translation is correct. Jahāngīr had married his daughter. Blochmann, 477, *n.* 2.

† This is the seesee partridge or *Ammoperdrix Bonhami* of Jerdon, p. 567 of first edition. Jerdon states that in Afghanistan it is called the teehoo, and that its flesh is said to be delicious.

‡ Apparently this is the *Hibiscus mutabilis*, for which the Bengali name is *thal padma* ("land lotus").

of the conquered province for a year, as a reward for this acceptable service. On Tuesday, the 14th, I halted at Ḥasan Abdāl. As the occurrences on this road and particulars of the stages have been related in detail in the account of the expedition to Kabul, I shall not repeat them. From this place as far as Kashmir, they will be written stage by stage, please Almighty God. From the date on which, disembarking from a boat, I reached Akbarpur in safety and prosperity, up to Ḥasan Abdāl, a distance of 178 koss, I took 69 days in 48 marches and 21 halts.* As at this place there is a spring full of water, and a cascade, and a very beautiful reservoir, I halted here two days, and on Thursday, the 16th (Isfandārmuz̲), the feast of my lunar weighing took place. The 53rd year, according to lunar calculation, of this suppliant at the throne commenced auspiciously. As beyond this stage, hills, passes, and many ups and downs were before us, the passage of the camp appeared a difficult matter, and it was settled that H. M. Maryamu-z-zamānī and the other Begams should delay for some days, and come on at leisure. Madāru-l-mulk I'timādu-d-daula al-K͟hāqānī, Ṣādiq K. Bak͟hs͟hī, and Irādat K. Mīr-Sāmān, with the directors of the buildings and other offices, should attend to their transit. At the same time Rustam Mīrzā Ṣafawī, K͟hān-A'ẓam, and a number of other servants, obtained leave to go by the Pūnch road, while the royal retinue went on with some privileged courtiers (*manẓūrān-i-bisāṭ-i-qarb*) and the necessary servants. On Friday, the 17th, we marched 3½ koss, and halted at the village of Sultanpur.† On this day came the news of the death of Rānā Amar Singh, who had died a natural death at Udaipur (become a traveller on the road of non-existence). Jagat Singh, his grandson, and Bhīm,‡ his son, who were in attendance on me, were presented with dresses of honour, and an order was given that Rāja Kis͟han Dās should proceed with a gracious farman conferring the

* The word for twenty is omitted in text, and also in Elliot, VI. 367.

† "On the southern bank of the Harroh River," Elliot, VI. 367.

‡ Bhīm was the younger brother of Karan (Tod). The passage is translated in Elliot, VI. 367.

title of Rānā, a dress of honour, a horse, and a private elephant for Kunār Karan, to perform the dues of condolence and congratulation. I heard* from people of this country that when it is not the rainy season, and there is no sign of a cloud or lightning, a noise like the voice of the clouds comes from this hill, which they called Garj (thunder). This noise is heard every year or at least every two years. I had repeatedly heard of this also when I was in attendance on the late king. I have written this as it is not devoid of strangeness,† but wisdom is from Allah. On Saturday, the 18th, marching 4½ koss, I halted at the village of Sanjī. From this stage I entered the pargana of Hazāra Qārlugh.‡ On Sunday, the 19th, marching 3¾ koss, I halted at the village of Naushahra.§ From this place we entered Dhantūr. As far as the eye could reach there were green meadows‖ interspersed with the *thal-kanwal* (hibiscus) and other flowers in bloom. It was a very beautiful sight. On Monday, the 20th, marching 3½ koss, the camp was pitched at the village of Salhar.¶ Mahābat K. presented as offerings jewels and inlaid vessels to the value of Rs. 60,000. In this country I saw a flower of the redness of fire, of the shape of *gul-i-khatmī*,** but smaller, and several flowers blooming together in one place, looked from a distance as if they were one flower. Its stem is of the size of the apricot-tree. On the hill-slopes here there are many wild violets,†† with a very sweet scent, but paler than the violet. On Tuesday, the 21st, marching 3 koss, I halted at the village of Mālgallī.‡‡ On this day I dismissed Mahābat K. to his duty in Bangash, and con-

* Elliot, VI. 368 and *n.* 1.

† Elliot, VI. 368, and note.

‡ Elliot has Hazāra Fārigh.

§ On the eastern bank of the Dhor. Elliot, *loc. cit.*

‖ Elliot has : "As far as the eye could reach, the blossoms of the *thal kanwal*, and other flowers were glowing between the green foliage. It was a beautiful scene."

¶ Salhar in text, but Sālhar in Elliot.

** Marsh-mallow of Steingass and Elliot. Query Hollyhock ?

†† The word violets occurs in MS. 181 and also in Elliot.

‡‡ The Bib. Ind. edition, Iqbāl-nāma, p. 135, changes this into Pakli. MS. 181 has Bankli (?) apparently. Pakli is probably not right, for the entrance to it is mentioned lower down.

ferred on him a special elephant and dress of honour with a *pūstīn* (sheepskin coat). This day there was a drizzling rain till the end of the march. On the eve of Wednesday, the 22nd, also there was rain. In the morning snow fell, and as most of the roads had become very slippery, the weak animals fell in every place, and could not rise again, and 25 of my own elephants were lent to assist* them. I halted for two days on account of the snow. On Thursday, the 23rd, Sulṭān Ḥusain, Zamindar of Pakli, had the good fortune to pay his respects: this is the entrance to the Pakli country. It is a strange thing that when H. M. Akbar came here it snowed at this stage, and it has now snowed as well. For many years no snow has fallen, and there has even been little rain. On Friday, the 24th, I marched 4 koss and pitched at the village of Sawādnagar.† On this road, too, there was much mud.‡ Apricot and peach trees were blooming on all sides, and fir-trees like cypresses rejoiced the eye. On Saturday, the 25th, having marched nearly 3½ koss, the camp was pitched near Pakli. On Sunday, the 26th, I rode out to hunt partridges (*kabak*), and at the end of the day, at the request of Sulṭān Ḥusain, went to his house, and increased his dignity among his equals and neighbours. H. M. Akbar had also gone to his house. He offered several kinds of horses, daggers, hawks, and falcons. I presented him with the horses and daggers. I ordered the hawks and falcons to be got ready§ (*kamar bar basta*), and shown everything

* *Taṣadduq shud*. This is how Mr. Rogers has translated the passage, and this seems to me to be right. Elliot has "lost," but surely Jahāngīr would not pass over so lightly the loss of 25 elephants. *Taṣadduq* is often used in the sense of almsgiving, or of granting a favour. The text 290, line 2, has *akṣar-i-rāh basta būd*. The word *basta* seems unintelligible, and in the corresponding passage of the Iqbāl-nāma, 135, the words are *akṣar-i-rāh ajama būd*. This word perhaps means "muddy," and this would fit the sense.

† Elliot has Tawādkar.

‡ *Achamba*. But MS. 305 has ajamat, and this may mean forest, or woods. Perhaps Elliot's "mud" is a clerical error for wood, but *ajamat* means pools as well as woods. Perhaps this is the same word as occurs in the Iqbāl-nāma, 135, and means "muddy."

§ So in text, but the MSS. *ba garaz basta* ("loosely tied"), so that they could be thrown off if any game appeared.

that might fly up. The Sarkar of Pakli is 35 koss in length and 25 in breadth. On the east, on two sides, is the hill country of Kashmir; on the west, Atak Benares (Atak); on the north, Kator; and on the south, the Gakkar country. At the time when Timur, after conquering Hindustan, turned his rein backwards towards the capital of Tūrān, they say that he placed in these regions this body of people, who were in attendance on the victorious stirrup. They say themselves that they are Qārlughs, but do not know for certain who was their leader at that time. In fact, they are pure Lāhaurīs, and speak the same language. The people of Dhantūr think the same thing. In the time of my father, one of the name of Shāhrukh was Zamindar of Dhantūr; now it is Bahādur, his son. Although they are all related to one another, there are always disputes, as is usual with Zamindars, about boundaries. They have always been loyal. Sulṭān Maḥmūd,. the father of Sulṭān Ḥusain, and Shāhrukh, both came to wait on me when I was prince. Although Sulṭān Ḥusain is seventy years old, to all outward appearance there is no diminution in his powers, and he can still ride and be as active as possible. In this country they make *būza* (a beverage) from bread and rice, which they call *sar.** It is much stronger than *būza*, and the older it is the better. This *sar* is their chief sustenance. They put this *sar* into a jar, and fastening it up, keep it for two or three years in the house. Then they take off the scum and call the liquor *āchhī*. The *āchhī* can be kept for ten years, and according to them, the older it is the better, and the shortest time in which they use it is a year. Sulṭān Maḥmūd used to take cup after cup of this *sar;* nay ! he would drink a jar of it. Sulṭān Ḥusain is also addicted to it, and brought me some of his choicest quality. I took some in order to try it. I had also drunk it before. Its intoxicating effects are aphrodisiac, but its taste is harsh. It appeared that they mix some *bhāng* (bang) with it, which increases its intoxicating power. If there were no wine, it could in case of necessity be used as a substitute. The fruits are apricots, peaches, and pears (?) (amrūd).

* Elliot has *sīr*.

As they do not cultivate them, but they spring up of themselves, they are harsh-flavoured and unpleasant. Their blossoms are a joy. Their houses are of wood, and are built after the Kashmiri fashion. They have hawks, and horses, camels, cattle, and buffaloes, and many goats and fowls. Their mules are small and are not fit for heavy loads. As it was represented to me that some stages farther on the cultivation was not such as to provide sufficient grain for the royal camp, I gave an order that they should only take a small advanced camp, sufficient for our needs and the necessary establishments, and diminish the number of elephants, and take with them provisions for three or four days; that they should take with them only some of the immediate attendants on the royal stirrup, and that the rest of the men should come on some stages behind under the command of Khwāja Abū-l-Ḥasan, the Bakhshi. In spite of precautions and injunctions, it was found necessary to have 700 elephants for the advanced camp and the establishments.

The mansab of Sulṭān Ḥusain was 400 personal and 300 horse; I now promoted him to 600 personal and 350 horse, and conferred on him a robe of honour, a jewelled dagger, and an elephant. Bahādur Dhantūrī was an auxiliary of the army of Bangash. An order was given that he should hold the mansab, original and increased, of 200 personal and 100 horse. On Wednesday, the 27th, having marched 5¼ koss, and crossing by bridges the Nainsukh,* I chose a halting-place. This Nainsukh (repose of the eyes) flows from the North, and comes down from the hills of Dārd† (?), which is between the country of Badakhshan and Tibet. As at this place it forms two branches, they had, according to order, prepared two wooden bridges for the crossing of the victorious army, one 18 cubits and the other 14 cubits in length, with a breadth each of 5 cubits. The way in which they make

* Now known as the Kunhār. It rises in Lake Lohusur at the head of the Kāgān glen. See I.G., old edition, VIII. 365, and ditto new edition, XIV. 272, for Kāgān Valley.

† Text Wārū. Iqbāl-nāma 136 has Kūh-i-Wāzūh. MS. 181 seems to have Dārd.

bridges in this country is to throw pine-trees* on the surface of the water, and fasten the two ends strongly to rocks, and having thrown on to these, thick planks of wood, make them firm with pegs and ropes, and these, with a little repair, last for years. Briefly, they made the elephants ford, whilst the horsemen and foot passed over by the bridge. Sulṭān Maḥmūd called this river Nainsukh—that is, "Repose of the eye." On Thursday, the 30th, having marched about 3½ koss, a halt was made on the bank of the Kis͟han Gangā. On this road there is a *kotal* of great height, the ascent being 1 koss, and the descent 1½ koss, which they call *Pīm darang*. The reason for this name is that in the language of Kashmir they call cotton (*pamba*) *pīm*. As the rulers of Kashmir had placed a superintendent there, who took duties from loads of cotton, and delay takes place here for the collection of the duty, it has become known as the *Pīm darang*† (cotton delay). After traversing the pass, there is a very fine and clear waterfall. Having drunk my usual cups on the edge of the water in the shade of the trees, I went on to my halting-place in the evening. There was an old bridge over this river, 54 yards long and 1½ yards wide, which footmen crossed by. According to orders, another bridge was prepared parallel to this, in length 53 yards and breadth 3 yards. As the water was deep and swift, they took the elephants across without loads, and the footmen and horses crossed by the bridge. By order of my father, a very strong saray of stone and lime was erected on the top of the ridge overlooking the river. One day before New Year's Day we had sent Mu'tamid K. forward to select a spot for the placing of the throne and preparing the New Year's entertainment. This had to be lofty and choice. By chance, as he crossed the bridge, there was a ridge overlooking the water, green and pleasant. On the top of this was a flat place of 50 cubits which one might say

* Text *shāk͟hdār* ("with branches"), but the true reading seems to be *nāj* ("pine"). Elliot has "sāl."

† This is a fanciful derivation. The word is not darang, but drang, which means a watch-station. See Stein, A.S.B.J., for 1899, p. 84. The Pamba-drang, however, was near the Kis͟han Gangā, and so is not the drang mentioned by Stein.

the rulers of fate had specially prepared for such a day. The aforesaid officer had made ready everything necessary for the New Year's feast on the top of that ridge, which was much approved. Mu'tamid K. was much applauded for this. The river Kis͟han Gangā comes from the south* and flows northwards. The Bihat (Jhelam) comes from the East, and joining the Kis͟han Gangā, flows to the North.

* A mistake. See Elliot, VI. 373, note.

THE FIFTEENTH NEW YEAR'S FEAST AFTER THE AUSPICIOUS ACCESSION

THE transit of the sun, that fulfils the hopes of the world, into his house of honour in Aries, took place on Friday, the 15th of the month of Rabī'u-s̤-s̤ānī in the Hijri year 1029, (10 March), 1620, after 12½ gharis, or 5 sidereal hours,* had passed, and the 15th year of the reign of this suppliant at the throne of Allah commenced happily and auspiciously. On Saturday, the 2nd (Farwardīn), having marched 4½ koss, I halted at the village of Bakkar. On this road there was no hill-pass (*kotal*), but it was rather stony. I saw peacocks, black partridges, and monkeys (*langūr*), such as exist in the Garmsīr country (Afghanistan). It is evident that these can also exist in cold countries. From this place to Kashmir the road is along the bank of the river Bihat. There are hills on both sides, and in the bottom of the valley the water flows with great force, boiling and raging. However large an elephant may be, he cannot hold his feet firmly in it, but immediately rolls over, and is carried away. There are also water-dogs† in the river. On Sunday, the 3rd, marching 4½ koss, I pitched at Mūsarān. On the eve of Friday the merchants who live in the pargana of Bāra Mūla came and paid their respects. I asked the reason of the name of Bāra mūla, and they represented that in the Hindi language they call a boar *Bārāh* (*Varaha*) and mūla

* Each sidereal hour being equal to 2½ gharis.

† *Sag-i-ābī.* Probably otters are meant, as a name for them is *pānī kuttā* ("water-dogs"). But in the dictionaries *sag-i-ābī* is given as meaning the beaver. The otter occurs in Kashmir, and is known as *wudar*. Lawrence, Valley of Kashmir, 111.

a place—that is, the boars' place. Among the incarnations that belong to the religion of the Hindus, one is the boar incarnation, and Bārāh mūla by constant use has become Bāra mūla. On Monday, the 4th, marching 2½ koss, I pitched at Bhūlbās. As they said these hills were very narrow and difficult (to pass), and they could be crossed by a crowd of men only with great trouble, I gave orders to Mu'tamid K. that, with the exception of Āṣaf K. and a few of the necessary attendants, no one should be allowed to march along with the prosperous stirrup (with the king personally), and the camp should be kept one stage behind. By chance, before this order was given, he had sent on his own tent. After this he wrote to his men that this order had been given with regard to him, and they should halt at whatever spot they had reached. His brothers heard this at the foot of the kotal of Bhūlbās,* and pitched their own tent there. When the royal host reached the place, snow and rain began to fall. One plain of the road had not been crossed when his tent became visible. Looking on this as a gift from the hidden world, I and the ladies alighted, and remained protected from the cold and snow and rain. His brothers, according to orders, sent someone in haste to summon him. When the news reached him that the elephants and the advance camp had arrived at the top of the *kotal*, and blocked up the road, as it was impossible to ride, *with great zeal*, he, not knowing his head from his feet, traversed a distance of 2½ koss on foot in two hours, and came to wait on me, and repeated this couplet with the tongue of gesture.†

VERSE.

"At midnight came the thought of thee. I was ashamed and resigned my life.
The poor man was abashed when suddenly the guest arrived."

---

* Properly Būlīyāsa. See Stein, A.S.B.J., for 1899, p. 85. It is the Peliasa of the maps. Later on, Jahāngīr indicates its position by saying that it is 11 koss on the Kashmir side of the Kishan Gangā.

† That is, I presume, he did not really utter the words, but his appearance represented them. The Iqbāl-nāma has, p. 138, *mihmān chū Bīga* ("a guest such as a Begam"). MS. 181 has *nāgah chū*

All that was in his store (*bisāṭ*) in the way of money and goods, of live stock or dead, he offered for me to tread upon. I gave them all back, and said: "What do worldly goods appear worth to the eye of our magnanimity? We buy the jewel of loyalty at a high figure. Such an event arising out of his devotion should be reckoned as the rising of his good star, in that a king like me with the people of his harem should remain in his house in comfort and at ease for a night and a day. It would be a cause of honour to him among his contemporaries and comrades." On Tuesday, the 5th, having traversed 2 koss, I alighted at the village of Kahā'ī.* I presented the dress (*sar u pāy*) I had on to Mu'tamid K., and an order was given assigning him the mansab of 1,500 personal and 1,500† horse. From this stage we entered within the boundary of Kashmīr. In the same kotal of Bhūlbās, Ya'qūb, s. Yūsuf K. Kashmīrī, fought with the victorious army of my father, of which Rāja Bhagwān Dās, father of Rāja Mān Singh, was the leader.

On this day, the news came that Suhrāb K., s. Rustam Mīrzā, had been drowned in the Jhelam. The details are as follows: He, according to orders, was coming up one stage in the rear, and on the road it came into his mind that he would have a bathe in the river, though warm water was ready. The people forbade him, and said that when the air was so cold, unnecessarily to get into a river so agitated and bloodthirsty that it would roll over a war-elephant, was contrary to the dictates of caution. He was not restrained by their words, and as the unavoidable destined time had arrived, got in. From excessive self-will and pride and carelessness, in reliance on his powers of swimming, in which art he was unequalled, he was more determined than ever, and with a *khidmatīyya* (Blochmann 252) and another servant, both of whom could swim, mounted a rock on the river bank

---

Sulṭān. I.O. MS. 305 has *nāgah chū mihmān*. The reading Bega or Begam certainly seems preferable! The text is wrong as usual, and has *mihān* ("the great"), unless it is to be read *mahān*, and taken in the sense of Moons—*i.e.*, ladies.

* The Iqbāl-nāma, 139, has Kahtā'ī.

† The Iqbāl-nāma, 139, has 500 horse.

and threw himself in. Immediately he fell, from the violent movement of the waves, he could not pull himself together or try to swim; to fall in and go were the same thing, and Suhrāb K.* and the *khidmatīyya* thus gave away the goods of their lives to the flood of destruction. The boatman,† with a hundred difficulties, brought the boat of his being (himself) in safety to the shore. Mīrzā Rustam was much attached to this son. On hearing of this fatal news on the Pūnch road, he rent the robe of patience, and showed great agitation. With all his dependants, clothed in mourning garments, with head and feet bare, he came to wait on me. What shall I write of the grief of the mother? Although the Mīrzā has other sons, his heart was bound up in this one. His age was twenty-six years. In shooting with a gun he was an excellent pupil of his father, and knew well how to drive elephants and carriages. On the expedition to Gujarat he was often ordered to ride on the front part of my private elephant, and he was an active soldier.‡

On Wednesday, the 6th, marching 3 koss, I pitched at the village of Rīwand. On Thursday, the 7th, crossing the *kotal* of Kuwārmat,§ which is the most difficult on this road (MS.), I alighted at the village of Wachaha (MS. and print differ). The distance of this stage is 4¼ koss. The *kotal* of Kuwārmat (Kulāmat in the MS.) is a difficult one, and is the last of the *kotals* on the road. On Friday, the 8th, having traversed nearly 4 koss, I halted at the village of Baltār.‖ There was

* The name of M. Rustam's son, who was drowned.

† *Kushtīgīr*, which means a wrestler. But Jahāngīr puns on the word as if it were *kishtīgīr* ("a boatman"). Perhaps kushtīgīr was his name. I presume that the person meant is the other servant. There was no boat there. The Iqbāl-nāma has either kishtīgīr, or kushtīgīr.

‡ There is an extraordinary account of the Mīrzā's death in Price's "Jahangir" which quite differs from the story told here. See Price, p. 138. It is also stated there that he had been married six months before to a daughter of I'timādu-d-daula. There is also an account of the accident in the Iqbāl-nāma, p. 139.

§ Or Kuwārmast.

‖ Perhaps we should read Būniyār. See Stein, *loc. cit*, p. 87. Jahāngīr seems to have crossed over to the left bank of the Jhelam in the course of his march. Perhaps he did so at Ooriu of the map (Ūrī). Būniyār seems to be the Bhaniar of the map. I.O. MS. 181 has Butiyār.

no *kotal* on this road. It was broad, and plain after plain, and mead after mead, of flowers. Sweet-smelling plants of narcissus, violet, and strange flowers that grow in this country, came to view. Among these flowers I saw (noticed especially) one extraordinary one. It had five or six orange flowers blooming with their heads downwards. From the middle of the flowers there came out some green leaves, as in the case* of the pineapple (?). This is the *būlānīk*† flower. There is another flower like the *pūy* (?), round which are small flowers of the shape and colour of the jessamine, some blue in colour and some red, with yellow points in the middle, exceedingly pretty in appearance: its name is "*ladar pūsh*." They call it *pūsh-i-'aliyyu-l-'umūm*‡ (the common *pūsh*?). There are many yellow *arghawān* (Judas-trees) on the road as well. The flowers of Kashmīr are beyond counting and calculation. Which shall I write of? And how many can I describe? I have only mentioned the most remarkable. There is a waterfall on this road, very high and fine. It flows down from a high place. No other waterfall of such beauty was seen on the road. I delayed a moment at it, and filled my eye and heart with gazing on it from a high spot. On Saturday, the 9th, I marched 4¾ koss, and crossed over at Bāramūla.§ It is one of the noted towns of Kashmīr, and 14 koss|| distant from the city, situated on the bank of the Bihat. A number of the merchants of Kashmir live in it, and have built houses and mosques on the bank of the river, and spend their days in ease and contentment. According to orders, before the arrival of the host of prosperity, they had prepared decorated

* The allusion may be to the tuft of leaves at the top of a pineapple.

† Perhaps *būlā nīk*.

‡ Pūsh means flower in Kashmiri. Does the name mean "flower of 'Alī the Perfect"?

§ Bāramūla is on the left bank of the Jhelam according to the I.G., new edition. But maps and travellers seem to place it on the right bank.

|| Fourteen koss seem too little. The distance to Srinagar seems to be 31 miles by the road. The old city Vāramūla was on the right bank. Stein, 201. It is 32 miles from Srinagar.

boats at the place. As* the hour for entry (into Srinagar) had been fixed for Monday, when two watches of the day had passed, on Sunday, the 10th, I entered S͟hihābu-d-dīn-pūr. On this day Dilāwar K. Kākar, the Governor of Kashmir, came from Kis͟htwār,† and had the good fortune to kiss the threshold. He was exalted with various royal favours and all kinds of imperial gratifications. He had done his duty here in an acceptable manner, and it is hoped that the great Giver of favours may light up the foreheads of all my servants with honour.

Kis͟htwār is to the south of Kashmir. From the city of Kashmir (Srinagar) to the stage of Alkah (?),‡ which is the capital of Kis͟htwār, the distance is 60 koss by measurement. On the 10th of the Ilāhī month of S͟hahriwar, in my 14th year, Dilāwar K., with 10,000 horse and foot, determined to conquer Kis͟htwār. He appointed his son, Ḥasan by name, with Gird ʻAlī *Mīr-baḥr* (admiral) to guard the city and administer the territory. And as Gohar Chak and Aiba Chak laid claim to Kashmir as heirs, and were stirring up strife in Kis͟htwār, and were wandering in the valley of confusion and ruin, he left Haibat, one of his brothers, with a force at Desū, which is near the *kotal* of Pīr Panjāl, by way of caution, and, dividing his forces at that place, he himself hastened with a force by the road of Sangīnpūr, sending his son Jalāl, with Naṣru-llah ʻArab, and ʻAlī Malik Kas͟hmīrī, and a band of Jahāngīrī servants by another road, and his elder son Jamāl with a band of zealous young men as an advanced guard to his own force. At the same time he placed two other forces to move forward on his right and left. As no horses could go on the road, by way of precaution he took some with him, but left

* There is an omission in the text here. The MSS. have: "As Monday had been fixed for entering Srinagar, I did not think it advisable to halt at this stage, but immediately entered boats with the ladies and proceeded on with blessings towards the goal. On Sunday, the 10th, when two watches of the day had passed, I arrived at S͟hihābu-d-dīn-pūr."

† See Jarrett, II. 310, *n*. 7.

‡ The MSS. have Lā ? Apparently the kah of text is a relative pronoun and not part of the name. Perhaps Lah in Ladakh is the place meant.

nearly* all his sipahis' horses behind, and sent them to Kashmir (*i.e.*, Srinagar). The young men girded the belt of duty on their waists, and went up the hills on foot. The *ghāzīs* of the army of Islam fought from post to post with the ill-fated unbelievers as far as Narkot, which was one of the enemy's strongholds. There the corps of Jalāl and Jamāl, which had been sent by different roads, met, and the enemy, not having the power to oppose them, took to flight. The brave ones who offered their lives traversed many ups and downs with the courage of determination, and hastened on to the Marū river. On the bank of that river the fire of slaughter was lighted, and the *ghāzīs* of the army of Islam displayed approved activity. The ill-fated Aiba Chak, with many of the people of ruin, were slain. By the death of Aiba the Raja became powerless and without heart, and took the road of flight, and, crossing by the bridge, stopped at Bhandarkoṭ, which is on the other side. A band of the brave ones (*bahādurān*) quickly advanced, wishing to cross the bridge. A great fight took place at its head, and some of the young men attained to martyrdom. In this way for twenty days and nights the servants of the Court tried to cross the river, and the unbelievers of darkened fortune did not fail to attack and try to drive them back, until Dilāwar K., after establishing *thānas* and arranging for the commissariat, arrived with his army. The Raja, by way of stratagem and vulpine trickery, sent his Vakils to Dilāwar K., and begged that he might send his brother with offerings to the Court, so that when his offences obtained pardon, and his mind were freed from fear and trouble, he could also himself proceed to the Court, the refuge of the world, and kiss the threshold. Dilāwar K. did not lend his ear to these deceitful words, and did not throw away from his hand the coin of opportunity. He dismissed the envoys of the Raja without the attainment of their object, and made every exertion to cross the bridge. His eldest son Jamāl, with a band of the crocodiles of the sea of bravery and valour, went up the river, and by bravely swimming it, although swollen, crossed over, and engaged in

* *Dar kull* ("in general, in bulk") (?).

a fierce battle with the enemy. The devoted servants of the Court made an attack from the other side, and made matters tight for these ruined people. These, when they found they had no longer the strength to oppose them, broke down the planking of the bridge, and took to flight. The victorious servants made the bridge strong again, and transported the remainder of the army. Dilāwar K͟hān drew up his forces at Bhandarkot. From the aforesaid river (the Marū) to the Chenāb, which is a strong support of these unfortunate people, is a distance of two bow-shots, and on the bank of the Chenāb there is a lofty hill. The crossing of the water is a difficult matter, and, with a view to the coming and going of people on foot, they attach strong ropes, and place planks of the width of a cubit between two ropes, and fasten one rope's end to the top of the hill, and the other on the other side of the water. Then they attach two other ropes a *gaz* higher than these, that foot-passengers may place their feet on the planks, and, taking hold of the upper ropes, may descend from the top of the hill to the bottom, and so cross the river. This bridge they call *zampa*, in the language of the people of the hill country. Wherever they apprehended that a rope bridge might be constructed, they stationed musketeers and archers and men-at-arms, and so felt secure. Dilāwar K. made rafts (*jhāla*), and, placing on them eighty of his valiant young men, sent them across the river at night. As the water was flowing with great violence, the rafts were carried down by the flood of destruction, and sixty-eight of these gallant men were drowned in the sea of non-existence, and obtained the renown of martyrdom, whilst ten, by the aid of swimming, reached the shore of safety (*i.e.*, returned), and two on the other side became prisoners in the hands of the infidels. In short, for four months and ten days Dilāwar K͟hān, having planted the foot of courage at Bhandarkoṭ, made endeavours to cross over; but the arrow of stratagem did not reach the target of intent until a Zamindar pointed out a place which the enemy had no idea of. There, having constructed a *zampah*, in the heart of night, Jalāl, Dilāwar K.'s son, with some of the servants of the Court and a band of

Afghans, about 200 in number, crossed over in safety, made unawares in the morning an attack on the Raja, and blew loudly the trumpets of victory. A few who were around and before the Raja rushed out, bewildered, half asleep and half awake, and most of them became the harvest of the blood-drinking sword, while the rest quickly withdrew themselves from that whirlpool of calamity. In that encounter one of the soldiers came upon the Raja, and wished to finish him with a sword. He called out: "I am the Raja; take me alive to Dilāwar Khān." The men rushed on him and made him prisoner. After the Raja was made prisoner, his people all fled. When Dilāwar Khān heard this good news of victory, he prostrated himself in thankfulness to Allah, and, having crossed the river with the victorious army, came to Mandal Badr,* which was the capital of the country, and is 3 koss from the river. The daughter† of Sangrām Raja of Jammu, and the daughter of the abandoned Sūraj Mal, s. Rāja Bāso, were in the Raja's house (*i.e.*, married to him). By Sangrām's daughter he had children. Before the victory he had, by way of caution, sent his family for refuge to the Raja of Jaswāl and other Zamindars. When my victorious retinue approached, Dilāwar Khān, according to order, took the Raja with him, and came to kiss the threshold, leaving Naṣru-llah 'Arab with a body of horse and foot to guard the country.

In Kishtwār there are produced much wheat, barley, lentils, millet, and pulse. Differing from Kashmir, it produces little rice. Its saffron is finer than that of Kashmir. About a hundred hawks and falcons are caught there (annually). Oranges, citrons, and water-melons of the finest kind are obtained. Its melons are of the same kind as those of Kashmir, and other fruits, such as grapes, apricots, peaches, and sour pears, are grown. If they were cultivated, it is possible they would improve. A coin‡ of the name of *sanhasī*§ is a relic of the old rulers of Kashmir, one and a half of which

* The MSS. have also Mandal Badr. They have not Mulk after Badr as in text.

† Sister in MSS.

‡ *Zar* here does not, I think, mean gold.

§ The silver *sāsnū* of Jarrett, II. 354, and *n.* 2.

equal a rupee. In their business transactions they reckon fifteen *sanhasī*, or ten rupees, as one *pādshāhī* muhar. They call two seers of Hindustani weight a *man* (maund). It is not the custom for the Raja to take revenue from cultivation; he takes annually six *sanhasī*—that is, four rupees—from each house. All the saffron is assigned, as pay, to a body of Rajputs and to 700 musketeers (*tūpchī*) who are old retainers. When the saffron is sold, four rupees per maund, or two seers, are taken from the purchaser. The whole income of the Raja consists of fines, and for a small offence he takes a heavy sum. From whomsoever is wealthy and in comfortable circumstances the Raja, on some pretext, clears out all that he has. From all sources his income is about Rs. 100,000. In time of war 6,000 or 7,000 men on foot collect together; there are but few horses among them. The Raja and the chief men have about fifty between them. I bestowed a year's revenue on Dilāwar K. by way of reward. By conjecture, his jagir was worth about 1,000 personal and 1,000 horse, according to the *Jahāngīrī* rules. When the chief diwans calculate the allowances to the jagirdars, the exact amount will be ascertained.

On Monday, the 11th, after two watches and four gharis had passed, the royal cortège alighted auspiciously and happily at the buildings lately erected on the bank of the lake (the Dal lake). By order of my father, a very strong fort of stone and lime had been built. It is not quite completed, one side being unfinished. It is hoped that hereafter it will be completed. From Ḥasan Abdāl to Kashmir by the road I came is a distance of 75 koss; this was accomplished in nineteen marches and six halts—that is, in twenty-five days. From Agra to Kashmir, in the space of 168 days, a distance of 376 koss was traversed in 102 marches and 63 halts. By land* and the ordinary route the distance is 304½ koss.

On Tuesday, the 12th, Dilāwar K., according to order, brought the Raja† of Kishtwār, chained, into my presence, and did homage. He (the Raja) is not wanting in dignity.

* Jahāngīr went part of the way by water.

† Perhaps he is the Raja Bhagwān Singh mentioned by Drew in his book on Kashmir, p. 119.

His dress is after the Indian fashion, and he knows both the Hindi and the Kashmiri languages. Contrary to other Zamindars of these regions, he looked like the inhabitant of a town. I told him that, notwithstanding his offences, if he would bring his sons to Court, he should be released from confinement, and might live at ease under the shadow of the eternal State, or else he would be imprisoned in one of the forts of Hindustan. He said that he would bring his people, his family, and his sons to wait on me, and was hopeful of my clemency.

I shall now give a brief account of the country of Kashmir and of its peculiarities.

Kashmir* belongs to the fourth climate. Its latitude is 35° N., and its longitude, from the White Islands, 105°. In old times the country was in the possession of Rajas. Their dynasty lasted for 4,000 years. An account of them, and a list of their names, are given in the Rāja-tarang, which, by my father's order, was translated† from the Sanskrit (Hindi in text) into Persian. In the Hijri year 712 (1312-13) Kashmir was illumined by the religion of Islam. Thirty-two Muhammadan princes reigned over it for 282 years, until, in 994 (1586), my father conquered it. From that date till now, being a period of thirty-five years, the country has been in the possession of the Crown. Kashmir, from the Pass of Buliyasa‡ to Qambarbar, is 56 *Jahāngīrī* koss long, and its

* Abū-l-Faẓl, Jarrett, II. 347, puts Kashmir into the third and fourth climates, but at Vol. III., p. 89, he puts Kashmir into the fourth climate. Probably both he and Jahāngīr mean by Kashmir Srinagar. The appellation "White Islands" is probably a mistake for "The Fortunate Islands," *safīd* (white) being written instead of *sa'āda*, which is the word in the Iqbāl-nāma. *Jazā'ir-i-Sa'āda* ("The Fortunate Isles") is also the expression used in the Ẓafar-nāma, II. 178, which is probably the source of the Āyīn and the Tūzuk. In the extract from the Ẓafar-nāma given in the T. Rashīdī translation, 430, the longitude is given as 105° from the "Fortunate Islands." The *text* of the Āyīn, Bib. Ind. edition, II. 42, gives 105·40° as the longitude.

† See Rieu, I. 296. The translator was Mullā Shāh Muḥ. of Shāhābād. See also Blochmann, 106.

‡ The Peliasa of the maps and the Bolvasaka of Stein. Qambarbar is Farūtar in text. The Iqbāl-nāma, 147, has Qambarbar. It is

breadth is never more than 27 koss, or less than 10 koss. S͟haik͟h Abū-l-Faẓl has, in the Akbar-nāma, stated, by guess and conjecture, that the length of Kashmir from the Kis͟han Gangā to Qambarbar is 120 koss, and its breadth from 10 to 25 koss. I, out of prudence and caution, appointed a number of trustworthy and intelligent men to measure the length and breadth with ropes (*ṭanāb*). The result was that what the Shaikh wrote as 120 koss came out as 67. As it is agreed that the boundary of a country is the place up to which people speak the language of that country, it follows that the boundary of Kashmir is Buliyāsa, which is 11 koss on this side (*i.e.*, east) of the Kis͟han Gangā. So, according to the preceding figures, the length of Kashmir is 56 (67 – 11) koss. The variations in breadth were found to be not more than 2 koss. The koss* which is in use during my reign is that prescribed by my father. That is, a koss is 5,000 yards, and the yard is 2 *s͟har'ī* yards, each of the latter (yards) being 24 digits† (*angus͟ht*). Wherever the koss or *gaz* is mentioned, the reference is to the above koss and the above *gaz*. The name of the city is Srīnagar, and the Bihat river flows

---

evidently the Qambarber of Jarrett, II. 347 and 361. It lies in the south-east of Kashmir. Measured by the compass, Jahāngīr's 67 is much more correct than Abū-l-Faẓl's 120. The I.G. new edition gives the area of Kashmir and Jammu as 80,900 square miles. Lawrence states the approximate length of the valley as 84 miles, and the breadth as from 20 to 25 miles.

* The word used by Jahāngīr is *dara'*, which is given by Steingass as Arabic, and as meaning a yard. *Z̲ara'* again, is given as equal to a cubit. Clearly Jahāngīr uses the word here as equivalent to a *gaz* or yard, for he says that there are 5,000 *dara'* in the koss adopted by himself and his father, and Abū-l-Faẓl in the Āyīn (Jarrett, II. 414) says the koss is 5,000 *gaz*. The word *dara'* is also rendered *gaz* in the Hindustani translation of the Memoirs. There is an important discrepancy between the two I.O. MSS. and the printed text of the Memoirs. The former, instead of saying that the *dara'* or yard is = 2 *s͟har'ī dara'*, say that 1¼ *dara'* are = 2 *s͟har'ī dara'*. In the Āyīn (Jarrett, II. 417) the *gaz* is given as equal to 24 digits. See later on, p. 303 of text, where, in describing S͟hāh S͟hujā's accident, 7 *dara'* are said to be equal to 10 *s͟har'ī*, or ordinary, *gaz*.

† See text (thirteenth year), p. 234, where it is stated that the *Ilāhī* gaz is 40 finger-breadths.

through the midst of it. They call its fountain-head Vīr-nāg.* It is 14 koss to the south. By my order they have made a building and a garden at that source. There have been built in the city four very strong stone and wooden bridges, over which people come and go. They call a bridge in the language of this country *kadal.* There is a very lofty mosque in the city, one of the marks of Sulṭān Sikandar,† made in 795 (1393). After a time it was burnt, but was rebuilt by Sulṭān Ḥusain. It had not been completed when the mansion of his life fell down. In 909 (1503-04) Ibrāhīm Māqrī, Vizier of Sulṭān Ḥusain, finished it handsomely. From that day till now it is 120 years since it has been in existence. From the *Miḥrāb* to the eastern wall it is 145 yards, and its breadth is 144 yards, containing four (*ṭāq*) alcoves. On all sides of the hall they have erected beautiful cloisters and pillars. In short, no better memorial of the rulers of Kashmir has been left than this. Mīr Sayyid 'Alī of Hamadan (may his grave be sanctified!) was for some time in this city. There is a monastery‡ to his memory. Near the city there are two§ large lakes full of water all the year round. Their flavour|| does not vary; they are the means for coming and going of the people, and for the conveyance of grain and firewood on boats. In the city and parganas there are 5,700 boats, with 7,400¶ boatmen.

* Vīr is willow, so Vīr-nāg means Willow-fountain.

† Jarrett, II. 387. The I.G., XXIII. 100, says it was built by Zainu-l-'ābidīn. The inscription shows that Zainu-l-'ābidīn built it (Lawrence, 290). It is stated there that it was also burnt in 1029, A.H.—*i.e.*, in the year of Jahāngīr's visit.

‡ *Khānaqāhī.* Lawrence, 292.

§ So in text and MSS., but perhaps *dū* is a mistake for Dal. However, the I.G. speaks of two lakes, the Dal and the Anchar (north of Srīnagar). See also Lawrence, 20 and 36.

|| Probably the meaning is that the water never causes indigestion. Abū-l-Faẓl speaks of the streams being khūsh-guwār—*i.e.*, their water is digestible.

¶ The number of boatmen, when compared with the number of boats, seems very small, but the figures are the same in the I.O. MSS. and in the Iqbāl-nāma, 149. Perhaps the word *bīst*, 20, has been omitted, and we should read 27,400 boatmen. Lawrence states the number of boatmen at 33,870, and the boats, exclusive of private

The country of Kashmir has thirty-eight parganas. It is divided into two provinces; the territory on the upper part of the river they call *Marrāj*, and that on the lower *Kāmrāj*. It is not the custom to use gold and silver for payment of the revenue from land or in commerce, except for a portion of the cesses (*sā'ir-jihāt*).* They reckon the value of things in *kharwārs* of rice, each *kharwār* being three maunds and eight seers of the current weight. The Kashmiris reckon two seers as one maund, and four maunds, or eight seers, make one *tark*. The revenue of Kashmir is 30,63,050 *kharwārs* and 11 *tarks*, which in cash represents 7,46,70,000 *dāms*. Ordinarily it maintains 8,500 horse. It is very difficult to enter Kashmir. The routes by Bhimbhar† and Paklī are the best. Though that by Bhimbhar is the shorter, yet if one wishes to find spring in Kashmir, he is confined to the road by Paklī, for the other roads at this season are blocked with snow. If one were to take to praise Kashmir, whole books would have to be written. Accordingly a mere summary will be recorded.

Kashmir is a garden‡ of eternal spring, or an iron fort to a palace of kings—a delightful flower-bed, and a heart-expanding heritage for dervishes. Its pleasant meads and enchanting cascades are beyond all description. There are running streams and fountains beyond count. Wherever the eye reaches, there are verdure and running water. The red rose, the violet, and the narcissus grow of themselves; in the fields,

---

ones, at 2,417. The revenue of Kashmir, as stated by Jahāngīr, is that mentioned in the Āyīn, Jarrett, II. 366, and is according to the assessment of Qāẓī 'Alī. In the two I.O. MSS. the corresponding number of dāms is given as 7,46,70,400 (Rs. 1,866,760), being only 11 less than that given in Jarrett, II. 367, line 3. The figures given in Lawrence, 234, are taken apparently from the Persian text (compare Bib. Ind. edition, I. 571), corresponding to Jarrett, II. 368. The pargana Der, which Lawrence failed to trace, is a mistake for the well-known Ver, *dal* having been written or read by mistake for *wa*.

* Compare Jarrett, II. 366. "Some part of the Sair Jihat cesses are taken in cash."

† Jarrett, II. 347.

‡ Compare Jarrett, II. 348, where we have "the country is enchanting, and might be fittingly called a garden of perpetual spring surrounding a citadel terraced to the skies."

there are all kinds of flowers and all sorts of sweet-scented herbs more than can be calculated. In the soul-enchanting spring the hills and plains are filled with blossoms; the gates, the walls, the courts, the roofs, are lighted up by the torches of banquet-adorning tulips. What shall we say of these things or of the wide meadows (*julgahā*) and the fragrant trefoil ?

VERSE.

"The garden-nymphs* were brilliant,
Their cheeks shone like lamps ;
There were fragrant buds on their stems (or 'under their rind'),
Like dark amulets on the arms of the beloved.
The wakeful, ode-rehearsing nightingale
Whetted the desires of wine-drinkers ;
At each fountain the duck dipped his beak
Like golden scissors cutting silk ;
There were flower-carpets and fresh rosebuds,
The wind fanned the lamps of the roses,
The violet braided her locks,
The buds tied a knot in the heart."

The finest inflorescence is that of the almond and the peach. Outside the hill-country the commencement of blossoming is the 1st Isfandārmuz̲ (February 10). In the territory of Kashmir it is 1st Farwardīn (March 10), and in the city gardens it is the 9th and 10th of that month, and the end of their blooming joins on to the commencement of that of the blue jessamine. In attendance on my revered father I frequently went round the saffron fields, and beheld the spectacle of the autumn. Thank God that on this occasion I beheld the beauties† of the spring. The beauties of the autumn shall be described in their place. The buildings of Kashmir are all of wood; they make them two-, three-, and four-storied, and covering the roofs with earth, they plant bulbs of the *chaughās̲h̲ī*‡ tulip, which blooms year after year

* That is, the flowers.

† Text *jawānīhā*, but I.O. MSS. have *k̲h̲ūbīhā*.

‡ Apparently the proper spelling is jūg̲h̲ās̲h̲ī. See Vullers' s. v. and Bahār-i-'ajam, 368, col. a. It is a black tulip. Sir George King thought it might be the *Fritillaria imperialis*. See Jarrett, 349, and *n*. 1.

in the spring season, and is exceedingly beautiful. This custom is peculiar to the people of Kashmir. This year, in the little garden* of the palace and on the roof of the chief mosque, the tulips blossomed luxuriantly. There are many blue jessamines in the gardens, and the white jessamines that the people of India call *chambīlī* are sweet-scented. Another kind is of the colour of sandal-wood, and this is also very sweet-scented. This is special to Kashmir. I saw several sorts of red roses: one is specially sweet-scented, and another is a flower of the colour of sandal (light yellow), with an exceedingly delicate scent. It (the scent ?) is of the nature of (that of) the red rose, and its stem is like that of the red rose. There are two kinds of lilies. That which is grown in gardens is vigorous (*bālīda*) and fresh (lit. green) coloured, the other is a wild kind. Although the latter has less colour it is very sweet-scented. The flower of the *Ja'farī*† (a yellow flower) is large and sweet-scented; its stem is above a man's height, but in some years, when it has grown large and has flowered, a worm is produced, and spreads over the flower a kind of spider's web, and destroys it and dries up its stem. This year it has so happened. The flowers that are seen in the territories of Kashmir are beyond all calculation. Those that Nādiru-l-'aṣrī Ustād Manṣūr,‡ has painted are more than 100. Before my father's time there were no *s͟hāh-ālū* (cherries).§ Muḥammad|| Qulī Afs͟hār brought them from Kabul and planted them, and there are now ten or fifteen fruit-bearing trees. There were also some apricot-trees. The aforesaid made them known in this country, and now there are many of them. In fact, the apricot¶ of Kashmir is good.

* Nūr-afzā garden. See *infra*.

† *Tagetes patula*. The genda of Bengal ?

‡ Compare text, p. 235.

§ Compare Jarrett, II. 349, where the words "Besides plums and mulberries" should be "except cherries (s͟hāh-ālū) and s͟hāh-tūt" (a large mulberry).

|| Blochmann, 411. Abū-l-Faẓl, Āyīn, Blochmann, 65, speaks of cherries coming from Kabul. But cherries both sweet and sour are mentioned in the T. Ras͟hīdī as growing in Kashmir (Translation, p. 425).

¶ Zard-ālū-i-paiwandī.

There was a tree in the Shahr-ārā garden at Kabul, called *Mīrzā'ī*, better fruit than which I had not eaten, but in Kashmir there are trees equal to this in the gardens. There are pears (*nāshpātī*) of the best kind, better than those of Kabul, or Badakhshan, and nearly equal to those of Samarkand. The apples of Kashmir are celebrated for their goodness. The guavas (*amrūd*) are middling. Grapes are plentiful, but most of them are harsh and inferior, and the pomegranates are not worth much. Water-melons of the best kind can be obtained. The melons are very sweet and creased, (? *shikananda*)*, but for the most part when they become ripe a worm is found in them that spoils them. If by chance they are preserved from this misfortune they are very delicate. There are no *shāh-tūt*† (some kind of large mulberry), but there are other (*tūt*) mulberries everywhere. From the foot of every mulberry-tree a vine-creeper grows‡ up. In fact, the mulberries of Kashmir are not fit to eat, with the exception of some on trees grown in gardens, but the leaves are used to feed the silkworm. They bring the silkworms' eggs from Gilgit and Tibet. There is plenty of wine and vinegar, but the wine is sour and inferior, and in the Kashmir language is called *mas*. After they take cups of it some heat of head ensues. They make various pickles with the vinegar. As the garlic of Kashmir is good, the best pickle is that of garlic. There are all kinds of crops except peas. If they sow peas, they give a crop the first year, in the second they are inferior, and in the third year they are like *mushang*.§ Rice is the principal crop. Probably there are three parts under rice and one under all other grains. The chief food of the people of Kashmir is rice, but it is inferior. They boil it fresh,|| and allow it to get cold, and then eat it, and call it *batha*. It is not usual to

* *Shikananda*, query, melting. The word occurs also in Iqbāl-nāma, 152. Possibly it means "with good markings."

† But see I.G., XV. 124, where shāh-tūt is mentioned. See also Lawrence, 348.

‡ Compare Jarrett, II. 349.

§ *Mushang* or *mushanj*, a small pea ("pisum arvense").

|| Text *khushka-tar*. MSS. have *khushka narm*. Perhaps we should translate "it is inferior and dry. They boil till it is soft, etc." The Iqbāl-nāma has *khushka narm mī-pazand*.

take their food warm, but people of small means keep a portion of the *batha* for a night, and eat it next day. Salt is brought from India. It is not the custom to put salt into the *batha*. They boil vegetables in water, and throw in a little salt in order to alter the flavour, and then eat them along with the *batha*. Those who want to have something tasty put a little walnut-oil into the vegetables. Walnut-oil soon becomes bitter and evil-flavoured. They also use cow-oil (*raughan*—*i.e.*, *ghi*), but this is taken fresh, and fresh from newly-made butter (*maska*). They throw this into the food, and call it "sadā-pāk" in the Kashmiri language. As the atmosphere is cold and damp, it becomes altered by being kept for three or four days. There are no buffaloes, and the cattle are small and inferior. The wheat* is small and of little substance (*kam maghz*). It is not the custom to eat bread (*nān*). There are tailless sheep, resembling the *kadī*† (or *gaddī*) of India. They are called *handū*, and their flesh is not without flavour. Fowls, geese, and ducks (*murghābī*)—golden and others—are plentiful. There are all kinds of fish, both with and without scales, but they are inferior. The woollen cloths are well known. Men and women wear a woollen tunic (*kurtā*), and call it *paṭṭū*. If they do not put on a tunic, they believe that the air affects them, and even that it is impossible to digest their food without it. The shawls of Kashmir, to which my father gave the name of *parm-narm*, are very famous: there is no need to praise them. Another kind is *taharma* (*naharma* in the printed version); it is thicker than a shawl, and soft.‡

* The sentence about wheat is omitted in the text.

† Text *kūhī* ("hill"); but this is opposed to the MSS and also to the Āyīn-i-Akbarī which Jahangir is evidently copying. See Jarrett, II. 350, and *n.* 3, and Persian text, I. 563. The I.O. MSS. of Tūzuk have *kaddī* or *gaddī*. *Gaddī* is the name of a pastoral tribe (see Lawrence, 12), and there is a Turkish word *kedī* meaning a cat, and a word *gaddī* which means "horned." The Iqbāl-nāma, 153, has "*kadī-i-Hindustān*." Jarrett, *loc. cit*, states that *handū* in Kashmiri means a domestic ram. The word for tailless is *bī-dumba*, and perhaps means that the sheep have not the enormously thick tails of some kinds of hill sheep.

‡ Possibly *nahrma* ("like a river"), is right, for the garment is said to be *mauj-dār* ("having waves"). The word *mauj-dār* occurs in the Iqbāl-nāma, 153, and in the two I.O. MSS.

Another is called *darma*. It is like a *jul-i-khirsak*,* and is put over carpets. With the exception of shawls they make other woollen materials better in Tibet. Though they bring the wool for the shawls from Tibet they do not make them there. The wool for shawls comes from a goat which is peculiar to Tibet. In Kashmir they weave the *paṭṭū* shawl from wool, and sewing two shawls together they smooth them into a kind of *saqarlāt* (broad-cloth), which is not bad for a rain-coat. The men of Kashmir shave the head and put on a round turban, and the common women do not wear clean, washed clothes. They use a tunic of *paṭṭū* for three or four years; they bring it unwashed from the house of the weaver, and sew it into a tunic, and it does not reach the water till it falls to pieces. It is considered wrong to wear drawers (*izār*); they wear the tunic long and ample as far as the head and falling down to the feet, and they also wear† a belt. Although most of the houses are on the river-bank not a drop of water touches their bodies. In short, they are as dirty outside as inside, without any cleanliness. In the time of Mīrzā Ḥaidar there were many skilled people there. They were skilled in music, and their lutes, dulcimers, harps, drums, and flutes were celebrated. In former times they had a musical instrument like a lute, and used to sing in the Kashmirī language compositions according to Hindi musical modes, there being even two or three modes combined together. Moreover, many sing together in chorus. In fact, Kashmir is much indebted to Mīrzā Ḥaidar for its excellencies. Before the reign of my father the chief method by which the people of these parts rode was on *gūnts* (ponies). They had no large horses, but used to bring 'Irāq and Turki horses by way of rare gifts for their rulers. *Gūnt* means a *yābū*‡ (pony).

* *Jul* is a coverlet, and *khirsak* means a little bear, but is applied to a rough woollen coverlet—a drugget. *Darma* is a name in Bengal for a reed mat.

† Perhaps "tie it at the waist." But see Lawrence, 252: "The Panditana wears a girdle, but no drawers."

‡ The MSS. have *ṭaṭṭū*. Both they and the text have also the words *chahār shāna ba-zamīn nazdīk*. *Chahār shāna* means a dwarf. Literally it means "four shoulders," and Vullers following, the Bahār-i-

They have thick shoulders, and are low in the body. They are common in other of the hill-countries of India. For the most part they are vicious* and hard-mouthed. When this God-created flower-garden acquired eternal beauty under the auspices of the State, and by the blessing of the teaching of the Alexander-minded K͟hāqān, many of the Aimāqs (cavalry) were presented with jagirs in this Subah, and herds of 'Irāqī and Turkī horses were given them to breed from (*kih kurra bagīrand*). The soldiers also brought horses† on their own account, and in a short time horses were obtainable, so that many Kashmiri horses were bought and sold for 200 and Rs. 300, and even for Rs. 1,000.

The merchants and artificers of this country are mostly Sunnis, while the soldiers are Imāmiyya Shias. There is also the sect of Nūr-bak͟hs͟hīs.‡ There is also a body of Faqirs whom they call *Rīs͟hīs*.§ Though they have not religious knowledge or learning of any sort, yet they possess simplicity, and are without pretence. They abuse no one, they restrain

---

'Ajam, defines it as a man of small stature with thick shoulders. Evidently the words *ba-zamīn nazdīk* are meant as an explanation or addition to *Chahār-s͟hāna*, and signify that the *yābū* or *ṭaṭṭū* has his withers near the ground. The words also occur in the Iqbāl-nāma, 154.

* *Jangrah u s͟hak͟h-jilau*. *Jangrah*, however, may refer to their gait, and may mean that they don't go straight, and very likely we should read *changrah* "going crookedly." *Shak͟h-jilau* is not in the dictionaries, and I only guess at the meaning. The phrase is also in the Iqbāl-nāma, 154.

† Text *īlchī-i-sāmān*. The real word is *īlk͟hī*, which is also spelt *īlqī* and *īlghī*, and is a Turki word meaning a horse, and also a troop of horses. See Pavet de Courteille Dictionary, p. 132, and Vullers I. 149*b*, who refers to the Burhān-i-qāṭi', Appendix. See also Zenker, p. 152. The Iqbāl-nāma, p. 155, top line, wrongly has *balk͟hhā* (from Balkh?).

‡ Jarrett, II. 352, and *n*. 1, also T. Ras͟hīdī, translation, 435. But perhaps all that is meant is the followers of the national saint S͟haik͟h Nūru-d-dīn. Lawrence, 287.

§ Taken from the Āyīn, see Jarrett, II. 353. There they are called brahmans, but this seems to be an error of the Bib. Ind. text. Gladwin has "Rishi." The Rīs͟hīs were Muhammadans. See Jarrett, II. 359, where mention is made of Bābā Zainu-d-dīn Ris͟hī. See also Colonel Newall's paper on the Rīs͟hīs or Hermits of Kashmir, A.S.B.J., 1870, p. 265.

the tongue of desire, and the foot of seeking; they eat no flesh, they have no wives, and always plant fruit-bearing trees in the fields, so that men may benefit by them, themselves deriving no advantage. There are about 2,000 of these people. There is also a body of brahmans living from of old in this country, who still remain there and talk in the Kashmiri tongue. Outwardly one cannot distinguish them from Mussulmans. They have, however, books in the Sanskrit language, and read them. They carry into practice whatever relates to the worship of idols. Sanskrit is a language in which the learned of India have composed books, and esteem them greatly. The lofty idol temples which were built before the manifestation of Islam are still in existence, and are all built of stones, which from foundation to roof are large, and weigh 30 or 40 maunds, placed one on the other. Near the city there is a small hill which they call Kūh-i-Mārān* ("The Wicked Hill," Lawrence 298), as well as Harī Parbat. On the east side of the hill there is the Dal Lake, which measures round a little more than 6½ koss.† My father (may the lights of Allah be his testimony!) gave an order that they should build in this place a very strong fort of stone and lime; this has been nearly completed during the reign of this suppliant, so that the little hill has been brought into the midst of the fortifications, and the wall of the fort built round it. The lake is close to the fort, and the palace overlooks the water. In the palace there was a little garden, with a small building in it in which my revered father used constantly to sit. At this period it appeared to me to be very much out of order and ruinous. As it was the place where that veritable *qibla* (place turned towards in prayer) and visible Deity used to sit, and it is really a place of prostration for this suppliant, therefore its neglected state did not appear right to me. I ordered Mu'tamid K., who is a servant who knows my temperament,

* Text Bārān. MSS. have Mārān, and Eastwick has Koh-i-Mahran. He calls it an isolated hill 250 feet high. It is on the north outskirts of the city. See also Lawrence, 184, and *n.* 2, and Stein, 147-48.

† The Dal Lake is 3·87 miles long and 2·58 broad, the Ānchar Dal is 3·51 miles long and 2·15 broad. Lawrence, 20.

to make every effort to put the little garden in order and repair the buildings. In a short space of time, through his great assiduity, it acquired new beauty. In the garden he put up a lofty terrace 32 yards square, in three divisions (*qiṭ'a*), and having repaired the building he adorned it with pictures by masterhands, and so made it the envy of the picture gallery of China. I called this garden *Nūr-afzā* (light increasing).

On Friday, the 15th of the Divine month of Farwardīn, two *quṭās* oxen, out of the offerings of the Zamindar of Tibet, were brought before me. In form and appearance they closely resemble the buffalo. All the limbs are covered with wool which properly belongs to animals in a cold country. For instance, the *rang* goats (ibex), which they brought from the country of Bhakkar (Sind) and the hill-country of the Garmsīr (in Afghanistan) were very handsome, and had but little wool, and those that are met with in these hills, on account of the excessive cold and snow, are covered with hair and ugly. The Kashmiris call the rang *kapal.** On this day they brought a musk deer as an offering. As I had not tasted its flesh, I ordered it to be cooked; it appeared very tasteless and bad for food. The flesh of no other wild animal is so inferior. The musk-bag when fresh has no scent, but when it is left for some days and becomes dry, it is sweet-scented. The female has no musk-bag. In these two or three days I frequently embarked in a boat, and was delighted to go† round and look at the flowers of Phāk and Shālamār. Phāk is the name of a pargana situated on the other side of the lake. Shālamār is near the lake. It has a pleasant stream, which comes down from the hills, and flows into the Dal Lake. I bade my son Khurram dam it up and make a waterfall, which it would be a pleasure to behold. This place is one of the sights of Kashmir.

On Sunday, the 17th, a strange affair took place. Shāh Shujā' was playing in the buildings of the palace. By chance there was a window with a screen in front of it looking towards

* MSS. have *kīl*, and so has the Iqbāl-nāma. *Kīl* is given in Lawrence, 114, as the Kashmir name for the ibex.

† Jarrett, II. 360.

the river. They had put a screen in front, but had not fastened the door, and the prince in play went towards the window to look out. As soon as he arrived there he fell headlong. By chance they had laid down a carpet below the wall, and a farrāsh (carpet-spreader) was sitting near it. The child's head fell on this carpet, and his feet on the back and shoulders of the farrāsh, and so came to the ground. Though the height was 7 yards* (*dara'*), the compassion of God, the Great and Glorious, came to his aid, and the carpet and the farrāsh became the means of saving his life. God forbid, but if it had not been so it would have been a serious matter for him. At the time Rāy Mān, the head of the Khidmatiyya † piyādas, was standing below the *jharoka*. He immediately ran and picked him up, and holding him in his arms, was taking him upstairs. In that condition he asked: "Whither are you carrying me?" He replied: "Into the presence of His Majesty." Then weakness overcame him, and he could speak no more. I was lying down when this alarming news reached me, and ran out in a state of bewilderment. When I saw him in this state my senses forsook me, and for a long time holding him in my affectionate embrace I was distracted with this favour from Allah. When a child of four years of age falls headlong from a place ten ordinary (*shar'ī*) gaz in height, and no harm happens to his limbs, it is a cause for amazement. Having performed my prostrations for this fresh act of goodness, I distributed alms; and ordered that deserving people and the poor who lived in the city should be brought before me in order that I might assure them their means of livelihood. A strange thing was that three or four months before this event Jotik Rāy, the astrologer, who is one of the most skilled of the class in astrology, had represented to me, without any intermediary, that it was predicted from the Prince's horoscope that these three or four months were unpropitious to him, and it was possible he might fall down from some high place, but that the dust of calamity would not settle on the skirt of his life. As his prognostications had repeatedly proved correct, this dread dwelt in

* This is the *Ilāhī gaz*.

† Blochmann, 252, and note.

my mind, and on these dangerous roads and difficult mountain passes I was never for a moment forgetful of that nursling of the *parterre* of Fortune. I continually kept him in sight, and took the greatest precautions with regard to him. When I arrived in Kashmir this unavoidable* catastrophe occurred. His nurses (*anagahā*) and wet-nurses must have been very careless. God be praised that it ended well!

In the garden of ʻAishābād† (abode of pleasure) I saw a tree which had numerous‡ blossoms. They were very large and beautiful, but the apples that the tree produced were bitter.

As excellent service had been done by Dilāwar K. Kākar, I promoted him to the mansab of 4,000 personal and 3,000 horse, and also conferred mansabs on his sons. Shaikh Farīd, s. Quṭbu-d-dīn K. was raised to the mansab of 1,000 personal and 400 horse. The mansab of Sar-barāh K. was ordered to be 700 personal and 250 horse, and I promoted Nūru-llah Kurkīrāq (in charge of furriery ?) to that of 600 personal and 100 horse, bestowing on him the title of Tashrīf K. The offerings of Thursday, the 21st, were handed over as a reward to Qiyām K., the chief huntsman. As Allah-dād Afghan, s. the Tārīkī,§ had repented of his evil deeds and come to Court at the request of Iʻtmādu-d-daula I pardoned his offences; the signs of disgrace and shame were evident on his forehead and, according to the previous arrangement, I bestowed on him the mansab of 2,500 and 200 horse. Mīrak Jalāyir, one of the auxiliaries of Bengal, was promoted to the mansab of 1,000 personal and 400 horse.

As it was reported that the *jūghāsī* (*i.e.*, black) tulips were in good bloom on the roof of the Jāmiʻ mosque, on Saturday, the 23rd, I went to see them. In truth, one side of that

* So called because in Shujāʻ's horoscope.

† A village called ʻAish-maqām is mentioned in Jarrett, II. 359, *n*. 1, but it is probably not the ʻAishābād here mentioned, for ʻAish-maqām was on the Lidar and a long way S.S.E. Srinagar.

‡ *Shigūfa-i-sad-barg* ("the blossoms of the hundred-leaved rose"?).

§ Allah-dād was s. Jalālu-d-dīn Tārīkī, also called Raushānī, and he became a distinguished officer of Shāh-Jahān under the title of Rashīd K. See Ma'āṣir, II. 248, and Dabistān, 390.

flower-garden was very beautiful. The parganas of Mau* and Mihrī (?) (text has Maud Mihrī), which previously to this had been granted to Rāja Bāso, and afterwards continued to his rebel son Sūraj Mal, were now bestowed on Jagat Singh, his brother, who had not obtained the *tīka* (mark of royal succession), and I gave the pargana of Jammū to Rāja Sangrām. On Monday, the 1st of Urdībihisht, I went to the house of Khurram, and entered his bath-house, and when I came out he presented his offerings. Of these I accepted a trifle in order to please him. On Thursday, the 4th, Mīr Jumla was promoted to the mansab of 2,000 personal and 300 horse. On Sunday, the 7th, I rode to the village of Chārdara,† which is the native country of Ḥaidar Malik, to hunt partridges. In truth this is a very pleasant spot of ground, and has flowing streams and lofty plane-trees. At his request I gave it the name of Nūrpūr‡ (city of light). On the road there was a tree§ called *halthal;* when one takes one of the branches and shakes it, the whole of the tree comes into movement. The common people believe that this movement is peculiar to that tree. By chance in the said village I saw another tree of the same kind, which was in similar movement, and I ascertained that it was common to that species of tree, and not confined to one tree. In the village of Rāwalpūr, 2½ koss from the city towards Hindustan, there is a plane-tree, burnt in the inside. Twenty-five years before this, when I myself

* There are different readings. No. 181 has Maud and Mihrī. Apparently it is the Mau and Nabah of Jarrett, II. 319, where also there are various readings. See also Tūzuk, 263, where the text has Mau u shahra.

† Or Chārvara. See Rieu. Catalogue, I. 297. Ḥaidar Malik wrote a history of Kashmir. It was he who protected Nūr-Jahān after her first husband's murder. Stein has Cadura, *recte* Isādur, p. 43; it is 10 miles south of Srinagar.

‡ An allusion to Nūr-Jahān and to Nūru-d-dīn Jahāngīr.

§ See Akbar-nāma, III. 542, and Ṭabaqāt-i-Akbarī extract in Appendix, translation of Tārikh-i-Rashīdī, p. 490. The place was Khānpūr or near it. Perhaps the tree is the Adansonïa. See also Jarrett, II. 363. According to Stein, 191, Halthal is the name of the village, and is a corruption of Salasthala. This agrees with the Āyīn I. 569, but not with Akbar-nāma III. 542, where *halthal* is given as the name of the tree.

was riding on a horse, with five other saddled horses and two eunuchs, we went inside it. Whenever I had chanced to mention this people were surprised. This time I again ordered some of the men to go inside, and what I had in my mind came to pass in the same manner. It has been noted in the Akbar-nāma that my father took* thirty-four people inside and made them stand close to each other.

On this day it was represented to me that Prithī-chand, s. Rāy Manohar, who was one of the auxiliaries of the army against Kāngra, had sacrificed his life in a useless (*bī-ṣarfa*†) battle with the enemy.

On Thursday, the 11th, certain servants of the State were promoted in the following manner: Tātār K. to 2,000 personal and 500 horse; 'Abdu-l-'Azīz K. to 2,000 personal and 1,000 horse; Debī Chand of Gwalior to 1,500 personal and 500 horse; Mīr Khān, s. Abū-l-Qāsim K. Namakīn to 1,000 personal and 600 horse; Mīrzā Muḥammad to 700 personal and 300 horse; Luṭfu-llah to 300 personal and 500 horse; Naṣru-llah 'Arab to 500 personal and 250 horse; and Tahawwur K. was appointed to the faujdarship of Mewāt. On Thursday, the 25th, Sayyid Bāyazīd Bukhārī, faujdar of Bhakkar, raised his head of honour with the Subadarship of Sind, and his mansab, original and increased, was fixed at 2,000 personal and 1,500 horse, and he was also presented with a standard. Shajā'at K. 'Arab obtained the honour of exaltation to the mansab of 2,500 personal and 2,000 horse. Anīrā'ī Singh-dalan, at the request of Mahābat K., was appointed to Bangash. Jān-sipār K. was promoted to the mansab of 2,000 personal and 1,500 horse.

At this time, on the representation of the Commander-in-Chief, Khān-Khānān, and all the loyal people, it was shown to me that 'Ambar, the black-fated one (he was an Abyssinian), had again placed his foot beyond the bounds of good behaviour,

* I have not found this passage in the Akbar-nāma. The Iqbāl-nāma, 159, says that 70 people stood erect inside of the trunk. Rāwal-pūr is marked on the map of Kashmir, a little to the south of Srinagar. Niẓāmu-d-dīn, in his chapter on Kashmir in the Ṭabaqāt-i-Akbarī, speaks of a tree under the shade of which 200 horsemen could stand.

† Possibly *bī-ṣarfa* only means "unsuccessful." But it is used lower down (text 308, line 8), in the sense of immoderate or unprofitable.

and had, according to his nature, laid a foundation for trouble and sedition, and as the victorious army had proceeded to a distant part of the country, he, considering it a good opportunity, had broken the pledges he had given to the servants of the Court, and had stretched out his hand to take possession of royal territory. It is hoped that he will soon be entangled in the disgrace of his deeds. As he (the Commander-in-Chief) had asked for treasure, it was ordered that the diwans of Agra should send Rs. 20,00,000 to the Commander-in-Chief. Close upon this news came that the Amirs had left their posts, and come together to Dārāb K., and that the *Bargīs** (the Mahrattas) were surrounding his camp, and that K͟hanjar K. had taken refuge in Aḥmadnagar. Two or three battles had already taken place between the rebels and the servants of the Court, and each time the enemy had been defeated, and many of them killed. On the last occasion Dārāb K., taking with him well-mounted young men, attacked the rebels' camp. A fierce battle ensued, and the enemy being defeated turned the face of ruin towards the valley of flight. Their camp had been plundered, and the victorious army had returned in safety to their camp. As difficulty and distress had fallen on the victorious army, those who were loyal came to the conclusion that they should go down by the Pass of Rohangaṛh† and remain below the *ghāt*, so that forage and grain might be easily obtained, and the men not incur any labour or distress. Having no choice, they prepared the army of prosperity at Bālāpūr, and the rebels of black fortune, with impertinence and importunity, appeared near Bālāpūr. Rāja Bīr Singh Deo, with some of the devoted servants, plucking up courage in order to beat back the enemy, slew many of them. An Abyssinian of the name of Manṣūr, who was in the rebel army, fell into their hands, and although they wished to put him on an elephant (see Iqbāl-nāma 161, the text wrongly has *zīr* "under"), he would not agree, and was insolent.‡ Rāja Bīr Singh Deo ordered them to separate his

* Text has Turks (Turkiyān).

† Apparently the Rohankhed of I.G., XXI. 304.

‡ Literally, "raised the foot of ignorance."

head from his body. It is hoped that the circling sphere will lay the recompense of improper deeds on the skirt of life of all who do not recognize the right.

On the 3rd Urdībihis͟ht I rode to see the Sukh Nāg.* It is a beautiful summer residence (īlāq). This waterfall is in the midst of a valley, and flows down from a lofty place. There was still ice on its sides. The entertainment of Thursday was arranged for in that flower-land, and I was delighted at drinking my usual cups on the edge of the water. In this stream I saw a bird like a *sāj*.† A *sāj* is of a black colour and has white spots, while this bird is of the same colour as a *bulbul* with white spots, and it dives and remains for a long time underneath, and then comes up from a different place. I ordered them to catch and bring two or three of these birds, that I might ascertain whether they were waterfowl and were web-footed, or had open feet like land birds. They caught two and brought them. One died immediately, and the other lived for a day. Its feet were not webbed like a duck's. I ordered Nādiru-l-'aṣr Ustād Manṣūr to draw its likeness. The Kashmiris call it *galkar*‡—that is, "water sāj."

On this day the Qazi and the Chief Justice represented to me that 'Abdu-l-Wahhāb, the son of Ḥakīm 'Alī, claimed Rs. 80,000 from the Sayyids of Lahore, and produced a bond with the seal of Qāẓī Nūru-llah. He said that his father had placed that sum in deposit with Sāyyid Walī, the father of these men, who denied it.§ If an order were given, the

* Perhaps Sukh Nāg is the Shakar Nāg of Jarrett, II. 361. The Sukh Nāg River is mentioned in Lawrence, 16. It may also be the waterfall mentioned by Bernier, which he says Jahangir visited and levelled a rock in order to see properly.

† From Dr. Scully's list it appears that this is the sāch, the rose-coloured starling, *Pastor roseus.* See also Vullers, Dictionary, s. v. The bird seen by Jahangir may have been a dipper, Lawrence, 153.

‡ The MSS. have *kulhai*.

§ According to the two I.O. MSS.—which are corroborated by the Iqbāl-nāma—the text has here omitted an important part of the report—presumably a written one—submitted by the Qazi and the Mīr 'Adl. After the words "denied it," there comes in the MSS. the statement: "The Ḥakīm-zāda (Ḥakīm's son) produced two witnesses in court. The Sayyids invalidated (or impeached) the testimony of one of them, and the Ḥakīm-zāda brought a third witness

Ḥakīm's son, by way of caution,* would swear an oath on the Qoran, and would take what was his due from them. I told them to do whatever was right by the Divine Law. The next day Mu'tamid Khān represented that the Sayyids showed great humility and submissiveness. The matter was a complicated† one. The greater reflection shown in ascertaining the truth in the matter the better. I accordingly ordered that Āṣaf K. should take exceeding trouble and forethought in ascertaining the truth of this quarrel, and point out such a way (of unravelling it) that no doubt whatever should remain. With all this, if it could not be cleared up, I would examine them in my own presence. Immediately he heard these words, the Ḥakīm's son lost both his hands and his heart in the affair, and made a number of his friends intercessors, and proposed a withdrawal. His representation was that if the Sayyids would not‡ refer the matter to Āṣaf K. he would give a release, and that hereafter he would have no right against nor claim from them. Whenever Āṣaf K. sent to fetch him, as he was a low deceiver, he passed his time in making excuses, and did not appear until he handed over the deed of release to one of his friends, and the true state of affairs became evident to Āṣaf K. They brought him by force into the place of examination, and, having no choice, he confessed that the deed had been prepared by one of his servants, who himself witnessed it, and had misled him. He gave a writing to this effect. When Āṣaf K. informed me of the real state of matters, I took away his mansab and jagir, and cast him out of my presence, and gave the Sayyids leave to return to Lahore in all honour and respect.

---

and proved his case according to law." The Iqbāl-nāma, p. 161, has not the whole of this, and it has *khārij* instead of *jāriḥ*, but it has the words *guwāh-i-ṣāliṣ* ("a third witness").

* The meaning seems to be that he would in corroboration and *ex cautela* take the oath. He had already proved his claim in the ordinary way by witnesses and the production of the bond. See the account in the Iqbāl-nāma, 160-63, which is fuller than that in text.

† *Mu'āmala-i-kullī ast.* "The case was involved" (like a bud ?), or perhaps "the case was important."

‡ The text wrongly omits the negative. See Iqbāl-nāma, I. 62.

On Mubārak-shamba (Thursday), the 8th of Khūrdād, I'tiqād Khān was promoted to the mansab of 4,000 personal and 1,500 horse, and Ṣādiq Khān to that of 2,500 personal and 1,400 horse. Zainu-l-'ābidīn, son of the deceased Āṣaf Khān (Ja'far), was promoted to be Bakhshi of *Aḥadīs*. Rāja Bīr Singh Deo Bandīla raised his head of honour with the high mansab of 5,000 personal and horse.

In Kashmir the most juicy(?) fruit is the *ashkan* (?) (*askamī* in the MSS.). It is subacid (*mai-khūsh*), smaller than the *ālū bālū* (sour cherry), much better flavoured, and more delicate. When drinking wine, one cannot eat more than three or four *ālū bālū*, but of these one can take as many as a hundred in twenty-four hours, especially of the *paiwandī* (?) sort. I ordered that the *ashkan* should hereafter be called the *khūshkan*. It grows in the hills of Badakhshan and in Khurasan; the people there call it *jamdamī*. The largest of them weigh ½ *misqāl*. The *shāh-ālū* (cherry), on the 4th Urdībihisht, appeared of the size of a grain of pulse; on the 27th it reddened, and on the 15th Khūrdād it was ripe, and new fruit (*nau-bar*) had formed (?). The *shāh-ālū* (cherry), to my taste, is better than most fruits. Four trees had borne fruit in the Nūr-afzā garden. I called one of these *Shīrīn-bār*, the second *Khūsh-guwār*, the third, which bore the most fruit, *Pur-bār*, and the fourth, which had less, *Kam-bār*. One tree in Khurram's garden had also borne fruit, and I called it *Shāhwār*. There was a young plant in the little garden of *'Ishrat-afzā* (joy enhancing), and this I called *Nau-bār* (new fruit). Every day I plucked with my own hand sufficient to give a flavour to my cups. Although they sent them by runners from Kabul as well, yet to pick them oneself from one's home garden gave additional sweetness. The *shāh-ālū* of Kashmir is not inferior to that of Kabul; it is even better grown. The largest of them weighed one *tānk*, five *surkhs*.

On Tuesday, the 21st, Pādshāh* Bānū Begam died (became a sitter in the bridal chamber of the permanent world), and

*Apparently this was Ṣāliḥa Bānū d. Qā'im K. Blochmann, 371, and 477, *n.* 2. She had the name of Pādshāh-maḥall. See Hawkins' account in Purchas, IV. 31, and Khāfī K. I. 259. He calls the father Qāsim.

grief for this heart-rending event laid a heavy load on my mind. I hope that Almighty God may give her a place near his own forgiveness. A strange thing is—that Jotik Rāy, the astrologer, two months before this, had informed some of my servants that one of the chief sitters in the harem of chastity would hasten to the hidden abode of non-existence. He had discovered this from the horoscope of my destiny, and it fell out accordingly.

One of the events (that now took place) was the martyrdom of Sayyid 'Izzat* K. and of Jalāl K. Gakhar in the army of Bangash. The particulars of this are that when the season for the collection of revenue arrived, Mahābat K. appointed a force to go into the hill-country to eat up the crops of the Afghans, and not omit one tittle of raiding and plundering, and killing and binding. When the servants of the Court arrived at the foot of the Pass the ill-fated Afghans attacked them from all sides, and took the head of the Pass, and fortified it. Jalāl K., who was an experienced man, and an old man that had undergone labours, thought it better to delay for a few days, so that the Afghans might expend the few days' provisions they had brought with them on their backs, and necessarily disperse of their own accord; that then his men would be able to cross with ease over the head of the difficult Pass. When he once passed the head of the defile they would be unable to do any more, and would be punished. 'Izzat K., who was a battle-lighting flame and a foe-burning lightning, did not fall in with Jalāl K.'s idea, and excited the steed of courage of some of the Sayyids of Bārha. The Afghans, swarming round on all sides, like ants and locusts, attacked him, and caught him in their midst. Though the battle-field was not fit for cavalry, yet wherever the forehead of his wrath shone, he consumed many with the fire of his sword. In the midst of the fighting they hamstringed his horse, but he fought on foot and as long as he had breath, and at last fell bravely. At the time when 'Izzat K. made his attack, Jalāl K. Gakhar† and Mas'ūd, s. Aḥmad Beg K., and Bīzan

* It is Ghairat K. in I.O. MS., 181.

† For Jalāl K., see Blochmann, 455 and 486. He was grandson of Sulṭān Ādam.

(or Bīzhan), s. Nād 'Alī Maidānī, and other servants, lost restraint, and rushed on from all sides of the pass, and the rebels seized the tops of the hills, and fought with stones and arrows. The devoted young men, both of the servants of the Court and the retainers of Mahābat K., performed the duties of valour, and slaughtered many of the Afghans. In this contest Jalāl K. and Mas'ūd, with many other brave men, sacrificed their lives. Owing to the rashness of 'Izzat K. such a disaster as this befell the Imperial army.

When Mahābat K. heard this fearful news, he sent a fresh body of men to assist, and strengthened the posts. Wherever they found a trace of those ill-fortuned ones, they did not fail to slay or bind them. When I heard this news, I summoned Akbar Qulī, s. Jalāl K., who had been told off for duty in the conquest of the fort of Kāngra, to my presence, and gave him the mansab of 1,000 personal and 1,000 horse, and confirmed to him, according to custom, his hereditary territory (the Gakhar country) in jagir, presented him with a dress of honour and a horse, and sent him to the support of the army of Bangash. As 'Izzat K. had left a son of very tender years, keeping before my eyes, that discerned the truth, his life-sacrifice, I gave him (the child) a mansab and a jagir, so that those left behind should not be scattered abroad, and others might have increased hope.

On this day Shaikh Aḥmad of Sirhind, who had for some time been placed in the prison of correction on account of his pretentiousness (literally, adorning his shop and selling himself) and immoderate language, was summoned to my presence, and I released him, giving him a dress of honour and Rs. 1,000 for expenses, and making him free to go or remain. He justly represented that his punishment had really been a valuable lesson to him, and that his desire was to wait on me.

On the 27th Khūrdād apricots arrived* (from Kabul). The picture-gallery in the garden had been ordered to be repaired; it was now adorned with pictures by master hands. In the

* *Rasīd.* See lower down text 308, where it is noted that the cherries came to an end.

most honoured positions were the likenesses of Humāyūn and of my father opposite to my own, and that of my brother Shāh 'Abbās. After them were the likenesses of Mīrzā Kāmrān, Mīrzā Muḥammad Ḥakīm, Shāh Murād, and Sulṭān Dāniyāl. On the second storey (row ?) were the likenesses of the Amirs and special servants. On walls of the outer hall the stages of the road to Kashmir were recorded in the order in which I had come to them. A poet fixed the date by this hemistich:

Pictures of kings of Solomon-like glory.*

On Thursday, the 4th of the Ilāhī month of Tīr, the Feast of *būriyā-kūbī*† took place. On this day the Kashmir cherries came to an end. From the four trees of the Nūr-afzā garden, 1,500, and from other trees 500 had been plucked. I strictly ordered the officials of Kashmir to plant *shāh-ālū* (cherry) trees in all the gardens. On this day Bhīm, s. Rānā Amar Singh, was honoured with the title of Raja, and Dilīr K., brother of the brave 'Izzat K., was promoted to the mansab of 1,000 personal and 800 horse, Muḥammad Sa'īd, s. Aḥmad Beg K., to that of 600 personal and 400 horse, and Mukhliṣ-ullah, his brother, to that of 500 personal and 250 horse. On Sayyid Aḥmad Ṣadr the mansab of 1,000, and on Mīrzā Ḥusain, s. Mīrzā Rustam Ṣafawī, that of 1,000 personal and 500 horse, were bestowed, and the last-named was despatched for duty to the Deccan. On Sunday, the 14th of the Divine month of Tīr, Ḥasan 'Alī Turkmān was made Governor of Orissa, and his personal and horse mansab was raised to 3,000. On this day Bahādur K., Governor of Qandahar, sent offerings of nine Iraq horses, some nine pieces of gold brocade, some brocaded satin, and some marten‡ skins, and other things; these were laid before me.

On Monday, the 15th, I rode to see the summer quarters

* This represents A.H. 1029, or 1620.

† Mat-treading or beating=house-warming. This was in honour of the new picture-gallery.

‡ *Dānahā-i-kīsh*. See Vullers, s.v. Kesh. The *kīsh* is a marten of whose skin neckcloths, etc., are made. This note corrects the one at p. 321 of translation, as also the text there.

of Tūsī-marg* (?). Arriving in two marches at the foot of the *kotal,* on Wednesday, the 17th, I reached the top of the pass. For a distance of 2 koss very elevated ground was crossed with difficulty. From the top of the *kotal* to the *Īlāq* (summer quarters) was another koss of high and low land. Although here and there flowers of various colours had bloomed, yet I did not see so many as they had represented to me, and as I had expected. I heard that in this neighbourhood there was a very beautiful valley, and on Thursday, the 18th, I went to see it. Undoubtedly, whatever praise they might use in speaking of that flowery land would be permissible. As far as the eye reached flowers of all colours were blooming. There were picked fifty kinds of flowers in my presence. Probably there were others that I did not see. At the end of the day I turned my reins in order to return. That night an account was given in my presence of the siege of Ahmadnagar. Khān-Jahān told a strange tale, which I had also heard before, and it is written on account of its strangeness. At the time when my brother Dāniyāl was besieging the fort of Ahmadnagar, one day the garrison laid the gun *Malik-maidān*† (king of the plain) against the Prince's camp, and fired it. The ball reached nearly to the Prince's tent; from that place it bounded (ricocheted), and went to the lodging of Qāẓī Bāyazīd, who was one of the Prince's companions, and fell there. They had tied up the Qazi's horse at a distance of 3 or 4 gaz. As the ball touched the ground, the horse's tongue‡ was torn out by the root and fell on the ground. The ball was of stone, weighing 10 maunds as current in Hindustan, or 80 Khurasan maunds. The said gun is so large that a man can sit comfortably in it.

On this day I promoted Abu-l-Ḥasan, the chief Bakshi, to the mansab of 5,000 personal and 2,000 horse, Mubāriz K. to that of 2,000 personal and 1,700 horse, Bīzan (or Bīzhan),

* It is Būsī-marg in the I.O. MSS. But perhaps the text is right, and the place is the Tosh Maidān of Lawrence, 16.

† The gun is now at Bijapur, I.G., VIII. 186.

‡ Compare Iqbāl-nāma, 163-64. The text has *rān* ("thigh") instead of *zabān*.

s. Nād 'Alī, to that of 1,000 personal and 500 horse, and Amānat K. to that of 2,000 personal and 400 horse. On Thursday, the 25th, I gave Nawāzish K., s. Sa'īd K., the mansab of 3,000 personal and 2,000 horse, Himmat K. that of 2,000 personal and 1,500 horse, and Sayyid Ya'qūb K., s. Sayyid Kamāl Bukhārī, that of 800 personal and 500 horse. Mīr 'Alī 'Askar,* s. Mīr 'Alī Akbar Mūsawī, was dignified with the title of Mūsawī K. As I had repeatedly heard praise of the *Īlāq* of Kūrī-marg,† I felt much disposed to visit it at this time, and on Tuesday, the 7th Amurdād, rode in that direction. How shall I write its praise? As far as the eye could reach flowers of various hue were blooming, and in the midst of the flowers and verdure beautiful streams of water were flowing: one might say it was a page that the painter of destiny had drawn with the pencil of creation. The buds of hearts break into flower from beholding it. Undoubtedly there is no comparison between this and other *Īlāqs*, and it may be said to be the place most worth seeing in Kashmir.

In Hindustan (*i.e.*, Upper India) there is a bird called *Papīhā*,‡ of a sweet voice, which in the rainy season utters soul-piercing (*jān-sūz*, lit. soul-burning) laments. As the *koyal* lays its egg in the nest of the crow, and the latter brings up its young, so I have seen in Kashmir that the *papīhā* lays its egg in the nest of the *ghaughā'ī* § (ring-dove ?) and the *ghaughā'ī* brings up its young.

* Blochmann, 382. The name of the son is given in the MSS. as Mīr 'Alī Aṣghar.

† Perhaps this is the Gurais Valley of Lawrence, 16, for Kūrī may be read Gūrī.

‡ See Jarrett, III. 121 and *n.* 5. The bird is either the common hawk-cuckoo of Jerdon (*Hierococcyx varius*) or his *Coccystes melanoleucos*—*i.e.*, the pied-crested cuckoo, for both birds seem to have the native name of *Papīhā*. The *Hierococcyx varius* is the "brain-fever" bird of the Anglo-Indian, I.G., I. 250. The pied-crested cuckoo occurs in Kashmir, and so also apparently does a bird of the genus *Hierococcyx*. Lawrence, pp. 138, 139.

§ I am not sure what bird this is. *Ghaughā'ī* means a turtle dove in Bengal, but I doubt if this be the bird meant by Jahāngir. *Ghaughā'ī* would mean a noisy bird, and perhaps is the Bengal Babbler

On Thursday, the 17th, Fidā'ī K. was promoted to the mansab of 1,500 personal and 700 horse. On this day the ambassador of 'Izzat* K., ruler of Ūrganj, by name Muḥammad Zāhid, came to the Court, and presented a petition, accompanied with some trifling presents, and recalled the existence of hereditary relations (lit., shook the chain of hereditary connection). I distinguished him with the eye of kindness, and on the spur of the moment gave the ambassador 10,000 darbs (Rs. 5,000) as a present, and ordered the officials of the buyūtāt (household) to prepare and send (by him) such things as he might ask for.

At this time a strange act of grace occurred to my son† Khān-Jahān (Lodī). He had become very ill from the madness of wine, and from the overpowering of this man-destroying intoxication things had come to such a pass that it threatened his precious life. Suddenly he reformed, and God directed him, and he made a vow that thereafter he would not defile the fringe of his lip with wine. Although I warned him that it was not good to give it up all at once, and that he should leave it off gradually, he would not consent, but gave it up manfully.

On the 25th of Amurdād Bahādur K., Governor of Qandahar, was promoted to the mansab of 5,000 personal and 4,000 horse, and on the 2nd of the Divine month of Shahrīwar, Mān Singh, s. Rāwat Shankar, to that of 1,500 and 800 horse, Mīr Ḥusāmu-d-dīn to that of 1,500 and 500 horse, and Karamu-llah, s. 'Alī Mardān. K.‡ to that of 600 with 300 horse.

---

of Jerdon, or the *Sāt Bhā'ī* (seven brothers) of the Indians. It belongs to the *Malacocircus* genus, and Jerdon, I. 340, states that the pied-crested cuckoo generally lays her egg in the nest of the *Malacocirci*. The babbling thrushes occur in Kashmir. In Blochmann, 296, there is an account of how *ghaughā'īs* are caught.

* MS. 305 has Ghairat K., but No. 181 has 'Arab K., and this agrees with Stanley Lane Poole's Muhammadan dynasties (p. 279), which has 'Arab Muḥammad as ruling down to 1623. Ūrganj is in Khīva.

† Jahāngir called Khān-Jahān his *farzand* (son).

‡ Not the famous 'Alī Mardān, but 'Alī Mardān, who was killed in the Deccan. Blochmann, 496.

As at this time I was much inclined to parti-coloured* veined teeth, the great Amirs exerted themselves greatly in looking out for them. Of these, 'Abdu-l-'Azīz K. Naqshbandī sent a servant of the name of 'Abdu-llah with a letter to Khwāja Ḥasan and Khwāja 'Abdu-r-Raḥīm, ss. Khwāja Kalān Jūybārī, who are to-day the leading holy men of Transoxiana, containing a request for these things. By chance, Khwāja Ḥasan had a perfect tooth, exceedingly delicate, and immediately sent it with the aforesaid (servant) to the Court, which it reached this day. I was greatly pleased, and ordered them to send the value of Rs. 30,000 in choice goods to the Khwājas, a service for which Mīr Baraka Bukhārī was fixed upon. On Thursday, the 12th Shahrīwar, Mīr Mīrān obtained leave to take up the faujdarship of Mewāt, and his mansab, original and increased, was fixed at 2,000 with 1,500 horse. I gave him a special horse, with a dress of honour and a sword.

At this time it was made clear from a report of Sundar† that Jauhar Mal, the rebel, had delivered his soul to the lords of hell (had died). It was also reported that a force sent against one of the Ẕamindars had abandoned the path of caution, and without fortifying the way of entrance and exit, or taking possession of the hill-tops, had entered into the fastnesses of the hills, and had fought without any good result. As the day drew towards its close, they had turned their reins with their object unaccomplished, and in turning back, had made every haste. Many people had been killed. especially those who would not put up with the disgrace of flight. They purchased martyrdom with their lives. Out of them Shāh-bāz K. Dalūmānī‡ (?), which is a tribe of Lodī

* *Dandān-i-ablaq-i-jauhar-dār*. *Jauhar-dār* here does not mean "jewelled," but veined or striped. See Vullers, I. 542*a*. Walrus-teeth may be meant by Jahāngir, but tortoise-shell is more likely.

† Sundar is another name for Rāja Bikramājīt, and the reference must be to the Siege of Kāngṛa. Jauhar Mal was a son of Rāja Bāso, and appears to be the same person as Suraj Mal. It is Jauhar in I.O. MS., 181.

‡ Deotānī in No. 181. Blochmann has the name Dutānī, apparently as a tribal name (p. 504), and Elphinstone speaks in vol. ii., p. 82, of a small tribe called Dumtauny.

Afghans, sacrificed his life with a band of his servants and tribesmen. In truth he was a good servant, and had intelligence combined with modesty. Another report was that Jamāl Afghān, Rustam, his brother, Sayyid Naṣīb Bārha, and some others had come in wounded. It was also reported that the siege (of Kāngṛa) had become a close one, and the affair was going hard with the besieged. They had sent (literally thrown out) men as mediators, and had asked for quarter. It was hoped that by the blessing of increasing fortune the fort would be subdued.

On Wednesday, the 18th of the same month (Shahrīwar), Dilāwar K. Kākar died a natural death. Beyond all the other Amirs of high rank, he combined valour with leadership and knowledge of affairs, and from the time when I was a prince carried away from all the ball of superiority in my service. He acted constantly with the perfection of sincerity and the jewel of doing right, and had thus arrived at the dignity of Amirship. In the end of his life God Almighty bestowed grace upon him, and the conquest of Kishtwār, which was an exemplary service, was accomplished by his courage. It is hoped he may be one of the pardoned. His sons and the others that he left behind him I exalted with all kinds of favours and patronage, and enrolled those of his people who were fit for mansabs amongst the servants of the Court. I ordered the rest, to remain as usual with his sons, so that his company might not be split up.

On this day Qūr Yasāwul came with a diamond that Ibrāhīm K. Fatḥ-jang had obtained from the Bengal mine, and waited on me. Wazīr K., dīwan of Bengal, who was an old servant of the Court, died a natural death.

On the night of Thursday, the 19th, the Kashmiris had lined with lamps both sides of the Bihat. It is an ancient custom that every year on this day everyone, whether rich or poor, whoever has a house on the bank of the river, should light lamps as on the Shab-i-barāt. I asked the brahmans the reason of this, and they said that on this day the fountain-head of the Jhelam was disclosed, and the custom had come down from old days that on this date must take place the feast of *Veth tarwāh.** Veth means the Jhelam, and they call thirteen *tarwāh;* as this day is the 13th of Shawwāl, they light lamps. In this way they call it the *Veth tarwāh.* Undoubtedly the lamp-lighting was good. I sate in a boat and went round to see it. On this day the feast of my solar weighing took place, and according to the usual custom, I weighed myself against gold and other things, which I distributed among deserving people. The 51st year of the age of this suppliant at the throne of Allah came to an end; the 52nd year lit up the face of expectation. It is hoped that the period of my life will be spent in pleasing God. The entertainment of Thursday, the 26th, was held in the lodging of Āṣaf K. (Nūr-Jahān's brother), and that pillar of the Sultanate fulfilled the duties of homage, and of offerings, and thereby acquired eternal bliss.

On 1 Shahrīwar (about 11 August) ducks (*murghābī*) appeared on the Wular lake, and on the 24th of that month they appeared on the Dal lake. The following is the list of birds which are *not* met with in Kashmir:

LIST.

1. Crane† (*kulang*).
2. Sāras (grus Antigone).
3. Peacock.

---

* Veth is the Kashmiri name for the Jhelam (Lawrence, 18). It is contracted from Vitasta. It is curious that the date of the festival should be given according to a Muhammadan month (Shawwāl), which must recur at different seasons. Apparently the meaning is that the birth of the Jhelam took place on that day.

Apparently the festival is not much celebrated nowadays, for it is not mentioned by Lawrence (264-266), except that in a note to p. 266 the Vathtrwah is mentioned as a day on which daughters receive presents. The 19th Shahrīwar, the corresponding date mentioned by Jahāngir, would answer to the end of August or beginning of September, and to the Hindu month of Āsin. 13 Shawwāl, 1029, would correspond to 1 September, 1620. Possibly the Shawwāl of text is a mistake for the Hindu month Sāwan—*i.e.*, Srāvan. The legend of the birth of the Jhelam is told in Stein, 97. Possibly Shawwāl does not here mean the month, and we should read *shaghal-i-chirāghān*, "the business of lamps."

† The crane visits Kashmir in winter, but Jahāngir was never there in that season.

4. Bustard (*jarz* or *charz*).
5. Stork (*laglag*).
6. Bustard (*tughdarī*).
7. Bustard (*tughdāgh*).
8. Karwānak (kind of crane ?).
9. Zard-ṭilak (golden oriole ?).
10. Nuqra-pāy (silver-foot).
11. 'Azam-pāy.
12. Boza laglag (royal curlew).
13. Pelican (*hawāsil*).
14. Makisa (Ardea indica ?).
15. Baghlā (paddy-bird).
16. Goose (*qāz*).
17. Konkla (*kokilā*, the black cuckoo ?).
18. Partridge (*durrāj*).
19. Shāvak (starling).
20. Nol-i-surkh (redbeak, [parrot] ?).
21. Mūsīcha (wood-pigeon ?).
22. Hariyal (green pigeon ?).
23. Dhīng (adjutant).
24. Koyal (Eudynamys Orientalis).
25. Shakar-khwāra (sugar-eater, [parrot] ?).
26. Mahokhā (cuculus castaneus ?).
27. Mahirlāt (?).
28. Dhanesh (hornbill).
29. Gulchaṛī (quail ?).
30. Ṭaṭīrī, which the Turks call (blank in MSS.) and I have named *bad-āwāz*, "evil-voiced." (It is perhaps the sandpiper.)

As the Persian names of some of these are not known, or rather, these birds don't exist in Persia (*Wilāyat*), I have written the Hindi names.* The names of the carnivorous

* The text wrongly gives this as a list of birds which are found in Kashmir. The Iqbāl-nāma 159 and the MSS. show that the text has omitted a negative, and that the list consists of Indian birds which are *not* met with in Kashmir. Several of the names do not occur in the dictionaries. No 2 (the sāras) is described in Babur's Memoirs, 321. No. 4 is the florikan, or *Otis Bengalensis*. For Nos. 5-7 see Babur's Memoirs, 321. Karawān is a crane in Arabic, apparently, and so Karwānak should be a little crane. It is also described as a kind of partridge. Perhaps the Karwānak is the demoiselle crane. No. 9 may be the oriole, or mango-bird, but that, too, is common in Kashmīr. For No. 12, which may be the ibis, see Babur's Memoirs, 322. For No. 14 see Babur's Memoirs, p. 321, and for No. 18 Babur's Memoirs, 320. For the Shārak (No. 19), see Babur's Memoirs, 319. No 22 may

and herbivorous animals that are *not* in Kashmir are as follows: The tiger, the panther (*yūz*), the rhinoceros,* the wild buffalo, the black antelope, the gazelle, the *kotāh pācha* (hog-deer), the *nīl-gāw*, the wild ass, the hare, the lynx, the wild cat, the *mūshak-i-karbalā'ī* (?),† the porpoise, and the porcupine.

On this day peaches came from Kabul by runners. The largest of these weighed 26 *tolas*,‡ or 65 *misqāls*. As long as their season lasted, such a number came that I gave them to most of the Amirs, and to the private servants fed from the royal table.

On Friday,§ the 27th, I went out to see Vīrnāg,‖ the source of the Bihat. Going up the river 5 koss in a boat, I alighted at the village of Pāmpūr.

On this day unpleasant news came from Kishtwār. The details of this are that when Dilāwar K. conquered it and returned to Court, he left Naṣru-llah 'Arab, with some of the mansabdars to guard it. Naṣru-llah made two mistakes. One was that he treated the Zamindars and the people of the place harshly, and did not observe a conciliatory demeanour towards them. The second was that the forces sent as auxiliaries to him, in expectation of increase of mansab, asked him for leave to go to Court and transact their affairs. He yielded to their representations,¶ and gave them leave one

---

possibly be the bee-eater (*Merops viridis*). For No. 23 see Babur's Memoirs, 267 and 321. No. 25 may be one of the parrots, as Ḥāfiẓ called the Indian parrots and poets *ṭuṭiyān-i-shakar-shikan*. See Āyīn-i-Akbarī, Persian text, I. 415, and Jarrett, II. 150. The ṭaṭīrī, No. 30, is apparently the black partridge *Francolinus vulgaris*. The names of the birds seem to be often wrong in the text, and so I have followed the I.O. MSS.

* Kurg, but perhaps Gurg, "the wolf," is meant. The wolf is very rare in Kashmīr (Lawrence, 109).

† Query, mūshak-i-kūr—*i.e.*, mole.

‡ According to Wilson's Glossary, the tola is = 180 grains Troy, and the misqāl = $63\frac{1}{2}$ grains Troy.

§ Elliot, vi. 373, and Iqbāl-nāma 165.

‖ Vernag of Lawrence, 23.

¶ Text *u ān*; in MSS. ū.

after the other. When only a small force was left with him, the Zamindars, whose hearts had been wounded by him, and were on the look out for a disturbance, found their opportunity and made an attack from all quarters. Having burnt the bridge by which the army had crossed, and by which assistance could come, they lighted the fire of disturbance and sedition. Naṣru-llah shut himself up, and for two or three days defended himself with the greatest difficulty (literally, with a thousand life-extractions). As he had no provisions, and they had closed the road, he determined to accept martyrdom, and manfully, with some of those who were with him, performed the dues of bravery and valour until most of his men were killed, and some became captives in the hands of destiny.

When this news reached my ear, I appointed Jalāl, s. Dilāwar K., on whose forehead the traces of bravery and ambition were manifest, and who had done good service in the conquest of Kis͟htwār, with the mansab of 1,000 personal and 600 horse, giving him the attendants of his father who were enrolled among the servants of the Court, and an army of the soldiers of Kashmir, with many of the Zamindars and men on foot with muskets, to assist him in overcoming that mob, doomed to a vile end. An order was also given that Rāja Sangrām, the Zamindar of Jammu, with his own men, should come in by the hill-road from Jammu. It is hoped that the rebels will quickly obtain the recompense for their deeds.

On Saturday, the 28th, I marched 4½ koss. Passing one koss beyond Kākāpūr, I came to the bank of the river. The *bang** (*bhang*) of Kākāpūr is well-known. It grows wild on the bank of the river in quantities. On Sunday, the 29th, I halted at the village of Panj Brāra.† This village‡ has been bestowed on my fortunate son S͟hāh Parwīz. His Vakils had prepared a small building and a little garden overlooking the river. In the neighbourhood of Panj Brāra there is a

* Lawrence, 67.

† Jarrett, II. 356, where it is written Vej Brára.

‡ Iqbāl-nāma, 164.

meadow (*julga*)* exceedingly clean and pleasant, with seven lofty plane-trees in the middle of it, and a stream of the river flowing round it. The Kashmiris call it *Sathā Bhūlī* (?)† It is one of the great resorts of Kashmir.

On this day arrived the news of the death of Khān Daurān,‡ who died a natural death at Lahore. He had nearly reached ninety years of age. He was one of the brave men of the age and valiant in the battlefield. He combined bravery with leadership. He performed great services for the dynasty. It is hoped that he will be among the pardoned ones. He left four sons, but none of them was worthy to be his son. He left about Rs. 400,000 in cash and goods, which were given to his sons.

On Monday, the 30th, I first visited the fountain of Inch. This village had been given by my father to Rām Dās Kachhwāha,§ and he had erected buildings and basins at the spring. Undoubtedly, it is an exceedingly sweet and delightful place. Its water is perfectly clear and pure, and many fish swim in it.

VERSE.

So clear the water that the grains of sand at bottom
Could be counted at midnight by a blind man.

As I gave || the village to my son Khān Jahān, he prepared an entertainment there, and presented offerings. I chose a trifle in order to please him. Half a koss from this spring, there is a fountain that they call Machhī Bhawan,¶ above which Rāy Bihārī Chand, one of the servants of my father,

* This must be the Nandīmarg of Jarrett II. 357 and of Akbar-nāma III. 551. In the Āyīn (Jarrett II. 356), mention is made of a place where there are seven *fountains*. Stein, 182, speaks of a spring sacred to the seven Rīshīs. Is it possible that *chashma* in the A.N. (Persian text, I. 565) is a mistake for *chinār*?

† Satha phūlī? Seven fountains?

‡ Khān Daurān is the Shāh-Beg K. Arghūn of Blochmann, 377.

§ See Ma'āṣir, II. 155, and Blochmann, 483, for an account of Rām Dās. Inch is mentioned in Jarrett, II. 356. Perhaps Inch is the Yech pargana of Stein, 190-191.

|| Rām Dās had died eight years before this.

¶ Akbar-nāma, III. 725, last line; Lawrence, 298; Stein, *loc. cit.*, 176, 177.

built an idol-temple. The beauty of this spring is more than one can describe, and large trees of ancient years, planes, white and black poplars, have grown up round it. I passed the night at this place, and on Tuesday, the 31st, pitched at the fountain of Achval.* The water of this spring is more plentiful than that of the other, and it has a fine waterfall. Around it lofty plane-trees and graceful white poplars, bringing their heads together, have made enchanting places to sit in. As far as one could see, in a beautiful garden, *Ja'farī* flowers had bloomed, so that one might say it was a piece of Paradise. On Wednesday, the 1st of Mihr, marching from Achval, I pitched camp near the fountain of Virnag.† On Thursday, the 2nd, the feast of cups was prepared at the spring. I gave my private attendants permission to sit down. Filling brimming cups, I gave them Kabul peaches as a relish, and in the evening they returned drunk (*mastān*, exhilarated ?) to their abodes. This spring is the source of the River Bihat, and is situated at the foot of a hill, the soil of which, from the abundance of trees and the extent of green and grass, is not seen. When I was a prince, I had given an order that they should erect a building at this spring suitable to the place. It was now completed. There was a reservoir of an octagonal shape, forty-two yards in area and fourteen‡ gaz in depth. Its water, from the reflection of the grass and plants on the hill, had assumed a hue of verdure. Many fish swam in it, round it halls with domes had been erected, and there was a garden in front of them. From the edge of the pond to the gate§ of the garden there was a canal 4 gaz in width and 180|| gaz in length, and 2 gaz in depth. Round the reservoir was a stone walk (*khiyābān-i-sang*).

* The Achh Dal of Jarrett, II. 358, and the Achabal of Lawrence, 22.

† Jarrett, II. 361. The Dīr Nāg of Iqbāl-nāma, 165. See also Jarrett, II. 361. The Vernag of Lawrence, 23. Jahāngir interpolates an account of Vīrnāg into the annals of the second year. See p. 92 of translation.

‡ So in text, but a few lines lower down the depth is spoken of as four gaz. The Ibqāl-nāma has "fourteen yards."

§ The Iqbāl-nāma has " to the end of the garden."

|| Iqbāl-nāma, 165, has "186 yards."

The water of the reservoir was so clear that, notwithstanding its 4 gaz of depth, if a pea had fallen into it, it could have been seen. Of the trimness of the canal and the verdure of the grass that grew below the fountain, what can one write ? Various* sorts of plants and sweet-smelling herbs grew there in profusion, and among them was seen a stem (*būṭā*), which had exactly the appearance of the variegated tail of a peacock. It waved about in the ripple, and bore flowers here and there. In short, in the whole of Kashmir there is no sight of such beauty and enchanting character. It appears to me that what is upstream† in Kashmir bears no comparison with (*i.e.*, is far superior to) what is downstream. One should stay some days in these regions, and go round them so as to enjoy oneself thoroughly. As the hour for marching was near, and snow was beginning to fall at the head of the passes, I had not the leisure to linger there, and was obliged to turn my rein towards the city. I gave an order that plane-trees should be planted on both sides, on the banks of the canal above mentioned. On Saturday, the 4th, I encamped at the spring of Loka Bhawan.‡ This spring is also a pleasant spot. Although at present it is not equal to the others, if it were to be repaired it would be very good. I ordered them to construct a building worthy of the place, and to repair the reservoir in front of it. On the road I passed by a spring which they call Andha Nāg§ (blind fountain. *See* Iqbāl-nāma, 166). It is well known that the fish in this fountain are blind. I delayed a while near this spring, and threw in a net and caught twelve of the fish. Of these, three were blind and nine had eyes. Evidently the water of this spring has the effect of making them blind. Certainly this is not devoid of strangeness. On Sunday, the 5th, I again passed by

* Compare Iqbāl-nāma, 166.

† The meaning is that the Marāj (or Marrāj), the upper part of Kashmir, is superior to the lower part, or Kāmrāj. See Tūzuk, 298.

‡ Iqbāl-nāma, 166. Perhaps the Bawan Send of Jarrett, II. 361. Loka Bhavan (bhavan means "abode") is mentioned in Stein, 180. It is the Lokapūnya of the Rājataranginī. It is five miles south of Achbal.

§ Is this a corruption of Ānantanāg—*i.e.*, Islāmābād ?

the springs of Machhī Bhawan and Inch, and went to the city.

On Wednesday, the 8th, news arrived of the death of Hāshim, s. Qāsim K. On Thursday, the 9th, Irādat K. was promoted to the governorship of Kashmir. Mīr Jumla in his place was chosen for the duty of *Khānsāmān*, and Mu'tamid* K. to that of *'Arz-muqarrir*. The mansab of 2,000 personal and 500 horse was ordered for Mīr Jumla. On the night of Saturday, the 11th, I entered the city. Āṣaf K. was appointed to the duty of Diwan of Gujarat. Sangrām, Raja of Jammu, was promoted to the mansab of 1,500 personal and 1,000 horse.

On this day I saw an unusual kind of fishing on the part of the fishermen of Kashmir. In a place where the water was up to a man's chest, they propelled two boats that were side by side, and so that at one end they were in contact, and at the other end they were 14 or 15 yards apart. Two boatmen held long poles in their hands, and sate on the outside edge of each boat (?) so as to regulate the space between each boat, and that they should proceed equally. Then ten or twelve boatmen got down into the water, and laying hold of the ends of the two boats that were joined† together with their hands, trampled the bottom with their feet, and moved on. The fish which were between the boats wanted to get out of the narrow space, and came against the feet of the boatmen. Immediately one of the boatmen dived, and another one pressed upon his back, and with his two hands kept him from coming to the surface. The latter caught a fish and produced it. Some who are skilful in the art catch two fish with their hands, and bring them to the surface. Among them was an old boatman, who generally at each dive brought up two fish. This kind of fishing occurs at Panj Brāra,‡ and is peculiar to the Jhelam. It is not used in

* Author of Iqbāl-nāma, 166. The appointment was that of examiner of petitions.

† I presume that the ends laid hold of by the boatmen were the disengaged ends—*i.e.*, the ends 14 or 15 yards apart. But see Iqbāl-nāma, 166-167.

‡ Text Panj Hazāra. The MSS. are not clear. It may be the Sendbrary of Bernier.

ponds or in other streams. It also only takes place in the spring when the water is not cold or impetuous (*gazanda*, "biting" ?).

On Monday, the 13th, the feast of the Dasahṛa took place. According to the annual custom, they decorated the horses in the special stables, and those that had been entrusted to Amirs, and brought them out. At this time I experienced in myself a shortness of breath and difficulty in breathing. I hope that in the end, please God, it may all go well.

On Wednesday, the 15th, I went to make an autumn tour in the direction of Ṣafāpūr and the valley of Lār, situated downstream of the Kashmir River. In Ṣafāpūr there is a fine tank, and on the north side of it a hill full of trees. It being the beginning of autumn, it had a wonderful appearance, with trees of all colours, such as the planes, the apricot, and others, reflected in the middle of the tank, and very beautiful. Undoubtedly the beauties of autumn are not less than those of spring.

VERSE.

There's no exhilaration in decay, but to the eye
The glory of autumn is more brilliant than the Spring.

As the time was short and the hour of marching near, I took a short circuit and returned. These few days I passed pleasantly in catching* ducks. One day, in the midst of the sport, a boatman caught and brought me a young *qarqara* (the demoiselle crane, *Ardea virgo*). It was very thin and miserable. It did not live longer than one night. The *qarqara* does not live in Kashmir. This had become ill and thin at the time of coming from, or going to, Hindustan, and fallen there.

On Friday news came of the death of Mīrzā Raḥmān-dād, s. the Khān-khānān. He died a natural death at Bālāpūr. It appears that he had been suffering from fever for some days. When he was recovering, the Deccanis one day appeared with an army. His elder brother, Dārāb K., mounted with the intention of fighting. When the news

* The word is *shikār*, but, as he had renounced shooting, netting is probably what is meant.

reached Raḥmān-dād, with great bravery, notwithstanding his weakness and failing health, he went to his brother. After he had beaten the enemy, he returned and in taking off his *jubba* (quilted waistcoat) was not sufficiently careful. The wind immediately caught him, and he was seized with convulsions, and his tongue became powerless to speak. He remained two or three days in this state and died. He was a good and brave youth, was fond of sword-play, and was very zealous. In every place it was his idea to display his skill with the sword. Although fire burns equally what is green and what is dry, yet it appeared very grievous to me, and what must it have been to his broken-hearted old father? Hardly had the wound from the calamity of Shāh-nawāz K. healed, when he received this fresh wound. I trust that God Almighty may give him patience and resignation.

On Thursday, the 16th, Khanjar K. was promoted to the mansab of 3,000 personal and horse, Qāsim K. to that of 2,000 personal and 1,000 horse, and Muḥammad Ḥusain, brother of Khwāja Jahān, who held the post of Bakhshī to the army of Kāngra, that of 800 personal and horse. On the night* of Monday, the 27th of the Divine month of Mihr, after one watch and seven gharis had passed, the royal standards were raised auspiciously and happily to return towards Hindustan. As the saffron had blossomed, a march was made from the neighbourhood of the city to the village of Pāmpūr.† In the whole country of Kashmir there is saffron only in this place. On Thursday, the 30th, the feast of cups was held in a saffron field. Groves on groves, and plains on plains were in bloom. The breeze in that place scented one's brain. The stem is attached (close?) to the ground. The flower has four petals, and its colour is that of a violet. It is of the size of a *champa* flower, and from the middle of it three stigmas of saffron grow. They plant the bulbs, and in a good year obtain 400 maunds of the current

* Iqbāl-nāma, 169.

† Or Pāmpar, the ancient Padmapūra. See Stein, J.A.S.B. for 1899, p. 167; Elliot, VI. 375. But the passage, as in Elliot, does not come directly from the Tūzuk or the Iqbāl-nāma.

weight or 3,002* Khurasan maunds. The custom is for half to go to the government, and half to the cultivators. A seer is bought and sold for Rs. 10. Occasionally its market price is more or less, and it is an established custom that they bring the saffron flowers plucked, and according to the plan they have adopted from of old, they take half its weight in salt as wages. There is no salt in Kashmir, and they bring it from Hindustan. Again, among the excellencies of Kashmir are the plumes of feathers (*kalgī*) and the hawks (*jānwar-i-s̲h̲ikārī*). As much as 10,700 feathers are yearly obtained. Hawks and falcons are taken in nets to the number of 260. It has also nest sparrow-hawks (*bās̲h̲a*),† and the nest sparrow-hawk is not bad. On Friday, the 1st of the divine month of Ābān, marching from Pāmpūr, I pitched my camp at K̲h̲ānpūr. As it was reported to me that Zambīl‡ Beg, ambassador from my brother S̲h̲āh 'Abbās, had reached the neighbourhood of Lahore, a dress of honour and Rs. 30,000 for expenses were sent to him by Mīr Ḥusāmu-d-dīn s. 'Aẓudu-d-daula Injū.§ I ordered that whatever he might expend on entertaining the ambassador should be sent to him to the extent of Rs. 5,000.|| Before this I had directed that from Kashmir to the end of the hilly country buildings should be erected at each stage for the accommodation of myself and the ladies, for in the cold weather one should not be in tents. Although the buildings at this stage had been completed, as they were still damp and there was a smell of lime, we put up in tents. On Saturday, the 2nd, I halted at Kalampūr. As it had repeatedly been represented to me that in the neighbourhood of Hīrāpūr there was a waterfall¶ very high and wonderful, as it was 3 or 4 koss off on the left

* MSS. have 3,200.

† *I.e.*, hawks taken from the nest, and not born in captivity.

‡ Iqbāl-nāma, 169.

§ This is Mīr Jamālu-d-dīn, the dictionary-maker and friend of Sir Thomas Roe.

|| The sentence appears obscure, but probably it was an order to the authorities at Lahore to supply Ḥusāmu-d-dīn with the cost of entertaining the ambassador up to the amount of Rs. 5,000.

¶ Perhaps the waterfall described by Bernier in his ninth letter, and mentioned as having been admired by Jahāngir.

of the road, I hastened there to see it. What can be written in its praise? The water pours down in three or four gradations (?). I had never seen such a beautiful waterfall. Without hesitation, it is a sight to be seen, very strange and wonderful. I passed the time there in enjoyment till the third watch of the day, and filled my eye and heart with the sight; but in the cloudy and rainy season it is not devoid of wildness. After the third watch had passed, in the evening I rode back to Hīrāpūr,* and passed the night at that stage. On Monday, the 4th, crossing over the *kotal* of Bārī Brārī,† I chose Pīrpanjal, at the head of the *kotal*, for a halting-place. Of the roughnesses of the pass and the difficulties of this road what shall I write? It is difficult for thought even to cross it. In these last few days snow had repeatedly fallen, the hills had become white, and in the middle of the path in some places ice had formed, so that the hoof of a horse had no hold, and a rider could only pass with difficulty. God Almighty bestowed upon us His mercy, for it did not snow on this day. The advantage was for those who went on in front. Those who followed came in for snow. On Tuesday, the 5th, going by the pass of Pīrpanjal the camp was pitched at Poshāna. Although on this side there is a descent, yet as it is high, most of the people passed it on foot. On Wednesday, the 6th, we pitched at Bahramgalla. Near this village there is a waterfall and a very fine spring. According to orders, they had made a terrace for me to sit upon; indeed, this is a sight to be seen. I ordered that they should engrave on a stone tablet the date of the crossing, and place it on the top of the terrace (*ṣuffa*). Bī-badal K.‡ composed some couplets, and this mark of my fortune remains on the path of poetry as a memorial on the tablet of Time (?). There are two Zamindars on this road in whose charge are the arrange-

* Hīrāpūr is Hūrapūr and the ancient Sūrapūra.

† Marī or Nārī Brāra in the MSS.

‡ Bī-badal K. is the name given by Jahāngir to Sa'īdā or Shaidā, who was chief goldsmith. See end of 15th year, p. 326 of text. For Shaidā, who died in Kashmir in 1080 (A.D. 1669-70), see Rieu, III. 1083*a*, and I. 251, and Supp. Catalogue, p. 207, and Sprenger's Catalogue 124.

ments for the traffic on it, and they are in reality the keys of the country of Kashmir. They call one Mahdī Nāyak and the other Ḥusain Nāyak. The charge of the road from Hīrāpūr to Bahramgalla is in their hands. Bahrām Nāyak, the father of Mahdī Nāyak, during the Kashmiri government, was an important person. When the authority passed to the imperial servants, Mīrzā Yūsuf K., during his government, made Bahrām Nāyak a traveller to the country of non-existence. It is now equally in the possession and charge of the two.* Although outwardly they are on good terms, they really bear great enmity towards each other. On this day Shaikh Ibn Yamīn, who was one of the old trusted servants, went to the neighbourhood of God's mercy (died).† On account of my great reliance on him, my opium and drinking water‡ were in his charge. On the night when we were encamped above the *kotal* of Pīrpanjal, the tents and furniture had not arrived. He was rather infirm and the cold affected him, and he became cramped so that he could not speak. He remained alive for two days in this state and then died. I gave over the private opium to Khawāṣṣ K., and the *āb-dār-khāna* (the water department) to Mūsawī K. On Thursday, the 7th, the village of Thāna§ became the encamping place. Many monkeys (*maimūn*) were seen in Bahramgalla, and from that stage a great difference was apparent in the climate, the language, the clothing, the animals, and whatever properly belongs to a warm country. The people here speak both Persian and Hindi. Evidently Hindi is their real language, and they have acquired Kashmiri on account of the proximity of Kashmir. Briefly, one enters India at this place. The women do not wear woollen clothing, and like Indian women, they wear nose-rings.

On Friday, the 8th, Rājaur was the camping-ground. The

* Text calls them brothers, but the MSS. show that *birādar* is a mistake for *barābar*, "equally."

† The MSS. add: "He was a good youth (*jawān*) and without guile."

‡ Āb-i-ḥayāt, "water of life," a name given by Akbar to his āb-dār-khāna, or supply of drinking-water, etc. See Blochmann, 51.

§ Text wrongly has Thaṭṭa.

people of this country were in old times Hindus, and the landholders are called Rajas. Sulṭān Fīrūz made them Muhammadans, but they are still called Rajas. They still have the marks of the times of ignorance. One of these is that just as some Hindu women burn themselves along with their husbands (bodies), so these women (the Rājaur women) are put into the grave along with their (dead) husbands. I heard that recently they put alive into the grave a girl of ten or twelve along with her (dead) husband, who was of the same age. Also, when a daughter is born to a man without means, they put her to death by strangulation.* They ally themselves with Hindus, and both give and take girls. Taking them is good, but giving them, God forbid! I gave an order that hereafter they should not do such things, and whoever was guilty of them, should be capitally punished. There is a river at Rājaur. Its water during the rainy season becomes much poisoned. Many of the people there get a swelling (*būghma*) under the throat, and are yellow and weak. The rice of Rājaur is much† better than the rice of Kashmir. There are self-grown and sweet-scented violets in this skirt of the hills.

On Sunday, the 10th, I encamped at Naushahra. At this place, by order of my father, they had built a stone fort, and there is constantly here, by way of a station (*thāna*), a body of men from the governor of Kashmir. On Monday the camp was at Chaukī Hattī. A *chela* named Murād had exerted himself to complete the buildings at this place, and had done it well. In the middle of the royal abode there was a fine terrace, superior to those of other stages. I increased his mansab. On Tuesday, the 12th, I halted at Bhīmbar. Passing this day out of *kotals* and hills, we entered the broad plains of Hindustan. The hunters had previously been dispatched to form *qamurghas*, so as to prepare *jirgas* (hunting rings) in Bhīmbar and Girjhāk‡ and Makhiyāla. On Wednes-

* Elliott, VI. 376. Apparently *Satī* was not practised by burning, but by burying.

† Bisyār bihtar, MS., 181.

‡ Girjhāk is said to be the Hindu name for Jalālpūr, and the probable site of Bukephala, Jarrett, II. 324. Mākhiyāla is also mentioned there.

day and Thursday they drove in the game. On Friday I rejoiced in a hunt. Hill *qūchqār*,* etc., to the number of 56 head were taken. On this day Rāja Sārang Deo, who was one of the intimate attendants, was promoted to the mansab of 800 personal and 400 horse. On Saturday, the 16th, I went towards Girjhāk, and in five marches encamped on the bank of the Bihat. On Thursday, the 21st, I hunted in the hunting-ring of Girjhāk. Less game than usual was taken, and I was not satisfied. On Monday, the 25th, I hunted with much enjoyment in the hunting-ring of Makhiyāla,† thence in ten stages I encamped at the stage of the hunting-place of Jahāngīrābād. When I was prince, this was my hunting-place. Afterwards, I founded a village with my own name, and erecting a small building, placed it in charge of Sikandar Mu'īn, who was one of my best huntsmen. After I came to the throne I made a pargana of it, and bestowed it as a jagir on him. I gave an order that they should construct there a building as a royal residence, with a tank and a minaret‡ (manāra). After his death this pargana was given in jagir to Irādat K., and the charge of the buildings was given to him. It has now been handsomely completed. Undoubtedly the tank was very broad,§ and in the middle there is a delightful building. Altogether the buildings here cost Rs. 1,50,000. Really it is a kingly hunting-place. On Thursday and Friday, having halted, I enjoyed myself with various kinds of sport. Qāsim K., who was honoured with the charge of Lahore, had the good fortune to pay his respects to me, and presented 50 muhars.

In one march after this stage I encamped at the garden of Mūmin 'Ishq-bāz,|| which is on the bank of the Lahore River

---

It seems that Mūkhyāla is the famous Mānikiyāla, where the Buddhist tope is which was first described by Elphinstone. Abūl-l-Fazl says in the Āyīn that it was a place of worship. See I.G., new ed., XVII. 182.

* Mountain-sheep. Apparently three rings were made.

† The I.O. MSS. add here 76 head of *mārkhwur*, etc., were taken.

‡ Perhaps the reference is to the tomb he formerly put up over a favourite deer.

§ MSS. have "is very noble."

|| Pigeon-fancier. He belonged to Herat, and is mentioned in Blochmann, 302.

(the Ravi), and has some lofty plane-trees and handsome cypresses. It is certainly a rare garden. On Monday, the 9th of the Divine month of Āẕar, corresponding with the 5th Muḥarram of A.H. 1030* (20 November, 1620), mounting an elephant of the name of Indra, I went towards the city, scattering coin as I proceeded. After three watches and two gharis of day had passed, at the selected auspicious hour, having entered the royal residence, I alighted happily and auspiciously at the building recently brought to completion and finished handsomely by the exertions of Maʻmūr K. Without exaggeration, charming residences and soul-exciting sitting places had been erected in great beauty and delicacy, adorned and embellished with paintings by rare artists. Pleasant green gardens with all kinds of flowers and sweet-scented herbs deceived the sight.

VERSE.†

From head to foot, wherever I look,
A glance plucks at the heart's skirt (saying),
"This is the place" (to stop at).

Altogether, there had been expended on these buildings the sum of Rs. 700,000 or 23,000 current tumans of Persia.‡

On this day the joy-enhancing news of the conquest of the fort of Kāngṛa rejoiced our mind. In thankfulness for this great boon and important victory, which was one of the renewed favours of the Bestower of Gifts, I bowed the head of humility at the throne of the merciful Creator, and beat with loud sounds the drum of gladness and pleasure. Kāngṛa is an ancient fort to the North of Lahore, situated in the midst of the hill country, famous for its strength and the difficulty of conquering it. Who was the founder of this fort God only knows. The belief of the Zamindars of the province of the Panjab is that, during this period the said fort has never passed to any other tribe, and no stranger has stretched out to it the hand of dominion. Wisdom is from

* Text wrongly has 1031. It should be 1030, as in the Iqbāl-nāma, 171.

† The couplet is given in Iqbāl-nāma, 171, with some verbal differences.

‡ Elliott, VI. 374.

Allah! But certainly from the time when the voice of Islam and the sound of the established religion of Muḥammad reached Hindustan, not one of the Sultans of lofty dignity has obtained the victory over it. Sulṭān Fīrūz-shāh, with all his power and might, himself went to conquer it, and besieged it for a long time. As he knew that the strength of the fort was such that as long as the means for holding it and provisions were with the besieged, victory over them was unattainable, *nolens volens* he was contented with the coming of the Raja to pay his respects to him, and withheld his hand. They say that the Raja prepared an offering and an entertainment, and at his request took the Sultan inside the fort. The Sultan, after going round and inspecting it, said to the Raja that to bring a king like him inside the fort was not according to the dictates of caution. What could he do if the body of men who were in attendance were to attack him and take possession of the fort? The Raja made a sign to his men, and instantaneously an army of valiant men armed and accoutred, came out from a concealed place and saluted the Sultan. The Sultan became suspicious and anxious about an attack from these men, and suspected some stratagem. The Raja came forward and kissed the ground of service, and said: "I have no thought but that of service and obedience, but as has been spoken by the auspicious tongue, I observe far-sighted caution, for all times are not the same." The Sultan applauded him. The Raja, having accompanied him for some stages, obtained leave to return. After this, whoever sat on the throne of Delhi sent an army to subdue Kāngṛa, but the thing went no further. My revered father also sent a large army once under the leadership of Ḥusain Qulī K., who, after approved service, was honoured with the title of Khān Jahān. Whilst the siege was in progress, the outbreak of Ibrāhīm Ḥusain Mīrzā took place That ingrate fled from Gujarat, and raised the flag of rebellion and calamity towards the Panjab. Khān Jahān was compelled to raise the siege, and to turn to extinguish the flame of his sedition. Thus the acquisition of the fort fell into the knot of delay. The thought was continually lurking in the royal mind: "The longed-for Fair one does not show her face from the secret place of Destiny." When by the Grace of the Glorious God the throne of the State was adorned by the existence of this suppliant, this was one of the holy wars which I considered incumbent on me. In the first instance I dispatched Murtaẓā K., who was governor of the Panjab, with a force of brave men skilled in war, to conquer the fort. This important matter had not been completed when Murtaẓā K. attained to the mercy of God (died). After this Jauhar Mal,* s. Rāja Bāso, undertook this duty. I sent him, giving him the command of the army. That wicked one, taking to evil revolt and ingratitude, committed sin, and dispersion found its way into that army, and the acquisition of the fort fell into the knot of delay. No long time elapsed before that ingrate received the recompense of his deeds and went to hell, as has been described in its own place.† In fine, at this time Khurram undertook that duty, and sent his own servant Sundar‡ with all haste, and many of the royal servants obtained leave to go to his support. On the 16th Shawwāl, A.H. 1029, (5 September, 1620), the armies, having invested the fort, erected batteries. Looking to the ways of entrance into and exit from the fort with the eye of caution, they closed the road for the entrance of provisions. By degrees the besieged became straitened, and when there remained in the fort no grain that they could eat, for four months more they boiled dry grasses§ with salt and ate it. When destruction was imminent, and no hope of escape was left, they asked for quarter and surrendered the fort.

On Thursday, the 1st Muḥarram, A.H. 1030,|| Hijrī (16 November, 1620), the victory unattainable by all preceding

* Jauhar Mal is mentioned at p. 310. Perhaps he was not Sūraj Mal, but it looks as if he was the same person. *Cf.* corresponding passage in Iqbāl-nāma, 173, where he is called Sūraj Mal.

† P. 310 of text.

‡ Rājā Bikramājīt. See *ante*, p. 310.

§ Text wrongly has *ghalla* grain, instead of *'alafhā* fodder, grasses, etc. See MSS. and Iqbāl-nāma, 174.

|| Text wrongly has 1031, but it is 1031 in the MSS. and in Elliot, VI., 375. See, however, Elliot, VI. 378, and text, 326, which shew that the 16th year began in 1030.

Sultans of lofty dignity, and which appeared distant to the short-sighted, God Almighty of His own grace and mercy granted to this suppliant. The troops, who had displayed praiseworthy activity in this service, were exalted according to their exertions and fitness by increase of mansab and dignities.

On Thursday, the 11th, I went, at the request of Khurram, to his newly-built house. I took those of his offerings that pleased me. Three elephants were placed in the private stud. On the same day I appointed 'Abdu-l-'Azīz K. Naqshbandī to the faujdarship of the district of Kāngṛa, and his mansab was fixed at 2,000 personal and 1,500 horse. I gave a private elephant to I'tiqād K. Alf K. Qiyām-khānī K. obtained leave to take charge of the fort of Kāngṛa, and his mansab, original and increased, was fixed at 1,500 personal and 1,000 horse. Shaikh Faiẓu-llah, son-in-law of Murtaẓā K., was appointed in company with him to stay at the top of the fort (*bālā-i-qil'a*).

On the night of Saturday, the 13th of the same month, a lunar eclipse took place. Having performed the dues of humility at the throne of the highest and most powerful God, cash and goods were distributed by way of charity among the faqirs and poor, and deserving people. On this day Zambīl Beg, ambassador of the ruler of Persia, had the good fortune to kiss the threshold. After performing salutation, he laid before me the gracious letter of that brother of high degree, containing expressions of sincerity and perfect friendship. He presented 12 '*Abbāsī** (coin) as *nazar*, four horses with trappings, three *tūyghūn* (white) falcons, five mules, five camels, nine bows, and nine scimitars. The Shah had given him leave, in company with Khān 'Ālam, but for certain necessary matters he could not come with him. On this day he arrived at Court. I presented him with a superb dress of honour, with a plume and a jewelled turban fringe, and a jewelled dagger. Wiṣāl Beg and Ḥājī Ni'mat, who had come with

* The '*Abbāsī* is also the name of a dress. The MSS. have fourteen, instead of four, horses. Apparently the presents were Zambil's own offering, not that of his master. See below.

him, were honoured by waiting on me. Amānu-llah, s. Mahābat K., was promoted to the mansab, original and increased, of 2,000 and 1,500 horse. At the request of Mahābat K., I added 300 horse to the mansab of Mubāriz K. Afghān, and brought it up to 2,000 personal and 1,700 horse. One hundred horse were also added to the mansab of Kabak* (?). I sent winter dresses of honour to 'Abdu-llah K. and Lashkar K. At the request of Qāsim K. I went to his garden in the neighbourhood of the city, and in the course of the procession, scattered 10,000 *charans* (4-anna pieces). Out of his offerings I selected one ruby and one diamond, and some cloths.

On the night of Sunday, the 21st, the advanced camp proceeded auspiciously and happily towards Agra. Barqandāz K. was appointed superintendent of artillery with the army of the Deccan. Shaikh Isḥāq (Isaac) was appointed to duty at Kāngṛa. The brother of Allah-dād, the Afghan, I released from prison, and made him a present of Rs. 10,000. I gave also a *tūyghūn* falcon to Khurram. On Thursday, the 26th, the usual entertainment took place. The presents from the ruler of Persia, which had been sent by Zambīl Beg, were laid before me. I gave an elephant to Sulṭān Ḥusain, and made a present of Rs. 1,000 to Mullā Muḥammad Kashmīrī.† The mansab of Sardār Afghān, at the request of Mahābat K., was fixed at 1,000 personal and 400 horse. As Rāja Rūp Chand of Gwalior‡ had been very active in his service at Kāngṛa, an order was given to the chief diwans to hand over half of his native place to him in free gift, and the remaining half as a *tankhwāh* jagir.

On the 3rd I demanded in marriage for my son Shahriyār the daughter's daughter§ of Madāru-l-mulk I'timādu-d-daula, and sent Rs. 100,000 in cash and goods by way of *sāchaq*

* *Mansab-i-kabak.* Perhaps we should read *katak*, and regard the increase as made to the office of guarding the palace. It is *katak*, apparently, in I.O. MSS. It may, however, be *Kang* or *Gang* and a man's name.

† Apparently the translator of the Rājatarangini.

‡ Doubtless the Gwalior in the Panjab.

§ Nūr Jahān's daughter by Shīr-afgan. The date of the asking is given in the text as the third, but should be the 30th, as in the I.O. MSS.

(dowry given as part of the marriage rites). Most of the Amirs and the chief servants went to his house with gifts. He prepared a grand entertainment with much ceremony. It is hoped that it may be auspicious to him. As that Chief of the State had erected lofty buildings, and highly decorated bowers in his house, he invited me to an entertainment. I went there with the ladies. He had prepared a great feast, and laid before me appropriate offerings of all kinds. In order to please him, I took such as I approved of. On this day Rs. 50,000 were presented to Zambīl Beg, the ambassador. The mansab of Zabar-dast K. was fixed at 1,000 personal and 500 horse, original and increased. Maqṣūd, brother of Qāsim K., was promoted to the mansab of 500 personal and 300 horse, and Mīrzā Dakhanī, s. Mīrzā Rustam, to that of 500 personal and 200 horse.

At this auspicious time* when the standards of victory and conquest were in Kashmir, the province of eternal spring, happily employed in sight-seeing and sport, representations constantly came from the officials in the Southern territories to the effect that when the victorious standards went to a distance from the centre of the Khalifate, the rulers of the Deccan, owing to their wickedness, broke their promises and raised their heads by giving trouble and exciting sedition, and placing their feet beyond their own boundary, took possession of many of the districts of Ahmadnagar and Berar. It was constantly reported that the chief object of these evil-fortuned ones was to plunder and ruin the cultivated fields and the grazing-lands. When at the first time the world-opening standards had proceeded to the conquest of the regions of the south and the overthrow of that band, and K͟hurram, with the vanguard, had gone to Burhanpur, they, by feline tricks suitable to such seditious people, made him their intercessor and evacuated the royal dominions. They also sent by way of tribute large sums in cash and goods, and promised that they would not let loose from their hands the rope of service, and would not place their feet beyond the boundary of respect, as has been recorded in the preceding

* Elliot, VI. 376.

pages. At the request of Khurram, I had halted for a few days at the Fort of Shādī'ābād Māndū, and at his intercession, and on their humiliation and bewailing, they were pardoned.

As they had now broken their agreement through evil disposition and quarrelsomeness, and had turned back from the way of obedience and service, I sent off the hosts of good fortune again under his leadership, that they might receive retribution for their evil deeds, and be an example to all those of crooked fortune and turned heads. But as the important business of Kāngṛa had been entrusted to him, he had sent most of his experienced men there. For some days, accordingly, he could not arrange the matter. At last, report followed on report one after another, that the enemy had gathered strength, and that nearly 60,000 vagabond horsemen had collected together and taken possession of royal territory, and wherever there were posts, had removed them, and joined together in the town of Mahakar. For three months the imperialists had passed their days in strife and fighting with their rascally enemies, and during this time three pitched battles had taken place, and each time the self-sacrificing servants (of the State) had proved superior to the evil-fortuned rebels. As grain and provisions could not reach the camp by any road, and the enemy was plundering on all sides of the army of good fortune, a great scarcity of grain resulted, and the animals were in bad plight. Having no choice, they came down from the Bālāghāt, and took up their position at Bālāpūr. The rebels, waxing valiant in their pursuit, engaged in plundering in the neighbourhood of Bālāpūr. Of the servants of the Court 6,000 or 7,000 horsemen, well mounted, were selected, and they made an attack on the enemy's camp. They (the enemy) numbered about 60,000 cavalry. Briefly, a great fight took place, and their camp was plundered. Having killed and taken prisoners many of them, they returned in safety and with plunder. When they turned back those wretches again attacked them from all sides, and they came on, fighting as far as the camp. On both sides about 1,000 were killed. After this fight they (the imperialists) remained about four months at Bālāpūr. When the scarcity of grain became excessive, many of the qulaqchīs (servants) ran away and joined the enemy, and constantly bands of them, taking to the road of disloyalty, were enrolled among the rebels. On this account, not considering it advisable to delay any longer, they (the imperialists) came to Burhanpur. Again, those wretches followed them and besieged Burhanpur, and they were six months shut up there. Many parganas of the provinces of Berar and Khandesh passed into their possession, and they stretched out the hand of oppression over the cultivators and poor, and engaged in collecting the revenues. As the army had undergone great hardships and the animals had fallen into bad condition, they could not leave the city to inflict substantial punishment. Thus the pride and conceit of those short-sighted ones became greater. Just at this time the royal standards returned to the capital, and by the grace of God Kāngṛa was conquered.

Accordingly, on Friday, the 4th of Dai, I despatched Khurram in that direction, bestowing on him a dress of honour, a sword, and an elephant. Nūr Jahān Begam also gave him an elephant. I told him after he had conquered the province of the Deccan he should take as a reward two* crores of dams from the conquered country. 650 mansabdars, 1,000 *Aḥadīs*, 1,000 Turkish musketeers, and 1,000† gunners on foot, in addition to the 31,000 horse already in that quarter, and a large force of artillery, and many elephants, were appointed to accompany him. I also gave him a crore of rupees for the expenses of the victorious army. The servants (of the Court) who were appointed on this duty received each, according to his standing as a reward, horses, elephants, and dresses of honour.

At the same auspicious hour and favourable time, the standards of the expedition were turned toward Agra, and a halt was made at Naushahr.‡ Muḥammad Riẓā Jābiri

* The Iqbāl-nāma, 176, has "ten crores."

† The MSS. have 5,000. The word for "gunners" is *tūpchī*.

‡ The MSS., instead of Naushahr, have *sawād-i-shahr*, "the environs of the city" (*cf.* Lahore ?).

was appointed Diwan to Bengal, and K͟hwāja Mulkī to the post of Bakhshi in the same, and were promoted in mansab. Jagat Singh, s. Rānā Karan, came from his native place, and had the good fortune to kiss the threshold. On the 6th of the same month the open space on the bank of Rāja Todar Mal's tank* became the alighting place of the Court of good fortune. Here I halted for four days. On this day some of the mansabdars who had obtained leave to go to the conquest of the Deccan were promoted as follows: Zāhid K. held the mansab of 1,000 and 400 horse; he received that of 1,000 and 500 horse; Hardī Nārāyan Hāḍā I promoted to 900 and 600 horse, original and increased; Ya'qūb, s. K͟hān Daurān, was given that of 800 and 400 horse, and in the same manner a great number of the servants of the State received increase of mansab according to their capabilities. Mu'tamid K. was appointed to the post of Bakhshi and newswriter to the royal army, and was honoured with a *tūgh*. The offering of Lachmī Chand, Raja of Kumaon, consisting of hawks and falcons and other hunting animals, was brought before me. Jagat Singh, s. Rānā Karan, obtained leave to proceed as an auxiliary to the army of the Deccan, being presented with a private horse and saddle. Rāja Rūp Chand, having been honoured with the gift of an elephant and a horse, took leave to go to his jagir. On the 12th my son K͟hān Jahān (Lodī) was made governor of Multan, and was given leave. There were conferred on him a complete dress together with a *nādirī* (a robe of Jahangir's invention), a jewelled dagger, a special elephant with trappings, a female elephant, a special horse of the name of K͟hadang (*i.e.*, Arrow), and a pair of hawks. Sayyid Hizabr K. held the mansab of 1,000 and 400 horse. Increasing these by 500 and 200 horse, I gave him leave to accompany K͟hān Jahān. Muḥammad Shafī' was appointed Bakhshi and newswriter to the Subah of Multan. Bhawāl (or Bahwāl), who was one of the old servants, was made *As͟hraf-i-tūp-k͟hāna* (head of the artillery ?), and received the title of Rāy. On the 13th the bank of the river Gobindwāl became the camp of the army of prosperity,

* It was in the vicinity of Lahore. Akbar-nāma, III. 569.

and a halt of four days was made. A special elephant called Jai Singh, with a female, were given to Mahābat K., and sent to him by Ṣafiyyā his servant. Robes of honour were also forwarded to the Amirs of the Subah of Bangash by 'Īsā Beg.

On the 17th* the feast of my lunar weighing took place. As Mu'tamid K. had been appointed Bakhshi to the army of the Deccan and given leave, the post of 'Arẓ-muqarrir was given to Khwāja Qāsim. Mīr Sharaf was made Bakhshi of the Aḥadīs, and Fāẓil Beg made Bakhshi of the Panjab. As Bahādur K., governor of Qandahar, in consequence of a disease in his eyes, had requested to be allowed to kiss the threshold, entrusting the government of Qandahar this day to 'Abdu-l-'Azīz K., an order was issued to Bahādur K., that when he arrived he should hand over the fort to him and come himself to Court. On the 21st of the same month I took up my quarters at Nūr-sarāy.† At this spot the Vakils of Nūr Jahān Begam had built a lofty house, and made a royal garden. It was now completed. On this account the Begam, having begged for an entertainment, prepared a grand feast, and by way of offering, with great pains produced all kinds of delicate and rare things. In order to please her, I took what I approved. I halted two days at this place. It was settled that the officials of the Panjab should send Rs. 200,000, in addition to the Rs. 60,000 already ordered for provisions for the fort of Qandahar. Mīr Qiwāmu-d-dīn, the diwan of the Panjab, obtained leave to go to Lahore, and received a dress of honour. Qāsim K., with a view to punish the

* But the next page of text records another feast of the lunar weighment. Can it be that the lunar weighment refers to Nūr Jahān's birthday, not to Jahāngir's? The 17th here mentioned is the 17th of the solar month of Dai, and corresponded to about December 28, 1620. In the following page (324) we are told that the lunar weighment took place on 30 Bahman, corresponding to 25 Rabī'u-l-awwal —*i.e.*, February 8, 1621. Jahāngir's birthday was on Rabī'u-l-awwal 17. so the anniversary fell this year on 22 Bahman. Consequently, if he celebrated it, as stated on p. 323, on 17 Dai, he did so more than a month too soon! Evidently there is a mistake somewhere.

† This place is mentioned again in the account of the 16th year, p. 338. It evidently received its name from Nūr Jahān.

seditious in the neighbourhood of Kāngṛa, and to preserve order in those regions, was given leave to go, and I presented him with a special *nādirī*, a horse, a dagger, and an elephant. His mansab, original and increased, was fixed at 2,000 personal and 500 horse. At his request, I allowed Rāja Sangrām (of Jammu) to proceed to that region, conferring on him a robe of honour, a horse, and an elephant.

On Thursday the camp was pitched outside the town of Sihrind. I halted one day, and amused myself with going round the garden. On Sunday, the 4th, Abū-l-Ḥasan was sent on service for the conquest of the Deccan. A dress of honour, with a *nādirī*, a special shawl, an elephant named Ṣubḥ-dam (breath of morn), a horsetail banner, and drums, being given him. I gave leave to Mu'tamid K., presenting him with a dress of honour, and a special horse called Ṣubḥ-i-ṣādiq (the true dawn). On the 7th of the same month the bank of the river Sarasatī (Saraswatī) was the place of encampment of good fortune in the neighbourhood of the *qaṣba* of muṣṭafā'ābād. The next day I encamped at Akbarpūr,* whence I sat in a boat on the river Jumna, to reach my object. On this day 'Izzat K. Chāchī,† with the faujdar of that region, had the good fortune to kiss the threshold. Giving Muḥammad S̲h̲afī' leave to proceed to Multan, I presented him with a horse, a dress of honour, and a *nūr-s̲h̲āhī muhar*, and sent by him a special turban (*chīra*) to K̲h̲ān Jahān, my son (*farzand*).

Thence, in five marches, I reached the pargana of Kirāna, the native country of Muqarrab K., and the Court encamped there. By way of offering, his Vakils laid before me 91 rubies‡ and 4 diamonds, 1,000 gaz of *mik̲h̲mal* (satin) as a *pā-andāz* (foot-carpet), with a petition from him, presenting also 100 camels as charity. I ordered them to be distributed among deserving people. From this place, in five marches Delhi

* Akbarpūr, twelve miles N.W. Mathurā. J. Sarkar's India of Aurangzeb, 171.

† That is, of Chāch in Transoxiana, but according to I.O. MS. 181, the word is K̲h̲āfī—*i.e.*, from K̲h̲āf or K̲h̲wāf.

‡ Ninety-one rubies is surely a mistake. The Iqbāl-nāma, 177, only speaks of one. It is, however, 91 *yāqūt* in I.O. MS., 181.

became the halting-place of the standards of good fortune. I sent It'imādu-d-daula to my fortunate son Shāh Parwīz with a special *farjī* (a dress), for him, and it was settled that he should return in the space of one month and wait on me. Having halted for two days at Salīmgaṛh, on Thursday, the 23rd, I passed through the district of Delhi with the intention of hunting in the pargana of Pālam, and halted on the bank of the Shamsī tank. On the road I scattered 4,000 *charans* (Rs. 1,000) with my own hand. Twenty-two elephants, male and female, had arrived from Bengal as an offering from Allah-yār, s. Iftikhār K., and were passed before me.

Ẕū-l-Qarnain* obtained leave to proceed to the faujdarship of Sambhar. He is the son of Iskandar, the Armenian, and his father had the good fortune to be in the service of 'Arsh-āshyānī (Akbar), who gave him in marriage the daughter of 'Abdu-l-Ḥayy,† the Armenian, who was in service in the royal harem. By her he had two sons. One was Ẕū-l-Qarnain, who was intelligent and fond of work, and to him, during my reign, the chief diwans had entrusted the charge of the government salt works at Sambhar, a duty which he performed efficiently. He was now appointed to the faudjarship of that region. He is an accomplished composer of Hindi songs. His method in this art was correct, and his compositions were frequently brought to my notice and were approved. La'l Beg‡ was selected for the daroghahship of the records in the place of Nūru-d-dīn Qulī. I passed four days pleasantly in sporting in the neighbourhood of Pālam and returned to Salīmgaṛh. On the 29th, 19 elephants,

* This is the Armenian of whom so much is said by Father Botelho and other missionaries. It is mentioned in M. Wāriṡ's continuation of the Pādishāh-nāma, p. 392, of B.M. MS., that Ẕū-l-Qarnain Farangī came from Bengal and presented poems which he had composed on Shāh Jahān's name, and got a present of Rs. 4,000. He it was, probably, who entertained Coryat. The passage in the text seems to show that Akbar had an Armenian wife.

† He is mentioned in some MSS. of the Akbar-nāma, vol. iii., as taking part in the religious discussions.

‡ Probably this is the La'l Beg who wrote a book about the Naqshbandī order. See Ma'āṡiru-l-Umarā, II., 382.

2 eunuchs,* 1 slave, 41† fighting cocks, 12 bullocks, and 7 buffaloes were brought before me as offerings from Ibrāhīm K. Fatḥ-jang. On Thursday, the 30th, corresponding with the 25th Rabī'u-l-awwal, the ceremony of my lunar weighing‡ was performed. I had sent Koka K. to the Khān-khānān, and forwarded some messages by him. On this day a petition from him arrived. Mīr Mīrān, who had been appointed to the faujdārship of Mewāt, on this day came and paid his respects, and was dignified with the governorship of Delhi, in the room of Sayyid Bahwa.

On this day Āqā Beg and Muḥibb 'Alī, the envoys of the ruler of Persia, paid their respects, and presented a loving letter from that noble brother, together with a black and white plume (*kalgī-i-ablaq*), valued by the jewellers at Rs. 50,000. My brother also sent me a ruby weighing 12 *tānks*,§ which had belonged to the jewel-chamber of M. Ulugh Beg, the successor of M. Shāh-rukh. In the course of time, and by the revolutions of fate, it had come into the hands of the Ṣafawī family. On this ruby there were engraved in the *Naskh*|| character the words: "Ulugh Beg b. M. Shāh-rukh Bahādur b. Mīr Tīmūr Gūrgān." My brother, Shāh 'Abbās, directed that in another corner they should cut the words:

Banda-i-Shāh-i-Wilāyat¶ 'Abbās
"The slave of the King of Holiness, 'Abbās."

in the *Nasta'līq* character. He had this ruby inserted in a *jīgha* (turban ornament), and sent to me as a souvenir. As the ruby bore the names of my ancestors, I took it as a blessing for myself, and bade Sa'īdā, the superintendent of the gold-

* The Iqbāl-nāma has "42 eunuchs."

† The MSS. have 40 cocks, 12 buffaloes, and 7 buffalo-horns. The text also has *shākh*, horns, but this has been taken as a pleonasm.

‡ But there was such a ceremony a few days before (see p. 323 of text).

§ For *tānk* see Blochmann, 16 *n*. The Iqbāl-nāma, 178, has "twelve miṣqāls."

|| For the *Naskh* character see Blochmann, 99-100, and for the *Nasta'līq*, 101. See also the elaborate article on Writing in Hughes' Dictionary of Islam.

¶ By *Shāh-i-Wilāyat* is meant the Caliph 'Alī b. Abī Ṭālib.

smith's department, engrave in another corner the words "Jahāngīr Shāh b. Akbar Shāh," and the current date. After some days, when the news of the conquest of the Deccan arrived, I gave that ruby to Khurram, and sent it to him.

On Saturday, the 1st of Isfandārmuz, I marched from Salīmgarh, and going first to the glorious mausoleum of Humāyūn (may the lights of Allah be his testimony!), performed the dues of humility, and presented 2,000 quarter rupees (*charan*) to those who sat in seclusion in that pure cemetery. I encamped twice on the bank of the Jumna in the environs of the city. Sayyid Hizabr K.,* who had been appointed an auxiliary to Khān Jahān, was sent off with the distinction of a dress of honour, a sword, a dagger, a horse, and a standard. Sayyids 'Ālim and 'Abdu-l-Hādī, his brothers, were also each honoured with a horse and a dress of honour. Mīr Baraka Bukhārī was allowed to go to Transoxiana. I entrusted Rs. 10,000 to him, 5,000 of them to be conveyed to Khwāja Ṣāliḥ Dihbīdī, who from his fathers was one of the well-wishers of this State, and the other 5,000 to be divided among the *mujāwirs* (custodians) attached to the tomb of Tīmūr (may the lights of Allah be his testimony!). I also gave a special turban (*chīra*) to Mahābat K., and sent it to him by Mīr Baraka. I also ordered Mīr Baraka to make every effort to procure mottled fish-teeth, and to procure them from any possible quarter, and at any price.

I went by boat from Delhi, and in six stages reached the plain of Brindāban. I gave an elephant to Mīr Mīrān, and permitted him to go to Delhi. Zabar-dast K. was selected to be Mīr Tūzuk (master of ceremonies) in the place of Fidā'ī K., and I presented him with a special shawl (*parm-narm*). Next day, Gokul† was the place of encampment. At this stage, Lashkar K., the governor of Agra, 'Abdu-l-Wahhāb Dīwān, Rāja Nath Mal, Khiẓr K. Fārūqī, ruler (deposed) of Āsīr and Burhanpur, Aḥmad K., his brother; the Qāẓī, the Muftī, and other chief men of the city (of Agra), had the good fortune

* The Houshabarchan of Hawkins.

† Mahāban, five or six miles from Mathura.

to wait* on me. On the 11th I halted auspiciously at the Nūr-afs͟hān† garden, which is on the opposite side of the Jumna. As the auspicious hour for entering the city had been fixed for the 14th, I halted here, and at the selected auspicious hour proceeded to the fort, and entered the palace happily and victoriously. The propitious journey from Lahore to Agra was accomplished in the period of two months and two‡ days, with 49 marches and 21 halts. No day either of marching or halting, on land or water, passed without sport. 114 deer, 51 duck, 4 heron (*kārwānak*), 10 black partridge (*durrāj*), and 200 *bodna*§ were taken on the way.

As Las͟hkar K. had satisfactorily performed his duties at Agra, I increased his mansab by 1,000 personal and 500 horse, and made it 4,000 personal and 2,500 horse, and sent him as an auxiliary to the army of the Deccan. Sa'īdā, superintendent of the goldsmith's department, was dignified with the title of Bī-badal K. Four horses, some silver ornaments and cloths, which the ruler of Persia had sent me by Āqā Beg and Muḥammad Muḥibb 'Alī, were produced before me on this day. The entertainment of Thursday, the 20th, took place in the Nūr-manzil garden. I gave a present of Rs. 1,00,000 to my son S͟hahriyār. Muẓaffar K., according to order, came from Thatta, and had the good fortune to wait on me. He offered 100 muhars and Rs. 100. Las͟hkar K. produced a ruby as an offering. It was valued at Rs. 4,000. A special horse of the name of Muṣāḥib (companion) was given to 'Abdu-llah K. 'Abdu-s-Salām, s. Mu'aẓẓam K., having arrived from Orissa, had the good fortune to wait on me: 100 muhars and Rs. 100 were laid before me as his *nazar*. The mansab of Dūst Beg, s. Tūlak K., was fixed at

* They had made an *istiqbāl*, or visit of welcome, from Agra.

† This was Babar's garden. It was on the opposite side of the Jumna to Agra.

‡ So in text, but two (*dū*) must be a mistake for "ten," as 2 months, 2 days=62, and the marches and halts 49+21 amount to 70, or 8 more. It is 10 in I.O. MSS.

§ The *būdna*, or *bodna*, is a species of quail. See Babar's Memoirs, Erskine, p. 320, where it is spelt *budinah*. There is a description in the Āyīn, Blochmann, 296, of the mode of catching them.

900 personal and 400 horse. The entertainment of Thursday, the 27th, was held in the Nūr-afs͟hān garden. A special dress of honour was given to M. Rustam, and a horse to his son, who was called Dakhanī, and a special horse and an elephant to Las͟hkar K.

On Friday, the 28th, I went to hunt to the village of Samonagar, and returned at night. Seven Persian horses, with their trappings, were laid before me as an offering from Āqā Beg and Muḥibb 'Alī. I presented Zambīl Beg, the ambassador, with a Nūr-jahānī muhar of the weight of 100 *tolas*, and gave a jewelled penholder to Ṣādiq K., the chief Bakhshi. I also gave a village* in Agra, by way of *in'ām,* to K͟hiẓr K. Fārūqī. In this year 85,000 *bīghās* of land, 3,325 *k͟har-wārs* (of rice), 4 villages, 2 ploughs (of land), and a garden, Rs. 2,327, 1 *muhar,* 6,200 *darbs* (half rupees), 7,880 quarter rupees (*charan*), 1,512 *tolas* of gold and silver, and 10,000 dams from the treasury were given, in my presence, as alms to faqīrs and necessitous people. Thirty-eight elephants, of the value of Rs. 2,41,000,† were presented as offerings, and were placed in the special elephant house, whilst 51 were presented by me to the great Amirs and the servants of the Court.

* The word "village" is omitted in both the I.O. MSS.

† This gives an average of Rs. 6,342 for each animal.

THE SIXTEENTH NEW YEAR'S FEAST AFTER THE AUSPICIOUS ACCESSION

On Monday,* the 27th Rabī'u-l-ākhir, A.H. 1030 (10 March, 1621), the sun that bestows bounty on the world lit up the abode of fortune of Aries with his world-illuminating light, and gladdened the world and its inhabitants. The sixteenth year of the reign of this suppliant at the throne of Allah commenced with gladness and victory, and at the auspicious hour and blessed time I sat on the throne of success in the capital of Agra. On this joy-enhancing day my fortunate son Shahriyār lifted up his head with the honour of the mansab of 8,000 and 4,000 horse. My revered father bestowed, for the first time, this mansab† on my brothers. It is hoped that in the shadow of my education and in carrying out my pleasure, he may reach the extreme of life and prosperity. On this day Bāqir K. arrayed his men and passed them before me in order. The great Bakhshis recorded (the number as) 1,000 horse and 2,000 foot, and reported to me. Having promoted him to the mansab of 2,000 personal and 1,000 horse, I entrusted the duties of faujdar of Agra to him.

On Wednesday, together with the ladies seated in a boat, I went to the Nūr-afshān garden, and rested there at night. As the garden belongs to the establishment of Nūr Jahān B., on Thursday, the 4th, she held the royal‡ entertainment and

* The I.O. MSS. have "Saturday." But Monday seems right, as Thursday was 4 Farwardīn.

† In the Āyīn, which was composed in the 40th year of Akbar's reign, Salīm's rank is given as 10,000, Murād's as 8,000, and Dāniyāl's as 7,000 (p. 308).

‡ In celebration of the commencement of the 16th year of the reign.

presented great offerings. Of jewels, jewelled ornaments, and all sorts of precious goods, I selected what I approved of, of the value of Rs. 100,000. During these days, every day after midday I embarked in a boat, and went to Samonagar, 4 koss distant from the city, for sport, returning to the palace at night. Sending Rāja Sārang Deo to my prosperous son Shāh Parwīz, I sent with him a special dress of honour, with a jewelled belt, which contained a sapphire* and several rubies. As I had given Behar to that son in the place of Muqarrab K., I started off a *sazāwul* to conduct him from Allahabad to Behar. Mīr Zāhid,† son-in-law of Muẕaffar K., having come from Thatta, waited on me. As Mīr 'Aẕudu-d-daula‡ had become very old and decrepit, he could not carry out the duties of the camp and his jagir. I released him from the trouble of service and active work. I ordered that he should receive Rs. 4,000 every month out of the public treasury, and living at ease and in comfort at Agra or Lahore, or wherever he wished, should employ himself in prayers for my increased life and welfare.

On the 9th Farwardīn the offering of I'tibār K. was laid before me. Of jewels, cloths, etc., the value of Rs. 70,000, was accepted, and I returned the remainder to him. Muḥibb 'Alī and Āqā Beg, envoys of the ruler of Persia, presented twenty-four horses, two mules, three camels, seven greyhounds (*sag-i-tāzī*), twenty-seven pieces (*ṭāq*) of brocade, a *shamāma* § of ambergris, two pairs of carpets, and two *namad takya* || (woollen coverlets). Two mares with foals that my brother had sent with them were also brought before me.

On Thursday, at the request of Āṣaf K., I went to his house with the ladies. Having prepared a grand entertainment, he submitted to me many delicate gems and wonders in cloths, and rare gifts. Choosing out of these to the value of Rs. 130,000, I gave the rest to him. Mukarram K., governor

* *Yāqūt-i-kabūd*, "a blue ruby."

† The I.O. MSS. have Mīrza Muḥammad.

‡ Jamālu-d-dīn Ḥusain Injū.

§ See Vullers, s.v. It is a smelling-bottle or case containing ambergris.

|| Blochmann, 55.

of Orissa, sent by way of offering thirty-two elephants, male and female, and these had the honour of being accepted. At this time I saw a wild ass * (*gūr-khar*), exceedingly strange in appearance, exactly like a lion. From the tip of the nose to the end of the tail, and from the point of the ear to the top of the hoof, black markings, large or small, suitable to their position, were seen on it. Round the eyes there was an exceedingly fine black line. One might say the painter of fate, with a strange brush, had left it on the page of the world. As it was strange, some people imagined that it had been coloured. After minute inquiry into the truth, it became known that the Lord of the world was the Creator thereof. As it was a rarity, it was included among the royal gifts sent to my brother Shāh 'Abbās. Bahādur K. Uzbeg had sent as an offering some tipchāq horses and cloth stuffs from 'Irāq, and they were produced before me. Dresses of honour for the winter were sent for Ibrāhīm K. Fatḥ-jang and the Amirs of Bengal by Mūmin Shīrāzī. On the 15th the offering of Ṣādiq K. was produced. It was of all sorts. Having taken what was worth Rs. 15,000, I gave the remainder to him. Fāẓil K. on this day also gave an offering according to his condition. Of this a trifle was taken. On Thursday (19th Farwardīn) the feast of the culmination was held, and when two watches and one ghari of the day had passed, I took my seat on the throne. According to the request of Madār-ul-mulk I'timādu-d-daula, the feast of the culmination was held in his house. He presented a remarkable offering of rare and choice things from all countries. Altogether I took the value of Rs. 138,000. On this day I gave Zambil Beg, the ambassador, a muhar† equal to 200 *tolas* in weight. At this time Ibrāhīm K. had sent some eunuchs from Bengal. One of these was a hermaphrodite. Among the offerings of the above-mentioned were two boats

* Apparently a zebra. See Iqbāl-nāma, 179, where it is stated that it was brought by sea. The text of the Tūzuk is wrong, as usual. What we should read is: "It was like a tiger (MS. 181 and Iqbāl-nāma have *shīr*, not *babar*), but the markings on a tiger are black and yellow, and these were black and white."

† Perhaps this is the muhar now in Germany.

made in Bengal, of a very pleasant shape, on the decoration of which a sum of Rs. 10,000 had been expended. They were really kingly boats. Having made Shaikh Qāsim K. governor of Allahabad, I honoured him with the title of Muḥtashim K. and the mansab of 5,000, and gave an order that the Diwans should give him an increase to his jagir out of the unappropriated (*maḥāll-i-ghair-i-'amalī*) estates. Rāja Shyām Singh, Zamindar of Srīnagar (in Garhwāl) was given a horse and an elephant.

At this time it was reported to me that Yūsuf K., s. Ḥusain K.,* had died in the victorious army of the Deccan a sudden death. The report said that when he was at his jagir he had become so fat that he got out of breath with the least exertion. One day when he was paying his respects to Khurram, in coming and going his breathing† became difficult. When a dress of honour was given him, in putting it on and saluting he became helpless, and a trembling affected all his limbs, and with a hundred labours and exertions he saluted and stumbled out and fell under the shelter of the tent enclosure, and became unconscious. His servants placed him in a palanquin, and took him home, and as he arrived, the messenger of death came also. He received his command, and left his heavy lump of earth in the perishable dustbin. On 1st Urdībihisht, I gave a special dagger to Zambil Beg, the ambassador. On the 4th of the same month the feast of the *kār-i-khair* (consummation of marriage) of my son Shahriyār increased the joy of my heart. The Ḥinna-bandī (putting on henna) assembly took place in the palace of Maryamu-z-zamānī. The feast of the *nikāḥ* (marriage) was held in the house of I'timādu-d-daula. I myself went there with the ladies and adorned the feast of joy. After seven gharis of night had passed, on Friday‡ the marriage took place with rejoicings. I hope that it will be propitious to this daily-increasing State. On Tuesday, the 19th, in the Nūr-afshān garden, I presented my son Shahriyār with a jewelled *chārqab* (coat), with a turban and waist-belt (*kamar-band*),

* Ḥusain K. Tukrīya.

† *Nafs mī-sūzad.*

‡ Thursday night or Friday eve is what is meant.

and two horses, one an 'Īrāqī, with a gold saddle, and the other a Turkī, with an embroidered saddle.

In these days Shāh Shujā' had an eruption so violent that water would not go down his throat, and his life was despaired of. As it had been recorded in his father's horoscope that his son would die this year, all the astrologers were unanimous that he would not live, but Jotik Rāy said, on the contrary, that the dust of calamity would not settle on the skirt of his life. I asked: "By what proof?" He said that in the horoscope of my destiny it was recorded that in this year no distress or trouble would find its way to the royal mind from any road, and as I had a great affection for the child, it behoved that no calamity should happen to him, and some other child would die. It came to pass as he said, and he carried his life out of this deadly place, and a son that he (Shāh Jahān) had by the daughter of Shāh-nawāz K., died at Burhanpur. Besides this, many of Jotik Rāy's judgments (aḥkām) turned out correct. This is not without strangeness, and it is therefore recorded in these memoirs. I accordingly ordered him (Jotik Rāy) to be weighed against money and the weight came to Rs. 6,500. This was given him as a reward.

Muḥammad Ḥusain Jābirī was appointed Bakhshi and newswriter of the Subah of Orissa. The mansab of Lāchīn Munajjim (astrologer) Qāqshāl, at the request of Mahābat K., was fixed, original and increased, at 1,000 personal and 500 horse. Muḥammad Ḥusain, brother of Khwāja Jahān, came from Kāngṛa and waited on me. Having presented an elephant to Bahādur K. Uzbeg, I sent it with his Vakil. Hurmuz and Hūshang, grandsons of the asylum of pardon Mīrzā Muḥammad Ḥakīm, by reason of the caution that is fitting to rulers, had been imprisoned in the fort of Gwalior. At this time, having summoned them into my presence, I ordered them to remain in Agra, and a daily allowance sufficient for their expenses was allowed for them. At this time a brahman of the name of Rūdar Bhattachāraj, who was one of the learned ones of this caste, and was engaged at Benares in teaching, had the good fortune to pay his respects to me. In truth, he has studied well, both in the rational and traditional sciences, and is perfect in his own line.

One of the strange events of this time* was that on 30 Farwardīn (about 10 April, 1621) in the present year, in a certain village of the pargana of Jālandhar, in the morning, a terrible noise arose from the East, such that its inhabitants, from fright at that terror-increasing sound, nearly deserted their bodies. Whilst this noise and disturbance were going on, a light fell from above on the ground, and the people thought that fire was raining down from heaven. After a moment, when that noise ceased, and their troubled hearts recovered from their bewilderment and terror, they sent a quick runner to the collector (*'āmil*) Muḥammad Sa'īd, and informed him of what had occurred. He immediately rode there himself, and went to look at the spot. For ten or twelve yards in length and breadth the land was so burnt that no trace of any grass or green was left, and there were still signs of heat and burning. He ordered them to dig up the soil, and the more they dug the greater the heat appeared to be till they came to a place where a piece of heated iron appeared. It was as hot as if it had been taken out of a furnace. After a while it became cold, and taking it up, he conveyed it to his house, and placing it in a *k͟harīṭa* (cover), which he sealed, he sent it to Court. I ordered them to weigh it in my presence, and it came to 160 *tolas*. I ordered Master (Ustād) Dā'ūd† to make a sword, a dagger, and a knife of it, and bring them to me. He represented that it would not stand below the hammer, and fell to pieces. I told him in that case to mix it with other iron and make use of it. As I had told him, he mixed three parts of lightning-iron and one of other iron, and having made two swords, one dagger, and one knife, brought them to me. From the mixing of other iron he had brought out its quality (watering). According to the manner of the excellent swords of Yaman‡ and the South, it could be bent, and became straight again. I ordered them to test

* Elliot, VI. 378.

† King David was said to be a maker of cuirasses.

‡ *Yamānī.* Elliot has *almāsī* (adamant-like).

it in my presence. It cut very well, equal to true swords. I called one the Shamshīr-i-qāṭi' (keen sword) and the other Barq-sirisht (lightning-natured). Bī-badal K. composed a quatrain which demonstrated* these particulars, and recited it:

> By Shāh Jahāngīr the world acquired order.
> There fell in his reign raw iron from lightning.
> From that iron were made by his world-taking command,
> A dagger, a knife, and two scimitars.

And "Spark of royal lightning" gave the date (A.H. 1030).

At this time Rāja Sārang Deo, who had gone to my fortunate son Shāh Parwīz, came and waited on me. Parwīz represented that he, according to order, had proceeded from Allahabad to Behar. I hope he will be prosperous (there). Qāsim K. was dignified with the gift of drums. On this day one 'Alīmu-d-dīn, a servant of Khurram, brought a report from him containing the good news of the victory, with a jewelled thumbstall (*shast*, perhaps a ring), which he had sent as *nazar*. I gave him leave, sending by him a dress of honour. Amīr Beg, brother of Fāẓil Beg. K., was appointed Diwan to my son Shahriyār and Muḥammad Ḥusain, brother of Khwāja Jahān, was made Bakhshi, and Ma'ṣūm was appointed *Mīr-Sāmān*. Sayyid Ḥājī obtained leave to go as an axuiliary to the army of the Deccan, and I gave him a horse. Muẓaffar K., was also promoted to the post of Bakhshi.

As at this time the mother† of Imām-qulī K., the ruler of Tūrān, had sent to Nūr Jahān Begam a letter containing expressions of good will and the dues of acquaintanceship, and sent some rarities from that country, Khwāja Naṣīr, who was one of the old servants and one of my attendants from the time when I was a prince, was sent by way of embassy on the part of Nūr Jahān Begam with a letter, with choice gifts from this country. At the time when the ladies were

* See Blochmann's translation and remarks in Proceedings A.S.B. for 1869, p. 167. It is there stated that the date of the fall of the meteorite was Friday, April 10, 1621, O.S., and that the weight would be nearly 5·271 pounds troy.

† A widow of Bāqī Muḥammad.

staying in the Nūr-afs͟hān garden, a *rang* (ibex) fawn eight days old, jumped down from the terrace of the palace, which is 8 gaz in height, on to the ground, and began to leap about, no sign of injury or pain being perceptible in it.

On the 4th of the Divine month* of K͟hurdād, Afẓal K., K͟hurram's Diwan brought a letter from him containing the good news of his victory, and kissed the threshold. The details are as follows: When the victorious army reached Ujain, a band of the servants of the Court, who were in the fort of Māndū, sent a report that an army of the rebels, putting forward the foot of audacity, had crossed the Narbadā, and burning several villages that were under† the fort, were busy with rapine and plunder. Madāru-l-mahāmm K͟hwāja Abū-l-Ḥasan, with 5,000 cavalry, were appointed to go in all haste and inflict punishment on that vain lot of people. The K͟hwāja made a night march, and at the dawn of day reached the bank of the Narbadā. When the enemy learnt this, they in one moment threw themselves into the river and reached the bank of safety. The brave cavalry galloped after them, and pursued them for nearly 4 koss,‡ and with the sword of vengeance, made many of them travellers on the road of non-existence. The ill-fated rebels did not turn back the reins of haste till they reached Burhanpur. K͟hurram wrote to Abū-l-Ḥasan to remain on that (the South) side of the river till he came. Soon he, with his army, joined this advanced force, and hastened on, march by march, till he reached Burhanpur. The graceless rebels were still keeping§ their ground, and were encamped round the city.

* Elliot, VI. 379.

† Elliot, VI. 379, has "in sight of the fort." Perhaps the meaning is that the villages were in the jurisdiction of the fort.

‡ The Iqbāl-nāma, 181, has "fourteen."

§ The account of S͟hāh Jahān's spirited attack on the Deccanis is in some places rather obscurely worded, and the printed edition is not always correct. Help can be obtained from the Iqbāl-nāma, 181, etc., and from Elliot, VI. 379. The text has *firār*, "flight," and this has been followed by Elliot, who has "on their approach the rebels took to flight, and removed to a distance from Burhanpur." But the true reading, as shown by the Iqbāl-nāma, is *qarār*, "firmness," not *firār*, and the words are *bar daur-i-s͟hahr*, "round the city," not *bar dūr*, "far

As the imperial servants had been contending with the rebels for two years, they had suffered much hardship from want of land (*bī-jāgīrī*,* non-possession of fiefs, landlessness) and scarcity of corn, and their horses were worn out by continued service. Accordingly, they had to delay nine days in order to recruit. During this period, thirty lakhs of rupees and many cuirasses† were distributed among the soldiers, and *sazāwuls* had been sent out and had brought many men out of the city (Burhanpur). The gallant troops had not yet put their hands to the work, when the black-fated rebels felt that they could not resist, and scattered like "the daughters of the Bier" (the stars of the constellation of the Great Bear, which are dispersed over the heavens, instead of being clustered like the Pleiades). The brave and swift cavaliers followed them, and with the sword of vengeance cast many of them upon the earth of perdition. They gave them no rest, but smiting and slaying them, pursued them as far as Khirkī, which was the residence of the Niẓāmu-l-mulk and the other rebels. One day before this the ill-starred one (Malik 'Ambar) had got information of the approach of the imperialists, and had removed the Niẓāmu-l-mulk and his family and effects to the fort of Daulatabad. There he had encamped, with his back resting on the fort, while in front of him there were marshes and quagmires.‡ Most of his men became scattered in all directions. The leaders of the victorious army, with their vengeance-seeking soldiers, halted three days in the town of Khirkī, and so destroyed a city

from." The rebels were, as the Iqbāl-nāma states, "in the environs of the city," "*dar sawād-i-shahr*," but apparently not in such force as to prevent Shāh Jahān's *sazāwuls*—*i.e.*, his apparitors and summoners—from going into the city and bringing out recruits.

* In the I.O. MSS. the word looks like *bī-jāgarī* (want of settled home or residence.?).

† Text has *chasa*. The word may be *jushsha*, given in Vullers, 516*b*, as meaning robes or garments, and this is the meaning given to it by Elliot, but the Iqbāl-nāma has *jubba*, "cuirasses," and this I have adopted. It is *jubba* in I.O. No. 181.

‡ Text, *chihla u khamcha*. The last word should, I think, be *jamjama*. *Chihlā* in Hindustani means a "slimy place." It is *jamjama* in I.O. MS., No. 181.

which had taken twenty years to build, that it is not known if it will regain its splendour in other twenty years. In fine, after throwing down its buildings, all agreed in opinion that as an army of rebels was still besieging Ahmadnagar, they must at once go there, and inflict condign punishment on the originators of the disturbance, renew the supplies (of the Ahmadnagar garrison), and leave assistance there, and then return. With this view they set out, and came as far as the town of Patan (in Berar, Jarrett II. 233). Meanwhile, the crafty 'Ambar* sent agents and officers, and said: "After this I will not drop the thread of service and loyalty from my hand, nor put out my foot beyond orders, and will regard whatever tribute and fine be commanded as a favour, and will send it to the government." It happened that just then there was great scarcity in the camp in consequence of the dearness of provisions, and also that news came that the rebel force which was besieging Ahmadnagar had withdrawn on hearing of the approach of the imperialists. Accordingly, a force was sent to help Khanjar K. (the governor of Fort Ahmadnagar), and a sum of money for his charges. Thereupon the imperialists were relieved from all anxiety and returned (across the Narbadā ?). After much entreaty and lamentation (on the part of 'Ambar) it was settled that in addition to the territory which of old had belonged to the empire, the rebels should surrender 14 koss of the adjoining country, and should pay into the public treasury fifty lakhs of rupees as tribute.

I gave Afẓal K. (Shāh Jahān's diwan) leave to return, and sent with him, for Khurram, the ruby plume (*kalgī-i-la'lī*) which the King of Persia had sent to me, and which has been already described, and I gave to the aforesaid (Afẓal) a dress of honour, an elephant, an inkpot, and a jewelled pen. Khanjar K., who, when besieged in the Fort of Ahmadnagar, had performed approved services, and shown proper activity, was promoted to the mansab of 4,000 personal and 1,000 horse.

Mukarram K., having come by order from Orissa, had,

* Text has *ghair* instead of 'Ambar.

with his brothers, the good fortune to wait upon me. He presented a string of pearls by way of offering. Muẕaffaru-l-mulk, s. Bahāduru-l-mulk, was honoured with the title of Nuṣrat K. A standard was conferred on Ūdā Rām, Dakhanī, and to 'Azīzu-llah, s. Yūsuf K., was given the mansab of 1,000 personal and 500 horse. On Thursday, the 21st, Muqarrab K. arrived from Behar, and had the good fortune to wait upon me. At this time Āqā 'Alī, Muḥibb 'Alī Beg, Ḥājī Beg, and Fāẕil Beg, the envoys of the ruler of Persia, who had come at different times, were allowed to depart. To Āqā Beg I made a present of a dress of honour, a jewelled dagger, and Rs. 40,000 in cash; to Muḥibb 'Alī Beg a dress of honour and Rs. 30,000; and to the others in the same way I presented gifts according to their positions. I also sent a suitable souvenir by them to my brother. On this day Mukarram K. was appointed Subahdar of Delhi, and faujdar of Mewat. Shajā'āt K. 'Arab was dignified with the mansab of 3,000 personal and 2,500 horse, original and increased; Sharza K. with that of 2,000 and 1,000 horse; Girdhar, s. Rāy Sāl Kachhwāha, with that of 1,200 and 900 horse.

On the 29th, Qāsim Beg, an envoy of the ruler of Persia, came and waited on me, bringing a letter from that brother of lofty dignity, containing expressions of sincerity and friendship. What he had sent by way of royal gifts was laid before me. On the 1st of Tīr, I sent a special elephant called Gaj Ratan, for my son (*farzand*) Khān Jahān. Naẕar Beg, a servant of Khurram, laid before me a letter from him asking for the gift of horses. I ordered Rāja Kishan Dās, the mushrif (accountant) to prepare within fifteen days 1,000 horses from the royal stables, and to send them off with him. I sent to Khurram as a present a horse of the name of Rūm-ratan* ("the jewel of Turkey"), which the ruler of Persia had sent me out of the spoils of the Turkish camp.

On this day a servant of Irādat K., of the name of Ghiyāṣu-d-dīn, laid before me a report from him containing the good news of his victory. In the preceding pages there has been

* Text wrongly has *Rūp-ratan*.

written with the pen of demonstration an account of the rebellion of the Zamindars of Kishtwār and of the despatch of Jalāl, s. Dilāwar K. As this important matter had not been properly managed by him, an order was given to Irādat K. to hasten to take up that duty, and to inflict severe punishment on the rebels, and make such arrangements in the hill-country that the dust of dispersion and calamity might not settle on its frontiers. He, as ordered, hastened there and did approved service, and the people of sedition and disturbance, having turned their heads towards the desert of exile, escaped half dead. Thus once more was the thorn of calamity and mischief rooted out of that country, and having established the officials and established posts, he returned to Kashmir. As a reward for this service I added 500 horse to his mansab.

As Khwāja Abū-l-Ḥasan had done good service and shown proper activity in the affair of the Deccan, I increased his mansab by 1,000 horse. Aḥmad Beg, nephew of Ibrāhīm K. Fatḥ-jang, being exalted to the Subahdarship of Orissa, was dignified with the title of *Khān*, and had given him a standard and drums. His mansab also was raised to 2,000 with 500 horse.

As I had often heard of the virtues and good qualities of Qāẓī Naṣīr of Burhanpur, my truth-seeking mind had a desire for his society. At this time he came, according to summons, to the Court. Doing honour to his learning, I paid him great regard. The Qāẓī is one of the unique of the age for rational and traditional sciences, and there are few books that he has not read, but his exterior did not agree with his interior, and I could not be delighted with his company. As I found him much devoted to being a dervish and seclusion, I respected his feelings, and did not give him the trouble of serving me. I gave him Rs. 5,000, and dismissed him to his native country to pass his days in ease.

On the 1st of the Divine month of Amurdād Bāqir K. was promoted to the mansab of 2,000 personal and 1,200 horse, and of the Amirs and royal servants who had distinguished themselves in the conquest of the Deccan, thirty-two individuals were exalted by having their mansabs raised. 'Abdu-l-'Azīz K. Naqshbandī, who had been appointed to the governorship of Qandahar at the request of my son Khān Jahān, was promoted to that of 3,000 personal and 2,000 horse. On the 1st Shahrīwār I gave the ambassador Zambil Beg a jewelled sword, and also presented him with a village under the jurisdiction of the capital, the revenue of which was Rs. 16,000.

At this time, knowing that he was unfit for duty on account of his bad temper and want of knowledge, I dismissed Ḥakīm Ruknā,* and told him he might go wherever he wished. As it was reported to me that Hūshang, the brother's son of Khān 'Ālam, had committed an unjust murder, having summoned him to my presence, I investigated the charge, and after it was established, gave an order for his execution. God forbid that in such affairs I should consider princes, and far less that I should consider Amirs. I hope that the grace of God may support me in this. On 1st Shahrīwar, at the request of Āṣaf K., I went to his house and bathed in the bath-house that he has lately built. It is beautifully finished. After I had done bathing he laid before me offerings fit for a *naẓar*. I took what I approved of and gave him the rest. The *Waẓīfa* (pension) of Khiẓr Khān (late ruler) of Khandesh, was fixed at Rs. 30,000,† original and increased.

At this time it was reported to me that a blacksmith of the name of Kalyān was much in love with a woman of his own caste, and was always laying his head at her feet, and showing symptoms of infatuation. The woman, though she was a widow, would in no way consent to accept him, and the love of this wretch who had given his heart to her made no impression on her. Having summoned both of them into my presence, I cross-examined them, and however much I advised her to unite herself to him, she did not agree. At this time the blacksmith said that if he could make sure that I would‡ give her to him, he would throw himself down from

* Pādishāh-nāma, I., Part II., p. 349.

† The text wrongly has 1,000.

‡ The Bib. Ind. ed. of Iqbāl-nāma, 184, inserts a negative here, but this seems wrong. In a MS. in my possession there is no negative.

the Shāh-burj of the fort. I said by way of jest: "Never mind the Shāh-burj; if your love be genuine, fling yourself from the roof of this house, and I'll make her submit herself to you." I had not ended before he ran like lightning and threw himself down. When he fell, blood began to flow from his eyes and mouth. I repented myself greatly of that jest, and was grieved in my mind, and bade Āṣaf Khān take him to his house and look after him. As the cup of his life was brimming over, he died from the injury.

VERSE.

The life-sacrificing lover who stood on that threshold
Gave up his life with joy and regarded death as a trifle.

At the request of Mahābat K. the mansab of Lāchīn Qāqshāl, original and increased, was fixed at 1,000 personal and 500 horse.

It has been mentioned* that on the day of the Dasahara festival in Kashmir, I had perceived in myself a catching and shortness of breath. Briefly, from excessive rain and the dampness of the air, a difficulty in drawing breath showed itself on my left side near the heart. This by degrees increased and became intensified. Of the physicians who were in waiting on me, Ḥakīm Rūḥu-llah first tried his remedies, and for some time warm, soothing medicines were of use, for there was evidently a slight diminution (of the symptoms). When I came down from the hills, they came on again violently. This time for some days I took goats' milk, and again camel's milk, but I found no profit whatever from them. About this time Ḥakīm Ruknā, who had been excused from the journey to Kashmir, and whom I had left at Agra, joined me, and confidently and with a show of power, undertook my cure, and relied on warm and dry medicines. From his remedies, too, I derived no advantage; on the contrary, they appeared to increase the heat and dryness of my brain and temperament, and I became very weak. The disease increased and the pain was prolonged. At such a time and in this state, at which a heart of stone would have burnt

* Elliot, VI. 380.

(been distressed) about me, Ṣadrā,* s. Ḥakīm Mīrzā Muḥammad, who was one of the chief physicians of Persia (was in attendance on me). He had come from Persia in the reign of my revered father, and after the throne of rule had been adorned by this suppliant, as he was distinguished above all others by natural skill and experience (*taṣarruf-i-ṭabī'at*), I was attended to by him, and I distinguished him with the title of Masīḥu-z-zamān (Messiah of the Age). I made his position more honourable than that of the other Court-physicians, with the idea that at some crisis he would help me. That ungrateful man, in spite of the claims which I had on him, though he saw me in such a state, did not give me medicines or treat me. Notwithstanding that I distinguished him beyond all the physicians who were waiting on me, he would not undertake my cure. However great attention I showed him and troubled myself to soothe him, he became more obstinate (*ṣullab*), and said: "I have no such reliance on my knowledge that I can undertake the cure." It was the same with Ḥakīm Abū-l-Qāsim, s. Ḥakīmu-l-mulk, notwithstanding his being a k͟hānazād, and what was due for his bringing up; he professed himself suspicious and afraid, and that considering the matter in his mind, he was terrified and vexed, and how, then, could he prescribe a remedy? As there was no help for it, I gave them all up, and weaning my heart from all visible remedies, gave myself up to the Supreme Physician. As drinking alleviated my sufferings, I took to it in the daytime, contrary to my habit, and gradually I carried this to excess. When the weather became hot, the evil effects of this increased, and my weakness and laboured breathing were augmented. Nūr Jahān Begam, whose skill and experience are greater than those of the physicians, especially as they are brought to bear through affection and sympathy, endeavoured to diminish the number of my cups, and to carry out the remedies that appeared appropriate to the time, and soothing to the condition. Although previously to this she had approved of the remedies

* Elliot, VI. 448, the Ma'āṣiru-l-Umarā, I. 577, and Pādis͟hah-nāma I., Part II., 347.

made use of by the physicians, yet at this time I relied on her kindness. She, by degrees, lessened my wine, and kept me from things that did not suit me, and food that disagreed with me. I hope that the True Physician will grant me perfect recovery from the hospital of the hidden world.

On Monday, the 22nd* of the same month, corresponding with the 25th of Shawwāl, A.H. 1030 (2 September, 1621), the feast of my solar weighing took place auspiciously and happily. As in the past year (of my life) I had suffered from severe illness, I had passed it in continuous pain and trouble. In thankfulness that such a year ended well and in safety, and that in the commencement of the present year the signs of health became apparent, Nūr Jahān Begam begged that her Vakils might make the arrangements for the entertainment (of the solar weighment). In truth, they prepared one which increased the astonishment of beholders. From the date on which Nūr Jahān Begam entered into the bond of marriage with this suppliant, although in all weighing entertainments, both solar and lunar, she had made such arrangements as were becoming to the State, and knew what were the requirements of good fortune and prosperity; yet on this occasion she had paid greater attention than ever to adorn the assembly, and arrange the feast. All the servants of approved service and the domestics who knew my temperament, who in that time of weakness had constantly been present and been ready to sacrifice their lives, and had fluttered round my head like moths, were now honoured with suitable kindnesses, such as dresses of honour, jewelled sword-belts, jewelled daggers, horses, elephants, and trays full of money, each according to their positions. And though the physicians had not done good service, yet in consideration of the slight contempt† with which they had been treated for two or three days, they

* Text wrongly has 12th. Jahāngir's birthday was on the 18th Shahrīwar.

† *Khiffatī.* I am not sure of the reading. One B.M. MS. seems to have *ḥaqqī*, and perhaps the meaning is that the physicians had already been abundantly recompensed for their labour for two or three days, *ḥaqqī* being taken as equal to *ḥaqq-i-sa'ī*.

received various favours, and on the occasion of this feast also, they received presents in jewels and cash.

After the conclusion of the weighment, trays of gold and silver were poured out by way of *niṣār* (coin-scattering) into the hope-skirts of the ministers of amusement (*ahl-i-nis͟hāṭ*), and of the poor. Jotik Rāy, astrologer, who had given the glad news of my recovery and restoration to health, I had weighed against muhars and rupees, and by this method a present was made* him of 500 muhars and 7,000 rupees. At the end of the entertainment the offerings she (Nūr Jahān) had prepared for me were produced. Of the jewels, jewelled ornaments, cloths and various rarities I selected what I approved of. Altogether the cost of this great entertainment which Nūr Jahān Begam gave was recorded to be two lacs of rupees, exclusive of what she laid before me as offerings. In previous years, when I was in health, I weighed 3 maunds and 1 or 2 seers more or less, but this year, as a result of my weakness and leanness, I was only 2 maunds and 27 seers.

On Thursday, the 1st of the Divine month of Mihr, I'tiqād K., the Governor of Kashmir, was promoted to the mansab of 4,000 and 2,500 horse, and Rāja Gaj Singh to that of 4,000 and 3,000 horse. When the news of my illness reached my son, S͟hāh Parwīz, without waiting for a farman he came to see me, being unable to restrain himself. On the 14th† of the same month (September 25, 1621), at an auspicious hour and propitious time, that fortunate son had the good fortune to kiss the threshold, and went three times round the couch (*tak͟ht*). However much I adjured him and forbade him to do so, he insisted the more in lamentation and importunity. I took him by the hand and drew him towards me, and by way of kindness and affection held him fast in an embrace, and displayed great love to him. I hope that he may enjoy a long life with prosperity.

At this time Rs. 20,00,000 were sent to K͟hurram for the expenses of the army of the Deccan by Allah-dād K., who

* A little before his weight came only to Rs. 6,500 (p. 329 of text). But possibly Jahāngir means that he had himself weighed for Jotik's benefit.

† Elliot, VI. 381.

was honoured with an elephant and a standard. On the 28th Qiyām K., chief huntsman, died a natural death. He was a confidential servant, and apart from his skill in hunting, looked over every trifling detail relating to it, and consulted my pleasure in it. In short, I was much grieved at this event. I hope that God may grant him forgiveness.

On the 29th the mother of Nūr Jahān Begam died. Of the amiable qualities of this matron (*Kad-bānū*) of the family of chastity what can I write? Without exaggeration, in purity of disposition and in wisdom and the excellencies that are the ornament of women no Mother of the Age* was ever born equal to her, and I did not value† her less than my own mother. With regard to the attachment that I'timādu-d-daula bore towards her it is certain that no husband was equal to him. Here one must imagine what had happened to that grief-stricken old man. Also with regard to the attachment of Nūr Jahān Begam to her mother what can one write? A son like Āṣaf K., exceedingly intelligent and clever, rent in pieces his robe of patience and left off the dress of men of the social state (lit., men of dependence, or connection). At the sight of his dear son, the grief and sorrow of the father, wounded at heart, increased more and more. However much we admonished him, it had no result. On the day on which I went to condole with him, as the disturbance of his mind and grief of his heart had commenced, I spoke a few words of admonition by way of affection and kindness, but did not urge him. I left him until (the sense of) his calamity should abate. After some days I ministered to his inward wound the balm of kindness, and brought him back to the position of sociable beings. Although in order to please me and satisfy my mind he outwardly controlled himself, and made a show of resignation, yet with regard to his affection for her what resignation could there be?

* *Mādar-i-dahr.*

† Text and MSS. have *mādar-i-ūrā,* "her mother" (?). Perhaps we should read *mā ūrā,* "we (esteemed) her not less than our own mother." Or it may be that the "her" means Nūr Jāhan, and that Jahāngir means he esteemed his mother-in-law as much as his own mother.

On the 1st of the Divine month of Abān, Sar-buland K., Jān-sipār K., and Bāqī K., were honoured with the gift of drums. 'Abdu-llah K. had gone to his jagir without the leave of the Subahdar* of the Deccan: I accordingly told the Chief Diwans to deprive him of his jagir, and I'timād Rāy was ordered to act as a *sazāwul*, and to send him back to the Deccan.

It has been recorded with regard to the case of Masīḥu-z-zamān (Ḥakīm Ṣadrā) that, notwithstanding what was due from him for his bringing-up and my kindness to him, he had not the grace to attend upon me in such an illness, and more strange still is it that he suddenly threw off the veil of modesty and asked for leave to undertake a journey to the Hijaz, and make a pilgrimage to the holy house. Inasmuch as at all times and under all circumstances the reliance of this suppliant is on the Lord, that needs no return, and the gracious Creator, I gave him leave with an open brow. Though he had all kinds of things (for the journey) I made him a present of Rs. 20,000 in aid of his expenses, and I hope that the Supreme Physician, without the assistance of physicians and the means of medicine, may grant this suppliant complete recovery from the Dispensary of His mercy.

As the air of Agra, in consequence of the increase of the temperature, did not agree with me, on Monday, the 13th of the Divine month of Abān and 16th year (of my reign), the standards were raised to go towards the hill country of the North, so that if the air of that quarter should be equable, I might choose some spot of ground on the bank of the River Ganges, and found a city there, to make a permanent place of residence for the hot weather, or else turn the reins of purpose in the direction of Kashmir. Leaving Muzaffar K. to guard and administer Agra, I dignified him with drums, a horse, and an elephant. Having appointed his nephew, M. Muḥammad faujdar of the city, I gave him the title of Asad K., and selected him for increase of mansab. Having exalted Bāqir K. to the duty of the Subah of Oudh, I dismissed him. On the 26th of the said month my prosperous son S͟hāh Parwīz

* That is, S͟hāh Jahān (see Iqbāl-nāma, 186).

obtained leave to proceed from Mathura to Bihar and his jagir. I gave him leave after presenting him with a special dress of honour, a *nādirī*, a jewelled dagger, a horse, and an elephant. I hope that he may enjoy long life. On 4 Āẕar, Mukarram K., governor of Delhi, was exalted with the good fortune of paying his respects. On the 6th I alighted at Delhi, and having halted two days in Salīmgarh I employed myself with the pleasure of sport. At this time it was reported to me that Jādo Rāy Kaitha (or Kathiya), who is one of the leading Sardars of the Deccan, by the guidance of good fortune and reliance on God, had elected for loyalty, and had been enrolled amongst the loyal servants. Bestowing on him a dress of honour and a jewelled dagger, I sent a gracious farman to him by the hand of Narāyan Dās Rāthor. On the 1st of the Divine month of Dai, corresponding with the 7th Ṣafar, A.H. 1031, Maqṣūd, brother of Qāsim K., was honoured with the title of Hāshim K. and Hāshim Beg Khūshī* with that of Jān-niṣār K.

On the 7th of the same month the camp was pitched at Hardwār on the bank of the Ganges. It is one of the most famous places of worship of the Hindus, and many brahmans and recluses have chosen a corner of retirement in this place and worship God according to the rule of their religion. I gave alms in cash and goods to each of them according to his requirements. As the climate of this skirt of the hills was not approved by me, and I could not see a spot of ground on which to make a permanent residence, I proceeded towards the skirt of the hill country of Jammu and Kāngra.

At this time it was reported to me that Rāja Bhāo Singh had died in the Deccan (become a traveller on the road of non-existence). From excess of wine-drinking he had become very weak and low. Suddenly a faintness came over him. However much the physicians tried remedies for him and burnt scars on the top of his head, he did not come to his senses: for a night and a day he lay without perception, and died the next day. Two wives and eight concubines burnt themselves in the fire of fidelity for him. Jagat Singh, his elder brother, and Mahā Singh, his nephew, had spent the

* The MSS. seem to have Khostī—*i.e.*, of Khost.

coin of their lives in the wine-business, and the aforesaid, not taking warning from them, sold sweet life for bitter fluid. He was of very good disposition and sedate. From the days when I was a prince he was constantly in my service, and by the blessing of my education had reached the high rank of 5,000. As he left no son, I dignified the grandson of his elder brother, though of tender years, with the title of Raja, and gave him the mansab of 2,000 personal and 1,000 horse. The pargana of Amber, his native place, was assigned to him as jagir, according to former custom, in order that his family might not be dispersed. Aṣālat K., s. K͟hān Jahān, was promoted to the mansab of 1,000 personal and 500 horse. On the 20th* of the same month I halted at the saray of Alwātū.† As I am constantly engaged in the pleasure of hunting, and the flesh of animals I have killed with my own hand is very much to my taste, in consequence of the suspicions and caution that I have in such matters, I order them to be cleaned in my presence, and myself inspect their stomachs to see what they have eaten and what the food of the animals is. If by chance I see anything to which I have a dislike I forbear from eating the flesh. Before this I was not inclined towards any kind of waterfowl except the *sona* (golden duck ?). When I was at Ajmir I saw a tame *sona* duck eating horrible worms. From seeing this, my taste turned against it, and I gave up eating tame *sona* ducks until now, when a duck was caught, and I ordered them to clean it in my presence. From its crop there first came out a small‡ fish: after this there appeared a bug § so large that I could not believe till I saw it with my own eye that it could swallow a thing of such a size. Briefly I this day determined that I would not eat waterfowl. K͟hān 'Ālam represented that the flesh of the white heron (*'uqāb-i-safīd*) was very delicious and tender. I accordingly sent for a white heron, and ordered them to clean it in my presence. By chance there came out of its crop ten

* Text 8th, but should be 20th.

† Alwanū in MSS. It appears to be Aluwa, 11 m. S.-E. of Sirhind.

‡ Text *pahangī*, which seems unintelligible. The MSS. have *māhīki*(?)-*i*-*k͟hūrd*, "a small fish."

§ *Baqqa.*

bugs in a manner disgusting to me, at the remembrance of which I am distressed and disgusted.

On the 21st the garden of Sirhind brought joy to my senses, and on the day of halt there I delighted myself by going round and looking at it. At this time Khwāja Abū-l-Ḥasan came from the Deccan, and had the good fortune to wait on me. He had great favour shown him. On the 1st of the Divine month of Bahman I halted at Nūr-Sarāy.* The mansab of Mu'tamid K., original and increased, was ordered to be 2,000 personal and 600 horse. Khān 'Ālam was made governor of Allahabad,† and having been presented with a horse, a dress of honour, and a jewelled sword, took his leave. Muqarrab K. was selected for the mansab of 5,000 personal and horse. On Thursday, when I was encamped on the bank of the Biyāh (Beās), Qāsim K. came from Lahore, and had the good fortune to wait on me. Hāshim K., his brother, with the Zamindars of the country bordering on the hills, had the honour of kissing the threshold.

Bāso'ī,‡ the zamindar of Talwāra, brought me a bird, which the hill-people call *jān-bahan.* Its tail resembles the tail of the *qirqāwul* (pheasant), which is also called the *tazrū*, and its colour is exactly like that of the hen-pheasant, but it is half as large again. The circle round the eyes of this bird is red, while the orbit of the pheasant is white. The said Bāso'ī stated that this bird lived in the snow-mountains, and that its food was grass and other stuff. I have kept pheasants and have reared young ones, and have often eaten the flesh both of young birds and of mature ones. One may say that there is no comparison between the flesh of the pheasant and this bird. The flesh of the latter is much more delicate. Among the birds which I saw in the hill-country one was the *phūl-paikār,* § which the Kashmiris call *sonlū.* It is one-

* Founded by Nūr Jahān (see Cunningham, "Archæological Reports," XIV. 62).

† Spelt Ilah-bās.

‡ I have translated this passage from the MSS., which differ a good deal from the text. Talwāra was in the Bārī Dū'āb Sarkār (Jarrett, II. 318.)

§ Apparently this is the *pulpaikar* of Bābar (Erskine, 320), though the two descriptions do not altogether agree. Perhaps it is a hornbill.

eighth (*nīm sawā'ī ?*) less than a pea-hen. The back, tail, and wings resemble those of the bustard, and are blackish, with white spots. The breast to the end of the bosom is black, with white spots, and some red ones. The ends of the feathers are fiery red, and very lustrous and beautiful. From the end of the back of the neck it is also brilliantly black. On the top of its head it has two fleshy horns of a turquoise colour. The skin of its orbits and round its mouth is red. Below its throat there is skin round it enough to cover the palms of two hands, and in the middle of this the skin is of a violet colour of the size of a hand, with blue spots in the middle. Around it each streak is of a blue colour, consisting of eight plumes; round the blue streak it is red to the breadth of two fingers, like the peach flower, and again round its neck is that blue-coloured streak: it has red legs also. The live bird, which was weighed, came to 152 tolahs. After it was killed and cleaned it weighed 139 tolahs. Another bird is of a golden colour: this the people of Lahore call *S̲h̲an** (?) and the Kashmiris *pūṭ*. Its colour is like that of a peacock's breast. Above its head is a tuft (*kākul*). Its tail of the width of five fingers is yellow, and is like the long feather (*s̲h̲ah-par*) of the peacock, and its body as large as that of a goose. The neck of the goose is long and shapeless: that of this one is short, and has a shape.

My brother, S̲h̲āh 'Abbās, had asked for golden birds,† and I sent some to him by his ambassador. On Monday‡ the ceremony of my lunar weighing took place. At this entertainment Nūr Jahān Begam gave dresses of honour to forty-five of the great Amirs and private servants. On the 14th of the same month the camp was pitched at the village of Bahlwan § belonging to the Sībā district. As I constantly longed for the

* The MSS. have *sal* and *lūt*. Is it the *s̲h̲ām* of Bābar ? (Erskine, 320).

† *Murg̲h̲-i-zarīn*, goldfinch or golden oriole (?).

‡ The date and month are not mentioned, but it appears from the Iqbāl-nāma, which gives the next entry as 14 Bahman, that the month was Bahman, and that the date was probably about 20 January, 1622.

§ The Bhalon of Jarrett, II. 316. Sībah is mentioned at p. 317, *ibid.* The text has Sītā.

air of Kāngra and the hill-country above-mentioned, I left the large camp at this place, and proceeded to inspect the said fort with some of my special servants and attendants. As I'timādu-d-daula was ill I left him in the camp, and kept Ṣādiq K., the chief Bakhshi, there to look after him and guard the camp. The next day news came that his state had undergone a change, and that the signs of hopelessness were apparent. I could not bear the agitation of Nūr Jahān Begam, and, considering the affection which I bore towards him, I returned to the camp. At the end of the day I went to see him. It was the hour of his death agony. Sometimes he became unconscious and sometimes came back to his senses. Nūr Jahān Begam indicated me, and said: "Do you recognise (him)?" At such a time he recited this couplet of Anwarī:

> Were a mother-born blind man present
> He'd recognise Majesty in the World-Adorner.

I was for two hours at his pillow. Whenever he was conscious, whatever he said was intelligent and rational. In fine, on the 17th of the said month (Bahman) (about the end of January, 1622), after three gharis had passed he attained to eternal mercy. What shall I say about my feelings through this terrible event? He was a wise and perfect Vizier, and a learned and affectionate companion.

VERSE.*

> By the reckoning of the eye, there's one frame less:
> By Wisdom's reckoning, the lessening is more than thousands.

Though the weight of such a kingdom was on his shoulders, and it is not possible for or within the power of a mortal to make everyone contented, yet no one ever went to I'timādu-d-daula with a petition or on business who turned from him in an injured frame of mind. He showed loyalty to the sovereign, and yet left pleased and hopeful him who was in need. In fact, this was a speciality of his. From the day on which his companion (his wife) attained to the mercy of God he cared no longer for himself, but melted away from

* The couplet comes from Budags's elegy on Abu-l-Ḥasan Nahid Balkhi. See Aufi's *Lababu-l-Albab*. Browne's ed, Part II., p. 3.

day to day. Although outwardly he looked after the affairs of the kingdom, and taking pains with the ordering of civil matters, did not withdraw his hand from business, yet in his heart he grieved at the separation, and at last, after three months and twenty days, he passed away. The next day I went to condole with his sons and sons-in-law, and, presenting 41 of his children and connections and 12 of his dependents with dresses of honour, I took them out of their mourning garments.

The next day I marched with the same purpose (as before), and went to see the fort of Kāngra. In four stages the camp was pitched at the river Bānganga. Alf K. and Shaikh Faiẓullah, the guards of the fort, had the good fortune to pay their respects. At this stage the offering of the Raja of Chamba* was laid before me. His country is 25 koss beyond Kāngra. There is no greater Zamindari in these hills than this. The country is the asylum of all the Zamindars of the country. It has passes (*'aqabahā*) difficult to cross. Until now he had not obeyed any king nor sent offerings. His brother also was honoured by paying his respects, and on his part performed the dues of service and loyalty. He seemed to me to be reasonable and intelligent and urbane. I exalted him with all kinds of patronage and favour.

On the 24th† of the same month I went to see the fort of Kāngra, and gave an order that the Qāẓī, the Chief Justice (*Mīr 'Adl*), and other learned men of Islam should accompany me and carry out in the fort whatever was customary, according to the religion of Muḥammad. Briefly, having traversed about one koss, I went up to the top of the fort, and by the grace of God, the call to prayer and the reading of the *Khuṭba* and the slaughter of a bullock, which had not taken place from the commencement of the building of the fort till now, were carried out in my presence. I prostrated myself in thanksgiving for this great gift, which no king had hoped to receive, and ordered a lofty mosque to be built inside the fort. The fort of Kāngra is situated on a high hill, and is so strong that if furnished with provisions and the necessaries for a fort

* Text wrongly has Chītā. Chamba is N.-W. of Kāngra.

† Elliot, VI. 382.

the hand of force cannot reach its skirt, and the noose of stratagem must fall short of it. Although there are heights (*sar-kūbhā*) in some places, and guns and muskets might reach (the fort) from them, yet no harm would accrue to the garrison, for they could move to another part of the fort,* and be safe. It has 23 bastions and seven gates. Its inner circumference is 1 koss and 15 ropes, its length is ¼ koss and 2 ropes (*ṭanāb*), its breadth not more than 22 ropes nor less than 15. Its height is 114 cubits. There are two reservoirs inside the fort, one 2 ropes long and 1½ broad; the other is of the same length (?).†

After going round the fort I went to see the temple of Durgā, which is known as Bhawan.‡ A world has here wandered in the desert of error. Setting aside the infidels whose custom is the worship of idols, crowds on crowds of the people of Islam, traversing long distances, bring their offerings and pray to the black stone (image). Near the temple, and on the slope of the hill there is a sulphur-mine (*kān*), and its heat causes flames to continually burst forth. They call it Jwālā Mukhī§ (Flame-Face or Burning Mouth), and regard it as one of the idol's miracles. In fact, Hindus, while knowing the truth,|| deceive the common people. Hindus say¶ that when the life of Mahādeo's wife came to an end and she drank the draught of death, Mahādeo, in his great love and attachment

* The fort was destroyed by the earthquake of 1905 (I.G., XIV. 397). Presumably Jahāngir's mosque was also destroyed then.

† The breadth of the second tank is not mentioned in the MSS.

‡ "The present temple of Bajreswari Devi is at Bhawan, a suburb of Kāngra" (I.G., XIV. 386).

§ See I.G., XIV. 86, and Jarrett, II. 314 and n. 1. Jarrett states that Jwālā Mukhī is two days' journey from Kāngra. Apparently Jahāngir took his statement from the Āyīn, which has the words "in the vicinity" (Jarrett, *ibid.*). Jarrett's statement that Jwālā Mukhī is two days' journey from Kāngra is taken from Tieffenthaler, I. 108. Tieffenthaler adds that the distance is 14 to 15 *milles* (leagues, or kosses). He speaks of the Fort of Kangra as being only one-fourth of a *mille* in circumference. The image, he states, was that of Bhowani, and represented the lower part of the goddess's body. The head was alleged to be at Jwālā Mukhī.

|| *I.e.*, know the physical cause of the flame. The MSS. do not mention Hindus in this clause.

¶ See Jarrett, II. 313, and note 2.

to her, took her dead body on his back, and went about the world carrying her corpse. When some time had passed in this manner, her form dissolved and dropped asunder, and each limb fell in a different place: they give honour and dignity to the place according to the dignity and grace of the member. As the breast, which when compared with other members has the greatest dignity, fell in this place, they hold it more precious than any other. Some maintain that this stone, which is now a place of worship for the vile infidels, is not the stone which was there originally, but that a body of the people* of Islam came and carried off the original stone, and threw it into the bottom of the river, with the intent that no one could get at it. For a long time the tumult of the infidels and idol-worshippers had died away in the world, till a lying brahman hid a stone for his own ends, and going to the Raja of the time said: "I saw Durgā in a dream, and she said to me: 'They have thrown me into a certain place: quickly go and take me up.'" The Raja, in the simplicity of his heart, and greedy for the offerings of gold that would come to him, accepted the tale of the brahman, and sent a number of people with him, and brought that stone, and kept it in this place with honour, and started again the shop of error and misleading. But God only knows!

From the temple I went to see the valley which is known as Kūh-i-Madār.† It is a delightful place. From its climate, the freshness of its verdure, and its delightful position it is a place of pleasure worthy to be seen. There is a waterfall here which pours down water from the top of the hill. I ordered them to put up a symmetrical building there. On the 25th

* The temple was sacked by Maḥmūd of Ghaznīn.

† This might be Koh-i-Mandār, the hill which was used as a churning-stick by the gods. There is a hill of this name in Bhagalpur district which is known as Mandārgirī. But probably Kūh-i-Madār here means the centre-hill, for in the Bib. Ind. text of the Āyīn-i-Akbarī, I. 538, two lines from foot, it is said that the place is called Jālandharī, and a note (7) gives the various reading, "this spot is regarded as the centre," "*sar-i-zamīn-rā madār pindārand.*" Apparently it is regarded as the central place because the breast fell here, Jarrett, II. 314, n. According to the list given there the right breast fell at Jālandhara and the tongue at Jwālā Mukhī.

of the month the standards were turned back to return. Having presented Alf K. and Shaikh Faiẓu-llah with horses and elephants I left them to defend the fort. Next day I encamped at the fort of Nūrpūr.* It was reported to me that in this neighbourhood there were many jungle fowl. As I had never yet caught these, I made a halt of another day, and enjoyed myself with the sport, having caught four. One cannot distinguish them in shape and colour from domestic fowls. One of the peculiarities of these birds is that if they are caught by the feet and turned upside down, wherever they are taken they make no sound, and remain silent, contrary to the domestic fowl, which makes an outcry. Until the domestic fowl is plunged into hot water its feathers do not come off easily. The jungle fowl, like the partridge and *podna*,† can be plucked when dry. I ordered them to roast them. It was found that the flesh of the full-grown ones was very tasteless and dry. The chickens had some juiciness, but were not good to eat. They cannot fly farther than a bow-shot. The cock‡ is chiefly red, and the hen black and yellow. There are many in this Nūrpūr jungle. The ancient name of Nūrpūr is Dhamerī.§ Since Rāja Bāso built the fort and made houses and gardens they call it Nūrpūr, after my name. About Rs. 30,000 were expended on the building. Certes, the buildings Hindus construct after their fashion, however much they decorate them, are not pleasant. As the place was fit and the locality enchanting, I ordered them to spend Rs. 1,00,000 out of the public treasury, and to erect buildings at it, and to make lofty edifices suited to the spot.

At this time it was reported to me that there was a *Sannyāsī Motī*‖ in the neighbourhood who had entirely renounced

* I.G., new ed., XIX. 232.

† *Podna*, or *būdana*. The quail.

‡ Text *khirdash*, which I presume is a mistake for *khurūs*.

§ Dhameri. See I.G., XIX. 232.

‖ *Mautī* might mean "dead," but probably the word means "Pearl," and was the title assumed by a tribe or family among the Sannyāsīs. See *infra*. The statement that this order put themselves into the figure of a cross doubtless means that they belong to the Urdu *bāhū* (arms-aloft) sect—*i.e.*, the sect who raise their arms above their heads.

control over himself. I ordered them to bring him that I might ascertain the real state of affairs. They call Hindu devotees *Sarb bāsī*.* By usage the word has become *Sannyāsī* (laying down everything). There are many degrees among them, and there are several orders among the Sarb bāsī. Among them there is the *Motī* order. They put themselves into the figure of a cross (?)(*ṣalb ikhtiyār mīkunand*) and surrender themselves (*taslīm*† *mīsāzand*). For instance, they never speak. If for ten days and nights they stand in one place, they do not move their feet forwards or backwards; in fact, make no movement at all, and remain like fossils. When he came into my presence I examined him, and found a wonderful state of persistence. It occurred to me that in a state of drunkenness and absence of mind and delirium, some change might be wrought in him. Accordingly I ordered them to give him some cups of spirit (*'araq*) of double strength. This was done in royal fashion (liberally ?), but not the least change took place, and he remained in the same impassive state. At last his senses left him, and they carried him out like a corpse. God Almighty granted him mercy so that he did not lose his life. Certainly there was great persistence in his nature.

At this time Bī-badal K. presented me with the chronogram of the conquest of Kāngra, and that of the foundation of the mosque which I had ordered. As he had hit it off well, I here record it:

VERSE.

World-gripper, World-giver, World-holder, World-king,
With the sword of *ghāzī*-ship he conquered this fort.
Wisdom spoke the date "The Jahangiri Fortune opened this fort."

---

in the figure of a cross. In Tavernier, II. 378, of ed. of 1676, this is the 8th posture of ascetics, and at that page and at 376 there are figures of such ascetics. The I.O. MSS. have *salab*, "mourning," instead of *ṣalb*.

* *Sarva vāsī* means "all-abiding." Perhaps the word should be *Sarva nāsī*, "all destroying."

† For *taslīm*, see Hughes' Dict. of Islam. Possibly we should read *taṣlīb*, "make the sign of the cross."

He composed the chronogram* of the building of the mosque as follows:

VERSE.

Nūru-d-dīn Shāh Jahāngīr s. Shāh Akbar
Is a king who in the Age hath no equal.
He took Fort Kangra by the aid of God.
A drop from the cloud of his sword is a tempest.
As by his order this illumined mosque was built,
May his forehead shine by his prostration.
A hidden messenger said: "In seeking for the date
(Say) The mosque of Shāh Jahāngīr was illumined."†

On the first of the Divine month of Isfandārmuz I gave the establishment and everything belonging to the government and Amirship of I'timādu-d-daula to Nūr Jahān Begam, and ordered that her drums and orchestra should be sounded after those of the king. On the 4th of the same month I pitched in the neighbourhood of the pargana of Kashhūna.‡ On this day Khwāja Abū-l-Ḥasan was raised to the lofty dignity of supreme Diwan. I conferred dresses of honour on 32 individuals of the Deccan Amirs. Abū Sa'īd, grandson of I'timādu-d-daula, was raised to the mansab of 1,000 personal and 500 horse. At this time a report came from Khurram that Khusrau, on the 8th§ (20th) of the month, had died of the disease of colic pains (*qūlanj*), and gone to the mercy of God.

On the 19th of the month I pitched on the bank of the Bihat (Jhelam). Qāsim K. was raised to the mansab of 3,000 personal and 2,000 horse. Rāja Kishan Dās was selected for the duty of faujdar of Delhi, and his mansab was fixed at 2,000 personal and 500 horse, original and increased.

* The chronogram of the taking of the fort yields 1029, and that of the building of the mosque 1031.

† *Nūrānī*, "illumined," an allusion to Jahangir's name.

‡ The MSS. have Kahtūma apparently. ? Kahūta in Rāwalpindī district.

§ This should be, I think, the 20th, and though the name of the month is not given, it should be Bahman. See MSS. and Iqbālnāma, 191. Khusrau died in the Deccan, and presumably at Burhanpur or Āsīr. 20 Bahman, 1031, corresponds to January 29, 1622, O.S. But the date of his death has not been quite determined. See J.R.A.S. for 1907, p. 601.

Previously to this, huntsmen and *yasāwulān* (guards) had been ordered to prepare a *jarga* (hunting-ring) in the *shikār-gāh* (hunting-place of) Girjhāk. When it was reported to me that they had brought the game into the enclosure, on the 24th of the month I went out to hunt with some of my special servants. Of hill *quchqār* (rams ?) and gazelles 124* head were taken. On this day it was reported that Ẓafar K. s. Zain K., had died. I promoted Sa'ādat Umīd, his son, to the mansab of 800 personal and 400 horse.

* The I.O. MSS. have 121 instead of 124, and they add to the information about Ẓafar K. that he died in Ghaznin. They also give his son's name as Sa'ādatu-llah. The Iqbāl-nāma, p. 191, has 121 hill sheep, mārkhūr and deer.

THE SEVENTEENTH NEW YEAR'S FEAST AFTER THE AUSPICIOUS ACCESSION

On the eve of Monday, the ——,* of the month of Jumāda-l-awwal, A.H. 1031, March 10-12, 1622, after one watch, five gharis and a fraction had passed, the sun that illuminates the world lighted the mansion of Aries, and the 17th year of the reign of this suppliant began auspiciously and happily. On this joy-increasing day Āṣaf K. was promoted to the mansab of 6,000 personal and horse. Having given Qāsim K. leave to proceed to the government of the Panjab, I presented him with a horse, an elephant, and a dress of honour. Eighty thousand darbs were given to Zambīl Beg, ambassador of the ruler of Persia. On the 6th of the same month (Farwardīn) the royal camp was at Rāwalpindī. Fāẓil K. was promoted to the post of Bakhshi. Zambīl Beg was ordered to remain at ease in Lahore until the return of the victorious army from Kashmir. An elephant was conferred on Akbar-qulī K. Gakkar.

At this time I frequently heard that the ruler of Persia had hastened from Khurasan for the purpose of conquering Qandahar. Although looking to our previous and present connections, it appeared very unlikely, and beyond all calculation, that such a great king should entertain such light and crude ideas, and himself come against one of my humble slaves who was in Qandahar with 300 or 400† servants, yet as

* Date not given. The Iqbāl-nāma, 191, has "the 8th."

† The Iqbāl-nāma, p. 192, speaks of a report of K͟hān Jahān that K͟hwāja 'Abdu-l-'Azīz Naqs͟hbandī, the governor of Qandahar, had a garrison of 3,000 men.

caution is one of the duties of a ruler and becoming to a king, I sent Zainu-l-'Ābidīn, Bakhshi of *Aḥadīs*, with a gracious farman to Khurram to come and wait on me with all possible speed with a victorious host, and elephants of mountain hugeness, and the numerous artillery that were assigned for his support in that Subah. So that, if these words should be near the truth, he might come and be despatched with an innumerable army and countless treasure, in order that he (the king of Persia) might discover the result of breaking faith and of wrong-doing.

On the 8th I halted at the fountain of Ḥasan Abdāl. Fidā'ī K. was promoted to the mansab of 2,000 personal and 1,000 horse, and Badī'u-z-zamān was appointed Bakhshi of the Aḥadīs. On Friday, the 12th, Mahābat K., having come from Kabul, waited on me and had the good fortune to pay his respects, and became the recipient of daily-increasing favours. He presented 100 muhrs as a present and Rs. 10,000 as alms. Khwāja Abū-l-Ḥasan passed his followers before me in review; 2,500 well-horsed cavalry were enrolled, of whom 400 were matchlock men. At this stage a *qamurgha* hunt was arranged, and I shot* 33 hill *qūchqār* (mountain sheep), etc. At this time Ḥakīm Mūminā, at the recommendation of the pillar of the State, Mahābat K., had the good fortune to wait on me. With power and courage he undertook my cure, and I hope that his coming may prove auspicious to me. The mansab of Amānu-llah, s. Mahābat K., was fixed at 2,000 personal and 1,800 horse. On the 19th I encamped near Pakhlī, and the feast of the culmination was held there. Having given Mahābat K. leave to return to Kabul, I gave him a horse, an elephant, and a dress of honour. The mansab of I'tibār K. was ordered to be 5,000 personal and 4,000 horse. As he was an old servant, and had become very weak and old, I promoted him to the Subah of Agra, and entrusted to him the defence of the fort and the treasury, and, presenting him with an elephant, a horse, and a dress of

* Jahangir appears on this occasion to have forgotten the vow he made in the 13th year. See Elliot, VI. 362. Jahangir's words are clear: "*ba tīr u tufang andākhtam.*"

honour, dismissed him. At the Pass of Kunwar* Mast, Irādat K. came from Kashmir, and had the good fortune to kiss the threshold. On the 2nd of the Divine month of Urdībihisht, I entered the enchanting region of Kashmir. Mīr Mīrān was promoted to the mansab of 2,500 personal and 1,400 horse. At this time, in order to ease the condition of the ryots and soldiery, I did away with the faujdari cess, and gave an order that in the whole of my dominions they should not impose anything on account of faujdari. Zabar-dast K., Master of the Ceremonies (Mīr Tūzuk), was promoted to the mansab of 2,000 personal and 700 horse. On the 13th, by the advice of the physicians, and especially of Ḥakīm Mūminā, I was lightened by being bled from my left leg. A present of a dress of honour was made to Muqarrab K., and one of 1,000 darbs to Ḥakīm Mūminā. At the request of Khurram the mansab of 'Abdu-llah K. was fixed at 6,000. Sar-farāz† K. was honoured with the gift of drums. Bahādur K. Uzbeg, having come from Qandahar, had the good fortune to pay his respects: by way of nazar he gave 100 muhrs, and by way of charity offered Rs. 4,000. Muṣṭafā K., governor of Thatta, had sent as an offering a Shāh-nāma and a Khamsa (quintet) of Shaikh Niẓāmī illustrated by masters (of painting), along with other presents: these were laid before me. On the 1st of the Divine month of Khurdād Lashkar K. was exalted to the mansab of 4,000 personal and 3,000 horse, and to Mīr Jumla was given that of 2,500 personal and 1,000 horse. Some of the Amirs of the Deccan were similarly honoured with an increase of mansab. Promotion was also given as follows: Sardār K., 3,000 and 2,500 horse; Sar-buland K., 2,500 personal and 2,200 horse; Bāqī K., 2,500 and 2,000 horse; Sharza K., 2,500 and 1,200 horse; Jān-sipār K., 2,000 personal and 2,000 horse; Mīrzā Wālī, 2,500 and 1,000 horse; Mīrzā Badī'u-z-zamān s. Mīrzā Shāhrukh, 1,500 personal and horse; Zāhid K., 1,500 and 700 horse; 'Aqīdat K., 1,200 and 300

* Apparently this is the Barahmūla Pass. It is mentioned in the Akbar-nāma, III. 480-81 and 558, but does not appear on modern maps. Jahangir refers to it in the account of the 15th year, p. 294, and says it is the last of the passes.

† Sar-afrāz in No. 181.

horse; Ibrāhīm Ḥusain Kās͟hg͟harī, 1,200 and 600 horse; and Z̲ū-l-faqār K., 1,000 personal and 500 horse. Rāja Gaj Singh and Himmat K. were selected for drums. On the 2nd of the Divine month of Tīr, Sayyid Bāyazīd was honoured with the title of Muṣṭafā K., and was also presented with drums. At this time Tahawwur K., who is one of the personal servants, was despatched with a gracious farman to summon my fortunate son S͟hāh Parwīz.

Some days before this, petitions came from the officials in Qandahar reporting the intention of the ruler of Persia to conquer Qandahar, but my mind, which is actuated by sincerity, looking to past and present relations, placed no reliance on the truth of this until the report of my son K͟hān Jahān arrived that S͟hāh ʻAbbās, with the armies of Iraq and Khurasan, had come and besieged Qandahar. I ordered them to fix an hour for leaving Kashmir. Khwāja Abū-l-Ḥasan, the Diwan, and Bak͟hs͟hi Ṣādiq K. hastened to Lahore in advance of the victorious army to expedite the arrival of the princes of high degree with the armies of the Deccan, Gujarat, Bengal, and Behar, and to send on the Amirs who were present with the victorious stirrups, and those who one after another should come in from the districts of their jagirs to my son K͟han Jāhān at Multan. At the same time the artillery, with the strings of warlike elephants, and the armoury* were to be prepared and forwarded. As there was little cultivation between Multan and Qandahar, the despatch of a large army without provisions was not to be thought of. It was therefore decided to encourage the grain-sellers, who in the language of India are called *banjārā*, and, providing them with money, to take them along with the victorious army, so that there might be no difficulty about supplies. The Banjārās† are a tribe. Some of them have 1,000 bullocks, and some more or less. They take grain from different districts (*bulūkāt*) into the towns and sell it. They go along with the armies, and with such an army there would be

* The I.O. MS., No. 181, adds "and treasure."

† "Wilson" Glossary, p. 60. Elliot, Supp. Glossary, I. 52. The word seems connected with *barinj*, "rice."

100,000 bullocks or more. It is hoped that by the grace of the Creator, the army will be furnished with numbers and arms so that there may be no delay or hesitation until it reach Isfahan, which is his (the Shah's) capital. A farman was sent to Khān Jahān to beware and not start in that direction (Qandahar) from Multan before the arrival of the victorious army, and not be disturbed, but attend to orders. Bahādur K. Uzbeg was selected to go as an auxiliary to the army of Qandahar, and favoured with a horse and dress of honour. Fāẓil K. was given the mansab of 2,000 personal and 750 horse.

As it had been brought to notice that the poor of Kashmir suffer hardships in the winter from the excessive cold, and live with difficulty, I ordered that a village of the rental of Rs. 3,000 or Rs. 4,000 should be entrusted to Mullā Ṭālib Iṣfahānī,* to be expended in providing clothes for the poor, and for warming water, for purposes of ablution, in the mosques.

As it was reported that the Zamindars of Kishtwar had again raised their heads in disobedience and sin, and engaged in sedition and disturbance, Irādat K. was ordered to proceed hot-foot, before they had time to establish themselves firmly, and having inflicted condign punishment on them to tear up the root of sedition. On this day Zainu-l-'Ābidīn, who had been sent to summon Khurram, came and waited on me, and reported that the stipulation he made was that he should pass the rainy season in the fort of Māndū, and then come to Court. His report was read. I† did not like the style of its purport nor the request he made, and, on the contrary, the traces of disloyalty (*bī-daulatī*) were apparent. There being no remedy, an order was given that as he proposed to come after the rains, he should despatch the great Amirs, the servants of the Court who were employed in assisting him, and especially the Sayyids of Bārha and Bukhara, the Shaikh-zādas, the Afghans, and the Rajputs. Mīrzā Rustam and I'tiqād K. were ordered to go to Lahore in advance, and assist the army

* This is the poet Bābā Ṭālib Iṣfahānī of Blochmann, 607.

† Elliot, VI. 383.

of Qandahar. Rs. 1,00,000 were given them as advance of pay, and I also granted drums to 'Ināyat K. and I'timād K. Irādat K., who had hastened to punish the rebels of Kishtwar, having killed many of them and regained the mastery and established himself firmly, returned to duty. Mu'tamid K. had been appointed Bakhshi to the army of the Deccan. As that matter was over* he was sent for at his own request. He came on this day, and on his arrival kissed the threshold.

It is a strange thing that when a pearl of the value of Rs. 14,000 or 15,000 was lost in the harem, Jotik Rāy, the astrologer, represented that it would be found in two or three days. Ṣādiq K. Rammāl (soothsayer) represented that in the same two or three days it would come from a place which was perfectly clean and pure, such as the place of worship or oratory. A female soothsayer represented that it would soon be found, and that a woman with white skin would bring it in a state of ecstasy, and give it into the hand of the Ḥaẓrat (the king). It happened that on the third day one of the Turkish girls found it in the oratory, and all in smiles and in a happy frame of mind gave it to me. As the words of all three came true each one was favoured with an acceptable reward. This is written because it is not devoid of strangeness.

At this time I appointed Kaukab and Khidmatgār K., and others to the number of twelve in all, of the familiar servants to be *sazāwuls* of the Amirs in the Deccan in order that they might exert themselves and send them forward as soon as possible to Court, so that they (the Amīrs) might be sent to the victorious army at Qandahar.† At this time it was frequently reported to me that Khurram had taken into his possession some of the estates of the jagir of Nūr Jahān Begam and Shahriyār, and especially the pargana of Dholpur, which had by the High Diwan been assigned to Shahriyār,

* Not that the question of the Deccan had been settled, but that Shāh Jahān had left Burhanpur and come to Māndū. See Iqbāl-nāma, 193.

† Elliot, VI. 383.

and had sent there an Afghan of the name of Daryā, one of his own servants, with a body of men. Daryā fought with Sharīfu-l-mulk, a servant of Shahriyār, who had been appointed to the faujdari of that region, and many were killed on both sides. Although in consequence of his (Khurram's) remaining in the fort of Māndū, and the unreasonable requests made in his letter it appeared that his reason was turned, yet from hearing this news it became clear that he was unworthy of all the favours and cherishing I had bestowed on him, and that his brain had gone wrong. Accordingly I sent Rāja Rūz-afzūn, who was a confidential servant, to him, and made inquiries as to the cause of this boldness. He was ordered hereafter to behave properly, and not place his foot beyond the path of reasonableness and the high road of politeness, and content himself with the districts of his own jagir that he had obtained from the High Diwan. He must also beware not to form any intention of coming to wait upon me, but to send the body of the servants of the State I had requisitioned on account of the disturbance at Qandahar to the Court. If anything contrary to this order should come to notice, he would repent it.

At this time Mīr Ẓahīru-d-dīn, the grandson of Mīr Mīrān, s. the famous Shāh Ni'matu-llah, came from Persia and waited on me, and received as a present a dress of honour and 8,000 darbs. Ujālā Dakhanī obtained leave to go to Rāja Bīr Singh Deo with a gracious farman in order that he should act as *sazāwul* and collect the men. Previously to this, on account of the great regard and abundant affection I bore to Khurram and his sons, at the time when his son (Shujā') was very ill, I had determined that if God Almighty would grant him to me I would not again sport with a gun, and would inflict no injury on a living thing with my own hand. Notwithstanding my inclination and love for hunting, especially with a gun, I had given it up for five years. At this time, when I was greatly distressed at his unkind behaviour, I took again to sporting with a gun, and gave orders that nobody should remain in the palace without one. In a short time most of the servants took a liking to shooting with guns, and the archers,* in order to perform their duties, became cavalry soldiers.

On the 25th of the month, corresponding with the 7th Shawwāl, at the favourable hour that had been chosen, I turned towards Lahore from Kashmir (apparently means Srinagar, the capital). I sent Bihārī Dās Brahman with a gracious farman to Rānā Karan to the effect that he should bring his son with a body of men to pay his respects to me. Mīr Ẓahīru-d-dīn was promoted to the mansab of 1,000 personal and 400 horse. As he represented to me that he was in debt, I made him a present of Rs. 10,000. On the 1st of Shahrīwar I encamped at the fountain of Achbal,† and on Thursday I had a feast of cups beside the fountain.‡ On this auspicious day my fortunate son Shahriyār was appointed to the Qandahar expedition, and was promoted to the mansab of 12,000 personal and 8,000 horse. A special dress of honour, with a *nādirī* with pearl buttons, was also given him. At this time a merchant had brought two large pearls from the country of Turkey, one of them weighing 1¼ *miṣqāls*, and the second 1 *surkh* less. Nūr Jahān Begam bought the two for Rs. 60,000, and presented them to me as an offering on the same day. On Friday, the 10th, by the advice of Ḥakīm Mūminā,§ I was relieved by bleeding from the arm. Muqarrab K., who has great skill in this art, always used to bleed me, and possibly never failed before, but now failed twice. Afterwards Qāsim, his nephew, bled me. I gave him a dress of honour and Rs. 2,000, and gave 1,000 darbs to Ḥakīm Mūminā. Mīr Khān, at the request of Khān Jahān, was promoted to the mansab of 1,500 and 900 horse.

* *Tarkash-bandān*, literally quiver-holders. Apparently the meaning is that the archers who were footmen (see Blochmann, 254, about *Dākhilī* troops) lost their vocation when guns came into use, and became cavalry soldiers. But the meaning in text may be that the archers took to practising with bows and arrows on horseback. It appears from a Dastūru-l-'amal in the I.O., No. 1,855 (E. 2736) that the *tarkash-bands* were an inferior order of servants receiving 1,000 dams or less a year. They probably were not necessarily archers.

† The Achh Dal of the Āyīn, Jarrett, II. 358.

‡ No. 181 has "at Vīrnāg."

§ Pādshāh-nāma, I., Part II., p. 349.

On the 21st of the month the feast of my solar weighing took place, and the 54th year of the age of this suppliant at the throne of God began auspiciously and happily. I hope that the whole of my life will be spent in fulfilling the will of God. On the 28th, I went to see the waterfall of Áshar* (?). As this spring is famous for its sweetness and agreeable flavour, I weighed it in my presence against Ganges water, and that† of the valley of Lār. The water of Ashar was 3 *māsha* heavier than that of the Ganges, and the latter was ½ *māsha* lighter than that of the valley of Lār. On the 30th the camp was at Hīrāpūr. Though Irādat K. had done his duty in Kishtwar well, yet as the ryots and inhabitants of Kashmir complained of his treatment of them, I promoted I'tiqād K. to the governorship of Kashmir. I bestowed on him a horse, a dress of honour, and a special enemy-piercing‡ sword, and appointed Irādat K. to do duty with the army of Qandahar. Having brought Kunwar Singh, the Raja of Kishtwar, out of the fortress of Gwalior, where he was imprisoned, I bestowed Kishtwar on him, and gave him a horse and a dress of honour, with the title of Raja. I sent Ḥaidar Malik to Kashmir (*i.e.*, Srinagar) to bring a canal from the valley of Lār to the Nūr-afzā garden, giving him Rs. 30,000 for the materials and labour. On the 12th of the month I came down from the hill country of Jammū, and pitched at Bhimbhar. The next day I had a *qamurgha* hunt. To Dāwar-bakhsh, s. Khusrau, I gave the mansab of 5,000 personal and 2,000 horse. On the 24th I crossed the Chenab.§ Mīrzā Rustam came from Lahore, and waited on me. On the same day Afẓal|| K., Khurram's Diwan, bringing a petition from him, waited on me. He had clothed his immoderate acts in the garment of apology, and had sent him with the idea that perhaps he might carry his point by flattery and smooth

* May also be read Uhar and Adhar. It is Adhar or Udhar in I.O. MSS.

† The Sind River of Kashmir is meant. Jarrett II. 364.

‡ This seems a translation of Akbar's word *arīnās* (enemy-destroying).

§ Elliot, VI. 384, where Jhelam is a mistake.

|| Pādshāh-nāma, I., Part II., p. 339. His name was Mullā Shukrullah, and he was from Shiraz. He is the Mirza Sorocolla of Roe.

speeches, and so correct his improprieties. I* paid no attention, and did not listen to him. The Diwan Khwāja Abū-l-Ḥasan and Ṣādiq K. Bakhshi, who had hastened to Lahore to make provision for the army of Qandahar, had the good fortune to kiss the threshold. On the 1st of the Divine month of Ābān, Amānu-llah, s. Mahābat K., was promoted to the mansab of 3,000 personal and 1,700 horse. A gracious farman was sent to summon Mahābat K. At this time 'Abdu-llah K., whom I had sent for for service at Qandahar, having come from the district of his jagir, paid his respects. On the 4th of the same month I entered the city of Lahore auspiciously and happily. Alf K. was promoted to the mansab of 2,000 and 1,500 horse. I gave† an order to the chief Diwans to levy the pay of the force of servants of the State who had been appointed for service at Qandahar out of the jagirs of Khurram, which were in the Sarkar of Ḥiṣār, and in the Dū-āb and those regions. In the place of these he might take possession of districts from the Subah of Malwa and the Deccan, and Gujarat and Khandesh, wherever he wished. Presenting Afẓal K. with a dress of honour I gave him leave to go. An order was passed that the Subahs of Gujarat, Malwa, the Deccan and Khandesh should be handed over to him (Khurram), and he might take up a permanent residence wherever he might wish, and employ himself in the administration of those regions. He was to send quickly the sazāwuls who had been appointed to bring the servants of the State who had been summoned to my presence on account of the disturbance at Qandahar. After that he was to look after his own charge, and not depart from order: otherwise, he would repent. On this day I gave the best *tipchāq* horse that was in my private stable to 'Abdu-llah K. On the 26th Ḥaidar Beg and Walī Beg, envoys of the ruler of Persia, had an audience. After performing the ceremony of salutation they produced a letter from the Shah. My son Khān Jahān,

* Compare Iqbāl-nāma, 194 and 196. It is stated there that Nūr Jahān would not allow Afẓal K. to have an audience, and that he was dismissed without gaining his object.

† See Iqbāl-nāma, 196, where it is said that these orders were not really given by Jahangir, but were Nūr Jahān's.

according to order, having come post from Multan, waited on me. He presented as offerings 1,000 muhrs, 1,000 rupees, and 18 horses. Mahābat K. was promoted to the mansab of 6,000 personal and 5,000 horse. I gave an elephant to Mīrzā Rustam. Rāja Sārang Deo was appointed sazāwul to Rāja Bir Singh Deo. I told him to produce him at Court as quickly as possible. On* the 7th of the Divine month of Āẕar the ambassadors of S͟hāh 'Abbās, who had come at different times, were presented with dresses of honour and their expenses, and given leave to go. The letter he had sent by Ḥaidar Beg making excuses in the matter of Qandahar has been given in this record of good fortune (Iqbāl-nāma) along with my reply.

Letter of the King of Persia.

(After compliments, and good wishes for that "brother dear as life" the letter proceeds as follows):

"You will be aware that after the death of the Nawāb S͟hāh Jannat-makān (S͟hāh Ṭahmāsp) great misfortunes befel Persia. Many territories which belonged to our saintly family passed out of possession, but when this suppliant at the throne of Grace became sovereign, he, by God's help, and the excellent measures of friends, recovered the hereditary lands which were in the possession of enemies. As Qandahar was held by the agents of your lofty family, I regarded you as myself, and did not make any objection. From feelings of unity and brotherhood we waited, thinking that you would, after the manner of your ancestors† who are in Paradise, voluntarily take the matter into your consideration. When you neglected to do this, I repeatedly, by writing and verbal messages, directly and indirectly, asked for the disposal of the question, thinking that perhaps that petty country (Qandahar) was not regarded as worthy of your notice. You said several times that by making over the territory to our family, the notions of enemies and censurers would be disposed of, and

* Elliot, VI. 280.

† This alludes to the facts that Humāyūn promised S͟hāh Ṭahmāsp that he would restore the fort after he had conquered India, and that Akbar had acknowledged the justice of Persia's claim.

praters, enviers, and fault-finders would be put to silence. A faction* formerly delayed the settlement of this matter. As the truth of the affair was known to friends and enemies, and as no clear answer, either of refusal or concession, came from you, it occurred to me that I would go to Qandahar to see it, and to hunt. In this way the agents of my distinguished brother, in accordance with the ties of friendship which exist between us, might welcome us and wait upon us. By this means the relationship of union would be renewed, and would be made evident to the world, and the tongues of the envious and the evil-speaking be shortened. With this view, I set off without apparatus for taking forts, and when I came to Farāh I sent a rescript to the governor of Qandahar, mentioning that I intended to see the place and hunt there. I did this in order that he might treat me as a guest. We also called the honourable K͟hwāja Bāqī Kurkarāq, and sent a message to the governor and the other officers in the fort to the effect that there was no difference between Your Majesty and ourselves, and that we were aware of each other's territories, and that we were coming to see the country. Therefore they were not to act in such a way as to give umbrage or to vex anyone. They did not receive the conciliatory order and message in the proper way, but showed obstinacy and a rebellious spirit. When I came to the fort I again called the honourable aforesaid (K. Bāqī), and sent him with the message that I had directed my troops not to invest the fort till the lapse of ten days. They did not receive the wholesome advice, and were stubborn in their opposition. As there was nothing more to be done, the Persian army set about taking the fort, though it was in want of appliances, and soon levelled the walls and bastions with the ground. The garrison became straitened, and asked for quarter. We, too, maintained the ties of love which had existed from of old between the two exalted dynasties, and the brotherly relation which was formed between you and me when you were prince (Mīrzā), and which was an object of envy to contemporary sovereigns,

* The clause is very obscure. Perhaps it is part of what Jahangir had said.

and from my innate kindness forgave their errors and offences. Encompassing them with favours, I sent them safe and sound to your Court along with Ḥaidar Beg Qūrbās͟hī, who is one of the sincere Ṣūfīs of this family. Of a truth, the foundation of love and union, both inherited and acquired, on the part of this seeker after affection, has not grown old or decayed, and is strong so that no rupture in it can take place on account of any things which may have transpired owing to the action of Fate.

VERSE.

Between us and you there cannot be trouble,
There can be naught but love and trust.

"It is hoped that you, too, will preserve your affection for us, and that you will not approve of certain strange actions, and that if any suspicion about friendship arise you will endeavour by your innate goodness and continual love to efface it. May the ever-vernal flower of union and cordiality remain in bloom, and every effort be made to strengthen the foundations of concord, and to cleanse the fountains of agreement which regulate temperaments and territories. You will regard all our dominions as belonging to you, and will extend your friendship to everyone (in them ?), and will proclaim that it (Qandahar) has been given up to him ('Abbās) without any objection, and that such trifles are of no importance, and that though the governor and officers who were in the fort did some things which were obstacles to friendship, yet what took place was done by you and me. They performed the duties of service and life devotion. It is certain, too, that Your Majesty will be gracious to them, and will treat them with royal kindness, and will not shame me before them. What more need I write ? May thy star-brushing standards ever be associated with the Divine aids !"

Reply to the Letter of Shah 'Abbas.

"Unfeigned thanks, and pure thanksgivings are due to the sole object of worship (God) for that the maintenance of the compacts and treaties of great princes is the cause of the order of Creation and the repose of mankind. A proof of this is the harmony and unity which existed between us and the exalted family (of Persia), and which were increased during our time. These things were the envy of contemporary sovereigns. The glorious Shah—the star of heaven's army, the ruler of the nations, the adorner of the Kayānī tiara, the fitting occupant of the throne of Chosroes, the fruitful tree of the gardens of sovereignty, the splendid nursling of the parterres of prophecy and saintship, the cream of the Ṣafawī dynasty—hath without ground or reason, engaged in disturbing the rose-garden of love and friendship and brotherhood in which for long periods there has been no possibility of a breath of confusion. Clearly the methods of union and concord among princes require that they make oaths of friendship to one another, and that there should be perfect spiritual agreement between them. There should be no need of physical contact, and still less should there be any necessity for visiting one another's countries for 'shooting and spectacle' (*sair u shikār*).

VERSE.

Alas, a hundred times for the love passing thought!

"By the arrival of your loving letter apologizing for the 'spectacle and shooting' (*sair u shikār*) of Qandahar, which came with the honourable Ḥaidar Beg and Walī Beg, I became apprised of the bodily health of your angelic personality, and the flowers of joy were scattered over the world. Let it not be hidden from the world-adorning mind of my exalted and prosperous brother that until the arrival of the letter and messages brought by Zambīl Beg no mention had been made by you in letters or verbal messages of your wish for Qandahar. At the time when we were engaged in visiting the delightful land of Kashmir, the Deccan lords, in their shortsightedness, extended their feet beyond the limits of obedience, and trod the path of rebellion. Accordingly it became necessary for me to chastise them. I moved my standards to Lahore, and appointed my worthy* son Shāh Jāhān to proceed against them with a victorious army. I myself was proceeding to

* *Farzand-i-barkhūrdār.*

Agra when Zambīl Beg arrived, and produced your loving letter. I took it as a good omen, and went off to Agra to put down the enemies and the rebels. In the jewelled and pearl-dropping letter there was no mention of a wish for Qandahar. It was mentioned verbally by Zambīl Beg. In reply, I said to him that I made no difficulty with regard to anything that my brother wished. Please God, after settling the Deccan affair, I would send him back in a manner suitable to my sovereignty. I also said that as he had made long marches he should repose for some days in Lahore, and that I would afterwards send for him. After coming to Agra, I sent for him and gave him leave to depart. As the favour of God attaches to this suppliant, I withdrew my mind from victories and proceeded to the Panjab. My intention was to send him away, but after disposing of some necessary matters I went to Kashmir on account of the hot weather. After coming there I sent for Zambīl Beg in order to give him his leave. I also wished to show him something of that delightful country. Meanwhile news came that my prosperous brother had come to take Qandahar. This idea had never entered my mind, and I was entirely astonished. What could there be in a petty village that he should set out to take it, and that he should shut his eyes to so much friendship and brotherly feeling? Though truthful reporters sent the news, I could not credit it! When it became certain I immediately gave orders to 'Abdu-l-'Azīz K. not to transgress in any way the good pleasure of that prosperous brother. Up to now the relationship of brotherhood stands firm, and I do not value the world in comparison therewith, nor do I consider any gift equal to it. But it would have been right and brotherly that he should have waited till the arrival of the ambassador. Perhaps he would be successful in the object* and claim for

* It is noteworthy that Jahangir does not attempt to controvert the statement of Shāh 'Abbās that Qandahar rightfully belonged to Persia. There is a very long account in the 'Ālam-ārā'ī of the claims of Persia to Qandahar, and of the various attempts made to realize them, until at last it was taken by Shāh 'Abbās. See the account of the 35th year in the Teheran lithograph, p. 682, etc. The fort of Qandahar surrendered on 11 Sha'bān, 1031, or June 11, 1622. The Shah's letter

which he had come. When he ('Abbās) takes such steps before the return of the ambassador, to whom will mankind ascribe the merit of keeping compacts and of preserving the capital of humanity and liberality! May God preserve you at all times!"

After I had given leave to the ambassadors, I devoted all my energy to urging on the Qandahar force, and presented my son Khān Jahān, who had been sent for for certain matters, with an elephant, a special horse, a jewelled sword and dagger, and a dress of honour. I sent him on as an advance guard, and directed him to remain in Multan until the arrival of Prince Shahriyār with the victorious army. Bāqir K., who was faujdar of Multan, was summoned to Court, and I appointed 'Alī-qulī Beg Darman to assist him (Khān Jahān), and raised him to the mansab of 1,500. In the same manner, having raised M. Rustam to the mansab of 5,000, I appointed him to the duty of assisting that son with the (Qandahar) army. Lashkar K. came from the Deccan, and waited on me, and was also attached to that army. Allah-dād K. Afghān, M. 'Īsā Tarkhān, Mukarram K., Ikrām K., and other Amirs, who had come from the Deccan and from their fiefs, after being presented with horses and dresses of honour, were sent with Khān Jahān. 'Umdatu-s-salṭana Āṣaf K. was sent to Agra to bring to Court the whole of the treasure in muhrs and rupees which had accumulated from the beginning of the reign of my father. Aṣālat K., s. Khān Jahān, was promoted to the mansab of 2,000 and 1,000 horse. Muḥammad Shafī'ā, Bakhshi of Multan, had the title of Khan conferred on him. I gave leave to Sharīf, Vakil of my fortunate son Shāh Parwīz, to go with all possible haste, and bring my son to wait on me with the army of Behar, and writing a gracious farman with my own hand I urged him to come.

On this day Mīr Mīrān, the grandson of Shāh Ni'matu-llah, died suddenly. I hope that he will be among the pardoned.

---

announcing the fact and explaining his procedure was presented by Ḥaidar Beg on 26 Ābān, 1031—*i.e.*, early in November, 1622. He brought the officers of the garrison with him. See 'Ālam-ārā'ī and the Tūzuk text, 348 (annals of the 17th year).

A raging elephant threw down the huntsman Mīrzā Beg and killed him: I assigned his duties to Imām-wirdī.

As in consequence of the weakness that came over me two years ago and still continues, heart and brain do not accord. I cannot* make notes of events and occurrences. Now that Mu'tamid K. has come from the Deccan, and has had the good fortune to kiss the threshold, as he is a servant who knows my temperament and understands my words, and was also formerly entrusted with this duty, I gave an order that from the date which I have written he shall hereafter write them with his own hand, and attach them to my Memoranda. Whatever events may occur hereafter he should note after the manner of a diary, and submit them for my verification, and then they should be copied into a book.

From this Place the Notes are Written by Mu'tamid Khān.†

As the whole of my world-opening mind was taken up with the preparation of the Qandahar army, and the remedy for that business, the unpleasant news that reached me of a change in the condition of Khurram, and his want of moderation, became a cause for aversion and dissension. I accordingly sent Mūsawī K., who is one of the sincere servants who knows my temperament, to that wretch (*bī-daulat*) to lay before him the threatening messages and my wishes, and to give admonitions that might sharpen his intelligence, so that by the guidance of good fortune he might awake from the dream of carelessness and pride, and that he (Mūsawī) having gained a (true) knowledge of his futile ideas and aims might hasten to my presence, and carry out whatever appeared to be necessary. On the 1st of the Divine month of Bahman the feast of my lunar weighing took place. At this auspicious ceremony Mahābat K., having come from Kabul, paid his respects, and was the recipient of special favours. I appointed

* Elliot, VI. 280.

† These words do not appear in the I.O. MSS. And what is written in this chapter about the fates of Khalīl and Muḥtarim, etc., does not agree with Mu'tamid's writing in Iqbāl-nāma.

Ya'qūb K. Badakhshī to Kabul, exalting him with the gift of drums. About this time report came from I'tibār K. from Agra that Khurram, with the army of adversity, had left Māndū and started in that direction. He had evidently heard the news that the treasure had been sent for, and fire had fallen into his mind, and having let fall from his hand the reins of self-control, had started (with the idea) that on the road he might lay hold of the treasure. Accordingly I thought it best to proceed for a tour, and in order to hunt to the bank of the river of Sulṭān-pūr (the Beas). If that wretch by the guidance of error should place his foot in the desert of audacity, I might hasten farther forward and place the punishment of his unbecoming behaviour in the skirt of his fortune. If matters turned out in any other way I might take steps accordingly. With this purpose, on the 17th of the same month, at an auspicious hour, I marched. Mahābat K. was dignified with a dress of honour. Rs. 1,00,000 were ordered to be given to Mīrzā Rustam and Rs. 2,00,000 to 'Abdu-llah K. by way of advance of pay. I sent Mīrzā Khān, s. Zain K., with a gracious farman to my fortunate son Shāh Parwīz, and renewed my urgency for his attendance. Rāja Sārang Deo had gone to summon Rāja Bir Singh Deo: he came, and having paid his respects, reported that the Rāja. with a proper force and an equipped army, would join me at Thanesar. At this time constant reports* came from I'tibār K. and other servants of the State from Agra that Khurram in revolt and disloyalty (*bī-daulatī*) had changed what was due by him for rearing into undutifulnesses,† and having placed the foot of ruin in the valley of ignorance and error, had started in that direction. They therefore did not consider it advisable to bring the treasure, and were engaged in strengthening the towers and gates, and providing things necessary for the defence of the fort. Similarly a report came from Āṣaf K. that the wretch had torn off the veil of respect, and turned his face towards the valley of ruin, and that the odour of good came not from the manner of his

* Elliot, VI. 384.

† *Ḥuqūq ba-'uqūq*, "rights into wrongs."

approach. As it was not for the advantage of the State to bring the treasure, he had entrusted it to God, and was himself on the way to wait on me. Accordingly, having crossed the river at Sulṭānpūr, by successive marches I proceeded to punish that one of dark fortune, and gave an order that henceforth they should call him *Bī-daulat* (wretch). Wherever in this record of fortune "Bī-daulat" is mentioned it will refer to him. From the kindnesses and favours bestowed upon him I can say that up till the present time no king has conferred such on his son. What my reverend father did for my brothers I have done for his servants, giving them titles, standards, and drums, as has been recorded in the preceding pages. It will not be hidden from the readers of this record of prosperity what affection and interest I have bestowed on him. My pen's tongue fails in ability to set them forth. What shall I say of my own sufferings? In pain and weakness, in a warm atmosphere that is extremely unsuited to my health, I must still ride and be active, and in this state must proceed against such an undutiful son. Many servants cherished by me for long years and raised to the dignity of nobility, whom I ought to employ to-day in war against the Uzbeg or the Persian, I must punish* for his vileness and destroy with my own hand. Thank God that he has given me such capacity to bear my burdens that I can put up with all this, and go on in the same path, and reckon them as light. But that which weighs heavily on my heart, and places my eager temperament in sorrow is this, that at such a time when my prosperous sons and loyal officers should be vying with each other in the service against Qandahar and Khurasan, which would be to the renown of the Sultanate, this inauspicious one has struck with an axe the foot of his own dominion, and become a stumbling-block in the path of the enterprise. The momentous affair of Qandahar must now be postponed, but I trust that Almighty God will remove these griefs from my heart.

* I rather think the meaning is "he by his baseness and illfatedness has capitally punished them, and has (as it were) slain them by his own hand," the meaning being that they will fall in the civil war about to take place.

At this time it was reported to me that Muḥtarim K., the eunuch, K͟halīl Beg Z̤ū-l-qadr, and Fidā'ī K., the Master of the Ceremonies, had allied themselves with Bī-daulat, and opened the gates of correspondence with him. As it was no time for mildness and winking at matters, I imprisoned all three, and as, after making inquiry into the circumstances, no doubt remained as to their falseness to their salt, and about the evil designs and malevolence of K͟halīl and Muḥtarim, and as Amirs like Mīrzā Rustam swore to the insincerity and malevolence of K͟halīl, having no remedy I punished them* capitally. Fidā'ī K., the dust of whose sincerity was free of suspicion and pure, I brought out of confinement and promoted. I sent Rāja Rūz-afzūn by post (*dāk-chaukī*) to my son S͟hāh Parwīz that he might bring him with all haste to wait on me; so that Bī-daulat might be brought to punishment for his improper conduct. Jawāhir K., the eunuch, was appointed to the post of *Ihtimām-i-darbār-i-maḥall* (superintendent of the harem).

On the 1st of Isfandārmūz̤ the royal army arrived at Nūr-sarāy. On this day a report came from I'tibār K., that Bī-daulat had arrived in all haste in the neighbourhood of Agra, in the hope that before the fort was strengthened, the gates of strife and mischief might be opened, and he might attain his end. When he arrived at Fatḥpūr, he found the gates closed against him, and, being struck with the disgrace of ruin, he had halted. The K͟hān-k͟hānān and his son and many of the royal Amirs attached to the Deccan and Gujarat had come with him as companions on the road of rebellion and ingratitude. Mūsawī K. saw him at Fatḥpūr, and showed him the royal orders, and it was settled that he should send his servant Qāz̤ī 'Abdu-l-'Azīz with him to Court to put his requests before me. He sent to Agra his servant Sundar,† who was the ringleader of the people of error and the chief of the seditious, to take possession of the treasures and hidden wealth of those servants of the State who were at Agra. Amongst‡

* Compare Iqbāl-nāma, 199.

† This is the man whom Jahangir had made Rāja Bikramājīt.

‡ Elliot, VI. 385.

others he entered the house of Lashkar K., and seized Rs. 9,00,000. In the same manner, wherever he suspected there was property in the houses of other servants (of the Court), he stretched out his hand to seize it, and took possession of all that he found. When nobles like Khān-khānān, who had been distinguished with the rank of Ātālīk and arrived at the age of seventy years, made their faces black with rebellion and ingratitude, how could one complain of others? It may be said that his very nature was seditious and ungrateful. His father (Bairām K.) at the end of his life behaved in the same unbecoming way towards my reverend father. He, following the example of his father, at his age made himself accursed and rejected to all eternity.

> In the end a wolf's cub becomes a wolf
> Although he grow up with man. (Sa'dī.)

On this day Mūsawī K. arrived with 'Abdu-l-'Azīz, the envoy of Bī-daulat. As his requests were unreasonable, I did not allow him to speak, but handed him over to Mahābat to be kept in prison. On the 5th of the month I pitched on the bank of the river of Lūdiyāna (the Sutlej). I promoted Khān A'ẓam to the mansab of 7,000 with 5,000 horse. Rāja Bhārat, the Bandīla, from the Deccan, and Dayānat K. from Agra, came and waited on me. I pardoned the offences of Dayānat K., and gave him the same mansab that he had previously held. Rājā Bhārat was raised to the mansab of 1,500 and 1,000 horse, and Mūsawī K. to that of 1,000 and 300 horse. On Thursday, the 12th, in the pargana of Thānesar, Rāja Bir Singh Deo, having waited on me, reviewed his army and elicited great praise. Rāja Sārang Deo was promoted to the mansab of 1,500 with 600 horse. In Karnāl Āṣaf K., coming from Agra, lifted up the head of honour in kissing my stirrup. His coming at this time was the herald of victory. Nawāzish K., s. Sa'īd K., having arrived from Gujarat, paid his respects. When Bī-daulat was at Burhanpur, at his request I had appointed Bāqī K. to Jūnāgaṛh. He had been ordered to come to Court, and now came and shared n my service. As my march from Lahore took place without previous notice, and time did not admit of delay or reflection, I came with the few Amirs who were in attendance. Until I arrived at Sihrind only a few men had the good fortune to accompany me, but after passing beyond it, great numbers of the army came in from all sides and quarters. Before arrival at Delhi such a force had come together that in any direction in which one looked the whole plain was occupied by troops.

As it was reported that Bī-daulat had left Fatḥpūr and was coming in this direction, and making continuous marches towards Delhi, I gave the victorious army orders to put on their *chiltas* (quilted coats). In this disturbance the pivot of the management of affairs and the arrangement of the army were entrusted to Mahābat K. The command of the vanguard was given to ‘Abdu-llah K. Of the selected young men and experienced *sipāhīs*, whoever was asked for by him was enrolled in his corps. I ordered him to march a koss ahead of the other forces. He was also entrusted with the intelligence department and the control of the routes. I was ignorant of the fact that he was in league with Bī-daulat, and that the real object of that evil-natured one was to send news from my army to him. Previously to this he used to bring long written slips of true and false news, saying that his spies had sent them from that place. The purport was that they (the spies) suspected some of my servants of being in league with Bī-daulat, and of sending him news. Had I been led away by his intrigues and become alarmed at this time when the wind of disturbance was blowing strongly I would have been obliged to destroy many of my servants. Although some faithful servants suspected his evil intentions and untruthfulness, the time was not one for removing the veil openly from the face of his deeds. I guarded my eye and tongue from doing anything which might carry terror into his evil mind, and showed him more attention and favour than before, with the idea that possibly he would be struck with shame, and might turn away from his evil deeds, and give up his evil nature and sedition. That rejected one to all eternity, in whom a tendency to vileness and falsity was natural, did not fail to do what was in accordance with himself, as will be related hereafter.

> The tree* that is bitter in its nature
> If you plant it in the garden of Paradise,
> And water it from the eternal stream thereof,
> If you pour on its root pure honey,
> In the end it shows its natural quality,
> And it bears the same bitter fruit.

In fine, when I was near Delhi, Sayyid Bahwa Bukhārī, Ṣadr K., and Rāja Kishan Dās came out of the city, and had the good fortune to kiss my stirrup. Bāqir K., faujdar of Oudh, also on this day came to the victorious camp. On the 25th of the month, passing by Delhi, I pitched my camp on the bank of the Jumna. Girdhar, s. Rāy Sāl Darbārī, having come from the Deccan, had the honour to pay his respects. He was promoted to the mansab of 2,000 and 1,500 horse, and obtained the title of Raja, and was clothed in a dress of honour. Zabar-dast K., Master of the Ceremonies, was honoured with a standard.

* The lines come from Firdūsī's satire on Maḥmūd of Ghazni.

THE EIGHTEENTH NEW YEAR'S FEAST AFTER THE AUSPICIOUS ACCESSION

On the eve of Tuesday, the 20th of Jumādā-l-awwal, A.H. 1032 (March 10, 1623), the sun that lights the world entered his house of honour in Aries, and the eighteenth year from the beginning of my reign commenced auspiciously and happily. On this day I heard that Bī-daulat, having gone to the neighbourhood of Mathura, had encamped the army tainted with ruin in the pargana of S͟hāhpūr, and reviewed 27,000 cavalry. It is hoped that they will soon be subdued and miserable. Rāja Jay Singh, grandson* of Rāja Mān Singh, came from his native country, and had the good fortune to kiss my stirrup. I dignified Rāja Bir Singh Deo, than whom in the Rajput caste there is no greater Amir, with the title of Maharaja, and promoted his son Jograj to the mansab of 2,000 with 1,000 horse. Sayyid Bahwa was presented with an elephant. As it was reported to me that Bī-daulat was coming by the bank of the Jumna, the march of the victorious army in that direction was also decided on. The array of the army that resembled the waves of the sea was divided into the van, the right and left wings, the *altmis͟h*, the *ṭaraḥ* (reserve), the *chandāwul* (rear), etc., and arranged in a manner suitable to the circumstances and according to the locality. Close upon this came the news that Bī-daulat, with the wretch K͟hān-k͟hānān, had turned his reins from the right road and gone towards the pargana Kotila, 20 koss towards the left, along with the brahman Sundar, who was his guide to the desert of

* He was the great-grandson, being the son of Mahā Singh s. Jagat Singh s. Mān Singh.

error, with Dārāb, s. Khān-khānān, and many of the Amirs who had accompanied him on the road of rebellion and rascality, such as Himmat K., Sar-buland K., Sharza K. 'Ābid K., Jādo Rāy, Ūday Rām, Ātash K., Manṣūr K., and other mansabdars, who were attached to the Deccan, Gujarat, and Malwa, the recital of whom would take too long, and all his own servants, such as Rāja Bhīm, s. Rānā, Rustam K., Bairam Beg, the Afghan Daryā, Taqī, and others whom he had left to confront the royal army. There were five* armies (corps ?). Although nominally the command was in the hands of the wretch (*bar-gashta-i-rūzgār*) Dārāb, yet in reality the leader and centre of the whole affair was Sundar, of evil deeds. These men of darkened fortune pitched in the neighbourhood of Balūchpūr to their ruin. On the 8th I pitched at Qabūlpūr. On this day the turn to take the rear fell upon Bāqir K. We had left him behind all the rest. A body of the rebels attacked him on the march, and stretched out the hand of plunder. Bāqir planted firmly the foot of courage, and succeeded in beating them back. Khwājā Abū-l-Ḥasan got news of this, and turned his reins to support him. Before the arrival of the Khwāja the rebels (*mardūdān*), not being able to stand, had taken to flight. On Wednesday, the 9th of the month, having separated 25,000 horse under the leadership of Āṣaf K., Khwāja Abū-l-Ḥasan, and 'Abdu-llah K., I sent them to attack the rebels who did not look to the end of things. Qāsim K., Lashkar K., Irādat K., Fidā'ī K., and other servants, to the number of 8,000 horse, were appointed to Āṣaf K.'s force. Bāqir K., Nūru-d-dīn Qulī, Ibrāhīm Ḥusain Kāshgharī, and others, to the number of 8,000 horse, were appointed to support Abū-l-Ḥasan. Nawāzish K., 'Abdu-l-'Azīz K., 'Azīzu-llah, and many of the Bārha and Amroha Sayyids, were ordered to accompany 'Abdu-llah. In this army 10,000 horse were enrolled. Sundar had arranged the army of ruin and put forward the foot of shamelessness. At this time I sent my special quiver

* *Panj fauj*. But perhaps the word is *binj*, or *bīkh*, "root." Or it may be *pīchhā fauj*, "the hinder army." Apparently the reference is to the arrangement of the royal army into five divisions.

by Zabar-dast K., Master of Ceremonies, to ʻAbdu-llah K., that it might be the means of animating his zeal. When the encounter of the two sides took place, that black-faced one to all eternity, in whom the tendency to rebellion and ingratitude was innate, taking to flight, joined the rebels. ʻAbdu-l-ʻAzīz K., the son of the Khān Daurān, God knows whether knowingly or not, went off with him. Nawāzish K., Zabar-dast K., and Shīr-ḥamla, who were in the corps of that shameless one (ʻAbdu-llah K.), planted firmly the foot of courage, and were not disturbed at his going. As the aid of Almighty God is ever near this suppliant, at this crisis, when a leader of the army such as ʻAdbu-llah K. threw 10,000 cavalry into confusion and joined the enemy, and there was nearly a great disaster, a shot from a mysterious hand reached Sundar. At his fall the pillars of the courage of the rebels shook. Khwāja Abū-l-Ḥasan also drove before him the army in front of him and defeated it. Āṣaf K., when Bāqir K. arrived, showing great activity, finished the affair, and a victory which might be the *ṭughrā* (sign manual) of the victories of the age showed its face of purpose from the hidden world. Zabar-dast K., Shīr-ḥamla, Shīr-bacha, his son, and the son of Asad K., the architect, and Muḥammad Ḥusain, brother of Khwāja Jahān, and a number of the Sayyids of Bārha who were in the corps of the black-faced ʻAbdu-llah, having tasted the sweet-flavoured wine of martyrdom, obtained everlasting life. ʻAzīzu-llah, grandson of Ḥusain K. (Tukriya), being wounded by a gun-shot, got off safely. Although at this time the desertion of that rejected hypocrite was a secret help, yet it is probable that if he had not performed this detestable action in the crisis of the battle, many of the rebel leaders would have been killed or captured. It chanced that he was known to the common people by the title of Laʻnatu-llah (God's curse), and as he had received this name from the hidden world I also called him by it. Hereafter, wherever the expression *Laʻnatu-llah* is used it refers to him. Briefly, after the rebels, whose end was evil, took to flight from the field of battle, and turned their faces towards the valley of ruin and could not reassemble, Laʻnatu-llah, with all the rebels, did not turn his rein till he reached Bī-daulat, who was at a distance of 20 koss.

When the news of the victory of the servants of the State reached this suppliant to God, he prostrated himself in thankfulness for this gift, which was from the renewed favour of Allah, and summoned the loyal ones into his presence. On the next day they brought before me the head of Sundar. It appeared that when the ball struck him he gave up his soul to the lords of hell, and they took his body to a neighbouring village to be burnt. When they were about to light the fire, an army appeared in the distance, and for fear lest they should be taken prisoners, everyone took to flight. The Muqaddam (head man) of the village cut off his head, and for his own acquittal took it to Khān A'ẓam, as it occurred in his jagir. He was brought to me (with the head): the head was quite recognizable and had as yet undergone no change, but they had cut off the ears for the sake of the pearls in them. No one knew by whose hand he had been shot. In consequence of his destruction, Bī-daulat did not gird his loins again. One might say his good fortune and courage and understanding lay in that dog of a Hindu. When, with a father like me, who in truth am his ostensible creator, and in my own lifetime have raised him to the great dignity of Sultanship, and denied him nothing, he acts in this manner, I appeal to the justice of Allah that He may never again regard him with favour. Those servants who in this disturbance had done fitting service were honoured with more and more favours, each according to his degree. Khwāja Abū-l-Ḥasan was raised to the mansab of 5,000, original and increased, Nawāzish K. to that of 4,000 and 3,000 horse, Bāqir K. to that of 3,000 and 500 horse, with drums, Ibrāhīm Ḥusain Kāshgharī to that of 2,000 and 1,000 horse, 'Azīzu-llah to that of 2,000 and 1,000 horse, Nūru-d-dīn Qulī to that of 2,000 and 700 horse, Rāja Rām Dās to that of 2,000 and 1,000 horse, Luṭfu-llah to that of 1,000 and 500 horse, Parwarish K. to that of 1,000 and 500 horse. If all the servants were to be written in detail it would take too long. Briefly I remained at that place one day and marched on the next. Khān 'Ālam, having marched from Allahabad, had the good fortune to kiss the threshold. On the 12th of the month I encamped at the village of Jhānsa (?).

On this day Sar-buland Rāy came from the Deccan and waited on me, and was honoured with a special jewelled dagger, with a *phūl katāra*. 'Abdu-l-'Azīz K. and some of those who had gone with La'natu-llah released themselves from the hand of Bī-daulat, and paid their respects, and represented that when La'natu-llah charged, they thought it was for a cavalry encounter. When they found themselves in the midst of the rebels they saw nothing for it but to submit and pay their respects, but now they had found an opportunity and had obtained the good fortune of kissing the threshold. Though they had taken 2,000 muhrs from Bī-daulat for their expenses, as the times were critical I made no inquiry, but accepted* their statement.

On the 19th the Feast of the culmination was held, and many of the servants of the State were raised in mansab, and had suitable favours conferred on them.

Mīr 'Aẓudu-d-daulah, having come from Agra, waited on me. He brought a vocabulary† of words that he had prepared. In truth he had taken much pains, and collected together all the words from the writings of ancient poets. There is no book like this in the science.

Rāja Jay Singh was raised to the mansab of 3,000 with 1,400 horse, and a special elephant was presented to my son Shahriyār. The post of *'Arẓ-mukarrir* (examiner of petitions) was conferred on Mūsawī K. Amānu-llah, s. Mahābat K., was given the title of Khān-zād Khān, was favoured with a mansab of 4,000 personal and horse, and was honoured with a flag and drums.

On the 1st of the Divine month of Urdībihisht I pitched on the bank of the lake at Fatḥpūr. I'tibār K. came from Agra and waited on me, and was graciously received. Muẓaffar K., Mukarram K., and his brother also came from Agra, and had the good fortune to wait on me. As I'tibār K. had done

* "Bought it as if it were genuine."

† The Farhang-i-Jahāngīrī, Rieu Cat., p. 496 b.

approved service in the charge of the Agra fort he was dignified with the title of Mumtāz K., and I gave him the mansab of 6,000 personal and 5,000 horse, and having bestowed on him a dress of honour, a jewelled sword, a horse, and a special elephant, I sent him back to his duty. Sayyid Bahwa was promoted to the mansab of 2,000 and 1,500 horse, Mukarram K. to that of 3,000 and 2,000 horse, and Khwāja Qāsim to that of 1,000 with 400 horse. On the 4th Manṣūr K. Farangī, whose circumstances have been recorded* in the proceding pages (?), with his brother† and Naubat‡ K. Dakhanī, by the guidance of good fortune separated themselves from Bī-daulat, and came into my service. I sent Khawāṣṣ K. to my fortunate son Shāh Parwīz. Mīrzā 'Īsā Tarkhān, having come from Multan, had the good fortune to kiss the threshold. A special sword was given to Mahābat K. On the 10th the camp was pitched in the pargana of Hindaun. Manṣūr K. (the Farangī) was raised to the mansab of 4,000 personal and 3,000 horse, and that of Naubat§ K. to that of 2,000 and 1,000 horse. On the 11th was a halt. As on this day a meeting with my fortunate son Shāh Parwīz had been arranged, I ordered that the powerful princes and the illustrious Amirs and all the devoted servants should go out to meet him, and bring him to wait on me in a fitting manner. After midday had passed, at an auspicious chosen hour he kissed the ground and illuminated the forehead of his sincerity. After the usual salutations had been performed and the customary ceremonies gone through I embraced my fortunate son with the greatest pleasure and affection, and loaded him with more and more favours. At this time news came that Bī-daulat, when he was passing through the township (*ḥawālī*) of the pargana of Amber, which was the hereditary abode of Rāja Mān Singh, had sent a band of scoundrels and plundered that cultivated spot.

* Where is this account ? He is mentioned later, p. 359 of text. Perhaps he is the Armenian mentioned in the 15th year as Zū-l-Qarnain. But an Armenian would hardly be called a Farangī.

† The MSS. have "his brother Maghrūr."

‡ The MSS. have a name that is not Naubat, and perhaps is Yūnas or Yūnash Khān.

§ Yūnas or Yūnash in MSS.

On the 12th I pitched outside the village of Sārwalī. I had previously sent Ḥabash K. (Abyssinian) to repair the buildings at Ajmir. I promoted my fortunate son Shāh Parwīz to the high mansab of 40,000 and 30,000 horse. As it was reported that Bī-daulat had sent off Jagat Singh, s. Rāja Bāso, to his own country to raise disturbances in the hills of the Panjab, I promoted Ṣādiq K., chief Bakhshi, to the governorship of that province, and ordered him to punish him, giving him a dress of honour, with a sword and an elephant, and making up his mansab, original and increased, to 4,000 personal and 3,000 horse. I also honoured him with a standard (*tūgh*) and drums.

At this time it was reported to me that the younger brothers of Mīrzā Badī'u-z-zamān, s. Mīrzā Shāhrukh, who was known as Fatḥpūrī, had attacked him unawares and killed him. About this time his brothers came to Court and paid their respects. His own mother also waited on me, but did not make a claim, as was proper, for her son's blood, and (so) proceedings* could not be taken according to law. Although his disposition was so bad that his murder was not to be regretted, but on the contrary was opportune and advantageous, yet, as these wretches had shown such audacity with regard to their elder brother, who was to them in the position of a father, I ordered them to be put in gaol, and afterwards what was deemed proper should be done to them. On the 21st Rāja Gaj Singh and Rāy Sūraj Singh arrived from their jagirs, and had the good fortune to kiss my stirrup. Mu'izzu-l-mulk, whom I had sent to Multan to summon my son Khān Jahān, came and waited on me, and presented me with a letter about his severe illness and weakness. He had sent his son Aṣālat K. with 1,000 horse to wait on me, and expressed great regret at being deprived of the honour of meeting me. As his apology was evidently sincere, I accepted it. On the 25th my fortunate son Prince Parwīz, with the victorious army, was sent in

* Perhaps it means that *qiṣāṣ* or retaliation could not be inflicted. See Ma'āṣiru-l-umarā, III. 335, and Iqbāl-nāma, 204. Evidently the mother did not want to prosecute. It is probable that his murderers were only his half-brothers.

pursuit to overthrow Bī-daulat. The reins of authority over the powerful Prince, and the centre of the ordering of the victorious army, were given into the hand of Mu'taminu-d-daula Mahābat K. Of the illustrious Amīrs and life-sacrificing brave men who were in attendance on the Prince of lofty fortune, this is the detail.

Khān 'Ālam, Mahārāja* Gaj Singh, Fāẓil K., Rashīd K., Rāja Girdhar, Rāja Rām Dās Kachhwāha, Khwāja Mīr 'Abdu-l-'Azīz, 'Azīzu-llah, Asad K., Parwarish K., Ikrām K., Sayyid Hizbar K., Luṭfu-llah, Rāy Narāyan Dās, and others to the number of 40,000 horse, with much artillery. Rs. 2,000,000 (twenty lakhs) of treasure were sent with them. At a propitious hour they were started with my son, and bridle to bridle with victory. Fāẓil K. was appointed Bakhshi and newswriter to the victorious army. A special dress of honour was bestowed on the Prince, with a *nādirī* of gold brocade, and pearls on the collar and skirt worth Rs. 41,000, prepared in the royal establishment, and a private elephant of the name Ratan Gaj, ten† female elephants, a private horse, and a jewelled sword, the value of the whole of which was Rs. 77,000. These were all given to the Prince. Nūr Jahān Begam also gave him a dress of honour, a horse, and an elephant, as is the custom. To Mahābat K. and the other Amirs, according to their standing, horses, elephants, and dresses of honour were presented. The immediate attendants of the prince were also honoured with favours. On this day Muẓaffar K. received a dress of honour on appointment to the post of chief Bakhshi. On the first of the Divine month of Khurdād Prince Dāwar-bakhsh, s. Khusrau, was appointed to Gujarat, and Khān A'ẓam to the high dignity of tutor to him. I conferred on the prince a horse, an elephant, a dress of honour, a private jewelled dagger, a standard (*tūgh*), and drums. Khān A'ẓam, Nawāzish K. and other servants were honoured with presents according to their standing. Irādat K. was appointed Bakhshi in place of Fāẓil K. Ruknu-s-salṭana

* The MSS. have Mahārāja Gaj Singh, and they also have the names Manṣūr Khān, Sar-buland Rāy and Lashkar K.

† "Two" in MSS.

Āṣaf K. exalted his head with the dignity of the Subadarship of Bengal and Orissa. A special dress of honour, with a jewelled sword, were conferred on him. Abū Ṭālib (*i.e.*, Shaista K.), his son, was appointed to accompany him, and promoted to the mansab of 2,000 with 1,000 horse. On Saturday, the 9th, corresponding with the 19th Rajab, A.H. 1032 (May 9, 1623), the camp was pitched at the Anā-Sāgar lake outside Ajmir. Prince Dāwar-bakhsh, being honoured with the mansab of 8,000, and 3,000 horse, was granted Rs. 2,00,000 of treasure for the expenses of the army which accompanied him. Rs. 1,00,000 I also gave as an advance to Khān A'ẓam. Allah-yār, s. Iftikhār Beg, who was in the service of my fortunate son Shāh Parwīz, was at his request granted a standard. Tātār K. took leave on his appointment to the charge of Fort Gwalior. Rāja Gaj Singh was appointed to the mansab of 5,000, with 4,000 horse.

On this day news came from Agra that Her Highness (ḥaẓrat) Maryamu-z-zamānī,* by the decree of God, had died. I trust that Almighty God will envelop her in the ocean of His mercy. Jagat Singh, s. Rānā Karan, having come from his native place, had the good fortune to pay his respects. Ibrāhīm K. Fatḥ-jang, governor of Bengal, had sent thirty-four elephants by way of offering, and they were submitted to me. Bāqir K. was appointed faujdar of Oudh, and Sādāt K. to the Dū-āb. The Mīr Mushrif was made Dīwān-i-buyūtāt.

On the 12th of the Divine month of Tīr a report came from the officials of Gujarat with the good news of victory and conquest. The particulars of this summary are that I had granted the Subah of Gujarat, the abode of Sultans of high dignity, to Bī-daulat as a reward for his victory over the Rānā, as has been fully related in the preceding pages. Sundar, the brahman, administered and protected the country. When futile ideas entered his ungrateful mind, he sent for that dog of a Hindu, who was always shaking the chain of enmity and perversity, along with Himmat K., Sharza K., Sar-afrāz K., and many of the royal servants who were fiefholders in the province. Sundar's brother Kunhar was appointed in his room.

* Jahangir's mother.

When Sundar was killed, and Bī-daulat retreated after his defeat to Māndū, the province of Gujarat was put in the charge of La'natu-llah as his fief, and Kunhar was sent for along with Ṣafī K., the diwan. At the same time the treasure, the jewelled throne on which five lakhs had been expended, and the *pardala* (belt) on which two lakhs had been spent—and which things had been prepared as a present for myself—were also sent for. Ṣafī K. was the brother's son (text says "brother") of Ja'far Beg, who received in my father's service the title of Āṣaf K., and was married to a daughter of Nūr Jahān's brother, who by my favour had received the title of Āṣaf K. An elder daughter was the wife of Bī-daulat. Both daughters were by one mother, and Bī-daulat expected that on account of this connection Ṣafī K. would be on his side. But an eternal decree had gone forth for Ṣafī K.'s loyalty and prosperity, and that he should attain to high rank! Accordingly, Almighty God made him loyal and the performer of good deeds, as will now be described. In short, the faithless (*bī-wafā*) La'natu-llah sent his eunuch named Wafā-dār to be governor of that country, and he, with a few ragamuffins (*bī-sar-u-pā*) entered Ahmadabad, and took possession of the city. As Ṣafī K. had made up his mind to be loyal, he courageously looked after the servants, and collected a force, and won the hearts of the people. Some days before Kunhar came out of the city he (Ṣafī) encamped on the bank of the Kankariyā lake, and thence hastened to Maḥmūdābād, giving out openly that he was going to Bī-daulat. Secretly, he opened communication and made arrangements to be loyal with Nāhir K., Sayyid Dilīr K., Nānū* K., Afghan, and other devoted servants of the State, who were waiting in their own jagirs. He awaited his opportunity. Ṣāliḥ, a servant of Bī-daulat, who was faujdar of the Sarkar of Pitlād, and had a good force with him, heard rumours that Ṣafī K. entertained other ideas. Kunhar† had also discovered this, but as Ṣafī K. soothed them and was very cautious and careful in his conduct,

* MS. 181 has Bābā Khān.

† MS. 181 has Kuhnar or Kunhar, and it seems that it is a name, and not merely "younger brother." The Iqbāl-nāma, 205, has Kunhar Dās.

they could not move hand or foot. Ṣāliḥ, for fear lest Ṣafī K., abandoning dissimulation, should stretch his hand towards the treasure, exercised foresight, and went farther on with the treasure, taking nearly Rs. 10,00,000 to Bī-daulat at Māndū. Kunhar (or the younger brother?) also, having seized the jewelled *pardala*, started after him, but could not take the throne on account of its weight. Ṣafī K., knowing this was his opportunity, changed his place from Maḥmūdābād to the pargana of Karang,* which is to the left of the usual road, where Nānū K. was, and arranged by letter and verbal messages with Nāhir K. and other loyal servants that each of them should ride from his jagir with the force that he had, and at the hour of sunrise, which was the morning of prosperity for people of good fortune, and the evening of ruin to those who practised villainy, enter the city by the gate to which each was opposite. He (Ṣafī) left his women in the aforesaid pargana, and, in company with Nānū (Bābū?) K., came at dawn to the outskirts of the city. He halted for a short time in the Sha'bān† garden until it had become light and friend could be distinguished from enemy. After the world-illuminating sun of good fortune (had risen), when he found the gate of prosperity open, though he could see no trace of Nāhir K. and the other loyalists, yet lest possibly the enemy might obtain information and fasten the gates of the fort, he placed his confidence in God who gives victory, and entered the city by the Sārangpūr gate. About this time Nāhir K. also arrived, and, entering by the gate, came into the city. The eunuch of La'natu-llah, having ascertained the unfailing good fortune of (Jahangir), took refuge in the house of Shaikh Ḥaidar, grandson of Niẓām Wajīhu-d-dīn. The royal servants

* Karīj in text. See Jarrett, II. 253. But perhaps it should be Kaira.

† It is Sha'bān in Nos. 181 and 305. The famous garden of Ahmadabad is the Shāhī, for which see the Bombay Gazetteer, vol. for Ahmadabad, p. 283. But besides being Sha'bān in the MSS. it is also Sha'bān in the Iqbāl-nāma, 207. The Shāhī garden lies to the north of Ahmadabad, and Ṣafī was at the south or south-east of the city. Perhaps the Sha'bān garden was near the Malik Sha'bān lake, which was east of the city, and is referred to in Bombay Gazetteer, p. 18. The Bāgh Sha'bān is also referred to in Bayley's Gujarat, 236.

of approved service, having proclaimed their victory with loud voices, set to work to strengthen the towers and gates. They sent men to the houses of Muḥammad Taqī, Bī-daulat's diwan, and of Ḥasan Beg, his Bakhshi, and seized them. Shaikh Ḥaidar himself came and informed Ṣafī K. that the eunuch of La'natu-llah was in his house, and they tied his hands to his neck, and brought him. Having imprisoned a number of Bī-daulat's servants and dependants, they engaged in keeping order in the city. The jewelled throne, the cash of Rs. 2,00,000, and the property and effects of Bī-daulat and his men in the city, came into their possession. When this news reached Bī-daulat, he sent off La'natu-llah with Himmat K., Sharza K., Sar-afrāz K., Qābil Beg, Rustam Bahādur, Ṣāliḥ Badakhshī, and other criminals. What with royal servants and his own men, he had some 5,000 or 6,000 horse. Ṣafī K. and Nāhir K., becoming aware of this, planted firmly the foot of courage, and employed themselves in encouraging their men and collecting forces. Whatever cash and valuables they could obtain, even to the throne, which they broke up, they divided amongst both the old and new troopers as pay. Rāja Kalyān, Zamindar of Īdar (printed wrongly "Andūr"), and the son of Lāl Gopī (?)*, and all the Zamindars from every quarter, were summoned into the city. A good number was thus assembled. La'natu-llah did not wait for auxiliaries, and in the space of eight days came from Māndū to Baroda. The loyal party, by the guidance of their courage, and in reliance on God, came out of the city and encamped on the bank of the Kānkariyā Lake. It occurred to La'natu-llah that if he came on quickly, the rope of order of the loyal might be broken. When he obtained news of the coming out of the loyal servants, drawing in the reins of ruin, he delayed in Baroda till the arrival of help. After the evil-ending criminals collected together at that chief place of mischief, he put forward the foot of error and deviation from the right path, and the loyal party, marching from the Kānkariyā tank, encamped outside the village of Batoh, near the mausoleum of

* Name very doubtful. MSS. seem to have Pīr Lāl Kolī, or it may be Bīr Lāl

Quṭb 'Ālam. La'natu-llah traversed a road of three days in two,* and arrived at Maḥmūdābād. As Sayyid Dilīr K. had seized the women of Sharza K. and brought them from Baroda to the city, and the women of Sar-afrāz K. were also in the city, Ṣafī K. sent a secret message to both of them that if by the guidance of good fortune they would rub off the stain of sin (rebellion) from the tablet of their foreheads, and would enrol themselves among the loyal servants, their position in the present and future worlds would approach salvation; otherwise he would subject their wives and children to all kinds of indignities. Hearing this, La'natu-llah sent for Sar-afrāz K. on some excuse to his house, and imprisoned him. As Sharza K., Himmat K., and Ṣāliḥ Badakhshī were in league together, and had alighted at the same place, he could not get Sharza K. into his hands. Briefly, on the 21st of Sha'bān, A.H. 1032, June 10, 1623, La'natu-llah mounted and arrayed the forces tinged with calamity. Those who were loyal also arrayed their forces and prepared for the fight. It occurred to La'natu-llah that if he were to go, their foot of courage would not stand firm, and, without a battle taking place, they would be dispersed in a miserable condition. When he saw the firm attitude of the loyal, he could not screw up his courage (*tāb nayāwarda*), but turned his rein towards the left, and gave out that they had hidden gunpowder under the ground of that plain, and that his men would be destroyed by it—that it would therefore be better to go into the plain of Sarkhej and deliver battle there. These futile ideas were due to the aid of good fortune, for on the turning back of his rein a rumour of his defeat was spread abroad, and the horsemen of the plain of victory attacked him in flank, and that ill-omened one was unable to reach Sarkhej, and halted in the village of Nāranja. The loyal party arranged their forces in the village of Bālūd, which is nearly three koss off. At dawn on the next day they went to battle after the approved manner, their forces being drawn up in this way. In the vanguard were Nāhir K., Rāja Kalyān, the Zamindar of Īdar, and other valiant men; on the left wing Sayyid Dilīr K., Sayyid Sīdū,

* The MSS. have "in ten."

and other loyal servants were stationed; and on the right wing Nānū K., Sayyid Ya'qūb, Sayyid Ghulām Muḥammad, and the rest of the life-sacrificing devoted ones, whilst in the centre were Ṣafī K., Kifāyat K. Bakhshī, and some other servants of approved service. It so happened, fortunately, that in the place where La'natu-llah had halted, the land was undulating, full of thorn brakes and narrow lanes. The forces, accordingly, were not in compact order. He had sent on most of the experienced men with Rustam Bahādur, and Himmat K., and Ṣāliḥ Beg were amongst the foremost in (the ranks of) error. The army doomed to calamity first of all came in contact with Nāhir K. and Shams K., and a notable fight took place. By chance Himmat K. fell in the dust of destruction from a gun-shot wound, and a fight ensued between Ṣāliḥ Beg, and Nānū K., Sayyid Ya'qūb, Sayyid Ghulām Muḥammad, and other servants. In the height of the battle the elephant of Sayyid Ghulām Muḥammad came and threw him (Ṣāliḥ) from his horse; he fell severely wounded to the ground, and about a hundred of his men were slain. At this moment an elephant which was in the van of the rebel army turned round at the noise of the rockets and the lightning of the guns, and got into a narrow lane, on both sides of which were thorn brakes, and trod down many of the rebels. By the turning back of the elephant the ranks of the enemy were disordered. At this moment Sayyid Dilīr K. came fighting from the right wing. La'natu-llah did not know of the killing of Himmat K. and Ṣāliḥ, and, with the idea of helping them, urged on the steed of ruin. As the brave ones in the van, having displayed activity, had been mostly wounded, they could not stand the onset of La'natu-llah, and turned back their rein, and it nearly happened that there was a great disaster. At this time the assistance of God displayed itself, and Ṣafī K. hastened from the centre to the support of the van. Just then La'natu-llah heard of the killing of Himmat K. and Ṣāliḥ Beg, and, on the appearance of the centre and the attack of Safī K., his courage failed him, and he became a vagabond in the desert of defeat and disaster. Sayyid Dilīr K. pursued him for a koss, and made many of the defeated the harvest of the sword of vengeance. Qābil Beg, unfaithful to his salt, with a body of rebels, became captives in the claws of retribution. As La'natu-llah was not sure about Sar-afrāz K., he on the day of battle placed him in chains on an elephant and put him in charge of one of his slaves, with orders that if a defeat occurred he should kill him. In like manner he placed in chains on one of the elephants Bahādur, s. Sulṭān Aḥmad, and gave permission to kill him. When the fight took place the man in charge of Sulṭān Aḥmad's son put him to death with a dagger, but Sar-afrāz K. threw himself down off the elephant. The man in charge of him in that confusion aimed a blow at him in his bewilderment, but it was not effectual. Ṣafī K., finding him in the fight, sent him into the city. La'natu-llah did not turn back till he arrived at Baroda. As the women of S͟harza K. were captives of those who were loyal, he was helpless, and came and waited upon Ṣafī K. Briefly, La'natu-llah hastened from Baroda to Broach. The sons of Himmat K. were in the fort there. Although they did not admit him, yet they sent him 5,000 *maḥmūdīs* by way of maintenance. For three days he remained outside the fort of Broach in a wretched state, and on the fourth went to Surat by sea. For nearly two months he remained there assembling his scattered men. As Surat was in Bī-daulat's jagir, he took nearly 4 lakhs of *maḥmūdīs* from his officials there, and took possession of whatever he could by oppression and injustice. He again collected together those whose fortune was reversed and whose stars had been burnt, and betook himself to Bī-daulat at Burhanpur.

In fine, when this approved service performed by Ṣafī K. and other loyal servants in Gujarat became known, each one was exalted with favours and kindnesses. Ṣafī K. held the mansab of 700 personal and 300 horse: having given him that of 3,000 personal and 2,000 horse, I honoured him with the title of Saif K. Jahāngīr-s͟hāhī, and conferred on him a standard and drums. Nāhir K. had 1,000 with 200 horse; having given him the mansab of 3,000 with 2,000 horse, I bestowed on him the title of S͟hīr K., and raised his head of honour with a horse, an elephant, and a jewelled sword. He is the (descendant ?)

grandson of (?)*, the brother of Pūran Mal Lūlū (?), who was governor of Rāysīn and Chanderī. When Shīr K., the Afghan (*i.e.*, Shīr Shāh), besieged the fort of Rāysīn, it is well known that he killed him (Pūran Mal) after promising him quarter, and that his women burnt themselves, committing "*Johar*," according to the Hindu custom, in the fire of fame and modesty, so that the hand of no unlawful person should touch the skirt of their chastity. His sons and caste fellows went off to various† places. The father of Nāhir K., whose title was Khān Jahān, having gone to Muḥammad K., governor of Āsīr and Burhanpur, became a Musalman, and when Muḥammad K. died, Ḥasan, his son, when in tender years, succeeded him. Rāja 'Alī K., brother of Muḥammad K., put the child in confinement, and took possession of the government. After some time news reached Rāja 'Alī K. that Khān Jahān and a body of the servants of Muḥammad K. had leagued together to attack him, and had determined to take Ḥasan K. out of the fort and raise him to power. He was beforehand with them, and sent Ḥayāt Khān Ḥabashī, with many brave men, to the house of Khān Jahān, either to take him alike or to kill him. He, planting his foot firmly on his good fame, took to fighting, and when things went badly with him committed *Johar*, and passed from this borrowed life. At that time Nāhir K. was very young. Ḥayāt Khān Abyssinian, having asked 'Alī K.'s permission, adopted him as his son, and made him a Musalman. After his death Rāja 'Alī K. brought up Nāhir K., and took good care of him. When my revered father conquered Āsīr, Nāhir K. joined his service. He (Akbar) discerned the signs of bravery on his forehead, and raised him to a suitable mansab, and gave him in jagir the pargana of Muḥammadpūr in Malwa. In my service he advanced more and more. Now that the grace of gratitude has been bestowed upon him, he has found the advantage of doing what was right.

* Text, Nar Singh Deo. But the MSS. seem to have another name, Silhadi Deo (?) The name Lūlū is also doubtful. The MSS. seem to have Bulur. In Elliot, IV. 402, Pūran Mal is called Bhaia.

† *Har kudām ba-ṭarafī aftādand.*

Sayyid Dilīr K. is of the Sayyids of Bārha; formerly his name was Sayyid 'Abdu-l-Wahhāb. I raised him from the mansab of 1,000 and 800 horse to 2,000 and 1,200 horse, and presented him with a standard. They call twelve *bāra* in Hindi. As in the Dū-āb there are twelve villages near each other which are the native country of these Sayyids, they have become known as the Sayyids of Bārha. Some people make remarks about their lineage, but their bravery is a convincing proof of their being Sayyids, for there has never been a battle in this reign in which they have not been conspicuous, and in which some have not been killed. Mīrzā 'Azīz Koka always said the Sayyids of Bārha were the averters of calamity from this dominion, and such is in reality the case.

Nānū K. Afghan held the mansab of 800 personal and horse: it was ordered to be one of 1,500 personal and 1,200 horse. In the same manner the other loyal servants, according to their services and sacrifices, were promoted to high mansabs, and obtained the desire of their hearts in lofty employments. At this time Aṣālat K., s. Khān Jahān, was deputed to the assistance of my son (grandson) Dāwar-bakhsh in Gujarat, and I sent Nūru-d-dīn Qulī into the Subah to bring Sharza K., Sar-afrāz K., and the other leaders of the rebel army who had been made captive in the land of retribution, chained, to the Court.

On this day it was reported to me that Minū-chihr, s. Shāh-nawāz K., had separated himself from Bī-daulat under the guidance of good fortune, and had joined the service of my fortunate son Shāh Parwīz. I'tiqād K., governor of Kashmir, was promoted to the mansab of 4,000 personal and 3,000 horse.

As the huntsmen brought news that in this neighbourhood a tiger had made its appearance, I felt disposed to hunt it. After entering the forest three other tigers became visible. Having killed all four, I returned to the palace. I have such a liking for tiger shooting that whilst I can get it I do not go after other sport. Sulṭān Mas'ūd, s. Sulṭān Maḥmūd (of Ghaznin) (may the lights of Allah be his testimony!), was also much inclined to tiger shooting. With regard to his killing of tigers strange tales have been recorded, especially in the history of Baihaqī,* who has kept a diary of what he saw with his own eyes. Among these things he writes that one day he (Mas'ūd) went to hunt tigers in the borders of Hindustan, and was riding an elephant. A very large tiger came out from the wood, and made for the elephant. He threw a javelin (*khisht*) and struck the tiger's chest. The tiger, enraged at the pain, came up on the elephant's back, and the Amir knelt down and struck him such a blow with his sword that he cut off both the tiger's fore-feet, and the tiger fell backwards and died. It happened to me once when I was prince that I had gone out in the Punjab to hunt tigers. A powerful tiger appeared out of the wood. I fired at him from the elephant, and the tiger in great fury rose and came on the elephant's back, and I had not time to put down my gun and seize my sword. Inverting the gun, I knelt, and with both hands struck him with the stock over the head and face so that he fell on to the ground and died.

One of the strange things that happened was that one day I was on an elephant, and was hunting wolves in Aligarh† in the Nūh forest. A wolf appeared, and I struck it with a bullet on its face (*mana*) near the lobe of the ear. The bullet penetrated for about a span. From that bullet it fell and gave up its life. It has often happened in my presence that powerful (*jawānān*) men, good shots with the bow, have shot twenty or thirty arrows at them, and not killed. As it is not right to write about oneself, I must restrain the tongue of my pen from saying more.

On the 29th of the month I presented a string of pearls to Jagat Singh, s. Rānā Karan. At this time it was reported to

* Rieu, Cat., I. 158 b.

† Text has Kūh-i-Kūl. But the I.O. MSS. show that the true reading is Kūl Nūh ban, and it appears from the Ayin, Jarrett, II. 186, that Nūh is a district in Kūl—*i.e.*, Aligarh. *Gurg* is a wolf, and *Kurag* a rhinoceros, but probably a wolf is here meant. It is not likely that there were rhinoceros in Aligarh, though Abū-l-faẓl says there were rhinoceros in Sambhal (Jarrett, II. 281). Tīr means an arrow as well as a bullet. The word *mana*, "face," is not in text, but occurs in both the I.O. MSS.

me that Sulṭān Ḥusain, Zamindar of Paklī, had died. I gave his mansab and jagir to Shādmān, his eldest son.

On the 7th of the month of Amurdād Ibrāhīm Ḥusain, a servant of my fortunate son Shāh Parwīz, came from the victorious army, and brought news of the victory of the chiefs of the everlasting State. The report of my son laid before me the particulars of the fight, and the exertions of the brave and distinguished men in it. I performed the dues of thanksgiving for this favour, which was of God's grace alone. The details of this are as follows: When the royal troops in the army of the prince of high degree crossed the pass of Chāndā,* and entered the province of Malwa, Bī-daulat, with 20,000 horse, 300 fighting elephants, and a large force of artillery, left Māndū in order to fight. He dispatched a body of the Bargīs (Mahrattas) of the Deccan with Jādū Rāy and Ūday Rām, Ālash K., and other rebels to make a raid (*qazzāqī*) on the royal camp. Mahābat K. made proper arrangements. He placed the illustrious prince in the *ghaul* (centre), and he himself proceeded with the whole army, and in marching and in halting observed the conditions of caution. The Bargīs kept at a great distance, and did not put forward the foot of bravery. One day it was Manṣūr K. Farangī's turn to be with the rear-guard. At the time of pitching the camp Mahābat K., by way of caution, was standing with his army drawn up outside the camp, in order that the men might fence it in at their ease. As Manṣūr K. had been drinking on the road, he was coming to the stage drunk with the wine of pride. It happened an army was seen in the distance, and the wine put the idea into his head that he must charge. Without telling his brothers or his men, he mounted and charged, and drove off two or three Bargīs, and came to where Jādū Rāy and Ūday Rām were standing with two or three thousand cavalry drawn up. As was their custom, they attacked him from all sides and surrounded him. He fought as long as there was breath in his body, and gave up his life on the path of loyalty.

During these days Mahābat K. was continually capturing, by messages and letters, the afflicted hearts of a number of

* Chāndā Ghāt between Ajmere and Malwa.

men who out of timidity and confusion had accompanied Bī-daulat. When men read the lines of despair on the page of his (Shāh Jahān's) condition, letters also came from that side, asking for agreements (*qaul*). After Bī-daulat came out of the fort of Māndū, he in the first instance sent forward a body of Bargīs, and after them he sent Rustam K., Taqī, and Barq-andāz K. with a body of musketeers. Then he sent Dārāb K., Bhīm, Bairam Beg, and his other active men. As he could not resolve to give battle in person, he was continually looking backwards. He crossed the war-elephants over the Narbadda with the artillery waggons, and went himself unattended behind Dārāb and Bhīm, turning his face of ruin towards the battle. On the day when the royal camp was pitched at Kāliyādaha, Bī-daulat sent his army against the victorious forces, and stationed himself with Khān-khānān and a few men at the distance of a koss in the rear. Barq-andāz K., who had made an agreement with Mahābat K., was lying in wait. When the armies were ranged opposite to each other, he got his opportunity, and attacked with a body of musketeers, and joined the royal army, crying out, "Success to King Jahāngīr!" When he reached Mahābat K., the latter took him to wait on my fortunate son Parwīz, who bestowed royal favours upon him. Previously he bore the name of Bahā'u-d-dīn, and was a servant of Zain K. After the latter's death he enlisted among the Turkish gunners. As he was active in the performance of his duty, and had a band of men with him, considering him worthy of patronage, I gave him the title of Barq-andāz K. When I sent Bī-daulat to the Deccan, I put him at the head of the artillery, and sent him with him. Although in the beginning he placed the scar of curse on the forehead of his obedience, yet in the end he turned out well and came at a good time. On the same day Rustam, who was one of his (Shāh Jahān's) chief servants, and on whom he had perfect reliance, when he found that Fortune had turned away from him, made a compact with Mahābat K. By the guidance of good fortune and reliance on God, he, with Muḥammad Murād Badakhshī and other mansabdars, left the ill-fated army, and joined that of the illustrious prince. Bī-daulat's hand and heart were paralyzed on hearing this news, and he suspected all his own servants, and still more the royal servants he had with him, of faithlessness and unreliability. During the night he sent for the men who were in front, and decided on flight, and in bewilderment crossed the Narbadda. At this time, again, some of his servants took the opportunity of separating themselves from him, and joined the service of my fortunate son. Each of them received favours according to his condition. On the day that he crossed the river Narbadda, a letter fell into the hand of one of his men, that Mahābat K. had written in answer to Zāhid's K. letter, making him hopeful of the royal favour, and urging him to come in. This they sent direct to Bī-daulat, and he, becoming suspicious of Zāhid K., imprisoned him with his three sons. Zāhid K. is s. Shajā'at K., who was one of the Amirs and trusted servants of my revered father. I had patronized this wretch in consideration of his claims of service and of his position as a house-born one (*khāna-zād*), and given him the title of Khan and the rank of 1,500, and had sent him with Bī-daulat for the conquest of the Deccan. When I summoned the Amirs of that quarter on account of the business of Qandahar, although a special farman of urgency was sent to him, the wretch did not come to Court, and gave himself out as an adherent and devoted servant of Bī-daulat. After the defeat near Delhi, he turned back. Though* he had not a family, he had not the good fortune to pay his respects, or to cleanse the dust of shame and the stain of sin from the tablet of his forehead. At last the True Recompenser caught him on this day, and his property, to the extent of one lac and Rs. 30,000, was confiscated by Bī-daulat.

When† thou hast done evil, think not thyself free of calamities
For retribution is according to natural law.

---

* Apparently the meaning is that he had no family with Shāh Jahān's army, and so could not be deterred from leaving Shāh Jahān through fear of their fate. See below, the reference to S. Ṣalābat's arrangements about his family.

† This couplet comes from Niẓāmī's Khusrau u Shīrīn, and is quoted by Bābur.

Briefly, Bī-daulat having quickly crossed the Narbadda, drew all the boats over to that side, and having secured the fords with men that he trusted, he left Bairam Beg, his Bakhshi, with a force of trustworthy men and a body of the Bargīs from the Deccan on the bank of the river. Taking the artillery-waggons, he himself went towards the fort of Āsīr and to Burhanpur. Meanwhile Taqī, his servant, caught the runner whom Khān-khānān had sent to Mahābat K., and took him to Bī-daulat. This couplet was written on the margin of the letter:

Hundreds are watching me
Otherwise I'd fly away from trouble.

Bī-daulat sent for him with his sons from his quarters, and showed him the writing. Although he made excuses, he could give no answer that could be listened to. In short, he kept him with Dārāb and his other sons in surveillance near his own station, and the lot he had himself drawn—viz., that hundreds were watching him—happened to him. At this time I gave Ibrāhīm Ḥusain, the servant of my prosperous son who had brought the report of the victory, the title of Khūsh-khabar K., with a dress of honour, and an elephant, and sent a gracious farman to the Prince and Mahābat K. by Khawāṣṣ K. I also sent with him a *pahūnchī** (bracelet) of great value to my son (Parwīz) and a jewelled sword to Mahābat K. As Mahābat K. had done approved service, I gave him the mansab of 7,000 personal and horse.

Sayyid Ṣalābat K., having come from the Deccan, had the good fortune to pay his respects, and received special favours. He was one of those employed in the Deccan. When Bī-daulat, having been defeated near Delhi, went to the fort of Māndū, he placed his children in independent territory under the protection of God, and went off by secret routes to pay his respects (to me). Mīrzā Ḥasan, s. Mīrzā Rustam Ṣafawī, having obtained leave to proceed to his appointment as faujdar of Bahraich, was given the mansab of 1,500 personal and 500 horse, original and increased. Having sent La'l Beg, Superintendent of the Record Department, to my fortunate son

* See Ja'far Sharīf's Qānūn-i-Islām. App., p. xxiv.

Shāh Parwīz, I sent with him a special dress of honour and a *nādirī* for him, and a turban for Mahābat K. Khawāṣṣ K., who had previously been sent to him and had returned, waited upon me with good news (of him). Khāna-zād K., s. Mahābat K., was given the mansab of 5,000 personal and horse.

At this time I enjoyed myself for a day with hunting nīlgāw. Whilst I was hunting I saw a snake the length of which was 2½ yards, and its girth equal to three cubits (*dast*). He had swallowed half a hare, and was in the act of swallowing the other half. When the huntsmen picked him up and brought him to me, the hare fell out of his mouth. I ordered them to put it into its mouth again, but they could not do it, however much they exerted themselves; but by using great violence the corner of his mouth was torn to pieces. After this I ordered them to open its belly. Thereupon another entire hare came out. They call this kind of snake *chītal** in Hindustan, and it grows so large that it swallows a hog-deer (*kotāh-pācha*) entire; but it is not poisonous, and does not bite. One day during the same hunt I shot a female nīlgāw, and two fully formed young ones were found inside. As I heard that the flesh of nīlgāw fawns was delicate and delicious, I ordered the royal cooks to prepare a *dū-piyāza*† (a kind of rich fricassee). Certainly it was not without flavour.

On the 15th of the Divine month of Shahrīwar Rustam K., Muḥammad Murād, and several other servants of Bī-daulat, who under the guidance of good luck had separated themselves from him and entered the service of my fortunate son Shāh Parwīz, according to orders came to Court, and had the good fortune to kiss the threshold. Having promoted Rustam K. to the mansab of 5,000 personal and 4,000 horse, and Muḥammad Murād to that of 1,000 personal and 500 horse, I made them hopeful of daily increasing favours. Rustam K. by extraction is a Badakhshī. His name was Yūsuf Beg. He is connected with Muḥammad-qulī of Isfahan, who was agent for and prime minister of Mīrzā Sulaimān (of Badakhshan). He was first of all in the service of the Court,

* Dhāmin, python (?)

† See Blochmann, 60.

and passed his days mostly in the Subahs. He was included among the smaller mansabdars. Having been deprived of his jagir for some reason, he came to Bī-daulat, and entered his service. He had a perfect knowledge of tiger-hunting. He also did good service with him, especially in the affair of the Rānā. Bī-daulat selected him out of all his servants, and made him an Amir. As I bestowed much favour on him (Shāh Jahān), at his request I gave him the title of Khan, with a standard and drums. For some time he conducted as his agent the government of Gujarat, and did not manage badly. Muḥammad Murād is the son of Maqṣūd Mīr-āb (butler), who was one of the old servants of Mīrzā Sulaimān and Mīrzā Shāh-rukh.

On this day Sayyid Bahwa came from Gujarat, and waited on me. Nūru-d-dīn Qulī brought in chains to the Court forty-one of the rebels, who had been taken prisoners at Ahmadabad. Sharza K. and Qābil Beg, who were ring-leaders of the seditious, I executed by throwing them under the feet of warlike (*mast*) elephants. On the 20th of the same month, corresponding with the 18th of the month of Zī-qa'da, a daughter was given by the grace of God to my son Shahriyār by the granddaughter* of I'timādu-d-daula. I hope that her advent† will be propitious and blessed to this State. On the 22nd of the month the feast of my solar weighment took place, and the 55th year of the age of this suppliant began auspiciously and happily. According to annual custom, I had myself weighed against gold and other valuables, and gave them to deserving people. Among these I gave Rs. 2,000 to Shaikh Aḥmad‡ of Sihrind. On the 1st of the Divine month of Mihr Mīr Jumla was promoted to the mansab of 3,000 personal and 300 horse. Muqīm, the Bakhshi of Gujarat, was given the title of Kifāyat K. As the innocence of Sar-farāz K.§ was established to my satisfaction, I took him

* Daughter of Nūr Jahān.

† Blochmann, p. 311, calls her Arzānī Begam. The Iqbāl-nāma (306) calls her Lāṛdilī Begam. A MS. of the Iqbāl-nāma in my possession calls her Walī Begam. She was born on September 4, 1623.

‡ The holy man formerly mentioned.

§ He had been captured in Gujarat when Ṣafī K. defeated 'Abdu-llah.

out of prison, and allowed him to pay his respects. At the request of my son Shahriyār, I went to his house. He had prepared a grand entertainment, and presented suitable offerings, and gave dresses of honour to most of the servants.

At this time a report came from my fortunate son Shāh Parwīz that Bī-daulat had crossed the river of Burhanpur (the Taptī), and was wandering in the desert of error. The particulars are that when he crossed the Narbadda and drew all the boats to that side. and fortified the banks of the river and the ferries with cannon and muskets, he left Bairam Beg on the bank with a large number of the rebels, and withdrew towards Āsīr and Burhanpur. The Khān-khānān and Dārāb he took with him under surveillance.

And now, for the sake of enlivening my narrative, a few words must be said about Āsīr. The said fort, in its great height and strength, is not in want of my praise. Before Bī-daulat went to the Deccan it was in the charge of Khwāja Naṣru-llah, s. Khwāja Fatḥu-llah, who was one of the household slaves and ancient servants. Afterwards, at the request of Bī-daulat, it was handed over to Mīr Ḥusāmu-d-dīn, s. Mīr Jamālu-d-dīn Ḥusain.* As the daughter of Nūr Jahān Begam's maternal uncle (*taghā'ī*) was married† to him, when Bī-daulat, having been defeated in the neighbourhood of Delhi, turned his rein towards Malwa and Māndū, Nūr Jahān Begam wrote to him and strictly urged him, saying: "Beware, a thousand times beware, not to allow Bī-daulat and his men to come near the fort, but strengthen the towers and gates, and do your duty, and do not act in such a manner that the stain of a curse and ingratitude for favours should fall on the honour or the forehead of a Sayyid." In truth, he strengthened it well, and the arrangements of the fort were not of such a sort that Bī-daulat's bird of thought could fly up to its border, or the conquest of it be quickly accomplished. In brief, when Bī-daulat sent one of his attendants, of the name

* The author of the dictionary.

† See Ma'āṣiru-l-Umarā, III. 382. His wife was the sister of Aḥmad Beg, the "brother's son of Ibrāhīm K. Fatḥ-jang. But if so would she not be the daughter of Sharīf and niece of Nūr Jahān? See Blochmann, 512.

of Sharīfā, to the above-mentioned, he (Sharīfā) seduced him by means of promises and threats, and it was settled (between Shāh Jahān and Sharīfā) that when Ḥusāmu-d-dīn should come down to take the letter and dress of honour which had been sent, he should not be allowed to go up again. That wretch, immediately Sharīfā arrived, put away on the shelf of forgetfulness what he owed on account of his bringing up and the favours conferred on him, and without opposition or effort handed over the fort to Sharīfā, and with his wife* and child went to Bī-daulat, who made him accursed of the Faith and in the world by bestowing on him the mansab of 4,000 personal, and a standard and drums, and the title of Murtaẓā K. —a disgraceful name to all eternity.

In short, when that one of reversed fortune reached the foot of the fort of Āsīr, he took with him Khān-khānān, Dārāb, and all his evil-minded offspring up to the fort, and remaining there for three or four days, and having set his mind at ease about provisions, etc., handed it over to one Gopāl Dās, a Rajput, who had formerly been an attendant of Sar-buland Rāy, and entered his service when he went to the Deccan. He left the women and his superfluous baggage, and took with him his three wives with their children and some maid-servants. At first he proposed to imprison Khān-khānān and Dārāb in the fort, but at last changed his mind, and bringing them down with him, hastened to Burhanpur. At this time La'natu-llah, after suffering disgrace and contempt, came from Surat and joined him. In great perplexity, Bī-daulat employed Sar-buland Rāy, the son of Rāy Bhoj Hārā, who is one of the brave Rajput servants, and who is fed from the royal table (?), as his mediator, and by letters and messages made proposals of peace. Mahābat K. said that until Khān-khānān came, peace was impossible. His (Mahābat's) sole purpose was by these means to separate from him that head of deceivers who was the ring-leader of trouble and sedition. Being helpless, Bī-daulat brought him (Khān-khānān) out of prison, and satisfied himself by taking an oath from him on the Qoran. In order to please him and strengthen his

* I.O. MS., 381, and the Iqbāl-nāma mention the wife.

promises and oath, he took him inside the female apartment and made a confidant* of him, and brought his own wife and son to him, and made use of all kinds of entreaty and lamentation. The gist of his (Shāh Jahān's) remarks was: "My times are hard, and my position difficult; I make myself over to you, and make you the guardian of my honour. You must act so that I no longer undergo contempt and confusion." The Khān-khānān, with a view to bring about peace, parted from Bī-daulat and proceeded to the royal army. It was settled that he should remain on the other side of the river, and arrange matters relating to peace in writing. According to fate, before Khān-khānān arrived on the bank of the river, some of the brave warriors and victorious youths one night found an opportunity and crossed over at a place where the rebels were careless. On hearing this news the pillars of their courage trembled, and Bairam Beg could not keep firm the foot of error and ignorance, or engage in driving them back. Whilst he was in this agitation† many crossed the river, and on the same night the rebels of evil fortune were separated from each other like the *Banātu-n-na'āsh*,‡ and took to flight. By the unfailing good fortune (of Jahāngīr) the Khān-khānān fell into perplexity (lit. fell into the *shash-dar* § position), and could neither go nor stay where he was. At this time again letters arrived from my prosperous son mingling threats with promises. The Khān-khānān, finding only despair and ruin in the page of Bī-daulat's affairs, hastened, through the mediation of Mahābat K., to wait upon my fortunate son. Bī-daulat, on hearing of the departure of Khān-khānān and the crossing of the Narbadda by the victorious army and the flight of Bairam Beg, lost courage, and, notwithstanding a flood in the river and the violence of the rain, crossed the Taptī in a state of wretchedness, and went off towards the Deccan. In this confusion many of the royal servants and his own attendants willingly or unwillingly separated, and

* *Maḥram sākht*, "made him one who could enter the Harem."

† The text wrongly has *ba-chand* instead of *ba-jambīd*.

‡ Daughters of the Bier—*i.e.*, the constellation of the Plough.

§ *Shash-dar* is the name of an *impasse* in the game of *nard*.

did not accompany him. As the native country of Jādo Rāy and Ūday Rām and Ātash K. was on the route, they thought it better for themselves to keep with him for some stages, but Jādo Rāy did not come into his camp, and followed him at the distance of one stage. He took possession of such property as the men in this confusion and fear for their lives abandoned. On the day he (Shāh Jahān) started from the other side of the river (the Taptī) he sent a message by one of his immediate attendants of the name of Ẕū-l-faqār K. Turkmān, summoning Sar-buland K. Afghan, with the message that it seemed to him contrary to courage and the due performance of his engagements that he had as yet not crossed the river. " Fidelity was the glory of men; the faithlessness of no one has touched me (Shāh Jahān) so much as yours." He (Sar-buland) was standing on horseback on the river-bank when Ẕū-l-faqār* K. came and delivered the message. Sar-buland did not give a precise answer, and was undecided as to whether to stay or go. In his perplexity and by way of objection he told Ẕū-l-faqār to let go his bridle. Ẕū-l-faqār drew his sword, and struck at his waist. At this crisis an Afghan interposed a short spear which the people of India call a *barchhā,* and the blow of the sword caught the shaft, and the point of the sword did not reach Sar-buland's waist. After swords were drawn, the Afghans attacked Ẕū-l-faqār and cut him in pieces. The son of Sulṭān Muḥammad, the treasurer, who was Bī-daulat's page, for friendship's sake had come (with Ẕū-l-faqār) without Bī-daulat's permission, and was also killed.

Briefly, when the news of his leaving Burhanpur and of the victorious army's approaching that city reached me, I sent Khawāṣṣ K. on the wings of haste to my loyal son, and strongly impressed upon him that he must not relax his efforts, but must determine either to take him alive or to drive him out of the imperial territory. It was said that if things went badly with him on this side, it was probable that he would throw himself by the road of Quṭbu-l-mulk's country into the provinces of Orissa and Bengal. This, too, was in accordance

* The Muḥammad Beg of Roe ?

with military plans. So out of caution, which is becoming to a ruler, I appointed Mīrzā Rustam to be governor of Allahabad and dismissed him with orders that if such circumstances should so occur (as Shāh Jahān's going to Bengal), he should rectify matters.

At this time my son (*farzand*) Khān Jahān came from Multan, and had the good fortune to pay his respects. By way of nazar he presented 1,000 muhrs and a ruby of the value of Rs. 100,000, a pearl, and other jewels. I gave an elephant to Rustam K. On the 9th of the Divine month of Ābān Khawāṣṣ K. brought a report from the prince and Mahābat K. to the effect that when my son (Parwīz) reached Burhanpur, though many of his men had remained behind in consequence of the heavy rains, he, according to orders, without delay had crossed the river (Taptī), and gone in pursuit of Bī-daulat. Bī-daulat, on hearing this terrible news, was marching on. On account of the heaviness of the rain and the excessive quantity of mud and constant marching his beasts of burden had become exhausted. If any baggage was left behind no inquiries were made, and he (Shāh Jahān) and his children and dependents thought themselves lucky to save their lives and did not trouble about their goods. The army of good fortune having come down the pass of Bhangar, hastened after him as far as the pargana of Ankot,* about forty koss from Burhanpur. Bī-daulat in this state reached the fort of Māhūr, and when he knew that Jādo Rāy and Ūday Rām and the other Dakhanis would not go with him any farther, he did not disgrace them, but let them go. Leaving the heavy elephants with the goods and chattels with Ūday Rām in the fort, he himself started for Quṭbu-l-mulk's territory. When his departure from the royal territory was ascertained, my fortunate son, with the approval of Mahābat K. and other loyalists, turned rein from that pargana. On the first of the Divine month of Ābān he entered Burhanpur. Rāja Sārang Deo was sent to my son with a gracious farman.

Qāsim K. was raised to the mansab of 4,000 personal and 2,000 horse. Mīrak Mu'īn, Bakhshi of Kabul, at the request

* Jarrett, II. 239.

of Mahābat K., was honoured with the title of Khan. Alf K. Qiyām-khānī, having come from the Subah of Patna, paid his respects, and was appointed to the charge of the fort of Kāngra. I presented him with a standard. On the 1st of the Divine month of Āzar Bāqi K. came from Jūnāgarh and waited on me.

As I was at ease with regard to the affair of Bī-daulat, and the heat of Hindustan did not agree with my constitution, on the 2nd of the month, corresponding with the 1st of Ṣafar* my camp started from Ajmir for a tour and to hunt in the pleasant regions of Kashmir. Before this I had appointed the chief of the state Āṣaf K. Subahdar of Bengal, and gave him leave. As I had taken a great liking to his society, and he was distinguished above all the other servants for ability and good disposition and tact, and is moreover unequalled in all kinds of propriety, and I regretted separation from him, I had broken through that purpose, and had sent for him to wait upon me. He came on this day, and had the good fortune to kiss the threshold. Jagat Singh, s. Rānā Karan, took leave on his return to his native country, and was given a dress of honour and a jewelled dagger. Rāja Sārang Deo brought a report from my fortunate son Shāh Parwīz and Mahābat K. Madāru-s-salṭana, and kissed the threshold. It was written that their minds were at ease with regard to the affair of Bī-daulat, and that the rulers of the Deccan, willingly or unwillingly, were performing the dues of obedience and submission. His Majesty (Jahāngīr) might make his mind at ease about that quarter and enjoy himself in hunting and travelling in whatever place in the royal dominions he might approve of and which was good for his health. On the 20th of the month Mīrzā Wālī, having come from Sironj, waited on me. Ḥakīm Mūminā was raised to the mansab of 1,000. Aṣālat K., s. Khān Jahān, according to order, came from Gujarat, and had the good fortune to pay his respects.

At this time a report came from 'Aqīdat K., Bakhshi of the Deccan, containing the news of Rāja Girdhar's having been

* 1 Ṣafar, 1033 = November 14, 1623.

killed. The particulars of this event are that one of the brothers of Sayyid Kabīr Bārha, who was an attendant of my fortunate son Shāh Parwīz, gave his sword to brighten and put on the wheel (to sharpen) to a cutler who had a shop close to the house of Rāja Girdhar. The next day, when he came to fetch his sword, a conversation took place as to the charge for the work, and the people of the Sayyid struck the cutler some blows with a stick. The Raja's people in supporting him used their whips on them. By chance two or three young Sayyids of Bārha had lodgings in that neighbourhood, and hearing of this disturbance, went to the assistance of the aforesaid Sayyid. The fire of strife was lighted, and a fight took place between the Sayyids and Rajputs, ending in an encounter with arrows and swords. Sayyid Kabīr, becoming aware of this, came to assist with thirty or forty horsemen, and at this time Rāja Girdhar, with a body of Rajputs and his caste people, according to the custom of the Hindus, were sitting barebodied and eating their food. Becoming aware of the coming of Sayyid Kabīr and the violence of the Sayyids, he brought his men inside the house and firmly closed the door. The Sayyids, setting fire to the door, forced their way inside and the fight went to such a length that Rāja Girdhar and twenty-six of his servants were killed and forty others wounded. Four of the Sayyids were also killed. After Rāja Girdhar was killed, Sayyid Kabīr took the horses out of his stable to his own house and returned. The Rajput officers, when informed of the slaying of Rāja Girdhar, came on horse-back in great numbers from their houses, and all the Bārha Sayyids came to the aid of Sayyid Kabīr. They assembled in the plain outside the citadel, and the fire of trouble and calamity increased, and it nearly came to a great disturbance. Mahābat K., being informed of it, immediately mounted and went there, and bringing the Sayyids into the citadel, and soothing the Rajputs in a manner suitable to the occasion, took some of their chief men with him and went to the house of Khān 'Ālam, which was near there. He soothed them down in a proper way, and promised and became security for an inquiry into the matter. When this news reached the prince he also went to the quarters of the K͟hān 'Ālam, and soothed them with words appropriate to the state of affairs, and sent the Rajputs to their own houses. Next day Mahābat K. went to the house of Rāja Girdhar, condoled and sympathized with his sons, and having contrived to get hold of Sayyid Kabīr put him into confinement. As the Rajputs would not be consoled without his being put to death, after a few days he executed him.

On the 23rd I appointed Muḥammad Murād faujdar of Ajmir, and sent him off. On this road I continually enjoyed myself in sporting. One day, while hunting, a *tūyg͟hūn* (albino) partridge, which till now I had never seen, came to my sight, and I caught it with a hawk. By chance the hawk that caught it was also a *tūyg͟hūn*. I ascertained by trial that the flesh of the black partridge was better than that of the white, and that the flesh of the large quail (*būdana*), which the people of India call *ghāghar*,* is better than that of the quail, which is a fighter. I compared the flesh of a fat kid with that of a lamb; the flesh of the fat kid is more delicious. By way of test I ordered them both to be cooked in the same way, so that I might discern the matter accurately. On this account I have recorded it.

On the 10th of the month of Dai, in the neighbourhood of the pargana of Raḥīmābād,† the huntsmen brought in news of a tiger. I ordered Irādat K. and Fidā'ī K. to take with them some of the guards (*ahl-i-yātis͟h*) and surround the wood, and mounting (an elephant) I followed them and went towards the hunt. From the number of trees and thickness of the jungle it could not be well seen. Driving the elephant forward, the tiger's flank came into view, and with one wound from my gun he fell and gave up his life. Of all the tigers I have shot from the time when I was a prince until now I never saw a tiger like this for size and majesty and the symmetry of its limbs. I ordered the artists to take its portrait according to its real form and body. He weighed 8½ Jahāngīrī maunds;

* Jerdon states that the black partridge is called *ghāghar* about Benares.

† Probably Raḥīmābād in the Bārī Dū-āb. Jarrett, II. 332.

his length, from the top of his head to the end of his tail, was 3½ cubits* and 2 *ṭassū* ($\frac{1}{24}$ of a yard).

On the 16th it was reported that Mumtāz† K., the governor of Agra, had died. At first he was in the service of Bahādur K., the brother of Khān Zamān. After they were killed he entered the service of my revered father. When I placed my foot in the world of existence that revered person favoured me with making him the Nāẓir (Superintendent) of my establishment. For a period of fifty-six years he served me sincerely and zealously and in a manner to please me, and at no time did a speck of dust from him settle on the fringe of my heart. What is due to him for the excellence of his service is more than a clerk could write. May God Almighty overwhelm him in the ocean of His forgiveness!

Having conferred on Muqarrab K., who is one of the old officials,‡ the government and administration of Agra, I gave him his leave. In the neighbourhood of Fatḥpūr, Mukarram K. and his brother 'Abdu-s-Salām had the good fortune to pay their respects. On the 22nd the entertainment for my lunar weighment took place in the town of Mathura, and the fifty-seventh year of my age began auspiciously and happily. At Mathura I went on by boat seeing what was to be seen, and hunting. On the way the huntsmen reported that a tigress with three cubs had appeared. Disembarking from the boat I engaged in the pleasure of sport. As the cubs were small I ordered them to be taken by hand, and killed the mother with my gun. At this time it was reported to me that the villagers § and cultivators on the other side of the river Jumna had not given up stealing and highway robbery, and, passing their time in the shelter of thick jungles and difficult strong places in stubbornness and fearlessness, would not pay their rents to the jagirdars. I gave an order to Khān Jahān to take a

* *Dara'* or *zara'*, yards? The text gives his weight as 20½, but *bīst* must be a mistake for *hasht*.

† He was a eunuch, and originally had the name of I'tibār K. He received the title of Mumtāz K. in this year. Tūzuk, 359. See Blochmann, 433.

‡ *Az qadīmān u bābariyān* (properly *bairiyān*).

§ *Ganwārān u muzāri'ān*.

force of mansabdars with him and give them exemplary punishment, and having slaughtered, imprisoned, and plundered them, raze to the ground their strongholds and forts, and tear up from the root their thorn-brakes of mischief and disturbance. The next day the force crossed the river and made a hot attack on them. As they had no time for escape by flight they planted firmly the foot of folly, and showed fight. Many of them were slaughtered: their women and children were taken prisoners, and much booty fell into the hands of the victorious army.

On 1st Bahman, having promoted Rustam K. to the faujdarship of the Sarkar of Qanauj, I sent him there.

On the 2nd 'Abdu-llah, s. Ḥakīm Nūru-d-dīn, of Teheran, was ordered to be capitally punished in my presence. The explanation of this brief announcement is as follows: When the ruler of Persia, on suspicion of his having money and other property, tortured his father, the aforesaid fled from Persia, and with a hundred miseries and adversities threw himself into Hindustan, and by the patronage of I'timādu-d-daula was enrolled among the servants of the Court. By the aid of good fortune, having in a short time become well known, he was included among those who were in immediate attendance, and obtained a mansab of 500 and a fertile jagir, but as his capacity was small (lit., his digestion was narrow) he could not stand such great good fortune, and assumed ingratitude and unthankfulnes; and constantly defiled his tongue with abuse* of his lord and master. At this time it was continually reported to me that as my kindness to him and observance of what was due to him increased, that ungrateful one blamed and abused me the more. When I considered the favours I had bestowed upon him, I could not believe these stories about him, but at last I heard from impartial and disinterested persons the disrespectful language which he had used with respect to me in assemblies and companies.

* Text *ba shukr u shukūh*, but the Iqbāl-nāma, 213, has *ba-shakwa*, "with complaints," and this must be correct. 'Abdu-llah indulged in abuse of his lord and master, *khudā u khudāwand-i-khwīsh* —*i.e.*, Jahangir.

The charge was thus confirmed, and accordingly I summoned him to my presence and had him executed.*

"A red† tongue gives the green head to the winds." As the huntsmen reported that there was a tigress in this neighbourhood, by the mischief caused by which the inhabitants were oppressed, I ordered Fidā'ī K. to take elephants with him and surround it. Mounting myself, I followed him into the forest. It soon came to view, and with one shot from my gun its affairs were finished. One day I was enjoying myself with sport, and caught a black partridge with a hawk. I ordered them to open its crop in my presence. A mouse it had swallowed whole came out of its crop, and which was not yet digested. I was greatly astonished that the pipe of its gullet, small as it was, should swallow a whole mouse and how it had done so. Without exaggeration, if anyone had told me the tale I should not have believed it. As I saw this myself I have recorded it on account of its strangeness. On the 6th of the month Delhi became the abode of good fortune.

As Jagat Singh, s. Rāja Bāso, at the instigation of Bī-daulat, had gone out into the hills in the north of the Panjab, which are his hereditary abode, and raised a disturbance there, I appointed Ṣādiq K. to punish him, as has been related in the preceding pages. At this time Mādho Singh, his younger brother, was promoted to the title of Raja, and given a horse and robe of honour. An order was given for him to go to Ṣādiq K. and attack the rebels with him.

Next day I marched from the outskirts of the city, and alighted at Salīmgarh. As the house of Rāja Kis̲h̲an Dās was on the road, and he had made great efforts and entreated me to do so, I at his request threw the shadow of prosperity on his dwelling, and gratified the desire of that old servant. A few of his offerings were accepted in order to dignify him. Marching on the 20th from Salīmgarh, I appointed Sayyid Baḥwa Buk̲h̲ārī to the governorship of Delhi, which is his ordinary

* *Cf.* Iqbāl-nāma, 213-214.

† A proverbial expression. It is quoted by Niẓāmu-d-dīn in the Ṭabaqāt.

residence. In fact, he had already done this service well, and I had given him high rank.

At this time 'Alī Muḥammad, s. 'Alī Rāy,* ruler of Tibet, by his father's order came to Court, and had the good fortune to pay his respects. It was clear that 'Alī Rāy had a great affection for and attachment to this son, and held him dearer than his other children. He wished to make him his successor, and he was consequently envied by his brothers, and disputes arose between them. Abdāl, s. 'Alī Rāy, who was the eldest of his children, through this jealousy sought the patronage of the Khan of Kashghar and made him his protector, so that when 'Ali Rāy, who was very old and decrepit, should die, he might, under the protection of the Wāli of Kashghar, become ruler of Tibet. 'Alī Rāy, suspecting that the brothers might attack 'Alī Muḥammad, and a disturbance might arise in his country, sent him to Court, his desire being that he might be attached to this Court, and his affairs might prosper by service to and kindness shown by the Court.

On the 1st of the Ilāhī month of Isfandārmuz I pitched in the pargana of Umbala. La<u>sh</u>karī, s. Imām-wirdī, who had run away from Bī-daulat, and joined the service of my auspicious son <u>Sh</u>āh Parwīz, having come on this date to Court, kissed the threshold. A report came from my son and Mahābat K. It contained the recommendation and the offer of service of 'Ādil K., with a letter which he had sent to Mahābat, in which were set forth his submissiveness and loyalty. La<u>sh</u>karī was sent back to Parwīz with a dress of honour, a *nādirī* with pearl buttons for the prince, and a dress of honour for <u>Kh</u>ān 'Ālam and Mahābat K. At the request of my son I wrote a gracious farman to 'Ādil K. showing great favour to him, and sent him a robe of honour with a special *nādirī*. I gave an order that if they thought fit they should send the above-mentioned† to 'Ādil K.

On the 5th I alighted at the garden of Sihrind. On the

* 'Alī Rāy was ruler of Little Tibet (Baltistan). Jahangir had married his daughter. Blochmann, 310, and Akbar-nāma, III. 603. The marriage took place in A.H. 1000 (1592).

† That is, La<u>sh</u>karī.

bank of the Beas Ṣādiq K., Mukhtār K., Isfandiyār, Rāja Rūp Chand of Gwalior, and other Amirs who had been appointed to support him, having succeeded in restoring order in the northern hill-country, had the good fortune to kiss the threshold. The facts, briefly, are that Jagat Singh, at the instigation of Bī-daulat, had taken to the hills above-mentioned, and engaged in stirring up sedition and strife. As the field was clear (*i.e.*, there was no one to oppose him) he passed over difficult mountains and defiles, and by attacking and plundering peasantry and the weak, heaped misfortune on them until Ṣādiq K. arrived. He brought the Zamindars under control by means of fears and hopes, and made the overthrow of that wretched creature the object of his exertions. Jagat Singh strengthened the fort of Mau, and was protected by it. Whenever he found an opportunity he left that fortress and fought with the royal servants. At last his provisions were exhausted, and he came to despair of assistance from the other Zamindars. The elevation of his younger brother became a source of disturbance and anxiety to him. Helplessly he then sought for patronage, and begged the protection of Nūr Jahān Begam, expressing shame and contrition, and sought a refuge in her mediation. In order to please and satisfy her, the pen of pardon was drawn through the record of his faults.

On this day reports came in from the officials in the Deccan that Bī-daulat, with La'natu-llah, Dārāb, and other wretched (with broken wing and feathers) creatures in miserable condition, with blackened faces, had gone from the borders of Quṭbu-l-mulk's territory towards Orissa and Bengal. In this journey great loss fell on him and his companions, many of whom, when a chance offered, with bare heads and feet, and having washed their hands of life (desperate), took to flight. Out of these one day Mīrzā Muḥammad, s. Afẓal K., his Diwan, with his mother and his family, ran away during the march, and when the news reached Bī-daulat, he sent Ja'far and Khān-qulī Uzbeg and some others of his confidential men in pursuit of him, that, if they could take him alive, well and good, or otherwise they should cut off his head and bring it into his presence. They with all speed proceeded and caught him up on the road. Becoming aware of this, he sent his mother and family into the jungles and hid them there, and himself with a body of young men whom he relied on as companions, planted manfully the foot of courage and stood with their bows. In front of them there was a canal and a swamp (*chihlā*). Sayyid Ja'far K. wished to approach near him and take him with him by deceiving him, but however much he tried to persuade him by threatening and holding out hopes, it had no effect, and he answered him with life-taking arrows. He made a good fight of it, and sent Khān-qulī and some others of Bī-daulat's men to hell. Sayyid Ja'far also was wounded. Finally Mīrzā Muḥammad received severe wounds and gambled away the cash of his life. But as long as he had breath he deprived many thereof. After he was killed, they cut off his head and took it to Bī-daulat.

When Bī-daulat was defeated near Delhi and went to Mandu, he sent Afẓal K. to get assistance and support from 'Ādil K. and others, forwarding with him an armlet (*bāzū-band*) for 'Ādil K., and a horse, an elephant, and a jewelled sword for 'Ambar. He first went to 'Ambar. After delivering his message he produced what Bī-daulat had sent for him, but 'Ambar would not accept them, saying he was the servant of 'Ādil K., who was at present the head of those in power in the Deccan: he should go first to him and explain what he desired. If he agreed, his slave would ally himself to and obey him, and in that case he would take whatever was sent, otherwise not. Afẓal K. went to 'Ādil K., who received him very badly, and for a long time kept him outside the city and did not look into his affair, but put all kinds of slights upon him, but secretly asked for what Bī-daulat had sent for him and 'Ambar, and took possession of it. The aforesaid (Afẓal K.) was there when he heard the news of the killing of his son and the ruin of his family, and so fell upon evil days. In short, Bī-daulat, in spite of all his (original) good fortune and happy auspices, undertook a long and distant journey, and came to the port of Machhlī Patan (Masulipatam), which belongs to

Quṭbu-l-mulk. Before reaching this place, he sent some of his men to Quṭbu-l-mulk, and besought him for all sorts of assistance and companionship. Quṭbu-l-mulk sent him a small amount of cash and goods for his support, and wrote to the warden of his frontier to conduct him in safety out of his territory, and encourage the grain-sellers and Zamindars to send grain and all other necessaries to his camp.

On the 27th of the month a strange event took place. Returning from the hunting-place, I had come back to the camp at night. By chance I crossed a stream of water, the bed of which was very rocky and the water running violently. One of the servants of the *sharbat-khāna* (wine-cellar) was conveying a huntsman's relish. He had a gold tray, which contained a salver and five cups. There were covers to the cups, and the whole was in a cotton bag. When he was crossing, his foot slipped and the tray fell out of his hand. As the water was deep and running rapidly, however much they searched and beat their hands and feet (exerted themselves), no trace of it could be found. Next day the state of the case was reported to me, and I ordered a number of boatmen and huntsmen to go to the place and make a careful search, and it perhaps might appear. By chance, in the place where it had fallen it was found, and more strange still, it had not been turned upside down, and not a drop of water had got into the cups. This affair is similar to what happened when Hādī was seated on the throne of the Khalifate. A ruby ring had been inherited by Hārūn from his father. Hādī sent a slave to Hārūn and asked for it. It happened that at that time Hārūn was seated on the bank of the Tigris. The slave gave the message, and Hārūn, enraged, said: "I have allowed thee* to have the Khalifate, and thou dost not allow me one ring." In his rage he threw the ring into the Tigris. After some months by the decree of fate Hādī died, and the turn of the Khalifate came to Hārūn. He ordered divers to look for the ring in the place where he had thrown it. By the chances of destiny, and the aid of good fortune, at the first dive the ring was found, and brought and given into Hārūn's hand!

* Hādī was Hārūnu-r-Rashīd's elder brother.

At this time one day on the hunting ground the chief huntsman Imām-wirdī brought before me a partridge that had a spur on one leg and not on the other. As the way to distinguish the female lies in the spur, by way of testing me he asked whether this was a male or a female. I said at once "A female." When they opened it an egg appeared inside (*pīshīna*) its belly. The people who were in attendance asked with surprise by what sign I had discovered this: I said that the head and beak of the female are shorter than the male's. By investigation and often seeing (the birds) I had acquired this dexterity.* It is a strange thing that the windpipe in all animals (*ḥaiwānāt*), which the Turks call *ḥalq*,† is single from the top of the throat to the crop (*chīna-dān*), while in the case of the bustard (*jarz*) it is different. In the bustard it is for four finger-breadths from the top of the throat single and then it divides into two branches and in this form reaches the crop. Also at the place where it divides into two branches there is a stoppage (*sar-band*) and a knot (*girih*) is felt by the hand. In the *kulang* (crane) it is still stranger. In it the windpipe passes in a serpentine manner between the bones of the breast to the rump and then turns back from there and joins the throat. The *jarz* or *charz* (bustard) is of two kinds: one is a mottled black and the other *būr* (a kind of dun colour). I now‡ discovered that there are not two kinds, but that which is a mottled black is the male, and that which is dun-coloured is the female. The proof of it is this, that in the piebald there are testicles and in the dun one there are eggs; this has been repeatedly found on examination.

I have a great liking for fish, and all kinds of good fish are brought for me; the best fish in Hindustan is the *rohū*, and

* Text *mulka*. Perhaps the word may be *malka-i-ān*, "possession of it"—*i.e.*, possession of such knowledge. The MSS. have *ān* after *malka*.

† Text *ḥanaq*. But the MSS. have merely *ḥaqq*, and it is said in the dictionaries that there is a bird called the *ḥaqq*.

‡ This corrects a previous statement to the effect that the black and red bustards were two species.

after that the *barīn*.* Both have scales, and in appearance and shape are like each other. Everyone cannot at once distinguish between them. The difference in their flesh also is very small, but the connoisseur discovers that the flesh of the *rohū* is rather more agreeable of the two.

* The MSS. have either barīn or parīn. I cannot find the name in the dictionaries, but my friend Sir K. C. Gupta suggests that the word may be *bāns* (*Labeo calbasa*). This fish is also a carp, and resembles the *rohū* (*L. rohita*), but is smaller. It may also be the catla.

THE NINETEENTH NEW YEAR'S FEAST AFTER THE AUSPICIOUS ACCESSION

On Wednesday, the 29th Jumādā-l-awwal, A.H. 1033, March 10, 1624, after one watch and two gharis of day had passed, the sun, that bestows bounty on the world, passed into its house of honour in Aries. The royal servants obtained promotions and increase of mansab. Aḥsanu-llah, s. Khwāja Abū-l-Ḥasan, received as original and increase that of 1,000 and 300 horse. Muḥammad Sa'īd, s. Aḥmad Beg K. Kābulī, the same, Mīr Sharaf Diwān-i-buyūtāt, and Khawāṣṣ K., each of them that of 1,000. Sardār K., having come from Kangra, had the good fortune to pay his respects. At this time I gave orders to the *yasāwuls* and men of the *yasāq* (guards) that hereafter at the time when I came out of the palace they should keep away defective people, such as the blind, and those whose noses and ears had been cut off, the leprous and the maimed, and all kinds of sick people, and not permit them to be seen. On the 19th the feast of the culmination was held. Ilāh-wirdī, the brother of Imām-wirdī, had run away from Bī-daulat and came to Court, and was honoured with great favours.

As the news of Bī-daulat's coming to the border of Orissa was constantly repeated, a farman was issued to the prince and Mahābat K. and the Amirs who had been sent to the support of my son, that they should set their minds at ease about the administering the provinces (of the Deccan), and go quickly to Allahabad and Behar, and if the Subahdar of Bengal could not forestall him, and he should put forward the foot of audacity, he must be made a wanderer in the desert of disappointment by the blows of the victorious army which is in the shadow of the flag of my son. By way of precaution on the 2nd Urdībihis̲h̲t I gave my son K̲h̲ān Jahān leave to proceed to Agra to remain in that neighbourhood and wait for a sign. If there should happen to any necessity for a particular service and an order should be given him, he must act as occasion might require. I sent him a special dress of honour, with a *nādirī* with pearl buttons, a special jewelled sword, and to Aṣālat K., his son, a horse, and a dress of honour.

On this day a report came from 'Aqīdat K., Bakhshi of the Deccan. He wrote that, according to order, my prosperous son S̲h̲āh Parwīz had married the sister of Rāja Gaj Singh. I hope that her coming will be auspicious to the State. He also wrote that, having sent for Turkumān K. from Pattan he had appointed 'Azīzu-llah in his place. Jān-sipār K., also by order, came and waited on me. When Bī-daulat crossed the Burhanpur river and took the road of ruin, Mīr Ḥusāmu-d-dīn, considering his own evil deeds, could not remain at Burhanpur. Taking his children with him, he conveyed the goods of ruin to the Deccan, in order that he might pass his days under the protection of 'Ādil K. By chance, as he passed by Bīr, Jān-sipār K. obtained information, and sent a body of men to head him off. He seized him and his dependants, and brought them before Mahābat. Mahābat placed him in confinement, and took from him Rs. 1,00,000 in cash and goods. (Also) Jādo Rāy and Ūday Rām had taken the elephants which Bī-daulat had left in Burhanpur and brought them to the prince (Parwīz).

Qāẓī 'Abdu-l-'Azīz, who had come to Delhi from Bī-daulat in order to state his objects, had not been allowed by me an opportunity to speak and I had handed him over to Mahābat K. After his (Bī-daulat's) defeat and ruin Mahābat K. had made him his own servant. As he was an old friend of 'Ādil K., and was for some years at Bījāpūr as Vakil of K̲h̲ān Jahān, Mahābat K. now sent him again as his representative* to 'Ādil Khan, and the leading men of the Deccan, *nolentes*

* *Ba-rism-i-ḥajābat.*

volentes, looking to the necessities of the time and the upshot of affairs, were contented and professed loyalty and desire for service. The rebel 'Ambar sent one of his confidential men of the name of 'Alī Shīr, and displayed great humility. He ('Ambar) wrote in the capacity of a servant to Mahābat K., and engaged that he ('Ambar) should come to Dewalgāon* and wait upon Mahābat. He would make his eldest son a servant of the State, and keep him in the service of my auspicious son. About this time there arrived a letter from Qāẓī 'Abdu-l-'Azīz that 'Ādil K. from the bottom of his heart had elected for service and loyalty, and agreed that he would send Mullā Muḥammad Lārī, who was his principal agent and minister, and whom both in spoken and written messages he called Mullā Bābā, with 5,000 horse, that he might remain continually on duty, and they might know that other† troops would follow (?). Urgent farmans had been sent that my son should proceed to Allahabad and Behar in order to overthrow Bī-daulat. At this time news arrived that notwithstanding the rainy season and the violence of the rain, that son, on the 6th Farwardīn had marched out of Burhanpur with the army of fortune, and had taken up his quarters in Lāl Bāgh,‡ and that Mahābat K. was awaiting at Burhanpur the arrival of Mullā Muḥammad Lārī, so that when he arrived he would relieve himself of the care of the maintenance of order in that neighbourhood, and come with him (Muḥammad Lārī) to wait on my son. Lashkar K., Jādo Rāy, Ūday Rām, and other servants of the State had been ordered to go to the Bālāghāt (the country above the Ghats), and remain at Ẓafarnagar. Having given Jān-sipār K. leave as before, he (Parwīz) kept Asad K. Ma'mūrī at Elichpur. Minūchihr, s. Shāh-nawāz K., was appointed to Jālnāpūr. He sent Riẓawī K. to Thālner, to guard the province of Khandesh.

On this day news came that Lashkarī had taken the farman

* Dewalgāon is about 60 miles S. of Burhanpur, Elliot, VII. 11.

† Or, perhaps, they might be sure he was coming shortly.

‡ Lāl Bāgh was on the outskirts of Burhanpur. Though the rainy season is spoken of, the date Farwardīn is in March.

to 'Ādil K., and he, having decorated the city, had gone out four koss to meet him, and had performed salutations and prostrations for the farman and the dress of honour. On the 21st I sent dresses of honour for my son Dāwar-bakhsh and Khān A'ẓam and Ṣafī K. Having appointed Ṣādiq K. to the government of Lahore, and given him a dress of honour and an elephant, I gave him leave. An order was given that he should have the mansab of 400 personal and 400 horse. Multafat K., s. Mīrzā Rustam, raised the head of distinction with the mansab of 1,500 personal and 300 horse.

One day while hunting it was reported to me that a snake with a black hood (*kafcha*) had swallowed another hooded (*kafcha ?*) snake and gone into a hole. I ordered them to dig up the place and bring out the snake. Without exaggeration I had never seen a snake of this size. When they opened its belly, the hood of the snake that it had swallowed came out whole. Although this snake was of another kind, in length and girth little difference was visible.

At this time it was represented to me in a report* by the news writer of the Deccan that Mahābat K. had ordered 'Ārif s. Zāhid to be executed, and had put him (*i.e.*, Zāhid), with two other sons, in prison. It appeared that that wretched man had written with his own hand a petition to Bī-daulat representing on the part of his father and himself his loyalty, sincerity, repentance, and shame. By fate that letter fell into the hands of Mahābat K. Having sent for 'Ārif into his presence he showed him the letter. As he had written a decree for his own blood, he could not make any acceptable excuse, and of necessity he was executed, and his father and brothers imprisoned.

On the 1st Khurdād it was reported that Shajā'at K. 'Arab, had died a natural death in the Deccan.

* Perhaps the meaning is that Mahābat had imprisoned 'Ārif, the son of the Zāhid whom Jahangir had condemned to death, for in the 18th year Jahangir speaks of Zāhid as a rebel. But the sentence is not clear.

At this time a report came from Ibrāhīm K. Fatḥ-jang that Bī-daulat had entered Orissa. The particulars of this are that between the boundary* of Orissa and the Deccan there is a barrier. On one side there are lofty mountains, and on the other swamps and a river. The ruler of Golconda had also erected a wall (*dar-band*) and a fort, and armed it with muskets and cannon. The passage of men by that closed route was impracticable without the leave of Quṭbu-l-mulk. Bī-daulat, with the guidance of Quṭbu-l-mulk, having passed by that route, entered the country of Orissa. It happened that at this time Aḥmad Beg K., nephew of Ibrāhīm K., had attacked the Zamindars of Khurda. At this strange occurrence, which happened without precedent or news or information, he became confused and bewildered and without seeing a remedy gave up his campaign, and came to the village of Bulbulī† (Pīplī), the seat of the governor of that Subah (Orissa). He then took his women with him and hastened to Cuttack, which is 12 koss from Pīplī towards Bengal. As the time was short, he had not leisure to collect troops and arrange his affairs. He did not feel himself equal to a war with Bī-daulat, and he had not with him associates such as were necessary, so he went on from Cuttack to Bardwan, of which Ṣāliḥ, nephew of Āṣaf Ḳ. deceased, was the Jagirdar.

* Elliot, VI. 390. It seems probable that this is the place mentioned in the Ma'āṣiru-l-umarā, I. 410, in the biography of Bāqir K. Najm Ṣānī, and also in the Pādishāh-nāma, I. 333. It is called there "the Pass of Chhatar Diwār," and is described as the boundary between Orissa and Telingana, and is two koss from Khairapāra. One Manṣūr, a servant of Quṭbu-l-mulk, had built a fort there, and called it Manṣūr-garh.

† *Bulbulī.* I had supposed this to be Pīplī, but the latter place is in the Balasore district, and nearer Bengal than Cuttack. Curiously enough Pipli or Pippli is not given in the I.G. new ed., though it is given as Pippli in the old. There is also a Pipli in the Puri district (I.G., new ed., XX. 404). In the Ma'āṣiru-l-umarā, I. 137 and 194, in the biographies of Ibrāhīm Fatḥ K. and Aḥmad Beg, the place is taken to be Pipli. It is also Pipli in the Iqbāl-nāma, 217, where also Cuttack is described as being 12 koss off, towards Bengal. The maps show a Pipalgaon between Puri and Cuttack, and about 30 m. from the latter place. A Pipli in the Puri district is mentioned in the I.G., new ed.

At first Ṣāliḥ was astonished*, and did not believe that Bīdaulat was coming, until a letter came from La'natu-llah to conciliate him. Ṣāliḥ fortified Bardwan and remained in it. Ibrāhīm K. was surprised on hearing the terrible news. Though most of his auxiliaries and soldiers were scattered in the villages round about and unprocurable, he yet planted the foot of courage firmly in Akbarnagar (Rajmahal), and set himself to strengthen the fort and collect troops, and encourage the heads of tribes and retainers. He prepared the things necessary for his guns and other weapons and for battle. In the meanwhile a notice came to him from Bidaulat that by the decree of God and the ordinances of heaven what was not suitable to him had appeared from the womb of non-existence. By the revolving of crooked-moving time and the changes of night and day his passage towards these regions had come to pass. Although to the view of manly courage the extent and breadth of that country were not more than an exercising-ground, or rather than a rubbish-heap (*pur-kāhī*, "full of straw"), and his aims were higher, yet as he had to pass by this way, he could not pass for nothing. If it were Ibrāhīm's determination to go to the royal Court, he (Shāh Jahān) would hold back the hand of injury from him and his family, and he might go to Court with an easy mind. If he considered it advisable to stay, he would bestow upon him any corner of the country he might ask for.

* Text *isti'dād*, but the true reading is *istib'ād*. *Istib'ād namūda*, "regarded the thing as at a distance," or "was surprised." The I.O. MSS. end here, their last words being "Till at length there came a conciliatory letter from La'natu-llah ('Abdu-llah). The R.A.S. MS. continues with Muḥammad Hādī's supplement.

ADDENDUM BY MĪRZĀ MUḤAMMAD HĀDĪ, THE WRITER OF THE PREFACE

The MS. states: "Up to this place is the writing (*ta'līf*) of the deceased king Jahāngīr. The rest, up to the end of the book, is written by Muḥammad Hādī from some trustworthy MS. collected together to complete the book.

ADDENDUM

Mr. Berthold Laufer's paper on "Walrus and Narwhal Ivory," reprinted at Leyden, 1913, from the *Toung Pao*, throws light on Jāhāngīr's remarks about fish-tooth dagger-hilts. It now seems certain that they were made of the canine tooth of the walrus, or the horn of the narwhal. Possibly one reason why Jāhāngīr attached so much value to the fish-teeth was because they were supposed to be an antidote to poison. He was fond of such things, and one day, when he was heir-apparent, Father Jerome Xavier found him engaged at Fatḥpūr in extracting copper from peacocks' tails, on account of its supposed antitoxine properties.

It is stated in Mr. Laufer's paper, pp. 13 and 15, that walrus-teeth were supposed to be also useful in reducing swellings. As they were often made into knife-handles, it is not improbable that the knife which a Rajah of Cochin appears to have sent to Akbar in 1569 (Akbar-nāma, i. 342) was, wholly or in part, made of walrus ivory. The Rajah said that whenever it was applied to a swelling it reduced it, and Akbar told Abū-l-Faẓl that over 200 persons had benefited by touching it.

In the British Museum there is a fascinating set of chessmen made of walrus or narwhal ivory. They were discovered in the island of Lewis in 1831, but are supposed to be as old as the twelfth century.

INDEX

B

C

L

M

N

O

P

Q

R

S

T